Forbidden Knowledge
Information *They* Don't Want You To Know

Edited by Robert E. Bauman, JD

Forbidden Knowledge: Information They Don't Want You to Know

Robert E. Bauman and The Sovereign Society, Ltd. 2004

The Sovereign Society
5 Catherine Street
Waterford
Ireland

5th edition July 2004

ISBN 0-9547754-1-4
Printed by: Victor Graphics • 1211 Bernard Drive • Baltimore, MD 21223

Forbidden Knowledge
Information *They* Don't Want You To Know

Edited by Robert E. Bauman, JD

The Sovereign Society
5 Catherine Street
Waterford
Ireland

Table of Contents

Preface

*". . . just as the State has no money of its own, so it has no power of its own.
All the power it has society gives it, plus what it confiscates from time to time on one
pretext or another; there is no other source from which State power can be drawn.
Therefore every assumption of State power, whether by gift or seizure, leaves society
with so much less power; there is never, nor can be, any strengthening of State power
without a corresponding and equivalent depletion of social power."*
~Albert J. Nock (1935)

"Knowledge itself is power."
~Francis Bacon, Meditationes Sacrae (1597)

In the age-old struggle for individual liberty against the power of the state, there can be no question which side has triumphed throughout most of the twentieth century.

The one interest the state willingly sacrifices to the "common good" is personal liberty "the freedom to produce and create, to buy and sell, to speak and publish, to travel, to live freely. By diminishing liberty, government systematically subverts people's responsibility for their own lives. It robs those who produce in order to placate those who only consume. The result is economic stagnation, retrogression and political corruption.

Since the seventeenth century, in England, France and America, and more recently in Russia and eastern Europe, revolutions against this tyranny of the state were fought on behalf of an alternative we can call "natural liberty." At first successful, over time these revolutions cooled to complacency and hard-won freedom came to mean guaranteed entitlement to government largess.

True natural liberty means that each of us is the sole legitimate owner of our own life and destiny, free to act as we wish so long as we use no violence, fraud or other aggression against others. That same freedom dictates a free-market economy enjoying peaceful production and trade. It opposes government control by self-serving politicians.

No activity of statist government has diminished personal liberty more than the unchecked power to tax. In the United States, the United Kingdom and Germany the effective rate of personal taxes far exceeds 50 percent of earnings. In some nations, such as France and Sweden, it is higher still. Business is taxed at even greater levels. And everyone pays the ultimate price.

When government takes wealth from some and gives it to others, this forced redistribution diminishes the rights and well-being of the former, and often destroys the independence of the latter.

The issue of taxation involves nothing less than the human and natural right to own, use and enjoy private property, a "civil right" of the most basic kind. Property and wealth determine personal power to control our own lives, to make decisions, to raise a family, to live free.

As Albert Jay Nock noted, every additional tax imposed diminishes our freedom.

In an economic history of the Middle Ages, Paul Craig Roberts, the economist and columnist, showed that medieval serfs bound to the land and their masters rarely paid more then one-third of the value of their labors in taxes. For good reason: with very low productivity, serfs could not survive if forced to pay more taxes. With nothing to lose, they would revolt and kill the tax collectors.

Yet a half-millennium later, with capitalism's enormously increased productivity, we have even less right to our earnings than did those enslaved serfs. Says Roberts: "You are not free when you do not own the product of your own labor."

This book, *Forbidden Knowledge*, is a compendium of the acts and ideas of dynamic men and women who have exalted natural liberty in their own lives—and many who do so to this day.

Albert Camus said, "Revolutionaries are men who say no!"

These authors have said an emphatic "NO" to Big Brother government. These practical people refuse to bow down to government, to submit to bureaucratic demands for ever higher taxes, greater controls and increased regulation.

In some cases this has meant leaving the nation of their birth and moving to countries that still believe in and practice natural liberty. There are such places, as you will see. Some individuals you will meet in these pages call no single nation "home," spending the changing seasons of each year in many places where they do business, and enjoy the new experiences and the pleasures life has to give.

Drawing on their experience, you too can have a life of natural liberty. You too can live, work, invest and do business without having to pay taxes to any government anywhere. And you can do this legally and with maximum personal security and financial privacy.

To knowledgeable people, true financial security means:

- the maximum possible tax avoidance
- the strongest possible financial privacy
- the greatest degree of asset protection
- the most profitable investments

These goals, and how to achieve them, are spelled out in *Forbidden Knowledge*.

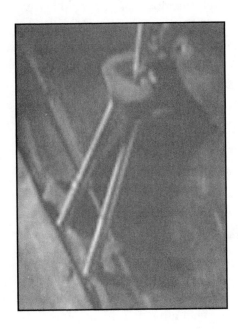

CHAPTER ONE

The Meaning of Natural Liberty

We are living in one of those times when civilization has become "a thin crust over a volcano of revolution." Unrecognized by most, the Old Order is dying, replaced by a new world economic structure built on free markets, massive technological change, instant communications, interlinked databases, electronic commerce and digital cash. These emerging systems weaken the power of traditional governments, even as they increase individual freedom, financial choice and personal privacy.

Today's politicians see what is coming and are clawing desperately to stay ahead of the inevitable tide. They'll fail, as did the corrupt leaders of a dying Soviet Union, brazenly trying to stop the spread of free ideas by outlawing fax and copying machines. As myopic nineteenth century Luddite workers failed to thwart the Industrial Revolution by destroying new laborsaving machinery.

As evidence, consider how shared, instantaneous information contributed to the collapse of Asian economies a few years ago, nations widely touted as world leaders of an unending boom. The resulting economic "correction" wasn't confined to Wall Street and the City. Nervous waves rippled daily through time zones and stock markets as CNN covered it live and Internet trading went wild, another example of irresistible techno-advances forcing a totally new financial and banking reality.

Consider too, the recent technology boom and bust on Wall Street and in other markets. Stock of corporations whose wealth existed only on paper or as future concepts rocketed up in price, and just as quickly, they disappeared.

A select few people long ago anticipated the revolution now at hand. These are the Sovereign Individuals, voluntary citizens of the world-at-large seeking freedom and fortune wherever they judge best.

Weary of oppressive governments and onerous taxes, they search the globe for personal liberty, for safe havens for their families, themselves and their wealth.

Now the rest of the world is coming to realize the successful strategies that the Sovereign Individual has known all along.

This first chapter highlights the basic principles of the freedom philosophy. This begins your guide to natural liberty.

On Becoming a Sovereign Individual
by John Pugsley, *The Sovereign Individual*, June 1999

The chairman of the Sovereign Society traces the evolution of freedom from serfdom into democracy, and now to a modern slavery by government in the name of democracy.

Since emerging from the caves and jungles of antiquity, mankind has been engaged in an epic struggle to discover the ultimate design for social organization, one that would allow civilization to progress in peace and ever increasing prosperity.

For thousands of years, the idea of monarchy reigned. The overwhelming majority accepted rule by an all-powerful government headed by a king appointed by God.

Then, about 200 years ago, an idea emerged that was to change the nature of government ... the idea that all men were born with equal rights to life, liberty and the pursuit of happiness. In short, all individuals were sovereign, and had both the right and the responsibility to rule themselves. The concept of the divine right of kings was cast aside and in its place democracy was born: citizens were free to elect their rulers. It was believed the era of oppressive government was over.

When democracy was embryonic, it seemed to work. Individual freedom from oppression led to a flourishing new world. Over the past few decades, however, there has been a steady growth of government as the masses of voters have learned that they can manipulate government to their advantage. They have found they can enrich themselves at the expense of the successful and thrifty.

This attack on the more affluent and productive individuals in countries like the United States, Canada, Germany and Great Britain has had the same effect as the repressive policies of King George had in the eighteenth century. It has led to a rising exodus of society's most productive people as they migrate to political environments that offer greater asset protection, privacy and lower taxation.

Many are moving only their assets offshore to countries that offer more financial privacy and low or no taxation. A smaller but rising number are electing to move themselves and their families offshore as well.

While a few officially disconnect from their nation of birth by renouncing their citizenship, others merely reside offshore while retaining their original citizenship. Still others acquire dual nationality by ancestral right or through financial citizenship programs offered by many countries. A few adopt the so-called "PT" lifestyle and become nomads, never staying long enough in one place to become subject to its taxes, thus becoming Permanent Tourists or Prior Taxpayers. But all are united in seeking privacy, freedom of movement, low or no taxes, safety of capital and minimal connection with big government. And in being Prepared Thoroughly for the unexpected.

The Sovereign Society

Over the years my study and writings on the subjects of political coercion, freedom and free markets has led to correspondence, affiliations and friendships with like-minded individuals from many disciplines and many countries.

In the past few months a group of us have formed The Sovereign Society, a group of the most creative thinkers on the subjects of personal and financial freedom, as well as individuals who are motivated to achieve personal independence for themselves. The aim of the Society is to create a network for developing strategies that individuals can use to wrest control of their lives and assets away from the menace of Big Brother.

I don't think of the Society as a club or organization but as a virtual society, an extra-national community existing all over the world in the hearts and minds of its citizen members. Essentially, it will offer members a new "passport," a whole new concept of citizenship in a country that takes its shape not on the basis of geography, but on the basis of ideology.

Through borderless cyberspace and with the security of encryption, members will be taught to carry on intellectual and financial commerce worldwide, 24 hours a day. Most important, citizen members will work with one another in their quest to find sanctuary from private and state snoops, bugs, swat teams, property seizures and other incursions on civil and economic liberties.

Our aim is to find free market alternatives to the services that governments today promise but fail to provide: security from crime and violence, education, old age security, health care, just enforcement of contracts.

We welcome all who share our views. For further information, contact The Sovereign Society, 5 Catherine Street, Waterford, Ireland, telephone +353 51 844 068, fax +353 51 304 561, U.S. Representative Service telephone +1 888 358 8125, U.S. Representative Service fax +1 410 230 1269, e-mail: info@thesovereignsociety.com, web: www.sovereignsociety.com.

The Evolution of Freedom
by John Pugsley, *The Sovereign Individual*, May 1999

If personal liberty is a natural choice, why do so many people surrender to tyranny?

I have long struggled to unravel the mystery of why the majority of intelligent, educated, successful people accept even the most irrational social customs of the society into which they are born. Why do people buy into the concept that government should solve their problems when history clearly demonstrates that the State worsens every problem that it is assigned to solve?

Most individuals go to great lengths to become model citizens. They dutifully follow the established religion of the group, the current economic system and the current political system. The majority experiences no urge to deviate from the customs, mores and taboos of the group and strives to be politically and socially correct.

Only a small minority views convention as a curious and irrational way to make choices. We question authority, ask for logical explanations of why particular rules should be followed, and, lacking a suitable explanation, do things our own way.

Why do most individuals march with the masses, while only a few of us march to our own drummers?

One close friend and colleague jokingly suspects a "socialism" gene that blinds people to the logic of the free market. He may be looking in the right area. Recently I've been reading a book by Dean Hamer and Peter Copeland titled *Living with Our Genes* that sheds breakthrough insights into the roots of individual behavior. The book is a fascinating investigation of the link between genes and social behavior.

Using DNA samples from a variety of sources in conjunction with psychological personality-typing questionnaires, Hamer and other scientists have isolated specific genes that regulate a variety of individual behaviors. Some of these bear heavily on an individual's propensity to follow social rules versus exploring on his or her own initiative.

Perhaps the slice of DNA most linked to the rule-following behavior in question is what psychiatrist Robert Cloninger has dubbed the "novelty-seeking" gene. The gene triggers the release of pleasure-creating chemicals in the brain when the individual is exposed to a new experience. Individuals carrying this gene tend to become bored with orderliness, precision and routine and have a higher-than-average propensity to be exploratory, seeking out new situations, new ideas, adventure, dangerous sports and unconventional pursuits. For individuals without the gene, new situations hold little reward and following routine and tradition would be more natural.

Other genes also influence social behavior. Hamer and other gene sleuths suspect a "harm-avoidance" gene causing feelings of increased anxiety when danger threatens. The presence of the harm-avoidance gene would thus ameliorate the effects of a gene that urges one to take risks.

Of course, genes influence our feelings but feelings alone don't determine behavior. Our feelings are tempered by our experiences and our accumulated experiences determine how our genetic propensities are played out.

How does the novelty-seeking gene help explain the mystery of why people support the idea of government control? Most people aren't drawn to experimentation and change, and follow the dictates of custom and tradition. I would wager that this majority doesn't carry the gene. The minority that do carry it become the engines of change in society. As I interpret the evidence, those with a high novelty-seeking score feel compelled to experiment outside the boundaries of tradition.

Does this indicate that those of us who struggle to live as sovereign individuals are doomed to remain in the minority, and that the growing trend toward big government is the fate of mankind?

Although the majority will always support the status quo, history also teaches us that the novelty-seekers, with their experimentation, do influence the course of history. Explorers like Columbus do discover new worlds, and intellectual adventurers like Thomas Paine do alter the course of society. In social evolution, just as in biological evolution, more efficient ideas eventually win the evolutionary contest.

There are two systems evolving, biological and social. Over millions of years, biological evolution has programmed each of us to be self-interested. This biological programming seduces individuals entrusted with political power to abuse that power. But social technology is the product of an evolutionary process, as well. In their quest for safety and security in societies, individuals have experimented with various forms of governments. All forms that have evolved to date grant power to some individual or small group of individuals. Our biological nature guarantees that individuals given political power will tend to be corrupted by that power, yet social evolution has not become sufficiently advanced to create systems of government that don't hand power to individuals.

Fortunately, evolution has also created the novelty-seeking gene, and the novelty-seekers, scattered throughout the human population, will continue to resist the status quo. We are also individually programmed to act in our own self-interest, so we resist being subjugated by the State.

I believe our experimentation will eventually lead to the evolution of a new social system in which the concept of government will change and a new status quo will be created. The majority will still accept the customs and traditions of the society into which they are born. However, those customs and traditions will no longer be that governments should have arbitrary powers over individuals. Rather, all individuals will be sovereign unto themselves.

The "PT" Life... Is It For YOU?

By John Pugsley, *The Sovereign Individual*, February 2002

More than a decade ago, an interesting character with the nom de plume of "Bill Hill" penned a popular escape manual for freedom advocates titled PT—The Perpetual Traveler. Hill had spent much of his life traveling the world, visiting the continents, regions, countries, and cities that interested him, while carefully avoiding staying in each place long enough to be considered a permanent resident and therefore subject to such unpleasantries as taxes, military service, and other local rules and regulations.

Hill argued that in a world in which every spot on the globe is under the forcible control of one gang of politicians or another, the answer for individual sovereignty is to avoid their control by becoming a "PT," an acronym for a Perpetual Traveler, Prior Taxpayer, or Permanent Tourist.

The ability to become a full-fledged Bill Hill style PT—i.e., living a life absolutely free of taxation, restrictions and obligations imposed by most governments—depends a great extent on your citizenship. U.S. citizens, for example, are liable for taxes on their worldwide income, wherever they travel or live. I've spent many years living outside the United States. But, because I haven't relinquished my U.S. citizenship (yet), living an expat lifestyle has provided very minimal tax advantages.

Most countries, however, impose tax on the basis of residency, not citizenship. Move abroad for at least a year or two and thereafter, the mother country ignores you, at least in reference to income tax. Therefore, for citizens of most countries, the PT lifestyle could legally eliminate income (and with proper planning, estate) taxes, along with along with achieving many other goals of individual sovereignty.

A dozen years ago I became friends with Paul and Vicki Terhorst, who could be considered a poster couple for the PT concept. Paul began his career as an accountant. After working his way up to a partnership in Peat Marwick, he and Vicki decided that what they really wanted in life was freedom from routine, and the opportunity to travel. Paul retired at age 35, and for the past 18 years Paul and Vicki have made do on a modest income from their investments, while leisurely wandering the world.

After retirement they spent eight years in Argentina, then lived in Mexico, London, Thailand, Bali, Australia, Paris, and even had a couple short stints in the United States. Often they just hit the road for several months, revisiting their favorite countries or exploring new ones. Right now, they're spending a few months in my current hometown of Carlsbad, California.

Since they've chosen to remain U.S. citizens, there are no significant tax advantages to their PT lifestyle. They file tax returns every year and meticulously declare all investment income, in spite of the fact that their investment accounts are offshore. And they are careful not to do anything that would constitute legal residence in any state with a personal income tax. Thus, they carry Nevada driver's licenses, and keep their financial records and mailing address in the state of Washington (several states including Nevada, Texas, Florida and Washington do not tax personal incomes).

To Paul and Vicki, the allure of the PT life has less to do with keeping out from under the scrutiny of Big Brother and minimizing taxes than with being free of the routines. Travel and exploration is their idea of the sovereign life.

If the PT life sounds attractive, it's probably more achievable than you might imagine. The communications revolution has dissolved the chains that bound many professions to urban offices. However, Paul and Vicki have demonstrated that if you're willing to trade the security of roots and possessions for travel and leisure, it can be done on a very modest income.

They've written about their own strategies to show the way. Paul's book, *Cashing In on The American Dream: How to Retire at 35* is presently out of print, but you can learn about their techniques and follow them in their travels through their Web site, www.geocities.com/TheTropics/Shores/5315.

While not everyone will find being a perpetual traveler fulfilling, it still makes sense to increase our personal sovereignty by adopting any of the elements of the PT concept that fit. The full PT plan includes holding citizenship in one country; maintaining official residence in a second; if not retired, domiciling your business in a third; and keeping investment accounts in one or more others. In each case, the country chosen should provide the best and most advanced laws for minimizing taxes, optimizing business and investment opportunities, and providing maximum privacy and legal protection from lawsuits.

Then, if your business permits and you enjoy travel, you can live the PT life by spending your time in the most interesting places around the world in their prime seasons—London or Aspen in July and August, January and February in the Bahamas or New Zealand, April and May in Paris, and so on.

The goal of every sovereign individual is to maintain control of his or her life and property, which coincide nicely with the PT concept. These are goals for which members of The Sovereign Society can strive to achieve.

PT: What's It All About?
PT, 1996

A philosophy and a way of life for those willing to roam the world seeking maximum freedom and personal liberty.

Do you want to escape the control over your life and property now held by modern Big Brother government? The PT concept could be called "individual sovereignty," because PTs look after themselves. We do not want or need authorities to dominate every aspect of our existence.

The PT concept is to break free. It is a coherent philosophy, a plan for a stress-free, healthy, prosperous life unlimited by government interference, threats of war, environmental contamination, litigation, domestic conflicts, taxation, persecution or harassment. PT offers escape. It is a way out of any negative situation. Many individuals choose to vent their frustrations with acts of violence. The PT merely avoids conflict by refusing to play where the rules are unfair.

What Does PT Mean?

PT stands for many things, Perpetual Traveler or Permanent Tourist, for instance. However, a PT need not always travel. The PT merely arranges his paperwork so that all governments consider him a tourist, a person just Passing Through. In the eyes of government officials, the PT is merely on a temporary sojourn, and as such is not subject to taxes, military service, lawsuits or persecution. Unlike most citizens or subjects, the PT will not be persecuted for his beliefs or lack of them.

PT is a concept, a way of life, a way of perceiving the universe and finding your place in it. One can be a dedicated PT all the time or part-time. PT is elegant, simple and requires no accountants, attorneys, offshore corporations or other complex arrangements. It's the Perfect Thing.

Governments, under the guise of protecting us, intrude into every area of life, taking our earnings in taxes and rewarding us with restrictions and harassment. Modern government has virtually eliminated individual privacy and continues to limit freedom of choice in many areas of human activity. The constitutions of most nations give lip-service to the absolute freedom to travel, but in practice governments severely limit travel with passport, visa and other requirements.

Personal finances, currency controls, domestic situations and job requirements make the freedom to go anywhere at anytime just a dream for most people. The properly equipped PT operates outside the usual rules, gaining perfect mobility and full human rights. PT is the logical and natural path to freedom from political whims and destructive bureaucracy.

Perpetual Traveler

PTs, People of Talent, can, at a few strokes of the pen, be truly free of Big Brother. Since oppressors and exploiters in the modern world exercise control with paperwork and computers, your prime objective is to disappear from all lists and registers of any kind. Once that is accomplished, your present government will lose interest in you. You have ceased to be a citizen or subject. It is the goal of the PT to achieve this invisibility by acquiring a new nationality and an offshore address.

PT freedom extends beyond monetary concerns. Neither the PT nor his family need be inconvenienced by government-instigated wars or military service. The flexibility and mobility of being a PT means you will never be an unwilling draftee, victim, inmate, casualty or refugee. PTs pick their fights and choose their surroundings. They are not swept along in torrents caused by forces beyond their control.

The PT remains comfortably beyond the reach of Big Brother's grasp. Governments cannot easily attack or wipe out an amorphous group with no consistent behavior patterns. Government officials see PTs as the most desirable kind of tourist, respectful of local authority, low profile and prosperous. Thus, unlike publicity-seeking tax rebels, a PT courts no danger and invites no confrontations.

Avoid Taxes Legally

By merely moving abroad and establishing a legally recognized residence and domicile in a tax haven, an investor can legally avoid handing over half of his income to the bureaucrats. He is free to roam the world, provided he does not remain anywhere long enough to be considered a resident for tax purposes. Thus, the PT avoids most income taxes without resorting to fraud, because fraud is unnecessary. In most cases a theoretically perfect PT need never file tax returns, government-required disclosure forms or other needless paperwork.

If you don't enjoy forcible extractions from your bank account or restrictions on your basic human rights, then you can easily move and declare yourself to be a legal resident of any place you please. No government has the legal right or ability to tax a PT who neither lives within its borders permanently nor has any assets there.

The PT is free to enrich the world with his talent, skills, invention, industry or artistry and then enjoy 100 percent of the fruits of his enterprise. Unlimited, untaxed wealth and the power to dispose of it as you please are two of the major benefits of becoming a PT. PTs can produce good things, be paid in full without withholdings or deductions and then spend their earnings as they please.

PT Possibilities

As PTs, only self-imposed restrictions can keep us from experiencing the wonders of the world. The PT can and will drive, fly or sail across international frontiers, moving freely without need of exit permits or entry visas. The PT is able to move fast and decisively, to disappear and resurface anywhere, anytime. PTs believe one must raise self-consciousness about the nature of freedom and rid one's self of limitations.

PT Means True Freedom

PTs can study any philosophy, raise and educate our children in our beliefs and opinions without contradiction from government-controlled school curriculum. We can pass on our knowledge according to our inner lights. We need not follow the dictates of an obtuse school commissar who bans books and forbids truths we find self-evident.

As PTs we are able to invent, reject or follow any religion, personal morality or way of life we choose. For those with unconventional thoughts, habits or beliefs, PT is the answer. PTs need not abide by regulations or laws they find offensive, inconvenient or immoral. PT is all about options. The more options, the greater the freedom.

This freedom does not mean a PT can be irresponsible, causing problems, injury or pain to others. As PTs we can vote with our feet, but the trip doesn't have to be irrevocable or permanent. The PT can leave until things get better, then return. The PT gains the world, while giving up nothing except the treadmill that is life as most people know it.

Follow Your Heart

by Gary Scott, *The Sovereign Individual*, July 1999

How two world travelers found just the right home simply by following the dictates of their hearts.

Those who choose to change residence to regain control over their lives often jump from the frying pan into the fire. Recently, I received a call from a reader who told me he was moving out of the United States to get away from Big Brother and reduce taxes.

"Have you ever lived abroad?" I asked. "Never have," he replied. "Visit first," was all I could add, knowing that it's usually cheaper to live in the United States and pay tax.

I have found there is a better process than checking tax regimes to figure out where to live. To start this process, look within, rather than without. Look for ways to do more of what you want and should do with people you like. The action you take in life is more important than money.

If you follow your heart (intuition) and invest and live in places that interest and attract you, your life gets better and your financial success will grow. When you are no longer consumed by money, it comes more easily. When you are on your own unique and correct path, synchronicity takes over and resolves issues that may formerly have appeared to be unresolvable.

Intuition Works!

To show how this works, allow me to share what happened to my wife, Merri, and me when we left the United States and began investing in and moving toward our dreams.

I have been concerned with the Y2K millennium bug for years. But what can one do? This computer problem is so complex no one knows what will really happen. How much should one do to prepare? I was grappling with this problem when our hearts became enthralled with the people who are Inca descendants and live in Ecuador. We became so involved in the Andes that I forgot about Y2K and started an Ecuadorian business. We followed our intuition and the monetary rewards became better than we could have ever imagined.

Exactly the right people, land, ideas and information popped up exactly when they were needed. Call it synchronicity, felicity or just good luck, but an extra financial power came along when we let go of our monetary motives and began to follow our dreams.

The magic worked in every way. For example, we had been trying for years to find a farm in North Carolina and nothing had seemed to work. Yet, when we decided with our Ecuadorian partners that we needed such a place in the Blue Ridge Mountains, a farm that the owners had previously refused to sell suddenly became available. But the deal was even better. Along with the 179 acres we expected and had tried to buy (without success) an extra 28 acres were thrown in free.

Suddenly the perfect plantation we needed in Ecuador also appeared at just the perfect altitude, the perfect location, perfect pure volcanic water and natural organic food supply and of course, the perfect price.

But the benefits of this approach reached into all levels. For example, Merri and I had no thought about the Y2K benefits when we started planning our Ecuadorian move, yet we ended up with a Y2K solution better than we could ever have conceived. We'll begin the new millennium living on land where we are self-sufficient in food, water and energy. Our Ecuadorian friends who live there with us are almost Y2K proof as their culture has lived beautifully without much technology for the last 500 years!

We started the venture because of our interest and not money or the need to protect ourselves from Y2K. Yet, we expect this venture to be very profitable and our Y2K needs have been resolved.

Apparent Tax Benefits

The benefits don't end there. My tax attorney told me that I had stumbled into one of the greatest tax benefits around. On the land, we are developing a center for longevity in a 50 percent partnership with local villagers. The center will offer ancient purification techniques that the Andeans have never before shared. Because this is half owned by non-Americans, the center can defer U.S. taxes on its business income. All we had to worry about was Ecuadorian tax.

We did not start this business as a tax shelter. Our goal was to help protect and preserve the wonderful valley where the center is situated, to help employ Ecuadorians, and to help share the wondrous Ecuadorian knowledge.

But the synchronicity didn't end there. A second incredible tax benefit appeared. Just as we began moving, Ecuador abolished all income and corporate tax. We'll live in Ecuador tax free!

When you follow your heart and not just your tax advisor you become more independent, self-sufficient, altruistic, connected, revitalized and respected, and gain a greater self-worth. You automatically become a better investor too!

You don't have to abandon your investing disciplines either. Quite the opposite. By narrowing your participation into areas you really enjoy, you'll have more time to apply greater economic sense and thought to your endeavors. Plus, you'll gain help from the universe you can't acquire in any other way. This can quickly put you on the path to personal sovereignty and wealth.

Big Brother's Tyranny
PT, 1996

There is not an adult alive who has not had unpleasant or annoying encounters with government bureaucrats. These experiences should serve as warnings of what to expect in more important matters. Serious, life-threatening troubles with government are like cancer. They strike unexpectedly. You could be lucky, but it is not always the guy next door who will be the victim, crushed by the grinding wheels of bureaucracy.

Government actions, not cancer, AIDS or heart attacks, have been the greatest killers throughout history. They are the primary cause of human injuries and premature death. Governments, not natural disasters, bear most of the blame for the suffering in the world. Vast numbers of good patriotic citizens are murdered in needless wars, displaced by government engineered relocations or starved by famines caused by government intentions or stupidity.

We do not have to look far to find examples of good, innocent people whose lives have been needlessly destroyed by oppressive systems. The former Soviet Union used to drug dissidents and confine them to mental wards. They were not alone.

Consider the case of the German-Jewish teenager whose biography I recently read. He was shipped to boarding school in England during the Hitler era. In England, he was not permitted to finish the schooling that had been prepaid for him, but instead was interned as an enemy alien for the duration of the war. No matter which way he turned, government, those seen by historians as both good and bad, sought only to take away his freedom or his life.

All extreme right- and left-wing governments are ruthless, inhuman and well-organized oppressors. They don't let civilized concepts of human rights stand in their way. Governments are, always have been and always will be dangerous, warlike and immoral institutions. No government is innocent of such proclivities, unless it is totally inept, powerless and inefficient. Belize, Portugal and Costa Rica come close to our ideal. After all, anarchy does permit the most individual freedom.

In war and in peace, in democracies or in dictatorships, under capitalists or under communists, strong centralized governments can make original thinking or succeeding visibly in any endeavor dangerous to your health. Governments are like fires, they can be useful. A fire can warm, if you can control it. A fire can also cook your goose. Sooner or later you will surely be involved in a confrontation with Big Brother. For those who have not read George Orwell's classic satire *1984*, in which the expression "Big Brother" was coined for the first time, get a copy and do so at once. Thus prepared, you will gain a better understanding of what I perceive as a clear and present danger: rampant government and big bureaucracy. In most democratic countries, there is the illusion that citizens control government, but the reality is that Big Brother is here today and will not be gone tomorrow.

Western man in our present day Big Brother world is nothing more than a dog on a leash. And that leash is getting shorter, due to the ridiculous and destructive laws that have been passed. The laws in most countries are so pervasive that one cannot get out of bed and engage in any economic activity for even a single day without breaking enough laws to go to prison. Everyone who is or has been in an executive position or who has owned his own business knows exactly what I am talking about.

Record-keeping requirements alone are almost impossible to maintain. Individuals of every occupation and profession, even those on the dole, are required to file a multitude of documents and papers, all within restricted time limits. A seemingly infinite number of worthless rules, laws, regulations and legal precedents can get even the most honest person into hot water.

Furthermore, many activities previously considered to be purely civil matters have been reclassified as criminal offenses. The difference between civil and criminal penalties is enormous. If you lose a civil case, you pay damages. If government is involved, civil damages usually take the form of back taxes or relatively reasonable fines. However, if criminal charges have been brought against you, jail may well be your next stop. No, you will not be allowed to pass go, but all of your assets will probably be confiscated. Also, as criminal cases are easier to win and offer more opportunities of career advancement for prosecutors, few civil cases remain purely civil these days. There are, unfortunately, few areas of human activity remaining that cannot in some way land you in jail when things go wrong.

Working in combination with this increase in senseless legislation is an alarming decline in personal privacy in most parts of the world. Nameless, faceless petty government officials can press a few buttons to find out what magazines you read, what videos you rent, where you travel, whom you call or who calls you. In the modern electronic world, it is a simple matter for government investigators to uncover every financial transaction you have ever made, or at least those that appear in your proper name with your proper taxpayer identification number.

Armed with such information, a skilled team of investigators can, if they wish, apply pressure or build a legal case against you for many victimless crimes from adultery to tax evasion, or for having failed to meet one of a myriad of technical requirements. Government or private investigators can and will quickly find out how much money you earn and where it is deposited or invested. They can also dig up quite a few damaging "facts" that are completely incorrect as a great deal of the information is culled from other people's files, intercepted mail and a mish-mash of unreliable sources and misinterpreted material. Unfortunately, you can never know for certain what they have in their mound of manure.

Although this proliferation of new and senseless laws and the accompanying decline in personal freedom may look accidental, there is method to the madness. As almost no one is in full 100 percent compliance with the various laws and regulations now in existence, we all become criminals by definition. Government prosecutors like a situation in which everyone is a potential criminal and thus a potential victim. The fact that we are not all prosecuted is due to luck and selective enforcement. The government cannot go after all law breakers. Big Brother can only shoot down those who provoke confrontations or otherwise stand out from the crowd.

Written in the Whirlwind

by Robert E. Bauman, JD, September 1998

There's an old saying about "straws in the wind" indicating future events. If true, the international monsoon directed against legal tax avoidance should tell us something about the future. What we're seeing is an official hurricane headed directly at legitimate offshore tax, business and banking haven nations. And if the tax-hungry bureaucrats have their way, national sovereignty and independence will top the casualty disaster list.

It's all part of a concerted battle Big Brother government is waging against personal liberty on many fronts. The Brussels bureaucrats running the European Union, under the hypocritical banner of "tax harmonization" (meaning "high taxes for all"), demand an EU-wide withholding tax on interest income earned by foreigners. Alternately they want a snitch-reporting system that informs a non-resident interest earner's home government of any and all offshore income.

In London, the Labour government demands "reform" of financial laws in the Channel Islands and on the Isle of Man. Never mind that these constitutionally independent territories have had the right to enact such laws as they see fit since the Norman Conquest. Whitehall bluntly has informed Jersey, Guernsey and the Isle of Man they must write foreign tax evasion into local law as a criminal offense. Similarly, U.K. pressure is mounting on offshore dependencies such as Bermuda and the Cayman Islands to enact "all crimes" money laundering laws (including tax evasion) that go far beyond anything ever envisioned as anti-drug measures. In defiance, the Caymans and the British Virgin Islands, bless them, have adopted statutes specifically excluding "fiscal crimes."

What should worry freedom lovers everywhere is that "tax avoidance" is now being rewritten to mean "tax evasion" both wrapped neatly into the all-purpose indictment of "money laundering." Throw in police forfeiture powers and you have a tax collectors' nirvana. Instant, self-financing government tax grabs.

At a June 1998 conference in New York, the United Nations sought to impose this expansive redefinition on the world at large. The draft UN report argues the common theme in financial crimes is the "enabling machinery" that exists in haven nations. The UN sees these haven nations (18 in the Caribbean, 16 in Europe, 11 in Asia and 6 in the Middle East and Africa) as "an enormous hole in the international legal and financial system" that must be plugged firmly and fast.

In effect, the UN wants to end and/or control the "proliferation" of offshore trusts and international business corporations, attorney-client privilege, use of free trade zones and the operation of gambling casinos. For good measure, they demand an enforceable international financial reporting system in which all nations will be forced to participate. Goodbye national sovereignty!

The UN minces few words in demanding that the world must "face the issue of the use of sovereignty by some countries to give citizens of other countries a way around the laws of their own society." Can we now expect to see multinational tax-collecting expeditions dispatched to Panama or the British Virgin Islands? Will CNN flash scenes of legions of armed accountants flooding ashore in the Cook Islands under the UN banner?

The *Wall Street Journal* editorially questioned Europe's lack of concerted action in foreign policy matters. "The EU's most obvious deficiency is that it lacks the military muscle to back up its declarations." It also needs political unanimity, which Switzerland and Luxembourg are unlikely to grant on most financial restriction issues.

But who knows what will happen? After years of talk, diplomats meeting in Rome on July 17, 1998 created an international court to punish those who commit "war crimes and atrocities." One-hundred twenty nations, including all those in Europe, voted for it; six (including the U.S., Israel, India and China) opposed; and 21 abstained. The court, destined for location in the Hague, the World Court's long-time hang out, will step in when a nation's justice system is deemed by other nations as being unable or unwilling to act.

The day may come when a gradual redefinition (as with money laundering) will expand the scope of "war crimes" to include the "war" against tax avoidance. The Nuremberg Trials will be child's play by comparison.

[**Ed. Note**: *In 2003 the world criminal court came into existence at The Hague, with the United States government refusing to participate or recognize its claimed jurisdiction over U.S. diplomats or members of the U.S. military.*]

Speaking of freedom, in 1976 the late U.S. Supreme Court justice, William O. Douglas, warned, "As nightfall does not come all at once, neither does oppression. In both instances, there is a twilight when everything remains seemingly unchanged. And it is in such twilight that we all must be most aware of change in the air 'however slight,' lest we become unwitting victims of the darkness."

Adopt a New Country
by Marshall J. Langer, *The Tax Exile Report*, 1997

A noted international tax expert shares with you his ideas about how to reduce your taxes to an absolute minimum—if you are willing to make a new home for yourself.

I personally believe you would be much better off moving to another country than you would be trying to roam the world just a step ahead of those who may pursue you.

Some advisers suggest that the best way to escape from Big Brother's tax clutches is to become a low-profile world traveler. I disagree. That may have worked well in the pre-computer days when people could simply disappear from the system never to surface again.

Today, if you are a significant taxpayer in any high-tax country, the government's computers should quickly notice your absence. The tax authorities may simply monitor your situation on an ongoing basis, waiting for the right time to pounce.

It is very difficult to become a true world traveler in today's computerized world. If you move from a high-tax country to a tax haven such as the Cayman Islands everyone will know exactly what you have done. If, on the other hand, you move from one high-tax country to another high-tax country you may not be watched nearly as closely. In fact, some high-tax countries treat new-comers rather well. I suggest that you consider establishing a new homeland in a hospitable high-tax country rather than moving to a notorious tax haven or wandering from place to place forever.

The Growing Sovereign Individual Movement
by Nicholas Pullen, 1998

Globalization of the world economy and the advent of immensely improved telecommunications have for many made it possible to live where we "want" to live rather than where we "have" to live. So says Roger Gallo in his excellent book, *Escape From America*. Though the title of the book suggests a work exclusively for U.S. citizens it is, in fact, an indispensable resource for any individual seeking to escape the negative impositions of any government. And every day more individuals are seeking to do just that.

Everywhere, people are choosing to escape restrictions, limitations and complications at "home" by physically relocating themselves and their affairs to countries where they can enjoy greater freedom.

Freedom Desired

The freedoms these people desire take many forms and depend as much on individual considerations as anything else. I have spoken to numerous individuals who have waved goodbye to their "home" government in order to enjoy their own particular brand of freedom. Their motivations were many and varied.

Some were sick and tired of paying high taxes. No longer prepared to be milked like cattle, they chose to relocate to countries where they get to keep more of their hard-earned wealth.

Some were tired of relentless government infringement and intrusion at home. So they relocated to countries where personal and financial privacy are still respected.

Some felt unsafe at home. They wanted to be free of high crime levels, avaricious litigants, malevolent bureaucrats and corrupt politicians. So they moved to countries offering security, political stability and social harmony.

Some felt they could secure better opportunities and a better future for their children than were available at home by relocating to younger, emerging countries with healthier economies.

Many people left their home shores to go in search of places where they could enjoy a significantly lower cost of living, cut-price real estate and service charges considerably less inflated than their equivalent at home. Others left home to enjoy a more attractive climate, a better environment, a more relaxed pace of life and, in one case I know about, better skiing and a thriving social scene.

Every expatriate I spoke to had cast off the shackles imposed by their home government for different reasons. But they all agree on one fundamental point: increased mobility and sophisticated technology make it perfectly practicable to live and conduct business, financial and personal affairs from almost anywhere in the world.

A computer, a modem and a telephone line make it perfectly feasible for anybody to stay in touch with friends and family, run a business, work and remain in contact with financial advisors, bankers and professionals worldwide at the touch of a button. And the rest of the world is never more than a flight away.

This is the gospel of the Sovereign Individual. And the word is spreading.

Flight from the U.S.

We only have to take a look at U.S. State Department figures issued toward the end of 1997. These illustrate how the principles of the Sovereign Individual are catching on in the U.S. There are now 3.3 million Americans living abroad (excluding government and military personnel). Over the last 30 years the number of Americans going offshore to seek out lower living costs, better lifestyles and more freedoms has quadrupled. And the rate of exit continues to accelerate. Every year, more and more Americans are waving farewell to Uncle Sam and relocating to every corner of the globe where freedoms remain available and intact.

The U.S. State Department used to publish annual statistics on the number of Americans renouncing their citizenship, but this information is no longer being made public. It isn't hard to figure out why. High tax bracket Americans must renounce their citizenship to escape from the U.S. tax net, which is imposed on all citizens regardless of residence. With countless thousands of Americans paying seven-digit tax bills while receiving little in the way of benefits to show for it, it isn't hard to understand why an exodus of the best and brightest has begun.

Flight from Europe

And it isn't just Americans turning their backs on their countries of origin. Every week I speak to Germans, Britons, Dutch, French, Scandinavians and individuals of every conceivable nationality who are unhappy with the services and rights their taxes buy at home. These people are looking for alternative governments, alternative service providers who offer cheaper services, less restrictions, more freedom and an improved quality of life.

Simply flipping through the papers on the desk in front of me and reading some of the reports and bulletins sent in by contacts, it becomes blatantly evident why so many people are disillusioned by life at "home."

The German government has been particularly busy attacking privacy lately. German police officers were awarded the right to bug private homes and eavesdrop on private conversations. Federal agencies in the U.S. have 15,000 "wild, out of control" informants on their payrolls. Now the Germans want to play follow-my-leader. The German tax department is eagerly awaiting the outcome of a Finance Ministry meeting which will consider awarding cash rewards to informants who squeal on tax evaders. It is easy to foresee the abuses to which such activities could lead.

In Switzerland, the police have been secretly following mobile phone users through a telephone computer company. In Britain, mobile phone companies are understood to have come to an arrangement with law enforcement agencies to provide coding information on individual phones used by suspected criminals. This will mean the police can track anybody who has their mobile phone switched on.

All over Europe, bank employees are being used as unpaid government informers, and cameras and surveillance equipment are springing up at seaports, airports, on roads, in the streets and in public buildings. We are told this development is to fight crime. But all too often in the past we have seen technology originally introduced to fight crime subsequently directed at private, non-criminal citizens.

If you live in the U.K., on any average day you are caught on camera up to 14 times. Many Western governments are working on and introducing technology capable of scanning individual faces and recording them. Pretty soon it will be difficult for Westerners to move without their government's surveillance network knowing about it and recording it.

And you won't need reminding that every day that ever dawns in the U.S. sees possibly innocent, unsuspecting individuals embroiled in the latest deployment of draconian civil asset forfeiture laws or predatory litigation. Every day sees fresh civil liberties violations. Every day sees the death of another freedom.

Exodus No Surprise

We shouldn't be surprised that people have had a gut full. We shouldn't be surprised that more and more individuals are voting with their feet. On the evidence of the above we should only be surprised that more Americans and Europeans aren't following the example.

Inevitably more will. This is the age of the Sovereign Individual. Increasing mobility and sophisticated telecommunications technology has made it possible to find freedom offshore without sacrificing earning potential, personal relationships or convenience.

When you relocate offshore the only things you sacrifice are your relationships with a government that doesn't respect your freedom and a tax authority that only has eyes for your personal wealth. I don't think the termination of either of these relationships is a sacrifice. I think of the end of such nightmarish associations as a blessing.

Your Own Escape Plan?

You may already be numbered among these sovereign individuals enjoying your new-found freedom. It may be that you are already considering escaping your government yourself.

If you fall into the latter category you may want to consider the findings of a study published by the Swiss-based Corporate Resource Group rating the best cities worldwide for expatriates to live in. The survey focuses on "quality of living issues" and rates cities for political and economic stability, crime, pollution, health, environment and schooling.

The top ten ranked cities for expatriates were, in descending order: Vancouver, Auckland, Toronto, Zurich, Geneva, Melbourne, Sydney, Helsinki, Vienna and Brussels.

If you're considering looking for a suitable destination to escape to or even weighing up the options just in case you need to move fast in the future, you might focus your initial research on these cities.

Are You a Libertarian?
by Vincent H. Miller, 1998

One of its American leaders recalls the history and growth of the Libertarian movement—and asks you to examine your own political conscience.

What is a libertarian? The catch phrase, "Fiscally conservative; socially liberal," explains it—sort of. But simplifications often lose the essence of what they describe. Basically a libertarian is a person who believes in individual liberty, an unregulated market economy and social tolerance for diverse lifestyles. It's a "live and let live" philosophy.

The foundation of libertarianism is the Non-Aggression Principle, which states that no one may initiate force or fraud against others. This is sometimes stated as, "First, do no harm," or in the biblical turn of phrase, "Thou shalt not aggress."

Many libertarians trace their roots back to the eighteenth and nineteenth century classical free trade liberals to England's Adam Smith, John Locke, John Cobden, Richard Bright, French philosopher Frederic Bastiat and others. Others look to nineteenth-century American individualist anarchists such as William Lloyd Garrison, Lysander Spooner, and Henry David Thoreau.

Modern Growth

The modern libertarian movement, however, has been most strongly influenced by the late Austrian economist Ludwig Von Mises, Mises' protege and Nobel Laureate, F. A. Hayek, and Nobel Laureate Milton Friedman of the University of Chicago.

Perhaps the most influential of all was the novelist and philosopher Ayn Rand, whose novels, plays, and essays strongly influenced the new wave of libertarians. The message of her epic novel *Atlas Shrugged* has been so powerful that a joint survey by the Book of the Month Club and the Library of Congress ranked *Atlas Shrugged* second only to the Bible as the book that had most influenced people's lives.

Although there have been pockets of libertarian influence throughout history, the modern movement began to gain momentum in the 1940s. With the founding of Leonard Read's Foundation for Economic Education at Irvington-on-Hudson, New York, and the near-simultaneous publication of Rand's *The Fountainhead*, Hayek's *The Road to Serfdom*, Isabel Paterson's *The God of the Machine*, Rose Wilder Lane's *The Discovery of Freedom* and Mises' *Human Action*, the modern libertarian movement took its first steps. It wasn't until the publication of *Atlas Shrugged* in 1957 that the Libertarian movement as we know it today regained its stride.

During those earliest years, a whole generation was inspired by Rand's libertarian message of individualism and uncompromising free-market capitalism. It was all the more amazing given that libertarianism began evolving during the era of President Roosevelt's socialist/fascist New Deal.

Libertarian pioneers such as author Rose Wilder Lane and H. L. Mencken, columnist for the Baltimore *Evening Sun*, vigorously attacked the socialism and collectivism of the New Deal and paved the way for a much larger and more influential movement which later developed.

A seminal moment of the modern libertarian movement was the 1969 convention of the pioneer young conservative group, Young Americans for Freedom (YAF) in St Louis, Missouri.

Since the founding in 1960 of this association of young Barry Goldwater conservatives, there had been an uneasy peace between YAF's traditionalist conservative wing and the libertarian-Randian wing. Libertarian opposition to the Vietnam War, the military draft and other human rights issues finally erupted into full-scale political war. This confrontation resulted in a purge of the libertarians, who left en masse and met under St. Louis Gateway Arch to found a new movement.

Luminaries such as Karl Hess, author of the 1960 Republican platform and a former Goldwater-Nixon-Ford speech writer, Leonard Liggio, who would later become president of the Institute for

Humane Studies, and most of the International Society for Individual Liberty's (ISIL) current board members were there. At this time ISIL's sister organization the Society for Individual Liberty (SIL) was formed as an umbrella group for disenfranchised libertarians.

From this new beginning the movement grew. SIL produced a comprehensive series of educational pamphlets which sold in the millions. They organized tax protest days, and created a network of activist student chapters in colleges and universities across the nation. In 1971, SIL member David F. Nolan founded the Libertarian Party in his Denver, Colorado, living room.

In the years following the historic 1969 conservative/libertarian split, many of the movement's intellectual institutions formed: Laissez Faire Books, *Reason* magazine and the Reason Foundation, the Cato Institute, the Institute for Humane Studies, the Ludwig von Mises Institute and more.

An Intellectual Force

Today libertarianism in America, if not a major success at the ballot box, is an intellectual force to be reckoned with.

One of the key contributions of the libertarian movement has been its critical examination and analysis of the proper role of government. This is a subject libertarians take very seriously. For many years the standard line was that since governments enjoy a monopoly on the use of force, its proper role should be limited to those agencies in which such powers seem appropriate, i.e., police, military and courts. Nothing else.

An impressive body of literature has arisen from the pens of libertarian scholars challenging the role of government in today's society. They have observed that it is difficult to find anything that governments touch that is not eventually turned into a cesspool of corruption, patronage and mind-boggling waste.

Competitive markets in a free economy, they assert, can provide most if not all the essential services currently provided by government.

Many in the movement, including David Friedman, son of Milton Friedman and author of a seminal book entitled *The Machinery of Freedom*, explain that virtually every function currently provided by governments can be provided better and more inexpensively—not to mention more compassionately—by competitive market institutions.

There are interesting arguments of great merit from both sides of this debate. How much better would it be, for example, if organizations like the United Way, churches or other charitable organizations handled welfare instead of government?

For example, in America the government wastes over 80 percent of its welfare dollars on mammoth bureaucracies and their palatial offices, whereas private charities reverse these figures. The Social Security system is bankrupt and inflicts a terrible tax burden on the younger generation. Why not take it out of the hands of corrupt politicians and privatize it? There is a vast library of literature on the privatization of most governmental functions by the world's leading scholars. For those interested, Laissez Faire Books can provide the proper research material. Their book service and informative catalogue is one of the treasures of the libertarian movement.

In 1980, I founded the Libertarian International in Ann Arbor, Michigan, with the assistance of Bruce Evoy of Toronto (founder of the Canadian Libertarian Party). In 1982, the first world conference of libertarians was held in Zurich, Switzerland. This event brought together widely diverse groups of classical liberals, libertarians and Ayn Rand Objectivists from all over Europe and the world (few of whom had been aware of their brothers and sisters in neighboring countries). A world network was established which attracted an amazingly powerful group of activists and intellectuals.

Former industrialist Hubert Jongen of Holland rapidly organized a network of European libertarians, which to this day meets quarterly in Amsterdam. He also organized the 1983 ISIL World Conference in Brussels.

In 1989 the Libertarian International and the original SIL merged to form the International

Society for Individual Liberty. The original founders of both of these pioneering organizations formed the board of the new educational foundation.

Since then, world conferences have been held in most European countries and, after the fall of the Berlin Wall, in many of the former Eastern Bloc countries—the Czech and Slovak Republics, Estonia and Russia. Economics and human rights conferences were held in Swaziland, Southeast Africa, Mexico's Yucatan—even one in San Francisco.

Our members became major figures in their home countries. South African advisory board members Leon Louw and Frances Kendall were nominated three times for the Nobel Peace Prize for their work to defuse the explosive environment in their country by installing a Swiss-styled cantonal system—and for setting up a law review project to repeal hundreds of the oppressive apartheid laws. They also had significant input into the drafting of a new Bill of Rights for South Africa.

In recent years, we have sponsored hundreds of struggling activists in the developing world, as well as the former countries of the Soviet Eastern Bloc.

Today, we are providing support for courageous individuals who are setting up free-market organizations in Belarus, Albania, Serbia and Croatia to name a few countries. We have sponsored translations of Rand's books into Russian and Romanian.

We believe that the world is in for a rough ride over the next decade, but that the twenty-first century holds the promise of a renaissance of freedom. Libertarians will remain on the front lines of the battle for free markets and free minds. We invite you to join us.

Ayn Rand: A Very Special Person
PT, 1996

An examination of the origins and theories put forth by the noted author and influential founder of the Objectivist philosophy.

Governments like the idea that innocent people suffer at the hands of new legislation. They know that in our modern world, anyone who achieves any degree of success also inherently becomes a lawbreaker along the way. As a result of this arrangement, they can prosecute almost anyone at almost any time.

The fact that the laws broken are silly, if not utterly ridiculous, does not in any way mitigate the severity of a conviction. Again, it seems that those responsible for shaping the movements of government have done their homework. Just as George Orwell demonstrated the need to have a fictitious enemy, Ayn Rand showed the benefits that a government can enjoy by transforming its entire population into ipso facto criminals.

A Russian expatriate who fled to the United States from Soviet Russia in the 1920s, Ayn Rand went on to become one of the leading authors of this century. Her success is based largely on the public acclaim she received for both her novels and philosophical volumes, but also comes from her general outlook on life.

In her view, life belongs exclusively to the individual who shall, in turn, be absolutely free to do with it whatever he pleases, as long as the rights of others are not transgressed. In 1957, Rand published her stunning and immensely significant novel *Atlas Shrugged* (out of print in Britain, it is still available from Signet Books, New York). In her work, Rand explains exactly how things work in the real world and what may happen if too many people lose sight of the facts. More terrifying still is the realization that much of what Rand predicted has already begun to happen in almost every western country.

Set in the U.S. (without mentioning any specific year), the backdrop for *Atlas Shrugged* is industry and the people who make it work. The heroes, according to Rand, are not unionized workers who alternate between whining for shorter hours and demanding more pay for less work, but rather a few, rare capitalists, without whose constant quest for efficiency and profit the engine of the world would stop. In the novel, a number of senseless laws are introduced by government. All are, officially, passed for the common good and public welfare. Competition is restricted by law, lest old and inefficient companies with bloated payrolls lose ground to new, ambitious upstarts. Plans are introduced to spread profits around, lest a few attain "excessive" riches.

An industrialist, Hank Rearden, invents a revolutionary metal, Rearden Metal. Suspicious, at first, over this new product, the world soon realizes that the invention holds supreme advantages over steel and will revolutionize just about every sector of industry. To make sure that Rearden does not discriminate against those customers who initially refused to buy his product, laws are passed that require him to put a quota-system into operation that ensures everyone will enjoy his state-guaranteed right to buy his "fair share" of the output. Even so, Rearden profits mightily due to his years of research and hard work. Soon rival mills, unable to compete against him with their old-fashioned steel, are driven to the brink of bankruptcy.

Making no excuses for his success, Rearden is in due course blackmailed by the government into giving up his patent rights so that all may share in the benefits of his invention. The following excerpt from the book is a verbal exchange between Rearden and Ferris, the emissary of Big Brother who visits the mills to announce the government blackmail.

"You honest men are such a headache, but we knew you'd slip up sooner or later—and this is just what we wanted."

"You seem to be pleased about it."

"Don't I have good reason to be?"

"But, after all, I did break one of your laws."

"Well, what do you think they're there for?"

Dr. Ferris did not notice the sudden look on Rearden's face, the look of a man hit by the first vision of that which he had sought to see. Dr. Ferris was past the stage of seeing; he was intent upon delivering the last blows to an animal caught in a trap.

"Did you really think that we want those laws to be observed?" said Dr. Ferris. "We want them broken. You'd better get it straight that it's not a bunch of boy scouts you're up against. We're after power and we mean it. You fellows were pikers, but we know the real trick, and you'd better get wise to it. There's no way to rule innocent men. The only power any government has is the power to crack down on criminals. Well, when there aren't enough criminals, one makes them. One declares so many things to be a crime that it becomes impossible for men to live without breaking laws. Who wants a nation of law-abiding citizens? What's there in that for anyone? But just pass the kind of laws that can neither be observed nor enforced nor objectively interpreted—and you create a nation of law-breakers—and then you cash in on guilt. Now that's the system, Mr. Rearden, that's the game, and once you understand it, you'll be much easier to deal with."

Translate this to modern-day politics and you quickly see that the so-called "war on drugs" is, in fact, nothing but an elaborate scare to make it legal for the state to invade everyone's privacy. A multitude of legislation introduced creates a situation where prosecutors can select and convict almost anyone of a drug-related crime.

If nothing else, *Atlas Shrugged* will open your eyes to what happens in both Europe and the U.S. once politicians, scheming intellectuals and over-ambitious bureaucrats are given too much of a say in your life.

The New Cold War: Wealth Is the Target

by Robert E. Bauman, JD, 1998

Knowledgeable U.S. lawyers, accountants and tax consultants will admit that the U.S. Internal Revenue Service (IRS) has declared war on Americans engaged in traditional offshore financial activity of nearly every kind.

It's a favorite IRS public relations tactic to issue dire "crack down" warnings and enforcement threats to keep taxpayers honest. In 1997, the IRS theme was stop "abusive trusts," both domestic and foreign, and those who sell them.

The IRS believes there is a host of alleged tax evaders and money launderers whom they presume guilty based on the financial tools the accused taxpayer uses. High on the prime IRS target list: those who set up and use international business corporations (IBCs), offshore trusts, and bank accounts in known "tax haven" nations, especially where financial privacy laws are strict.

This anti-wealth attack is coordinated with other federal agencies including the U.S. Department of Justice (DOJ), the Federal Reserve Board, the U.S. Treasury Department's Financial Crimes Enforcement Network (FinCEN), the Comptroller of the Currency, the Federal Bureau of Investigation, other appropriate police agencies, and sympathetic foreign governments like the U.K.

J. Richard Duke, Esq., a leading U.S. asset protection attorney from Birmingham, Alabama, sees the IRS agenda as "an indiscriminate attack on anyone who dares to shield wealth in ways that until now have been considered entirely legitimate."

Mr. Duke's view was echoed by Charles A. Cain of the U.K., editor of *Offshore Investment*, in a February 1998 editorial ("The New Cold War") in which he charged "the line between tax avoidance and tax evasion" is purposely being blurred by governments, with honest people (and their tax advisors) being jailed for "failed attempts at tax avoidance" while "tax evasion is put down on a moral level with heroine and cocaine pushing."

Among current programs IRS officials boast of:

- A computerized IRS "wire transfer project" that matches outbound and inbound wire transfers with individual income tax returns, or lack thereof. (Keep in mind the U.S. government has the ability to monitor virtually every electronic communication that occurs anywhere in the world.);

- A continuing review of suspicious IBCs, especially Panamanian IBCs using "bearer" shares;

- The "Offshore Internet Wagering Project" looking for unreported income from cyberspace gambling. Scores of people in the U.S. have been arrested for running Internet gambling operations;

- The auditing of tax returns of offshore trusts with U.S. offices primarily located in the Miami and Los Angeles areas; and

- A special effort by the IRS Criminal Investigation Division (CID) to search out "promoters" of alleged tax-evading legal structures, with the goal of indictment, as well as hitting their clients with back taxes due, penalties, interest and possible criminal charges.

IRS CID officials also revealed they now systematically train agents of the FBI, Central Intelligence Agency (CIA) and the U.S. Secret Service in tax aspects of international crime. They also train police agents from Russia, Spain, Mexico, Brazil, several Central American and Caribbean nations and have established formal "working relationships" with Canada, Germany and other nations.

Cold War Against Wealth

This is all part of a new international "Cold War," waged by government bureaucrats against anyone who seeks lower taxes and less financial regulation, especially those who choose to go off-shore. The IRS battle plan is a desperate grasp by Big Brother aimed at stopping those who rebel against heavy taxation and the transfer of wealth from productive citizens to unworthy tax consumers.

The tax collectors know the most talented citizens of the U.S., U.K. and other welfare states are deserting, setting up financial shop where they and their capital are treated best. This trend is intensified by the developing worldwide "cyber-economy" based on Internet technology and free communications unmediated by governments. What has been called the "permeability of financial frontiers" now empowers investors instantly to shift vast sums of money from one nation to another and from one currency to another. The 1998-99 "Asian crisis" demonstrated this heretofore unparalleled economic force.

Myopic liberals welcome these trends as the potential "collapse of nationhood," the chance to establish one-world government and control by institutions like the International Monetary Fund and the European Union.

Lovers of liberty with an acute sense of history see instead the potential for liberation of "the sovereign individual," the courageous person who declares independence from "decrepit and debilitating welfare states" as the *Wall Street Journal* described them. (For more on this debate, read *The Sovereign Individual*, by James Dale Davidson and Lord William Rees-Mogg, Simon & Schuster, US$25, 1997, an excellent book that explains the coming mass exodus of wealthy people from high tax nations.)

No wonder the U.K. Inland Revenue, the IRS and other tax hounds are worried. The Economist notes that "undeclared" (untaxed) work now exceeds 15 percent of Europe's combined gross domestic product (GDP), up from five percent in the 1970s. In the somewhat freer U.S., the underground "black market" economy accounts for nearly 10 percent of GDP. That means billions of dollars slipping through the eager hands of the tax man.

Why the growing black market? Confiscatory taxes, exorbitant labor costs, over regulation - all failures of big government. All things bureaucrats love.

This coordinated assault on wealth has a strong international dimension as well. The U.S., using its considerable powers, and the U.K., using old colonial ties, are turning the screws on national governments who fail or refuse to go along with the concerted anti-offshore wealth attack. Even greater pressure is being applied to international banks who do business in the U.S. or U.K., as well as in known tax and wealth "haven nations"—which means nearly every international bank.

As that firebrand of the American Revolution, Patrick Henry of Virginia said, "I am willing to know the whole truth, to know the worst, and to prepare for it. You have been forewarned and should act accordingly."

<hr>

Should You Become A Tax Exile?
by Marshall J. Langer, *The Tax Exile Report*, 1997

Most people are not likely to become tax exiles. Most Americans and some British are insular; they tend not to invest abroad and wouldn't think of moving to another country. This section is intended for those individuals who would consider obtaining a new citizenship and moving abroad.

A surprisingly large percentage of wealthy individuals seem to like the idea of being shorn like sheep. They live and work in high-tax countries and they allow their governments to take from them a substantial portion of everything they earn. They tolerate wealth taxes and transfer taxes that take away much of what they own, not only year-by-year but also when they try to transfer it to their loved ones by gift or inheritance. They sheepishly acquiesce as their governments use the power to tax to redistribute their wealth within the society. They tolerate an ever-increasing expansion of the Robin Hood theory of taxation, under which governments take from the middle class and the rich and give to the bureaucrats and some of the poor.

Taxes, Taxes, More Taxes

People generally understand that they have to pay some taxes if they expect to receive any services from their government. Most of us accept that taxes are the price we pay for a civilized society.

The problem is that many of us now feel—rightly I think—that we are being gouged by taxes, taxes on taxes, and more taxes. We pay federal taxes, state or provincial taxes and local taxes. We pay two levels of tax on corporate income—first at the corporate level and again at the shareholder level when dividends are paid. Salaries are subject to both a gross income tax (called social security) and a net income tax on the same earnings. Investment income is subject to two different forms of taxes—an income tax and inflation that strips away the value of the investment. Capital gains tax must often be paid not only on the real gain but also on the appreciation in value that is actually due to inflation.

Insular Americans

I have represented non-American clients for more than three decades. Many of my clients were either Europeans or former Europeans who had fled to Latin America just before the second World War. These people left nearly everything behind and struggled to build a new life in a new land. Most went to Latin America only because they couldn't get into the U.S. or Canada. Using their European know-how in third-world countries, some of them became immensely wealthy. One of their primary investment objectives was and still is international diversification. They keep perhaps one-third of their money in their new homeland and they divide the rest of it between Europe (mostly in Swiss banks) and North America. More recently, some of them have begun investing a small part of their wealth in the booming Pacific Basin.

Contrast this picture with Americans who typically invest all of their funds in the U.S. Until very recently, most Americans hesitated to put even a small percentage of their assets in as foreign a place as Canada. Anything more foreign than that was unthinkable. Only during the past two or three years have some Americans begun to buy U.S.-based mutual funds investing in the emerging markets of Asia and Latin America.

An article by Anatole Kaletsky in the *Times of London* discussed and tried to explain the insularity of Americans. Based on a study by Philip Tumer entitled *Capital Flows in the 1980s*, published by the Bank for International Settlements (BIS), Basel, Switzerland, the article asked:

> If Japanese, German and British investors have been diversifying their portfolios into dollars, why has this not been offset by American investors buying up assets in yen, marks and pounds? Financial analysts rarely stop to ask this obvious question. Perhaps it is because the answer, suggested in the BIS study, is too alarming, or simply too damaging to the financial markets' self-esteem.

The fact is that despite the apparently sophisticated and overdeveloped financial industry operating on Wall Street, American investors are among the most primitive and insular in the world. In 1990, American pension funds and life insurers each held only four percent of their portfolios in foreign assets. Among individual investors, international diversification is almost unheard of.

One reason for this is that, despite Washington's free-market rhetoric, America has some of the fiercest and most effective capital controls anywhere in the world. American banks make it almost impossible for individuals to hold foreign currencies, pension fund trustees frequently insist on "buy America" investment policies, and marketing restrictions imposed by the Securities and Exchange Commission make it illegal for American citizens to invest in most offshore equities, bonds and investment funds.

And, he didn't even discuss the nasty tax problems that arise when Americans acquire foreign shares or mutual funds.

Americans Stay and Pay

The U.S. Congress and the IRS both know that they have a captive market of taxpayers. Most Americans don't even think in terms of investing outside the U.S. They are incapable of moving abroad or becoming perpetual tourists. They are horrified at the thought that anyone would give up American citizenship either to avoid taxes or for any other reason.

Congress could double present tax rates and most Americans would simply grumble. Most of them would not even consider leaving. They would stay and pay.

Many Britons are like that too. During the last Labour government, investment income over about £20,000 a year was taxable at a whopping 98 percent.

In the late 1970s, I was asked to advise an elderly British woman how she could reduce her taxes. I suggested that she move to a tax haven such as Bermuda. Her response was: "Oh, but I wouldn't think of leaving London." She stayed and paid. She eventually got a reprieve in the form of lower taxes from Margaret Thatcher's Tory government.

Violence in Our Time
by John Pugsley, *The Sovereign Individual*, June 1999

April 1999 was the cruelest month, bringing unbearable heartbreak in Kosovo as well as in Littleton, Colorado. Both events unnerve and confound us. How can our civilization be so breath-takingly advanced, yet so frighteningly primitive?

There is a tendency to believe that we live in a more enlightened age, one in which advancing civilization has risen above the murderous behavior that characterized more primitive cultures. Yet, the facts destroy this illusion. The dark, violent side of human culture has not been subdued as civilization has aged. The twentieth century regimes of Hitler, Stalin, Pol Pot and now Milosevic are proof that our "advanced" civilization has not advanced in thousands of years.

Throughout history people in every nation have searched in vain for solutions to mass slaughter, but they have utterly failed. The historians debate past wars, pontificating on how each could have been avoided by better diplomacy or faster response. They place the blame on evil leaders, or they blame some genetic defect of the people, like the militarism of the Germans or the belligerent nature of the Serbs. Occasionally, they blame the meekness of the population for failing to stand up to the rising bullying of a dictator. Sometimes they flail themselves for failing to intervene in time.

All these ideas are "sound and fury signifying nothing." In truth, well-intentioned people have failed to stop wars because, in their anguish and frustration, they have not bored deep enough into the chain of causality to discover the ultimate root of war. The root of these murderous conflicts is not to be found in the evil nature of the leaders or the perpetrators, a flaw in the race, or strategic errors in responding to tyranny. I'm convinced that the cause of these conflicts lies in a fundamental defect in the concept of government.

The core premise of all governmental systems is that to satisfy the needs of the people for defense, protection or property, and securing of rights, power must be relinquished by the many and placed in the hands of a few. Those few, be they kings, dictators or elected representatives, are then expected to exercise that power on behalf of the governed. However, history proves that government inevitably grows corrupt, and that corruption leads to an increasing use of police and military force, both against foreign "enemies" and against its own citizens. Rising taxes, regulations, restrictions, conscriptions and war are built into the nature of government.

Why is this inevitable? The survival of the human species required the evolution of selfishness. To survive, individuals must be "hard-wired" to act first on behalf of their offspring and themselves, then on behalf of their close kin. Any system of social organization that expects individuals to act altruistically toward distant and unknown members of the tribe or nation, rather than considering their own immediate needs and wants, is certain to fail. Yet, that is exactly what is expected of those in government. It is only a matter of time in any nation until the power to tax, regulate and conscript is twisted and used to the personal gain of those in power. Eventually, the lure of power attracts those with the least integrity and greatest lust for personal gain.

How can the tragedy in Littleton be rooted in government? It is rooted in the existence of government power. When our youth are indoctrinated on a diet of propaganda glorifying violence and justifying the use of deadly force by the police or the armed forces against enemies of the State, then those few who feel oppressed and who simultaneously tend toward violence, will justify the use of force against their perceived oppressors. The violence presented in the media is a symptom of our culture's fascination with power, not a cause of the existence of either the power or the violence.

The endless wars and the mass murders will cease only when individuals learn that it is not necessary for them to seek safety and security through handing power to government. When there is no longer a belief that the group must hand power to someone, then there will no longer be the opportunity for a Milosevic or a Bill Clinton to use that power for his own benefit. When such power is no longer available, there will no longer be long lines of power-seekers waiting for their turn to grab it.

History and the study of human nature lead me unswervingly to the conclusion that the peaceful society will be one in which all individuals are sovereign unto themselves. It will be one in which both the right to self-regulation and the responsibility for personal survival and self-defense rest with each individual. As more and more people elect to become Sovereign Individuals, the world grows closer to the ultimate solution to events like Kosovo and Littleton.

It All Starts With Property Rights

By John Pugsley, *The Sovereign Individual*, January 2003

"To be controlled in our economic pursuits, means to be…controlled in everything."
—F. A. Hayek

The feelings that drive us to defend ourselves against government oppression are an expression of our innate compulsion to control our own property. Each of us shares the feeling that it is unjust and an outrage for our hard-earned wealth to be taken from us without our consent.

The drive to control our own property is not unique to modern man. Studies of animal species, observations of hunter-gatherer groups still in existence, and the written history of civilization leave no question that territorialism is a biological imperative. As socio-biologist E. O. Wilson argues, "The biological formula of territorialism translates easily into the ritual of modern property ownership." By the time our early hominid ancestors were wandering the African savannah millions of years ago, the genes that expressed the "property" instinct were firmly wired into mammalian DNA.

The Declaration of Independence suggests that the Founding Fathers sensed this aspect of human nature. It argued that all men "are endowed by their Creator with certain unalienable Rights, that among these are Life, Liberty and the pursuit of Happiness." Life, liberty and the pursuit of happiness, of course, are all aspects of property.

The long train of abuses and usurpations that drove the founding fathers to rebel were triggered by the same genes that give rise to your rage when someone burglarizes your home, steals your car or defrauds you. Those genes are equally activated when that attack comes from government.

Most would agree that the function of government is to safeguard the property and freedom of citizens. Yet, it must be clear by now that the single greatest threat to any citizen's property is its own government. In the United States, the combined burden of local, state and federal tax immediately confiscates between 30% and 60% of our annual incomes, and hits anything a person saves again at the point of death. And that's just the beginning.

Governments also hold monopolies on licenses and permits which, in many countries, prohibit rather than encourage business enterprise and wealth creation. Peruvian economist Hernando de Soto in his brilliant book *The Mystery of Capital* provides numerous examples of how governments around the world discourage private ownership and enterprise. "An Egyptian who wants to acquire and legally register a lot on state-owned desert land (which means, most land) must wend his way through at least 77 bureaucratic procedures at 31 public and private agencies," which can take from 5 to 14 years. "To build a legal dwelling on former agricultural land would require 6 to 11 years of bureaucratic wrangling."

"In Haiti," writes De Soto, "one way an ordinary person can settle legally on government land is first to lease it from the government for five years and then buy it. Working with associates in Haiti, our researchers found that to obtain such a lease took 65 bureaucratic steps requiring, on average, a little more than two years. All for the privilege of merely leasing the land for five years."

Of course such government restrictions have given rise to tremendous amounts of underground activity, but people are seldom able to do as well as they could if the activity was legal. "Extra legal businesses," De Soto explains, "are taxed by the lack of good property law and continually have to hide their operations from the authorities. Because they are not incorporated, extralegal entrepreneurs cannot lure investors by selling shares; they cannot get low-interest formal credit because they do not have legal addresses. They cannot reduce risks by declaring limited liability or obtaining insurance coverage...moreover, because extralegal entrepreneurs live in constant fear of government detection and extortion from corrupt officials, they are forced to split and compartmentalize their production facilities between many locations, thereby rarely achieving economies of scale."

Moreover, because illegal businesses are always on the lookout for police, they can forget about openly advertising to build their customer base or making less costly bulk deliveries. Underground businesses are also easy prey for local Mafias who know they don't have to fear official police protection of the illegal operation.

Failure to comply with the myriad laws, regulations, rules, codes and policies levies an additional cost. Fail to pay your taxes, allow a permit or license to expire, find your property in the way of a new public project, have any illegal drug found on your premises, violate a building code, deposit an unusual amount of cash into your bank account, have inadequate toilet facilities for handicapped employees, or paint your building a shocking color, and you may be fined, arrested, and have your property taken away by city, county, state, or federal authorities.

Attempt to resist and they'll take your "primordial property" (you). They will throw you in prison or even kill you.

Ultimately, protection of your property rests on protecting yourself from all threats, the biggest of which is government itself. The United States is considered by many the freest nation on earth and one in which private property is held in the highest regard. In fact, there are many nations in the Western world, the Pacific Basin, and elsewhere that recognize and respect private property to a much higher degree than the United States.

Prudent individuals diversify their financial portfolios to protect against market fluctuations, inflation, deflation, recession, depression, currency devaluation and even war. In the same way, they diversify internationally to protect against the abuses of government.

The function of The Sovereign Society is to help identify those political jurisdictions that offer the most effective and cost-efficient methods of property protection. Using offshore bank accounts, trusts, and real estate, as well as spreading business holdings among different countries, are practical ways to accomplish your primal need to defend and protect your property.

A Declaration of Independence for Sovereign Individuals

By John Pugsley, *The Sovereign Individual*, July 2002

For Americans, July 4, 2002, will be a particularly emotion-filled Independence Day. The first one since last September's terrorist attack, it strums an intensely patriotic chord in most citizens. That makes this an especially appropriate time to reflect on the principles of independence.

Revolts against despotic governments are a familiar motif of history. Almost all modern nations from Mexico to the Philippines and from Zaire to the Ukraine have their own national "independence" days, marking their emergence from under one group of tyrants and usually into the grip of another. Throughout history, independence and subjugation have chased each other around a revolving door. In light of the destruction of freedom in America since 9/11, it seems assured that the hopes of the founding fathers that their sacrifices could end this cyclical process are being dashed.

Understanding why the struggle for independence must be waged again and again requires us to step back and examine the social contract in the light of human nature. The rising specter of devastation from weapons of mass destruction make it clear that man had better solve this conundrum, and quickly, or risk annihilation.

Homo sapiens is a mewling infant on the evolutionary scene, arriving a mere 200,000 to 100,000 years ago. Our species is not physically imposing and would have been at a serious disadvantage in the struggle for survival except for a single evolutionary difference that catapulted it to dominance: a powerful forebrain. A single species was equipped with cognitive powers immensely greater than those available to all other life forms. With this formidable weapon, our forebears quickly spread around the globe, reproducing and expanding until we colonized every continent, adapted to every climate, and overwhelmed every physical and biological obstacle.

They did it by using their new cognitive powers for discovery and invention. Somewhere in the prehistoric dawn early humans invented language, captured fire, learned to make spears, fabricated the wheel, conceived agriculture, developed metallurgy, domesticated animals, and originated writing. Progress accelerated as they recorded instructions for making gunpowder, the catapult, the steam engine, electromagnetism, atomic energy, and the computer. Human "progress" has been built upon science and technology. We are the inheritors. But we are also faced with a terrible obstacle.

Our species has overcome all but one threat to long-term survival. As Pogo said, "We have met the enemy and he is us!" The urgent problem is to discover the social contract that will end the perpetual cycle of subjugation followed by independence once again leading to subjugation.

Man is, by nature, a social animal. Each individual is bound to his community, but is simultaneously bound by his genes to pursue individual survival and the well-being of his immediate kin. In the hunter-gatherer environment in which our ancestors evolved, the social contract was much simpler. In a tribal village of a few dozen members, everyone was kin, and although there were disputes over food and mates and other property, the resolution was simple. Everyone understood fairness. Everyone participated in the decisions.

In modern nations with millions of inhabitants, kin altruism does not extend even to the other side of the town, let alone to strangers across the country and certainly not to "foreigners." At the primal level of our brains, and in spite of all indoctrination to the contrary, strangers are non-kin, and are thus viewed either as potentially dangerous or to be exploited.

When political power is handed to distant persons, those individuals instinctively tend to use it to benefit themselves, their immediate kin, and those who support their power.

Simply declaring independence from a distant tyrant, however, does not solve the problem of despotism if the political system remains intact. It merely leaves the seat of political power open to be grabbed by a new despot. Thus, man's natural bias toward self-interest, programmed into his brain by eons of natural selection, eliminates the possibility of creating a workable, enduring social contract that is founded on investing power in unrelated individuals or groups.

All individuals, by the authority of the nature of man, should sign a personal Declaration of Independence. It should state that they are, and of right ought to be free, independent individuals, absolved from all allegiance to any of the arbitrary rules and restrictions forcefully imposed on them by politicians and bureaucrats who claim to be working selflessly in the public interest. Certainly, this is the right of Americans under the Declaration of Independence, although in the cycle of subjugation in which the United States is now mired, exercising our rights as "sovereign individuals" may bring retribution from an increasingly despotic government.

While nations will continue to pass in and out of the revolving door of independence and subjugation, the personal declaration of independence is for all time. It is the statement that you consider yourself a sovereign individual.

The day you sign your personal Declaration of Independence should become the most important holiday in your life. By adhering to the principle.

Security? What Security?

By Mark Nestmann, *The Sovereign Individual*, January 2003

"If the government always knows where you are, what job you are seeking, what doctor you're seeing, where you travel, how you spend your money, how you defend yourself, and what arguably unhealthy behavior you engage in, what do the rest of your rights really mean?"
— *Former U.S. Rep. Bob Barr, R-Ga.*

What civil liberties restrictions are you willing to accept to curtail "terrorism" and achieve "security?" The question has more than an academic importance as governments in supposedly "free" countries enact measures that are unprecedented in peacetime: In the United States, the newly enacted Homeland Security Act gives the government authority to collect and analyze data on individuals and groups, including databases that combine personal, governmental, and corporate records, including e-mails and web sites viewed.

In the European Union, a proposal that would require Internet service providers and phone companies to save the records of all phone calls and e-mails for a year or more seems almost certain to become law in 2003.

Do you want to live in a world where, to quote commentator William Safire, "...every purchase you make with a credit card, every magazine subscription you buy and medical prescription you fill, every web site you visit and e-mail you send or receive, every academic grade you receive, every bank deposit you make, every trip you book and every event you attend...will go into what the Defense Department describes as 'a virtual, centralized grand database?'"

Fortunately, this hellish vision is nowhere near fruition. Indeed, experts we have polled tell us it will take an effort comparable to the development of an anti-ballistic missile system to make surveillance this intensive a reality.

But this vision does show the shape of "things to come." It also makes the stakes for persons seeking greater freedom and sovereignty higher than ever as we enter 2003. In this environment, the international wealth building, wealth preservation and privacy preservation techniques outlined by The Sovereign Society have never been more important. Pay them heed, while you still can.

In the Name of Security

By John Pugsley, *The Sovereign Individual*, December 2003

"Far from having their rights to life, liberty, and property upheld by the federal government, Americans have been routinely deprived of such rights under declarations of emergency...Step by step, a ratcheting loss of rights will attend each episode of national emergency."
—Robert Higgs, *Reason Magazine*, 1987

History shows that if you do not act to preserve your personal liberty, the government will take it from you piece by piece. This is a trend that has only gotten stronger in the past century, with each new "emergency." In the 1930s the emergency was the Great Depression. In the 1940s, World War Two. In the 1950s, it was Korea; in the '60s Vietnam, and the '70s brought the Oil Crisis, followed by the War on Drugs. Today, of course, the emergency du jour is the War on Terrorism.

One thing has changed. The buzzword on which the politicians and bureaucrats hang their justification for government's usurping your liberties is no longer "emergency," it's "security." What hasn't changed is the justification for reduced freedoms. Rep. Richard Gephardt (D-Mo.) recited it for this emergency: "We're in a new world where we have to rebalance freedom and security." More accurately, we live in a world where, for the last 70 years, the government has infringed on our rights, supposedly in exchange for greater security.

Security? What security? Flying out of San Diego last month, I was relieved of my nail clippers, then watched a 4-year-old boy as he was instructed to take off his shoes so the federal inspector could check them for bombs. Two more potential terrorists foiled.

In the meantime, a 20-year-old student recently smuggled box-cutters and other tools that could be used as weapons onto an airplane and hid them in a lavatory. He left a note telling authorities how he did it. Rather than thanking him for highlighting a real vulnerability, they arrested him.

If these government-mandated procedures seem absurd, consider the "identity check," a critical strategy to thwart terrorists. Perhaps the politicians failed to note that terrorists don't use their own IDs when boarding planes. The September 11, 2001, hijackers obtained government-issued drivers licenses in fake names, by paying a corrupt state employee US$1,000 for each one.

Counterfeit or stolen passports are also easy to obtain, for a price. Better yet, get the government to issue you an official one in an assumed name. In the 1972 book The Day of the Jackal, by Frederick Forsyth, an assassin wanders around graveyards in Britain looking for a headstone belonging to a male born about the same time he was. After finding a suitable headstone, he applies for a birth certificate and, pretending to be that individual, gets a British passport in his name.

Apparently, 32 years after Forsyth first publicized this loophole, the Brits are about to close it. But for the moment, it's still available, and, according to a recent BBC report, easier to exploit than Forsyth described. British birth and death records are open to everyone at the Public Records office in London. Find the birth record of your choice, then apply for a birth certificate, no questions asked. A couple of relatively easy (but illegal) steps, and a month or so later your British passport will arrive in the mail, complete with your own picture!

The bottom line is that ID checks are worthless as security against terrorism. Nevertheless, government relentlessly expands the requirement for citizens to show identification. The U.S. Postal Service now wants to design a postage system in which you'll have to identify yourself every time you send a letter. "Most users of the Postal Service," a report on this initiative concludes, "would consider such a requirement a relatively modest concession to ensure their safety."

Enough modest concessions, of course, and all freedoms are surrendered. If security isn't really behind ID checks, why are they being pushed on us? Governments are composed of individuals, and individuals crave power. One of the best ways to exercise power is to control people, by tracking them, and their assets, continuously.

The government uses emergencies and the promise of security to achieve its goals. But it gets help. Often, the ideas originate or are lobbied for by the private sector. Take airline ID checks. Complex fare schedules in the airline industry result in vastly different fares being paid by travelers for identical seats. To prevent clever customers from buying and selling tickets to obtain cheaper seats, airlines lobbied the government to "require" positive ID for all flyers.

What's ahead? More "emergencies" and even more cries that we must surrender liberty for safety. Robert Higgs pinpointed the problem years ago, and nothing has changed since: "…citizens in the United States today, with only a few notable exceptions, have neither an

appreciation of this ratchet process nor a strong commitment to individual rights to life, liberty, and property."

Among the "few notable exceptions" are people like you who have joined The Sovereign Society. You have committed yourself to improving your own personal and financial security. It's an ongoing task, but by following the principles of individual sovereignty, the payoff is real   security, not the bogus kind mythologized by governments.

———————•◆•———————

The "War on Terror"—Surrender of Civil Liberties?
By Mark Nestmann, *The Sovereign Individual*, September 2002

Terrorism has been part of daily life in many parts of the world for decades. On September 11, 2001, Americans discovered that they are not immune to such attacks, which are virtually certain to recur. It is only prudent to adjust your portfolio and the way you live to deal with their anticipated effects.

"Freedom and human rights in America are doomed. The U.S. government will lead the American people and the West in general into an unbearable hell and a choking life."
—Osama bin Laden

Did Osama bin Laden win the "war" against the United States?

If "victory" means achieving his oft-voiced objective of removing foreign troops from the Mideast and ending U.S. support for Israel, the answer is no.

But if "victory" instead means ending the "American way of life," with its support for free markets, property rights and limited governmental powers, then terrorism has indeed triumphed.

In the wake of September 11:

- Hundreds of foreigners suspected of being terrorists or to have terrorist sympathies have been detained without being charged with any crime. The U.S. Department of Justice now asserts that U.S. citizens can also be held incommunicado as "enemy combatants."

- Military tribunals, operating in secret may be set up to try foreigners charged with terrorism. Millions of dollars in property has been confiscated from persons alleged to be terrorists, or to support terrorism. Most of the owners have not been charged with any crime.

- The FBI is eavesdropping on lawyers' conversations with clients, including people who have been not charged with any crime, when deemed necessary to prevent violence or terrorism.

- Restrictions on the FBI's ability to spy on religious and political organizations have also been relaxed.

- The FBI can monitor e-mail message "header" information (i.e., obtain source, destination and subject line information) and web browsing patterns merely by declaring that such spying "relevant" to an ongoing investigation. The same authority applies to materials checked out of libraries.

- Police can conduct secret searches of homes and businesses and implant electronic surveillance devices without informing the occupants.

- Restrictions on data sharing between federal agencies have been significantly relaxed.

- Immigration controls have been tightened, and issuance of visas restricted.

Other initiatives appear to have little relevance to terrorism, but are being justified as having an anti-terrorist purpose:

- The Treasury Secretary has the authority to unilaterally terminate all U.S. financial transactions with any country.

- The IRS is publishing the names of persons suspected of being engaged in aggressive tax avoidance strategies, smearing their reputations.

- A nationwide financial transaction-tracking network is under construction.

- Millions more businesses now must report "suspicious transactions" by their customers to law enforcement.

- Any person engaged in a trade or business must file the U.S. Treasury's Financial Crimes Enforcement Network if a customer makes one or more "related" currency transactions that exceed US$10,000.

- Carrying large amounts of cash has now become "bulk smuggling" and made a criminal offense.

- Persons living in low-tax jurisdictions who previously enjoyed visa-free travel to the United States now find it necessary to obtain a visa to do so.

One of the most disturbing aspects of these initiatives is the loose definition of "terrorism." Both the Declaration of National Emergency declared by President Bush in September 2001 and the USA PATRIOT Act (the primary legal authorities under which these initiatives have occurred) define "terrorism" as: "...an activity that—(i) involves a violent act or an act dangerous to human life, property, or infrastructure; and (ii) appears to be intended—(A) to intimidate or coerce a civilian population; (B) to influence the policy of a government by intimidation or coercion; or (C) to affect the conduct of a government by mass destruction, assassination, kidnapping, or hostage-taking."

This incredibly expansive definition allows the U.S. government to label practically all forms of domestic protest as "terrorism." One could certainly conclude that the words "intimidate" and "coerce" could apply to any group or organization that actively disapproves of official U.S. policy. Indeed, it could be argued that many forms of organized protest are designed to "intimidate or coerce" a change in government policy.

But these erosions in civil liberties aren't sufficient to fight the War on Terrorism, we are told. The Bush Administration now proposes:

- Issuing all Americans a "tamper proof" driver's license from their state—a de-facto national ID card. Without the federal ID, you likely will not be able to obtain health care, get a job, conduct bank transactions, board an airplane, purchase insurance, or obtain a passport.

- Asking millions of American workers who in the course of their job visit homes or businesses to report any suspicion of illegal activities there to police.

- Permitting any mail crossing a U.S. border to be searched for any reason.

- Using the military for domestic law enforcement purposes.

- Making the penalties for "attempting" to violate any federal law the same as actually violating it.

Nor is the United States acting alone:

- Throughout the European Union, Internet Service Providers must now install equipment that permits governments to monitor their client's e-mails and web browsing patterns.

- In Hong Kong, the government may now confiscate assets it believes are linked to terrorists. Anyone who has been wrongly accused must prove their innocence in court to reclaim their property.
- Citing terrorism as the cause, the United Kingdom has opted out of Article 5 of the European Convention on Human Rights, which bans detention without trial.
- The United Nations has proposed that every person in the world be fingerprinted and registered under a universal identification scheme to fight illegal immigration and terrorism.

A Better Way to Fight the "War on Terrorism"

In short, the "War on Terrorism" has been co-opted into a war against civil liberties.

Is there a better way to fight this war? Yes.

We have observed previously that it is the U.S. propensity to intervene in ethnic and religious struggles worldwide that makes it a terrorist target. Ending U.S. foreign intervention would dramatically reduce the terrorist threat against the United States and its allies.

Equally important is to narrow the focus of the fight against terrorism so that it does not require the wholesale destruction of civil liberties. Programs designed to collect information to administer taxes, for instance, should not come disguised in an anti-terrorist wrapper.

Obtaining the information about the financial activities of terrorists should have a higher priority than obtaining information for tax purposes.

The Roots of Terrorism

By John Pugsley, *The Sovereign Individual*, June 2002

June marks the beginning of the tenth month in the War on Terrorism, or as Doug Casey calls it, "the Forever War."

Forever seems to be an accurate description of war in general, as inter-tribal aggression has been a characteristic of Homo sapiens from the beginning. Anthropologists classify it as a general characteristic of hunter-gatherer social behavior.

Harvard professor Edward O. Wilson calls the practice of war "...a straightforward example of a hypertrophied biological predisposition [emphasis added]. With the rise of chiefdoms and states, this tendency became institutionalized, war was adopted as an instrument of policy of some of the new societies, and those that employed it best became, tragically, the most successful." As a result, 6,000 years of recorded history appears as an endless series of wars interspersed with brief periods of recuperation and rearmament.

Terrorism is the easiest if not the only strategy of war left open to a group that cannot directly attack or defend against a superior armed force.

The U.S. colonists who were confronted with the superior army of King George saw the futility of following the accepted rules of war. They fired from behind trees and walls, engaged in sabotage, tarred and feathered innocent Tories, and thus were denigrated as rabble terrorists by the British. In our day, the Israeli commandos who blew up the King David Hotel in Jerusalem in 1946 were called terrorists.

But the actors change costumes as power shifts. When 'terrorist' tactics succeed in overthrowing the incumbent power structure, terrorists are reclassified in the history books. Today Sam Adams and John Hancock are remembered not as terrorists but as heroic freedom fighters. Menachem Begin, who ordered the destruction of the King David Hotel, subsequently became Israel's Prime Minister and went on to win the Nobel Peace Prize.

The chameleon nature of "terrorists" and "freedom fighters" leaves politicians struggling to distinguish terrorism from their own strategies of aggression. The U.S. Department of Defense, for example, defines "terrorism" as "the calculated use of violence or the threat of violence to inculcate fear; intended to coerce or to intimidate governments or societies in the pursuit of goals that are generally political, religious, or ideological." It seems a perfect description of the U.S. military, or the armed forces of any major power.

Considering mankind's innate aggressive tendencies, can the War on Terrorism ever be won? Can we end the Forever War?

Yes. But it will never be accomplished through military victory. The solution to all forms of war, including terrorism, will be found in a deeper understanding of man's biological programming.

We are each endowed with powerful primal instincts that natural selection perfected as survival mechanisms long before Homo sapiens was a twinkle in evolution's eye. All life forms require two things: an instinct for self-preservation and for procreation. Two powerful primal instincts that support self-preservation and procreation are territoriality and hierarchy. Today, these instincts are permanently hardwired into all mammals. They dominate human behavior, and therefore hold the key to the solution of inter-tribal aggression.

The territorial instinct is the internal, subconscious program that urges almost all animals to mark the boundaries of their chosen habitats, defend against intrusions, and battle for food, lairs and mates. In humans, the territorial instinct pushes us to acquire property, and defend it against threats, theft, and trespassing. We "mark" our land with deeds, our bank accounts with name and number, and our mates with rings and contracts. We are angered and enraged when our property is taken.

The hierarchical instinct pushes us to seek approval, climb the social ladder, and achieve dominance among our peers. In the non-human animal world it is documented everywhere from the struggle for the position of alpha male in primate groups to the pecking order of chickens. In human culture, the drive for status creates the endless battle for political power and the insatiable desire for property.

Viewed through the lens of these two primal instincts, the root of all conflict is the innate, subconscious drive in all humans to acquire and defend resources. When individuals feel their territory has been attacked, they instinctively feel rage and seek vengeance. As Wilson notes, under the sway of our primal instincts we are "...strongly predisposed to slide into deep, irrational hostility."

Contrary to the nonsense perpetrated in the media, suicide bombers don't sacrifice their lives in hopes of a sexual paradise in the afterlife. Their irrational hostility boils up from deep within the limbic system of their brains. Their primal instincts take control. Such instincts are not devils that can be exorcized through fear or punishment. As long as people feel their property has been stolen from them, their primal instincts will urge them to seek revenge at any cost.

The answer to minimizing human conflict, and particularly war, will be the design of a social contract that protects every individual's property. Our innate human nature leads directly to the conclusion that the Forever War will end when all of us are sovereign individuals, and we feel securely in control of our individual lives and property.

Mirror, Mirror on the Wall, Where's the Freest Land of All?

By John Pugsley, *The Sovereign Individual*, January 2003

Each November, The Heritage Foundation and the *Wall Street Journal* release their annual "Index of Economic Freedom." Backed by voluminous comparative data on taxes, regulations, labor laws, property rights, judicial independence, sound money, international trade barriers, capital controls, etc., this index proposes to rank the world's nations in a descending order from most free to least free.

As has been the case in the past few years, Hong Kong received top billing as the world's freest nation; Singapore was second. The United States, usually rated around third or fourth, dropped to eighth. Heritage and the *Journal* are not alone in passing out freedom "Oscars." The Fraser Institute, a Canadian public-policy organization, cooperates with free-market research institutes in 56 countries to publish "The Economic Freedom Network Index," and the Cato Institute competes with its "Economic Freedom of the World" index.

It's a commendable effort, but unfortunately, as Pierre Lemieux, a member of The Sovereign Society Council of Experts, noted in a recent article in the *Financial Post*, "...in trying to measure it with simplistic index numbers, our friends unwittingly betray their cause...They give us a false sense of contentment...they provide our politicians and bureaucrats with another tool to persuade us that we live in 'the best of all worlds.'" The concept of indexing freedom has many flaws.

First, if polled, the hundreds of economists and other social "scientists" who compile these indexes wouldn't even agree on an exact definition of "freedom" let alone the way to measure it. As an example, at the recent Freedom Summit conference in Phoenix, Arizona, every speaker addressing the topic had a different definition for freedom. No science can progress without precise definitions of terms. If each auto manufacturer could make up its own definition of what constituted a gallon, or what length constituted a mile, every one would claim its vehicles got the best fuel mileage.

Nor does the principle of measurement apply to a condition such as freedom. One is either free or not free.

The late physicist Andrew Galambos provided the best and most precise definition of the word. He defined freedom as: "The societal condition that exists when every individual has 100% control of his own property."

There is no such thing as partial freedom. It's 100% or 0%.

Nor are indexes or averages even useful to us in our quest for freedom. As Chris Mayer pointed out in a recent essay for The Mises Institute on price indexes, "To speak about average prices is like talking about average precipitation to a golfer. It either rains during a specific time period or it doesn't. There is no average that is in anyway useful for an acting human being on a golf course. The only information that counts is what it is doing right now while he is teeing off."

The same fallacy attaches to the idea of indexing freedom.

Over and over I hear that the United States is among the freest nations on earth. Perhaps that's true, but it's tragic that after 10,000 years of civilization that "free" citizens have almost half of all their earnings confiscated, almost all of their exchanges scrutinized and regulated, and let those in power control what they're allowed to put into their bodies, whether, where and what they're allowed to inhale, and what they are allowed to say.

There are no free countries, only competing political enclaves where authorities with guns use differing degrees of coercion against their populations. The organizations that purport to monitor the level of government control over private action would serve their purpose much better if they changed the names of their reports to "Coercion Indexes" so as not to give the impression that people are enjoying something akin to real freedom.

A general freedom index has no meaning for someone who is facing the decision about where to live, invest, or start a business. Such decisions are based on specific levels of coercion—what is the income or capital gains tax rate, what tariffs are levied on goods, what licenses are required, etc. At best, such indexes serve only the purpose of gaining publicity for non-profit organizations that seek to demonstrate to their contributors that they are doing something worthwhile in the promotion of freedom. It's doubtful that they even have any effect on the public policies they are meant to affect.

The rational individual understands that the quest is, as Harry Browne put it in his classic book, *How to Find Freedom in an Unfree World*. Freedom will not be found in any single nation, regardless of how high that country may rise in any index of the freest places on earth. Finding freedom in this unfree world is a never-ending search for places and legal structures that provide the highest degree of privacy, asset protection, business and investment opportunity, and personal safety.

This quest is the real challenge to each individual who seeks sovereignty over his or her life, and is the purpose and mission of The Sovereign Society.

CHAPTER TWO

Second Passports & Dual Nationality

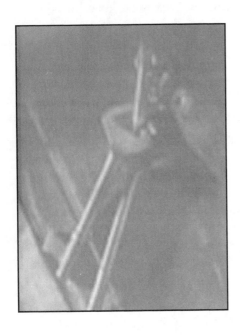

Almost anyone with determination and the financial means can become an international citizen. This is accomplished by acquiring a legal second citizenship, and with that enhanced status comes an official second passport. This new passport can expand your legal rights, allowing world travel unmolested by curious border guards and nosy customs and tax officials. It can open doors that otherwise would forever remain closed to you.

Best of all, a second citizenship/passport can serve as the key to reducing your taxes and protecting your assets—or even your life.

In Chapter 2 we explain how this second passport "magic" can work for you.

Passports Explained

by Robert E. Bauman, JD,

Complete Guide to Offshore Residency, Dual Citizenship and Second Passports, 2003 ("The Passport Book")

Foreign travel in the modern world means having to deal with all the inconveniences imposed by national sovereignty—international borders, customs officials, passports, visas and identity documents. It means having to put up with officious customs officers, bribe-seeking border guards and unreasonable, unexplained delays.

Passports, a Modern Invention

It may seem difficult to believe, but until shortly before the First World War (1914-1919), official passports were almost never required by most countries. In those slower times, document-free international travel was the general rule. Passports were usually special travel documents used to protect official emissaries of nation states at war with each other, allowing safe conduct for surrender or peace negotiations.

The first modern travel document, known as the "Nansen Passport," was issued to White Russian refugees in the prolonged civil war that followed the 1918 anti-Tsarist Russian Revolution led by the Bolsheviks.

That document took its name from Fritzjof Nansen, a Norwegian explorer, later a delegate to the ill-fated League of Nations in Geneva, who first proposed the passport concept. This passport, administered by the League, successfully served hundreds of thousands of refugees as a travel and identity document until the outbreak of World War II in September 1939. The International Refugee Organization (IRO) replaced the defunct League's Nansen Passport Office from 1930 to 1945, but had no authority to issue refugee documents.

In a 1951 treaty, the "Convention on the Status of Refugees", the United Nations attempted to defined the rights of international refugees. The CSR authorized signatory countries to issue travel documents for those they determine eligible for refugee status, applying the Convention's criteria. Since each nation interpreted the CSR in its own fashion, the world soon became cluttered with thousands of refugees fleeing from wars, ethnic conflicts, famine and pestilence. These unfortunates were admitted by some countries, rejected by others, and the result was misery on a grand scale in places as diverse as the Balkans, Israel and Palestine, Hong Kong, Viet Nam, Cambodia and Rwanda.

On the subject of the right of persons to travel freely, the United Nations Universal Declaration of Human Rights, Article 13 states:

Everyone has the right to freedom of movement and residence within the borders of each state. Everyone has the right to leave any country, including his own, and to return to his country.

Article 15 states:

Everyone has the right to a nationality. No one shall be arbitrarily deprived of his nationality nor denied the right to change his nationality.

It goes without saying these so-called "rights" of free movement, travel and residence have been, and are, systematically violated by almost every nation, including dictatorships and democracies. The United States and the United Kingdom are among the worst violators when it suits the political convenience of the government in power at the moment.

Politics dominates the recent history of world refugee problems.

In 1956 the U.S. government under President Dwight Eisenhower welcomed thousands of refugees from the failed Hungarian revolt against the Russian-backed Communists who then dominated that eastern European nation. During four decades of the Castro regime in Cuba, the U.S. has repeatedly admitted tens of thousands of Cuban refugees who, with their offspring, now constitute a majority of U.S. citizens in south Florida.

In contrast, in what has been called a racist policy, during the early 1990s the U.S. turned away thousands of Haitian "boat people" trying to escape dictatorship and poverty. In a shameful act, the British refused to give citizens of Hong Kong full U.K. citizenship when Communist China took over the colonial government in 1997, mainly because of a feared U.K. voter backlash against admitting more immigrants "of color."

More recently the Balkan wars involving Serbia, Bosnia, Albania and Kossovo have produced hundreds of thousands of refugees whose fate seemed the least concern of many national leaders, including their own.

Who Needs a Second Passport?

The English political philosopher Edmund Burke (1729-97) observed in another time: "Early and provident fear is the mother of safety."

That is still good advice for any potential world traveler. Having to be "politically correct" often means travel using a national passport that keeps the bearer as far away as possible from international controversy. It may be a fact of your political life that while your home nation's passport provides you little or no safety margin, another nation's passport will.

Some countries are more popular and accepted in the world than others. Some countries are respected in some parts of the world, reviled in others. Some countries are universally condemned and ostracized. Whichever categories your nation happens to fall into at the moment can determine when you present your passport.

Travel in the Middle East or the Balkans, parts of Russia or Asia using a U.S. passport can make you an instant target for terrorist groups. If your government is out of world favor at the moment, your passport could be confiscated, revoked or suspended at will, as happened to citizens of the Republic of South Africa during the apartheid years.

It's a fact of international political life that citizens of certain countries, the U.S. among them, find travel abroad difficult. For many reasons some countries impose strict visa requirements each time a foreign national wants to enter their country. It's their way of keeping out trouble makers and other supposed "undesirables."

When I served as a member of the United States Congress I was asked by a personal friend, a Catholic priest, to intercede with the South African embassy in Washington, D.C. so that he could obtain a visa to visit that nation. He wished to spend several months there working with members of his religious order, but the apartheid regime diplomats apparently suspected he might engage in anti-apartheid political activities. It required a personal phone call and my assurances in writing to the South African ambassador, a personal friend of mine, to obtain the visa.

Similar troubles can be expected by Americans who want to visit Cuba. For decades it has been illegal for U.S. citizens to visit Cuba because of the official U.S. embargo aimed at toppling Fidel Castro's Communist dictatorship. This is now easing however.

Even a national whose passport usually allows easy international access can find a visa denied due to temporary travel restrictions during trade sanctions or political disturbances. And even if you finally do obtain a desired visa, it can take weeks of procedural delays.

Holding second citizenship and a passport issued by a small, peaceful, non-controversial country can save your life when traveling in times of political unrest, civil war and in other delicate situations abroad. For good reasons, thousands of international businessmen and other travelers consider an alternative passport as their best life insurance.

In an unsettled world, acquiring a second citizenship can be an investment in your future. Your second citizenship is a choice for life and that protective shield can be extended to your spouse and children as well. And there is usually no need to surrender or change your present nationality while you enjoy the benefits of your second passport.

Home Government Coercion

There is another disturbing trend that makes a second passport a great value. In various ways governments increasingly use issuance of a passport to their own citizens as a means of coercion. In the United States, for example, a citizen can be denied a passport simply for being in debt to the Internal Revenue Service or because of problems with other federal government agencies.

Since 1986 the U.S. State Department has informed the IRS of all persons who renew their U.S. passports using a foreign address. Since passport renewals require an applicant's Social Security number, this is also used by the IRS to see if applicants have filed income tax returns. In 1998 an IRS official speaking in Zurich said a special effort was being made by the agency to track all U.S. citizens who renewed U.S. passports while living in Switzerland, for reason we can easily guess.

There is a growing tendency in important countries to follow the lead of the United States in taxing non-resident citizens. Alternative citizenship is therefore increasingly important as a powerful tool for truly international tax planning. As a national of two different countries you also can enjoy extra privacy in your banking and investment activities.

An even more immediate threat can arise from your own government. Depending on your nation's policies, your government may use your passport to restrict your right to travel, rather than to guarantee it. Use of your passport can be made contingent on payment of your taxes, however unreasonable, and on reporting of worldwide income and assets. Issuance of your passport allows your government to control, restrict, monitor and record your travels.

Now you can begin to see why a second passport may be highly useful. Your qualification for a second nation's passport, one that comes with no restrictive strings attached, can serve as your passport to freedom. It can be your key to a whole new world of free movement, expanded international investment, greater flexibility and adventure. And it can mean safe passage as compared to delay or even worse.

Dual Nationality

There is little doubt that government bureaucrats and tax collectors see dual nationality as a serious threat to their control over the citizenry they pretend to serve. As more U.S. citizens acquire dual nationality the debate is intensifying. Eager to work abroad free of red tape and restrictions, or to strengthen ties with their ancestral lands, record numbers are obtaining a second, foreign passport.

Dual nationality simply means that a person legally is a citizen of two countries at the same time, qualified as such under each nations law. This status may result automatically, as when a child born in a foreign country to U.S. citizen parents is both a U.S. citizen and a citizen of the country where he or she is born. Or it may result from operation of law, as when a U.S. citizen acquires foreign citizenship by marriage to a spouse from another nation, or a foreign person naturalized as a U.S. citizen retains the citizenship of his or her country of birth.

Under U.S. law, a second passport does not jeopardize American citizenship. U.S. citizens, including dual nationals, must use a U.S. passport to enter and leave the United States. Dual nationals may also be required by the foreign country to use its passport to enter and leave it. Use of the foreign passport does not endanger U.S. citizenship.

Many countries won't permit their citizens to hold a passport from another nation. This was the case in the U.S. until 1967, when the U.S. Supreme Court upheld the right of U.S. citizens to hold a second, foreign passport. Before that time the official rule was that a person acquiring second nationality automatically lost U.S. citizenship. Since 1967 the government generally presumes a U.S. citizen does not wish to surrender citizenship. Proof of that intention is required before expatriation is officially recognized. The burden of proof is on the government to show intentional abandonment of U.S. citizenship. This presumption is set forth in a U.S. Department of State publication, "Advice About Possible Loss of U.S. Citizenship and Dual Nationality" (1990). As a matter of policy the U.S. government recognizes dual nationality but does not encourage it because of what it views as problems and conflicts that may result.

No doubt legal tax avoidance is at the top of the U.S. government's list of major "problems" it sees resulting from Americans enjoying dual nationality.

The law of most countries holds that the exercise and acquisition of dual citizenship need not affect a person's original national legal status. Many people are automatically entitled to dual citizenship under the various nations' laws, as in case of American grandchildren of Irish grandparents. In addition, a growing number of countries now issue "economic citizenship" based on investment by a foreign national in the issuing country. This may confer limited or full citizenship status on the recipient, but it does not usually affect that person's original citizenship.

In the final analysis, it is the law of the nation which is seeking to impose its control over a dual national that determines whether expatriation, or loss of citizenship, occurs. Dual nationals owe allegiance and obedience to the laws of both countries of which they are citizens. Either country has the right to enforce its laws, especially when the person is physically within that country.

Some countries demand that a foreign national seeking citizenship formally renounce his or her original national allegiance. That in theory is the rule of the U.S. Although all naturalized U.S. citizens must take an oath which requires them to "renounce allegiance" to any other nation, in fact new U.S. citizens do not have to surrender their previous nationality or passports. But in varying degrees the renunciation rule is followed in Italy, France, Spain and Portugal. Other countries, notably Japan and the People's Republic of China, automatically exclude from citizenship any child born from the matrimonial union of one of their citizens and a parent from a foreign nation.

The trend toward multiple nationalities has the potential to turn upside down traditional notions of how people think of themselves, their careers and their communities. It's drawn a flurry of attention from scholars, many of whom believe nationalities are artificial and, thus, interchangeable. "Most academics are happy to declare the end of the nation-state," says T. Alexander Aleinikoff, who studied international migration trends for the Carnegie Endowment for International Peace. "Dual citizenship is seen as a part of that."

Some critics worry that the trend has dangerous implications for a unified society. "If people can become dual citizens, why not have allegiances to three, four or even eight countries?"asks Mark Krikorian, director of the Center for Immigration Studies, a conservative think tank in Washington, D.C. Mr. Krikorian worries that native-born Americans will be harmed by a loosening of the traditional notion of "us" and "them."

Fueling the soul-searching over identity and nationality is the rapid spread of capital and culture around the world. Fast transportation and instant communication links have redefined "home" for many people as anywhere they can plug in a modem or get a dial tone.

"Whether you're a migrant or a hi-tech worker, you can move around the globe and you're not boxed in to any one single notion of belonging or 'identity,'" said Noah Pickus, a professor of public policy at Duke University who edited a book on migration and citizenship in the twenty-first century. "This is an emotional issue that has far-reaching implications we can only begin to imagine at this point."

In recent years, Americans with dual nationality have served as officials in the governments of Yugoslavia, Armenia and Estonia. A retired U.S. government employee, Valdas Adanikus, was elected president of his native Lithuania, and a former New York City attorney served a term as president of the Dominican Republic.

France and the United Kingdom are among the major powers allowing dual nationality. In recent years, Colombia, Ecuador, Brazil and the Dominican Republic have allowed their citizens to hold a second passport. South Korea and the Philippines are considering it. And in a move expected to substantially boost the number of the world's dual citizens, Mexico on March 21, 1998 began allowing its nationals to hold a U.S. passport. Naturalized Mexican Americans are allowed to reclaim their Mexican passport, though they can only vote in Mexico in person.

Scholars say increasingly U.S. immigrants are maintaining their ties to their homelands, just as native-born Americans are reconnecting to roots overseas. "The old model of nationality is outmoded in this globalizing world," says Aiwa Ong, an anthropologist at the University of California at Berkeley. Ms. Ong, who wrote a book on the trend, calls the new way of living "flexible citizenship." Other scholars prefer the term "transnationals."

In the U.S., one of the questions most hotly debated by scholars is whether the oath of allegiance, required for all naturalized citizens, should be altered. The oath requires new citizens to swear off fidelity to other countries, but has little practical effect since the Immigration and the Naturalization Service doesn't even ask new citizens whether they retain the passport of their country of origin. In fact, no one knows just how many citizens claim a second nationality.

But millions of Americans are eligible to become dual citizens based on their family ties to foreign lands that themselves allow dual citizenship. The requirement for gaining citizenship in many countries is being born there, or the birth there of a parent or grandparent. Relying on U.S. Census data, some estimates say the pool of eligible American dual nationals grows by at least 500,000 each year, based on the number of U.S. children born to foreign-born parents.

In supporting dual citizenship, some governments have an economic incentive: to maintain, or even strengthen, ties with emigrants who settled in the U.S. or other wealthy countries. An estimated 30 percent of all Latino immigrants to the U.S. send money back to native countries, and governments fear these remittances may decline over time.

Do Americans Need a Second Passport?

People of means living in places where it seems civil war never ends, like the Balkans, home to the shattered pieces of the former Yugoslavia, or people facing continued political uncertainty, such as Hong Kong since the 1997 hand-over to Communist Beijing, obviously can use a safe refuge for escape. If besieged people enjoy the legal status afforded by a second nationality, their chance of safety is far more certain. In a time when threats turn into physical menace they simply head to their "other" country.

But what about American citizens? The "good old USA" has been the favorite destination of millions of refugees throughout its history, and remains so. The Statue of Liberty in New York harbor still welcomes those "huddled masses" from other shores who want to become Americans.

So why would any U.S. citizen need a second nationality, and the additional passport that goes with it? One very good reason: the growing restrictions imposed by the U.S. government on the freedoms the nation's Founders set down in the U.S. Constitution. For people of wealth in particular, there is now a wide web cast to catch persons the government decides may be doing something wrong. And the current definition of "wrong" is so expansive as to be all-inclusive in the bureaucratic mind.

Example: the mere fact that one has an offshore bank account, creates an offshore trust or owns shares in an international business corporation can suggest potential tax evasion to jaundiced IRS eyes.

What About the British?

The same holds true in the United Kingdom. It is estimated that in recent years 600,000 or more U.K. citizens have been driven into exile by high taxes. Once domiciled abroad, in Italy, Portugal, Singapore, or Bermuda, many Brits used to return home like migratory birds to spend six months annually "vacationing" in England. Stay one day more and under the law they would be liable to pay U.K. income taxes.

Realizing this, the tax collector, Her Majesty's Inland Revenue Service, adopted rules making long stays by former Brits more difficult. Today if a Brit maintains a home or apartment within the U.K., even a single day's visit results in full income taxes on all worldwide income. Without a U.K. home, the allowable non-taxable visit is 90 days per year, but only after an initial three-year continuous absence.

But consider the alternative using a second passport.

If former residents enter and leave the U.K. using a legitimate, non-British passport, entry and departure records produce no tax demands. The person comes and goes free from Inland Revenue's counting of days. That's because U.K. law allows unrestricted dual citizenship and does not dictate which passport you must use if you are lucky enough to have dual citizen status.

A similar "days-in, days-out" rule applies in the U.S. A foreigner who establishes residence in the U.S. for more than 122 days annually, and engages in what could be called "business activity," can be held liable for U.S. income taxes on all worldwide income. The IRS may decide he is a "U.S. person," as this legal status is called, for tax purposes. He may have to submit to an unpleasant grilling to get tax clearance before being permitted to leave. Any legal resident alien in the U.S. is also counted as a "U.S. person" for tax purposes by the IRS.

Multinational Corporations Do It

There is an apt analogy between multinational corporations doing business around the world, and individuals who legally hold dual or multiple citizenship, using their passports for world travel and business.

By registering and qualifying under local laws in more than one political jurisdiction, a corporation has the right to do business in each country where it qualifies. Or a corporation in one nation may choose to set up a subsidiary company in a foreign nation where it does business. The subsidiary may be owned by a foreign parent, but the local government treats it as a domestic corporation, i.e., as a local citizen.

In fact, to induce a foreign company to set up shop, many governments offer special concessions, tax holidays, discounts on energy and raw materials, free land, subsidized local labor, cash grants and other attractions. Why? Because ruling powers want to stay in office and that's easier to do when the local populace is employed and prosperous.

The major impetus to form multinational businesses, however, is not because of extravagant foreign inducements. This international movement didn't grow primarily to exploit profitable opportunities in foreign lands. Instead, explosive growth of the multinationals came about in part to evade undue business restrictions and confiscatory high taxes in the company's home nation.

Now the same pressures are forcing individual citizens to look elsewhere for protection from high taxes and excessive government control.

Until relatively recently many countries did not permit their citizens to have foreign bank accounts, own foreign currencies or hold foreign investments. Those that did allow these financial activities abroad still imposed strict reporting requirements, currency controls, costly exit permits and special transactions taxes. But "dual nationals," as dual citizens are also known, like multinational corporations, can move about the world in such a way as to minimize or avoid currency and other controls.

Dual nationality is not without its inherent contradictions. Members of the Rolling Stones rock group moved to France to escape high British income taxes. Yet many wealthy (and not so wealthy) Frenchmen have moved to the U.K. in order to avoid high French taxes. This anomaly exists because most high tax countries often exempt foreigners who reside within their borders less than six months a year.

A foreign citizen who winters in California for four months, travels or lives outside the U.S. for three months, then spends the remaining five months in his own country, may be able to avoid paying taxes anywhere! More importantly, this roaming individual can escape currency controls, investment restrictions and the burdensome paperwork that comes with permanent attachment to one place on the map.

In order to enter a foreign country and live there for six months as a tourist, one generally needs a passport. Some countries also require foreign tourists to obtain a "visa," a prior written permission to enter that country, which is attached to your passport. And in order to remain longer, to work or to purchase a home, a "residence permit" is needed. "Non-work residence permits" are typically granted to entrepreneurs and others who do not compete in the local job market.

Citizenship and Passports

Before going further, let's examine the elements of citizenship and the meaning of passports.

Citizenship can be loosely defined as the legal relationship between a person and the sovereign nation in which he lives, a status defined by the law of that nation, conferring or limiting the person's duties and rights. Only through the formal process of citizenship acquisition, called naturalization, can one legally acquire the right to a second passport.

A passport is a personal identification and travel document for international use issued by a sovereign nation, usually to its own citizens, but to others as well.

Most familiar are government-issued passports based on a person's national citizenship. However "official" they may appear to be, passports sold or "issued" by some commercial sellers may be illegal and therefore useless. Many governments designate attorneys and others to act as their official agents on second citizenship matters. Also there are special travel documents such as diplomatic passports and other temporary travel documents issued by international organizations or individual countries. Diplomatic passports are only legal if issued by the proper authorities of the nation or international organization and only if the passport holder is properly accredited in the receiving nation.

Dual or Alternative Citizenship

Under the laws of most countries it is legal and proper for some qualified persons to enjoy what is called "dual citizenship," sometime also called "alternative citizenship."

This dual status also may confer the right to have and use a second passport.

Legal grounds that can allow a person to have or acquire dual citizenship status are:

1. Being born within the borders of a nation's territory; the Fourteenth Amendment to the U.S. Constitution grants citizenship to any child born within American territory, regardless of the citizenship of the parents. Other countries conferring automatic citizenship on those born within their jurisdiction include Argentina, Australia, Barbados, Belize, Bolivia, Brazil, Canada, Chile, Cost Rica, the Dominican Republic, Ecuador, Greece, Honduras, Ireland, Israel, Italy, Jamaica, Lebanon, Malta, Mauritius, Mexico, New Zealand, Panama, Paraguay, Portugal, Spain, St. Kitts and Nevis, Thailand, Trinidad, Turkey, Uruguay and Venezuela.

2. Descent from a foreign citizen parent or grandparent, making ancestry a basis, as in Ireland, Germany, Spain or Greece;

3. Marriage to a foreign citizen;

4. Religion, as in Israel; or

5. Formal naturalization, meaning applying and qualifying for citizenship status. The process for receiving the privilege of naturalization varies among countries. Usually a certain period of residence is required (in the U.S. it is five years); good character and an absence of any criminal record may be among other requirements.

Some countries demand that a foreign national seeking naturalized citizenship formally renounce his or her original national allegiance. That is the U.S. law, but as we explained, it simply is not being enforced, even though the citizenship oath includes such a statement. The same rule is followed in varying degrees in Italy, France, Spain and Portugal. Other countries, notably Japan and the Peoples Republic of China, automatically exclude from citizenship any child born from the matrimonial union of one of their citizens and a parent from a foreign nation.

Second Passports: Important Considerations

The single most important consideration when evaluating the usefulness of an alternative citizenship is that it be legal in every respect. That fact may seem obvious, but the proliferation of fly-by-night passport fraud operations requires not only this reminder, but strict adherence to it when making second passport plans and decisions.

If you are going to expend a considerable sum of money to acquire a second citizenship and then use a second passport as your basis of personal international movement, you should demand that these documents and your status be in strict accord with the constitution and laws of the issuing nation.

A few countries actually do have provisions in law that give the head of government or other government ministers discretion regarding the granting of citizenship to foreign nationals in exceptional cases. But even then, if criminal bribery is involved, the person acquiring the passport may face revocation of this previously granted citizenship after a subsequent political change in government. Persons with such documents frequently are subject to blackmail by being forced to pay further "fees" later on. That is why it is imperative that second citizenship be based upon clear provisions in the existing law of the issuing nation.

The prospective second passport client most at risk is one lured into an "instant" or "immediate" passport deal that promises to waive residency requirements and grant quick citizenship. Immediate passports are a favorite lure for attracting unsuspecting and ill-informed would be buyers who need and want a quick passport but haven't done sufficient investigative groundwork.

And even legal passport programs can come and go swiftly, so a candidate must always determine what actually is current. Ireland had an immediate citizenship program for wealthy investors, but ended it in 1996. A similar Cape Verde economic citizenship program ended in 1997. The same year the Seychelles canceled their program in the face of European Union complaints about its questionable operation. Belize ended its program in January 2002.

A casual recent Internet search using the terms "second passport" and "economic citizenship program" produced scores of web sites offering allegedly "instant" passports from Argentina, Guatemala, Honduras, Tonga, Vanuatu, Western Samoa, Greece, Panama, Venezuela, Brazil, the Dominican Republic, Peru, Paraguay and Chile. None of these countries has such an official program. The reasonable implication is that what these sites offer is either fraudulent and/or illegal.

All this may also reflect the fact that the black market in forged and faked passports is both large and lucrative. In October 1997, forged Canadian passports were carried by two Israelis who took part in an unsuccessful assassination attempt in Jordan. And even legal passports can go astray. In 1998 the Western Samoan government announced 150 of its official passports simply had been "lost." Belgium admitted to losing thousands of its official passports during recent years.

Passport Fraud

In late 1999, had you read the classified advertisements in such respectable journals as the *International Herald Tribune* and *The Economist*, you would have seen an ad that promised to provide a "European Union passport, fully registered and renewable" for only US$19,500. A contact phone number in Ireland was listed.

When we made inquiries of this advertiser, the person who answered the phone said, yes, for a price his company could arrange "official citizenship" in the Netherlands and/or Switzerland. When we asked for citations to specific Dutch and Swiss laws authorizing the sale of such passports, the spokesperson gave several answers; a) the company had a special deal with senior Dutch and Swiss officials; b) they had arranged an accelerated naturalization process; c) their legal counsel who could explain more fully how all this worked was away at the moment.

Consular officers at both the Swiss and Dutch embassies were astonished when told about the company and their claims. The officials confirmed what we already knew. Neither nation has ever had an economic citizenship/passport program at any price. They assured us their national police authorities would be immediately alerted about this passport fraud and action taken to end it.

This example is typical of the passport frauds that abound in offshore publication ads, even in so well-respected publications as these. As mentioned, the Internet is loaded with hundreds of passport fraud web sites masquerading as legitimate passport services, many claiming to have official sanction from the countries whose "passports" they hawk.

International Recognition

Before you acquire it, be certain that the passport is one that commands widespread acceptance and prestige in the international community. If it is not likely to be recognized by all other countries, it is worthless from the start.

And in this age of instant communications, it takes only hours, certainly no more than a few days, before customs and immigration officials worldwide know when a passport is called into question. This happened in 1992 with official, but illegally issued Dominican Republic passports, mentioned above, and in 1999, with passports issued by Panama. In the latter case a high passport official resigned alleging she had been pressured into issuing passports to various foreign business associates of the outgoing president. At this writing an investigation continues, but you can be certain that when and if the facts are revealed, anyone holding such a passport will soon find it valueless.

Of course, if you intend to become a citizen of another nation, and possibly spend time there, your consideration should include geographic location, language, stability of the political and legal system, the banking and business environment, visa-free travel possibilities and of course, total initial and future costs.

Do You Need a Lawyer?

There is something to be said for dealing directly with the officials of the nation from which you seek a second citizenship. This can be done at the appropriate embassy in your nation's capital city or at a local consulate. Information and applications can be obtained by phone or fax. If you have the time, expertise and patience to go the often tedious bureaucratic route that can take months or even years, working directly with diplomatic and consular officials eliminates the middleman and probably lessens the chance of fraud or mistakes.

A better alternative is to employ an experienced attorney based in your own nation or in your intended country, an established, reputable professional who specializes in immigration and passport matters. These experts usually know the legitimate shortcuts and have personal acquaintances with the involved foreign nation officials. That can speed your application and approval process considerably.

Caution may dictate using an escrow agent, a trustworthy third party who holds your citizenship and passport fees until the transaction is complete. A bank, law firm, solicitor or other escrow agent can serve this purpose. The agent will hold your money, usually in the form of a certified check payable to the agent, will receive your passport or other documents, permitting you to inspect them before a final payment is made. If you are satisfied a genuine passport or other documents have been delivered, the escrow agent makes payment and delivers the passport to you. An agent's fee for services will range from one to ten per cent of the transaction value. In most second passport cases "advanced fees" should be avoided. If you are willing to place cash in escrow, expense advances should seldom be required.

The Sovereign Society Worldwide Immigration Assistance Program

By special arrangement with one of the world's leading international immigration service firms, Henley & Partners, and with selected attorneys, the Sovereign Society is able to offer its members considerably reduced fees on acquisition of permanent residency and second citizenship in almost every nation. These special fee reductions apply to economic citizenship programs, residency pending naturalization, naturalization and other programs offered by various countries to foreign nationals.

Henley & Partners is recognized as one of the world's leading service firms for international immigration and citizenship law. The firm also offers services in corporate location, international tax and estate planning. Henley & Partners, Inc. can advise you on all aspects of current residency and citizenship programs available in the nation of your choice. They offer expert information on second passports, the advantages and disadvantages of various options, special situations and current events affecting citizenship. They maintain offices and associates in all countries offering economic citizenship programs and as well as other major countries.

Henley & Partners maintains an international network of immigration specialist attorneys, tax consultants, investment advisors and other professionals who are experts in their fields. They emphasize practical and speedy solutions consistent with the best current advice available. Topics for which assistance is available include not only second passports and immigration, but also taxation, private law, insurance, real estate, corporate and personal relocation and government procedures in all countries.

All services and contacts are completely confidential and strict privacy is assured. Inquiries should be directed to: Mr. Christian H. Kalin, at Henley & Partners AG, Haus zum Engel, Kirchgasse 24, 8001 Zurich, Switzerland. **Tel:** +41-1-267 60 90. **Fax:** +41-1-267 60 91. **E-mail:** c.kalin@henleyglobal.com. **Website:** www.henleyglobal.com.

Recommended Attorney

Marshall J. Langer, JD, Shutts & Bowen, 43 Upper Grosvenor Street, London W1X 9PG U.K. **Tel:** +(44) 171 493 4840. **Fax:** +(44) 171 493 4299. **E-mail:** mjlanger@aol.com.

Recommended Visa Publication

Since 1963, the Travel Information Manual (TIM) has supplied the air travel industry with reliable and comprehensive up-to-date country destination information on entry and health requirements as well as visa, customs and currency regulations. The TIM booklet, issued monthly, offers a complete package to help travelers save time and avoid fines and delays. The TIM service costs US$166 annually. Contact: **Tel:** +31 (0) 20 316 3714. **Fax:** +31 (0) 20 316 3801. **E-mail:** mwesterwaal@iata.nl.

Citizenship & Tax Obligations

by Marshall J. Langer, *The Tax Exile Report*, 1997

Only a few countries impose taxes based on nationality. If you want to escape taxes in one of these countries, you may have to change your nationality. If you don't already have another nationality you must first acquire a second one. Then you can abandon your original nationality.

Unless you are a citizen of the United States, the Philippines, Eritrea, Finland, Greece, the Netherlands or Sweden, retaining your present citizenship should not cause tax problems after you move to another country or accept a second citizenship. These seem to be the only countries that try to impose any tax burden based on citizenship. And among these nations, the U.S. is the only country that makes a serious effort to collect taxes from its citizens that live abroad. Not content with that, the U.S. also tries to collect taxes from some of its former citizens.

Dual Nationality—A First Step

An American cannot become a "tax exile" if he remains an American citizen. If you think you might ever want to abandon your American citizenship, you will need to acquire another nationality as well as a passport on which to travel. The U.S. State Department now concedes an American citizen's right to have dual nationality and to acquire the other nationality voluntarily without automatically losing American citizenship. The first step is to acquire another nationality. Do it now while it is clear under U.S. law and policies that you can do so without problems.

There are many fine reasons for becoming a dual national if you can do so. For example, if you are fortunate enough to acquire citizenship in one of the 15 countries that is presently a member of the European Union (EU), you will have the right to live and work in any of those EU countries. You may be entitled to such a citizenship if your parents or any of your grandparents were born in an EU country. The rules are not uniform. They vary from one EU country to another.

Things to Think About

by Marshall J. Langer, *The Tax Exile Report*, 1997

The noted international tax and citizenship expert explains, step by step, just how you can obtain the very best arrangement to avoid maximum taxes—but that may entail some political sacrifices.

Now that you know expatriation may be required to lower your tax burden, you must determine whether it makes sense for you to become a tax exile. Only you can decide whether it is worthwhile for you to develop your own ultimate estate plan.

Examine your present will and estate plan. How much will you and your spouse pay in taxes when you pass your estate to your heirs? How much would these taxes be reduced if you became a tax exile? How much of your present income now goes to pay income taxes? How much would that income tax be reduced if you became a tax exile?

The Decision Is Yours

After you carefully analyze these questions and the answers you are likely to reach one of three conclusions:

1. You enjoyed learning about the possibilities, but becoming a tax exile would be too disruptive to your present and future lifestyle. You will stay and pay. Your children and grandchildren will have to make do with whatever is left after taxes.

2. You feel that the savings during your lifetime and to your heirs would be great but you can't afford to move now. You will begin to take steps that will make it possible for you to move when you can.

3. You are ready, willing and able to become a tax exile now. The after-tax savings will improve your lifestyle for the rest of your life, and the eventual savings to your family will be substantial.

If you have chosen either 2 or 3, you have further work to do. Sit down with your legal and tax advisers and work out your plan. This is an area where no two plans can ever be the same. You already have a general idea of the steps you must take to leave your present home country.

Residency Questions

At a minimum you must terminate your existing residency. You will want to determine whether you must sell or lease your home or whether you can keep it for visits.

Must you establish one specific home base or can you be a perpetual tourist with homes in several different places? Which country or countries will be best for you to move to? Have you already visited or lived in them or in similar foreign countries? Have you gathered all the information you possibly can concerning living conditions there? Are you satisfied that your new base has adequate facilities for health care and your other needs?

Should you terminate your present residence at or near the end of a tax year, or can you do it when it is most convenient for you? Are you subject to a departure tax if you leave? How many days a year can you spend visiting your friends and family in your present home country after you leave? Must you stay at a hotel or can you rent an apartment or home for your visits? Can you keep a car or should you rent one during your visits? Will it be safe for you to keep any bank accounts or investments in your present home country after you leave?

Domicile Questions

Must you also change your domicile? If so, how will you and your heirs be able to prove that you have made the change? What is your domicile of origin? What is your present domicile? What happens if you leave your present domicile without establishing a new one? Do you retain your present domicile? Do you revert to your domicile of origin? Must you change both your residency and your domicile at the same time or can you change your residency now and your domicile later?

Citizenship Questions

Can you retain your present citizenship? Even if you can, would you feel safer or more comfortable if you had a second nationality and another passport? Does your present passport make it difficult for you to travel to certain parts of the world that you would like to visit? Trace your family history and that of your spouse. Does your ancestry entitle you to obtain citizenship somewhere? Does your present country permit dual nationality? Does it make sense for you to obtain another nationality now so that you can terminate your present nationality when and if you consider it necessary to do so? Do you know where and how you can obtain another suitable nationality? If you keep your present nationality and passport must you use that passport to enter and leave your present country? Do you know how to terminate your present nationality when and if you decide to do so? Are you subject to a departure tax or ongoing taxation if you give up your citizenship?

Other Key Issues

Are you married and, if so, are your assets subject to community property rules? Are those rules consistent with your own wishes? Will your spouse take the same steps you do to become a tax exile? If you are not married, do you have an ongoing relationship with someone to whom you plan to leave part of your estate? Will that person be treated as unrelated for gift or inheritance tax purposes in your present or proposed future home country?

How much of your present income comes from sources in your present home country? Will you still be taxed on that income if you leave? If so, can you change the source of that income so as to reduce or eliminate such taxes? Can you use your new home country's tax treaties to reduce the tax at source on any of your income?

How much of your assets are located in your present home country? Will you still be taxed on gifts or other transfers of those assets after you leave? If so, can you change the location of those assets to reduce or eliminate gift and death taxes?

Do you know when to take each of the steps required to achieve the most beneficial results? Will most of your beneficiaries move with you or will some or all of them remain in your present home country? If they remain behind are there special steps you need to take to ensure that they are not pounced on for taxes on your estate after you are gone?

Your own personal circumstances may require you to take steps that are different than those that might be suitable for someone else. Check each step carefully. Develop your own ultimate estate plan. If you want to become a tax exile, do it right or don't do it.

The Hypothetical Family

To help you get started, let us take a look at Larry and Laura Latour. They are American citizens, resident and domiciled in California. Her estimated estate is $25 million and his is about $1 million. Since this is a second marriage for both of them and each has grown children from a prior marriage, they signed a premarital agreement under which their existing assets at the time of marriage remain separate property rather than community property. Their combined income averages about $2 million a year before taxes and they spend about $400,000 a year to live. If they remain in California, their federal and state income taxes will take at least $900,000 a year. Other taxes, including property taxes, may cost them another $100,000 a year. Thus, by leaving, they could save an extra $1 million a year.

If Laura dies first, she plans to leave Larry enough income to enable him to maintain his present lifestyle, but she expects to leave the bulk of her estate to her grown children from a prior marriage. Little, if any, of her estate would qualify for the estate tax marital deduction since she will not leave her estate to Larry outright nor will she give him the absolute power to choose who will receive it when he dies.

If she remains a U.S. citizen or retains her California domicile, her $25 million estate will pay a federal estate tax of around $13.75 million when she dies. If she tries to leave substantial sums to her grandchildren rather than her children, a further generation-skipping transfer tax will eat up most of the rest of the estate.

If Larry dies first, he plans to leave his entire estate to his children since Laura has no need for either capital or income from his estate. His estate will get the equivalent of a $600,000 exemption. Thus, if his taxable estate is $1 million, the estate tax would be $153,000. If his estate increases to $2 million, the estate tax would jump to $587,200. If it increases to $3 million, the estate tax would be $1,098,000.

Laura Latour has decided that she definitely wants to become a tax exile. She is prepared to terminate her residency, domicile and citizenship if that is what it takes. She has selected Bermuda as the best place for them to move to. Larry plans to move with her, and he is willing to change his domicile from California to Bermuda so there is no risk that Laura remains stuck with his California domicile despite her wish to change. He is also willing to obtain a second nationality, but he would prefer to retain his American citizenship even if Laura gives up hers.

They are investigating various ways to acquire another nationality and passports from that country. They plan to acquire a condominium apartment in Bermuda and to establish residency there before the end of the current year. They will also take whatever steps are needed to change their domicile at that time. They realize that it may take them some time to acquire a suitable new nationality. As soon as they can do so, Laura will relinquish her U.S. citizenship. Larry will decide whether to do so later.

Laura Latour and her advisers feel that she can convert a large part of her income into foreign-source income on which she will no longer be subject to U.S. income tax even if she is treated as a tax-motivated expatriate. Her remaining U.S.-source income may still be subject to U.S. federal income tax for ten years. Larry will remain taxable on his separate income from all sources if he remains a U.S. citizen.

Laura had planned to set up a British Virgin Islands (BVI) company shortly after she moved and relinquished her citizenship. She was going to transfer most of her U.S. securities into that company, Magnum Limited, in exchange for Magnum's shares. She had received preliminary advice from her advisers some time ago that she would not be taxed on the transfer but that she would be taxable if she sold the Magnum shares or liquidated the company within ten years after her expatriation. She had planned to keep the Magnum shares indefinitely. Magnum, however, was going to sell its U.S. securities and replace them with comparable foreign securities. That would not have resulted in any U.S. tax on either Magnum or Laura Latour since none of these securities was in real estate holding companies. Unfortunately, she did not leave in time to carry out this plan.

Laura and Larry estimate that it will cost them $100,000 a year more to live in Bermuda than it does now in California. This should cover their extra living expenses and the additional cost of travel for their visits to the children and the family's visits to Bermuda. They feel that this will be more than made up by the annual income tax saving.

If Laura dies within ten years after her expatriation owning the shares of Magnum, her estate may be taxable on any U.S. securities or property owned by Magnum at the time of her death, so she plans to keep these to a minimum. Laura would like to make some gifts to her children after she leaves the U.S., but she will confine these to foreign-situs assets.

Laura is concerned that if Larry does not relinquish his citizenship, she may face residual tax problems to the extent that any of their assets are considered to be community property. She is also concerned that Larry's continued citizenship may require him to file all kinds of information returns with the IRS and the Treasury Department including, for example, forms concerning bank accounts and securities accounts outside the U.S. on which he can sign and information returns concerning her foreign corporations. She has been told that a U.S. citizen married to a nonresident alien must theoretically file detailed information returns concerning foreign corporations owned by the alien spouse even if the citizen spouse doesn't actually own any of the shares of the foreign company. She asked whether Jackie Onassis ever filed such returns concerning all of the companies owned by her husband when Aristotle Onassis was still alive. Her advisers said they didn't know, but that under the law such returns may have been required. Because of these complications, Laura would prefer that Larry joins her in expatriating. He has promised to think about it.

What if someday they decide they have made a mistake and they want to move back to the U.S.? The easiest way would be for one of their adult children (over 21) to sponsor them for green cards. There is no quota and no wait for adult children who obtain green cards for their parents. If that were to present a problem, there are other possibilities such as obtaining a treaty investor visa or qualifying under an investor program. Laura has made up her mind. She is going to proceed with her ultimate estate plan.

———————◆———————

Relinquishing American Citizenship
by Marshall J. Langer, *The Tax Exile Report*, 1997

The world is full of dual nationals because each country has its own archaic and peculiar rules for determining citizenship. Most countries recognize dual nationality acquired at birth at least until a child becomes an adult. Then he may be required to make a choice of nationality. Such a person might lose one of his nationalities if he fails to meet that nation's requirements for compulsory military service. U.S. law does not require a U.S. citizen born with dual nationality to choose one nationality or the other at adulthood.

U.S. law states that a citizen loses his U.S. nationality by voluntarily being naturalized by a foreign country if he made application with the intention of relinquishing U.S. nationality. The key is the U.S. State Department's factual determination of that intent. In a typical situation, State brings a case to adjudicate loss of nationality when it learns a U.S. citizen has obtained a second citizenship. State must prove the person's intent to relinquishing U.S. citizenship. The U.S. State Department current standards of evidence governing such cases presumes that a U.S. citizen wants to retain his U.S. citizenship.

In the 1990 State Department publication, "Advice About Possible Loss of U.S. Citizenship and Dual Nationality," these were the highlights:

- Any of several different acts can result in loss of U.S. citizenship if done voluntarily and with the intent to relinquish U.S. citizenship.

- It is presumed a U.S. citizen intends to retain U.S. citizenship when naturalized in a foreign country, takes a routine oath of allegiance to a foreign country, or accepts non-policy level employment with a foreign government.

- When a U.S. consulate officer learns of such acts he may ask the U.S. citizen to complete a questionnaire. Unless the citizen affirmatively asserts intention to relinquish U.S. citizenship, the consul must certify the citizen's intention to retain his U.S. citizenship.

- The new premise does not apply when a U.S. citizen formally renounces U.S. citizenship before a consul, takes a policy-level position in a foreign government, or is convicted of treason.

- If a citizen performs any of the acts and wishes to relinquish his U.S. citizenship, he may affirm in writing to a consul that the act was done with the intent to relinquish U.S. citizenship.

- Individuals who previously lost U.S. citizenship may be able to have their cases reconsidered under the 1990 rules.

- The U.S. does not favor dual nationality, but it recognizes its existence in individual cases.

The State Department did not explain what is meant by a routine oath of allegiance, but apparently it is an oath that does not require renunciation of other nationalities. If you are considering signing an oath of allegiance to any country, check with the legal experts before you do sign.

Relinquishing U.S. Citizenship

If you wish to surrender U.S. citizenship you must make a formal renunciation before a U.S. Consulate officer in a foreign nation. The same result is achieved by giving the consul your completed questionnaire that concedes your intent to relinquish U.S. nationality.

With few exceptions, an American citizen who is a dual national must use his U.S. passport when entering or leaving the U.S. In all other countries, a U.S. dual national can use either passport he possesses.

Expatriation: The Ultimate Estate Plan

Robert E. Bauman, JD, from an Oxford Club special report, 2001

The legal dictionary definition of "expatriate" reads: "to voluntarily withdraw oneself from allegiance to one's native country: to renounce allegiance to one's country and abandon one's nationality voluntarily."

Admittedly, that sounds like fairly drastic action, especially to the ears of patriotic citizens of the United States or, for that matter, any nation.

Marshall Langer, a distinguished author and advisor to the Sovereign Society on asset protection issues, is an American lawyer who practices in London. In explaining why "expatriation" is so attractive to wealthy Americans, Mr. Langer argues from his practical experience: "Expatriation is the ultimate estate plan."

What Dr. Langer means is that, after taking well planned, prudent steps to rearrange his or her personal and business finances, a high net worth American could voluntarily surrender U.S. citizenship as a legal means to avoid all, or nearly all, U.S. taxes on personal and business income, including capital gains and estate taxes.

Yes, we mean "zero taxes"—as in not having ever again to pay taxes to the Internal Revenue Service. But how does this work?

Wealthy American citizens and permanent resident aliens can cut their income, capital gains and estate taxes to zero if they follow a planned, long-term expatriation strategy. But U.S. laws admittedly could make the price to accomplish that far too steep for all but heartiest of souls.

A 1996 U.S. law (Title 26, Section 877 of the Internal Revenue Code) imposed punitive higher taxes on individuals who relinquish U.S. citizenship "with the principal purpose of avoiding" taxes. For the purposes of this law tax avoidance is presumed to be the true purpose if, at the time of expatriation, an expatriate's net worth exceeds $552,000 or he or she pays an annual tax bill exceeding $110,000. (These figures are indexed for inflation annually.)

The U.S. also asserts tax jurisdiction over an expatriate and his or her assets for ten years after American citizenship ends. Permanent resident aliens ("green card" holders) are also covered by this law's provisions.

As a measure of just how "serious" a problem this may be, fewer than a thousand Americans, rich or poor, formally gave up citizenship in each of the last five years. In the first quarter 1999, for example, exactly 128 people quit U.S. citizenship, including J. Paul Getty's 31-year old grandson, Tara Getty (now an Irish citizen), who will enjoy his $400 million inheritance tax free as a result of abandoning American citizenship.

Why Expatriate?

Here's the compelling arithmetic: a very rich citizen of The Bahamas, for example, pays zero estate taxes; rich Americans, anyone with an estate worth $3 million or more, can pay 55 percent and up. A fairly stiff 37 percent marginal rate kicks in for Americans leaving as little as $675,000 to their children and heirs. The Bahamas has no capital gains taxes or income taxes on most offshore income and no estate taxes either. And the weather, golf, sailing, swimming and fishing usually are excellent year round, bar an occasional hurricane or two.

Now you can understand why expatriation to avoid U.S. taxes has been an intermittent hot button issue in American politics since 1994. All those rich folks getting away with tax avoidance murder! The very idea! Former U.S. Treasury Secretary Lawrence Summers, when in office during the Clinton reign, even went so far as to call such tax expatriates "traitors" to America. He later was forced to apologize.

Political History

It all began on November 24, 1994 when *Forbes* magazine published what turned out to be a sensational article entitled "The New Refugees," a supposed expose of wealthy Americans who had surrendered their citizenship to escape U.S. taxes.

Filled with juicy details (famous names, luxury offshore addresses, huge tax savings in the millions), the story described how clever ex-Americans who became citizens of certain foreign nations henceforth paid few or no U.S. federal and state income, estate and capital gains taxes.

To the average uninformed U.S. taxpayer, this unfamiliar expatriation gimmick seemed like just another rich man's tax loophole and/or rip off while the "little guys" left behind had to pay. Before *Forbes* raised the issue of expatriation, few people had even heard of the concept of formal surrender or loss of U.S. citizenship. Since that *Forbes* article, "expatriation" has remained a favorite issue kicked around when convenient by the American news media and "soak-the-rich" politicians.

Less than two years after the article, Public Law 104-191 was signed by then President Bill Clinton on August 21, 1996, imposing special taxes, penalties and claiming a continuing 10-year tax jurisdiction on persons who renounce U.S. citizenship with the intent to avoid U.S. taxes. The law covers both U.S. citizens and certain foreign aliens legally resident in the U.S. who permanently leave the U.S. For most of the law's provisions, the effective date was February 6, 1995.

As a national political issue, expatriation is hardly new in America.

In the bitter aftermath of the War Between the States (1860-65), Congress hotly debated the status of people in the southern states that formed the Confederacy. Ultimately, Congress decided "rebels" who swore allegiance could again become U.S. citizens. The "Expatriation Act of 1868" formally recognized that all Americans do have a right to give up their citizenship, if they so choose.

Almost a century later, in the Foreign Investors Tax Act of 1966, Congress again decided to make an issue of expatriation. In that Act lawmakers tried to impose onerous taxes on exiting wealthy Americans, but the law was so ambiguous it proved unenforceable. How could the IRS prove such "intent"? They couldn't and they didn't even try.

Expatriate Envy

The media and political furor following the 1994 *Forbes* article may have reflected collective envy as much as patriotic opposition to expatriation by American citizens.

After all, expatriation is hardly a serious a problem, with fewer than 800 Americans, rich or poor, formally giving up their citizenship in recent years. Most expatriates give up their U.S. citizenship due to family circumstances, such as marrying a foreign national, or moving abroad, rather than avoiding taxes.

In the 1996 anti-expatriation frenzy, some in the U.S. Congress wanted to forbid ex-Americans who renounce their U.S. citizenship by deed or formal act, from ever again legally entering the United States, if the government could prove they left to avoid paying taxes. And under the sponsorship of Senator Jack Reed (D-RI), this "no return" provision became law, slipped into a major appropriation bill with no debate hours before Congress adjourned for the year. Section 352 of the 1996 Immigration Reform Act adds expatriation to avoid tax as grounds for excluding former U.S. citizens from re-entry into the United States.

Weeks later when he discovered what the Senate had unknowingly done, then U.S. Senator Daniel Patrick Moynihan (D-NY) angrily denounced the provision supposedly exiling American tax expatriates noting that, Congress had without justification added such persons to a list that had until then included only "terrorists, convicted criminals, [and] those with communicable diseases..."

But as we said, the law has never been enforced and not one person has been excluded from U.S. re-entry under its onerous provisions.

It is worth noting that the expatriate tax punching bag is hauled out by demagogic U.S. politicians whenever it becomes politically convenient. In 2000 a new "soak the rich who run" gimmick was introduced in Congress by ultra leftist Rep. Charles Rangel (D-NY) as H.R.3099. It would have imposed a new, one-time capital gains tax on the assets of expatriates when they left the U.S., regardless of the taxpayer's motive for relinquishing U.S. citizenship. Gifts by offshore expatriates to relatives back home in the U.S. would also have been subject to new taxes. The bill died, but Rep. Rangel has promised to keep pushing his punitive proposal.

Save Millions Legally

In spite of possible punishment, for some high net worth U.S. individuals and their family members there are definite advantages in pursuing expatriation.

In 1962, John Templeton, respected international investor, businessman and philanthropist, surrendered his U.S. citizenship to become a citizen of The Bahamas. This move saved him more than $100 million when Templeton sold the well-known international investment fund that still bears his name. Twenty-three years after surrendering his U.S. citizenship, Templeton, a well-known philanthropist, told the *Wall Street Journal* the political frenzy over expatriation could happen "only in America."

Other wealthy ex-Americans who have taken their formal leave include billionaire Campbell Soup heir John (Ippy) Dorrance III (Ireland); Michael Dingman (The Bahamas), chairman of Abex and a Ford Motor director; J. Mark Mobious (Germany), one of the leading emerging market investment fund managers; Kenneth Dart (Belize), heir to the billion dollar Dart container fortune; Ted Arison (Israel), head of Carnival Cruise Lines; and millionaire head of Locktite Corp., Fred Kreible (Turks and Caicos Islands).

In truth, citizens of almost every other nation see maximum tax avoidance as a positive means for self-survival. In some countries, such as France and Italy, tax-dodging is said to be as much a part of the respective national character as a taste for vin rouge ordinaire or pasta.

Public Law 104-191 (26 USC 877)

The original 1966 U.S. anti-expatriation law, conceded to be unenforceable, was the first attempt by Congress to impose special, higher taxes on individuals who relinquished their U.S. citizenship "with the principal purpose of avoiding" U.S. taxes. That highly subjective intention was virtually impossible to prove. There are no known cases of it being enforced.

The later 1996 law imposed what might be called a "wealth means test." It assumes that an individual has a principal expatriation purpose to avoid tax if the individual's average net income tax liability for the five tax years ending before expatriation is greater than $110,000; or if the individual's net worth on the date of expatriation is $552,000 or more.

The 1996 law is so potentially punitive that thoughtful migration experts criticize what they see as the setting of a much broader and very dangerous U.S. precedent. They point out the law not only involves retaliatory government acts against resistance to high taxes, but poses possible human rights violations by limiting the right to international travel and migration, both guaranteed by traditional international law and the United Nations Charter.

The underlying punitive motive behind the 1996 law can be seen in its crass reversal of the normal burden of legal proof. Whereas the old 1966 law required the government to prove the expatriating U.S. citizen was renouncing citizenship to avoid taxes, the later law shifted the burden of proof to the taxpayer, who must prove he is not trying to avoid taxes.

On the broader issue of other, non-tax specific acts that might cause a loss of citizenship, as I have noted, U.S. government policy presumes an American citizen does not wish to surrender citizenship; therefore proof of that specific intention is required before expatriation is officially recognized.

The 1996 expatriation tax law does allow a few exceptions to this reversal of the traditional proof requirement described above. The law exempts:

- Persons born with dual citizenship, including U.S. citizenship;
- Cases in which a person acquires the nationality of his or her spouse, or that of the nation in which either of the person's parents were born;
- Persons who expatriate before reaching the age of 18;
- Persons who have been present in the U.S. less than 30 days in each of the last 10 years; and
- Persons to be exempted by as yet unwritten IRS regulations as the law requires.

On a related point, it worth noting that even for U.S. citizens there are still legal opportunities for substantial U.S. estate tax avoidance offshore not available within the U.S. Virtually every form of estate planning that can be done within the U.S. can be accomplished with an offshore structure, but with the added benefit that after the taxpayer's demise, the offshore estate moves outside the U.S. tax system and can then prosper free of U.S. income taxes.

Formal Expatriation

While the 1996 law applies only to those who voluntarily surrender their citizenship to avoid taxes, it is worth considering the acts by which Americans may jeopardize their legal standing as U.S. citizens.

In its irrevocable form, "expatriation" per se is caused by an individual's deliberate act of surrendering the native or acquired legal citizenship of their home country. The person must formally surrender U.S. citizenship before a diplomatic or consular officer of the U.S. under the Immigration and Nationality Act, sec. 349(a)(5), who then furnishes to the State Department a signed statement of voluntary relinquishment of U.S. citizenship confirming the performance of an act of expatriation under the Immigration and Nationality Act, sec. 349(a)(1)-(4). Practically, in the case of an American citizen, this means visiting a U.S. embassy or consulate abroad, filing out a standard questionnaire and signing a formal document under oath requesting an end to U.S. citizenship.

Subsequent U.S. State Department approval usually is granted as a matter of routine and it issues a "Certificate of Loss of Nationality." Since 1997 by law the IRS publishes quarterly lists of those who abandon U.S. citizenship for any reason. For names and interesting articles on this subject on the Internet see, http://www.frissell.com/taxpat/taxpats.html.

It goes without saying that surrender of U.S. citizenship should never be attempted unless, and until, a new national citizenship is formally, legally and securely in place. No one wants to replicate the perpetual agony described in Edward Everett Hale's classic short story, *The Man Without a Country*.

Acts Jeopardizing U.S. Citizenship

In addition to the formal renunciation described above, most nations, including the U.S., also have a developed body of statutory and judicial law describing various specific acts that may cause involuntary expatriation or possible loss of citizenship by their citizens.

Depending on the facts of each case, under U.S. law as formerly interpreted, these acts might include voluntary military service in the armed forces of a foreign nation, voting in foreign elections, swearing allegiance to, or accepting an official office in a foreign government. As we noted earlier, the U.S. legal presumption now is always in favor of an American citizen retaining citizenship in the absence of some definitive act of surrender.

In *Nishikawa v. Dulles*, 356 U.S. 129 (1958), the U.S. Supreme Court held the government must offer clear and convincing proof that a potentially expatriating act was done voluntarily before citizenship can be lost. In *Afroyim v. Rusk*, 387 U.S. 253 (1967), the Court said an American has a constitutional right to remain a citizen until voluntary relinquishment and that intent to relinquish must be proven by the government. In *Vance v. Terrazas*, 444 U.S. 252 (1980), the Court said such intention to relinquish citizenship must be proven by conduct or reasonable inferences. Mere long-term residence abroad does not cause loss of U.S. citizenship, *Schneider v. Rusk*, 377 U.S. 163 (1964). Even leaving the U.S. to evade the draft in time of war cannot end citizenship. *Kennedy v. Mendoza-Martinez*, 372 U.S. 144 (1963).

At various stages in U.S. history, reflecting the prejudice of the moment, U.S. law has stated that a non-native, naturalized U.S. citizen could lose acquired citizenship for re-establishing a permanent legal residence in his or her country of origin within one year after U.S. naturalization; by marriage to a Hindu or Chinese spouse; or by becoming a dues-paying member of the Communist Party (USA)!

Plan Ahead

Lost in the furor over expatriation stirred by politicians and the press are the practical aspects of expatriation.

Long before, even many years before, a wealthy American formally surrenders his or her citizenship, that person already will have reordered completely his or her financial affairs in such a way as to remove from possible government control and taxation most, if not all, of their assets.

Here are some of the steps a U.S. citizen who desires to avoid U.S. (and foreign) taxes to the maximum extent should consider:

- Move abroad and make your home in a no-tax foreign nation so you are no longer a "resident" for U.S. income taxes;
- Change your legal domicile (your intended home), to a no-tax foreign nation to avoid U.S. estate taxes;
- Arrange your affairs so that most or all of your income is derived from foreign sources; and
- Title your property ownership so that all or most of your assets are foreign-situs properties exempt from U.S. estate and gift taxes. Any property, including real estate, remaining within the U.S. is subject to potential judicial control by American courts and the IRS.

Conclusion

It's worth considering the advice of a recognized expert, Dr. Marshall Langer, on the decisions one must make if one is seriously considering adopting "the ultimate estate plan," expatriation.

Before making any move, consider all applicable Internal Revenue Code provisions and IRS rules, with expert technical and professional assistance at every step, giving special thought to the timing of each action, the impact on your beneficiaries and their tax status. Pay close attention to the legal status of your spouse, since that will affect the tax outcome, especially if jointly owned property is involved.

Consider informal expatriation as a last resort, but always make certain exactly what the law and regulations mean as they might apply to you specifically. Obviously, at every step, you should seek and obtain the assistance of the very best legal and tax advisors.

Questions for Aspiring Expatriates
by John Sturgeon, 1998

Here's a practical "how to" and "what to expect" test for those considering expatriation to a new country. It's not a course for the faint of heart.

I recently spoke with a colleague who resides in a continental European nation. The economy there is in a shambles and many young people have decamped to other parts of the world to seek better prospects. My colleague said he too would leave but he noted that an expatriate needs three things:

1. The ability to speak the language of his intended country;

2. To be able to work or have another source of income there; and

3. To have full family support for the move.

For my friend, these were all reasons not to leave. In my own experience, these perceived problems are easily overcome.

The Language Barrier

Life is easier when you're fluent in the tongue of your future home country. But that should not present an insurmountable barrier. A great many people have managed to learn the rudiments of a new language relatively quickly. Younger people, particularly children, are capable of learning a language very quickly if motivated. They don't suffer from the "I can't do it" syndrome, a condition that generally afflicts adults.

Instead of seeing a new language as a barrier, take it as a chance to enhance options and opportunities available to you. Colleges in most countries hold night classes in a variety of languages. After a few weeks, you will be surprised how quickly you have acquired a working knowledge of a language that seemed impenetrable.

Alternatively, there are numerous language courses on the market—cassettes and supplementary materials enabling you to study at your own pace, in the comfort of your own home, office or car. Shop around and find a course you like. For starters try Berlitz, telephone +44 171 915 0909. But the best way to familiarize yourself with a new language is to immerse yourself in it on a daily basis. You can do that when you're in the country where the language is spoken.

The Means Barrier

Employment or an alternative source of income is obviously important. A move overseas doesn't stop the bills coming in even if the cost of living may be cheaper in your intended destination. This needn't present the creative and flexible individual with a problem.

I've been impressed by how many expatriates, regardless of their origin, live in every country of the world. More than likely a group of expatriates from your current country already resides where you are going. This might be an ideal market for your skills, products or services or a source of leads for new work. Alternatively, it may be possible to work at your current profession on a long-distance basis. Modern communications, transport systems and sophisticated computer software make it possible to live in one country, retain clients and contacts in your old country, while developing new customers all over the world. With a portable office consisting of a laptop, a modem and a telephone, you are ready. Consequently, expatriation needn't adversely affect earnings potential and with organization and effort it can be enhanced.

The Family Barrier

It is true that if your family is not supportive, finding happiness in your new home is unlikely. Too many guides on expatriation fail to acknowledge family problems. They wrongly assume that expats seek a better place on their own or for their sole benefit. Many of those who move overseas do so because they want a better place for their family to grow and thrive. Obviously, you should include the whole family in the decision-making process.

The prospect of leaving friends, family and present lives behind induces a certain amount of hesitation regardless of where you plan to live. Advantages and disadvantages should be weighed up by the whole family.

A Million Dollar Question

Perhaps the most important question you must ask yourself is what you are seeking by moving to another nation. Naturally, personal preferences play a role in deciding where and how you wish to live. If you want to get away from "civilization" (i.e., crowds) there is no point considering large cities that offer little elbow room.

I recommend you commit your thoughts to writing, as a means of clarifying your goals. Never assume that people and things function in another country in same way they do at home. Local customs and attitudes develop over a long period. Make sure your religious views are tolerated in the new country. Remember you are the foreigner. Once you are there you will be expected to abide by local customs.

Go On A Fact-Finding Mission

Having narrowed your selection, you and your family should travel to your prospective country before you actually move there. You will soon learn whether that country is acceptable to you, or whether alternatives should be considered.

When you visit, don't stay in a big hotel that is part of an international chain. That won't provide an accurate picture of the country, its people or customs. Instead, stay in a small local hotel or bed and breakfast to learn about the locals, their food and habits.

While there, things you should investigate include:

- Availability of housing. Are there any restrictions on property ownership? Speak to lawyers experienced in real estate. They know the pitfalls and the best ways of getting things done.

- The infrastructure. How does it affect the way you intend to make a living?

- Schools for the children. Do they meet your expectations? Is alternative schooling available? Most schools are happy to allow an inspection.

- Medical and dentistry services. How do they measure up? As an expatriate will you get free care? Be sure you and your family will be adequately served.

- Are shopping and recreational facilities suitable and sufficient to your anticipated needs?

- Does the country really look and feel as you thought it would? Or has it engaged in clever self-promotion that fails to reflect reality?

- How do local people receive you? Do you feel comfortable around them?

- Are you free to practice your chosen religion or engage in activities you consider important?

- What level of government restriction will you have to overcome?

- How do you obtain a residence permit? What do you need to do? How long will the process take? What will it cost? Will you be able to obtain a work permit (restrictions will apply for your employment by others as well as for self-employment)?

- Will you be able to bring your household goods, cars, pets, etc. with you and, if so, under what conditions?

- Cost of living issues. How much will a tank of gas, food, local taxes, television licenses, postal stamps, telephone calls cost? Will you save as much as you anticipated or will moving overseas result in additional household expense?

Armed with this information you will be able to base your eventual decision on cold, hard facts. It is not bad to be overly critical about what you find in your chosen country, but realize no place on earth is perfect in every detail. Are you willing or able to overlook imperfections in light of what the country has to offer? Moving abroad is difficult but worth pursuing to obtain the lifestyle and standard of living you want.

A Tax Exile's Wish List
by Marshall J. Langer, *The Tax Exile Report*, 1997

A tax exile must generally establish a new country of residence and a new domicile, and may also need a new citizenship and passport.

The hypothetical Larry and Laura Latour have made a preliminary decision to become tax exiles. Where will they go? Before looking at individual countries, they must determine what they will require. How will they choose one country over another? What do they need and where will they find it?

More Than One Home Country

Until now, the Latours have been U.S. citizens, and they have been resident and domiciled in the U.S. There may not be any one other country that will immediately meet all of their needs. Their first choice of a country in which to reside may not permit them to become citizens for many years. Moreover, it may not be suitable as their permanent domicile. They may have to choose more than one new home country—one, or perhaps several, for residency, one for their permanent home or domicile, and still another for citizenship and passports with which to travel.

A Home Country for Residency

The Latours need at least one country in which they can actually live. Eventually, they may want one place where they can spend most of the year. Initially, however, they may choose to divide the year, spending a few months in each of several countries. This will give them the opportunity to try out several places. If they like some of them better than others they can spend more time there.

Any new home country for residency should be a safe place in which to live and it should have a good quality of life. It should also have a fair and reasonable tax system. They may consider any of the following:

- An island in the Caribbean or Atlantic with low or no taxes and an easy lifestyle. They should look at The Bahamas, Bermuda, Cayman, St. Kitts and Nevis, and Turks and Caicos. They might also look at Anguilla, Antigua, Costa Rica and either Curacao or St Maarten in the Netherlands Antilles.
- An English-speaking base in or near Europe from which they can easily travel. They should look at Britain, the Channel Islands, Cyprus, Gibraltar, Ireland, the Isle of Man, Israel and Malta.
- A "real country" in which they can establish roots and eventually obtain citizenship. They should consider Australia, Britain, Canada, Ireland and New Zealand.
- A toehold on the European continent from which they can readily travel around Europe by car or train. They should look at Britain (now that the Channel tunnel is open), Gibraltar, Monaco and Switzerland. They may also look at Andorra or Campione.

A Home Country for Domicile

The Latours need to choose one country that will be their new domicile. For practical purposes, it must be one of the countries that they have chosen for residency. It should be the one place that they will call their permanent home. They should be comfortable with its laws concerning the eventual descent and distribution of their assets. They will want to know whether it has community property and forced heirship rules and whether they can live with those rules. They will also want a place that does not have excessive taxes on lifetime gifts or at death.

They will begin the process by eliminating those countries that impose excessive death taxes on persons domiciled there. This will probably eliminate Britain and Ireland. Surprisingly perhaps, they can probably cope with the gift and death tax structures of any of the other countries. Some, like Canada or Switzerland, may require careful estate planning.

A Home Country for Citizenship and a Passport

The Latours will need a new citizenship and passports on which they can freely travel without undue hassle. Their new passports should give them visa-free travel to as many as possible of the places they like to visit.

Most of the countries whose citizenship and passports they would like will not give them immediate citizenship or passports. Some of the countries that they may consider for residency or domicile will never allow them to become citizens. Others will grant them citizenship only after several years of residency. Their biggest problem is the time factor. They need citizenship and passports now.

They may be lucky. One of them may have a parent or grandparent who was born in Ireland. If so, he or she would be entitled to Irish citizenship with its first-class passport. The other spouse would also be entitled to Irish citizenship based on the first spouse's citizenship. Similar, less publicized rights, may exist if their parents were born in other countries within the European Union (EU) or the larger European Economic Area (EEA).

If either of them is Jewish, he or she may be entitled to Israeli citizenship under that country's law of return. This comes with immediate citizenship and a laissez-passer; a full passport is issued after one year. An Israeli passport is a very good travel document for visa-free travel.

If none of these options applies, they will almost certainly have to consider one of the few countries with economic citizenship programs. Those countries with legal programs recently available include:

- *Dominica.* This is probably the best legal program at this time. Both spouses and one or two young children can qualify for full citizenship for a total outlay of US$75,000. The applicant donates US$50,000 to the Dominica government. The other US$25,000 covers all government fees, professional fees and miscellaneous expenses. Each eligible family member receives a British Commonwealth passport good for visa-free travel to more than 90 countries, including Canada, Switzerland, Britain and most other British Commonwealth countries. Estimated time: about two months after papers are filed.

- *St. Kitts and Nevis.* Both spouses can qualify for non-voting citizenship by purchasing a condominium costing at least US$250,000 or by investing US$200,000 in 10-year government bonds that pay no interest. Government registration fees and professional fees for the two of them would add about US$70,000 to the cost. Both spouses would receive Commonwealth passports good for visa-free travel to about 90 countries. Estimated time: about two months after papers are filed. At this writing Nevis is considering declaring its independence from St. Kitts as the national constitution permits. This should not affect the citizenship program, except a choice as to which island you prefer will have to be made. The more developed financial structure is located in Charles Town on Nevis.

The Latours must determine how much they need to invest to get a passport that will satisfy their travel requirements. This may depend on how much traveling they plan to do. If they expect to travel extensively, they may need one requiring a larger investment, such as Ireland (if available), Dominica, or St. Kitts and Nevis.

———————◆———————

Canada–Non-Resident Citizens Pay Zero Taxes
An interview with David Melnik, Q.C., *The Sovereign Individual*, June 2002

(**Ed. Note:** *Canada offers first-world amenities and one of the world's most desirable passports after only three years of residency. The Canadian government also has an official policy encouraging immigration. Taxes are high, but in this interview, tax attorney David Melnik outlines a strategy that immigrants can use to avoid tax on their non-Canadian income for five years after they arrive. Nor does Canada impose income taxes on non-resident citizens, as does the United States.*)

TSI: You're a lifelong resident of Canada. Can you give us a snapshot of life in Canada?

Melnik. Canada is one of the world's largest countries. It's sparsely populated, except for the southern regions close to the U.S. border and in our cities. The services and amenities in Canada are very similar to the United States. On the downside, Canada is essentially a socialist country.

Taxes are high and the quality of some of the "free" or low cost services provided by the government is not always the best.

Education is free through the secondary level (grade 12). A university education isn't cheap, but is much less expensive than in most U.S. schools. Typically tuition fees, excluding living costs, are around C$1,100 (US$700) per year. However, a professional school will have higher fees.

Health care is also "free," via a socialized medical system funded by the federal government. However, a de facto rationing system has developed and the quality of care is not always high. If you can wait to see the doctor, fine, but in an emergency, you may not be treated immediately. In addition, you can't purchase medical care privately, although there is increasing pressure to legalize private care. Many Canadians travel to the United States to receive medical treatment if they fall through the cracks of the system.

TSI: Is immigration to Canada encouraged by law?

Melnik. The Canadian government encourages immigration, especially from persons who have capital to bring into the country and who wish to employ Canadians in a business. If you have substantial assets and are in relatively good health, you stand an excellent chance of qualifying for "landed immigrant" status leading to permanent residency and eventual citizenship.

A points system applies to all prospective immigrants. The system takes into account your health, age, net worth, education, business experience and whether you're likely to go on welfare. Of these, the most important factor is whether or not you're likely to become a burden to the government.

You must come from outside Canada to achieve landed immigrant status. Unless you're a refugee, you can't live in Canada while your application is being processed. Immigration is run by the federal government, with the exception of the province of Quebec, which has its own immigration ministry.

TSI: What immigration programs are available?

Melnik. Quebec has the only investment program. If you buy C$250,000 (US$160,000) of Canadian government bonds, and are in good health, you will almost certainly receive landed immigrant status. Immigrant entrepreneurs are encouraged in all provinces. If you invest in an existing business, as long you have reasonably good health and have no criminal record, you should receive landed immigrant status in any province.

If you have family members in Canada, extra points are awarded. However, if you can't support yourself, you won't qualify unless your family in Canada agrees to support you.

There are also quotas from various countries. Quotas from wealthier and more populous countries—the United States, for instance—are much higher than for less wealthy countries. Certain occupations and skills are also in high demand. For instance, we have a serious shortage of doctors and nurses, especially in smaller communities. This is because salaries for medical professionals are very low by U.S. standards.

Anyone who speaks French as their first language will receive special consideration in Quebec. Retirees are welcome to immigrate to Canada if they can demonstrate that they will not be a burden to the state and are in good health.

TSI: What documents are needed to obtain landed immigrant status?

Melnik. You need a current passport, extra passport photos, a medical examination supervised through a Canadian consulate, a letter from the local police stating that you don't have a criminal record and a letter from broker or banker attesting to your net worth. You must also have a personal interview with a government official.

TSI: What family members can you bring with you?

Melnik: A husband, wife and their dependent children can all apply together. Children over the age of 18 must make their own application, although applications from adult children of landed immigrants are viewed favorably. You can also bring parents and grandparents but you must generally guarantee financial responsibility for them unless they have their own assets.

There is no official policy on same sex partners. In one case I handled, two female partners each made a separate application. Both achieved landed immigrant status since each of them worked in a high demand occupation.

TSI: Are there any restrictions on where you settle once you enter Canada?

Melnik. The only restrictions are if you qualify under Quebec immigration law. In that case, you're required by Quebec law to live in Quebec. However, this provision is difficult to enforce and, in practice, people settle wherever they wish.

TSI: What is the process for obtaining citizenship and passport?

Melnik. After you have lived in Canada for three years, you apply for citizenship through a citizenship court. Instant "economic citizenship" is not available. You must take a course in "Canadian civics" and pass a test, but I have never heard of anyone failing it. You subsequently apply for a Canadian passport. You can keep your old passport—dual nationality is permitted.

TSI: Could you compare the Canadian and U.S. passports?

Melnik. Canada has one of the world's best passports, on a par with Swiss, Austrian and U.S. passports. There are more places you can travel without a visa on a Canadian passport than on a U.S. passport. In addition, there are no travel prohibitions as with a U.S. passport–you can travel to Cuba, North Korea, Iran, etc. on a Canadian passport without violating any Canadian law.

TSI: Could you summarize the Canadian tax system?

Melnik. There are several layers of taxation in Canada. First, there are provincial and federal income taxes. The maximum combined rates are between 46% and 49.5%. You reach the top rate for an annual income exceeding C$60,000 (US$40,000). If you have a taxable income of C$100,000 (US$63,000), after various deductions, your total income tax would be about C$35,000 (US$23,000). However, there are fewer deductions for income tax available in Canada than in the United States. For instance, interest on home mortgages is not tax-deductible.

While income taxes generally cover the cost of medical care, if you are self-employed, you will pay as much as C$1,500/year in government medical insurance premiums. Employers and employees must also pay into the Canada Pension Plan (CPP), our form of social security, in the amount of approximately C$1,800 (US$1,100) each per year.

The application of capital gains tax is best illustrated through example. Let's say you had C$100,000 (US$63,000) of capital gains in 2002. Of the total gain, 50% is added to your 2002 tax return as ordinary income. So, if you're in the 50% combined tax bracket, then C$25,000 (US$16,000) would be paid in tax. The effective rate would be about 25%.

Each province also has a Provincial Sales Tax (PST) of 8% on most goods but not on services. Alberta is the only province without a PST. Finally, there is a Goods and Services Tax (GST) that is a federal government tax on most goods and services and the rate is 7%. Canada has no estate taxes at the federal level. However, several provinces do impose death taxes.

TSI: Is it possible for an immigrant to shelter some of their assets from Canadian taxation?

Melnik. This requires the formation of an offshore trust—a trust set up outside Canada—before you enter Canada. The income or capital gains in the trust is not taxable for your first five years in Canada. But U.S. citizens would still have to file tax returns on such a trust. Since you can obtain Canadian citizenship after three years of residency, this means you have two additional years where the assets in this trust are not subject to Canadian tax. Some wealthy persons who immigrate to Canada become Canadian non-residents after receiving their Canadian passport, but before the five-year period elapses. If you wait longer than five years, your worldwide assets become subject to a "deemed sale" provision when you become non-resident.

You add up the purchase price and current value of all your property, including the assets in your immigration trust, and calculate the capital gain. You then have to pay the capital gains tax due on the increase in value of those assets. Alternatively, you may post a security bond with the tax authorities equal to the tax liability.

Becoming a non-resident citizen involves more than simply living abroad. You must make a "clean" break from Canada by taking steps such as selling your home and personal effects in Canada, ending national health insurance coverage, etc.

TSI: Are there any proposals that would end this tax-favored status? Or that would penalize naturalized Canadian citizens who leave Canada?

Melnik. No, nothing like this has been proposed. Canada requires a large number of skilled immigrants to counter a severe and continuing "brain drain" to the United States where salaries are generally higher and taxes generally lower. Nor have their been any proposals to restrict the ability of naturalized Canadian citizens to become non-resident.

TSI: Many Americans who might be considering immigrating to Canada to operate a business are concerned about lawsuits. Are lawsuits common in Canada? Are punitive damages often awarded?

Melnik. Lawsuits in Canada are not nearly so common as in the United States and punitive damages are rarely awarded. One thing that limits lawsuits is that the provinces, other than British Colombia, don't permit contingency fees. Liability insurance premiums are lower as well.

TSI: What services do you offer for persons considering immigration to Canada?

Melnik. I work with another attorney who specializes in immigration work. He knows the point system and knows the people in the government who handle immigration. Our applicants tend to be processed quickly because of this, although they don't receive any favoritism from officials.

My job is to insure the assets are protected and that they don't run afoul of the tax provisions. We try to create a package that takes advantage of whatever fiscal incentives exist plus streamline the application process without skating on to any "thin ice." Due to the new Canadian money laundering legislation, I require that all new clients meet with me personally before beginning the application procedure.

The Best Places for Second Passports & Offshore Residency

by Robert Bauman, *The Sovereign Individual*, February 2004

Someone once wrote of "the kind of patriotism which consists of hating all other nations."

Here at The Sovereign Society, our friendly international outlook is well-established. We feel just as at home "offshore" as we do in our native lands. Sometimes even more so. We know from experience that offshore quite often offers more personal freedom, economic liberty and financial success than we can now obtain in the country of our birth.

I often write about obtaining a second passport or dual citizenship as a means to hedge one's bets against future events. The last century (and already this one) has witnessed horrors when individuals or entire groups have been forced to flee their homelands. Millions of citizens each year choose to change their residence to another nation for a variety of reasons.

The English political philosopher Edmund Burke (1729-1797) observed in another time: "Early and provident fear is the mother of safety." That's still good advice for world travelers or those who choose to make their home abroad.

Safety means using a national passport that keeps the bearer as far away as possible from controversy. Travel in many parts of the world using a U.S. passport may mean you're a target for terrorism. With a passport from any of the European Union countries you gain the aluable right to live, work and do business in every one of these nations. Second passports can be obtained as a matter of right based on your ancestors born in nations such as Ireland, Italy or even the United Kingdom.

If you're a U.S. citizen, there's no need to surrender your U.S. passport if you do acquire a second nationality. U.S. law fully supports the right of Americans to enjoy dual citizenship.

What About "Economic Citizenship"?

If you don't qualify for alternative citizenship based on your ancestry, "economic citizenship" can be obtained from the two nations that still make it available; Dominica and St. Kitts & Nevis.

In 2002, Dominica sharply increased both the fees and administrative hurdles applicants for economic citizenship must overcome, making St. Kitts & Nevis the most viable program. While costs are still slightly lower in Dominica, the St. Kitts & Nevis passport is now a far more attractive travel document.

To qualify for citizenship in St. Kitts & Nevis, you must make a real estate investment of at least US$250,000. There are also government fees of US$35,000 for a single applicant plus US$15,000 for each dependent. Finally, there are application fees of US$15,000 and due diligence fees, which vary depending on the number of persons included in an application. The Government recently increased these due diligence fees to US$ 2,500 per adult applicant.

These requirements make the program relatively expensive but also more exclusive. However, St. Kitts & Nevis is an attractive place to own real estate, and there are some excellent real estate developments approved under the citizenship program. Further, relatively few passports have been issued under the program.

As a result, St. Kitts & Nevis passports have and passport holders enjoy visa-free travel to more than 90 countries, including the United Kingdom, Canada, Switzerland, Sweden, and many others. St. Kitts & Nevis passport holders, unlike Dominica passport holders, still have visa-free access to Canada. As a citizen of St. Kitts & Nevis you can live and work in St. Kitts & Nevis anytime, and as a Commonwealth citizen you enjoy special rights and privileges in the United Kingdom. You are not liable to taxation in St. Kitts & Nevis as there are no income taxes there at all.

Finally, owning real estate in St. Kitts & Nevis, two of the most attractive islands in the Caribbean, is a good investment that you can use for your vacation, as a pied-a-terre, for future retirement or to generate rental income.

For more information, please visit www.henleyglobal.com/stkittsnevis. Sovereign Society members are eligible for a US$2,500 discount on the application fee for this program.

Eliminate State Tax, Pay Zero Estate Tax and Slash Your Income Tax to 10%

Short of becoming a citizen of a foreign nation, one might well consider the possibility of trying out a foreign homeland by first moving there and experiencing life as lived by the locals.

Several nations have residency programs especially designed to attract foreign citizens who may want to make their home abroad. These attractions include many special tax exemptions, some even total, reduced prices on many goods and services, plus home buying and building programs, also tax exempt.

Under a unique federal income tax arrangement applying only to the U.S. Territory of the Virgin Islands, it is possible for U.S. nationals and foreigners who make the islands their main residence to enjoy substantial personal and business tax benefits. These lower taxes make the islands an offshore tax haven option for wealthy U.S. citizens and for foreign nationals seeking U.S. citizenship. And for Americans, moving to the USVI is little more trouble than moving from one mainland state to another.

Like anyone else in the United States, USVI residents and corporations pay federal taxes on their worldwide income. However, they make their payments to the Virgin Islands Internal Revenue Bureau (IRB), not the U.S. Internal Revenue Service. This distinction has important legal consequences for those who are legal residents of the USVI or those who immigrate from outside the United States and become naturalized U.S. citizens while USVI-resident. For purposes of U.S.

federal gift and estate taxes, such individuals are treated as non-U.S. residents. Since the USVI has no estate or gift taxes, this means that upon death their estates owe zero federal or state estate or gift taxes.

That's just the beginning. To attract investment, the USVI government grants generous tax relief packages including a 90% exemption on corporate federal income taxes. This package usually is offered for 10-15 years (with possible five year extensions), and is available to USVI-chartered corporations, partnerships and limited liability companies on their worldwide income. This allows investors to live in their second home anywhere in United States for the spring, summer and fall, then come home to the USVI for the winter, to play golf, tennis, sail and swim.

You too may be able to enjoy the unique legal privilege of paying 10% of your federal income taxes and no state or local taxes. To find out more, contact:

U.S.V.I. Government Web site. Link: www.usvi.net/usvi/tax.html.
Attorney: Marjorie Rawls Roberts, PC, LLB, JD, AB
P.O. Box 8809, St. Thomas, U.S. Virgin Islands 00801.
Tel.: +1 (340) 776-7235. Fax: +1 (340) 776-7496.
E-mail: jorieroberts@worldnet.att.net. Link: www.lawyers.com/robertslaw.

Panama: Leading Retirement Haven

Despite its relatively advanced industrial and financial infrastructure, Panama remains an affordable place in which to live. A live-in maid earns about US$120 a month; first-run movies cost US$1.50. Unlike much of Central America, Panama boasts a first class health care system with low costs compared to the United State -- a doctor's office visit costs about $15.

The government makes retirement in Panama easy, and laws provide important tax advantages for foreigners who wish to become residents under its pensionado program. The only significant requirements are good health and a verifiable monthly income of at least US$500. There are no local taxes on foreign income and you can import your household goods tax-free.

Because of Panama's geographical diversity, there is considerable climatic variation. Panama City, the historical and financial center, has a year-round tropical climate. Yet only a few hundred miles away is a sub-tropical forest, with cascading waterfalls, mountainsides covered with flowers, and spring-like weather year-round. There are also many low-priced buys on condos and other real estate, particularly in Panama City and the surrounding areas. This is in part a byproduct of the U.S. government exodus after the Panamanian takeover of the Panama Canal in 1999.

For more information, contact: Greg Geurin, International Living (Panama), 17 Avenida Jose Gabriel Duque, La Cresta, Panama, Republic of Panama. Tel.: +(507) 264-2204.

Tax Free Residency in Belize

Since 2000, this Central American nation has welcomed offshore persons with its Retired Persons Incentive Act. The program, which resembles the popular *pensionado* program in Panama, is designed to attract foreign retirees and foreign capital.

Known as the "qualified retired persons" (QRP) program, the law offers significant tax incentives to those willing to become permanent residents (but not full citizens). The program is aimed primarily at residents of the United States, Canada and the United Kingdom, but is open to all.

As with Panama, a "qualified retired person" is exempted from all taxes on income from sources outside Belize. Import duties are waived for personal effects, household goods and for a motor vehicle or other transport, such as an airplane or boat. There is no minimum time that must be spent in Belize and you can maintain your QRP status so long as you maintain a permanent local residence, such as a small apartment or condo.

QRPs can also own and operate an international business based in Belize exempt from all local taxes. Local income earned within Belize is taxed at a graduated rate of 15%-45%. However, you will need a work permit to engage in purely domestic business activities.

To qualify for the QRP program, you must be 45 years of age or older and prove personal financial ability to support yourself and any dependants. Initial fees for the program are US$700, plus US$100 for an ID card upon application approval. A spouse and dependents (18 and younger) qualify along with the head of household at no extra cost. Minimum financial requirements include an annual income of at least US$24,000 (or equivalent) from a pension, annuity or from other sources outside Belize.

For more information on the QRP Program, contact:

* Belize Tourist Board, New Central Bank Building, Level 2, Gabourel Lane, P.O. Box 325, Belize City, Belize. Tel.: +(501) 231-913. Fax: +(501) 231-943. E-mail: info@travelbelize.org

* Ministry of Tourism, Constitution Drive, Belmopan, Belize. Tel.: +(501) 823-393. Fax: +(501) 823-815. E-mail: tourismdpt@btl.net

For More Information

In an unsettled world, acquiring a second citizenship is a wise decision, an investment in your future. It can be a choice for life and a protective shield for your spouse and children as well. But offshore residency also opens doors to, not only new worlds, but to a new life as well.

Besides the contacts already mentioned, we recommend:

Henley & Partners, AG. The Sovereign Society has a formal association with this firm. We highly recommend Mr. Chris Kälin, a member of The Sovereign Society Council of Experts, as a source of information and expert planning for alternative citizenship and residency. Contact Henley & Partners AG, Kirchgasse 24, 8001 Zurich, Switzerland. Tel.: +(41) 1 267 60 90. Fax: +(41) 1 267 60 91. E-mail: chris.kalin@henleyglobal.com. Link: www.henleyglobal.com.

The Complete Guide to Offshore Residency, Dual Citizenship and Second Passports. If you want to know more about second passports and offshore residency, visit www.sovereignsociety.com to obtain my latest book on these important subjects.

What is "Economic Citizenship?"
By Mark Nestmann, *The Sovereign Individual*, November 2002

Economic citizenship is the granting of citizenship by a sovereign government in exchange for a financial contribution to that government.

The Sovereign Society recommends economic citizenship only from countries where a statute clearly authorizes it to be granted. "Unofficial" documents purchased from corrupt government officials can lead to the arrest and incarceration of the purchaser.

Why seek economic citizenship? A second nationality is a hedge investment against the unknown events of tomorrow. If you are a citizen of a currently or potentially politically unstable country, your physical survival and self-preservation may require you to leave, quickly.

In addition, any number of unanticipated events could make it necessary for you to leave your home country, including divorce, government corruption, violence, etc. Your passport is the property of your government and a local court could order you to relinquish it. And in many countries, a court is the last place to expect justice!

A second nationality gives you the right to reside in the country granting it. The concept of residence is critical in international tax planning, and in most cases, permanent residency in that country is sufficient to eliminate income and capital gains tax liabilities at "home." (U.S. citizens, no matter where they live, must take the additional step of relinquishing their citizenship to avoid future liability for U.S. taxes.)

You may be able to acquire a second citizenship based on your ancestry, your marriage to a citizen of that country or your religious affiliation. If you qualify under any of these grounds, you should take advantage of them.

If you don't qualify on any of these grounds, your options are limited to obtaining citizenship through prolonged residency (anywhere from 2-10 years) or purchasing economic citizenship.

In recent years, economic citizenship programs have come under heavy criticism. There have been allegations that documents are being sold to international organized crime figures and terrorists. These allegations are false. In the surviving programs (Dominica and St. Kitts-Nevis), applicants must pass through a rigorous screening process involving checks with Interpol and other agencies before citizenship is granted.

Economic Citizenship—Programs in Transition
By Christian Kalin, *The Sovereign Individual*, November 2002

Only two countries now offer a legal and verifiable economic citizenship program: Dominica and St. Kitts & Nevis.

In just the last two years, Belize, Grenada and St. Vincent have either terminated or suspended their economic citizenship programs. Now, the government of Dominica has sharply increased both the fees and administrative hurdles that applicants for economic citizenship must overcome. In my opinion, this makes St. Kitts & Nevis the only viable program currently in existence.

In proposals that were to become effective July 1, 2002, the current (Labour) government of Dominica tripled the required government contribution as well as other fees under its economic citizenship program. The business community and the political opposition have criticized these new policies. It is currently unclear if and when the government will amend them. No new applications are being processed under the new requirements, as the costs are excessive and the procedural requirements too onerous.

It appears that the Dominica citizenship program will in the future be more costly, depending on the effective increase of costs in Dominica, than other programs, in particular the program of St. Kitts & Nevis.

In the Dominica government's new proposals, there are now two options for obtaining citizenship: a Family Option and a Single Option. The Family Option costs US$150,000 and qualifies the applicant, his or her spouse and two children under 18 for citizenship. An additional US$25,000 per child is required for each child under 25 years old. Under the Single Option, a single applicant pays US$100,000. In addition to the above substantially increased government contributions, additional application, agent and registration fees have been introduced. Besides these substantially increased costs, the government has also proposed more onerous procedural requirements, which would make the program less attractive compared to St. Kitts-Nevis.

To qualify for citizenship of St. Kitts & Nevis, the government requires a real estate investment of at least US$150,000. Because there are very few qualifying properties left in this price range, the required minimum investment in most cases is US$200,000. There are also government fees of US$35,000 for a single applicant plus US$15,000 for each dependent. Finally, there are application fees of US$15,000 (same as with Dominica) and a US$2,000 due diligence fee per adult applicant. These requirements make the program relatively expensive but more exclusive.

However, St. Kitts & Nevis is an attractive place to own real estate, and there are some excellent real estate developments approved under the citizenship program. Further, relatively few passports have been issued under the program. As a result, St. Kitts & Nevis passports have and passport holders enjoy visa-free travel to more than 90 countries, including the United Kingdom, Canada, Switzerland, Sweden, and many others. St. Kitts & Nevis passport holders, unlike Belize,

Dominica and Grenada passport holders, still have visa-free access to Canada.

As a citizen of St. Kitts & Nevis you can live and work in St. Kitts & Nevis anytime, and as Commonwealth citizen you enjoy special rights and privileges in the United Kingdom. You are not liable to taxation in St. Kitts & Nevis on any income earned outside of the country. Finally, owning real estate in St. Kitts & Nevis, two of the most attractive islands in the Caribbean, is a good investment that you can use for your vacation, as a pied-a-terre, for future retirement or to generate rental income.

For more information, please visit our web site at www.henleyglobal.com/stkittsnevis. Sovereign Society members are eligible for a US$2,500 discount on the application fee for this program.

Tax-Advantaged Residence in Switzerland

By Christian H. Kalin, *The Sovereign Individual*, July 2002

Switzerland is one of the most attractive countries in the world in which to live. Politically stable, wealthy, clean and safe, Switzerland offers excellent communication and transport, efficient public services, schools of international reputation, low tax rates, and many other advantages.

Switzerland also offers a unique opportunity for low-tax residency by virtue of a lump-sum taxation regime available to foreigners who are not gainfully employed in Switzerland.

Recent changes in Swiss immigration law based on the bilateral agreements signed between Switzerland and the European Union will make Switzerland an even more attractive residential alternative for wealthy EU citizens.

Foreigners who fulfill certain requirements can take advantage of a special tax arrangement whereby Swiss taxes are levied on the basis of expenditures and standard of living in Switzerland rather than on the usual worldwide income and assets. This arrangement is called "lump-sum taxation." Previously only known in certain cantons, it is now available throughout Switzerland, thanks to a federal tax harmonization law enacted in 1990.

To benefit from this special tax regime, you must not have been resident in Switzerland during the last ten years. Nor are you permitted to carry out a gainful occupation. These provisions are specifically aimed at financially independent persons who do not seek employment in Switzerland.

The tax regulations specify no age requirements or similar restrictions to qualify for lump-sum taxation. However, you must obtain a residence permit under one of the categories provided for by Swiss immigration law. The category of persons who do not intend to carry on a gainful occupation in Switzerland includes students, persons visiting Switzerland for medical treatment, and retired persons over 55 years old. Foreigners younger than 55 may still obtain a residence permit and benefit from the lump-sum taxation arrangements in some cantons. Other cantons, such as Zurich, do not permit this arrangement.

If you agree to pay a certain minimum in annual taxes, you may receive a residence permit under the annual cantonal residence permit quota after establishing a company in that canton. The annual payment varies from canton to canton, but is generally higher than that imposed on persons over 55. Again, you may not pursue a gainful occupation and must show that you can support yourself without working.

Immediate Access to Switzerland for Financially Independent EU Citizens

Recent changes in Swiss immigration law and regulations resulting from a series of seven agreements signed with the EU will expand the availability of residence permits for financially independent EU citizens. As the lump-sum taxation regime is unaffected by these changes, it will henceforth be possible for all EU citizens who can show sufficient financial means to become resident and benefit from lump-sum taxation in all cantons. Residence permits became available as soon as the agreements came into force June 1, 2002.

The categories of Swiss residence permits available to EU citizens have now changed. Basically, apart from cross-border commuter permits (to be gradually phased-out), there will be only two main categories of permits for EU citizens: short-term permits for up to one year, and long-term permits generally issued for five years. Residence permits will be issued to persons with a gainful occupation, and to persons who are not economically active but who have sufficient financial means to support themselves.

Essentially, all EU citizens who can show sufficient financial means to support themselves and their dependents and have adequate medical insurance will be permitted to live in Switzerland. Indeed, EU citizens who meet these conditions will have a right to move to Switzerland and will be entitled to obtain a five-year residence permit regardless of the canton in which they wish to settle. In principle, any EU citizen will be granted a permanent residence permit after five years residence in Switzerland.

No Need to Account for Foreign Assets

Under the lump-sum taxation regime, the Swiss tax authorities generally require the assessment of a minimum taxable income of at least five times the annual rental payments for your residence in Switzerland. If you own your residence, the annual rental value is the basis for this calculation.

If you are taxed on this basis, you will not be required to declare your worldwide income or assets. This offers wealthy individuals considerable privacy in their financial affairs. In addition, the lump-sum taxable income agreed upon with the tax authorities normally remains the same from year to year unless your personal circumstances change and warrant a re-negotiation of the agreement.

Suppose the annual rental value of your residence in Switzerland is SFR 50,000 (US$32,000). The taxable income is then calculated as five times this sum, or SFR 250,000. This amount serves as the hypothetical annual income on which the normal tax rates apply.

Although income tax rates differ widely between cantons and even between individual communes, for an income of SFR250,000, you may expect to pay approximately 40% in income tax, or about SFR 100,000 annually, plus social security contributions amounting to approximately SFR 12,000. In addition, five times the annual rental value will be capitalized to calculate a taxable hypothetical net wealth on which cantonal net wealth tax is applied, which for our example would amount to a total of about SFR 20,000.

These payments added together will yield the lump-sum tax payable to the tax authorities and represent your total tax liability, regardless of your worldwide income and assets. If you rent or own a large property in Switzerland, its rental value, and your total annual tax bill will consequently be higher.

The amount of tax effectively payable, however, must exceed the income tax that would be due on certain expenses in Switzerland. It is assumed that income was generated to meet these expenses, and tax must be paid on such income. The tax payable must also exceed the tax due on any Swiss source income as well as income for which a partial or total reduction of foreign taxes is requested by virtue of an international tax treaty. A comparative calculation must therefore be made on an annual basis for the most effective tax planning.

Other elements must be considered when calculating your total tax liability, namely whether assets or sources of income are located in Switzerland or if you claim tax treaty relief under one of the double tax treaties concluded by Switzerland. If the tax on such income exceeds the tax on the lump-sum amount agreed with the tax authorities, then the income tax for the respective year will be levied on the higher amount.

Income from all other sources is not relevant and therefore does not have to be disclosed to the Swiss tax authorities. In several double taxation agreements concluded by Switzerland, including the treaties with Belgium, France and Germany, treaty benefits are limited to foreign source income taxed at Switzerland's regular tax rates. Because these provisions would normally exclude persons taxed under a lump-sum arrangement, a modified lump-sum taxation regime has been introduced.

Limited or No Gift and Inheritance Taxes

Besides offering a unique lump-sum taxation regime that effectively caps the income and net wealth tax for qualifying foreigners, Switzerland has no federal inheritance or gift taxes. Each canton levies its own inheritance and gift taxes, which means that there are 26 different tax regimes. In addition, Swiss law allows foreigners living in Switzerland to choose whether to apply the inheritance law of Switzerland or of their country of origin.

The ability to select an inheritance and gift tax regime among 26 choices permits great flexibility. The Canton of Schwyz (adjacent to Zurich) dispenses entirely with such taxes, and many cantons do not levy inheritance taxes between spouses or between parents and children, or levy only a very modest tax of below 10% for descendants.

Cantons that levy these taxes do so on a progressive basis on real estate situated in the canton and on the worldwide estate of deceased persons or donors who had their last domicile in that canton. The highest tax rates apply to gifts and inheritances between unrelated persons and in such cases tax rates may reach approximately 50% in certain cantons.

Depending on the circumstances, it may also be necessary to take international tax issues into consideration. For example, while in many cantons there is no tax liability for spouses and close relatives, it may still be desirable to pay a very small percentage of gift or inheritance taxes to prevent the country of origin of the deceased, donor, heirs or recipients from taxing the estate or gift.

Moreover, some Swiss treaties provide for important exceptions to the general rule that Switzerland may levy inheritance and gift taxes on the worldwide estate of deceased persons or donors who had their last domicile in Switzerland. Germany is an example.

Swiss Residents Can Purchase a Home Without Restrictions

For decades, Switzerland has restricted the right of foreigners to purchase real estate. In principle, foreigners who wish to acquire Swiss residential real estate must obtain approval prior to their purchase. Such approval is difficult to obtain. However, since 1997, foreigners holding a Swiss residence permit have been allowed to purchase a reasonably sized house or apartment for their personal use with no need to seek prior approval. Even foreigners who subsequently leave the country can keep their property.

Further, the acquisition and holding of purely commercial real estate by foreigners or foreign entities is no longer restricted in Switzerland. As a result, there is ample scope for tax planning by foreigners and foreign entities wishing to invest in Swiss commercial real estate.

The possibility of lump-sum taxation, low or even zero gift and inheritance taxes and the high degree of privacy and personal security, already make Switzerland the residence of choice of many wealthy retirees and international celebrities.

The liberalization of the Swiss immigration regulations will make Switzerland an even more attractive residence for financially independent EU persons who wish to relocate to a milder tax climate.

EU Citizenship via a Latin American Back Door
The Passport Book, 2002

Everyone wants a passport from one of the European Union member nations. With that document in hand, you are free to roam, live and do business in any of the EU countries, no questions asked. EU member states don't give out citizenship and passports easily—but their ex-colonies often do! Few know it, but the quickest backdoor route to EU citizenship is through several South

American nations, long ago colonies of Spain and Portugal. And some of these poor nations literally sell passports to those who can pay the price.

Suppose you want to obtain the right to live, work or run a business in the European Union. All European Union countries, including Spain and Portugal, issue the new maroon colored EU passport. Qualify for one, and you can live and work in any EU country.

You could go there directly and apply for residence in one of the various EU countries, meaning that unless you qualify for either immediate citizenship or a reduced period of residence due to marriage or your ancestry, you would not become an EU citizen for anywhere from five to ten years.

Another option, which can greatly reduce this waiting period, is to approach the EU via a little-known back door. Two EU countries offer such an option, Spain and Portugal.

Spain will grant citizenship within two years after application to persons of Spanish blood or descendants of the Sephardic Jews. Spanish blood is normally taken for granted whenever an applicant is a citizen of a former Spanish colony, meaning most Central and South American nations, or has a Spanish surname and speaks Spanish. Spain also has a special treaty with Honduras and Guatemala that further reduces the Spanish residency period for their nation's citizens to just one year. Following the direct application route for Spanish citizenship, one must endure 10 full years on a Costa del Sol beach before being allowed to become officially Spanish.

The obvious fast-track, back door to Spain and, through it, to the EU, is the acquisition of instant citizenship available for a price from many Central and South American countries. A little bargaining goes a long way in that part of the world. Latin American passport in hand, the next step is acquisition of a house or apartment in Spain and a Spanish residence permit. After the special reduced period of residence based on your Latin American second citizenship, you can apply for a Spanish passport. Obviously, learning Spanish somewhere along the line is desirable.

This is a valid back door for the time being. However, in the passport world things change quickly, so act now while you still can get in this legal and quick route.

The other direct Spanish option is of the religious sort. To become a Sephardic Jew is not impossible, but it takes time and requires that you join a Sephardic congregation. This works much like the standard path to Israeli citizenship, which requires spending approximately one year in Israel. To later obtain Spanish nationality, you must also prove a Spanish connection. Sephardic Jews speak a language known as "Aladdin," a sort of Spanish written with Hebrew letters. It might work.

Try Portugal

Portugal also offers special considerations to members of its former colonies. Brazilian citizens qualify for Portuguese nationality after only three years of official residence; no visa is required to enter or take up residence in Portugal. Citizens of former Portuguese colonial enclaves in India (Goa, Daman and Diu), and parts of Asia, Timor (a former Indonesian colony) Macau and Africa (Cape Verde, Guinea-Bissau, Angola, Mozambique and Sao Tome-Principe) may also qualify for Portuguese citizenship. The same goes for Brazil, the biggest Portuguese ex-colony on the world map. But Brazilian citizenship is not cheap. Any one of these former colonies could be your short route into the EU.

Argentina's EU Loophole

An Argentinean passport is valid for five years, although a pending proposal would extend it to 10 years. As a travel document, the Argentinean passport allows visa-free travel to 33 countries, including most of Europe and nearly all of South and Central America. The Argentinean passport is also the first in South America that entitles its holder to visa-free entry into the U.S. Argentineans also qualify for a reduced, two-year residence period when seeking Spanish nationality. "Hola, EU!"

Or Guatemala

A Guatemalan passport is good for travel to most countries in Europe without a visa, and dual citizenship is common in the nation. Most upper-class Guatemalans hold U.S. and Spanish passports. Spain gives special consideration to Guatemalans, who by treaty need only two years of residence in Spain to acquire Spanish citizenship or vice versa.

Or Honduras

A Honduran passport would probably be best for someone who wanted to live far away from Central America, yet was willing to learn Spanish. It is a good back door for Spain because, being from a former colony, Hondurans can easily get Spanish residency. After two years of residency, a Spanish passport may be obtained. And Honduras has a reputation as one of the top choices for instant passports.

Become a Citizen of Spain
International Living, February 1998

The idea of becoming a citizen of the European Union appeals to many of us. Holders of this valuable passport enjoy the freedom of living and working in any member country, as well as the ability to move assets and holdings between countries with ease.

It is not a difficult process to become an EU citizen. You must simply become a citizen of one of the EU countries. Spain is one of the most attractive options. It offers year-round sunshine, one of the lowest costs of living in Europe, and many cultural and entertainment possibilities, making its residency requirements extremely easy to bear.

Post-Franco Spain is more popular than ever. The song goes the sun is always shining in Spain, but there's more than just good weather to be happy about here. The integration of Spain into the European Union has created another gateway to European citizenship.

It used to be that marriage provided the easiest means to citizenship in Spain. Under the old law, foreigners were able to apply if they were or had ever been married to a Spaniard, even if the marriage had been dissolved. Now, the rules have been tightened and a foreigner must be married to a Spaniard at the time of application and the marriage must have been in existence for at least one year.

Alternatively, you can still acquire Spanish citizenship if you were born in Spain or in certain Spanish territories at certain times. Or if one of your parents was born in Spain you can claim citizenship. To find out whether you might qualify, consult a respected Spanish lawyer. We recommend Malaret & Associates, 104 Pasedo de Gracia, 08008 Barcelona, telephone +34 32 17 1999, fax +34 32 15 1546. They have practical experience in nationality issues. Your embassy or consulate can provide you with a list of legal offices in different cities.

Ordinarily, you must first be a resident in Spain for a staggering 10 years before you can be naturalized. Refugees are granted citizenship after only five years residence. And citizens of some of Spain's former colonies can apply for a Spanish passport after a period of only two years of residence.

As there is no shortage of citizenships available from the former Spanish colonies, this can prove an easy path into the EU. Former Spanish colonies include most of Central and South America, except Brazil, which was a colony of Portugal. It is worth noting also that those of Spanish-Jewish descent can also apply for a Spanish passport after two years of residence.

Purchasing a home is not a requirement for obtaining citizenship. And with or without citizenship you'll likely have the legal right to work, though you may have to prove six months of residence.

To become a citizen, you will be expected to become a reasonable Spanish speaker and to maintain a real presence in the country. However, during your period of residence, which will be between two and 10 years depending on which category you fall under, your travel will be totally unrestricted. No one will count the days you are away, and, because you will be living in the EU, your movements through member countries will be entirely painless.

While there are no restrictions on travel during the required residence period, token residence is not acceptable. The Spanish police keep close tabs on foreigners and will actually visit your home and interview neighbors to make sure you really live there and are behaving yourself. It is worth remembering that the authorities will not hesitate to expel any resident alien they consider undesirable. But there's no need to worry. It's relatively easy to prove that you are living in the country through a renta, a permanent residence income tax form. All permanent residents also have an ID called an NIF that identifies them as Spanish taxpayers to EU tax officials.

Taxation in Spain

If you're a permanent resident of Spain, you'll be taxed on your worldwide income at rates in excess of 50 percent. Income is established by authorities based upon your home, car and lifestyle. It's not surprising then that many wealthy Spanish passport holders establish legal residence in a tax haven.

Spain has tax treaties with many non-EU countries, including the U.S. and Switzerland. These treaties tend to allow individuals to pay taxes in the country where the rate is lower. Wealthy foreigners are therefore advised to consider Spain as a fine place to spend some leisure time but not as a place to live tax-free after acquiring a passport.

Taxation on income and capital gains for nonresidents extends from 20 percent to 50 percent. Tax laws effective since 1992 state that individuals will be considered resident if they stay in the country for longer than 183 days annually or if their main center of professional or business activities for economic interest is in Spain. If your spouse or dependents remain resident, you will be considered a resident unless you can prove you were a resident for more than 183 days in another country. Temporary absences will be included in the authorities' calculations.

Income obtained by non-residents is deemed to be earned on the date it became due or when it was effectively collected. Unless you have a permanent establishment, you must appoint a fiscal representative in Spain and notify the tax authorities. Non-residents that own only one holiday home need not worry about this requirement. Tax-haven corporations that own villas are charged with a special tax of five percent of each villa's value per year.

Despite these tax implications, a Spanish passport is a very good one to hold. A Spaniard can travel visa-free to a dozen more places than an American can. In addition, Spain has a superb relationship with its former colonies in the same way the U.K. does with the Commonwealth. And remember, Spain does not tax its non-resident citizens.

EU nationals can remain in Spain for up to six months without a residency permit, non-EU nationals for three months. Requirements for obtaining a permit are payment of a small fee, plus four passport photos, a residency visa from the Spanish consulate in your home nation, proof of income or pension, the Form E111 endorsed by Spanish health authorities or proof of medical insurance, a certificate that you have registered with your nation's consulate in Spain, and an escritura (rental contract).

<hr />

An Automatic Ancestral Passport

by Nicholas Pullen, *The Sovereign Individual*, December 1998

All it takes is a few phone calls, a bit of paper work, and one in every six Americans (and lots of others, too) is instantly eligible for a European passport, but most folks just don't know it.

It's difficult to believe, but you may be able to acquire a second citizenship and a European passport at little cost and in a very short time. It all depends on where your parents or grandparents come from. If any one of them is or was a native of Ireland, you have the luck of the Irish on your side, for sure.

Here's how it works. The Irish Nationality and Citizenship Acts of 1956 and 1986 provide that any individual, regardless of current location or national status, who has Irish-born parents or grandparents (alive or deceased) can qualify for Irish citizenship. That includes those born in Northern Ireland as well, even though it is technically part of the United Kingdom.

Along with Irish citizenship comes an official Irish passport that gives you free access to every nation within the European Union (EU). That valuable passport entitles you to the EU fast-track—the right to live, travel, work and do business anywhere in the European Union without having to obtain visas or other permits.

Irish citizenship is automatic if you qualify based on your ancestry. The current (1999) required fee to cover the cost of registration is £88/US$145. With proof of ancestry, it's just a matter of completing the necessary application and supplying supporting documentation. This can be done at any Irish embassy or consulate anywhere in the world.

Only Irish parents or grandparents can qualify you for Irish citizenship status. At one time an Irish citizenship claim could also be based on a great-grandparent born in Ireland, but that was abolished in 1986. If you qualify for Irish status, register your application with the Irish authorities as soon as possible. Don't miss the boat. It won't be possible to back-date an application if or when these rules are rescinded. If they are changed, it's unlikely such an opportunity will exist again.

Dual Nationality Is OK

As do both the U.S. and UK, Ireland recognizes dual nationality, so you aren't required to relinquish your current national status if you wish to retain it. There is no residency requirement that you must live in Ireland. In fact, because of high Irish incomes taxes (a graduated 24 percent to 46 percent), you probably won't want to do more than visit. Besides, living outside of Ireland doesn't diminish your Irish citizen rights. And non-residence means you are only liable for taxes on income actually earned within Ireland.

Security and Mobility

Acquisition of Irish nationality can turn out to be first-class insurance against future uncertainties. Perhaps you don't feel a need for alternative citizenship and a second passport now, but you may be very glad to have this option at some future time. You can hold your Irish citizenship in reserve until you need it. No matter what threat or upheaval occurs elsewhere, your Irish citizenship guarantees you and your family a home (permanent or temporary). And it gives you a safe haven in a modern nation with up-to-date infrastructure and amenities, excellent communications and a high standard of living.

With an Irish passport come other real benefits. It is an excellent stand-by document offering visa-free travel to an extensive range of countries, including most first world destinations. It is recognized internationally and causes minimal delay at border crossings. As the travel document of a small country with a low international profile, the Irish passport also may provide more personal security than, for example, its U.K. or U.S. equivalent. Terrorists, kidnappers and hostage takers are less likely to be interested in an Irishman, than an American or an Englishman.

Application Process

The application process is known as the Foreign Birth Registration. Applications—and requests for detailed information regarding the rules and procedures—should be made through your local Irish Consulate or Embassy.

The application forms will require the names, birth places, dates of birth, marriages, deaths and other details of your Irish forebears. Conclusive proof of your Irish lineage is required. That means you must supply original documents such as:

- Your own birth certificate showing your parent's names;

- Your marriage certificate, if appropriate;
- The birth certificate of the parent or grandparent through whom you claim your Irish citizenship;
- Your parent's or grandparent's death certificate if appropriate, or alternatively, a copy of their passport, driving license, voting card, etc.
- Your parents' or grandparents' civil marriage certificate showing the age of each one at the time of marriage and the name of at least one of their parents; and
- Your own present passport (which will be returned to you).

Some documents may prove difficult to obtain. Many churches, public buildings and court records were destroyed during the Irish struggle for independence from Britain. If you encounter difficulty, before hiring an expert, look at the Genealogical Supplement published by the group Inside Ireland. This pamphlet gives detailed information on tracing your Irish roots and family history. Inside Ireland also offers consultations and introductions to qualified Irish genealogists.

Once you submit the requisite information and documentation, it takes from six to eight weeks to process your citizenship application. With that in hand, you can next apply for your Irish passport.

An acquired Irish citizenship can be passed on by an adult to children born subsequently, but those born before obtaining your Irish status must make their own application via the Foreign Birth Registration process. These applications must be accompanied by the child's birth certificate, their parent's birth and marriage certificates, and the original of your own Irish Foreign Birth Registration certificate. It is definitely worth the extra paperwork since an alternative citizenship status and passport is a wonderfully protective gift for your child in these uncertain times.

Contacts

- U.S. citizens can obtain Foreign Birth Registration application forms from: *Embassy of Ireland*, 2234 Massachusetts Avenue NW, Washington, DC 20008, USA. **Tel.**: +1 202 462 3939. **Fax:** +1 202 232 5993.
- U.K. citizens: *Irish Embassy*, 17 Grosvenor Place, London SW1X 7HR, UK. **Tel:** +44 171 235 2171. **Fax:** +44 171 245 6961.

For tax information

- *Office of the Revenue Commissioners*, Department of Justice, Immigration and Citizenship Division, 72/76 St. Stephen's Green, Dublin 2, Ireland. **Tel.**: +353 1679 22777.

Resources

- *Inside Ireland*, PO Box 1886, Dublin 16, Ireland, contact: Brenda Weir.
- *Irish Ancestral Research Association*, http://tiara.ie. This website links to useful resources for researching your Irish ancestry, including general information, national, local and regional resources, emigration and passenger lists, family and clan associations, databases and search engines, referrals to professional researchers and commercial services.

Why I Gave Up My U.S. Citizenship
By P. T. Freeman, *The Sovereign Individual*, March 2002

Have you ever been to Key West, Florida?

A landmark in Key West is a marker at the corner of Whitehead and South Streets that says in big letters: "Southernmost Point Continental United States." Above it reads in smaller letters: "90 miles to Cuba." Visiting this concrete marker recently made me pause and reflect upon a major decision that I made a few years earlier: the choice to give up my U.S. citizenship.

This process started when I found that because of my U.S. citizenship, there were many restrictions on my ability to travel or do business outside the United States. For instance, I had a real desire to visit the Republic of Cuba, but because of my citizenship, I could not do so. Canadians, Mexicans, Europeans and every other nationality could travel and do business there, but with limited exceptions, U.S. citizens have not been allowed to do so for more than 40 years.

As I thought about this prohibition and the many others established by statute or executive order, I became outraged. Finally, in 1994, I read a story that galvanized me to take action. The story was about a group called the "Freedom to Travel Campaign" that sought to end these travel restrictions and which challenged Treasury Department regulations prohibiting such travel.

Business Opportunities Forbidden U.S. Citizens

However, the U.S. Justice Department, apparently fearing that juries would side with these "tourist lawbreakers," declined to prosecute the cases. This emboldened me. I decided to go to Nassau, The Bahamas and secretly visit Cuba by using the daily direct flight on Cubana de Aviacion, Cuba's national air carrier.

In reaction to the failure of the Justice Department to prosecute "tourist lawbreakers," the U.S. Treasury Department amended the regulations to make it possible to fine persons violating travel restrictions through an administrative process, without going to court. The U.S. Treasury Department administers these and other sanctions programs through the Office of Foreign Assets Control (OFAC)—http://www.ustreas.gov/ofac.

While in Cuba, I discovered a wealth of business opportunities. This was the height of the "Special Period in Peace" when, due to the collapse of the Soviet Union and the end of Soviet aid, the Cuban economy was in a tailspin. There was a serious need for outside investment on favorable terms. I decided that I wanted to participate in those investments. Returning a few days later to Nassau, I passed through U.S. Customs pre-flight inspection without revealing that I had visited Cuba. (The Customs inspector did not ask me if I had done so, and the customs forms in those days did not ask, "countries visited on this trip prior to U.S. arrival," as they do now.)

Upon my return to the United States, I began to read the U.S. Treasury regulations regarding Cuba. I learned that they prohibited virtually all contact with Cuba by any person "subject to U.S. jurisdiction." This included: "all U.S. citizens and permanent residents wherever they are located, all people and organizations physically in the United States or its territories, and all branches and subsidiaries of U.S. organizations throughout the world, corporations, wherever they are located throughout the world."

In the case of Cuba, criminal penalties for violating the sanctions range up to 10 years in prison, US$1 million in corporate fines, and US$250,000 in individual fines. Civil penalties up to US$55,000 per violation may also be imposed. The only way to legally travel to or do business with Cuba, or any other sanctioned country, was (and still is) to obtain a license issued by OFAC. For business, it was almost impossible to obtain a license, although journalists and a few other classifications of individuals are permitted to travel to sanctioned countries.

The only other option was not to be a U.S. citizen. At that moment, I was not prepared to take that step. Instead, I decided to explore the possibility of living outside the United States. However, I quickly discovered that doing so did not exempt me from OFAC regulations. I also learned that there was no escape from the obligation of U.S. citizens to pay tax on their worldwide income, even if they physically resided outside the United States. I began to seriously wonder if my "little blue book" (my U.S. passport) was really worth keeping.

Next, I began looking into ways of obtaining an alternative citizenship and passport. I conducted some research on the Internet; but then, as now, many of the companies offering passports were thinly disguised scams offering unofficial or even stolen documents. However, there were, at that time, a few Caribbean countries that offered legitimate "economic citizenship" programs.

With the aid of an attorney, I began to conduct research into which program would best suit me. I looked at cost, the availability of visa free travel, credibility, and the desirability of that country as a residence.

"Economic Citizenship" Is Not Second-Class Citizenship

After considerable research, I chose a country (which shall remain nameless since it has discontinued its economic citizenship program) and visited it. I liked the country and decided to possibly settle there, or at least maintain a residence or business presence. I paid the necessary fees to obtain economic citizenship and met with some government officials. Several weeks later, after an extensive background check, I swore an oath of allegiance to this country, was granted citizenship and subsequently obtained my passport.

A major concern was whether persons who had obtained economic citizenship from this country would be subject to discrimination, either from its residents or at border crossings. I found that there were no real problems in either case. Indeed, my passport was identical to those issued native-born citizens. While I ultimately made to decision to settle elsewhere, I still maintain a residence in my new country and also invest there.

Later, based on other factors, I was able to obtain another passport that offered superior visa free travel than did the passport obtained through economic citizenship. After obtaining this third passport, at the advice of my attorney, I decided to take the biggest step of all: giving up my U.S. citizenship.

Walking up to the U.S. embassy, my heart was pounding. I feared that I was going to be called a traitor. I had also been advised that individuals who gave up their U.S. citizenship for tax reasons could be permanently excluded from ever returning to the United States. (**Ed. Note:** This provision is part of the 1996 immigration bill, but has never been enforced due to questions about its constitutionality). However, the process went smoothly. I signed a form stating that I was not insane and that I was exercising my rights of citizenship. The embassy official took my U.S. passport, as well as the form. He also made a copy of one of my new passports to prove that I would not be a "stateless person" upon giving up U.S. citizenship. This was necessary because the United States has signed treaties obligating it not to permit its citizens to become "stateless persons."

The entire process took about 20 minutes, about 17 of which were waiting for copies to be made and other administrative processes. I was told that the U.S. Department of State reviews these copies and subsequently issues a "Certificate of Loss of Nationality of the United States" if it concludes that the person concerned did, in fact, lose his or her nationality. Until then, I was still considered a U.S. citizen.

About two months after I visited the embassy, I received my "Certificate of Loss of Nationality" by mail. Attached was a letter explaining that I could appeal my loss of nationality, if I chose to do so, directly to the Attorney General. I took this certificate back to the U.S. Embassy and applied for a visa to visit the United States. After convincing a consular officer that I did not intend to resettle in the United States, I was granted a multiple entry U.S. visa. This gave me the right to visit the United States, although not to live there. Of course, I had no intention of living in the United States and thus becoming subject to the jurisdiction of OFAC and the IRS!

While I completed these steps only a few years ago, I have already experienced enormous benefits both personally and in business. I can travel anywhere in the world with my new passport. And I now have extensive business interests in Cuba and other countries subject to U.S. sanctions.

As I stood at the marker in Key West, looking over the Straits of Florida, I turned around and saw a group of tourists who had disembarked from a trolley tour and were snapping pictures of the marker. None of those tourists who are U.S. citizens or residents can visit Cuba. I can. Those who are U.S. citizens or residents also have to file an annual tax return with the IRS. I don't.

That's what you call true liberation—or if you prefer, being a "sovereign individual."

(**Ed. Note**: "P.T. Freeman" is a former U.S. citizen living in a Caribbean country and doing business throughout the world, including countries subject to U.S. sanctions. U.S. law now contains a rebuttable presumption that U.S. persons who surrender their citizenship are presumed to do so for reasons of tax avoidance if; 1) they have an average annual income tax obligation exceeding US$100,000 and/or; 2) they have a net worth exceeding US$500,000. Such persons are required to pay tax on certain income for 10 years after they give up U.S. citizenship. It is therefore critically important to obtain expert tax advice before expatriation. For more information, see "Expatriation: The Ultimate Estate Plan" in this chapter).

Know Your MLATs!

by Mark Nestmann, *The Sovereign Individual*, December 1998

In which we learn more than, hopefully, we will ever need to know about MLATs—Mutual Legal Assistance Treaties.

Mutual Legal Assistance Treaties (MLATs) are bilateral agreements between governments that simplify evidence gathering and forfeitures. Early MLATs, such as the U.S.-Swiss agreement of 1973, applied only to a short list of serious offenses that were crimes in both the U.S.A. and Switzerland. However, most MLATs today cover "all crimes." In some MLATs (e.g., the U.S.-Cayman agreement), pure tax offenses are excluded, unless committed in conjunction with other crimes. In more recent MLATs, tax and other "fiscal" offenses are covered as any other crime. The new U.S.-Austrian MLAT is an example.

The U.S. has the most extensive network of MLATs in the world. Australia, Canada and the United Kingdom also have extensive MLAT networks.

You May be a Criminal

Because of their sweeping application, MLATs can represent a threat to legitimate investors and businesses that, for whatever reason, come under investigation for a crime. And don't be too certain that you're not a criminal. In the U.S. alone, according to the December 5, 1997 issue of *Forbes* magazine, "There are well over 3,000 federal crimes, including 1,700 that cover minor or regulatory matters. Beyond that, 10,000-plus actions have been made into crimes by regulators."

Example: Filling in a puddle on your own property that a bureaucrat later classifies as a "wetland" is a crime. Any assets you've conveyed to an asset haven to protect yourself from whatever fines or forfeiture results from this or any other "crime" could conceivably be forfeited under all-crimes MLATs.

MLATs May Override Bank Secrecy

MLATs also override local confidentiality laws. For instance, the MLAT between the United States and the U.K.'s Overseas Territory of the Turks and Caicos Islands states: "A person who divulges any confidential information or gives any testimony in conformity with the [MLAT] request shall be deemed not to commit any offense under the Confidential Relationships Ordinance 1979..."

Most MLATs do not require a judicial or administrative finding of probable cause to be invoked. Reasonable suspicion, essentially, not much more than a hunch. is sufficient. In effect, MLATs reduce the requisite burden of proof for a warrant for international evidence-gathering. Further, MLATs typically provide the subject of a confiscation order no right of appeal.

MLATs Help Forfeiture

One of the most frightening provisions of MLATs is that they provide the U.S. and other governments the authority to order international forfeitures, often on the flimsiest pretext.

The U.S.-Switzerland MLAT is typical. It requires Swiss authorities to freeze assets in Switzerland following a MLAT request "as long as the investigation relates to conduct which might be dealt with by the criminal courts of the United States." [Emphasis added.] Virtually any offense, including running a stop sign, fits this definition. Nor is it reassuring to learn that the Swiss Federal Supreme Court has declared: "If judicial assistance is requested by the United States, it cannot be denied just on the basis of deficiencies in the American proceedings, because the treaty does not contain any corresponding provision. Even alleged violations of human rights in the American proceedings form no basis for denying judicial assistance." [Emphasis added.]

Nor is it sufficient for a U.S. court to order the funds unfrozen. The Department of Justice itself must make the request to unfreeze the funds, something it has refused to do even when faced with a court order to the contrary.

U.S. MLAT Network

As of January 1999, the United States had MLATs in effect with Anguilla, Antigua-Barbuda, Argentina, Austria, Australia, The Bahamas, Barbados, Belgium, Brazil, British Virgin Islands, Canada, Cayman Islands, the Czech Republic, Dominica, Estonia, Grenada, Hong Kong, Israel, Italy, Jamaica, Latvia, Lithuania, Luxembourg, Mexico, Montserrat, Morocco, the Netherlands, Panama, Poland, Spain, St. Kitts & Nevis, St. Lucia, St. Vincent & the Grenadines, Switzerland, Thailand, Turkey, the Turks & Caicos Islands, Trinidad & Tobago, Venezuela and the United Kingdom. MLATs are pending with Colombia, Hungary, Nigeria, the Philippines, South Korea and Uruguay.

Even lacking a MLAT, however, judicial assistance may be rendered in many countries. For instance, in response to an inquiry to the U.K.'s Judicial Cooperation Unit, located within the Organized and International Crime Directorate of the Home Office, we received the following reply: "The U.K. is able to provide a full range of legal assistance in criminal matters to judicial and prosecuting authorities in other countries under Part I of the Criminal Justice (International Cooperation) Act 1990, the U.K.'s principal mutual legal assistance legislation. The 1990 Act does not require any treaty or agreement to be in place before assistance may be given in obtaining evidence in criminal proceedings or investigations. The U.K. can assist any country (or territory) in the world, whether or not that country is able to assist the U.K."

MLAT Targets Have Limited Defense

While the U.S. government has used MLATs for more than 20 years to gather evidence in foreign countries against criminal defendants, it systematically refuses to permit investigative targets to use these agreements to gather evidence for their defense, even after indictment. U.S. courts have concluded that individuals lack standing (i.e., the right to litigate) in asserting violations of treaties. Individuals may use treaties on their own behalf only if the agreement explicitly or implicitly provides this right.

This position appears to violate the U.S. Constitution, applicable foreign law and international treaties to which the United States is a party, but it nevertheless remains official U.S. policy.

Doing Business in MLAT Jurisdictions

The best way to avoid the impact of MLATs is to do business or invest in jurisdictions that don't have MLATs with your home country. For instance, the Cook Islands, Cypress, Labuan, Liechtenstein, Madeira, Malta, Mauritius and the Seychelles lack MLATs with the U.S. Nor do the U.K. Overseas Territories of Bermuda and Gibraltar have MLATs with the U.S., nor the Crown Dependencies of Jersey, Guernsey and the Isle of Man.

However, U.K. Overseas Territories and Crown Dependencies could conceivably come under the authority of the U.S.-U.K. "all-crimes" MLAT. And even countries without a MLAT will cooperate with foreign authorities to investigate allegations of serious crime.

If you do business or invest in a jurisdiction with a MLAT that could apply to you, consider the following strategies to reduce your vulnerability:

• Review the relevant MLAT or MLATs to determine what "crimes" are covered, and whether the offenses covered must be an offense in both jurisdictions to apply (dual criminality). This determination should ideally be made in consultation with your attorney.

- Review with your attorney whether assets conveyed to a foreign trust or other structure may be frozen or forfeited in a MLAT proceeding. This must be a separate determination from the normal evaluation of potential vulnerability to civil judgments, fraudulent conveyance claims, etc.

- Monitor changes in MLAT language or definitions of criminal activity when published.

- Prepare "flight clauses" in trust documents and/or Articles of Incorporation that permit the domicile of the trust or corporation to be changed if the MLAT is amended or reinterpreted in any manner that would threaten the existence of the entity, or its assets.

Extradition: Could It Happen to You?

by Robert E. Bauman, JD, *The Sovereign Individual*, 1999

Extradition is the formal legal process, established in a bilateral treaty between nations, by which the government of one country (called the sanctuary nation), at the request of another country (the requesting nation), decides whether or not to surrender a fugitive who is located within its territory. Usually the fugitive is either accused of, or already has been convicted of, a serious crime under the laws of the requesting country.

This process differs from deportation, which usually is a matter of applying a nation's immigration laws. Unlike deportation, extradition usually requires a court hearing and judicial determination of the alleged fugitive's status.

The Library of Congress estimates that ". . .the United States is party to over 100 bilateral extradition treaties . . .[and] there are many countries with which we have no extradition treaty . . . those countries are not under any obligation to extradite an individual to the U.S. under any circumstances." Among all nations, currently there are some 300 bilateral extradition treaties.

Common Law vs. Civil Law

These treaties differ considerably in content and scope. The resulting confusion in applying treaties is worsened by a basic extradition policy split among nations. The international divide is between the common law countries and civil law countries with legal systems based on the Napoleonic Code.

Common law countries as a general rule do not exempt their own nationals from extradition. The U.S. extradition law expressly permits extradition of U.S. citizens. Civil law countries generally are more protective of their citizens when it comes to extradition, but differ greatly in their approach. Some flatly prohibit any extradition of their nationals (Germany, France, the Netherlands, Switzerland, Denmark and Colombia). Others allow the government to decide on a case by case basis (Spain). Still others permit conditional or limited extraditions of nationals. Some allow their nationals who are fugitives from justice in other countries to be tried locally in lieu of extradition. Colombia included a provision to this effect in its 1991 Constitution, no doubt under heavy pressure from nervous drug lords.

Extradition is firmly established in the Anglo-American legal systems. In former times an arrest warrant issued by any British Commonwealth country was valid in all other member nations. In theory this was a unitary legal system headed by the monarch, so Scotland Yard could nab their man anywhere the sun hadn't yet set on the British Empire. Commonwealth countries still have these procedures, but more often extradition is an informal process, handled much as it is between states of the U.S.

The Pinochet Affair

Recently extradition has made headlines because of a highly unusual request made last November by a Spanish judge, Baltasar Garzon. He asked the United Kingdom to extradite 84-year-old General Augusto Pinochet of Chile, to be tried in Spain for crimes allegedly committed when he headed the Chilean government for 17 years from 1973 to 1990. Pinochet was in England on October 16, 1998 recuperating from back surgery at a London clinic when in a surprise move, the Labour government honored the Spanish request and detained him. He now remains under house arrest until the issue of extradition to Spain can be resolved by U.K. courts. British law is generous in allowing appeals in the lengthy extradition process, and experts say it could be another year before Pinochet finally might be released or ordered to stand trial in Madrid. [**Ed. Note:** As of this writing, the elderly Gen. Pinochet is back in Chile, released in late 2000 by the U.K. due to ill health and permitted to return home. The precarious state of his mental and physical health appears to bar any future Chilean prosecution for his alleged crimes.]

What is so unusual about the Pinochet case is the absence of any alleged crimes committed in the requesting nation, Spain. Extradition is being sought on grounds that Spanish citizens were killed, tortured and held hostage in Chile during the Pinochet regime by officials of his government. U.K. Home Secretary Jack Straw declined to sustain charges of genocide and murder because he said they did not fit the legal definitions of extraditable crimes under Britain's Extradition Act of 1989. However he matched accusations by the Spanish judge, with equivalent British criminal charges of attempted murder, conspiracy to murder and torture and hostage-taking.

Consider the international legal precedent if General Pinochet is extradited to Spain. Every living former U.S. president and ex-heads of state from most nations will be harassed by zealots seeking extradition on spurious grounds of alleged criminal activity. (Already another Spanish court has rejected a request from Cuban exiles to have Fidel Castro extradited to Spain for trial on charges of 40 years of murder, genocide and criminal acts.)

Extradition Until Now

As a general rule (until now), nations do not permit extradition for minor crimes or most non-criminal civil matters, such as unpaid taxes or private debts, failure to pay alimony or child support or fiscal offenses such as currency control violation. Victimless crimes such as prohibited sexual relations, slandering the state or refusing to abide by restrictions imposed upon racial or religious minorities, are also not included among extraditable crimes.

In theory, political offenses are not a basis for extradition, but defining "political" can be difficult. Tax offenses also generally have not been extraditable. However, fraud per se is an extraditable offense, and so a government that wants to pursue a tax case claims "tax fraud."

Extradition Expanding

Despite these past limitation, an ominous international trend is developing that, if successful, could broaden the scope of extradition beyond anything seen before. The U.S. and U.K. governments are frothing at the mouth in their zeal to make legitimate tax avoidance (tax bureaucrats call it "tax evasion") a basis for criminal proceedings in any nation where an accused citizen may be found. This campaign is aimed squarely at people who seek lower taxes and less financial regulation by choosing to go offshore.

The tax collectors know the most talented citizens of the U.S., U.K. and other welfare states are deserting, setting up financial shop where they and their capital are treated best. This trend is intensified by the developing worldwide cyber-economy based on Internet technology and free communications unmediated by governments.

Small wonder the U.K. Inland Revenue, the U.S. IRS and other tax hounds are worried. In 1998, undeclared (untaxed) work exceeded 15 percent of Europe's combined gross domestic product (GDP), up from only five percent in the 1970s. In the U.S. the underground "black market" economy accounts for nearly 10 percent of GDP. That means billions of dollars slipping through the eager hands of the taxman.

If the legal definition of an "extraditable" offense starts to expand, every world traveler must be fully aware of exactly what this means. And they must also know what nations are safe, and those that are not.

For those who may scoff, I'm not and never will be in need of protection from extradition think again. In the U.S., the U.K. and other statist nations, a whole host of laws now impose criminal penalties for what used to be civil offenses, ranging from improper toxic waste disposal and water pollution to the ever-expanding, catch-all crime of money laundering. Even without your knowledge, some past corporate or personal transgression might be used as a basis for a criminal charge, followed by a warrant for arrest seeking extradition. A knock on the door may be your first notice.

Informal Extradition

In most cases extradition is carried out informally using unofficial methods. It happens at U.S.-Mexican and Canadian border control points when immigration officers arrest a fugitive working in one or the other country without a legal permit, then hand the accused over to police across the border.

Without regard to formal extradition procedures, some fugitives have been abducted forcibly from a foreign country and taken to another nation for trial and/or punishment. A famous example of this kind of informal extradition occurred in 1960 when Adolf Eichmann was kidnapped from Argentina by Israeli agents. He was returned to stand trial in Israel for Nazi war atrocities committed during the Second World War, was convicted and executed.

U.S. Kidnapping Ruled Legal

The same kind of tactic was used by the U.S. Drug Enforcement Agency (DEA) in Mexico. On April 2, 1990, Dr. Humberto Alvarez Maccan was kidnapped from his medical office in Guadalajara, Mexico, and forcibly brought to Los Angeles to stand trial for the 1985 murder of DEA agent Enrique Coumarouna. A U.S. court found that Alvarez was abducted at gunpoint in Mexico by paid agents of the United States, physically and psychologically tortured by his abductors and injected with mind altering drugs. He and his family were threatened and he feared for his life throughout his ordeal.

In a highly embarrassing outcome, within months Dr. Alvarez Maccan returned to Mexico a free man. Presiding U.S. District Judge Edward Rafeedie denounced the government's weak case and found his kidnapping violated the Extradition Treaty between the United States and Mexico. The judge accused U.S. prosecutors of irresponsible and unethical conduct in using six Mexican criminals who were allegedly paid by the U.S. to testify against Alvarez.

After acquittal, the Mexican attorney general demanded the extradition of two DEA agents on charges of kidnapping, but the U.S. ignored the demand. The fiasco outraged Mexican authorities and sparked international condemnation.

In August 1990, Judge Rafeedie dismissed the case against Dr. Alvarez. In 1992, the Supreme Court reversed this decision, but by then the doctor was back home in Mexico. In this extraordinary decision the Court ruled, in effect, it is legal for U.S. agents to carry out kidnapping anywhere in the world.

Shortly afterwards, President George Bush issued a presidential Executive Order specifically authorizing U.S. agents to do just that. Since then the Order has not been challenged successfully in court. In the same year U.S. armed forces took the deposed Panamanian dictator, Manuel Noriega, prisoner during the short-lived military attack on Panama. He was transported to Miami, where he was tried and convicted of federal drug and other criminal charges, in spite of defenses based in part on extradition law and treaties between the two nations.

The Extradition Process

Formal extradition, by comparison, is a complex process governed by the terms of bilateral treaties between the nations involved. It begins when a diplomatic agent requests that a named individual be surrendered by the nation in which the person is located. The government investigates the situation and, even if there is an extradition treaty between the two nations, the sanctuary nation does not necessarily surrender the individual. Their decision will depend on their interpretation of the treaties.

In formal extradition the legal principles of specialty and dual criminality apply.

The principle of specialty means if extradition is granted, the requesting State has the right to put the fugitive on trial only for those specific offenses on which the extradition request was based. Of course once an accused is returned to his home country, there is little a foreign government can do, except protest, if the extradited person is tried for every offense under the sun.

Dual criminality requires that extradition be granted only when the acts of which the fugitive is accused are recognized as statutory crimes in both countries. Often an absence of this factor serves as the basis for refusal of an extradition request.

Canada as Example

The Canadian federal law on extradition is typical of many nation's laws. It requires that:

1. The requesting country must have jurisdiction over the offense charged. Where the crime is committed on the territory of the requesting country, there's no problem. But where the case involves jurisdiction over nationals for crimes committed outside the territory of the requesting state, things get complicated, as in the Pinochet matter.

2. The offense must constitute a crime in the requesting country.

3. The offense must constitute a crime if committed in Canada.

4. The crime must be named specifically in the extradition treaty between Canada and the requesting country.

U.S. MLATs Are Spreading

Extradition of fugitives to the U.S. is governed by traditional treaties, but augmented by a newer series of so-called Mutual Legal Assistance Treaties (MLATs). These agreements promote cooperation in the exchange of information and evidence in criminal investigations.

U.S. prosecutors have gained real power with MLATs in their arsenal. They can request search warrants be served in foreign jurisdictions, the freezing of foreign-owned assets before trial, and demand access to financial records located abroad. U.S. prosecutor's power is greatest under MLATs with Argentina, Spain and Uruguay, and all governments willing to assist the U.S., even if their local laws do not consider the fugitive's offenses to be criminal.

However, it is worth noting that The Bahamas, Panama, the U.K. and many of the U.K.'s former Caribbean colonies and Uruguay are not obliged, under MLATs with the U.S., to assist U.S. prosecutors who pursue an individual for tax offenses. This policy is changing in the U.K., where the government now is insisting that its still dependent former colonies, including Bermuda, the Cayman Islands and the Turks and Caicos adopt "all crimes" laws that includes tax offenses as crimes. One can assume these laws will eventually be used as a basis for extradition requests. Only months ago the Cayman Islands caved into these demands.

The U.K. is also a signatory to the European Convention on Extradition, which governs all European Union nations, as well as several that have voluntarily agreed to participate.

Nations with U.S. Extradition Treaties

Antigua-Barbuda, Argentina, Austria, Barbados, Belgium, British Virgin Islands (U.K.), Canada, Cayman Islands (U.K.), Cyprus, Dominica, France, Grenada, India, Italy, Luxembourg, Mexico, Morocco, Poland, Spain, St. Kitts and Nevis, St. Lucia, St. Vincent and the Grenadines, Trinidad-Tobago, Switzerland, Turks and Caicos Islands (U.K.), United Kingdom and Zimbabwe.

Nations with U.S. Diplomatic Relations but NO Extradition Treaties

Afghanistan, Algeria, Armenia, Bahrain, Bangladesh, Brunei, Burkina Faso, Burundi, Cameroon, Cape Verde, Central African Republic, Chad, People's Republic of China, the Comoros, Djibouti, Equatorial Guinea, Ethiopia, Gabon, Guinea, Guinea-Bissau, Indonesia, Ivory Coast, Jordan, South Korea, Kuwait, Laos, Lebanon, Madagascar, Mali, Marshall Islands, Mauritania, Micronesia, Moldavia, Mongolia, Mozambique, Myanmar, Namibia, Nepal, Niger, Oman, Philippines, Principe and San Tome, Qatar, the Russian Federation, Rwanda, Saudi Arabia, Senegal, Sudan, Syria, Togo, Tunisia, Uganda, Vietnam, Western Samoa, Yemen and Zaire.

Nations with NO Diplomatic Relations and NO Extradition Treaties with the U.S.

Andorra, Angola, Bhutan, Bosnia, Cambodia, Cuba, Iran, North Korea, Libya, Maldives, Serbia, Somalia, Taiwan and Vanuatu.

Nations with U.K. Extradition Treaties

Albania, Argentina, Austria, Belgium, Bolivia, Brazil, Bolivia, Chile, Colombia, Cuba, Czechoslovakia, Denmark, Ecuador, Finland, France, Germany, Greece, Guatemala, Haiti, Hungary, Iceland, India, Iraq, Israel, Italy, Liberia, Luxembourg, Mexico, Monaco, the Netherlands, Nicaragua, Norway, Panama, Paraguay, Peru, Poland, Portugal, Romania, Salvador, San Marino, Spain, Sweden, Switzerland, Thailand, USA, Uruguay and Yugoslavia.

EU Extradition Convention Nations

Austria, Belgium, Bulgaria, Croatia, Cyprus, Czech Republic, Denmark, Estonia, Finland, France, Germany, Greece, Hungary, Iceland, Irish Republic, Israel, Italy, Liechtenstein, Lithuania, Luxembourg, Malta, Moldova, the Netherlands, Norway, Poland, Portugal, Romania, Slovak Republic, Slovenia, Spain, Sweden, Switzerland, Turkey, United Kingdom, Isle of Man and the Channel Islands.

Viewed in comparison with the long list of countries who have MLATs with the U.S., the U.K. list seems small. Until now the U.K. government has not been as zealous as its U.S. counterpart when it comes to limiting the options of fleeing fugitives. Depending on the outcome of the Pinochet case, and the pressure on former U.K. colonies, this policy may change drastically.

The U.K. has no extradition treaty of any kind with Costa Rica, Korea, Russia, Tanzania, Mongolia, Indonesia or Jordan.

U.S. as Safe Haven

For a foreign national considering the U.S. as a safe haven, chances are mixed. Foreign governments requesting extradition of an individual from within the U.S. need demonstrate only "probable cause" that a crime has been committed by the accused. Based on that showing, most U.S. courts will automatically issue an order for the arrest and detention of the accused while the issue of extradition is reviewed.

In November 1995, a Federal Appeals Court in San Francisco threw up a major roadblock to America's quick and easy extradition of foreign citizens. The case was not appealed by the government and has weakened a decades-old quirk of American extradition law the U.S. government's power to arrest and detain a foreign citizen for extradition without showing probable cause that the accused committed an alleged crime abroad. Up until this ruling the government could jail a foreigner based on nothing more than a request from a foreign government alleging a crime.

In October 1995, Giancarlo Paretti, a jet-set Italian financier, was arrested in his Los Angeles lawyer's office while attending a deposition concerning his highly leveraged purchase of MGM-United Artists entertainment group. The French government wanted him for alleged bank fraud. When released on bond, he jumped bail and went home to Italy. But as a result of his case, in support of an extradition request, now the U.S. government must produce affidavits or other substantial proof from which a court can find probable cause to believe the person sought actually committed the crime alleged by a foreign government.

What About You?

So how might this tangled web of extradition affect a foreign citizen living abroad?

As we said, extradition procedures are covered by a network of bilateral treaties among nations, constantly under revision. In recent years the U.S. government has led demands for a broad definition of criminal acts warranting extradition. Newer U.S. treaties and MLATs include mail fraud and money laundering as "extraditable offenses." (The American government always presses for mail fraud as an included offense since most nations will not extradite for what the U.S. claims is "tax evasion.")

There's also an international movement to expand extradition law. In 1997, the then prime minister of India, hosting the 66th annual meeting of the International Criminal Police Organization, better known as "Interpol," demanded the adoption of a universal extradition treaty and a common code of conduct "to check international crime and corruption and to prevent criminals from taking shelter in foreign countries and laundering wealth acquired through corrupt means." You can read between those lines and easily see tax matters on such a list.

Such an agreement would fit nicely into United Nations demands that tax haven nations be forced to abrogate their financial privacy laws and turn over information about foreigners who have bank accounts, trusts and international business corporations offshore. The UN formally adopted that demand in May 1998.

Light in the Tunnel

There still is some hope.

A leading international tax consultant in Washington, D.C. told us (off the record, since he must deal with the IRS constantly), most nations just don't have stiff criminal tax penalties like the U.S. and are reluctant to change. That's because "...foreign tax laws usually apply criminal penalties only to intentional fraud, such as false filings. Many treat failure to file as negligence, since their systems require filing of an estimated income statement. On that statement the government bases tax bills that are sent later."

Broadened tax law extradition became an issue in 1996 when the U.S. and Switzerland revised their mutual tax treaty. Boastful "unnamed U.S. sources" claimed the new treaty made it easier for the IRS to get information on which to base requests for extradition from the Swiss. The Swiss government quickly echoed a ruling of the nation's highest court holding that unless fraud was shown as defined by Swiss tax laws, the Swiss would continue to deny information and extradition based on broader U.S. tax laws.

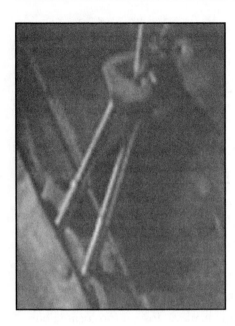

CHAPTER THREE
Offshore Banking: Privacy & Asset Protection

The prime requirement for achieving iron-clad financial privacy and asset protection is to get your cash and property out of what the late admiral of the U.S. Navy John Paul Jones correctly described in a military sense as "harm's way." This simply means you must move a large part of your financial activity "offshore"—out of, and away from, the high-tax nation you call home, whether it be the U.S., U.K. or any other state bent upon confiscating your hard-earned wealth.

Here we present articles and ideas that explain how to establish and use a bank account in a financial institution located in a foreign nation. Also explained are U.S. laws governing banking, money laundering and reporting of offshore cash transfers, a touchy matter under the current state of the law.

Part One—Offshore Accounts
The Advantages of Offshore Banking
Banking in Silence, 1998

The best first step in your quest for financial privacy is to move at least some of your cash away from the prying hands of Big Brother. In the modern world this does not mean burying gold coins in your backyard, then carefully guarding your secret stash. Instead, financial freedom flows from making use of one or more offshore banking facilities. (And not telling anyone where your hard-earned cash is stashed is still good advice, especially in this age of "cyber-banking.")

What exactly is an offshore banking facility? Quite simply, any banking institution located outside of your home country.

The process of opening an offshore bank account is neither daunting or intimidating. It is often just as simple, if not easier, than opening a bank account in your home town. Don't think the offshore option is only viable for the incredibly wealthy with a jet-set lifestyle. Ordinary people from many countries have discovered the advantages of offshore banking.

Even if you have only a few thousand to squirrel away, why not start up your international portfolio today? Once your money is liberated from home soil, it will be free to grow offshore unrestricted by your home government's restraints.

Free From Government Interference

The major advantage of offshore banking is the power to say goodbye to unwanted government interference, where banks are subjected to a myriad of restrictive regulations. These rules are designed to strip you of banking privacy and lay your affairs open to government scrutiny.

The good news is that by making use of offshore bank accounts you need not surrender your financial privacy. Funneling assets offshore means at the very least your government faces a complicated diplomatic hassle to get its hands on your bank records. The average small investor will be passed over by bureaucrats who would rather chase after the big fish. Catching multimillionaire tax evaders means big revenue for government, but also ensures prestige and promotions for those underlings responsible.

At the same time, those same bureaucrats tend to focus on easy targets. In other words, if you combine the basic PT principle of low profile with banking privacy, your financial affairs will stay private even in our over-regulated world.

Finally, remember that although the U.S. has had some success in prying the lid off of banking secrecy in world tax havens, it has also met with a great deal of resistance. The war is not lost yet. Countries offering banking secrecy understand they cannot appear too weak in the face of U.S. demands. It is in their best interest to protect your banking privacy, for if they fail much of their business will quickly evaporate. Furthermore, if you use the right techniques, your banking records can achieve a level of privacy considered by many to be all but lost in the modern world. [**Ed. Note**: Since this was written in 1996, many tax havens have weakened financial privacy protections, under pressure from various sources. Elsewhere in these pages you will find described those havens (see Chapter 8) that still protect privacy to a high degree (Panama, Switzerland, Austria, Andorra, Liechtenstein) and those that have surrendered to Big Brother's anti-secrecy demands (The Bahamas, the Channel Islands, the Isle of Man, among them.)

Greater Profitability

Many who venture into the world of offshore banking seek greater banking privacy. However, the benefits go much further. Freedom from Big Brother snooping into your affairs also means market forces are left to work freely. The myriad of laws imposed in many countries not only means extra hassles for you and your banker, it renders banks far less profitable. In the U.S., between 10 and 20 percent of bank earnings now pay for regulatory compliance alone, a staggering US$100 billion per year for the U.S. banking community.

Of course, banks are not forced to pay this exorbitant bill. As any business would, your local bank does not hesitate to pass on such costs to you, whether in the form of increased fees or reduced interest rates. In the end, you lose money by banking exclusively with the bank around the corner.

Government interference costs you a whole lot more. The U.S. Federal Reserve System further restricts banking activities, demanding banks hold back a certain amount of their funds.

Who hangs on to these funds for safekeeping? You guessed it, Big Brother. Does he pay any interest on these deposits that he ties up and renders useless? Of course not. On the other hand, offshore banks need not comply with these restrictions and can therefore make use of a larger percentage of their holdings. With more of their capital invested, they can in turn pass on greater profits to you.

Offshore banks are not required to lend money to certain borrowers at below-market rates. They need not purchase certain types of debts or securities, such as government debt. They are not affected by credit ceilings that prohibit onshore competitors from seeking certain types of profitable business. There are no limits on the rates at which they can borrow and lend money, meaning that the bank itself is free to decide the interest rates it offers.

Greater Flexibility

Offshore banks enjoy a degree of flexibility that is the envy of their onshore competitors. For example, although its repeal is now being considered, the Glass-Steagall Act prohibits U.S. banks from brokering or dealing in securities or offering investment counsel. [**Ed. Note**: Recent changes in the U.S. banking laws now have removed many of these prohibitions].

Conversely, banking havens such as Switzerland and Panama have universal banking laws that allow banks to engage in many types of investment activity, such as investment and trust management or precious metals brokering.

By using an offshore bank you can develop a personal rapport with one individual who can oversee the bulk of your financial affairs. Your bank is no longer merely a place to stash your cash, paying hefty fees for the privilege, then paying more to your stockbroker or portfolio manager. Offshore banks offer a multitude of investment services, including mutual funds, precious metal funds, currency funds, foreign government bonds and managed accounts.

Furthermore, your bank is free to invest your money in a more varied portfolio with better returns. Many domestic banks are restricted from investing in certain areas, such as real estate or commodities. Your portfolio manager cannot move funds quickly, reaping rewards of investment savvy. But offshore, regulation-free banking allows your money to achieve its full potential.

Finally, offshore banks are free to engage in business ventures that would make their more conservative onshore counterparts shy away. They can finance new businesses dealing in unexplored areas of opportunity. They can provide insurance services covering such "risky" areas of investment. Malpractice insurance premiums have skyrocketed. By using commissions to offset prices, offshore banks can offer such insurance to clients at a price often lower than their domestic competition. Such gambles mean huge profits.

Low Or No Taxes

Ben Franklin said it first: "In this world nothing can be said to be certain except death and taxes." Ben may be right about death, but taxes are far from certain. Offshore banks can set up shop in whatever jurisdiction they please, and so they go where they can avoid the burden of taxation.

The figures speak for themselves. The industry as a whole pays a negative two percent in tax. Whereas most businesses are saddled with close to 50 percent tax rates, in many nations the offshore banking industry is on the receiving end of government subsidy and promotional programs.

This means your offshore bank can pass on these tremendous savings to you. Even if you are legally required to declare interest that you earn on an offshore account and pay taxes on this income to your home government, you will still reduce your level of overall taxation by banking offshore. When invested offshore, the profit your money generates is not taxed twice as in the U.S., first on the bank's earned profits, then again on the interest you earn. With imaginative thinking all of your money earned offshore in a tax-free jurisdiction can remain in the possession of the person most entitled to it—you.

By their nature, offshore banks are nimble. They can quickly move and set up shop wherever the sun happens to be shining the brightest. A few banking haven nations have been around for a long time, other new ones sprout up in far flung places. They all understand the minute liberal banking policies are gone, the money will also go, fleeing to safer pastures.

Higher Interest Rates

Freedom enjoyed by offshore banks translates into more money for you. In some over-regulated nations it is five times more expensive to start an investment fund than it is offshore. In fact, the large number of offshore banks competing for deposits means interest rates offered are always going to be higher than domestic rates.

Few or No Currency Restrictions

Offshore banking opens up new windows of opportunity. Many countries prohibit citizens from holding any currency other than the national currency. Countries that do allow foreign currency accounts often impose heavy taxes that negate any advantage.

By moving your money offshore into stronger currencies you effectively liberate it from senseless national policies. No single currency is always best for all your cash assets. As in any good investment plan, diversity is the key. By opening at least one offshore account in a friendly, no-tax jurisdiction, your eggs are no longer stuck in a single basket.

An offshore bank account can be your safety valve if your government prohibits or restricts taking cash out of your homeland. The safety valve process uses what are known as back-to-back or parallel loans. You lend your controlled currency to a company in your home country, while its affiliate in a foreign land arranges a loan to you. If you want to liberate Brazilian cruzeiros from restrictive local policies, you lend them to Widgets of Rio de Janeiro. In turn, the London branch of Widgets lends a U.K. company you control a similar amount in pounds sterling. Presto, your money is out of the currency control country, free to roost wherever you desire.

True, many governments that impose currency restrictions are aware of such schemes and have laws prohibiting them. But countries that are so shaky as to need currency restrictions also need favorable relations with foreign banking entities. In short, the government has no choice but to look favorably on any loan you arrange with an offshore bank.

Stash some of your money in a secure offshore banking environment and you escape senseless government restrictions. Political upheaval and consequent currency fluctuations no longer affect you. Currency restrictions or government cash confiscation stops at the water's edge. Banking offshore, your funds can be denominated in secure currencies in various havens around the globe, guaranteeing your financial future whatever happens tomorrow.

Opening and Using an Offshore Bank Account
by Nicholas Pullen, 1997

To many people "offshore banking" evokes images of criminals in dark glasses, funneling black cash through fraudulent accounts in countries with questionable banking laws. But these negative images are simply the product of government demonizing programs aided and abetted by sensationalist media coverage.

Offshore banking is neither unpatriotic or illegal. Moving cash offshore protects your financial well-being and ensures your money works best for you, rather than for your government.

Choosing a Secure Banking Haven

Before dispatching your cash to the safe-keeping of an offshore banking institution, you must consider which safe haven nation you are going to choose. Not all countries offering so-called "offshore financial services" are suitable. In some places your cash is at risk from corruption, mismanagement, and downright fraud. Fortunately, there are some well-established offshore banking havens with long histories of excellent service and maximum privacy.

Evaluate each haven according to these simple criteria.

Stability—Only select havens with a long history of political, financial and judicial stability. They should have no history of confiscations or nationalization of foreign cash/bank accounts and should offer depositor insurance. The local economy should be dependent to a great extent on the continued presence of foreign cash and the on-going development of an attractive environment for foreign capital. Banana republics where dictators and governments change like the weather are definitely out.

Secrecy—The best havens have non-intrusive governments prepared to impose stiff penalties on local professionals who dare to breach bank secrecy/confidentiality laws. Go for havens with solid banking privacy legislation and a reputation for upholding and defending it.

Local Attitudes—Consider local attitudes toward high net worth individuals. If there is a high proportion of anti-wealth zealots, find another haven. You don't want to be the scapegoat for tomorrow's domestic problems. Consider how the government behaves towards the local population. If it treats them badly or has a poor human rights records, it is not likely to treat you any better when push comes to shove. If you don't like what you find—look elsewhere.

Low Profile—Pay special attention to haven nations you can enter without obtaining an entry visa. Visa stamps can betray your interest in a region and governments are particularly interested in those with regular business in a tax haven. No visa stamp—no obvious evidence of your movements.

Based on the above criteria and years of experience here are some of the best nations: Switzerland, Austria, Liechtenstein, Luxembourg, St. Kitts and Nevis, Panama, and the Cook Islands. For certain purposes we also recommend the British Channel Islands and the Isle of Man, but keep in mind these jurisdictions have weakened their financial privacy even though they offer others useful services such as insurance, annuities and financial planning.

Opening Your Account

Never have information from offshore banks sent to your home or office. Mail snoops record details and tamper with mail deemed suspicious. Postmarks, stamps from offshore centers and foreign bank envelopes all figure highly on the suspect list. Overly conscientious postmen, nosy colleagues and curious family members can all compromise security.

Use a mail drop, preferably one outside your own country. For example, U.S. citizens should use Canadian mail drops, Europeans should use mail drops in a neighboring country. Collect mail in person or have it sent on under plain cover to another mail drop where you can collect—why trust the mail drop operator with your home address? Use mail drops offering personal boxes and a key with 24-hour access. Collect mail at times when no one else is around to see you.

Don't necessarily use your real name when first approaching offshore banking institutions to make inquiries. Why surrender personal information to an institution you may never use? An alias is legal unless you use it to defraud. But don't try to open an account using a false name. Banks in most jurisdictions will want to see a copy of your passport for verification of ID at the very least. Havens with strong secrecy laws will not divulge this information to anybody.

Don't open an account with a bank that is based in, or has branches located in, your home country. Governments can put pressure on home country branches to force offshore counterparts to release account details or initiate seizures. For example, a U.K. citizen wanting to bank in the Caribbean should use the Netherlands Antilles as opposed to the Cayman Islands, which is a British overseas territory. A U.K. citizen should choose a Dutch/Danish/Swiss account.

Nothing is better, in terms of the ability to leave no paper trail, than using cash. A few alternatives to cash are legally allowable amounts of bank drafts, bank checks, postal money orders or traveler's checks, preferably purchased anonymously. Beware exceeding purchases of these instruments in amounts that trigger reporting requirements—$10,000 or more in the U.S.

Be sure the bank you choose does not perform its account data processing in your home country. Ask and make sure all banking records are kept and maintained offshore out of harm's way.

If you have an offshore account denominated in your home country currency, these funds usually will be stored or at least cleared by the offshore bank in a correspondent account located in your home country. It is better to hold offshore accounts denominated in currencies which can't be grabbed by the authorities at home.

If possible move funds into your offshore account in a manner that leaves no paper trail. Do not use any form of electronic transfer or checks drawn directly on already existing home country accounts. There are still a few ways to move assets abroad both anonymously and legally. The most common is with cold, hard cash. Withdraw cash from your existing account then travel to your haven to bank it. Make future deposits in a similar manner. By breaking the paper trail you leave no telltale links between home and offshore accounts. Keep in mind that U.S. laws require the reporting to Customs of the transport of more than $10,000 in or out of the country.

For a list of international bankers, consult the *Polk World Bank Directory* (International Edition), Polk's Bank Services, P.O. Box 305100, Nashville, TN 37230-5100, USA. **Fax:** + 1 615 885 3081. On the net, http://www.qualisteam.com lists almost every bank web site in the world. Sites are classified by country, banking services and additional information.

Maintaining Privacy

The precautions you take while investigating and opening offshore accounts count for nothing if that is where your low-profile techniques end. Once your account is opened you need to work constantly to maintain secrecy.

Don't tell anybody about your offshore arrangements. Telling ex-spouses, family members, friends, colleagues and business partners about your offshore nest egg can have expensive consequences. Too often, the people closest to you are those most likely to play lead roles in separating you from your assets. Many tax inspections and seizure cases start as the result of a tip-off from a disgruntled acquaintance, family member or ex-friend.

Keep contacts with your offshore bank to a minimum. Give government watchers and listeners as few chances as possible to intercept information relating to offshore accounts you hold. If you need to receive mail from the bank use a mail drop. If at all possible, don't call your bank by telephone. By minimizing phone contact you ensure your voice, codes, account numbers or transfer details cannot be recorded. If you must phone your bank, use pre-paid disposable phone cards and destroy them after use. If you send/receive faxes use a copy shop.

Don't leave evidence of offshore accounts lying around in your briefcase, at home or in the office—the first places to which investigators are drawn. Keep all such information in a safe place. Consider opening a safety deposit box outside your home country.

Stay abreast of the political situation in your chosen haven country via newspapers, the media and subscriptions to specialty offshore financial newsletters.

If using a credit card issued by your offshore bank, be careful where you use it. Never use it in your home country to avoid a paper trail traceable back to your offshore bank. Unusual cards can attract the wrong type of interest. Remember, if using your bank or credit card at ATMs, surveillance cameras are always watching.

Spend cash wisely at home. Preferably, you should try to spend it carefully abroad like a tourist. Extravagance at home attracts tax hounds. If your home accounts seem to contradict your observable lifestyle, the tax authorities will take an interest.

Whatever else you may do, make certain none of your activities violates the laws of the country in which you are resident. You don't want to lose your home base.

Profitable Investing in Your Offshore Bank Account

By Mark Nestmann, *The Sovereign Individual*, January 2004

An offshore bank account can give you almost unlimited access to offshore investments. But for many investors, the idea of an "offshore bank account" is shrouded in mystery.

Here I'll help you clear up the mystery. I'll help you decide what type of offshore account is best for you, where you should open it, what information you'll need to disclose to get started, the best way to transfer money to and from your account and a few of the possible investments you can make with it. Plus, I'll show you some ways you can reduce the fees associated with an offshore account.

How to Choose the Right Offshore Bank

Most offshore banks specialize in one of the following areas: 1. Taking money on deposit and lending it to businesses (commercial banks) 2. Taking money on deposit and lending it to private individuals (savings and loans) 3. Buying and holding investments for private individuals (private banks).

The type of account you need depends on your objectives. If you just want a small offshore nest egg, and don't plan to actively trade with your account, your best option is to use an offshore building society or savings and loan, or a commercial bank. Interest rates are usually higher and the fees are much lower.

If you are doing business offshore, you will likely need an offshore commercial bank that specializes in business financing, multiple currency dealings and merchant payment solutions. However, if you are like most members of The Sovereign Society, and are an active investor, you'll want to use a private bank. The Sovereign Society has established working relationships with private banks in Austria and Denmark. During the coming year, we anticipate establishing such relationships with private banks in other offshore centers.

Once you decide on a bank, here are the questions you must ask:

What types of accounts are available for international investors?

Are there any investments that nationals of your country are not permitted to purchase?

What taxes will be withheld from my investments?

What investments are considered part of the bank's balance sheet and thus available to the bank's creditors (including depositors) in the event of the bank's insolvency?

What are the fees for securities transactions and custody?

What other fees apply to the account?

Is my account insured against losses in the event of the bank's insolvency?

How can I transact business with the bank? Are telephone, fax or e-mail orders accepted?

Is Online banking available? If so, is this service available in English?

You'll also want to check out the financial standing of the bank. A convenient service for this purpose is at www.fitchratings.com.

Opening and Funding the Account

Banks worldwide now require customers to identify both themselves fully and the source of their funds before opening an account. However, information you provide a bank outside your own country will not be easily available to someone in your home jurisdiction. Indeed, in some countries, such as Austria, Panama and Switzerland, bank secrecy laws assure that information about your account will only be released in the event of a criminal investigation, and even then only with the order of a local court.

For private banks, information you must provide will include: a detailed application, including your name and address; what type of account you wish to open; what currency in which you wish it to be denominated; and whether you wish to apply for a debit card. To satisfy the "know your customer" regulations, you'll need to present a copy of your passport and possibly a utility bill to confirm your residential address.

Investor profile. The bank will ask that you specify your investment objectives, investment experience and the investment risk approach you prefer.

Source of funds. You will be asked to specify the source of your funds, and in some cases, obtain a reference letter from a bank in your home country stipulating that the funds have been earned legitimately.

Choice of beneficiary. Without proper planning, it's possible that upon your death, your account assets will not be made available to your loved ones without a complex and expensive legal proceeding. The best way to avoid this is to list your spouse, partner or other person as an account beneficiary. This designation is revocable—you can always designate a new beneficiary. For banks that don't have this option available, an alternative is to make your intended beneficiary a co-owner of the account.

A wire transfer is the fastest way to fund your account. Your account is also credited much more quickly than with a check. Just ask your domestic bank for wiring instructions.

Most offshore banks also accept personal or business checks. The disadvantage is that it takes a considerable length of time for a check to clear. You can also fund your offshore account with pension assets. In most offshore jurisdictions funding accounts with cash is discouraged and in some cases prohibited altogether.

What Kind of Account?

Offshore banks offer the same types of accounts as domestic banks, although the name of the account and the way it's used may differ.

When you first deposit funds, your offshore bank will open a current account. The account will earn no interest or a very low interest rate, and the assets will be held on the bank's balance sheet.

Certificates of deposit are available at most foreign banks, in almost any currency. You earn more interest for a larger investment or for a longer commitment. The interest rate also varies depending on the credit quality of the issuer and the currency. Interest rates tend to be slightly lower than those published in financial newspapers, such as The Wall Street Journal or Financial

Times. Depending on the bank's policy, CDs may or may not remain part of the balance sheet.

Securities accounts permit you to purchase stocks, bonds or funds, anywhere in the world. The purchase price for each trade, less commissions, is debited from your account and credited to a custodial account maintained by the bank. Your securities are usually segregated from the bank's assets and are not available to meet claims by the bank's creditors. But inquire to make sure this is the bank's policy.

As with a domestic securities account, you may issue limit orders, stop loss orders, etc. You may also buy and sell put and call options on many foreign securities, although the rules may be different than in your home country. For instance, with European-style options, you can only cash out on the last business day before expiration.

Dividend and interest payments may be subject to withholding tax, depending on the country in which they are issued. You can often reclaim withholding tax under a tax treaty between your country and whatever jurisdiction has imposed it. The United States, for instance, has tax treaties with more than 50 countries.

While it is common for offshore banks to purchase U.S. securities on behalf of their clients, we don't recommend this strategy, due to the IRS "qualified intermediary" (QI) regulations. These legal provisions strip away all privacy for U.S. securities holdings purchased through a foreign bank by requiring the bank to report to the IRS.

Precious metals accounts have purchase options similar to those available for securities. Depending on the type of custody you choose, the metals you purchase may or may not be part of the bank's balance sheet.

Managed accounts are available if you have the equivalent of US$250,000 (more at some banks) to invest. The stated portfolio management minimums of most private banking departments are negotiable, depending on the client. You can choose to have your portfolio managed for growth, income, or a combination of growth and income.

Buying Foreign Currencies

One of the advantages of a foreign account is that it gives you easy access to foreign currency markets. Here's an example of how this strategy might pay off.

Let's say that you purchased a one-year CD denominated in euros with U.S. dollars on Jan. 1, 2001. You invested US$10,000 in the CD, which had an interest rate of 4.0%. On that date, US$10,000 would purchase EUR$9,414. One year later, on Jan. 1, 2002, you rolled over the CD for another year, this time at 2.5%. And you did the same Jan. 3, 2003, at an interest rate of 2%.

On Jan. 1, 2004, your CD will be worth EUR10,236. But in the meantime, the euro has appreciated against the U.S. dollar. We went to press Dec. 9, 2003, so we don't know the year-end euro-dollar exchange rate. But if it's around what it is today—1.22—if you cashed out your CD on Jan. 1, 2004, and converted it back to dollars, you would have US$12,488, less foreign exchange fees.

Because of your currency gains, your total three-year return nearly tripled—from 9% to 25%.

Of course, the euro could have just as easily gone down against the U.S. dollar. But since the long-term trend of the dollar's value is down, investing in global currencies may be an intelligent diversification.

Account Fees You'll Pay

There's no getting around it—fees in offshore accounts are higher than they are in U.S. accounts.

This is a consequence, in part, to the fact that foreign laws generally prohibit financial institutions from disclosing any information about individual accounts to outside sources. In contrast, U.S. banks and brokerages can freely sell or exchange information about your account to third parties.

Greater privacy, though, comes with a price. Fees and commissions you can anticipate paying offshore include:

* Currency conversion fees and hidden spreads. Commissions for currency conversions generally are about 0.15%-0.5%, but beware of conversions that don't occur at or near the interbank rate, but at a less favorable "retail rate" that may mask a hidden charge of 2% or more.

* An account maintenance fee. This varies from a flat rate equivalent to about US$50/year to a percentage of your account—as high as 0.25%/year.

* A statement preparation fee. Each time the bank executes a transaction, it charges a fee to print and mail you a statement.

* Commissions offshore are significantly higher than in the United States. Expect to pay 0.15% or more for each bond trade and 0.3% or more for each stock you purchase. Commissions for precious metals generally are about 1%. You may even be charged a commission of 0.15%-0.5% to purchase a CD (although generally not to roll it over). The good news, though, is that commissions are coming down due to greater competition.

* Loads and management fees. When you purchase offshore funds, you can anticipate paying a front end load of 5% or more, plus annual management fees as much as 3%. Even offshore funds without a front-end load may impose a rear end load if you sell before a specified number of years have elapsed.

* Safe custody fees. For securities the bank purchases for your account, you will pay a custody fee from 0.15%-0.5% per annum based on their market value. As custodian, the bank collects dividends, coupon payments and, if the security has a maturity date, the value of its principal when it matures. These fees are for collective custody. This means your holdings are not segregated from alike and interchangeable securities of other investors. Higher fees apply for individual custody, in which case your holdings are segregated and placed in secure storage under your name. In both types of custody, your holdings are generally not part of the bank's balance sheet.

* Portfolio management fees. A typical portfolio management fee is 1% per annum. This fee does not include fees and commissions for trades on the account.

* Other fees. Many services provided at no charge by domestic banks or brokerages are only available for a fee at offshore banks. To avoid surprises, before ordering a service, ask about the fee associated with it.

Six Fee-Saving Strategies

Here are a few ideas to reduce fees in your offshore account.

1. Limit securities purchases to blue chip issues that you plan to hold for an extended period. This reduces commissions for securities trading.

2. Purchase closed end funds that trade like stocks on a securities exchange. This eliminates the loads imposed by many offshore funds. Your bank will purchase and sell the fund at the market price, which may represent a premium or discount to the value of the underlying assets. You pay the same commissions as you would for any other security. Note: We generally do notecommend paying premiums for exchange-traded funds.

3. Take delivery of your securities and precious metals and maintain custody in a safety deposit box or private vault. This avoids custodial fees, but you will be responsible for collecting dividends, coupon payments, etc. If you want to sell your securities, you will need to find a   broker willing to execute the trade and then arrange to have the certificates or metals securely conveyed.

4. Use intermediaries for currency conversions. If your bank will not conduct a trade at or near the interbank rate, you may want to use a foreign currency account or trade currencies through an intermediary foreign exchange broker. One such intermediary is Asset Strategies International, headed up by Council of Experts member Michael Checkan (www.assetstrategies.com). Another foreign exchange service is www.customhouse.com, with an online affiliate at www.xe.com/fx.

5. Instruct your bank not to mail you account statements. This will eliminate or substantially reduce statement fees. At some banks, you can arrange to access them Online.

6. Ask for a lower fee. If you are a good customer, and believe that a fee for a trade or service is too high, just say so. Chances are the bank will reduce it to a more reasonable level.

Tapping Your Offshore Nest-Egg

It's generally best to leave your offshore assets "offshore" unless you need to tap into them in an emergency. This keeps the assets off the domestic "radar screen." But if you require access to these assets, the same methods used to fund foreign investments may also be used to reclaim them.

The easiest and most convenient way to obtain payments from an offshore bank is via wire transfer. It may also be possible to have a check issued in your domestic currency by a correspondent bank located in your country.

If you open a large enough account (approximately US$5,000 at commercial banks, higher at private banks), you can apply for a debit card to withdraw funds. Ask whether the card can be used outside the country of origin and what the fees are for using it. Also find out if the bank or credit card network imposes a currency conversion fee if you need to withdraw funds in another currency.

However, don't use a debit card if you are seeking privacy from your government. The U.S. government has obtained the credit card records of hundreds of thousands of Americans. Some of these Americans allegedly used offshore debit cards tied to bank accounts that the IRS says were never reported to the U.S. government and for which taxes were never paid.

Where to Open Your Foreign Account

Banks are part of modern commerce in every country. But The Sovereign Society's top country picks for offshore banking are Austria, Denmark, Panama, Switzerland, and Liechtenstein. We recommend these jurisdictions because they offer favorable laws to foreigners investing or doing business there, including (in most cases) zero taxes for non-resident investors.

We also recommend these countries because, in two of them, we have set up "Convenient Account" relationships with local service providers—and we plan to establish other such relationships in 2004. As a member of The Sovereign Society, you can immediately activate a Convenient Account with a top-notch private bank, with a professional, English-speaking staff. The minimum necessary to open the most basic account is US$14,000. All you need to do is complete the application you received when you became a Sovereign Society member.

Here are the contact addresses for Convenient Accounts in our recommended jurisdictions:

Austria. Anglo Irish Bank (Austria) AG, Rathausstrasse 20, 1010 Vienna, Austria. Tel.: +(43) 1 406-6161. Fax: +(43) 1 405-8142. E-mail: welcome.desk@angloirishbank.at. Link: www.angloirishbank.at. (minimum investment: US$25,000; US$100,000 for companies and trusts).

Denmark. Jyske Bank, Vesterbrograde 9, DK-1780 Copenhagen V, Denmark. Contact: Thomas Fischer. Tel.: +45 (33) 787-812. Fax: +45 (33) 787-833. E-mail: fischer@jyskebank.dk. Link: www.jbpb.com. (minimum investment: US$14,000).

Don't have US$14,000 to invest? Don't worry. Many foreign commercial banks accept much lower minimums, even from non-resident investors, although you won't get the personalized service that you would from a private bank. One such bank is Bank Austria. You can log on to their web site at www.ba-ca.com/en/index.html.

How Secret Is an Offshore Bank Account?
by John Pugsley, *The Sovereign Individual*, June 1998

Over the years I've had many bank accounts in the U.S. and other countries, and have often telephoned my bank to verify my balance. Occasionally, I have been asked for my mother's maiden name or my social security number to get the information. All too often, I've needed to give nothing more than my name and account number.

Getting information over the telephone about anyone's account in U.S. banks is simple. Your bank account numbers are printed on every check you write, and required information for disclosure, such as your Social Security number or your mother's name, can easily be found.

It's not difficult for any private individual to find out the details of your U.S. bank accounts if they hire a well connected private investigator, but for government agencies, it's even simpler. Financial institutions must pony up every detail of your account history any time the IRS (or any other government agency) requests it, and no court order is required. Furthermore, banks are prohibited from even telling you about the inquiry. If Uncle Sam wants the money in your account, he can simply take it. You won't know it until after the fact. Increasingly, the situation is the same in the U.K., Canada and other industrialized countries. It's "seize now, ask questions later."

If you're outraged by the lack of bank privacy in your own country, an offshore bank account is one answer. Numerous countries, including Switzerland, Austria and Liechtenstein, as well as most of the "tax haven" countries like Panama have laws that prohibit banks and other financial institutions from divulging any information about customer accounts without a court order.

Indeed, it is a crime for anyone working in one of these institutions to divulge customer information. The bank can only release information if a local court orders it to do so. And such an order can be obtained only if it receives evidence that the account holder is suspected of criminal activity.

The popular belief is that in asset havens, no one, including agencies of the U.S., U.K. or Canadian governments, can break through these barriers. Typically a foreign banker will tell you that if a foreign agency, such as the IRS or Revenue Canada, demands to see the bank records of a depositor who is suspected of tax evasion, it would be sent packing. It couldn't get a court order.

Bank secrecy laws and the assurances of financial institutions that customer information would never be revealed unless a non-tax crime was involved, have led hordes of people to hide funds in "secret" accounts. Without doubt, many persons fail to disclose the existence of these accounts and don't report any income earned on them. In the case of a U.S. person this is clearly illegal. They feel they're safe because of bank secrecy. Are they?

Don't bet your freedom on it. It would be very foolish to rely on such bank secrecy as an unbreakable barrier to your account information. Many people have been prosecuted for tax evasion because their "secret" offshore accounts were discovered.

How Tax Agencies Find Unreported Foreign Accounts

This information can be obtained many ways. Some poor souls are languishing in jail because they inadvertently left a paper trail to their accounts. They deposited checks into the accounts, wire transferred the funds or left some other paper evidence that was discovered on a routine audit. In other cases, they telephoned their banker from home and the national tax agency obtained a record of the call's existence from their long distance bill. In the USA, the IRS needs a warrant to obtain this information, but need not establish probable cause to get it, only that an inquiry is underway.

Other persons with "secret" offshore accounts have been betrayed because they revealed the account's existence to someone they trusted but shouldn't have. A nasty divorce, a business dispute or an angered friend resulted in betrayal. In many cases, a trusted friend or associate was threatened with prosecution and forfeiture if he or she didn't become a turncoat. In others, the "friend" became a paid informant.

Of course, it's possible to open an account and tell no one. Some depositors simply give the foreign bank or trust company a letter of instructions telling it what to do at their death. This eliminates the chance of betrayal, but it still doesn't guarantee that the account won't be discovered.

Some secret accounts have been discovered when bank employees were bribed to disclose information. Also, the tax agencies plant undercover agents in foreign banks. One gentleman I know was visiting the head of a Swiss bank in the banker's office above the bank floor. The banker pulled back the curtain and pointed to a teller and to another person sitting behind a desk. "We believe," he said, "that those two both secretly work for the IRS."

Cloak-and-dagger techniques are another threat. In one case, the IRS wanted information about suspected tax evaders that it believed had secret accounts at a bank in The Bahamas. The IRS agent in charge of the investigation learned that one of the bank officers was coming to the U.S. to meet with a number of clients, including the suspect.

The agent set up a "chance" meeting between the banker and a beautiful woman, herself an IRS informant. She invited the banker to visit her in her hotel room. While the banker was with her, the IRS agent broke into his hotel room, opened his locked briefcase, and copied all of the documents. With this information, they were able to successfully prosecute a number of U.S. citizens who had secret accounts at the bank.

Was this theft illegal? Of course, but the Supreme Court upheld the prosecution of one of the victims. This gave the IRS carte blanche to engage in similar operations.

I have described some of the practical privacy advantages of an offshore bank account. But that doesn't mean you can count on "absolute secrecy" in any account. Governments of high-tax countries regularly seek to penetrate bank secrecy. But government agents aren't the only threat. Consider the following:

Betrayal in Liechtenstein

A few years ago a foreign employee of a trust company in Liechtenstein copied the financial records of a large number of the trust company's German clients and offered to sell them to a German magazine for US$250,000.

Had it been a bank, the exposure of bank account records would have been less serious, as most bank accounts are in the name of corporations, trusts or nominees. That these were trust company records made their exposure particularly grave, as they contained the names of the beneficial owners of corporations and trusts, as well as the links to the bank accounts held in the name of these structures.

In this case, the thief fled Liechtenstein to avoid being arrested for violating its secrecy laws. Needless to say, he won't be able to return.

The scandal has ignited a furor, and the German publisher has been debating whether to buy the records. If it does, not only will many Germans who relied on financial privacy as a shield from tax evasion be prosecuted, but also thousands of employees of financial institutions in asset havens may begin calculating the risk/reward ratio of betraying their employers.

You can be certain of one thing: The tax man won't for a microsecond debate the issue of the morality of buying stolen records. The point is that the much-vaunted financial privacy laws of the tax haven countries are no guarantee your "secret" offshore account won't be discovered.

Offshore Debit Cards

Many offshore financial advisors have suggested that one way to withdraw money from a secret offshore bank account would be to have the bank issue a debit card, and then use the debit card to get cash from ATM machines, either in the U.S. or offshore.

The managing director of the British Virgin Islands branch of VP Bank, an international investment bank headquartered in Liechtenstein, warned me about the privacy risks associated with Visa, MasterCard and Eurocard (the European issuer of MasterCard).

VP bank doesn't offer any credit cards because it's a dead giveaway that the individual has a foreign bank account. According to my B.V.I. contact, the IRS and perhaps other tax agencies have access through an agreement with Visa and MasterCard and can easily determine who has been issued a card. Nor is it that difficult for an investigator to learn of the existence of a bank issued card, including Eurocards.

Just holding a card is evidence you have a foreign account. The first six digits of the card number identify the country of origin and obviously prove that somewhere in this country an account exists. If those digits show a Swiss bank issued the credit card, it's obvious that the holder has a Swiss bank account. Nor does it help if the card is a corporate or company card, if you're a signatory on the account on which it's drawn. You still have to reveal the existence of the account to the tax man.

If you want to hold a foreign credit card without having a foreign bank account, Eurocard issues "bank neutral" cards, such as airline credit cards, as well as bank-related cards. (You can also have a credit card listing only the name of your offshore corporation.)

Play It Safe

Seeking privacy with offshore financial structures is a wise decision. However, it should be done legally, and not in hopes of keeping unreported accounts secret from the tax man. Why risk jail to save on taxes? There are many advantages to taking your assets offshore other than illegally saving taxes. Simply structure your offshore dealings legitimately, and follow the law. You'll sleep better.

On the other hand, what if you have a "secret" account that you no longer wish to keep secret? Do not contact the tax authorities directly if you find yourself in this situation. Revealing the presence of this account on your own may subject you and your property to criminal and civil sanctions. Instead, contact a tax attorney.

Uncle Sam Wants to Look Into Your Bank Account

By Mark Nestmann, *The Sovereign Individual*, March 2002

What do governments do when their policies fail? They enhance their power, ostensibly to "solve" the problem. The reaction by the U.S. government to the events of September 11, 2001, confirms this trend. For instance, financial transactions in the United States have been monitored for years to combat crime. But that monitoring didn't detect nine small U.S. bank accounts used by those individuals who blew up the World Trade Center and the Pentagon.

To correct the situation, the government is doing more of the same things that haven't worked in the past. Law-enforcement agencies now run daily checks on individuals or groups with suspected connections to terror networks against the databases of America's largest banks.

The Treasury Department's intelligence division, the Financial Crimes Enforcement Network (FinCEN) (www.ustreas.gov/fincen), reviews all matches. Assets in suspect accounts can be frozen instantly.

However, this system is even less likely to detect "terrorist" activity than those already in place to fight money laundering. U.S. banks are already required to submit many reports to FinCEN, including reports of "suspicious transactions" engaged in by their customers.

Between 1987 and 1995, banks sent FinCEN over 77 million "Suspicious Activity Reports" (SARs). Only 580 convictions resulted from these reports—a "success" rate of one conviction per 133,000 SARs.

Trying to find transactions tied to terrorism is even more difficult, because the sums involved are much smaller. According to the International Monetary Fund, drug dealers launder approximately US$1.5 trillion per year. In contrast, it cost only about US$500,000 to conduct the attacks of September 11, 2001.

Further, most terrorist groups reportedly use Hawala or "flying money" networks (*TSI* 7/00), an underground banking system that is not affected by this initiative (although the government is trying to shut down Hawala networks as well). Thus, the daily checks by FinCEN against suspect terrorist accounts are probably doomed to failure. And in that event, FinCEN is likely to propose a far more comprehensive "Deposit Tracking System" (DTS).

The idea for a DTS first surfaced in 1993, when the CIA proposed a system that could instantaneously track transactions in all U.S. bank and credit card accounts and create continuously updated financial dossiers based on the data. Once the DTS is developed, FinCEN would presumably share data from it with other governments. Indeed, FinCEN's participation in a secretive organization called the "Egmont Group" gives it access to a "secure web server" designed to facilitate data exchange. Using data from DTS systems in other countries, the goal is clearly for FinCEN and its Egmont affiliates to monitor financial transactions as they occur, anywhere in the world.

If a DTS would be ineffective at fighting crime or terrorism, how could it be used? I believe that it could present an inviting mechanism for quieting unwanted dissent. Consider the definition of "terrorism" in the USA PATRIOT Act enacted by Congress in November 2001: "...[A]n activity that-(i) involves a violent act or an act dangerous to human life, property, or infrastructure; and (ii) appears to be intended—(A) to intimidate or coerce a civilian population; (B) to influence the policy of a government by intimidation or coercion; or (C) to affect the conduct of a government by mass destruction, assassination, kidnapping, or hostage-taking."

This definition allows the U.S. government to label virtually any form of social protest as "terrorism." According to J. Bradley Jansen, an analyst with the conservative Free Congress Foundation, "All of the groups here (in Washington) that are active in public policy could by that definition be considered terrorist."

Then there is the matter of persons caught in this financial dragnet. For instance, in December 2001, federal agents raided the suburban Chicago offices of Global Relief Foundation, a Muslim charity. They carted away files, froze bank accounts and put the charity's founder in jail. However, the government sealed all documents justifying the action. According to Global Relief's attorney, "They've said nothing to us except that they have a reason for what they did, and it's classified."

Four Strategies to Deal with Financial Surveillance

1. *Take your assets offshore.* It is highly unlikely, for instance, that Switzerland or Austria (the jurisdictions in which the Sovereign Society has established Convenient Bank Account relationships) would cooperate in a global DTS, since doing so would violate the bank secrecy laws in these jurisdictions.

For assets and transactions in the United States:

2. *Use currency for small transactions that, for whatever reason, might look "suspicious" if viewed out of context.* For instance, if you are an avid reader of books dealing with Islamic fundamentalism, purchase them at a local bookstore with currency, not on the Internet using a credit card. (And don't check them out of a library; the USA PATRIOT Act requires libraries to surrender patron records with no notification to the people affected.)

3. *Volunteer to complete any "paperwork" for transactions that might be viewed as suspicious.* For instance: you just sold a vehicle for US$8,000 in currency. You bring the currency to the bank to deposit it, but have never deposited more than US$200 in currency previously. This might be viewed as a suspicious transaction, since it doesn't match your previous account history—but not if you make the deposit at the teller window, explain where the money came from and offer to complete any "paperwork" that might be necessary. (For this transaction, no reporting should be necessary, as the reporting threshold for currency transactions is US$10,000 per transaction or series of "related" transactions).

4. *If you own or operate a U.S.-based business, follow the recommendations in "Seven Essential Strategies to Cope with U.S. Emergency Controls."*

The last thing you need is for your business to suffer the same fate as the ill-fated Global Relief Foundation.

How To Achieve the Maximum Privacy in Your Offshore Account

By Mark Nestmann, *The Sovereign Individual*, August 2003

In the minds of most Americans, there is nothing so mysterious, so enticing, as an "offshore bank account."

The very phrase, particularly among the wine and brie crowd, brings up images of exotic and possibly illegal financial dealings in a tropical setting, accompanied by absolute bank privacy.

The movie The Firm, which was popular a few years ago, greatly reinforced these stereotypes. It portrayed the Cayman Islands as a jurisdiction where you could simply land a plane stuffed with bags of cash and deposit that cash directly into a local bank account.

However, those days, if they ever existed at all, are long gone. The truth about offshore bank accounts is very different from what you hear at parties or see at the movies. In this column, I'm going to separate fact from fiction, and give you six recommendations that will allow you to legally protect the privacy of your offshore account.

The Truth About "Bank Secrecy"

For better or worse, the concept of "bank secrecy" has changed greatly in recent years. Thirty years ago, it was possible to hire an attorney in one of several offshore jurisdictions—including Switzerland, Liechtenstein or The Bahamas—and have the attorney open up an offshore bank account, in his name, and operate it for you without the bank knowing your real identity.

In those days, secrecy was virtually absolute. No one—including agents of the U.S. government—could penetrate it, except in very unusual circumstances.

All this began to change in the 1970s, when the United States signed its first "Mutual Legal Assistance Treaty" (MLAT) with Switzerland. This agreement obligated Swiss authorities to waive bank secrecy when the U.S. government presented them with evidence that money tied to a serious crime in the United States was held being in Switzerland. Tax offenses, with the exception of tax fraud, were not covered.

Since then, the United States has ratified nearly 50 additional MLATs, most with expanded provisions in comparison to the Swiss agreement. In addition, various international organizations, including the Organization for Economic Cooperation and Development (OECD) and its stepchild, the Financial Action Task Force (FATF), have prepared "blacklists" of countries in which "excessive financial secrecy" prevails, and tried to impose sanctions against those countries not agreeing to severely restrict it.

But bank secrecy has not been "eliminated," as some press reports would imply. The best way to view bank secrecy today is as a bulwark against prying eyes peering into your financial affairs, unless you are suspected of committing a serious crime.

No doubt, bank secrecy occasionally shields lawbreakers. But more often than not, it is used for legitimate purposes—to shield individuals and their families from retribution by corrupt or totalitarian governments; to give them access to investments forbidden or restricted in their own countries; or to hide wealth from kidnappers who typically target persons with visible wealth.

And today, even if some of the more powerful tools individuals and companies could once use to keep their financial affairs secret have been severely restricted, there remain opportunities for financial privacy "offshore" that simply don't exist domestically. You just have to be realistic in your expectations.

Offshore Bank Accounts and Privacy

While it's become more difficult to move money offshore, you can still take your domestic wealth off the radar screen to achieve practical, if not necessarily impenetrable, privacy.

The single best reason to move assets outside your own country is to protect yourself from the global litigation epidemic. The United States is unique in its approach to "tort liability," in which both sides in a lawsuit pay their own expenses, no matter who wins, and where lawyers are permitted to finance lawsuits, no matter how ridiculous the claim. In recent months, doctors have actually gone on strike in several states to protest skyrocketing malpractice premiums resulting from increased exposure to lawsuits.

However, truly frivolous litigation is no longer a U.S.-only phenomenon. The U.K. and Canadian legal systems are also undergoing quiet, yet revolutionary transformations that dramatically increase the odds of being sued and losing. (See http://overlawyered.com/places/canada.html for some mind-boggling Canadian lawsuits, including "Father files suit after son fails to make MVP award.")

An offshore bank account provides substantial protection from frivolous lawsuits. Since lawyers size up targets for lawsuits by looking for their money, someone considering suing you may decide to find a target with more visible wealth. This is one reason why The Sovereign Society developed its "Offshore Convenient Account" member benefit. Unfortunately, the availability of offshore bank accounts with low minimums is rapidly diminishing. This is a direct consequence of the escalating cost of banks performing "due diligence" on their customers to comply with new initiatives from the OECD and FATF. However, minimum deposits for the Offshore Convenient Account still may start as low as US$15,000.

Six Recommendations for Offshore Banking Secrecy

The advantages of dealing offshore—privacy, asset protection and investment diversification—remain in place, but only if you follow a few simple rules.

1. Choose the right jurisdiction. As we described in our annual review of offshore havens (TSI 6/03), we believe the top offshore jurisdictions to be Switzerland, Panama, Liechtenstein and Hong Kong. First class offshore banking services are also available in Austria. Denmark offers low-cost offshore banking, but no privacy with regards to foreign tax authorities.

2. Understand foreign "due diligence" requirements. Along with the end of anonymous accounts in most offshore jurisdictions, most offshore banks now require prospective customers to prove their identity with a certified copy of their passport or other official document. You may also face questions regarding the origin of the funds you are placing into the account. Don't be afraid to answer these questions—the application for your account along with all documentation you provide is subject to whatever bank secrecy laws prevail in the jurisdiction you've chosen.

3. Don't try to cheat the tax man. Most high-tax countries impose taxes on the worldwide income of their residents. While domestic tax authorities don't generally have the authority to go on offshore "fishing expeditions" to uncover unreported offshore income, the momentum is clearly toward greater disclosure. There's also little doubt that the tools that governments are giving themselves to fight "terrorism" will ultimately be used to augment tax collection. Our recommendation is to report the existence of the account to your domestic tax authorities and pay whatever taxes are due. Doing so will not generally raise a red flag and will not negate the privacy advantages of the account with respect to prospective litigants. At least in the case of the IRS, there have been many more prosecutions for failing to report an offshore transaction than for engaging in an allegedly illegal transaction that was reported.

4. Don't open an account at the foreign branch of a U.S. bank, or a foreign bank that has U.S. branches. Either of these factors places the bank under the jurisdiction of U.S. courts, thus providing litigants with additional opportunities to penetrate offshore banking secrecy.

5. Don't use offshore accounts to hold U.S. dollar denominated investments, including U.S. securities. The USA PATRIOT Act gives U.S. authorities the right to demand to know the identity of individuals with interests in the U.S. "correspondent accounts" offshore banks maintain for their customers who maintain U.S. dollar investments. In addition, the U.S. government is beginning to confiscate the proceeds of such accounts under the notorious "civil forfeiture" statutes.

Finally, IRS "qualified intermediary" (QI) regulations enmesh correspondent accounts in a maze of red tape. U.S. depositors in foreign banks who purchase U.S. securities and refuse to identify themselves to the IRS under the QI regulations are subject to a 31% withholding tax—not just on income from the account, but on their entire investment. So make sure to set up your offshore account(s) so that you can use them to purchase U.S. securities or other dollar-denominated assets without actually holding them in U.S. dollars (sounds complicated, but it really is easy to do).

6. Keep it simple. It's a good idea never to get involved in an investment you don't understand, and this is doubly true for investments you make outside your own country. Ultimately, the value of offshore investing is to create a "nest egg" that can survive lawsuits; changes in public policy; even a collapse in the value of your domestic currency. You don't need complex investments to achieve these goals.

Seven Essential Strategies to Cope with U.S. Emergency Controls
by Mark Nestmann, *The Sovereign Individual*, December 2001

The U.S. Congress has given the president and executive agencies the authority to seize the assets of anyone suspected of many types of crimes. These powers are at their strongest during times of war or national emergency, but have been in almost continuous effect in some form for more than 80 years.

Since the events of September 11, 2001, the impact of U.S. emergency financial controls is becoming clear as millions of dollars of suspect "terrorist" assets are seized, a consequence of an executive order signed by President Bush on September 24, 2001.

Emergency financial controls have a long history. There are more than 20 sets of such controls currently in effect, not only against assets owned by or connected to Osama bin Laden and the Taliban regime in Afghanistan, but also against Cuba, North Korea, Libya, Iraq, Iran, the UNITA faction in Angola, and designated "narcotics kingpins."

With narrow exceptions, all persons and entities subject to U.S. law are forbidden from having any commercial contact with these countries and more than 5,000 additional "specially designated nationals"—individuals and companies on a constantly-expanding watch list maintained by the Treasury Department's Office of Foreign Asset Control at www.treas.gov/ofac.

If your assets are frozen by OFAC, you must apply for a "license" (exemption) to recover them. In some cases, it takes OFAC years to process a claim, with the entire process shrouded in secrecy.

Gossip Can Get Your Assets Frozen

The authority to designate you or your company as "terrorists" or "terrorist sympathizers" can easily be misused:

1. A subscriber to an investment service purchased "put" options on American Airlines and Morgan Stanley just days before the September 11 attacks. (Purchasers of put options are betting that prices of particular securities or indices will fall.). He funded the contracts with an offshore account. OFAC used this as justification to order an emergency freeze of the entire account. The foreign government complied with this request.

2. Mohammed Ahmad, who lives in Maryland, had his account at Citibank blocked after OFAC published the first list of people with suspected financial ties to alleged terrorists. One person on that list was known as "Mustafa Muhammad Ahmad." Citibank would not tell the Maryland Ahmad for several days why his account was frozen. Then, he was required to prove that he was not on the list by submitting documentation to show that his name was different.

3. In 1998, the United States attacked and destroyed a pharmaceutical plant in Sudan with

cruise missiles. The Clinton administration claimed that the owner, Saleh Idris, was laundering money for terrorists and froze US$24 million in Idris' London bank accounts. Idris sued to recover his money as well as compensation for his plant. In May 1999, after failing to produce evidence to connect Idris or his plant to terrorism, the United States unfroze Idris' accounts and announced it would not contest his US$50 million lawsuit.

However, if Mr. Idris had been identified as a "narcotics kingpin," he would have had no right to contest that designation in court. The "Foreign Narcotics Kingpin Designation Act" states: "The determinations, identifications, findings, and designations made pursuant to [this act] shall not be subject to judicial review."

How does the government determine who a "terrorist" is? It can rely on reports from intelligence agencies, third-hand accounts, press clippings, hearsay and material posted on the Internet to make its decision. Inflammatory gossip or anonymous news group postings could provide legal authority for your assets to be frozen.

While banks are perhaps the institutions most heavily impacted by OFAC controls, other businesses that must be aware of them include securities and commodities broker/dealers; investment companies; currency exchanges; issuers, redeemers, and cashiers of traveler's checks, checks, money orders, or similar instruments; credit card system operators; insurance companies; dealers in precious metals, stones or jewels; pawnbrokers; loan and finance companies; travel agencies; money transmitters; telegraph companies; businesses engaged in vehicle sales; persons involved in real estate closings or settlements; and casinos.

These businesses are NOT permitted to reject suspect transactions. Let's say that you instruct your bank to wire US$50,000 to a U.K. company that you do business with, but which, unknown to you, has been added to OFAC's list. Your bank must accept the transaction, then deduct US$50,000 from your account and place it in a master "blocked account."

Five Key Strategies for Businesses

Most major banks have turned to name-recognition software to block questionable transactions automatically. Vendors include JMJ Consulting (www.jmjconsulting.com/jmjcons2.htm) and OFAC Compliance (www.ofaccompliance.com). However, there may be dozens or even hundreds of "false positive" matches for each legitimate match.

If you or your company does not routinely engage in international financial transactions, it may not be economical to purchase interdict software. In that event, OFAC advises paying attention to the following factors:

1. Is the account party, beneficiary, issuing bank or confirming bank blocked?

2. Is the underlying trade transaction prohibited?

3. Does the bill of lading indicate that goods were shipped by a blocked shipping company or aboard a blocked merchant vessel?

4. Does the certificate of origin reveal that the goods originated from a target country?

5. Does the invoice tip you off that a blocked company supplied the goods to the seller? If the answer to any of these questions is "yes," do NOT process the transaction, as it will be subject to the emergency controls administered by OFAC.

Two Vital Tactics for Investors

1. Use U.S. accounts to make U.S. investments. Don't risk having your foreign assets frozen simply because the government decides it doesn't like a trade you made through an offshore account.

2. Confer with competent legal counsel to provide you with sound suggestions and recommendations in light of the new laws and government policies being enacted in response to terrorism. One expert we can recommend—a member of the OFAC Practitioners Forum and edi-

tor of the International Enforcement Law Reporter (www.ielr.com)—is attorney Bruce Zagaris (**Tel.**: +1 (202) 293-5555. **E-mail**: bzagaris@bcr-dc.com)

If, despite these precautions, your assets are frozen, download Treasury Form TDF 90-22.54 from www.treas.gov/ofac/legal/forms/license.pdf, complete it and send it in for consideration. Just don't be in a hurry—OFAC has a huge backlog of cases.

Types of Accounts Available at Offshore Banks
Banking in Silence, 1998

The offshore banking industry offers a much wider range of account types than most onshore banking jurisdictions. The options vary from simple savings accounts to accounts designed for the sole purpose of tax avoidance to accounts where the bank invests and oversees your money on your behalf.

The various types of accounts can be grouped into a few categories. Although the names may change from bank to bank, the basic design behind each account type is more or less the same. They are as follows:

Current accounts are the most common type of account. They generally come with a check book or debit card and can sometimes be linked with a credit card. The required starting balance is low, but the interest rate is also generally low. Some banks allow for multi-currency accounts, meaning that you can deposit and withdraw funds in any of a number of currencies. You can also easily change either all or part of your account into the currency of your choice.

Deposit accounts are generally a good place to store money over the slightly longer term. They offer higher interest rates, but restrict your ability to get at your money by requiring that you provide sufficient notice or sacrifice the interest earned. Starting balances are also generally higher with many banks requiring a minimum deposit of somewhere in the region of US$10,000. The interest rate depends upon the amount deposited, as well as the time period for which it will stay in the account. It also depends on the currency in which the account is denominated, stronger currencies paying less interest.

Twin accounts basically combine a high-interest deposit account with the convenience of a current account under one all-inclusive number. The bulk of the funds on deposit is kept in the high interest account while a smaller amount is kept in the current account for day to day use. If you one day find yourself overdrawn, the bank would then merely transfer money from the deposit account into the current account. Thus, the need to maintain two different accounts is eliminated.

Fiduciary accounts allow you to invest anonymously in high-tax markets, even in your home country, by using your bank as a proxy investor. For example, if you maintain an account in a Liechtenstein bank but wish to hold part of your overall portfolio in German marks, you could instruct your banker to open an account in Germany on your behalf. The marks would be purchased in Frankfurt and then held there in the bank's name, although the interest earned is paid to you in Liechtenstein. For the record, it appears as if the bank is acting on its own initiative, meaning that if you happen to be German you would no longer be liable for German tax. Of course, the bank charges a fee, usually one quarter of one percent of your principal, for providing you with such anonymity. You also receive a slightly lower interest payment than you would if you made the deposit on your own.

Certificates of deposit (CDs) are a way to earn much higher interest rates than those on offer through deposit accounts. In short, your funds are loaned to the Euro currency market at the current rate for the currency in which the CD is denominated. CDs usually come in bearer form, meaning that they can be freely and anonymously traded. They enjoy a large and active secondary market. They vary a great deal in terms of the maturity of the investment, ranging from almost overnight to up to five years. Best of all, banks do not withhold any tax on the CDs that they issue, meaning that with a little creative planning your money can earn hefty interest payments tax free.

Precious metal accounts allow you to invest in precious metals via your bank. The bank will then store the metal in its vault on your behalf. The advantage of opening up this type of account is that by combining your resources with those of other bank clients, you can purchase precious metals at a far more competitive price. Of course, such an account does not generate any income but should be seen as a safety net. The bank generally charges an annual storage fee usually in the region of one half of one percent of the value of the metals on deposit.

Investment accounts are usually only offered by larger banks. They allow you to invest your funds in commodity markets with the help of your bank. They usually take the form of a mutual fund in stocks, bonds and other commodities and are overseen by the bank itself. The required starting balance is somewhat hefty, generally US$50,000. These accounts usually come with rather high front-end costs as well as significant management fees. But as long as the markets are performing well a good investment account will on average prove to be more profitable than a simple deposit account.

Managed accounts work much like investment accounts but allow you to choose where to invest your funds. Instructions of what to buy and sell are sent to the bank by phone or fax. It is possible to hold the commodities purchased in the bank's name rather than your own for an extra layer of privacy. The price for such convenience takes the form of a minimum deposit requirement of approximately US$250,000.

Safekeeping accounts allow you to deposit bonds, stocks and other valuables. The bank will then manage the overall portfolio deposited, redeeming the bonds when they mature and doing whatever need be done with the valuables entrusted to them. Of course, such convenience comes with a price tag, usually a fee of approximately .015 percent of the market value of the portfolio they are maintaining.

Safety Deposit Boxes Offshore
by Mark Nestmann, *The Sovereign Individual*, May 1999

When most of us think of an offshore account, we usually associate it with the purchase of certificates of deposit (CDs) or securities or asset management. But behind the scenes, any bank—offshore or otherwise—must take precautions to insure the safe custody of the investments it holds for you. And it's also possible—and in some cases preferable—to maintain your own "safe custody" in an offshore safety deposit box.

Custodial Accounts

Many offshore banks provide convenient accounts that maintain custody of securities or precious metals they purchase on your behalf or that you turn over for safekeeping. The assets in such a "custodial account" are not available to creditors of the bank. You can also turn over documents or valuables in a sealed envelope or box to the bank. Numbered custodial accounts are also available at some banks.

You may specify "fungible" or "non-fungible" storage for these assets. Fungible storage means that when you redeem your securities or precious metals, you receive "like-kind" assets, although not necessarily the identical assets. In other words, the numbers on the securities you receive back may be different from that on those you deposited. Non-fungible storage means that the bank will return to you the exact securities or metals—or the sealed envelope—you deposited.

A custodial account is fully integrated with your other account(s) with the bank. You receive regular statements about the assets held in custody and all charges are deducted from the account balance. If you have instructions relating to the assets in the custodial account, you can relay these to the bank through normal channels; i.e., via letter, fax or phone.

If you merely use a custodial account to hold assets that do not generate income, there are no tax or reporting consequences in most countries, including the United Kingdom. However, this integration and convenience comes at a price to U.S. depositors: a custodial account is a reportable "foreign financial account" if the aggregate value of the account and all other "foreign financial accounts" exceeds US$10,000. The existence of all such accounts must be acknowledged on Schedule B of your U.S. tax return and on Treasury Form TD F 90.22-1.

Offshore Safety Deposit Boxes

As an alternative to a custodial account, consider a safety deposit box to maintain custody of securities, precious metals or other valuables. The main advantage of a safety deposit box is privacy. The bank does not know what you keep in the box, although you must agree not to store dangerous or illegal materials in it. Further, the bank does not exercise authority over the box. Thus, the rental of a safety deposit box in a foreign bank does not in itself appear to constitute an account relationship. A U.S. person can make the argument that the box does not constitute a "foreign financial account."

To avoid having to personally visit the box each time valuables are to be added or removed, you may give an attorney or other trusted intermediary a limited power of attorney or other legal authority necessary to perform this function.

You can use the combination of an offshore account and a safety deposit box to control assets worth many times the US$10,000 reporting threshold. For instance, you could make a series of securities purchases through the bank, then take personal delivery of the securities to place in your safety deposit box. Or have your attorney or other designated person take delivery. However, the funds to purchase these securities will leave a paper trail, particularly if they have a domestic origin.

Materials held in a safety deposit box are not ordinarily insured against theft or other loss. Where this protection is available, the limits are generally low. Supplemental insurance is available, but will compromise privacy. Contact the bank for details.

Safekeeping Precious Metals Offshore
by Mark Nestmann, *The Sovereign Individual*, June 1999

Warehouse receipts—documents providing title to a specified quantity of goods—are a convenient and low profile way to own precious metals.

I know of two warehouse-receipt programs that provide title to a specified quantity of precious metals held offshore—the Mocatta Delivery Order (MDO) and the Perth Mint Certificate Program (PMCP). Warehouse receipts do not generate income nor do they constitute an "account relationship." Therefore, in most countries, including the United States, their ownership does not appear to be a reportable "foreign account." An exception would be Canada, where assets held offshore in warehouse receipt form appear to be reportable if the aggregate value of all offshore assets exceeds C$100,000.

But while warehouse receipts allow you to take assets "off the radar screen," thus making life more difficult for asset predators and Big Brother, the MDO and PMCP are not anonymous. Neither is available in bearer form; both must be registered to an individual or individuals, company or trust.

Mocatta Delivery Orders

Mocatta Delivery Orders are warehouse receipts issued by ScotiaMocatta Metals of New York City, providing legal title to a specified quantity of gold, silver or platinum. The metals are stored in the United States or in the Free Trade Zone at the Zurich (Switzerland) airport at the warehouse of Mat Securitas, one of Europe's largest precious metals vaults. However, transaction records remain in New York and are subject to U.S. jurisdiction. To take delivery of the metals, you present your MDO to the custodian.

You can purchase MDOs from any ScotiaMocatta-approved dealer. Contact ScotiaMocatta for the list at telephone +1 800 662 2882 (toll-free in the U.S. and Canada) or +1 212 912 8500. The minimum purchase is 10 ounces of gold coins, 20 ounces of platinum coins or 1,000 ounces of silver bullion. Storage fees are 0.5 percent annually, based on the market value of the metals. The cost is US$100 per certificate.

Each MDO lists a serial number for your gold or silver bars or coins and their storage location. Your metals are not mixed with those belonging to anyone else or with the custodian's assets. They cannot be seized to satisfy creditor claims against the custodian. Such "allocated" or "non-fungible" storage is in contrast to warehouse receipts that provide for "unallocated" storage. Unallocated warehouse receipts are merely a call upon a collective asset pool that may easily be dissipated, and have in the past been associated with various scams, such as the International Gold Bullion Exchange (IGBE) scandal of the 1980s.

However, the MDO isn't perfect. For starters, the document is preprinted in specific amounts. Therefore, you must make the transaction conform to the document size. The largest MDO available is a 400-ounce gold bar, which is worth approximately US$107,000.

You also can't put metals you already own into a MDO. Doing so would require a liquidation of the metals and a subsequent purchase of a MDO. To ensure that all metals it handles are genuine, ScotiaMocatta buys only from the refiners and mints that it represents.

ScotiaMocatta also has not appointed any approved dealers outside the United States. Deliveries at MAT Securitas in Switzerland must be coordinated through New York. This can cause needless delays, fees and disclosures.

An Improved Warehouse Receipt?

MDOs have been around for nearly 25 years, according to Glen Kirsch, Executive Vice President of Asset Strategies International, Inc., an MDO-approved dealer. But to deal with some of the shortcomings of this instrument, ASI has developed a warehouse receipt that in some respects appears to be a major improvement over the MDO—the Perth Mint Certificate Program.

The PMCP can be issued for gold, silver, platinum or palladium under authority of the Western Australian government with storage in Australia at the Perth Mint. The cost per certificate is US$50, and the certificate can be for any quantity of metal.

Both allocated and unallocated storage is available. Allocated storage is slightly more expensive than an MDO. Unallocated storage, however, is free. Kirsch believes that by working with the Perth Mint, the risks of unallocated storage are minimized. The PMCP will also be marketed worldwide, which means there will be approved dealers outside the U.S. To my knowledge, this is the only government-guaranteed program of its kind in the world.

Australia, of course, does not have the reputation as a privacy haven that Switzerland does. And you may prefer to avoid having the Australian government being a partner to your "private" offshore investments. But the convenience and low maintenance cost of the PMCP make it attractive.

For more information on the PMCP, contact *Asset Strategies International, Inc.*, 1700 Rockville Pike, Suite 400, Rockville, MD 20852-1631, USA. **Tel.**: +1 800 831 0007 (toll-free in the U.S. and Canada) or +1 301 881 8600. **Fax**: +1 301 881 1936. **E-mail**: assetsi@assetstrategies.com.

From a privacy standpoint, one of the disadvantages of both the MDO and the PCMP is that ownership must be registered. The certificates are not issued in bearer form, so that whoever is in possession of the certificate would be able to take delivery of whatever quantity of metals are noted on it. There are obvious security risks to this approach, but no greater than those that exist for existing bearer stocks and bonds.

Offshore Bank Deposit Insurance
by Mark Nestmann, *The Sovereign Individual*, July 2001

There is no evidence that investing in an offshore financial institution is riskier than a domestic financial institution. You can lose money even in an insured deposit account when account interest is adjusted for inflation/opportunity cost. But in the event of isolated fraud or mismanagement, offshore insurance schemes are comforting.

Deposit insurance systems are designed to protect investors against isolated bank failures, not a systemic financial collapse. For instance, in the United States, the Federal Deposit Insurance Corporation's Bank Insurance Fund had a balance of US$29.6 billion at year-end 1999. This sum represents only a little more than 1 percent of funds on deposit in U.S. credit institutions.

The need for deposit insurance is a consequence of the fractional reserve banking system. In a 100 percent reserve banking system, there would be little or no need for deposit insurance, because banks could not loan out more money than they had on deposit.

Outside the United States, competition has forced banks to develop nationwide branch networks and to diversify into lines of business forbidden to U.S. banks until very recently. Despite a fractional-reserve banking system, this has resulted in large banks that are relatively secure because they spread their risks among many regions and activities. Examples are Canada (five major banks with an overwhelming percentage of domestic business) or Switzerland (where competition has left just two major nationwide banks).

Foreign deposit insurance systems encourage depositors to monitor the health of their banks, which the U.S. system does not. Limits are much lower, from one-half to one-tenth as much, and the insurance may not pay for 100 percent of depositor losses. The possibility of suffering losses encourages depositors to entrust their money only to well-managed banks.

A handful of banks, mainly in Switzerland, maintain 100 percent reserves. These are the Swiss "private banks," in which owners have unlimited liability up to the amount of each customer's assets. Their numbers have fallen sharply in recent years due to the greater profits available in rising markets for institutions that leverage their assets, and the reluctance of owners to continue to shoulder unlimited liability.

Ireland offers deposit insurance for deposits in Irish Pounds (Euros after 2002), on the following basis per depositor: 80 percent of the first £5000 (US$5,700), 70 percent of deposits from £5000-10,000 (US$5,700-11,300) and 50 percent of deposits from £10,000-15,000 (US$11,300-17,000). There is a deposit insurance fund, premiums for which are paid by banks at the rate of 0.2 percent of monies on deposit.

Deposits not eligible for cover include: interbank deposits; certificates of deposit; deposits in respect of which a money laundering offense has been committed; deposits by a company connected to the credit institution or who had responsibility for or who profited from the failure of the credit institution; deposits by insurance companies; deposits by mutual funds; deposits by pension and retirement funds; debt securities; and deposits by large companies (as defined under companies legislation).

Austria has offered deposit insurance since 1979. Coverage extends to deposits by non-residents, in any currency, to a maximum of maximum of ATS 200,000 (US$13,000) per depositor. There is no deposit insurance "fund"; banks are assessed for premiums on an as-needed basis. Exclusions from coverage are similar to those in effect in Ireland.

Luxembourg has also offered deposit insurance since 1989. Coverage extends to all deposits, in any currency, to a maximum of LF500,000 (US$11,100) per depositor. There is no deposit insurance "fund"; banks are assessed for premiums on an as-needed basis based on the percentage of loss to be met. Exclusions from coverage are similar to those in effect in Ireland.

On the Isle of Man, a Depositors Compensation Scheme provides protection up to 75 percent of the first £20,000 sterling (US$27,628) or its equivalent in other currencies. Banks are assessed a premium of 0.2 percent of funds on deposit. Exemptions from coverage are similar to those in effect in Ireland, except that investments in qualifying mutual funds are covered to £48,000 (100 percent of the first £30,000 plus 90 percent of the next £20,000). Further, insurance policies underwritten by a Manx company are covered without limit, although payment is generally limited to 90 percent.

On Gibraltar, deposit protection is in line with the EC Directive on Deposit Guarantee Schemes (94/19/EC). The scheme covers qualifying deposits in most European currencies, with qualifying deposits and currencies are defined in the Ordinance. Coverage extends to the lesser of 90 percent of the total amount of all the claimant's qualifying deposits or £18,000.

In Switzerland, banks owned by cantons (the equivalent of states or provinces) are covered by a deposit insurance scheme. Coverage in cantonal banks extends to all deposits to a maximum of Sfr30,000 (US$17,300).

A dodgy bank won't be magically converted into a legitimate one just because it is supposedly "guaranteed" by deposit insurance. The recent collapse of the First International Bank of Grenada (FIBG) is an example. FIBG guaranteed its customers returns of 30 percent or more annually in "prime bank instruments" and other questionable investments. To assure depositors that their investments were safe, FIBG claimed that a private company called International Deposit Insurance Corporation backed deposits. However, IDIC never made good on its depositor guarantees and is now the subject of extensive litigation.

While there is no reason that a private company could not provide deposit insurance, in FIBG's case, the promised guarantees simply didn't exist. As always, caveat emptor.

There Are Ways
by Robert E. Bauman, JD & David Melnik, QC, *The Offshore Money Manual*, 1998

International Wire Transfers

American banks are notoriously inept at handling international cash transfers. You need a reputable professional to handle the process if you want it done correctly.

We recommend Michael Checkan and Glen O. Kirsch of Asset Strategies International (see page __ for contact information). They provide wire transfer services to almost every country in the world. Simply telephone ASI and they will confirm the currency exchange rate and transaction costs involved with the transfer. Once these rates are established, you order your bank to wire money directly to ASI. (Grand Bank, Rockville, MD, ABA # 055-001-711, c/o Asset Strategies International, account number 10-077-85, FBO, client name.)

Upon receipt, ASI converts the dollar amount into the foreign currency at the guaranteed quoted rate. They will wire payment in whatever currency you choose, directly to your offshore account. No foreign wire transaction appears in your bank records, only the domestic wire transfer to ASI's bank account. ASI charges 1.5 percent for transfers up to US$9,999.99, one percent for amounts between US$10,000 and US$49,999.99, and 0.5 percent for amounts over US$50,000.

The ASI procedure has the advantage of locking in the currency exchange rate. Otherwise, your offshore bank decides the rate when the wire arrives. An important note: call ASI before wiring funds so they know it's on the way. This will reduce confusion immensely.

U.S. Treasury rules now require banks and currency brokers to keep records of all domestic and international wire transfers exceeding US$3,000 or more. In addition, transfers over US$10,000 must be officially reported. These records must show the exact amount and date of the transaction.

Also required are instructions, name, address, social security and employer's identification number (EIN). This information must be made available to government agents who present judicially-approved subpoenas or search warrants. Although these records will exist, you may find it more private to have a transfer record with ASI or another exchange broker, than to have it recorded at your own bank.

Portable Privacy

U.S. law says you must also report the movement of precious metals across borders if valued at US$10,000 or more. But this is not the only difficulty in many such assets overseas. Obviously, large quantities of gold and other metals are cumbersome, making them difficult to transport physically. "Gold certificates" offer an alternative way to transfer such assets out of the country privately.

The two best precious metals certificate programs available in North America are the ScotiaMocatta Delivery Order (SMDO) and the Perth Mint Certificate Program (PMCP). Both programs are similar but there are some differences in minimum amounts, fees and flexibility.

Both programs issue a certificate in the purchaser's name, or the name of a designated existing legal entity. The certificate serves as legal evidence of ownership of a certain number of coins or bars of precious metals. These metals are stored in locations in different parts of the world. The security and safety of the actual metals is fully insured by Lloyds of London and other underwriters. If you really want to see your precious metals, you can arrange an appointment to visit the vaults. A lost certificate can be replaced, unlike a bearer instrument.

The precious metals certificates include legal powers that easily entitle you to sell, assign or collateralize the identified metal. They also provide the protection of "non-negotiability." Since precious metals certificates are non-negotiable, under laws they are not considered cash or cash equivalent. Therefore, you are not required to report the purchase or transfer of precious metals certificates.

The minimum order for a PMCP is US$25,000. The SMDO can be purchased for as little as the cost of 10 one ounce gold coins. In general, the PMCP is less expensive than the SMDO. The PMCP is also more flexible for delivery and storage in other parts of the world.

Each certificate program offers coins and bars in gold, silver and platinum. In addition, the PMCP offers coins in palladium. There is storage available primarily at the Perth Mint in Perth, Australia for the PMCP, and at Mats Securitas in Zurich, Switzerland for SMDO.

For more information about precious metals certificate, contact Michael Checkan, Rich Checkan or Glen Kirsch at Asset Strategies International, Inc. at the numbers above.

Reporting Foreign Bank Accounts

So you have gotten your assets offshore. Now what? Do you have to tell the government that you have opened an offshore account? The law says:

Each United States person who has a financial interest in, or signature authority over bank, securities, or other financial accounts in a foreign country which exceeds US$10,000 in aggregate value, must report the relationship each calendar year by filing Treasury Department Form 90-22.1 before June 30 of the succeeding year. There's a line on your annual income tax Form 1040 where that notice must be filed.

The US$10,000 account limit includes the total value of cash, CDs and negotiable securities held in your name in any offshore bank accounts. It excludes foreign investments held separately from the bank account itself. So long as the foreign bank account does not exceed US$10,000 at any point in time during the taxable year, no IRS report is required. There's no prohibition in the Bank Secrecy Act against the sort of "structuring" outlawed by the Anti-Money Laundering Act of 1986. Consequently, you can have a number of offshore accounts in your name. As long as each stays under the US$10,000 limit, you have no responsibility to report them.

Keeping each account below the US$10,000 limit might appear relatively easy at first glance, until you consider the disturbing influence of exchange rates. Currency exchange rates change daily, and occasionally swing drastically. Such shifts might push your account balance above the US$10,000 limit. The law says you must make your calculations based on the official rates for each currency as determined by the Federal Reserve Bank of New York. Naturally, these figures are published only once annually at year's end. By then it may be too late to make downward adjustments in your balance.

The solution is simple enough; keep your account balance well below the US$10,000 limit. This will provide a buffer against interest income and currency appreciation. It will require you to set up more accounts, but in the end you will come out ahead.

Part Two—The Law, Privacy and Asset Protection

The End of Ordinary Money

by J. Orlin Grabbe, *The Cyberpayments Revolution*, 1999

Here you learn the extent to which government has destroyed almost all financial privacy; how computers and bureaucrats track your every banking move; how the war on drugs and terrorism has become carte blanche for government snoops to spy on you.

It was bright lights and balmy action. Thomas Constantine, the head of the U.S. Drug Enforcement Administration (DEA), claimed we've entered a "new world order of law enforcement." He meant the cooperation of British, Italian, and Spanish authorities in setting up a fake bank in Anguilla, in the Caribbean. It was a sting to trap money launderers. Like all pirate organizations, the group calculated success by the amount of booty seized. And this cleverly code-named "Operation Dinero" added US$52 million, nine tons of cocaine, and a number of paintings (including works by Reynolds, Reuben, and Picasso) to official coffers. There were also 88 arrests. In many ways it was a great scam in classic DEA style: government officials got to keep the goods, while taxpayers got to pay for the incarceration of up to 88 people.

The British Foreign Office—those wacky guys who, you will recall, conveniently released a barrage of information about Nazis in Argentina at the outbreak of the Falklands (Malvinas) war, and who also helped coordinate Operation Dinero—have since made a propaganda video about this official foray into fraudulent banking. Among others it stars Tony Baldry, junior minister.

Be prepared for more of the same. The nine tons of coke should enable the British Foreign Office and the nosy DEA to burn the midnight oil for months to come, planning other booty-gathering raids and video thrillers. After all, the European Organization for Economic Cooperation and Development's Financial Action Task Force (FATF) report of 1990 encouraged international banking stings like this one. But it isn't just the pseudo-bankers you should worry about.

The Banker as Snitch: the Brave New World of Law Enforcement

One of the precepts of the Church of the Subgenius is: You will pay to know what you really think. But in the world of money laundering, you will pay your thankless banker to turn you in to the government. In 1993 a Federal judge in Providence, Rhode Island, issued the longest sentence ever given for a non-violent legal offense: he sentenced a man to 600 years in prison for money laundering. The individual was fingered by his Rhode Island bankers, who then cooperated with federal agents in building a case against him, even while the same bankers received fees for banking services.

American Express was recently fined US$7 million for failing to detect money laundering, and agreed to forfeit to the U.S. Justice Department another US$7 million. As part of the settlement, the bank will spend a further US$3 million in employee education, teaching them recommended procedures for spying on customer transactions.

In a book about banker Edmond Safra, author Bryan Burrough notes: "To truly defeat money launderers, banks must know not only their own customers—by no means an easy task—but their customers' customers, and in many cases their customers' customers' customers." And then, as part of an argument clearing Safra's Republic National Bank of money laundering charges, Burrough recounts how he visited the office of the Financial Crimes Enforcement Network (FinCEN) and talked with one of its top officials. The official said that, on the contrary, Republic had made "some solid suggestions about new ways the government could track dirty money."

Most have still not gotten the message that their banker is a spy. They are still stuck in yesterday's world, where legislation like the Right to Financial Privacy Act of 1978 allowed banks, on the one hand, to monitor their own records and inform the government when there were suspicious transactions in an account. On the other hand, the bank was prohibited from identifying either the account number or the account's owner. But the Privacy Act was effectively gutted by the Annunzio-Wylie Anti-Money Laundering Act of 1992, which gives protection from civil liability to any financial institution, director, officer or employee who makes a suspicious transaction report under any federal, state or local law. The latter act essentially implies banks can reveal to the government any information they want to about their customers, without fear of prosecution.

Money Laundering—What Is It, Anyway?

There's a specter haunting the international financial markets: the specter of crime by nomenclature, by theological semantics. To be sure, the faceless piece of transaction information that makes money "money"—a useful medium of exchange, whereby we exchange everything for it, and avoid the direct bartering of wheelbarrows for oranges—has been under attack before.

The 1960s brought us "euro"-dollars, and the 1970s "petro"-dollars. Now we have "narco"-dollars, "terror"-dollars, and (who knows?) maybe "kiddie-porn"-dollars. For some of the data bits stored in banks' computers comprise "clean" money and others "dirty" money, the latter legalistically smitten with original sin. Since the governmental powers that be can't do much about drug-dealing or terrorism—if only because they themselves are the chief drug dealers and the chief terrorists—they have transferred these and other (often alleged) sins to the money supply. And since every dollar is a potential "narco" dollar or "terror" dollar, they must track each one as best they can. The fact that monetary monitoring has done nothing to diminish either drug-dealing or terrorism is treated of no importance, because it's all part of a larger game. All the players can easily see that this same financial tracking yields political side benefits in the form of social control and government revenue enhancement.

Anyone who has studied the evolution of money laundering statutes in the United States and elsewhere will realize that the "crime" of money laundering boils down to a single, basic prohibited act: Doing something and not telling the government about it. But since the real Big-Brotherly motive is a Thing That Cannot Be Named, the laws are bogged down in prolix circumlocution, forming a hodge-podge of lawyers' fingers inserted here and there into the financial channels of the monetary system.

U.S. legislation includes the Bank Secrecy Act of 1970, the Comprehensive Crime Control Act of 1984, the Money Laundering Control Act of 1986, the Anti-Drug Abuse Act of 1988, the Annunzio-Wylie Anti-Money Laundering Act of 1992, and the Money Laundering Suppression Act of 1994. International efforts include the UN Convention Against Illicit Traffic in Narcotic Drugs and Psychotropic Substances of 1988; the Basle Committee on Banking Regulations and Supervisory Practices Statement of Principles of December 1988; the Financial Action Task Force (FATF) Report of April, 1990 (with its 40 recommendations for action); the Council of Europe Convention on Laundering, Search, Seizure and Confiscation of Proceeds of Crime of September 8, 1990; the 61 recommendations of the Caribbean Drug Money Laundering Conference of June, 1990; the agreement on EC legislation by the European Community's Ministers for Economy and

Finance of December 17, 1990; the Organization of American States Model Regulations on Crimes Related to Laundering of Property and Proceeds Related to Drug Trafficking of March 1992; and a tangled bouillabaisse of Mutual Legal Assistance Treaties (MLATs).

"Most economically motivated criminals always have wanted to appear legitimate," says attorney Kirk Munroe. "What is new is the criminalization of money laundering. The process itself now is a crime separate from the crime that produced the money."

Money laundering is said to be the "process by which one conceals the existence, illegal source, or illegal application of income, and then disguises that income to make it appear legitimate" (emphasis added). Notice the word "existence." The sentence could be construed to mean that simply disguising the existence of income is money laundering. But whatever money laundering is, in practice U.S. law purports to detect it through the mandatory reporting of cash transactions greater than or equal to a threshold amount of US$10,000. For countries in Europe the figure ranges from ECU7,200 to 16,000.

In the United States, Section 5313 of the Banking Secrecy Act (BSA) requires a Currency Transaction Report (CTR) of cash deposits or transactions of US$10,000 and above, which is IRS Form 4789, and a Currency Transaction Report by Casinos (CTRC), which is IRS Form 8362. Section 5316 of BSA also requires a Currency or Monetary Instrument Report (CMIR) for transport of US$10,000 or more of currency in or out of the United States. This is Customs Form 4790. Section 5314(a) of BSA requires reporting of foreign bank or financial accounts whose value exceeds US$10,000 at any time during the preceding year. This is called a Foreign Bank Account Report (FBAR) and is Treasury Form TDR 90-22-1. Section 60501 of the IRS Code requires the reporting of business transactions involving more than US$10,000 cash. These are reported on IRS Form 8300.

Suppose you need a criminal lawyer. The lawyer charges a modest US$200 an hour, so the first month you pay him US$7,000 in cash. The next month you pay him US$4,000 in cash. Under current U.S. law, the lawyer is required to report complete information about you, including the US$11,000 total cash payment, on IRS Form 8300, and ship it off to the IRS Computing Center in Detroit, Michigan, within 15 days of receiving the second payment (which put the total above the reporting threshold). Never mind if either you or your lawyer thinks filing such a form violates attorney-client privilege, the Sixth Amendment right to counsel, or the Fifth Amendment right to be free from self-incrimination. For if the report is not made, and the IRS finds out about it and penalizes and/or prosecutes your lawyer, the courts will most probably back up the IRS.

The scope and arrogance of the money laundering statutes knows no bounds. The Kerry Amendment to the Anti-Drug Abuse Act of 1988 demands that foreign nations must also require financial institutions to report deposits of US$10,000 or greater, and to make this information available to U.S. law enforcement. Otherwise, the President is directed to impose sanctions against non-cooperative countries.

Having extended the concept of evil to a vaguely defined practice called "money laundering," and having put in a detection system to help trace it, the laws have proceeded to make evasion of the monitoring system evil also. This tertiary evil may be found in the practice of "smurfing" or "structuring," which is basically any method of spreading cash among accounts or across time to avoid the US$10,000 reporting threshold. Structuring is defined in a 1991 amendment to the Bank Secrecy Act thusly:

Structure (structuring)… a person structures a transaction if that person, acting alone, or in conjunction with, or on behalf of other persons, conducts or attempts to conduct one or more transactions in currency in any amount, at one or more financial institutions, on one or more days in any manner, for the purpose of evading the reporting requirements… 'In any manner' includes, but is not limited to, the breaking down of a single sum of currency exceeding US$10,000 into smaller sums, including sums at or below US$10,000, or the conduct of a transaction or series of transactions, including transactions at or below US$10,000. The transaction or transactions need not exceed the US$10,000 reporting threshold at any single financial institution on any single day in order to constitute structuring within the meaning of this definition.

And what does the government do with the information it collects? When your lawyer's Form 8300 reaches the IRS Computing Center in Detroit, it will be entered into the Treasury Financial Data Base (TFDB). Similarly, if you cross a U.S. border with more than US$10,000 cash, you will fill out Customs Form 4790. This form will be sent off to customs' San Diego Data Center, and it too will eventually show up in TFDB. These and other forms will now be available on-line in the Treasury Enforcement Communications System (TECS II). The TFDB data will also be processed through the FinCEN Artificial Intelligence (AI) System, which is trained to identify suspicious transaction patterns.

So, when you deal in cash, expect to give a note to the government, a crumb to the friendly FinCEN AI. But AI has a voracious appetite, so the reporting doesn't stop with cash. The heart of any modern monetary system is the digital transfer of electronic money through the telecommunication links among bank computers. Internationally, banks are connected by a computer messaging system operated by the Society for Worldwide Interbank Financial Telecommunication (SWIFT). Domestically, banks within a country use equivalents of the U.S. clearing systems operated by the Federal Reserve (Fedwire) and the Clearing House Interbank Payments System (CHIPS). A Federal Reserve Policy Statement of December 23, 1992, asks financial institutions to include (if possible) complete information on the sender and recipient of large payment orders sent through Fedwire, CHIPS and SWIFT. "Historically, law enforcement efforts to curtail money laundering activities have focused on the identification and documentation of currency-based transactions; however, recent investigations have focused on the use of funds transfer systems," the statement notes.

The focus on funds transfer brings in the resources of the U.S. National Security Agency (NSA). The NSA has been monitoring civilian communications ever since it installed IBM computers at Menwith Hill in the U.K. in the early 1960s to keep track of international telex messages. NSA tentacles are now ensconced not only in transatlantic communications, but also in Pacific satellite transmissions, the regional Bell System telephone offices, the SWIFT messaging system, the CHIPS clearing computers in Manhattan, and Fedwire.

In addition, a satellite surveillance system picks up high frequency transmissions of specially constructed computer chips which are activated by certain types of transactions-oriented financial software. U.S. agencies are not alone in financial monitoring. As a trivial additional example, the Council of Europe has recommended Interpol be given access to SWIFT to assist in money-laundering detection.

The Bank Secrecy Act of 1970
Banking in Silence, 1998

The official name for this U.S. statute is the "Financial Record Keeping, Currency and Foreign Transactions Reporting Act." How exactly it became known widely as the Bank Secrecy Act is a mystery. It is a prime example of what is meant by "newspeak," where a government says one thing while doing the exact opposite.

This act has absolutely nothing to do with bank secrecy. In fact, it explicitly sets out to provide the U.S. government easy access to all American bank records. Of course, the pretty name undoubtedly contributed to the lack of resistance Big Brother experienced in passing the legislation.

The Bank Secrecy Act formed the first volley in the war on financial privacy. It called for the monitoring of financial affairs in three specific areas:

1. The dreaded Currency Transaction Report (CTR), or form 4789, was brought into existence. This form must be filed with the IRS by all banks and financial institutions for each deposit,

withdrawal or exchange of currency or other monetary instruments in excess of US$10,000.

2. Customs form 4790 was born. This form must be filled out whenever in excess of US$5,000 (later raised to US$10,000) in cash, negotiable securities or certain monetary instruments are carried across U.S. borders. This applies both when entering and leaving the country.

3. Any individual American who either owns or controls a financial account outside of the U.S. must inform the IRS of the existence of this account. If the total amount of funds owned or controlled offshore exceeds US$10,000, form 90-22.1, which forces one to provide explicit detail as to the nature and location of such accounts, must also be filed. These provisions marked the beginning of the end of banking privacy. As far as the government is concerned, your relationship with your bank is as much its business as yours.

The effect of the law has been absolutely crippling on U.S. banks. They are now required to maintain detailed records of almost every transaction, including copies of all deposit slips and copies of the front and back of all checks drawn for over US$100. Most banks routinely microfilm all of the checks that you write. In addition, banks are required to keep permanent records of all loans issued for over US$5,000, with the exception of loans on property.

Your bank is also required to keep your social security number on file. If you fail to provide this number within 45 days of opening an account, your name, address and account number will be put on a special list that will in turn be given to the Treasury Department.

In short, Big Brother wants to know exactly how much you have in the bank. This act has assured him easy access to not only this information, but to detailed figures for virtually all of your banking activities as each of your accounts is now permanently linked to your taxpayer identification number.

To make matters worse, the legislation goes on to accomplish a whole lot more than just turning your bank into a government spy. Almost any institution that you do business with has been enlisted by the government as an unpaid and, in many cases, unwilling accomplice. Any and all businesses considered to be "financial institutions" must also comply with the above reporting requirements.

What exactly is a financial institution? As would be expected, Big Brother uses a fairly loose definition, meaning that all of the following suffice:

- All securities brokers and dealers

- Investment companies

- Currency exchange houses

- Anyone who sells cashier's checks, traveler's checks or money orders

- Anyone who operates a credit card system

- All accountants and attorneys

- The U.S. Post Office

- All automobile, aircraft and boat dealers, as well as property dealers and settlement agents

- And just for good measure, any other institution that the government determines either constitutes a financial institution, or from which such reports would provide "a high degree of usefulness in criminal, tax or regulatory matters."

[**Ed. Note**: The USA PATRIOT Act became law in October 2001 in the wake of the terrorist attacks in New York City and on The Pentagon in Washington, D.C. This law mandated the issuance of a series of regulations governing all of the categories of "financial institutions" named above, as well as others. Most of these new rules are now in effect.]

In short, anyone that Big Brother would like to squeeze information from could easily fall within the parameters of this very loosely worded legislation. With the passage of this single act, the

U.S. government successfully cracked open the financial practices of everyone who lives in or does business in the U.S.

Is This Constitutional?

Although the bulk of the populace accepted the ridiculous provisions of the Bank Secrecy Act with little hesitation, a few saw through the political rhetoric and questioned its legality. The matter soon made its way to the Supreme Court, but in each case the court sided with the government. This really should come as little surprise when one considers who writes the large paychecks received by each of the judges involved. After all, if government revenue were to suddenly take a nose dive, many of those in the employ of government would soon have to start looking for work, perhaps even legitimate work.

The Bank Secrecy Act was first challenged in the case of *California Bankers Association v. Schultz*. Schultz had brought legal action against his bank because it had turned over his records to the federal government. He claimed that in doing so, both his Fifth Amendment rights, that which protects one from compulsory self-incrimination, and his Fourth Amendment rights, that which prohibits unreasonable search and seizure, had been violated.

The courts failed to agree, saying that the records belonged to the bank, not the customer. In other words, as the records were the property of the bank, the rights of its customer cannot be used to prevent the release of such information. The opinion was not unanimous, however. Justice William O. Douglas lodged a dissent which stated the various problems he saw with the act. It reads in part: "It is, I submit, sheer nonsense to agree with the Secretary [of the Treasury] that all bank records of every citizen "have a high degree of usefulness in criminal, tax, or regulatory investigations or proceedings." That is unadulterated nonsense unless we are to assume that every citizen is a crook, an assumption I cannot make."

Since the banking transactions of an individual give a fairly accurate account of his religion, ideology, opinions and interests, a regulation impounding them and making them automatically available to all federal investigative agencies is a sledge-hammer approach to a problem that only a delicate scalpel can manage. Bank accounts at times harbor criminal plans. But we only rush with the crowd when we vent on our banks and their customers the devastating and leveling requirements of the current act. I am not yet ready to agree that America is so possessed with evil that we must level all constitutional barriers to give our civil authorities the tools to catch criminals.

Justice Douglas goes on to compare the requirements of the act with those that would require book stores to keep tabs on the books purchased by customers or the phone company to keep recordings of all calls made. Although I admire his opinion, I only hope that he has not given the bureaucrats yet more ideas on how to limit our freedom.

The second case to examine this act again succeeded in narrowing the basic rights enjoyed by U.S. citizens. In *U.S. v. Miller*, the court found that bank customers have no legal right to prevent the release of financial information held by third parties. The court also found that Miller, or any other depositor for that matter, does not even have standing to bring such matters before the court. The court claimed that if anything, it is the bank that should protest against the release of such records. Yet, in Schultz the court had previously found that the bank could not invoke the rights of its clients.

In short, the court had successfully closed off all possible avenues to prevent the release of such information. This is particularly alarming as such records would not even have existed in the first place had the government not forced banks to start maintaining them.

The death blow came in the case of *Payner v. U.S.* This case came to light because the IRS used illegal means to gather evidence. After distracting a Bahamian bank customer (a female agent invited him to dinner), the IRS broke into his hotel room and stole his briefcase. In the briefcase evidence was found that was later used to convict Payner of tax evasion.

Did the court have a problem with such subversive tactics? No. In the eyes of the court it was all perfectly legal. If nothing else, this case clearly shows that Big Brother will stop at nothing to get his hands on your money. He makes the rules and then expects you to follow them. Whether or not he complies is an entirely different issue.

Government Money Madness

by Robert E. Bauman, *The Sovereign Society Offshore A-Letter*, February 2003

Shortly after the terrorist attacks of September 11, 2001, the USA PATRIOT Act, was rushed through the U.S. Congress sight unseen by most members. The 342-page law gave the FBI and police many new powers, including the unchecked ability to conduct Internet surveillance without a court order and secretly to search homes and offices without notifying the owner.

Tacked on to this law in the anti-terror frenzy were numerous new powers over domestic and offshore financial activity, based on alleged massive offshore terror financial activity that to this day never has been proven. The sleeper in the law was an expansive definition of "financial institutions."

In recent months stock brokers, hedge funds, mutual funds, insurance brokers, financial advisors and other financial activities have suddenly been confronted with rules making all of them government money spies. Now the federal rule makers have issued preliminary regulations for travel agencies, auto dealers and precious metals dealers and refiners, jewelry manufacturers, loose gemstone merchants and retail stores that also act as a dealer in such items.

It is estimated that US$856.6 billion was laundered worldwide in 2002. The total will grow at an annual rate of 2.7% to reach US$926.6 billion by 2006. Large institutions will spend a total of US$845 million and mid-tier firms a total of US$2.2 billion on anti-ML programs up to 2005. Small sized financial institutions will spend an aggregate of US$7.9 billion. You pay the bill for all this in increased fees.

Yet terrorist groups account for only one quarter of 1% of all money laundering activity.

Where will this government madness end?

The Money Laundering Control Act of 1986

Banking in Silence, 1998

In 1985 and 1986, it came to light that, in spite of the government's many and varied efforts, a large number of banks and financial institutions were simply ignoring the restrictive requirements of the Bank Secrecy Act and its accompanying legislation. Many individuals felt that the government really had no right to such information and proceeded according to their own beliefs rather than those of the bureaucratic system. Understandably, this practice caused a great deal of embarrassment for the federal government and inevitably led to a crackdown.

Banks were forced into compliance through the use of several highly publicized and large fines. The Bank of Boston was the first to fall, fined US$500,000. This was quickly followed by fines against Seafirst Bank for US$697,000, the Bank of New England for US$1.2 million, Crocker National Bank for US$2.25 million and the Bank of America for US$4.75 million. Banks across the country took notice; no longer was this myriad of regulations a matter to be taken lightly. The government's precious forms started to roll in and Big Brother found himself buried in an avalanche of paperwork.

Next came another decisive blow against financial privacy with the Money Laundering Control Act of 1986. This single act is responsible for the loss of more American liberties than any other piece of legislation. Again, to keep the public from realizing what was really going on behind the scenes, the actual provisions of the act were encoded in pretty language and political rhetoric. The fact of the matter is that the act set about dismantling the basic rights of Americans in three separate ways:

1. Money laundering was made into a federal crime for the first time anywhere in the world.

2. It became a federal crime to engage in any transaction involving the proceeds of any "specified unlawful activity."

3. Structuring transactions so as to avoid any federal reporting requirements was made illegal.

The fines and penalties for violations of this act are some of the harshest possible in all U.S. legislation. Money laundering, an activity that was perfectly legal in the U.S. until 1986, has been put on a par with murder, espionage and racketeering. The fines and jail terms handed down are often more severe than those given to rapists. Fines can be levied for up to US$500,000 or twice the value of the transactions involved.

Furthermore, the law provides Big Brother with powers to seize any property involved in or even related to an illegal transaction. If convicted of money laundering conspiracy, fines can reach up to US$25 million and can include forfeiture of all assets, not just those criminally derived. Often a money laundering conviction is linked with a charge under the Racketeer Influenced and Corrupt Organizations (RICO) Act, which permits the federal government to seize all monies "laundered" as well as all assets derived through these funds.

In addition, a fine of up to three times the amount laundered is permissible. For example, in 1988 when Lee Chan-Hong, an investor who went by the name of Fred Lee, was convicted of insider trading, he was fined a total of US$77.6 million, four times the US$19.4 million he supposedly made from his specified illegal activity.

What Is Money Laundering?

The term "money laundering" is certainly not lacking in connotations. It brings to mind images of suitcases stuffed with cash carried by men wearing pin-striped suits who speak in raspy whispers. In the eyes of the public, money laundering is one and the same with drug smuggling and violent crime. The government and the mainstream media foster this image. The truth is far less exciting, as money laundering is one of the most boring crimes on record.

The actual legal definition of money laundering is found in Section 1956 of the Money Laundering Control Act. It states that it is illegal to make any transaction with the proceeds of specified unlawful activity:

A. with the intent to promote that activity; or

B. knowing that the transaction is designed in whole or in part—

(i) to conceal or disguise the nature, the location, the source, the ownership, or the control of the proceeds of specified unlawful activity; or

(ii) to avoid a transaction reporting requirement under state or federal law.

What falls within the bounds of specified illegal activity? Of course tax evasion appears at the top of the list. Simply depositing or using money on which taxes have not been paid is now legally defined as money laundering. Opening a foreign bank account and establishing a small nest egg offshore without notifying the government of your activities can now be classified as money laundering.

Prosecutions for money laundering are soaring and often lead to confiscations of all funds concerned. Prison terms of up to 20 years are frequently issued. Not to mention the fact that a conviction of money laundering all but ruins the reputation of the individual involved.

Such tactics are clearly primarily intended to succeed in routing yet more money in the direction of the government. They are akin to a 100 percent tax on those individuals smart enough to realize that governments are not to be trusted. The moral of the story? Do not be surprised if what originally appeared to be a simple tax investigation by the IRS turns into a money laundering conviction.

More alarming, the government does not stop there and goes on to define a host of other specified unlawful activities; at last count more than 150 such activities appear on the growing list. Have you ever heard of the Emergency Economic Powers Act of 1977 or the Trading With the Enemy Act of 1977? Violating either of these acts could land you in jail for money laundering. Recently, even violations of environmental laws have been added to the list. In short, it seems that almost any activity that involves money and financial transactions, or in other words just about any business activity, could be linked to a money laundering charge. As a money laundering conviction tends to be easier to achieve and also manages to bring much larger sums into the government kitty, it is really no wonder that the list of prohibited activities just keeps on growing.

Furthermore, you need not even directly participate in any of these activities to take the fall. Merely doing business with or accepting cash or other monetary instruments from the public could also set you up for a conviction of money laundering. According to Section 1957 of the Money Laundering Control Act, it is illegal for a merchant to accept funds that he suspects have been derived from any of the growing list of specified unlawful activities.

[**Ed. Note:** It is estimated that there are now over 200 federal statutes, and many more state laws, that allow forfeiture of cash or property associated with prohibited criminal activities. The trend is to add on "money laundering" criminal charges against persons engaged in all crimes if evidence shows cash dealings as part of the criminal activity.]

If you would like an indication of the level of commitment expected from you in Big Brother's war, consider the comments of then Florida Congressman Bill McCollum (R-Fla.): The corner grocer in a community is aware of the reputation of the local drug trafficker. That person comes to the store and buys five pounds of hamburger. The grocer has to know that he is coming in to buy groceries with what is indeed the money derived from a particular designated crime. I don't have any problem whatsoever holding the grocer accountable for money laundering.

Apparently Congressman McCollum had never heard of the idea of the right to a fair trial, or for that matter of the concept of innocent until proven guilty. Instead, he wanted the public to act as prosecutor, judge, jury and executioner. Businessmen and bankers have been instructed to discriminate against anyone who even appears to be guilty of a crime. If Congressman McCollum has his way, anyone unfortunate enough to be labeled as a criminal, whether correctly or not, will basically be sentenced to death without a trial. If no one is willing to do business with this individual or even sell food to him, he will be left with no alternative but to become destitute and homeless. This is not such an unlikely scenario, as anyone not willing to participate in Big Brother's campaign risks forfeiture of his assets as well as up to 10 years in prison.

Even more damaging is that the merchant need not even be aware that the activities of which the person is suspected of committing are criminal. According to Section 1957, the government need not prove that "the defendant knew that the offense from which the criminally derived property was derived was a specified unlawful activity." As already mentioned, this growing list contains many activities that most individuals would never even imagine could be linked with a money laundering conviction. Should every corner grocer in the U.S. consult a competent attorney on a weekly basis so that he can find out which customers he is allowed to sell hamburger to and which ones he must turn away? If he wishes to stay entirely inside the law, this is his only option.

Even criminal lawyers almost automatically risk entering into a criminal conspiracy just by agreeing to represent a client. Under common law, one must both have knowledge of an illegal activity and the intent to encourage it to be convicted of criminal conspiracy. Under Section 1957, neither is required, as one can be convicted of conspiracy for merely not taking a person's reputation into account before doing business with him. If an attorney even suspects that his client is guilty, he may well go to jail for merely representing him.

Placed under such restrictions, many attorneys will choose not to represent individuals solely because they are known to have a bad reputation. In other words, Congress has yet again succeeded in turning over a basic civil liberty, that of the right to legal representation as promised by the Sixth Amendment.

About the only saving grace is that Section 1957 only applies to amounts in excess of US$10,000. However, related transactions over a 12-month period that exceed US$10,000 are also enforceable. Be warned: many in Congress would like to further restrict American liberties and reduce the limit to only US$3,000.

What Is Structuring?

The new crime of structuring was brought into existence by the Money Laundering Control Act. It came to the attention of the government that many individuals interested in laundering large amounts of money simply changed tactics to circumvent reporting requirements. They developed a process that became known as "smurfing." This procedure simply involved large number of couriers, known as "smurfs," making several deposits a day at various locations. Each smurf would deposit an amount just below US$10,000, meaning that in the end no CTRs would need to be filed. Over a relatively short period of time, very large amounts of cash could make their way into the banking system.

The Money Laundering Control Act brought an end to all of this. Transactions structured in such a way were made illegal. However, like most of the legislation introduced to curb money laundering and to snare drug traffickers, the act has failed miserably. Once smurfing became illegal, professional criminals changed their tactics again. Instead of using banks, today's launderers feed dirty money into the system through other financial operators, such as money exchanges, money transmitters and check cashing services.

In reality, the new legislation has only really succeeded in stealing the assets of innocent individuals. For the most part, those prosecuted for structuring first hear of the crime's existence when they are arrested. According to a 1991 Treasury Department analysis, over 75 percent of assets seized as a result of the anti-structuring laws were originally the property of individuals not involved in any illegal activities. In the modern over-legislated world, the question of guilt or innocence increasingly seems to be a thing of the past.

The major problem with anti-structuring laws is that no underlying illegal intent need be proven by the government. Merely depositing US$9,000 in cash into an account on two consecutive days is now a crime. The penalties for such infractions are severe. The funds involved almost automatically become the property of the government. Criminal violations may well bring an additional fine of US$250,000 as well as a five-year stint in jail. Civil penalties for "willful" violation are a bit less severe, but still claim either US$25,000 or the full amount of the funds involved, whichever is greater. You can be convicted of willfully violating the law even if you are unaware of its existence. Finally, if you are convicted of structuring in conjunction with a violation of any other law, the fine can escalate to a cool half a million as well as 10 years in jail.

The Financial Crimes Enforcement Network (FinCEN
July 1994

Because you have lots of money, you are automatically guilty until proven innocent. That, at least, seems to be the view of FinCEN, the Financial Crimes Enforcement Network of the U.S. Department of the Treasury, a quasi-secretive federal sleuthing operation whose brief is to unearth money secrets.

The U.S. government is lining up the computer big guns ostensibly to defeat drug barons and criminals but, in reality, frightening links are being developed between the data systems of the IRS, the FBI, the Secret Service, similar policing groups and FinCEN.

The following scenario is an example of the capacity to delve into an individual's past. A drugs dealer is found by police with the word "John" and a phone number scribbled on a piece of paper but no other evidence of the suspected drugs supplier. The local police turned to FinCEN. When FinCEN received the request, the digital hunt was on. First, the telephone number was checked against listed businesses, and was quickly found to belong to a restaurant.

Next, the computer operator entered the Currency and Banking Database of the IRS to check currency transaction reports, which note all transactions of more than US$10,000. Within the database, the operator requested a list of "suspicious" requests made by banks and other institutions. It came up with a number of suspect deposits in the area of the restaurant's ZIP code. The suspicious requests were made because a series of US$9,500 deposits, just below the official reportable threshold had been made. They were made by someone whose first name was John.

Through one of those suspicious Currency Transaction Reports, the computer operator was able to ask for personal details on the depositor and the machine came up with data including a full name, social security number, date of birth, home address, driver's license number and bank account numbers. When the IRS computer was accessed again, it came up with more suspicious and non-suspicious reports on John, who listed his occupation as being involved in a restaurant with a telephone number identical to that found originally. Turning to commercial and government databases, John's restaurant was discovered to have a substantially smaller income than that being deposited on its behalf. Cross-checks found other suspect transactions by John's other businesses. Within an hour of the first police inquiry, FinCEN had enough evidence to make a case against John on charges of money laundering and conspiracy to traffic narcotics.

Since its inception in 1990, under the auspices of the Treasury Department, FinCEN has become one of the world's most effective financial crime investigation units. Its 1993 tally of cases being probed totaled 40,000, plus longer-term reports on 16,000 other individuals or organizations.

Although its major successes have been in the field of drugs and money laundering, what is worrying civil liberties activists is FinCEN's close links with the CIA and the Defense Intelligence Agency, which enable it to act with immense power and breadth of operation. The consummate ease with which computer boffins can tap into linked databases can mean the world is an oyster ripe for opening—or a nest of vipers, depending on your viewpoint.

Operation Gateway is a new system implemented by the U.S. government in all 50 states. Gateway gives state and local law enforcement officers access to the federal financial database containing 28 years of records filed under the Bank Secrecy Act. The results from all queries are written into a constantly-updated master file for cross-indexing purposes. The financial database contains only records on major money movements and is not a threat to individual privacy. However there is worse to come.

When implemented, this computer system can be used to probe all 400 million bank accounts and their holders in the U.S. The government says it is wanted to assess the funding needed for federal deposit insurance, and to locate assets of individuals ordered by courts to make restitution for financial crimes.

The deposit tracking system has attracted civil liberties criticism at a high level. The federal law enforcement agencies and intelligence agencies see the system as a valuable addition to economic intelligence gathering, such as monitoring foreign financial dealings in the U.S. The present system has successfully identified previous unknown criminal organizations and activities because of deposit flows and patterns.

Watch Out for Cash Reporting Requirements

Banking in Silence, 1998

For privately moving money into your offshore account you must use a method consistent with the reporting requirements in effect in your home country. These laws are designed to inform the government when large amounts of cash are moved, and to reveal the purpose of these transfers. Of course, these Big Brother laws destroy banking and financial privacy, but ignoring them means possible fines, jail and confiscation of your cash.

Once you understand the obstacle course you can adapt your game to suit your particular circumstances. Big Brother knows all too well that once money is converted into cash it becomes very difficult to monitor. Acting on behalf of the government, banks are now forced to monitor all transactions, especially those in cash. Bank staff is always on the lookout for customer behavior that warrants a "suspicious activity report."

Banks have been instructed to look for individuals who frequently deposit or withdraw large amounts of cash. Unless your business requires it (and the bank knows this in advance), changing a large number of small bills into larger bills could mark you as a criminal suspect. Making a cash deposit just below the amount covered by reporting requirements may also get attention from your banker. Buying an excessive amount of cashier's checks, money orders or traveler's checks could cause a red flag on your account. Under the new rules purchasers of these instruments must identify themselves fully and often must be a bank customer in order to be eligible to buy. Just about any cash transaction that looks odd could get you caught in the expanding government net.

Big Brother has been thorough in blocking all possible routes to bank secrecy. But the massive reporting requirements have buried banks and bureaucrats in mountains of unread reports, useless unless properly sorted and analyzed. Under government threat of severe penalties, banks have adopted the practice of filing "defensive" reports. In addition to mandatory reporting of all cash transactions of US$10,000 or more, bank managers tell employees any activity even remotely suspicious should be written up. This information glut insulates the bank from possible reprisals and clogs government computerized data banks.

As frightening as this sounds, the sheer volume serves to dilute the overall effectiveness of reporting requirements. A surge in the quantity of cash banking reports filed in the U.S. does little to boost the number of individuals prosecuted for money-laundering offenses. The U.S. Treasury Department's Financial Crimes Enforcement Network (FinCEN) is several years behind in examining the flood of reports (approximately eight million annually) that it demands from all and sundry.

One individual in New York filed nearly 1,700 such reports before Big Brother noticed him. A random computer search revealed a large number of reports filed within a single zip code and then the government agents became interested. Further analysis showed all these reports had been filed by one individual in one bank. This suggests that properly filed reports are generally ignored. This has led many professional money launderers to adopt what is known as the "file and forget it" approach.

Once Big Brother finally focuses on these precious reports he looks for certain patterns of behavior rather than single incidents. In other words, if you want to move a large amount of your money offshore in cash, withdraw it in one lump sum and file the appropriate report. That's the least you can do to join the war against drugs. After all, no sacrifice is too great for the welfare of our children.

The worst thing one can do is to fail to file a report or even appear to be disturbed when the reporting requirement is mentioned. Such behavior sets off alarm bells and makes your banker assume the worst about you. That a free person might wish to move legally earned money into a safe offshore account seems indeed foreign to government agents. But once you have soothed the bureaucratic mind by filing their beloved reports, you have your cash in hand and can put it wherever you wish.

The next worst mistake when withdrawing cash from a bank is known as "structuring." This is simply making several withdrawals in lesser sums than the total amount that comes within the reporting requirements. Many bank computers are now programmed to detect such cash activity patterns so the bank can alert government officials. The act of structuring in and of itself is illegal and allows not only the forfeiture of all funds involved, but of any other funds held in the accounts used. In the U.S, fines up to US$250,000 and five years in jail can follow conviction of this and other non-reporting crimes.

It is much better to file a report, especially if both you and your assets are headed out of your home country for good. With a new passport in hand, you can freely wander the globe and enjoy the finer things in life while your former tax collector wrings his hands over his useless reporting forms.

Exempt Yourself

If you insist on staying in your home country, there may be a way to avoid reporting requirements in certain situations. Even government bureaucrats realized that too many reports would be as useless as no reports at all, thus certain types of businesses are granted exemptions from reporting requirements.

For example, in the U.S. exemptions may be granted to owners and operators of a sports arena, race track, amusement park, vending machine company or theater, all businesses in which large amounts of cash are collected on a daily basis. Exemptions may be given to large companies and banks on behalf of known customers who reasonably require them. If you own a business that falls within the narrowly defined limits you might be freed from most reporting requirements. Avoid investing in automobile, airplane or boat dealerships since these business are specifically denied exemptions from cash reporting.

Whatever method you choose, once you successfully convert your assets into either cash or other untraceable instruments, you face the task of moving money out of your home country and into your offshore account.

Restrictions on Transporting Cash

There are no exchange control restrictions on the free flow of capital in and out of most countries at the present time. This freedom to transfer assets abroad exists in almost every democracy including the U.S., Australia, Japan and most of Europe. Reporting requirements are, however, a different matter entirely. For example, the U.S. Currency and Foreign Transactions Reporting Act requires everyone "who transports or causes to be transported into or out of the United States currency or certain monetary instruments in the amount of exceeding US$10,000 or more" is required to file a report (IRS Form 4790) with U.S. Customs Bureau agents at the time of entry or departure, or on or before the date of sending or receiving, if the currency or monetary instrument is mailed or shipped.

Thus the government not only wants to know when your money is withdrawn from your bank, but also when you actually transport your cash to safer offshore pastures. The U.S. reporting requirements cover not only cash but any negotiable monetary instruments that can be converted into cash. This includes anything in bearer form, bonds, securities and investments. Similarly, cashier's checks, money orders or traveler's checks on which the name of the payee has been omitted or which have been endorsed must also be reported. Some countries are only concerned with the movement of large quantities of cash and not monetary instruments. Check the situation in your home country and any countries where you may be traveling.

Never ignore reporting requirements. Non-reporting penalties are severe and ignorance of the law is no excuse. Big Brother will seize money from an innocent traveler completely unaware of the law as easily as from an international drug lord. Thanks to political terrorists, you can expect heavy airport security every time you board an international flight. Carry-on as well as checked luggage will be x-rayed before it is allowed on the plane. It is also increasingly common for passengers to be frisked as they pass through airport security.

The bottom line: if you travel with a large amount of cash before boarding an international flight, government agents will know about it. Any unreported large amount of cash will automatically lead to forfeiture of all funds in your possession.

One easier way to avoid reporting is to move cash into your offshore account in the form of cashier's checks, money orders or traveler's checks. Although you must report buying such monetary instruments, you need not report transporting them if they are made payable to a specific person or entity—in other words, they are in non-negotiable form. You can make such instruments payable to your offshore bank, instructing the bank to cash them and deposit the funds in your account. There is no paper trail if such instruments are purchased anonymously with cash, though that may be difficult to do.

Another method is to use personal or business checks payable to you or your business from third party payers. By endorsing such checks over to your offshore bank and directing them to make deposits in your offshore account, you can legally avoid reporting the fund transfer. Be sure not to place a simple endorsement on the check since that makes it a reportable bearer instrument. You must make the check payable to a named party. By making your offshore bank the payee, your offshore account stays out of the picture but your bank is known. When the check is returned after clearance to the original check drawer he or she will be privy to banking information best known only to you. Be sure you can trust that person or avoid using their third party check.

Happily, full-fledged currency restrictions that prohibit going abroad with your money are now largely in the past. However, in many third world countries business may still be hampered by currency controls. Nonetheless, as with all reporting requirements, currency restrictions can be circumvented legally. Talk to resident foreigners in business. They usually know the easiest way to get money in and out of the country. Wealthy residents are usually knowledgeable about ways of beating the system. A quiet talk in private with local American Express office staff can also produce results.

U.S. Government Grabs Offshore Cash in Secret

By Robert E. Bauman, JD. *The Sovereign Individual*, July 2003

It gives me no pleasure to say we told you so. But what is happening was inevitable, given the blind reaction by the U.S. Congress to the terror attacks on Washington, D.C. and New York City in the aftermath of September 11, 2001.

On May 30, 2003, the New York Times reported: "The Justice Department has begun using its expanded counter terrorism powers to seize millions of dollars from foreign banks that do business in the United States...Officials at the State Department, however, have raised concerns over the practice, in part because most of the seizures have involved fraud and money-laundering investigations that are unrelated to terrorism."

The Times explained: "A little-noticed provision in the sweeping antiterrorism legislation passed in October 2001, gave federal authorities in such cases the power to seize money that passes through banks in the United States without notifying the foreign government. Most overseas banks maintain what are called 'correspondent accounts' in American banks, allowing them to exchange American currency and handle other financial transactions in this country. Section 319 of the Patriot Act, as the legislation that grew out of the Sept. 11 attacks is known, allows federal authorities to seize money from the foreign bank's correspondent account if they can convince a judge that the money deposited overseas at the bank was obtained illicitly."

So only now, for some uninformed people, is it becoming known just how far reaching the PATRIOT Act is.

Small wonder since the Congress passed the law without even knowing what was in it. In less than six weeks after the terrorists horror, the Congress rammed through a 362-page law, sight unseen, with few members having the courage to oppose one of the worst attacks on the American liberties ever enacted into law.

Writing in our sister publication, The Sovereign Society Offshore A-Letter, on November 2, 2001, I said: "The 'USA PATRIOT ACT'—Public Law No. 107-56, signed by Pres. Bush on Oct. 26—devotes 125 of its 362 pages to U.S. and offshore banking and finance under the banner of 'anti-money laundering.' In the wake of the Sept. 11 horror, 'anti-terrorism' is the patriotic fig leaf, but, as the fine print makes painfully clear, the real objective is massive expansion of the all purpose prosecutorial crime of money laundering, with tax collection an equal, if unstated, goal."

Previously, on October 2, 2001, I had said: "Using the newly created terror imperative as their cover, leftist US politicians are scurrying to hang their favorite anti-offshore nostrums on the catch-all terrorist legislation about to sail though Congress...these opportunists want to ban much ofU.S.-offshore correspondent banking and give the Treasury power to cut off foreign nations from the U.S. banking system, a radical Clinton proposal that failed in Congress last year. These totalitarian proposals have as their true goals abolition of financial privacy and increased tax collection. The lie is that this is sold as fighting money laundering and terrorism."

So now, it is happening, and thanks to federal judges who seal the records of the pending cases, America knows little about these cash seizures from the U.S. correspondent accounts of foreign banks.

Law enforcement officials said the U.S. Justice Department had employed the new tool in about a half-dozen investigations, seizing money from at least 15 bank accounts. Most of those came in recent months and involved alleged fraud and money laundering cases that had nothing to do with anti-terrorism.

Here's how it works.

In one case, the U.S. government seized $1.7 million in funds from a correspondent account in the U.S. belonging to the Bank of Belize. A U.S. lawyer, James Gibson, was accused of bilking clients out of millions of dollars, then fleeing to Belize where he deposited some of the money.

Although the government of Belize initially agreed to freeze the money, a court there blocked the move, but U.S. prosecutors said they believed that Mr. Gibson and his wife were looting the accounts to buy yachts and other luxury items. After passage of the PATRIOT Act, the Justice Department moved within weeks in late 2001 to seize the money from the Belizean banks' correspondent accounts in the United States.

Using this drastic procedure, the U.S. government ignores mutual legal assistance treaties with other nations which they have used in the past and which do contain procedural safeguards. They do not have to prove guilt or even show probable cause. They simply demand that the U.S. correspondent bank hand over sums they claim to be the result of alleged illegal activity of someone who has funds in the offshore bank. Once the U.S. bank surrenders the cash, the offshore bank is left holding the bag. They either deduct it from the accused's account, or sustain the loss. Banks in New York City that hold correspondent accounts for Citibank, Standard Chartered Bank, Deutsche Bank and HSBC Bank USA have all been hit.

We would not be surprised to see this unconstitutional tactic used in tax cases by the IRS. Until the Congress or the courts curb this wholesale money grab sans proof or due process, you can expect to see more.

These developments place even greater wisdom on our repeated advice; choose an offshore bank without any U.S. branches, which only makes seizures easier. Maintain your funds outside the

U.S. dollar so that there is no need for the bank to maintain your funds in a U.S dollar correspondent account.

But with the inter-related world banking system as it is, this new government seizure tool confirms the Nazification of the U.S. financial system. The day has now come where government money police, on their say so, can loot banks of funds belonging to people who have never been tried or convicted of any crime.

Welcome to the new Amerika.

———————◆●◆———————

Unreported Offshore Accounts
by Donald McPherson, *The Sovereign Individual*, June 2001

It's 7 p.m. on a Friday evening. Relaxing at home, you are finishing your second martini when the doorbell rings. Two IRS Criminal Investigation Division (CID) agents (the ones that carry guns), announce that they have credit card records which prove that you have been maintaining an unreported offshore account.

The agents claim that you "obviously" acted willfully, and thus, committed federal crimes. They ask you to sign a plea agreement stipulating that you will forfeit your home, business and retirement accounts and that you spend the next four years in a federal prison. If you fight them in court, they say you could spend the next 20 years in prison.

What are your options? What, if anything, is the solution?

Any U.S. person with signatory or other authority over one or more foreign "bank, securities or other financial accounts" that contain, in aggregate, US$10,000 or more, is required to acknowledge those accounts on Schedule B of Form 1040, and separately, on Treasury Form TD F 90-22.1. You must make these disclosures if you have effective control over the account—e.g., if someone else controls an offshore account on your behalf, you must acknowledge the account.

If you failed to make these disclosures, the possible scenarios vary from bad to worse. The situation is less serious if the unreported account(s) contain after-tax dollars and you have paid taxes on any earnings from the accounts. At worst, the unreported accounts contain substantial pre-tax dollars with intent to evade assessment or collection of income tax.

The situation has in recent months become more serious due to the disclosures made by John Mathewson, former head of Guardian Bank in the Cayman Islands. To avoid prison, Mathewson provided the IRS with detailed records of more than 2,000 client accounts, thereby violating Cayman Islands bank secrecy laws. Armed with the Mathewson information and details of his modus operandi, which included an offshore bank account, trust, corporation, and credit card, the IRS has prosecuted numerous Guardian depositors.

Based on Mathewson's testimony, the IRS has also obtained a court order to obtain data on transactions with American Express and MasterCard cards issued through bank accounts in the Caymans, Bahamas, and Antigua and Barbuda. The IRS hopes to use this data to identify additional U.S. persons with unreported offshore accounts. So far, the card companies haven't complied, although it's probably just a matter of time before they do.

Possible Crimes—and Punishments

Depending on how large the tax loss from fraud or evasion is, possible federal charges range from filing a false tax return and tax evasion to conspiracy and money laundering—all of which are felonies. In less serious circumstances, misdemeanor charges may be brought.

The likely punishment is not the statutory maximum, but within the range allowed under the Federal Sentencing Guidelines. This range depends on the "tax loss," or in laundering cases, the amount laundered. Without adjustments, the following sentencing ranges in months apply:

US$50,000 (12-18); US$150,000 (18-24); US$550,000 (23-33). Money laundering sentencing guidelines begin at 46-57 months and increase depending upon the amount laundered.

In a tax-conspiracy case, an upward adjustment is made for "sophisticated concealment" (use of an offshore trust, corporation, bank, or credit card) and "role in the offense." Assuming a tax loss of US$250,000 plus these adjustments, the range is 41-51 months.

However, negotiated settlements with taxpayers whose foreign accounts were revealed in the Guardian Bank probe have been lower than these guidelines. None have been charged with money laundering.

A computer executive who evaded US$2.2 million in taxes was sentenced to five months in jail, five months home detention, and a US$60,000 fine.

A Brooklyn golf pro deposited US$150,000 in money orders in a Cayman corporation. He was sentenced to six months home detention, three years probation and 600 hours of community service. The court recommended golf lessons to inner city children and a US$50,000 fine to be paid within 90 days.

On the other hand, prison sentences under the IRS's "abusive trust program" (TSI 5/99) have been extremely harsh.

If you fight an IRS criminal prosecution in court, you can expect to spend tens of thousands of dollars, or more, in legal fees, assuming that you have the means to hire an attorney and don't need to rely on court-appointed counsel. More than 95 percent of defendants lose, and the sentencing guidelines definitely apply. However, the government must prove beyond a reasonable doubt that you acted knowingly and willfully.

Ignorance of the law is an excuse/defense to technical crimes such as tax offenses.

Willfulness means that you intentionally violated a known legal duty. Good faith reliance, misunderstanding of the law, or reliance on others, especially professionals—such as an offshore promoter, banker, or your accountant—can provide a viable defense.

"Willful blindness" negates a willfulness defense. This might be the case if you rely on the promises of an offshore promoter without asking an accountant or tax preparer for an opinion.

What are the chances of being caught? Detection for depositors in Guardian Bank appears a certainty. Detection of credit card users tied to offshore bank accounts may depend on cooperation by offshore banks.

The Bahamian Central Bank has informed card-issuing banks that future audits must itemize their credit and debit card activity; a step that would permit the offshore banks to assemble the records required to identify individual depositors. The IRS can be expected to request this information once a pending U.S.-Bahamas Tax Information Exchange Agreement is signed, if not before.

The real question: by what method will IRS select individuals for audit?

In the Guardian investigation, it is believed the names of all 2,000 account holders were turned over to CID, at least initially. In the subpoena of offshore credit card holders, only taxpayers with accounts larger than US$10,000 are likely to be investigated.

If the tax loss is zero or very low, one might assume that chances of being selected are low. But for "deterrence" (interpret: reign of fear), the IRS prosecutes tax loss cases as low as US$1,000. Recently, a client, a Colorado chiropractor, was charged for use of a trust for three years with a total tax loss of only US$15,000.

Another unknown is whether the federal courts will uphold the procedures by which IRS obtained the Guardian Bank information, including use of the fruits of Mathewson's violations of Cayman law. Given a recent district court's decision in the Guardian case in favor of the IRS, it appears likely that the courts will uphold them.

But the IRS has limited resources. Audits are at an all-time low. The CID brings only about 600 criminal tax prosecutions each year (although for every prosecution there may be dozens of "settlements," where a taxpayer ends up paying and serving time on a plea deal). And there may be tens or even hundreds of thousands of unreported offshore accounts.

Is It Too Late To Say You're Sorry?

The five main choices for persons at risk of an IRS criminal investigation for non-reporting of offshore accounts are: (1) Do nothing. (2) File the delinquent reporting forms. (3) #2 plus an amended return, 1040X for the last three years, and pay all the back tax, interest and penalties. Amended returns, however, cannot be filed beyond three years from the due date or filing date, whichever is later. A sub-option to (3) is to pay all tax, interest and penalties for all years. (4) Pay back tax, interest and penalty anonymously, through your attorney, under cover of the attorney-client privilege. (5) Proceed through counsel with an informal request to the CID, which need not involve disclosure of your identity, as described below.

There is no obvious "best" choice. Counsel must evaluate each case. Under no circumstances can the IRS promise immunity. At best, your attorney, after presenting a "hypothetical" case, might obtain a "reading" from the local CID chief. Yet promises are not likely, much less binding.

What about "voluntary disclosure" to the IRS? The Internal Revenue Manual states: "When faced with a taxpayer who wants to make a voluntary disclosure, the special agent should inform the taxpayer of the following: 'It is the practice of the Internal Revenue Service that a voluntary disclosure does not bar criminal prosecution, but rather is a factor to be considered when deciding to recommend prosecution.'"

The IRS requires five elements in a voluntary disclosure to avoid prosecution: truthfulness, timeliness, completeness, cooperation and legal income. A voluntary disclosure may not be done anonymously. A disclosure is timely only if received prior to IRS's initiation of any inquiry that "is likely to lead to the taxpayer and the taxpayer is reasonably thought to be aware of that investigative activity."

If "some event known by the taxpayer" has occurred which is "likely to cause an audit into the taxpayer's liabilities," it's too late to say you're sorry. This is particularly relevant since the knowledge that offshore credit card information soon will be in the hands of IRS investigators is a matter of public record.

An amended return (1040X) and payment of back tax, interest and penalty demonstrates contrition and offers an argument of mitigation and no prosecution, to which the IRS may respond, "Thanks, sign the plea agreement here." A major disadvantage to an amended return is that it starts running a new civil and criminal statute of limitations; and, if filed correctly, may identify other problems.

However, a 1040X does not include a revision of information on Schedule B, which asks if you control an offshore account(s). Nor does it identify the source of unreported income; it merely shows the old 1040 numbers, the new numbers, and the difference.

The general statute of limitations for a civil tax audit is three years from the due date of the return or the filing of the return, whichever is later, unless gross income is unreported by 25 percent or more, in which case IRS has six years. In the case of civil fraud there is no statute of limitation, but the IRS must prove fraud by clear and convincing evidence.

In a criminal case, there is a six-year limitation for tax crimes; generally five years for conspiracy and other crimes. However, conspiracy runs five years from the last overt act in furtherance of the conspiracy, which might be last week's phone conversation with a Cayman banker.

Meanwhile, Congress is about to enact a new bankruptcy law that will reduce options for discharging tax debts through bankruptcy. Time is on the government's side.

Summary and Conclusion

The answer is: there is no answer. There are only choices, some perhaps more viable than others, depending on particular facts and circumstances. Those with a gambler's heart and patience may wish to do nothing. Others hate dealing with the unknown and want to get it over with, and on with their life, without fear of the knock at the door. If the financial loss to the government is small, prison is unlikely, but the government may insist on a felony rather than a misdemeanor plea.

Competent, experienced counsel can review the specific facts and discuss the options, make a recommendation, and ride herd on the case. IRS websites and answers to Freedom of Information requests concerning the offshore credit card project may prove fruitful.

And finally, do NOT sign a plea agreement with the IRS unless advised to do so by an experienced tax attorney.

IRS's Qualified Intermediary (QI) Regulations
Center for Freedom and Prosperity, March 2001

The IRS has decided to implement new regulations governing money that is invested in America from overseas. These so-called QI (Qualified Intermediary) regulations, which will impose costly reporting requirements on foreign institutions, are ostensibly designed to increase tax collections by catching U.S. taxpayers trying to hide income earned in America from the IRS by anonymously investing through foreign institutions. To the extent that such tax evasion exists, however, tax evaders can avoid the net by shifting investments out of the U.S. While failing to reduce tax evasion, the new regulations will have an impact. Unfortunately, that impact will be negative. Likely effects include capital flight out of the U.S. market, less future foreign investment in the U.S., a loss of privacy, a reduction in national sovereignty, a reduction in international commerce, and a discriminatory burden against medium- and small-sized businesses.

Equally important, the QI regulations create a disquieting precedent. In effect, the U.S. is trying to impose rules on the rest of the world. This will create an obligation on the part of the U.S. government to acquiesce to rules that foreign tax collectors will want to impose on U.S. citizens and businesses.

The QI regulations will be simultaneously costly but ineffective. Indeed, serious shortcomings already caused their enactment to be twice postponed. Yet, the legally required cost/benefit analysis is still lacking. And while significant adverse effects are a certainty, experts foresee no real dent on U.S. tax evasion. The IRS should thus withdraw the proposal and reconsider how best to tax the U.S. income earned by U.S. taxpayers and foreigners.

What are QI Regulations?

The IRS decided to change its withholding tax regime, enforcing new regulations effective January 1, 2001 that are aimed in particular at "U.S. persons"— i.e., U.S. citizens, dual nationals, green card holders, U.S. residents—who invest in the U.S. market through financial institutions abroad. Recipients of U.S.-source income are thus faced with the choice of either withdrawing their investments from the U.S. market or disclosing their identity to the IRS, under threat of a penalty of over 30 percent of their investment (not just the income, but 30 percent of any financial flow). The tax would be collected on behalf of the IRS by QI. Overseas financial institutions practicing IRS-approved know-your-customer rules (KYC) can apply to enter into an agreement with the IRS to directly enforce these new regulations as QIs, with IRS-approved and QI-paid fiduciaries serving as auditors acting under U.S. laws.

Are foreign investments an important component of the U.S. economy?

In its latest report, the U.S. Federal Reserve Board stated total foreign-held U.S. financial assets to be $6.3 trillion. The Institute for International Economics puts the figure at $10 trillion. These investments have helped trigger America's unprecedented prosperity. Yet the QI regulations will encourage both "U.S. persons" and foreign investors to reduce or eliminate their investments from the U.S. market. It appears that the IRS, so far, has published no studies analyzing the risks associated with the QI regulations. More specifically, it appears that the cost/benefit analysis required by the Administrative Procedures Act has not been completed.

What is the supposed need for QI?

Unlike many other nations, the United States asserts the right to tax the world-wide income and assets of its citizens and businesses residing abroad. The IRS worries that some U.S. taxpayers may be "hiding" income by anonymously investing through foreign financial institutions. The QI regulation is designed to catch these taxpayers.

Why are the QI Regulations misguided?

In effect, the IRS seeks to swat a fly with a sledgehammer. To the extent that U.S. taxpayers are trying to evade taxes by investing in the U.S., through foreign institutions, they will simply shift their investments out of U.S. assets to avoid the QI regulations. These untested IRS regulations, however, will inevitably cause significant collateral damage. For instance, they will be:

Bad for investment. The QI regulations create a damned-if-you-do, damned-if-you- don't quandary for overseas institutions and investors. Failure to qualify means higher withholding taxes, yet the decision to qualify forces the institutions and investors to endure considerable red tape and a costly regulatory burden. The easy way to avoid this catch-22 is to invest someplace other than America. Indeed, professionals and banking executives have warned that the new regulations "could trigger an exodus from U.S. securities."

The regulations would hit all persons investing in the U.S., especially non-U.S. firms.

Bad for privacy. The QI regulations, stripped of fancy rhetoric, represent an attempt by the IRS to export nosy and intrusive know-your-customer rules that force financial institutions to spy on their customers, i.e., to act contrary to their legal duties and traditional fiduciary obligations. American consumers revolted against similar provisions that regulators attempted to impose in the U.S. Yet the IRS seeks to get these invasive rules overseas.

Foreign institutions would be forced to engage in a massive data-collection exercise to determine whether or not their clients are "U.S. persons." This is a costly, time-consuming task, particularly given the complex rules governing dual citizens, green card holders, varying tax rules for different types of investments, and the use of multi-tiered structures and multi-country entities.

Bad for sovereignty. Using the threat of higher withholding taxes, the IRS is trying to deputize foreign institutions to assist in the collection of U.S. taxes. This puts long-term U.S. interests at risk as foreign taxmen will likely insist on and receive reciprocal treatment. The specter of foreign tax authorities having power over U.S. citizens and companies may not be to the liking of many U.S. lawmakers either—particularly since it would mean a costly new regulatory burden for U.S. institutions and investors.

A managing partner at one overseas bank justifiably complained that "The U.S. is trying to impose its own rules on the rest of the world." Indeed, this effort to impose U.S. information-gathering requirements on an extraterritorial basis is not seen to be in the U.S. interests. For it could badly backfire. And it could violate and generally undermine the respect for existing tax and other treaties.

The QI regulations interfere with nations that genuinely respect financial privacy.

Bad for free trade. The QI regulations are going to create a discriminatory system that imposes different tax rates on global investment. This favoritism is a violation of open trade rules. Moreover, the costs of compliance may simply lead many institutions to avoid the U.S. market altogether.

In order to fully comply, foreign institutions would have to endure large information technology costs, huge legal fees, and ongoing auditing costs.

These regulations would create a non-tariff barrier to non-U.S. investment custodians.

A regulatory burden. U.S. international tax specialists have criticized these regulations for their extraordinarily bewildering complexity. Needless to say, it will be almost impossible for foreign institutions and investors—particularly those from the non-English speaking world—to decipher the intricacies of U.S. regulations that cross-reference numerous provisions of the Internal Revenue Code.

The burden is particularly harsh for small- and medium-sized companies that lack the in-house legal assistance and/or the resources to engage costly outside counsel.

MLATs Threaten Offshore Assets

By Mark Nestmann, *The Sovereign Individual,* June 2002

Think your assets are safe just because you've placed them offshore?

Think again.

The United States (and other governments) have negotiated dozens of treaties that permit them to seize assets in dozens of offshore centers without a court hearing and (in some cases) with no right of appeal to any court. Instead, the head of a prosecuting entity in one country sends the request directly to his or her counterpart in the foreign country for execution.

Since the first "mutual legal assistance treaty" (MLAT) was signed in 1973, billions of dollars have been seized using them. The US splits the booty with the jurisdiction seizing it, giving both countries an incentive to cooperate.

MLATs override all bank secrecy or confidentiality laws that might otherwise apply. For instance, the U.S.-Turks & Caicos Islands MLAT states: "A person who divulges any confidential information or gives any testimony in conformity with the [MLAT] request shall be deemed not to commit any offense under the Confidential Relationships Ordinance 1979 ... sub-section (6) of section 16 of the Banking Ordinance 1979 ... [or] section 202 of the Companies Ordinance 1981."

Early MLATs applied only to a short list of serious offenses that were crimes in both the US and Switzerland. However, most MLATs today cover "all crimes," whether or not the "crime" in question is an offense in both countries.

In some MLATs (e.g., the U.S.-Switzerland, U.S.-Austria and U.S.-Luxembourg agreements), tax evasion is an excluded offense, but not tax fraud. This was once the case in MLATs with many of United Kingdom's current and former Caribbean colonies (e.g., the Bahamas, Cayman Islands, British Virgin Islands, etc.) although these jurisdictions have now signed or promised to sign agreements that open the books of banks and trust companies to the IRS in both civil and criminal tax investigations.

The use by the United States of MLATs to fight tax evasion in countries where it is not a crime has led to serious disruptions in the fight against other, more serious, types of crime, and particularly, terrorism. This has been documented in a recent study by the Center for Freedom and Prosperity (www.freedomandprosperity.org/ltr/president1/president1.shtml).

MLATs also allow prosecutors to dodge constitutional protections otherwise due the target of an investigation. Most MLATs may be invoked on the grounds of "reasonable suspicion" that a crime has been committed, a far less demanding standard than the "probable cause" demanded by the Fourth Amendment.

Nor are the U.S. subjects of MLAT requests permitted to challenge disclosure in U.S. courts. Indeed, most MLATs explicitly deny this option to investigative targets, leaving them with no redress to contest disclosure in the courts of the requesting jurisdiction. There have even been cases where the interaction of U.S. and foreign law make it impossible for the subject of a MLAT request to make an effective challenge in either country.

Further, a U.S. defendant—or that defendant's property—cannot challenge the admission of evidence gathered in a MLAT inquiry even if prosecuted for a different crime not covered by the applicable MLAT. This has been the case even when evidence to support the inquiry may have been fabricated by prosecutors.

The only saving grace is that MLATs are evidently not used with great frequency. A report from the Senate Foreign Relations Committee published in November 2000 states that the U.S. Department of Justice makes only about 500 MLAT requests annually.

However, this does not mean that foreign jurisdictions release information to U.S. law enforcement authorities only 500 times annually. U.S. authorities continue to use covert means to retrieve financial records "informally" in offshore centers, including bribery, and extortion. The U.S. Supreme Court has upheld convictions obtained through the use of such illegal investigative techniques.

As of January 1, 2002, MLATs are in effect with Anguilla, Antigua & Barbuda, Argentina, Australia, Austria, the Bahamas, Barbados, Belgium, Brazil, British Virgin Islands, Canada, Cayman Islands, Czech Republic, Dominica, Egypt, Estonia, Greece, Grenada, Hong Kong, Hungary, Israel, Italy, Jamaica, Latvia, Lithuania, Luxembourg, Mexico, Montserrat, Morocco, the Netherlands, Panama, the Philippines, Poland, Romania, Spain, St. Vincent & the Grenadines, South Africa, South Korea, St. Kitts & Nevis, St. Lucia, Switzerland, Thailand, Trinidad & Tobago, Turkey, Turks & Caicos Islands, Ukraine, United Kingdom, Uruguay and Venezuela.

Because of their sweeping application, MLATs can represent a threat to legitimate investors and businesses that, for whatever reason, come under criminal investigation.

And don't be too certain that you're NOT a criminal. In the US, there are well over 3,000 federal crimes. Beyond that, 10,000-plus actions have been made into crimes by regulators. For instance, filling in a puddle on your own property that a bureaucrat later classifies as a "wetland" is a crime. Any assets you've conveyed offshore to protect yourself from whatever fines or forfeiture results from this or any other "crime" could conceivably be forfeited under all-crimes MLATs.

If you do business or invest in a jurisdiction with a MLAT that could apply to you, consider the following strategies to reduce your vulnerability. Review the relevant MLAT or MLATs to determine what "crimes" are covered, and whether the offenses covered must be an offense in both jurisdictions to apply ("dual criminality").

This determination should ideally be made in consultation with your attorney. Review with your attorney whether assets conveyed to a foreign trust or other structure may be frozen or forfeited in a MLAT proceeding. This must be a separate determination from the normal evaluation of potential vulnerability to civil judgments, fraudulent conveyance claims, etc.

Prepare "flight clauses" in trust documents and/or Articles of Incorporation that permit the domicile of the trust or corporation to be changed if the MLAT is amended or reinterpreted in any manner that would threaten the existence of the entity, or its assets.

Canada's Anti-Laundering Law Threatens Privacy and Property

By Douglas Hendler, *The Sovereign Individual*, July 2002

The original justification for money-laundering legislation in Canada, first enacted in 1991, was to repress the black markets and criminal industry created by the ban on recreational drugs. As with anti-laundering legislation in most other countries, this justification has now expanded to include many other crimes. Canadian solicitor Douglas Hendler discusses Canada's newest anti-laundering legislation, enacted in 2001.

Under Canada's Criminal Code, money laundering involves concealing or converting property or money, knowing or believing that they were derived from the commission of specified offenses such as drug trafficking, bribery, child pornography, prostitution, theft, extortion, fraud, illegal gambling, murder, robbery and counterfeiting. Violations can result in fines of up to $2,000,000 (US$1.3 million), five years in prison and forfeiture of all laundered property.

Recent amendments to this legislation, intended to combat terrorist financing, together with provisions that came into effect in 2001, establish record keeping and reporting requirements to facilitate detection and prosecution of money laundering offenses.

Three categories of transactions give rise to mandatory reporting to a new bureaucracy called FinTRAC, the Financial Transactions and Reports Analysis Center: (1) suspicious transactions; (2) prescribed transactions; and (3) certain cross border currency and monetary instrument transactions.

Being in a Hurry is Suspicious

Suspicious transactions are the most difficult to identify because the category is broad and the guidelines nebulous. Any transaction that creates reasonable grounds to suspect that it is related to money laundering must be identified on a "Suspicious Transaction Report" (STR), regardless of how little money is involved. It is an offense to disclose to the affected party that you have filed a STR or to disclose the contents of the report.

Suspicious transactions may involve several factors that individually seem insignificant but together create suspicion of money laundering, including:

"Client insists a transaction be done quickly."

"Client attempts to develop close rapport with staff."

"Client has unusual knowledge of the law in relation to suspicious-transaction reporting."

"Client makes cash transactions of consistently rounded-off large amounts."

"Client runs large credit-card balances."

"Client shows uncommon curiosity about internal systems, controls and policies."

"Transaction seems to be inconsistent with the client's apparent financial standing or usual pattern of activities."

"Client refuses to produce personal-identification documents."

The act requires detailed reports about suspicious transactions from lawyers; banks, credit unions or trust and loan companies; life insurance companies; insurance brokers and agents; securities dealers; portfolio managers; investment counselors; foreign exchange dealers; money services businesses including Canada Post; accountants; real estate brokers and sales representatives; and casinos, along with the employees of any of these businesses.

For lawyers, these provisions require the disclosure of information that would normally be confidential between a solicitor and client. Where a conflict exists between solicitor-client confidentiality and the obligation to report, the obligation to report takes precedence unless the communication is clearly protected by privilege. It is likely that all or most of the information required in a suspicious or prescribed transaction report will not be protected by solicitor-client privilege.

Several types of "prescribed transactions" must also be reported. These include cash transactions of C$10,000 (US$6,500) or more, or its equivalent in a foreign currency, including two or more transactions totaling C$10,000 or more conducted on behalf of the same individual within 24 hours. Reports are also required for movements of cash or monetary instruments across the Canadian border for amounts of C$10,000 or more, or its equivalent.

Property Seizures With No Criminal Conviction

FINTRAC has been given the authority to search mail and to enter premises (other than a dwelling) without a search warrant. Currency and monetary instruments that are not reported to

FINTRAC may be seized and forfeited, without a criminal conviction. However, the currency or monetary instrument must be returned if the fine for non-reporting is paid unless FINTRAC believes that the money is from proceeds of crime. While confiscation can be appealed to the courts, the ability to seize property without convicting the owner of a crime is a dangerous escalation of the government's civil forfeiture authority.

(**Ed. Note:** It seems likely that FINTRAC, like the U.S. Treasury's financial intelligence agency, FinCEN, will be overwhelmed by STRs. The lack of a minimum threshold, together with the vague and all-encompassing list of suspicious behaviors and the draconian penalties for violations, are likely to encourage persons affected by the legislation to report any activity that is even remotely suspicious. Thus, as in the United States, where more than 99% of reports identifying "suspicious activities" turn out to be groundless, the reporting mechanism could actually make it more difficult to identify the financial activities of money launderers and terrorists by diverting the attention of law enforcement away from more credible suspects.]

The best way to deal with these requirements is to avoid the prescribed and cross border currency and monetary instrument transactions identified in the law. If a party covered by these requirements indicates that a transaction must be reported, advise them that they are free to do so. This will virtually eliminate the possibility that they will report your transactions as suspicious as you have expressed a willingness to be cooperative.

Asset Protection in a Post 9/11 Environment: New Considerations and New Solutions

By Ron Holland, *The Sovereign Individual*, March 2004

What can we learn from legal and jurisdictional attacks on our wealth since the events of September 11, 2001?

What are the loopholes used to attack the wealth of productive, working Americans and how do we build maximum protected wealth in a world of transparency?

Think back to a decade ago when asset protection was all the rage.

Tens of thousands of Americans were fleeing the lawsuit mania of the abusive U.S. legal system and putting their wealth into asset protection trusts and other structures offshore. It became fashionable to have an offshore trust, and the mainstream media, if not exactly approving of the concept, didn't attack it virulently.

For many, this was a prudent move, since productive Americans who had spent their lives building, saving and accumulating wealth did not want to risk having it stolen in a frivolous lawsuit or trumped-up asset forfeiture.

However in today's post 9/11 environment, increased attacks by theU.S. government on offshore jurisdictions, combined with a dramatic reduction in privacy, make it important to review wealth preservation structures and asset protection strategies to insure that they stand up to today's new threats to wealth.

Today's most effective asset protection structures contain so-called "duress clauses" and limit your access to the protected funds. These features, along with the confidentiality and protection offered by attorney-client privilege, effectively close most of the avenues that litigants and the government use to gain unwarranted access to your wealth. If your existing program doesn't take advantage of these features, you should consider bringing it up to date.

First: A Warning

Investors have used many techniques in the past to protect and defend their wealth. Some have worked well, others have been successful in specific circumstances and some were unwise, questionable choices that in time became illegal. Just remember that illegal actions will eventually catch up with you. It is better to have the peace of mind of being legal with your offshore products and strategies.

If in the past you engaged in questionable offshore activities, such as not reporting the existence of, or income from, a foreign financial account, you need to retain a criminal tax attorney immediately to protect yourself from possible civil or even criminal liability. Like it or not, we live in a world that demands complete transparency with invasive "know-your-customer" rules forced on the entire world. Wealth preservation plans that involve non-reported or non-tax-compliant structures place you, your wealth and your property at greater risk than if you did nothing at all.

A consequence of the 9/11 attacks and the subsequent passage of the USA PATRIOT Act is that every bank teller, investment advisor, stockbroker or insurance agent in America is a de facto federal agent. They are required to report any "suspicious transactions" in which you engage to the federal government, and are prohibited from informing you of that fact. In addition, the feds now consider lawyers and accountants as "gatekeepers" to the national and international financial system. These professionals are also required to help detect and deter money laundering, although they are not yet required to report "suspicious transactions" to the government.

Prevent Forced Distributions from Your Offshore Nest-Egg

Let's take a look at several of the ways the legal predators after your wealth have pierced existing wealth preservation programsand how you might thwart these actions in the future.

Duress provisions are important in order to keep the courts and others from forcing you to do what you would not have done on your own free will. Your asset protection strategy should not depend on permanent personal, business or family relationships because these often change, especially when large sums of money are involved. Remember, your best friend—and even your spouse—can quickly become your worst enemy.

For maximum asset protection, no one should have the right to receive distributions from the product or structure, except at pre-established intervals. Structures that can be terminated or that permit assets to be loaned back permit others to coerce, threaten or use contempt-of-court charges to steal the assets in your wealth preservation structure.

To prevent such coercion, many asset protection structures now include a duress clause. Such a clause allows a financial service provider, trustee and attorney to require a visit from the individual beneficial owner if there is any question whether a withdrawal or liquidation is voluntary—or is being made under coercion or duress from outside parties. The duress clause should still allow for investment strategies and portfolios to be changed anytime.

Everyone needs liquid funds, but you should never invest funds you might need to tap to meet immediate living expenses in an asset protection or wealth preservation structure. That's because if the program can meet short-term liquidity needs, this opens up your structure to outside attack. If you can easily obtain access to your funds in an asset protection structure through cancellation, a debit card, loans or early withdrawal, then so can a court.

Case Study: Contempt of Court. Learn about what can happen even with offshore protected wealth when a judge can prove you have access to the money in your offshore asset protection structure. Link: www.swissgnomes.com/book/casestudy/cs-5.htm.

Use Attorney-Client Privilege for Increased Confidentiality

For hundreds of years, the attorney-client privilege has helped to preserve the confidentiality of communications between lawyers and their clients. It exists because: 1) Clients need to be completely truthful with their legal counsel, so their advice is based on all the facts of a case; and 2) it helps to assure those needing legal counsel that their private affairs will not be disclosed.

Until 9/11, the privacy and confidentiality of what was said between a client and his lawyer was almost completely protected. But recent U.S. court rulings indicate that attorney-client privilege is being weakened, along with most other protections of confidentiality, liberty and wealth. In the United Kingdom attorney-client privilege has declined even further, as attorneys are now required to inform the government if they believe their client is engaged in illegal activity.

However, attorney-client privilege can still help to keep your communications and structures confidential. You just need to hire an attorney in a jurisdiction where attorney-client communications remain untouchable. The essential strategy is to consult with your local attorney on general matters, but when dealing offshore, consider using an offshore attorney to further enhance attorney-client privilege. Using this strategy, all communications, both written and oral, and subsequent attorney work-product, enjoy enhanced protection from any future disclosure orders of a U.S. court.

Note that attorney-client privilege does not extend to accountants, business associates, financial experts, consultants or anyone else either in the United States or offshore. For maximum privacy and confidentiality, all discussions regarding your specific objectives and asset protection goals, including investment decisions and structure questions, should be handled directly between you and your retained legal counsel. This provides a high level of confidentiality not available in many other structures where a promoter, salesperson or marketing group is positioned between you and the product or strategy.

With the exception of your retained attorney, all conversations, written or e-mail communications and records with any other individual or professional could be subject to subpoena in a lawsuit. Plus, the promoter or salesperson could even be forced into courts to testify against you and your wealth preservation program.

For Maximum Privacy, Hold All Documentation Offshore

Attorney-client confidentiality can be further enhanced through products and strategies requiring the minimal amount of legal reporting and by maintaining all documentation outside your own country.

Most asset protection and wealth preservation strategies allow contracts, trust documents, and certificates or indicia of ownership to be freely retained by the client and held in the client's home country. The problem with this arrangement is that during the discovery phase of litigation, armed with only a subpoena, a lawyer can obtain the documentation and learn how your offshore asset protection program is structured. This leaves your wealth defenses wide open for review and attack.

A better method is to maintain all documentation and account information securely offshore. You should of course retain the right to review this data in a personal visit, but you should not keep copies of it in the United States. Nor should you have online access to this information, since a court may compel such access, thereby fully disclosing your structure to your legal opponents.

When an attorney and/or trustee holds all account information offshore, a U.S. plaintiff must generally bring a lawsuit in that foreign jurisdiction to retrieve it. This will be an uphill battle, because in most offshore jurisdictions, attorney-client privilege is taken much more seriously than in the United States. In addition, offshore jurisdictions often require a plaintiff to pay a large deposit for the privilege of bringing a lawsuit and require a higher burden of proof to prevail than in the United States. In addition, the concept of "punitive damages" awarded by a jury is almost unknown outside the United States.

All of these factors tend to prevent lawsuits from even getting started. Your attackers will always be in the dark regarding your structure defense and legal protections, as this adds to their costs and uncertainty. Remember: there are plenty of "easy pickings" for individuals and their lawyers out to legally steal the wealth and property of others. They usually will not waste their time on a difficult case when an easier target is available.

"No Loans" Enhance Asset Protection

Many offshore structures and investments permit you to "borrow" some of the funds you have invested to meet immediate liquidity needs. However, such provisions can fatally weaken the structure. The solution is simple: when establishing your wealth preservation program, make sure that your trust, insurance contract or other structure does not allow for a loan provision.

Case Study: Variable Annuity Loans. Offshore fixed and variable annuity products can provide a high level of asset protection. However, if your foreign insurance contact has a loan provision, this can open up your protected wealth to creditors and place you in a dilemma of choosing between your money or jail time for contempt of court. Learn how this can occur. Link: www.swiss-gnomes.com/book/casestudy/cs-6.htm.

The offshore world has changed profoundly since the events of 9/11. You must either update your wealth preservation strategies or risk the loss of your protection and maybe your wealth!

(Ron Holland is a member of The Sovereign Society's Council of Experts and an internationally known financial consultant, author and public speaker. He is the editor of the SwissGnomes website which provides offshore alternative financial news and comment. Originally from North Carolina, Ron now lives and works in Geneva, Switzerland. Tel.: (800) 891-8332. E-mail: Ron@swissgnomes.com. Link: www.swissgnomes.com.

Part Three—Places
The Top Four Banking Havens of the World, 2001

These are the four safest money havens in the world, used by the super-rich for decades. Your cash will be protected by some of the strictest secrecy laws in existence. Interest rates are high, and tough banking laws keep bankers honest.

To help you decide about where best to locate your offshore bank account, we investigated and visited many of the world's banking havens, and narrowed the choices down to the four safest and most stable havens on the planet. We also include specific bank recommendations from each haven with their contact numbers and addresses. The banks selected are well known, established banks and are highly recommended for service and confidentiality.

Haven 4: Switzerland

Although Switzerland has succumbed to U.S. pressure to loosen its strict secrecy laws, for safe banking it still rates as one of the top havens.

Technically, any depositor will still be protected by Switzerland's secrecy laws. These laws were first enacted in 1934 and call for the punishment of anyone who releases information on any Swiss bank account holder without authorization. Offenders can receive a fine of more than Sfr50,000 and a six-month prison sentence.

However, Switzerland has entered into a number of treaties with other countries that allow for information to be released in cases involving a crime committed in another country that is also a crime under Swiss law. Tax evasion is not a crime under Swiss law, so foreign tax evaders are technically protected, but tax fraud is a crime.

At the very least, if any creditor or government wanted to come after your money they would have to go through a complicated and expensive process to get at it. But if you want strict banking privacy, you are probably better off to go to a haven that does not have any information-sharing treaties with your country.

Having said that, Switzerland is still the yardstick by which all other financial centers are measured. Swiss bankers enjoy an international reputation that is second to none. The country has been economically and politically stable for centuries. It enjoys a low rate of inflation, and the Swiss franc is one of the strongest currencies in the world.

Swiss banks are undoubtedly among the strongest and most stable financial institutions in the world. They offer a full range of services to investors, as well as a wide variety of investment opportunities in stocks, bonds, precious metals, insurance and most other financial services.

Switzerland does impose a 35 percent withholding tax on all interest and dividends earned within its borders, but this can be easily avoided by investing money through a fiduciary account. Also double-taxation treaties may cancel out the tax.

Switzerland has more than 500 banks from which to choose. The best banks, however, require very large deposits (up to and over US$500,000) and also require personal recommendations.

Anyone wishing to bank in Switzerland may do best to first go through a local advisor. We can recommend one company that can help you: Office Services, Jupiterstrasse 56, CH-8032 Zurich, Switzerland, telephone + 41 1 382 0356, fax 41 1 382 0153. They will let you do everything by mail. They will also send you their literature and information free.

Three banks we can recommend: Banque Union de Credit if you have US$50,000, Banque SCS Alliance if you have US$100,000, and Banque Julius Baer if you US$500,000. Each of these banks offers the full range of financial services.

Contacts

For a complete, up-to-date list of Swiss banks and other financial institutions, see Chapter 5.

Haven 3: Luxembourg

Luxembourg is one of the fastest-growing financial centers in the world and our third choice for international banking. It has seen a massive influx of capital in the last decade due to its new liberal banking and tax laws.

Located in central Europe bordering France, Germany and Belgium, it covers only about 1,000 square miles. Both a city and a country, it has one of the highest per capita incomes in Europe and enjoys an almost 100 percent employment rate.

Although its secrecy laws only date back to the early '80s, it has maintained a long tradition of banking confidentiality. Information will only be released to foreign governments if the depositor has been charged with a crime that is related to the account and is also a crime in Luxembourg. Tax evasion is not a crime in Luxembourg.

Luxembourg, however, does maintain international tax treaties with a slew of countries including the U.S., the UK, Germany and France.

Interest, dividends and capital gains earned in the country are totally free of tax. Accounts are insured by the government for amounts up to Luxembourg francs 500,000 (approximately US$15,000).

Luxembourg is also home to over 1,000 investment funds. Many of them are sponsored by major banks. Some are no-load, others charge as much as 7 percent commission.

More than 187 international banks have set up shop in Luxembourg. And nearly all bank employees are fluent in English and German. In fact, this is one of their prerequisites for employment.

Banque International à Luxembourg is our number one choice, for deposits of more than US$50,000. It is one of the largest banks in Luxembourg and is locally owned and operated.

Haven 2: Liechtenstein

Tucked in a beautiful mountain valley along the border between Austria and Switzerland, Liechtenstein is one of the smallest countries in the world. But its importance as a banking haven is almost unparalleled.

Liechtenstein has some of the strongest bank secrecy laws in existence. There is no withholding tax on interest. And all deposits, no matter what amount, are guaranteed by the state.

Considering Liechtenstein is one of the five richest countries in the world in per capita income and personal wealth, you can rest assured that the country will be able to stand by their promise.

Although Liechtenstein only has a few banks, each has a phenomenal growth rate and caters to the needs of foreign investors. Each bank offers their private investors an account called a Therma-Konto. The advantage of this account is that your funds are always immediately available, and you can use the account to buy shares, make payments, write Euro checks and pay credit card bills. Your funds are also held in one of the world's strongest currencies—the Swiss franc. Numbered accounts are also available to large depositors.

The Verwaltungs-und-Privatbank (VP-bank) is our bank of choice in Liechtenstein. This bank is accustomed to dealing with foreign investors. It even sends its customers a regular newsletter containing the latest investment news, recommended investments, securities and stocks, as well as information on Liechtenstein and the bank itself.

Contacts

- *Bank en Liechtenstein*, Herrenstrasse 12, P.O. Box 85, 9490, Vaduz. **Tel.:** +41 75 235 1122. **Fax:** +41 75 235 1522.

- *Liechtensteinische Landebank*, Städtle 44, Postfach 384, 9490, Vaduz. **Tel.:** +423 236 8811. **Fax:** +423 236 8822.

- *Verwaltungs-und-Privatbank*, Postfach 885, FL-9490, Vaduz. **Tel.:** +41 (75) 235 6655. **Fax:** +41 (75) 235 6500. **E-mail:** info@vpbank.li.

Haven 1: Austria

We have traveled to many of the world's banking havens and reviewed numerous offshore banks, but Austria in our opinion is one of the finest long-standing banking havens. Not only does it offer services and products comparable to Switzerland, but it has done well to preserve its long tradition of banking confidentiality.

Austria has strict bank secrecy laws, calling for the prosecution of any bank employee who divulges any information on a client's account. Information can only be released with a court order in connection with criminal proceedings. And that only includes activities that are considered crimes under Austrian law. It does not include tax evasion.

Austria ranks among the 10 richest countries in the world on a per capita basis. Its capital gold reserves rank third in the western world. Its political and economic stability is reflected in its currency. The Austrian schilling is a hard currency closely linked to the deutschemark. It has appreciated against the U.S. dollar by 150 percent in the last 20 years.

Austria's banking tradition is more than 200 hundred years old and is based on a universal banking system. Investments are available in all major currencies at competitive Euro-market interest rates. Currency conversions are a routine practice allowing investors to benefit from currency appreciations. The minimum requirement for operating an account is extremely modest by international standards. And Austrian banks are well known for their flexible and courteous service.

The banks are low-key operations that stay out of the banking limelight, and because of this they are able to offer their customers unique opportunities to invest secretly and anonymously. In fact, Austrian monetary authorities are reluctant to promote their investment opportunities to non-residents as they realize the European Union will put an end to them. This means that Austria can offer you a financial edge that you cannot get anywhere else on the planet.

Austrian banks are required by law to guarantee deposits up to 200,000 schillings. But several, such as the Raiffeisenbank, will insure the entire amount of your deposit.

At the Anglo Irish Bank (Austria), you can open an account for as little as US$5,000. You can bank in most major currencies, and they can buy securities for you from all over the world. They can also buy and hold gold, silver and other precious metals for you.

The bank also offers a unique "pooled account," which is like a mutual fund. This account may be able to offer you asset protection and tax deferral benefits. Be sure to inquire when you approach this bank.

Contacts: For complete, up-to-date information on Austrian banks, see Chapter 9.

———◆◆———

Asset Protection: A Canadian View
by David Melnik QC, & David Potts

The Canadian legal system is undergoing a quiet yet revolutionary transformation that dramatically increases the odds of being successfully sued.

This is particularly true in Ontario, which has shifted the balance to the plaintiff and made it easier for people to bring lawsuits and to move lawsuits through the courts more quickly. These changes, while well meaning in theory, are based on the assumption that most actions are legitimate and that justice delayed is justice denied.

In fact, sometimes there is a salutary value in delay, as it forces people to reassess their actions and determine whether they were really worth pursuing. Delay allows tempers to cool and compels people to seek more business-like methods in resolving disputes. Finally, the specter of delay can deter people from launching frivolous lawsuits.

Here are some of the changes that have occurred recently:

Class action lawsuits authorized. This is an action that can be brought on behalf of many individuals who claim to have suffered a particular wrong at the hands of a company. These actions are often used in product liability cases. In the United States, class-action lawsuits have been used against a wide variety of corporate defendants and are cited as a primary reason for the increased cost of—or in cases the cancellation of—business liability insurance.

Funding for lawsuits established. In an extraordinary development, an insurance company has announced that it will fund litigation for plaintiffs. An article in the January 2000 issue of *Canadian Lawyer* entitled "Insurance Makes Lawsuits a Sure Thing" discusses several new types of insurance policies for potential plaintiffs—contingent asset indemnity and insurance for plaintiffs' costs.

According to the brochure prepared by the underwriter, the contingent asset indemnity policy would be available to "plaintiffs who have an excellent chance of success in lawsuits instituted in Canada." The action must have a value greater than C$500,000.00. It is "an insurance vehicle which guarantees to a plaintiff a sum up to 75 percent of the likely award arising out of a lawsuit."

There is also a plaintiff costs indemnity policy that "reimburses the legal costs of a plaintiff in the event that the case is lost or that legal costs exceed the award or settlement."

Small claims procedures streamlined. Another development is that simplified rules have been enacted allowing claims for under C$25,000 to be brought to trial more quickly and less expensively. Examinations for discovery and pretrial court motions are not allowed. Actions can be placed on the trial list much more quickly than originally. (Rule 76 of the Rules of Civil Procedure for Ontario.)

Case management introduced. This is a fundamental change to the legal system. It shifts control of the pace of the litigation from the litigants to either court officers or judges. Again, this is done in the ostensible interest of streamlining and simplifying the legal system. In the fast track, an action can come to trial within 90 days from the date of the defense being filed. (Rule 77, Rules of Civil Procedure)

Contingency fees permitted. In a contingency fee arrangement, the plaintiff doesn't pay his lawyer unless the lawyer wins the lawsuit and collects a judgment. In theory, contingency fees are not allowed in Ontario. But contingency fee arrangements are used quite regularly, particularly in personal injury cases. (In other provinces, such as British Columbia, contingency fees are explicitly permitted.)

Mandatory mediation. This is being introduced under the belief that most actions can be settled. The problem is that it imposes another layer of costs on the parties whether they want it or not. It is another example where litigation is taken out of the hands of the parties and put in the hands of the courts. A party is obliged to attend a mandatory mediation session and pay a mediator for at least three hours. (Rule 77, Rules of Civil Procedure.)

From our experience, this again favors the plaintiffs. Since both sides hire the mediators, they don't want to send one side away empty-handed. It is easier to extract some money from the defendant and say, "you are lucky you weren't required to pay more" than to dismiss the claim. Mediators have many complicated and high-sounding theories, which ultimately boil down to one thing: compromise. In most cases, "compromise" means that someone with a deep pocket—the defendant or the defendant's insurance company—has to pay the claimant.

While some of these changes were intended to streamline and lower the cost of litigation, as a whole, they dramatically shift the balance in favor of a plaintiff bringing a lawsuit.

Canadians who have watched with horror the lawsuit epidemic in the United States and said, "It can't happen here" need to wake up. If you haven't done so already, you need to begin taking steps to protect your wealth from lawsuits.

The techniques and structures used are in many cases similar to the U.S. practice, albeit with some important differences. Corporations, limited liability companies and similar liability-isolating structures may be appropriate for some clients. Offshore structures are used as well, although as in most other high-tax countries, there are no longer significant tax advantages.

Is Swiss Bank Secrecy Still Alive?

by Robert E. Bauman JD, *The Sovereign Individual*, October 2001

A global survey of private bankers published a few years ago by Price Waterhouse Coopers found that the major attraction for any new customer is a bank's good reputation. In the past it also could be said that Switzerland's solid financial reputation was central to that nation's claim that it serves as "banker to the world."

For 250 years, as European empires and nations rose and fell, Swiss topography and determination combined to defend this Alpine redoubt, even as its citizens maintained political neutrality towards other nations. The result has been a haven trusted by the rich and powerful from around the world: King Louis XVI of France was reputed to have maintained Swiss accounts in the eighteenth century, as do many political leaders today.

In 1945, after World War II, the Swiss people overwhelmingly rejected membership in the United Nations. In national polls in 1992 and again in 2001, Swiss voters rejected membership in the European Union, fearing EU bureaucratic interference with their privacy and banking laws. The Swiss again said "no" to opening negotiations to join the EU by 77 percent to 23 percent on March 4, 2001, largely because they wanted to preserve bank secrecy.

A few years ago a national ballot soundly rejected a specific proposal to ease Swiss bank secrecy laws. More recently, in a June 2001 national opinion poll by the Swiss Bankers Association, over 80 percent of the Swiss continued to support the country's bank secrecy laws, but many (66 percent) also believed more can be done to combat money laundering.

After each of the earlier national plebiscites, even greater amounts of foreign cash flowed into Swiss banks, re-confirming the widespread belief that Switzerland is the place to safeguard your money. It's estimated that currently Swiss banks manage at least one-third of all assets held offshore by the world's wealthy. In books, movies and popular culture, Switzerland and its much-vaunted bank secrecy have become a modern cliché.

But in spite of Swiss popular support, just how safe is true financial privacy in Switzerland today?

The 1934 Bank Secrecy Law

The rise of Hitler's Germany in the early 1930s prompted the famous 1934 Swiss bank secrecy law that remains in force today. That law was a good faith effort to stop Nazi agents who were bribing bank employees for information about the accounts of German citizens and expatriates. The law protects foreign depositors from unwarranted intrusions into their bank privacy, although now it has been tempered in important ways by newer anti-money laundering statutes and tax information exchange treaties, noted below. But most foreigners don't understand the current nature and extent of Swiss financial and banking privacy.

A Swiss bank is prohibited by law from responding to inquiries about an individual account—whether from attorneys, credit rating services or foreign governments. The law punishes violations of bank secrecy with fines up to Sfr50,000 (US$30,000) and six months in prison. In most cases the Swiss government cannot obtain information about an account without a court order. To obtain an order it must be proven that Swiss law has been violated and that there is reason to believe the particular account at issue is involved in that law violation.

The Anti–Money Laundering Crusade

In spite of its reputation for bank secrecy, self-regulation began as far back as 1977 when Swiss bankers themselves adopted voluntary restrictions. They preferred to clean house rather than have government force them to act. This came after US$500 million in Italian investments mysteriously disappeared from the Chiasso branch of the Credit Suisse bank.

In 1990 Switzerland was one of the first European countries to make money laundering a criminal offense. The law forced the demise of the famous Swiss *compte anonyme*, as the French-speaking Swiss termed it. Previously, it was possible for an attorney or other nominee to open an account in which the identity of the beneficial owner need not be revealed to the bank. Instead, the nominee submitted a form to the bank attesting that the nominee knew the identity of the underlying client.

Since 1994 there has been a central office in Bern devoted exclusively to fighting organized crime. The Swiss Bankers Association has issued specific "know your customer" guidelines to be used by Swiss banks to investigate potential clients and decide their acceptability. The regulations call for banks to pay particular attention if a prospective client tries to open an account of more than Sfr25,000 (US$15,000) in cash, or if anyone tries to convert large amounts of cash into foreign currencies.

Court orders to obtain account information are issued only if evidence suggests that a criminal offense has occurred under Swiss law, without regard to whether the alleged offense is a crime in the home country of a foreign national. Non-payment of taxes is not a crime in Switzerland, but "tax fraud" is—and as you'll learn momentarily, that can be a rather elastic phrase.

On April 1, 1998, a new, stricter money laundering law took effect. This law transformed the face of Swiss banking in a fundamental way. Previously, bankers had the option of reporting suspicious transactions to police authorities. Now, under pressure from world governments pursuing corruption, drug cartels and organized crime, Switzerland has made bank non-reporting of suspicious activities a crime. Bankers now can go to jail for keeping secret the names and records of suspect clients. Before, they faced jail if they did reveal such information. The result has been a revolution in the previously top-secret world of Swiss banking.

Official figures show that in 2000 about 270 "money laundering" cases were reported to authorities, of which 70 percent led to investigations and 50 percent convictions or asset freezes.

Using these newer statutes, in some few cases Switzerland has released information that does not involve a crime under Swiss law. The government has shown its willingness to do this before an individual is convicted if the foreign government can demonstrate "reasonable suspicion" that the accused engaged in criminal conduct.

The list of offenses for which the Swiss government is willing to step in and order account freezes seems to grow longer. This has been particularly true in high-profile drug or corruption cases.

Ferdinand Marcos, the late Philippines dictator, was said to have stashed away up to US$20 billion in Swiss accounts. The Swiss government has cooperated for more than a decade in efforts by the present Filipino government to recover the assets. When the Haitian government asked that all private accounts held by Baby-Doc Duvalier be identified and frozen, it had no problems. Similarly, at the request of the American government, Switzerland froze all of the accounts owned by Panama's Manuel Noriega. And in one recent and infamous case, the U.S. split several hundred million dollars with the Swiss government for its assistance in freezing and confiscating that cash.

Despite these headline-grabbing asset freezes, several officials of the Swiss money laundering office resigned earlier this year to protest what they charge is lax enforcement of these laws. Add to this, pressure from the European Union to modify bank secrecy, plus repeated attacks by Socialist members of the French parliament who charge Switzerland harbors French tax cheats.

And outside pressure continues. In an effort to reach a tentative agreement on tax evasion policy with the European Union, Swiss finance minister Kaspar Villiger has suggested extending the 35 percent withholding tax on accounts belonging to EU citizens in Switzerland's banks until the year 2010, but the issue remains highly contentious.

But there are limits to how far the Swiss will go. In March 2001 a new, even stricter laundering bill was rejected by the Swiss parliament after the government announced that it considered the existing defenses against money laundering to be adequate.

Treaties Prevent Double Taxation, Sacrifice Secrecy

Treaties have also eroded Swiss secrecy. Switzerland has entered into many treaties with other countries allowing for information release where a crime committed in the other country is also a crime under Swiss law, the "dual criminality" principle. The most famous such treaty is the U.S.-Switzerland Mutual Legal Assistance Treaty, which came into effect in 1977. Since that time, it has been used on thousands of occasions to investigate alleged criminal activity, and in many cases, to confiscate assets allegedly derived from crime.

Switzerland has also signed many tax treaties, including a revised treaty with the United States in 1997. While this treaty has significant benefits—e.g., permitting U.S. persons purchasing Swiss insurance policies to forego paying a 1 percent U.S. excise tax that would otherwise apply—Article 26 of the treaty poses a significant threat to tax privacy. While nonpayment of taxes is not a crime in Switzerland, Article 26 permits the two governments to exchange information about alleged tax fraud. It also allows authorities to transfer information that may help in the "prevention of tax fraud and the like in relation to taxes."

Historically, the Swiss position was that tax evasion involved merely not listing all of one's income on a tax return. Tax fraud, on the other hand, involved the preparation or submission of false tax documents. However, the United States has consistently taken the position that signing a false tax return under penalty of perjury is, in fact, tax fraud. While the Swiss have not yet come around to this position, the new treaty makes the distinction very narrow.

Swiss Bankers Defend Secrecy

Swiss banking industry officials proclaim they will never abandon the country's bank secrecy, vowing to resist any pressure to weaken it. However, this statement must be taken in the context of market reality.

For instance, the 1998 merger of Swiss Bank Corp. and Union Bank of Switzerland, creating

UBS AG, involved the U.S. subsidiaries of both organizations, and was therefore subject to U.S. regulatory scrutiny. The merger was approved by the U.S. Federal Reserve only after the banking giant agreed to provide U.S. regulators with all information "necessary to determine and enforce compliance with …[U.S.] federal law." No exception was granted for U.S. tax laws. Rather than defend their clients' privacy rights, the bank compromised.

UBS compliance with this deal was bad news for financial privacy seekers. Obviously U.S. depositors considering Swiss banks should avoid UBS AG and any Swiss bank with U.S.-based branches, affiliates or actual banking operations, other than a mere "representative office."

But some doubt these claims. They say that Swiss bankers realize that secrecy has lost its positive image and that the bank secrecy law undercuts Switzerland's image of financial probity. "The secrecy concept is completely disappearing and can no longer be used to promote Switzerland as a private banking center," Carlo Lombardini, a Geneva lawyer specializing in banking, told the *International Herald Tribune* last year.

For finance minister Villiger, however, the crux of the matter is that the Swiss people simply do not want to give up their cherished banking secrecy. Says he: "A person's confidentiality is a very important principle, especially when new technology allows detailed profiles of everyone. Every person has a right to be protected. We Swiss have all the tools necessary to avoid abuses, and that is why it is legitimate to maintain this special professional secrecy. I'm convinced that even if the government proposed moving away from this system, the people would never say yes."

And so long as secrecy keeps the billions rolling in, neither will the Swiss government.

The Swiss Franc: End of an Era?

by Mark Nestmann, *The Sovereign Individual*, July 1999

In April 1999, voters in Switzerland approved a new constitution that ends the requirement that the Swiss franc be backed by gold. This is the end of an era. A world without a gold-backed franc is a world that seems without one of its fundamental economic pillars.

For decades, investors have sought financial refuge in the Swiss franc. And they have been rewarded by stellar performance verses other currencies. Even the mighty U.S. dollar—currently the world's strongest currency—is only worth about one-third as much in Swiss franc terms as it was in 1970.

Swiss voters are selfish. They're no different from voters anywhere else. And by reneging on gold backing for the franc, they sent a strong message to the politicians representing them.

Anyone who's ever visited Switzerland knows it's expensive to live, work or do business there. The main benefit that ordinary Swiss citizens obtain by having the world's strongest currency is that imports to Switzerland are relatively inexpensive.

Everything else in Switzerland costs more when the franc rises. Swiss businesses look abroad for investment and expansion opportunities—not in Switzerland. Swiss workers—at least those outside the financial sector—lose their jobs and see their income stagnate.

Swiss voters wouldn't mind seeing a weaker Swiss franc. However, despite their intentions, it's unlikely they'll get it.

Under the old constitution, every Swiss franc in circulation had to be backed by a minimum of 40 percent in gold reserves. But the government defined the "official" price of gold at Sfr142.90 (US$93.90) per ounce. Taking into account that gold trades at approximately US$268 per ounce, that meant the franc was effectively 100 percent backed by gold.

The new constitution stipulates that the Swiss National Bank, the nation's central bank, shall accumulate sufficient reserves to back the franc, a portion of which shall be in gold. It is left up to the SNB to determine how much of its reserves will be maintained in gold. It also for the first time mandates that the SNB shall operate free of political control.

No Mandate to Sell Gold

But the new constitution does not require that the SNB sell any gold, although the SNB has announced its intention to sell approximately 50 percent of Swiss gold reserves over the next decade.

This announcement was met with consternation by investors worldwide who assume that any reduction in Swiss gold holdings will adversely affect the value of the franc. Many of these investors had anticipated that the long-term rise in the value of the Swiss franc in relation to the U.S. dollar and other fiat (backed by nothing but paper) currencies would continue indefinitely.

For reasons I'll discuss momentarily, the Swiss franc is unlikely to decline significantly in value, despite the prospect of gold sales. But neither is it likely to rise appreciably—here's why:

Almost all the increase of the value of the franc versus the U.S. dollar occurred from 1970 to 1986, a highly inflationary period. Since 1986, the franc has fluctuated in a trading range between US$0.60 and US$0.87. It is currently trading at the lower end of this range. In a world gripped by deflation, not inflation, I don't expect massive increases in value in the franc, at least in U.S. dollar terms. On the other hand, modest gains are possible if the franc moves back to the higher end of its trading range.

Nor do I anticipate that the value of the franc will collapse, or that the SNB will permit Switzerland to debase its currency to the extent, for instance, that the U.S. Federal Reserve has with reference to the U.S. dollar. Quite the contrary.

Even if the Swiss "man in the street" is not particularly supportive of a strong franc, the financial engineers at the SNB are acutely aware of the need to maintain confidence in the Swiss franc. This allows Switzerland to purchase essential imported goods (e.g., food and fuel, neither of which the country produces enough to be self-sufficient). Not to mention the foreign exchange benefits that a strong franc provide and the continuing flow of capital to Swiss financial institutions. In short, the SNB is unlikely to do anything that would lead to a decline—and surely not a collapse—in the value of the franc.

The same holds true in relation to the amount of gold the SNB will retain. It has been acknowledged in Swiss academic circles that as gold is the only government-independent medium of payment, maintaining a substantial reserve of the metal is essential in preserving Swiss neutrality. It is unquestionable that gold will continue to play a crucial role in the SNB's portfolio.

Swiss Reserves World's Highest

According to the SNB, Switzerland currently owns 2,590 tons of gold—the fourth largest holding in the world (after the United States, France and Germany) and by far the highest reserves per capita. In addition, Switzerland holds Sfr53.2/US$34.5 billion in foreign currencies and Sfr3.3/US$2.15 billion in other reserves.

Every Swiss franc in circulation is backed by much more than gold. Indeed, the existence of non-gold reserves insures that holders of franc-denominated assets can easily exchange these holdings for yen, euros, dollars or any other freely traded currency. This shows the importance of foreign currency reserves in today's world where transactions rarely involve gold.

Again, these holdings are the world's largest relative to GDP. Relative to GDP, Swiss international reserves with gold valued at market prices amounted to 23 percent in 1997. Relative to yearly imports, Swiss international reserves amounts to 90 percent. Only Japan among the industrial countries is in the same league.

Viewed in this context, the SNB's plan to sell half of its gold reserves over the next 10 years—assuming the requisite laws to approve the sales are even passed—is not a particularly threatening development. Nor is it certain that gold will be sold outright. The SNB could conceivably issue gold-backed bonds or lend gold for revenue purposes. And so long as Switzerland keeps running surpluses in trade and other foreign transactions, it will have the ability to add to its total reserves.

Further, the size of a nation's reserves—gold or otherwise—is just one factor impacting the value of its currency. Its balance of payments, economic strength, market psychology and the openness of its markets each have an impact that is at least as important. In all of these factors, Switzerland passes with flying colors. And based on these parameters, I expect its currency will remain one of the strongest, if not the strongest, in the world.

A Candid American View of Civil Forfeiture
by Robert E. Bauman, JD, December 1998

During the last 15 years, police confiscation of private property has grown into a multi-billion dollar American scandal. Since the early 1980s, using the excuse of the failed "war against drugs," federal, state and local police have confiscated cash and property of every sort valued at over US$7 billion.

This blatant police grab occurs because of extraordinary powers granted by a U.S. legal doctrine that grew out of ancient English common law. That legal theory has been codified into statutory law by U.S. politicians eager to appear "tough on crime."

It's called "civil asset forfeiture" and property owners beware! Brenda Grantland, a prominent criminal defense attorney from California specializing in anti-forfeiture law, heads a national U.S. group, Forfeiture Endangers American Rights (FEAR). (Check the excellent FEAR Internet web site at www.fear.org).

Ms. Grantland says, "In America asset forfeiture has become a polite euphemism for government confiscation of private property. It allows government to seize property without paying for it, based solely on police accusation the property was or is somehow connected to criminal conduct."

Under U.S. forfeiture laws, a home or office building in which a crime allegedly occurs can be confiscated because use of that place is said to "facilitate" the crime. Motor vehicles driven to the place a transaction occurs also are said to "facilitate" crime, so they can be taken too. The government claims depositing $1.00 in criminally tainted money in a bank account allows them to forfeit (confiscate) all the cash in the account!

Property can be confiscated from innocent owners even for alleged crimes by other people. Even a totally innocent accused property owner must go through a lengthy court process and prove at trial they neither knew of, or consented to, illegal use of their property.

Constitutional "due process" guaranteed in other areas of U.S. criminal law is virtually unknown in asset forfeiture cases. Procedure is stacked against an innocent owner and in favor of government. The basic presumption of "innocent until proven guilty" is turned on its head; the burden is on the owner who, in order to reclaim the property must prove a negative, showing it was not used in a criminal act.

The government seizes property without a hearing and holds it until the case is finally decided in the courts, months or years later. Police often seize everything of value a person owns, so the accused has no money to hire a lawyer to fight the seizure. There is no right to court appointed counsel in forfeiture cases and typically the cost is a minimum of US$10,000 to US$15,000 in legal fees.

The record shows that in the U.S. forfeiture is aimed not so much at wealthy suspected drug traffickers, but in the great majority of cases, at more convenient targets—average people, many of them minorities, whose only "crime" is ownership of real and personal property (or cash) ripe for police taking. Today on-the-spot police confiscation of cash and assets is common. Mere suspicion has become a police license to steal.

In more than 80 percent of U.S. forfeiture cases the property owner is never charged with a crime, yet the police can and do keep the seized property.

In most cases there has been little or no proportionality between the crime alleged to justify forfeiture, and the punishment imposed. Under asset forfeiture, hotels are seized because one room was said to be used for a drug transaction, and landlords lose apartment houses because tenant drug deals allegedly occurred in some unspecified apartments.

The forfeiture of real estate is so attractive, routine police policy arranges "structured arrests." Whenever a drug deal is set to "go down," undercover agents make sure the transaction occurs inside a valuable building or on a high-priced tract of land—which then or later is confiscated by police. When even a small part of a larger parcel of land is the locus of an alleged drug crime, the entire tract is subject to forfeiture under the legal theory that the land's use "facilitates" the commission of the crime. When a drug deal takes place in a driveway, the government seizes the house and thirty acres of land as well. Marijuana found growing in the remote corner of a 500-acre farm, allows confiscation of the entire farm, even if the owner knew nothing about it.

Under threat of great financial loss, forfeiture law forces property owners to act as police agents and incriminate others; innocent owners are defenseless unless they prove not only that the alleged illegal activity occurred without their knowledge or consent—but also they did all they "reasonably could be expected to do to prevent the proscribed use of the property."

Forfeiture skirts the usual safeguards of the normal government appropriations process; billions of dollars worth of property and cash fall into police hands, then are spent with no supervision by elected officials and little or no accounting to anyone. Hundreds of police, prosecutors and officials themselves have been arrested for stealing or misusing forfeited cash and property—and for falsely arresting and confiscating property on trumped up charges. Millions of dollars have been awarded by courts to victims of this police misconduct.

That is one of the worst aspects of forfeiture; that police and prosecutorial authorities engage in criminal conduct themselves, corrupted by an illicit profit motive because the property and cash being expropriated from private citizens goes directly to police budgets, including salaries. This perverse conflict of interest is inherent; the more they seize, the more they get for "official use."

Former New York City Police Commissioner Patrick Murphy admitted, "The large monetary value of forfeitures . . . has created a great temptation for state and local police departments to target assets rather than criminal activity."

Small wonder police rape squads and murder details have been joined by official "forfeiture squads," cops out scouring the town to meet quotas, not for arrests and convictions, but for total dollar value confiscated. High-priced autos are a special police target. As the *Pittsburgh Press* so aptly put it, "The billions of dollars that forfeiture brings into law enforcement agencies is so blinding that it obscures the devastation it causes the innocent."

Not content with forfeiture for drug offenses, eager politicians and legislators have expanded this brutal punishment broadly. More than one hundred federal statutes now impose forfeiture for environmental crimes, health and safety law violations. A growing number of states, including Texas and Florida, now apply civil forfeiture to any and all criminal activity. Scores of federal government agencies now have statutory forfeiture power, including, of course, the Internal Revenue Service—plus more than 3,000 state and local police departments.

Used together with U.S. and state anti-money laundering laws, forfeiture has become a government cash cow that keeps on milking.

Americans courts, caught up in "drug war" fervor, generally have acquiesced in this police confiscation. While upholding forfeiture in principle, the U.S. Supreme Court has curbed some of its worst abuses. They held that until a court renders judgment, a property owner has title and the right to defend it; that civil forfeitures are subject to the constitutional prohibition against excessive fines or cruel and unusual punishments, and that forfeitures cannot be excessive in relation to the offense committed.

Ms. Grantland, FEAR president, is the author of an excellent book on how to avoid forfeiture of real and personal property. Entitled *Your House Is Under Arrest*, its subtitle tells it all: "How police can seize your home, car and business without a trial—and how to protect yourself."

Here are some of Grantland's practical anti-forfeiture measures:

- Homeowners must make sure absolutely no police-attracting or criminal activity takes place in their house, including drug use and/or parties that get out of hand.

- Landlords must take every precaution against criminal activities by tenants, warning and evicting problem tenants, even notifying police. Keep careful records of all you do. Owners of run-down rental property, so-called "slum lords," are particularly vulnerable. Governments use forfeiture as a kind of area "renewal."

- Time-sharing resort condo ownership is also apt to be risky because of joint-owner's inability to control renter's conduct. Think before you buy a share.

- Be certain your on-site property manager is strict in applying occupancy and other rules, and is himself clean in every respect.

- Don't buy, or if you own, sell, any public place such as a bar, night club, motel or hotel located in a high-crime area likely to be targeted by police.

- If you're a rural landowner, constantly make sure there is no illegal substances growing anywhere on your land.

- Think twice before investing in commercial real estate. Forfeiture police look for high-value buildings where owners may be lax on supervision and management.

- Watch out for business partners or co-investors who may have even the faintest link with criminal activity. Under forfeiture, your property co-interest is taken along with all others.

- Be especially wary of business with foreign investors who may violate currency reporting or other international cash movement restrictions.

[**Ed. Note:** In 1999 a significant anti-forfeiture legislative victory was achieved when the U.S. Congress passed reform law that rolled "back 30 years of criminal measures passed at the height of Government 'wars' on drugs and terrorism," as the *New York Times* phrased it. The law, sponsored by Rep. Henry Hyde (R-Ill.), imposed major restrictions on police forfeiture powers and bolsters property owners' rights. Unfortunately, many of the Hyde reforms were weakened by so-called "anti-terrorist" provisions of the USA PATRIOT Act adopted in October 2001.]

CHAPTER FOUR
The Matter of Cash

Cash is defined as "money or its equivalent." Until relatively recent times money meant paper currency backed by gold, or metal coins of gold or silver with intrinsic value. Today cash can be billions of binary digits controlled by computers that send it around the world with a speed once reserved for lightning bolts.

The Bible, in the First Book of Timothy, admonishes us, "The love of money is the root of all evil." In the modern world the manner in which you handle your money can result in evils befalling you worse than all the plagues described in both the Old and New Testaments.

In this chapter, we survey the state of money and its many new equivalents in what can be called a "money safety course"—the new money regime you must master to survive.

Illegal Tender: The War on Cash
by John Pugsley, *The Sovereign Individual*, December 2001

History teaches us that the most serious casualty of war is always liberty.

In "America's New War," this sad lesson is being demonstrated again. Each passing day we are told that in order to protect our freedoms we must relinquish them. George Orwell had a name for this: doublespeak.

Using the fear of terrorism as cover, world governments are cranking up an all-out assault on financial privacy. Their primary target: cash.

I'm old enough to remember when cash was the most common medium of exchange. Companies paid their employees in cash, and people used cash for most purchases, including large ones like cars and even houses.

Until the mid-20th century, bank accounts were the exception rather than the rule for individuals and even businesses worldwide. Credit cards were non-existent until the 1950s. The American Express card didn't appear until 1958.

Although wealthy individuals sometimes purchased stocks, for almost everyone else, savings were in the form of cash (or gold and silver coins) stashed "under the mattress." Cash was king. Large bills circulated in most countries. In the United States there were $500 and $1,000 notes, and even $10,000 and $100,000 bills. They're long gone, although they are still sold as collector's items. Now the U.S. government is working to eliminate $100s, and $50s are likely to follow.

Governments don't like cash. With cash, citizens can conduct exchanges without written records and in complete privacy. Cash leaves no trail. While we are told government is against cash because it facilitates crime, in fact they hate it because cash makes individuals, sovereign.

The objective is a "cashless society," where every financial transaction will be available for instant examination and comprehensive analysis in government-run data banks.

It has taken decades for governments to gradually lull the public into accepting the elimination of cash, but success is at hand. Citizens are learning through bitter experience that to accept, hold, transport and exchange relatively large amounts of cash is to risk forfeiture and even prison.

In bygone days, the danger in carrying cash was that you might be robbed. It still is. Only today the robber is most likely to wear a police uniform. The early signs of this war on cash came with the passage of the 1970 Bank Secrecy Act, which made it a federal crime for anyone to cross the U.S. border with more than $10,000 in cash without filing a report with the U.S. Customs Service.

Today, government agents can basically empty your wallet of cash anytime they want. Most people whose cash is seized are never formally charged with a crime. Some 90% never get their property back.

In Florida, the "Impact" unit, a force of 50 officers backed by nearly a dozen police agencies, funds itself entirely through asset seizures, and it doles out millions more stolen dollars to area police departments.

A Vietnamese immigrant forfeited US$80,000 in cash he was carrying despite the fact he was never charged with a crime after agents seized money from him during a train ride from California to Boston.

In Wayne County, Michigan, police confiscate the cash that people bring in to bail out friends or family members, simply by having a dog sniff it, supposedly "alerting" to the smell of drug residues on the currency. Such seizures continue, despite that numerous federal court cases have established that nearly all U.S. currency has enough such residues to excite a drug-sniffing dog.

Occasionally, the amount confiscated is large enough that the victim sues to recover it. In 1998, the U.S. Supreme Court said federal authorities could not keep the $357,144 in legally earned funds they had taken from Hosep Bajakajian for failure to declare it when exiting the country. The Court, for the first time in its 200-year history, invalidated the forfeiture because it would result in a punishment grossly disproportionate to the underlying offense to which Bajakajian had pleaded guilty, which would have resulted in a maximum fine of only US$5,000.

Not willing to be bound by the U.S. Constitution or by justice itself, the Bush administration successfully lobbied to change the Bajakajian type of offense from "failure to disclose" to "smuggling," a crime with a much stiffer maximum penalty. This change is part of the new U.S. anti-terrorist legislation. In the future, someone like Bajakajian will not be able to recover his legally earned after-tax money and could be sent to prison for up to five years.

Is the war on cash likely to end? Not a chance. The events of September 11 have given all the major governments new justification for their war on cash. Is there an answer for sovereign individuals? Yes. The ongoing battle between the sovereign state and sovereign individuals is moving to the next evolutionary step in money: electronic currencies.

The largest operation in existence is called e-gold (www.e-gold.com).

However, my preference is for GoldMoney (www.gold money.com), the patented cyber-gold payment system introduced this year by long-time gold advocate James Turk. This new concept completely eliminates the forfeiture and theft risks of transporting cash and is the perfect solution to moving money across borders. It also eliminates fraud and solves the collection problems and costs inherent with transferring money through checks, wires and credit cards. Best of all, GoldMoney (and e-gold) offer individuals the opportunity to bypass fiat currency.

As mediums of exchange that are fully backed by gold or other precious metals, these avant-garde systems are based on tangible wealth-in contrast to the "dollars" issued by the Federal Reserve which are backed by nothing but the "good faith" of politicians.

Each of us, like it or not, is at war to protect our dwindling liberties. As sovereign individuals we don't assemble, arm ourselves and march against the enemy. Instead, we search for strategies and products that protect our property, and deny our resources to the State.

Gold-backed electronic currencies are one more such tool.

What Is "CyberCash"?
by Mark Nestmann, *The CyberCash Report*, August 1999

What is "cybercash?" A working definition is that cybercash is any system that facilitates the transfer of money or other financial value electronically, potentially outside the banking system.

Cyberpayments can be made on the Internet or through "smart cards," which contain a microchip that stores value on the card. Such arrangements provide the transacting parties with an immediate, convenient, secure (i.e., encrypted) and potentially anonymous means by which to transfer value. Cyberpayments need not ever re-enter the banking network. They can move from consumer to consumer, consumer to point of sale, or point of sale to point of sale, just as cash does now, but at the speed of light.

Cyberpayments pose an unprecedented threat to the governmental monopoly on money and to the global surveillance system designed to prevent "money laundering," the metaphysical crime defined by one apologist as "a process which obscures the origin of money and its source." Under this definition, any action to maintain financial privacy is a crime. J. Orlin Grabbe masterfully explains how this system developed, and how cyberpayments will force it to unravel. (See below in this chapter).

Central to the cyberpayments revolution is the development of privately issued digital money that can be transferred outside the banking system, with no regulatory "choke points" to facilitate government surveillance.

To establish these choke points, governments will try to require that all cyberpayment transactions clear through a central authority. It will also try to ban anonymous transactions and require that a paper trail be established for cyberpayments similar to those recently imposed for transfers of cash.

In the words of the Financial Crimes Enforcement Network (FinCEN), the U.S. Treasury's financial intelligence unit, "Because most cyberpayment systems are being designed to operate internationally and in multiple currencies, it will be more difficult to determine the applicability of jurisdictional authority. The apparent and immediate erosion of international financial borders resulting from cyberpayment transactions mandates enhanced cooperation and efforts among international entities to ensure that there are consistent policies and standards. It will not deter financial crime if one country has extensive laws and regulations and another has none. The illicit money will merely move to the weakest link."

FinCEN and each of the more than 50 financial intelligence units around the world should be worried. An unregulated cyberpayments industry will make it far more difficult for governments to tax their most productive citizens. This revolutionary development, according to Davidson & Rees-

Mogg in *The Sovereign Individual*, may herald the end of big government, and indeed, of governments themselves:

> Cyberspace is the ultimate offshore jurisdiction When this greatest tax haven of them all is fully open for business, all funds will essentially be offshore funds at the discretion of their owner. This will have cascading consequences. The state has grown used to treating its taxpayers as a farmer treats his cows, keeping them in a field to be milked. Soon, the cows will have wings.

FinCEN thus proposes that cyberpayments be made subject to stringent anti-laundering legislation. However, the ability in the very near future to conduct encrypted financial transactions over the Internet outside the banking system will prove a powerful incentive for many individuals to bypass whatever regulations FinCEN imposes. Such actions will no doubt be illegal. But whatever regulations are issued to prevent anonymity, they will again prove the truth of the warning issued by the philosopher Tacitus, "The more corrupt the state, the more numerous the laws."

A Critical Look at E-Currencies
by Mark Nestmann, *The Sovereign Individual*, May 2001

Will privately issued e-currencies eventually replace government-issued currencies? In theory, e-currencies, particularly those backed 100 percent by gold or other precious metals, have much to offer. The biggest advantage is that consumers can choose to hold or do business in e-currencies that are backed by tangible assets rather than fiat money issued by a central bank.

E-currencies can also enhance privacy. Residing on your hard drive, on an Internet server or on a "stored value" card, e-currencies are transferable directly from one party to another, without using a bank as an intermediary. This system architecture also lowers transaction costs.

Businesses benefit because transactions can be settled more quickly than with a wire transfer, regardless of the location of buyer or seller. For instance, a North American buyer of Asian textiles can send funds to the seller online while the buyer's agent is at the seller's factory ready to take delivery. The entire transaction is completed in seconds and is not dependent on a bank being open during business hours.

Merchants benefit as well, because the fees associated with e-currencies are far lower than the 1.5-15% fees imposed by credit card companies.

The fees are also lower than those imposed for wire transfers. This makes small-value transactions attractive that otherwise would be infeasible. Further, transactions in most e-currencies cannot be repudiated. Unlike credit card transactions, payments are not subject to reversal or chargeback. (Conversely, "non-repudiation" makes these e-currencies less attractive to consumers.)

Despite these advantages, to date, e-currencies have not been particularly successful. The best-known e-currency scheme, DigiCash, declared bankruptcy in 1998. Three stored-value card e-cash schemes—Mondex, VisaCash and Proton—have been modestly successful, but can only be used for relatively small purchases. Various hybrid digital cash schemes, such as CyberCash (www.cybercash.com), E-Cash (www.digicash.com) and Billpoint (www.billpoint.com), also exist. CyberCash only works with a credit card (and recently declared bankruptcy); E-Cash and Billpoint both require a bank account.

There are several reasons for this lack of acceptance. One is hostility from governments. Since e-currencies don't depend on banks for their existence, regulations in most countries requiring banks to "know their customers" don't apply to their issuers. This has anti-laundering organizations such as the Financial Action Task Force (FATF) deeply concerned. As a result, most e-currencies haven't been designed to facilitate privacy or permit large transactions.

Nor do other banking regulations or depositor protections apply. While some e-currency firms insure their aggregate physical holdings from theft, there is no insurance on individual holdings corresponding to the U.S. Federal Deposit Insurance Corp. or similar guarantor with an implied government backing.

But a larger reason e-currencies haven't caught on is that there hasn't been much demand, given the convenience of credit cards. And since it is possible for buyers to stop payments on a credit card if sellers fail to deliver goods ordered via credit card, consumers feel relatively safe using credit cards over the Internet.

According to Gerald P. Dwyer, Jr., a Vice President at the Federal Reserve Bank of Atlanta: "Buyers will not acquire e-currency if few sellers accept it and sellers will not accept that currency if few buyers hold it. If few sellers accept electronic currency, there is little reason for buyers to tie up part of their assets in the currency. On the flip side, if few buyers hold electronic currency, there is little reason for sellers to bear the costs of accepting the currency. A successful e-currency ... will require an introduction that manages to overcome what otherwise is a catch-22."

Required Course: Electronic Finance 101
by J. Orlin Grabbe, *The Cyberpayments Revolution*, 1999

Many of the basic features of electronic cash—variously referred to as "e-cash," "digital cash," "digital money," and so on—may sound novel to those unfamiliar with the financial markets. But much of the financial system is already on an electronic basis, and has been so for years.

To see why, consider the foreign exchange market. This is a largely interbank market for trading the currency of one country for the currency of another: dollars for pounds, dollars for yen, and so on. But if I, as an interbank trader, sell U.S. dollars for British pounds, what are the actual logistics of the transfer?

Consider the problems that would be imposed by a cash-based market. The standard transaction size in the foreign exchange market is an amount of currency equivalent to US$1 million. A US$20 bill weighs about 1 gram. So, if transacted in cash, the US$1,000,000 (50,000 bills) would weigh approximately 50 kilograms or 110 pounds.

Imagine the cost involved in such a transaction if in order to sell dollars for pounds I had to fill up a suitcase with US$20 bills, lug the 110-pound suitcase to a Manhattan taxi, take a long ride to Kennedy Airport (New York City), fill out a CMIR form and check my baggage, arrive at Heathrow (London) seven hours later, retrieve my baggage, go through customs, and catch a cab to the appropriate British bank in central London. Once there I would pick up the equivalent in pounds sterling and reverse the whole process.

There's a problem with this scenario: transaction costs. Anyone trying to change dollars into pounds will go to some other bank where he doesn't have to pay for my plane tickets and cab fares, not to mention my courier salary and the lunch I had at the Savoy before I headed back to New York.

(In the present markets for cocaine and heroin, it is hard to reduce transactions costs, because the weight of the drugs is less than the weight of the cash proceeds. In the early 1980s, cash bills were actually loaded into suitcases and moved around. To save time and money, however, the cash wasn't counted. After a spot check of bills for denomination and authenticity, the suitcases were simply weighed to determined the total value. This measurement was accurate to within a few dollars—close enough. But foreign exchange trading isn't illegal and doesn't, and can't, happen this way.)

To see how international money transfers really work, consider the case of a Greek immigrant who has opened a restaurant in Boston, has made a little money, and wants to send some cash to the folks back home. In earlier days he probably would have gone down to the Western Union office and handed the attendant cash to "wire" to his mother in Athens. The Western Union office in Boston would put the cash in its safe, or perhaps deposit it in a Boston bank, and would meanwhile send a message to the Athens office, "Give so-and-so X dollars" (or, more likely, "Y drachmas"). That is, the cash received was not the same as the cash sent. All that was sent was a message. But no one cared, because cash itself is fungible: the dollar that is taken out is interchangeable with, but not the same as, the dollar that was put in. The bills are also not registered: no particular name is associated with any particular serial number.

In this example, bills were put into the safe at one end of the transaction, and different bills were taken out at the other. Consider now a slight modification to this scenario: Eurobond trading. Eurobonds are generally placed in the depository systems operated by Euroclear in Brussels or Cedel in Luxembourg. Once bonds are in the vault, they generally stay there, because of transactions costs. If a trader in Frankfurt sells a GM eurobond with a coupon of 7 1/8 percent and maturing in 2012 to a trader in London, they both send messages to Euroclear. Euroclear compares the two set of instructions, checks the cash balance of the London trader, then switches the computer label of ownership of the bond to the London trader, and the ownership of the requisite cash to the Frankfurt trader.

Again, however, the bonds are not registered, and are fungible within the parameters of a particular issue. There may be several thousand GM eurobonds with a coupon of 7 1/8 percent and maturing in 2012, and the London trader owns one of them, but his ownership is not attached to a particular bond serial number.

This is pretty much the way the foreign exchange market works. If a New York bank deals dollars for German owned euros [deutschemark] with a London bank, they send each other confirmations through SWIFT. Then the New York bank will turn over a dollar deposit in New York to the London bank, while the London bank will turn over a euro deposit in Frankfurt to the New York bank. The Frankfurt bank simply switches the name of the owner of the euros [deutschemarks] from the London bank to the New York bank. The New York bank now owns X-number of fungible, unregistered (but completely traceable) euros at the Frankfurt bank.

"I remember my shock when I learned that the fastest way for two banks in Hong Kong to settle a dollar transaction was to wire the money from Hong Kong to New York and back again," said Manhattan assistant district attorney John Moscow. He was shocked because he didn't understand how the process works. The "wired" dollars were sitting in New York all along as numbers in a bank computer, originally labeled as owned by the first Hong Kong bank. After the transaction is completed, they are still in the same place, but labeled as owned by the second Hong Kong bank. There is nothing mysterious about this at all.

Now let's modify the basic scenario again: Yankee bond trading. Yankee bonds are dollar-denominated bonds issued by non-U.S. citizens in the U.S. bond market. Yankee bonds are registered. If you buy a bond, your name is attached to a particular bond with a particular serial number. If someone steals the bond, he will not be able to receive interest or principal, because his name is not attached to the bond serial number. So when Yankee bonds are traded, the seller's name is removed from the serial number of the bond being sold, and the buyer's name is attached.

To this point we have talked about things that potentially exist in physical form. I can take a bond out of the vault, or I can cash in my electronic euros for printed bills. The final modification to these various scenarios is to get rid of the physical paper entirely. Such purely electronic creatures already exist: U.S. Treasury bills; short-term debt instruments issued by the U.S. government. You buy, for example, a $10,000 T-bill at a discount, and it pays $10,000 at maturity. But you don't see printed T-bill certificates, because there aren't any. T-bills are electronic entries in the books of the Federal Reserve System. You can trade your T-bill to someone else by having the Fed change the name of the owner, but you can't stuff one in your pocket. You can "wire" your T-bill from one bank to another, because the "wire" is just a message that tells the Federal Reserve bank to switch the name of the owner from one commercial bank to another.

Smart and Not-So-Smart Cards

In the previous section we saw that most of the financial system is already on an electronic basis. And we understand that "wiring" money doesn't at all correspond to the mental image of stuffing bills down an electrical wire or phone line. To bring this story closer to home, let's consider how most of us use a computer and a modem on a daily basis to make financial transactions. Even if we don't own a computer. Or a modem. Let's talk about smart and dumb cards—ATM cards, credit cards, phone cards, and much more.

Some smart cards have microprocessors and are actually smart (and relatively expensive). They are really computers, but missing a keyboard, video screen, and power supply. Others, such as laser optical cards and magnetic stripe cards, are chipless and only semi-smart.

Laser optical cards are popular in Japan, and can hold up to 4 megabytes of data—enough for your tax and medical files and extensive genealogical information besides. The cards are a sandwich, usually a highly reflective layer on top of a non-reflective layer. A laser beam is used to punch holes through the reflective layer, exposing the non-reflective layer underneath. The presence or absence of holes represents bits of information. A much weaker laser beam is then used to read the card data. You can later mark a file of information as deleted, or turn it into gibberish, but you can't reuse the area on the card.

Magnetic stripe cards, popular everywhere, doesn't hold much information. An ATM card is one example. Data is recorded on the magnetic stripe on the back of the card similar to the way an audio tape is recorded. There are three tracks—the first of which is reserved for airline ticketing. This track holds up to 79 alphanumeric characters including your name and personal account number (PAN). The ATM doesn't actually use the first track for transactions, but it may read off your name, as when it says, "Thank you, Joe Blowup, for allowing me to serve you." The second track contains up to 40 numerical digits, of which the first 19 are reserved for your PAN, which is followed by the expiration date. The third track will hold 107 numerical digits, starting again with your PAN, and perhaps information related to your PIN (personal identification number, or "secret password"), along with other information, all of which potentially gets rewritten every time the track is used.

The ATM machine into which you insert your card is itself a computer. The ATM typically has both hard and floppy drives, a PC mother-board which contains the microprocessor, and a power supply—as well as drawers for deposits, cash, and swallowed cards. If the ATM is Online (i.e., one that is connected to a distant central bank computer, which makes all the real decisions), then it also has a modem to communicate over phone lines with the central computer. When you make a request for cash, the ATM machine compares your password to the one you entered. If they are the same, it then takes your request and your PAN, encrypts (hopefully) the information, and sends it on to the central computer. The central computer decrypts the message, looks at your account information, and sends an encrypted message back to the ATM, telling it to dispense money, refuse the transaction, or eat your card.

In between the ATM and the authorizing bank is usually a controller, which services several ATMs. The controller monitors the transaction, and routes the message to the correct authorization processor (bank computer). Some transactions, for example, will involve banks in different ATM networks, and the transaction will have to be transferred to a different network for approval. The controller would also generally monitor the status of the different physical devices in the ATM—to see that they are operating properly and that the ATM is not being burglarized.

Are Smart Cards the Mark of the Beast?

Besides optical and magnetic stripe cards, there are two types of "chip" cards. Chip cards are basically any cards with electronic circuits embedded in the plastic. One type of chip card, called a memory (or "wired logic") card, doesn't have a microprocessor and isn't any smarter than the cards we discussed previously. Prepaid phone cards are of this type. They may have about 1K of memory, and can execute a set of instructions, but can't be reprogrammed.

Then there are the truly smart cards that have a microprocessor and several kilobytes of re-writeable memory. Smart cards allow for greatly increased security, since access to their data is controlled by the internal microprocessor. And there can be built-in encryption algorithms. This versatility has made smart cards controversial.

The negative reputation arises from certain cases where smart cards were imposed by force, as well as from smart-card storage of biometric data. The use of smart cards became a prerequisite for Marines to receive paychecks at Parris Island, South Carolina. Fingerprint-based smart card ID systems were implemented by the Los Angeles Department of Public Social Services and the U.S. Immigration and Naturalization Service. The "Childhood Immunization" bill, introduced by Sen. Ted Kennedy (D-MA), would have tracked vaccination of all children under six years of age, together with at least one parent, across geographical areas through smart cards. Access control at the U.S. Department of Energy Hanford Site requires smart card badges which store the cardholder's hand geometry. Security access through retinal scan patterns stored in smart card memory have been tested at the Sandia National Laboratory.

Visa announced plans for creating an "electronic purse." The purse would be a reloadable spending card. You would charge the card up at an ATM machine, where it would suck some cash value out of your account, and store it in memory. You would then use the card instead of cash to make small purchases. Visa is attracted by the estimate that consumer cash transactions in the United States are about five times the size of bank-assisted transactions (those that use checks, credit cards, and debit cards). Visa has been joined in this endeavor by a consortium that includes VeriFone, the leading supplier of point-of-sale transaction systems, and Gemplus, the leading manufacturer of smart cards.

There may be increased security in the use of an electronic purse, but it is not clear how replenishing one's card balance at an ATM is any more convenient for the user than getting cash at an ATM. Since Visa is not advertising the privacy aspects of electronic purse payments, one must assume this feature was omitted in the planning. Hence, a cynic could conclude that the electronic purse is little more than a Rube Goldberg device which, by substituting for cash, will create a better set of PROMIS-type transaction records.

These and other examples suggest possible uses of smart cards for more general surveillance and social control. The truly paranoid envision the use of a single smart card for every financial transaction, medical visit and telephone call. This information would be sent directly to a common PROMIS-like database, which would constitute a record of all your activities. In addition, your card could be programmed to transmit its identification code whenever you use it. So you (or your card, anyway) could be instantly located anywhere on earth via the satellite-based Global Positioning System.

But smart cards don't have to be used this way. Recall that mainframe computers once appeared destined to turn the average citizen into Organization Man, a creature to be folded, spindled and mutilated in lieu of IBM's punched cards. The advent of the personal computer, however, showed the same technology could be a tool of individual freedom and creativity.

There is nothing intrinsically evil in storing a great deal of information about ourselves, our finances, and our current and future plans. That is, after all, exactly why some of us carry around portable computers. But in this case the use of the computer is voluntary, and we ourselves control both access to, and the content of, the information. The same principle applies to smart cards. It is smart cards more than any other aspect of banking technology, I believe, that will allow for financial privacy through cryptology, for anonymous and secure digital cash transactions. It's simply a matter of taking control of the technology and using it to enhance personal freedom.

Bearer Shares & Bearer Bonds

Banking in Silence, 1998

Another alternative for transporting large amounts of money anonymously is by means of bearer securities. These are simply shares of companies or bonds that are issued to the "bearer." The issuing company maintains no record of the sale. By definition, these shares or bonds may be freely bought, sold, traded or given away without creating a paper trail. As far as banks or other financial institutions are concerned, such shares or bonds are legally owned by whoever actually has them in his or her physical possession. No central registration exists, meaning that for all intents and purposes, they are as untraceable as good old cash.

Bearer shares are issued by most offshore corporations. They are also used by banks, insurance companies and even countries, states and municipalities, which issue them to raise revenue. They can be purchased just about anywhere on the planet, with, of course, the exception of the U.S. Bearer shares and bonds were one of the first victims of the so-called war on drugs and are now illegal in this Big Brother stronghold. American corporations, even those based offshore, are now prohibited from issuing bearer bonds or shares. Even the U.S. government swallowed its own bitter pill and recently stopped issuing bearer T-Bills. Nonetheless, in spite of such ongoing efforts by Big Brother, such wonders of anonymity remain freely available in most of the rest of the world, at least for the moment.

Bearer bonds are considered by many privacy conscious investors to be the best invention since sliced bread. As a conduit for convening your cash and transporting it in the least conspicuous way, they are unbeatable. You can convert $1,000,000 into perhaps ten pieces of paper (ten bonds of $100,000 each) and carry them on your person. In many countries, a border guard has the legal authority to confiscate any cash you carry in excess of reporting requirements if you fail to declare it. (Why any country would make it difficult to import cash in the first place remains a mystery, but that's how the world works.) However, most countries will not give a second glance to $1,000,000 or even $2,000,000 as long as it is in the form of bearer shares or bonds. Again, the U.S. government swims against the tide and requires that you report any bearer instrument worth in excess of US$10,000.

ABCs of Bearer Bonds

Bearer bonds come in two versions: coupon and non-coupon. The former is a bond with a number of coupons attached to it. At specified intervals, these coupons may be cut out and redeemed for cash, either at a bank or by mailing them directly to whoever issued the bond in the first place. Rules vary, but will be stated on the back of the bond. This payment is usually interest, as the bond itself is redeemable at face value upon maturity. On the other hand, a non-coupon bond, as the name implies, does not have any coupons. This means that interest is not paid out as long as you hold the bond but is instead added to the overall value of the bond until it reaches maturity.

Let us say, for instance, that a bond is issued in the amount of US$100,000. The interest rate is set at 10 percent per annum and the date of maturity (the date when the bond may be redeemed at full face value of US$100,000) is seven years from the date of issue. Obviously, no one would pay US$100,000 for a bond just for the pleasure of owning it for seven years and then at the end of it all get the same amount back. In effect, that would mean receiving no interest payments on your funds. So, the bond is issued at a discount to face value. For the purpose of this example, I have set an interest rate of 10 percent per annum and a running time of seven years because an amount will double in seven years (plus a few weeks, anyway) if 10 percent annual interest is left to be compounded upon the good old interest on interest.

This means that when a bond is issued with a face value of US$100,000 it will be sold for US$50,000—a 50 percent discount on face value. No one in his right mind would pay the

US$100,000 face value before maturation date, seven years hence. Remember, there are no coupons on such a bond. In fact, interest for the entire seven-year period will be paid as part of a lump sum of US$100,000 at the end of it all—that's US$50,000 in interest as well as the original US$50,000 paid for the bond. Strictly speaking, one does not buy a bond but rather lends money and receives the bond as collateral for the loan.

So what happens if you need or want your money back before maturation date? No problem. You just find someone who wants to buy it. That is exactly the sort of thing that banks and brokerage houses do for a living. They make surprisingly small charges for their services. (Of course, if a low-quality junk bond is involved, there may be no buyers.) After one year, you will be able to sell the bond of the above example for US$55,000—the original outlay plus 10 percent interest. If your bearer bonds are not counterfeit or damaged, you will have no problem selling them. Just walk into any bank or stockbroker's office with your bond and they will happily buy it from you at the prevailing price.

It should be noted that bearer bonds are investments—places to put your money and earned interest. They can be just as fickle as ordinary bonds. If the interest rate quoted on your bearer bonds is 10 percent and general interest rates suddenly skyrocket to 20 percent, then the price of your bond will naturally slip by 50 percent. If, on the other hand, general interest rates plummet to five percent, your bearer bond will double in value because it promises a rate of interest (10 percent) that is double that obtainable elsewhere. Of course, for our purposes in this discussion, bearer shares and bonds are covered purely and simply because they are one of the easiest ways for you to move large amounts of money into your offshore account anonymously. Whether you hold on to bearer bonds until maturation or cash them in as soon as they arrive at your new account is entirely your decision.

Just remember that once deposited in your new account, you can easily instruct your bank either to hold on to bearer securities or to sell them and deal with the proceeds as directed. At home, be certain when purchasing bearer securities that you do so anonymously. Otherwise you may inadvertently create a paper trail (albeit one that is very difficult to follow) if you buy bearer securities in your own name through a stockbroker or bank. Explain to your stockbroker when making the purchase that confidentiality is your objective. A good stockbroker will arrange for an anonymous purchase.

Are Bearer Bonds Safe?

The major drawback to bearer bonds is the same as with cash—if you lose it, kiss your money goodbye. Yes, there is a way to get a duplicate bond to replace one that has been lost, stolen or destroyed, but this means that you must also purchase a "lost instrument surety bond" from an insurance company. This will cost about 12 percent of the value of your bearer bond. You will also have to wait about six months to get your money back after proving that the paper was lost or destroyed.

If you dread the risk, ask an insurance company for more information or seek out one of the very few bearer bonds that comes pre-insured. Alternatively, guard your bearer bonds closely, preferably keep them on your person or in a safety deposit box until you can get them to your bank and add them to the growing mother lode held securely offshore.

Another caveat about bearer bonds and shares is that, as there is no central registration of bonds, you could accidentally buy stolen shares. As stolen bearer bonds are almost always canceled bonds that have already been redeemed, again you can then kiss your money goodbye. The easiest way to avoid this is to buy bearer securities only from a major bank or broker. They supply you with a receipt and a guarantee that the paper is bona fide.

Con artists love everything that has a tad of mystique about it, whether this mystique is warranted or not. Every year, both banks and private investors are duped into either forking over money for worthless canceled bearer bonds or into extending large loans and taking physical possession of bogus bonds as collateral.

Usually, the way it works is that a crook somehow obtains, more often than not by theft, a number of bonds that have been redeemed but have not yet made their way to the incinerator. Sometimes the ruse is obvious to those who know what to look for, such as one or more tiny holes or perforations in a corner of the bond. (Those little holes, if undetected, may mean that the piece of paper you just paid £10,000 for is about as valuable as a piece of toilet tissue.) On other occasions, even bonds that have already been redeemed but for some reason were not perforated are peddled by more enterprising con artists. Be careful! Bearer bonds are extremely valuable as a monetary tool, but you should guard yourself against hoaxes by buying only from a bank or a large, thoroughly reputable brokerage house.

Don't be satisfied just because you have seen an ad for a brokerage house (or even a bank) in a newspaper and thus reckon that the outfit must be legit. Two decades ago, an unknown individual referred to by investigators as "Dr. No" placed ads in several international bank registers for The Bank of Sark, a bank that does not exist and has never existed. Dr. No did not do this to attract customers or business, but merely to make the name linger in the memories of bank managers everywhere. After buying and placing these ads for three consecutive years, he managed to pull off an international swindle with cashier's checks and bearer bonds based on the mere perception created as to the bank's existence. He got away with more than US$100,000,000. Both Interpol and a lot of banks and investors are still wringing their hands over the affair. Dr. No is still at large.

So, when you go to buy bearer bonds, check the scene out carefully and gather as much information as you possibly can. Place calls to good, old brokerage houses and merchant banks such as Manufacturers Hanover, Prudential Bathe, Merrill Lynch or Goldman Sachs. Check out everything before taking the plunge.

Bearer Bonds An Endangered Species?

On another note, although you can take steps to protect yourself from con artists when purchasing bearer bonds, there is little you can do to protect yourself from legislators.

For example, in 1992, the State Bank of Pakistan ran full page ads in the *International Herald Tribune*, the *Wall Street Journal* and other papers. They touted a new series of bearer certificates and proclaimed proudly that no questions would be asked as to the origin of funds used to buy the bonds. Of course, Big Brother saw this as nothing less than a direct assault against his ongoing war against banking privacy. He acted swiftly.

The U.S. government, acting as self-elected world cop, threatened to summarily arrest and prosecute all Pakistani bankers living or working in the United States for aiding and abetting drug dealers and money launderers, current and prospective. Talk about Nazi methods! But it worked. A short three weeks later, the State Bank of Pakistan ran new ads saying the bearer bonds offer was withdrawn. Big Brother had struck another blow against freedom. Pakistan then went on to sell its bearer bonds more discreetly as almost all nations and corporations do.

The U.S. government requested that Pakistani officials turn over names of all Americans who responded to the ads. The demand was not honored. However, one can learn from this story, particularly if you are an American interested in purchasing bearer securities. When requesting information about such commodities, make absolutely certain you use an address located outside of the U.S. If your government discovers you frequently buy and sell bearer securities you may well find yourself at the center of a very unfriendly investigation. Don't allow this to happen. Stay absolutely low-profile from the very outset.

Furthermore, this story also shows that you really do need to start thinking about how you intend to move large sums at some future date. This rule applies not only to Americans but to everyone, unless you have your mind set on spending the rest of your days in your present country no matter what may happen in the future. Bearer bonds exist now—use them before this door closes.

Cash is great but bulky. A million pounds doesn't buy what it used to, but it still takes up a lot of room. Even in Sfr1,000 notes we are talking about roughly 2,000 bills. If you are using US$100 bills, the equivalent number is about 15,000 greenbacks. In terms of keeping cash on your person, I reckon that you can get away with carrying 600 or perhaps even 1,000 bills of any denomination strapped to your legs and in a money belt. That's about the limit before you have to start carrying a brown paper shopping bag. (This is the preferred method of transporting large amounts of cash, low-profile style.)

How does gold compare? Not well.

Gertrude Stein would say that a pound of gold is a pound of gold is a pound of gold. Fine, but an ounce of gold is still only about US$360—making a pound of gold a measly US$5,500. With a bit of effort, you may be able to drag a suitcase filled with 50 kilos of gold but that is still only a bit more than US$550,000. Then you have to transport the stuff. The last time I moved a mere million dollars in gold it broke the axle of a heavy-duty baggage cart at Zurich airport. It took three porters to lift my suitcase. When leaving New York there were no reporting requirements at the time for gold and, likewise, Swiss customs didn't care if you imported 20 tons of the stuff.

Bearer bonds were born in a pre-computer world. Stock and bond exchanges around the world are slowly changing from bearer to registered shares. In other words, now that the world has got hooked on silicon chips instead of real money, the days of the bearer bonds may be numbered. Get yours and lock them in a box.

[**Ed. Note**: Since the above was written there has been a concerted international campaign by major high tax governments and related pro-tax groups to ban bearer shares entirely. This attack is based on the supposition that anonymous ownership of shares may conceal criminal financial activity or money laundering. In a few offshore havens, such as The Bahamas and the British Virgin Islands, this has resulted in restricting or banning bearer shares, but in others, such as Panama, bearer shares are still legal.]

Bearer Shares: Friend or Foe?

By Derek Sambrook, *The Sovereign Individual*, November 2002

Bearer shares and trusts have both suffered a similar fate: each has been used for purposes neither was ever intended for, in some instances in ignorance, but in most cases by deliberate design. Most abuse of bearer shares (as with trusts) has occurred offshore and, as a consequence, many onshore bankers, accountants and lawyers view bearer shares with suspicion.

Bearer shares were once the normal way in which ownership rights in companies were established. The certificate, with no investor's name recorded, was deemed to be owned by the person possessing the certificate, i.e., the bearer. Whoever possessed the certificate controlled ownership. Like cash, it was easy for a certificate to change hands.

Gradually, certificates bearing the name of the owner became the norm. Some countries, including many states in America, no longer permit the issue of bearer shares.

Today, shares are usually either certificated (registered in the owner's name) or held through nominees, or through a stockbrokers' depository, in either certificated or dematerialized form (i.e., as a book entry).

Bearer shares have a long history in Europe where banks have traditionally held them in safe custody and collected dividends on behalf of customers. I remember as a bank inspector visiting the vault of a bank in London in the 1970s and seeing long rows of filing cabinets filled with bearer bond and bearer share certificates, many of them issued by Asian, Latin American and European governments and corporations. The collective value of the investments represented must have been staggering. I was told that the vault door weighed the same as a London double-decker bus.

Clearly, bearer shares are the speediest form of transition of ownership, avoiding practically any paperwork, but they can be the most hazardous means of ownership if not properly protected. Inevitably, with their inappropriate use (particularly offshore), there are an increasing number of court cases in which ownership of bearer shares is fiercely contested.

However, most of the litigation could have been avoided if the parties had acted responsibly and been properly advised. One recent case heard in the Caribbean amply illustrates the point. It involved an offshore corporation whose entire issued share capital had been put in bearer form. The sole bearer share certificate had been delivered to the client, who was now deceased. The plaintiff was the deceased's widow, who contended that before her husband died he had handed the certificate to her, thus effecting a proper transmission of ownership. This transfer, she argued, made her the owner of the company.

The company, however, had been an asset of a trust established by the widow's late husband. The trustee told the court that the deceased husband had verbally asked for share certificate number 1 to be canceled and thereafter a replacement share certificate, number 2, was issued by the company and delivered to the trustee.

There were glaring errors made in the case, the most obvious one being the fundamental mistake that the trustee made of accepting the trusteeship before he had control of share certificate number 1. No wonder onshore professionals hold their hands up in dismay when they read about such cases.

It is one thing to buy bearer shares in XYZ Petroleum with which you have no relationship beyond an interest in profiting from its worldwide drilling activities. Such impersonal relationships lend themselves to bearer shares, provided that the share certificate is kept in a secure and safe location. But when bearer shares, in the guise of an offshore company, represent access to your own personal assets, a different perspective is needed.

Unfortunately, many corporations that are nothing more than an investor's alter ego have issued bearer shares. Well-experienced and properly trained offshore professionals can help clients avoid problems down the road (especially litigation) by making suggestions as to the type of share to be issued. If you believe in the tooth fairy you may think that anyone presenting bearer share certificates of an offshore corporation to the professionals managing it will be automatically recognized as the new owner and, therefore, of all its assets. This is not necessarily the case; presentation of all or some of the share certificates will not automatically bestow any ownership rights.

Even so, it might still be feasible to use bearer shares when there is perhaps one specific asset such as a piece of undeveloped land. Here, bearer shares may not only reduce paperwork and transfer costs, but can provide, if desired, a degree of confidentiality concerning the transfer of ownership.

And, despite bad publicity, bearer shares can also be useful in estate planning. If shares are put in either a client's name or a nominee's name, the client's executor will have to approve any post death transfer. But if the client wishes to create an offshore estate comprising the shares of the company which can be dealt with after his death, without the need for probate, bearer shares could be issued and held under a simple inexpensive revocable trust. The trust would act as an agency (bare trust) during the client's lifetime such that the client could have the share certificates at any time. After the client's death, if the trust has not been revoked, the trustee would transfer the shares to the beneficiaries named in the trust deed.

Bearer shares do have their place but you should always seek expert advice and think about double-decker buses when it comes to protecting them.

[**Ed. Note**: Panama, in which the author is based, is one of the few remaining jurisdictions permitting the use of bearer shares. For transactions involving U.S. citizens, bearer shares pose numerous potential problems. These include state or federal securities law violations and unintended federal tax consequences.]

Government Targets: Smart Cards & Digital Banking
by Robert E. Bauman, JD, September 1997

On May 21,1997, the U.S. Treasury Department's Financial Crimes Enforcement Network (FinCEN), in a little-noticed rule proposal, began the government's takeover of all forms of electronic and digital cash in America.

For the first time the U.S. government asserted direct control over all so-called "financial value systems," defined as "...funds or monetary value represented in stored digital format (whether or not encrypted) and stored, or capable of storage, on electronic media... as to be retrievable and transferable electronically." (Official text; 31 CFR Code of Federal Regulations, Part 103, May 21, 1997.) This definition covers so-called "smart cards," online Internet banking and any other cash transactions in electronic form.

Registration Requirement

The rule requires registration with FinCEN of all "money services businesses" (MSBs) and their agents that use "stored value systems," a broad definition that now replaces the former, narrower description of "non-bank financial institutions." MSBs include non-bank cash systems run by currency dealers, check cashing operations, money order sales, including the U.S. Post Office, and issuers of travelers' checks—accounting for US$200 billion in business in America each year.

The ominous grab for control over digital cash got lost in sensational news stories about another May 21 FinCEN regulation, aimed at South American drug money launderers who allegedly used storefront "money transmitters" in Texas and New York City. As a result, such operations now must report all transactions of US$750 or more.

At the heart of the stored value controversy are plastic digital smart cards, look-alike for what may soon be obsolete credit cards. A smart card's embedded chip holds 500 times more information than an ATM or credit card magnetic strip, allowing it to serve as a portable personal bank account in your wallet. These "electronic purses" store digital money that can be replenished with a phone call to your bank. In time, smart cards could replace the need for paper notes and coins.

Privacy—The Target

What worries tax-collecting, crime-fighting governments most is the smart card's privacy potential. Based on the U.S. Bank Secrecy Act, regulations now cover virtually all cash transactions, making non-reporting of specific money transfers criminal acts punishable by prison and fines of up to US$250,000. The official money laundering crusade that began a decade ago as part of the so-called "war on drugs," now criminalizes over 200 other financial activities, many far afield from illegal drug money.

Superior encryption technology makes possible one way cash transactions that record only deposit sources, but not where card payments go. Respected digital cash pioneers could be hampered by the new rules. Most smart cards are issued by banks that already operate under a mountain of restrictive government rules. This will add to the burden and cost.

Suspicious Activity?

Money laundering experts outside the U.S. government say i's unclear whether separate FinCEN registration of stored value cash systems means any stricter application of so-called "Suspicious Activity Reports (SARs) to digital cash account holders. These rules already require banks to monitor and report all customers and accounts suspected of possible criminal activity. A bank official says SAR rules, although difficult to enforce on digital cash accounts, already apply.

But he predicted a major outcry if FinCEN tries to impose a lower US$750 transaction reporting rule on smart card bank transfers. The present reportable amount for cash transfers is US$10,000 and above.

Whether all U.S. Bank Secrecy Act rules do apply to digital cash seems an open question. Treasury's Stanley E. Morris, director of FinCEN, expressed doubt to the *Wall Street Journal*, suggesting "technology that permits anonymous transactions outside the regulated banking sector" could destroy anti-money laundering efforts. Early this year the Paris-based, 26-nation member Financial Action Task Force warned against "the speed, security and anonymity" of digital banking, factors they see as having great potential use for cyber-criminals.

Deaf To Advice

The rush for expanded government control of digital financial transactions flies squarely in the face of opposite advice from U.S. Federal Reserve Board Chairman, Alan Greenspan. In a publication by the Cato Institute of Washington, DC, *The Future of Money in the Information Age* (Cato Books, $12.95,+1 800 767 1241), the Fed chairman expressed concern that government "...not attempt to impede unduly our newest innovation, electronic money or...our increasingly broad electronics payment system." Greenspan warned, "Government action can retard progress but almost certainly cannot ensure it."

A senior American banking expert sees the new FinCEN rules as further proof of an established trend. "Government agents already view almost anyone engaged in cash transfers as potential criminals. They started down this road 10 years ago," he said. "If these rules are approved in their present form, it's only a matter of time until the privacy potential of digital cash is dead in the United States."

Flying Money: The Global Financial Underground
by Mark Nestmann, *The Sovereign Individual*, July 2000

Services such as e-gold (www.e-gold.com) promise a future where individuals can transfer value between one another without using a bank or other government-regulated institution as an intermediary. And one where the currency used can't be manipulated or debased by any government.

This development is of profound concern to world governments. Their most important concern, as always, is tax collection. Monitoring such transactions, much less collecting taxes on them, will be difficult—if not impossible. This is the real reason why governments want to end Internet anonymity and force Internet Service Providers worldwide to maintain logs.

But governments face an even larger threat—the fusion of these new forms of "digital money" with a much older worldwide network through which billions of dollars is transferred each year, outside the banking system. This is the world of *fei-chien*, Chinese for "flying money."

Fei-chien predates western banking by centuries. More than 1,200 years ago, the growing tea trade between the south and the imperial capital emphasized the need for a medium of exchange to avoid physically transporting copper, silk or other valuables. Tea merchants deposited their proceeds to these courts. The courts applied a portion of the deposit for taxes due and issued a certificate representing the balance due the merchant. Upon returning home, the merchant presented the certificate to the provincial government to collect his money.

Centuries later, flying money moves hundreds of billions of dollars each year, almost invisibly. According to Temple University Professor Nikos Passos, "it is an efficient, speedy and cheap way of moving money, often for very legitimate porpoises." Today, flying money brokers, often doing business as a currency exchange, can be found in bazaars throughout Asia and the Middle East.

But the world's tax collectors are no longer sponsors. Despite its legitimate uses, law enforcement agencies consider flying money a major source of tax evasion, currency exchange violations and money laundering—and have vowed to shut it down. However, doing so presents a major challenge. According to police inspectors in Hong Kong: "The record keeping procedures of the underground banking system are nearly non-existent, with coded messages, chits and simple telephone calls used to transfer money from one country to another." One Hong Kong police official stated that he once seized a piece of paper with the picture of an elephant on it that represented the collection receipt for US$3 million at a Hong Kong gold shop. The system, nonetheless, has the ability to transfer funds from one country to another in hours, provide complete anonymity, total security, convert gold or other items into currency and convert currencies.

Indeed, a recent report from the Financial Action Task Force acknowledges that this money transfer system "costs less than moving money through the banking system, operates 24 hours per day and is virtually completely reliable. It also admits that in India, "up to 50 percent of the economy uses the Hawala system—yet it is prohibited." And with the Internet and encryption software, flying money underground bankers' can now transfer value with an encrypted e-mail message, from any telephone in the world.

If governments can't stop flying money cartels from moving billions of untraceable dollars, how can they prevent sovereign individuals from doing the same on the Internet? They can't, and their failure means that privately issued, anonymous, gold-backed electronic currencies may eventually compete with government-issued fractional reserve currencies.

With flying money combined with modern e-technology, sovereign individuals may yet triumph over the all-powerful state.

Suspicious Transactions
by Mark Nestmann, *The Sovereign Individual*, March 2001

Welcome to the "Snitch Society."

In the United States, and increasingly, in other countries, your children are encouraged to report their suspicions to teachers that you might be using illegal drugs. Tax authorities pay generous rewards for turning in tax cheats. Anyone who forwards a lead to police that property was used illegally is eligible for a reward if it is forfeited.

These aspects of snitch society, odious as they are, for the most part are voluntary. Yet with respect to our money, they are mandatory. U.S. law requires banks, casinos and money transmitting businesses to report "any suspicious transaction relevant to a possible violation of law or regulation" to the Financial Crimes Enforcement Network (FinCEN), the U.S. Treasury's financial intelligence unit.

These incredibly broad provisions, through the first half of 1998, led to 150,000 Suspicious Activity Reports (SARs) being filed. From these reports, a total of 337 money laundering, fraud, embezzlement, theft or narcotics prosecutions were initiated. More than 99.7 percent of these reports did not lead to a criminal investigation.

But the collateral damage is huge. In one case, a mistaken report caused the accounts of 1,100 innocent depositors to be frozen. And the reports keep coming: an additional 350,000 SARs were filed through October 2000.

SARs are available electronically to every U.S. Attorney's Office, 59 federal agencies and police in all 50 states. No suspicion of crime need be shown for disclosure. Since FinCEN is exempt from U.S. privacy legislation, it can maintain SARs indefinitely. In addition, SARs have been made available (illegally) to private investigators.

The more reports filed, the greater the chance for such foul-ups. Especially since FinCEN itself has trouble entering the data it gets accurately. A 1999 audit found that in one case, $5,000 was entered as $5 million.

But this is only the beginning. FinCEN notes approvingly the expansion of mandatory SAR requirements in other countries to all professionals that handle money as fiduciaries. U.K. law, for instance, requires lawyers to report transactions they believe are related to money laundering. Similar provisions are now in effect in many offshore centers.

FinCEN is already preparing new SAR rules for U.S. securities brokers and firms engaged in foreign trade. And it suggests extending the requirements to accountants, insurers and even appliance makers and consumer electronics stores.

It is possible that these new requirements will result in some crimes being solved that might otherwise have gone undetected. But at what cost?

The tradition of confidentiality in the conduct of one's financial affairs is more than 5,000 years old. The Code of Hammurabi, one of the first written system of laws, stipulated that the when persons entrusted their money to a banker, that transactions were not to be disclosed to outsiders.

The Justinian Code of the sixth century A.D. (that compilation of Roman Law on which most European legal systems are based) recognized that relationships between individuals and their lawyers should also be afforded secrecy. In English law, the principle was first mentioned in 1580.

The common thread in these traditions is that clients should feel free to make full disclosure, thus making it more likely that a professional advisor will provide good advice. Confidentiality makes us feel comfortable disclosing information that, if known to others, could be damaging.

But today, banks, attorneys and many other professionals owe their first duty to the state, not to their clients. We are rapidly approaching the Nazification of the global financial system, with our trusted advisors acting as spies against us in an illusory "War on Crime." We have no choice but to take responsibility for our own individual sovereignty.

The IRS Tries to Profile Card Holders

by Robert E. Bauman, JD, *The Offshore A-Letter*, August 2001

In October 2000 an unprecedented IRS fishing expedition was allowed by a U.S. District Judge in Miami. Under the guise of pursuing possible tax evasion, the IRS was granted broad subpoena power for the 1998-99 credit card records of American Express and MasterCard holders whose cards were issued by banks in The Bahamas, the Cayman Islands and Antigua. Since the card clearing houses are located in south Florida, the court asserted U.S. jurisdiction over the card charge records.

At the time I asked: "Will the credit card companies have the guts to stand up to the government and honor their obligation to protect the privacy of their cardholders?" Our question was posed after the card companies pledged "cooperation" with the IRS.

Now it appears, happily, we were wrong. It is reported that both AmEx and MasterCard have resisted turning over cardholder account information to the IRS, and have not done so. It is now possible that the card companies may continue to resist IRS demands, even to the point of appealing any adverse rulings in the courts.

As we see it, this IRS wholesale demand for thousands of persons' financial records is nothing less than another example of police "profiling." Add this illegal waiver of due process to the insulting racial and ethnic profiling commonly practiced by prejudiced American police. Now we have IRS "offshore" profiling.

The IRS Crackdown on Offshore Credit Cards

By Mark Nestmann, *The Sovereign Individual*, June 2002

Each year in the weeks leading up to the tax filing deadline of April 15, the IRS trots out a "celebrity victim" to demonstrate that no one is safe from its long arms.

This year, however, the IRS changed its strategy. Instead of targeting a single victim, it targeted an entire class of (mostly) wealthy individuals: taxpayers who use credit cards issued by foreign banks.

In its latest broadside against offshore investors, the IRS is demanding that VISA International turn over hundreds of millions of confidential transaction records. It has obtained authorization from a California federal district court to issue so-called "John Doe" summonses on VISA in an ongoing investigation of tax evasion using offshore credit and debit cards.

Did the IRS target these taxpayers because it is illegal for a U.S. person to use credit cards issued overseas? No, the IRS admits that this is perfectly legal.

Is it because the IRS had proof that even a single one of these individuals was guilty of tax evasion? No such proof exists—which is why the steps the IRS is taking to gather such evidence is so troublesome.

The court order, issued March 28, 2002, allows the IRS to examine the records of VISA credit or debit cards issued "by, through, or on behalf of banks or other financial institutions" in more than 30 offshore jurisdictions, including the Bahamas, Bermuda, Cayman Islands, the Channel Islands, Hong Kong, Isle of Man, Luxembourg, Panama, Singapore, and Switzerland. The IRS already has obtained 1.7 million offshore transaction records from MasterCard International Ltd. American Express Co. has agreed to release similar records.

VISA must provide "the names, addresses, Social Security numbers (or such other identifying information as driver license, passport or employer identification numbers) and telephone numbers of cardholders or card users of VISA cards issued by the banks and financial institutions in the subject jurisdictions where a U.S. citizen or U.S. resident had signature authority over the VISA card or account during the years ended December 31, 1999 through 2001."

IRS investigators plan to review car, boat and airline ticket purchases and hotel and car rentals to determine whether account holders were living beyond their reported incomes. Banks in the targeted jurisdictions require customers to open bank accounts before obtaining cards; obtaining the names of cardholders will produce the names of bank account holders as well.

In a "John Doe" summons, the IRS does not know the identity of the taxpayer(s) under investigation. The U.S. Supreme Court upheld such summonses in 1974, in a case where the IRS rummaged through a bank's customer records to discover the identity of a single individual suspected of tax evasion. Only Justices William J. Brennan and William O. Douglas dissented, finding this "a breathtaking expansion of the summons power ... any private economic transaction is now fair game for forced disclosure." Given that the IRS is now demanding hundreds of millions of transaction records of individuals not shown as being connected to any crime, these concerns are proven justified.

How many Americans are affected by the inquiry?

According to the IRS: "If the MasterCard information is representative of the industry, there could be one to two million U.S. citizens with debit/credit cards issued by offshore banks. This compares with only 170,000 Reports of Foreign Bank and Financial Accounts being filed in 2000, and only 117,000 individual 1040 filers indicating they had offshore bank accounts in tax year 1999."

Testimony of Convicted Money Launderer Basis for Investigation

The summons against VISA International granted by U.S. District Judge Phyllis Hamilton was issued on the basis of information provided by John Mathewson, former head of Guardian Bank in the Cayman Islands. In 1998, to avoid prison after being convicted of money laundering, Mathewson provided the IRS with detailed records of more than 2,000 client accounts, thereby violating Cayman Islands bank secrecy laws.

Armed with the Mathewson information and details of his modus operandi, the IRS prosecuted numerous Guardian depositors. The IRS also used Mathewson's testimony to support its application for a John Doe summons against MasterCard and American Express, which was granted in November 2000.

Relying on the testimony of a convicted felon to support its application for these records is bad enough. But the IRS also included a declaration from self-proclaimed offshore "expert" Jack A. Blum, who estimated the annual loss to the IRS by individual taxpayers holding unreported offshore accounts at $70 billion. Blum had a year earlier made the incredible statement before Congress that: "There is no legitimate reason for an American citizen to have an offshore account ...When you go offshore, you are doing so to evade rules, regulations, laws or taxes."

This statement belies Blum's own ignorance of the many advantages of dealing offshore, including access to investments effectively "banned in the USA," protection from ID theft, avoidance of frivolous lawsuits, etc. Given Blum's record for making patently absurd statements under oath, the $70 billion figure he cited for offshore tax evasion is highly questionable.

[**Ed. Note**: In 2002 the IRS Commissioner quietly admitted that fewer than 200,000 U.S. persons probably had offshore credit cards, and further, that the total estimates of lost taxes due to offshore credit card cheating was almost impossible to quantify. Nevertheless, the news media continue to use the inflated figures.]

How Offshore Credit/Debit Cards Operate

In its John Doe summons, the IRS is targeting U.S. taxpayers that open accounts in offshore financial centers, often in the name of a trust or an international business company (IBC). The taxpayer is then issued a credit or debit card by the bank with which he or she can withdraw funds from the account. Bills are paid directly from the account, so there is no paper trail in the United States directly linking the taxpayer to the account. Until now, because of offshore bank secrecy laws, there has been no practical way for the IRS to find out about the accounts.

However, transfers of assets or cash, directly or indirectly, to a foreign entity or trust require disclosure, with few exceptions. Further, tax must almost always be paid on income from such entities or accounts. According to tax attorney Richard Duke, "Failure to report these transactions, accounts and/or income may result in prosecution for tax evasion, tax fraud and even money laundering."

The penalties for these crimes are almost unbelievably harsh, although according to tax attorney Donald MacPherson: "The likely punishment is not the statutory maximum, but within the range allowed under the Federal Sentencing Guidelines, which were amended in November 2001 to make them more onerous with regards to tax offenses." This range depends on the "tax loss," or in laundering cases, the amount laundered. Without adjustments, the following sentencing ranges in months apply: US$30,000 (15-21) US$200,000 (27-33); US$1,000,000 (41-51). Money laundering sentencing guidelines begin at 46-57 months and increase depending upon the amount laundered. "In a tax-conspiracy case, an upward adjustment is made for 'sophisticated concealment' (use of an offshore trust, corporation, bank, or credit card) and "role in the offense." Assuming a tax loss of US$250,000 plus these adjustments, the range is 41-51 months. However, negotiated settlements with taxpayers whose foreign accounts were revealed in the Guardian Bank probe have been lower than these guidelines. None have been charged with money laundering."

Are You at Risk?

The real question is how useful will the information received from this investigation be to the IRS? And how will it be used to target individuals for audit?

According to MacPherson: "If the tax loss is zero or very low, one might assume that chances of being selected are low. But for "deterrence" (interpret: reign of fear), the IRS prosecutes tax loss cases as low as US$1,000." However, the IRS will be limited by both the terms of the agreements it concludes with VISA International and the quality of the information it receives from them:

Terms of agreement. The IRS accord with American Express calls for records to be released only for account holders with billing addresses in The Bahamas, Antigua & Barbuda, or the Cayman Islands. In addition, the cardholder must have had at least one authorization in the United States for a purchase of more than $2,500 in one of a handful of categories (including yachts, jewelry, and cars), and at least five authorizations in the United States during 1998 and 1999. Individuals who do not meet these requirements are not at risk for having data released, at least for now. In addition, the agreement permits the company to notify affected customers before handing over their data to the IRS.

Quality of information. While the IRS has already obtained 1.7 million offshore transaction records from MasterCard International Ltd., this data is likely to be useful only if it can be matched to information already in the hands of the IRS. Historically, MasterCard has not maintained a central database matching account numbers to the names of the people who hold them. In contrast, American Express both issues and processes its cards, and therefore knows the identity of every cardholder.

Strategies to Deal With the IRS Crackdown

If you have an unreported offshore account, and particularly if you have used a debit card or credit card tied to it to make purchases in the United States, you face a significant risk for audit.

According to MacPherson, the five major choices for persons potentially facing an IRS criminal investigation for non-reporting of offshore accounts are: "(1) Do nothing. (2) File the delinquent reporting forms. (3) #2 plus an amended return, 1040X for the last three years, and pay all the back tax, interest and penalties. Amended returns cannot be filed beyond three years from the due date or filing date, whichever is later. A sub-option to (3) is pay all tax, interest, and penalties for all years. (4) Anonymous payment of back tax, interest and penalty, paid through your attorney, under cover of the attorney-client privilege. (5) Proceed through counsel with an informal request to the Criminal Investigation Division (CID), which need not involve disclosure of your identity, as described below.

"There is no obvious best choice. The general statute of limitations for a civil tax audit is three years from the due date of the return or the filing of the return, whichever is later, unless gross income is unreported by 25% or more, in which case IRS has six years. In the case of civil fraud there is no statute of limitation, but the IRS must prove fraud by clear and convincing evidence.

"In a criminal case, there is a six-year limitation for tax crimes; generally five years for conspiracy and other crimes. However, conspiracy runs five years from the last overt act in furtherance of the conspiracy, which might be last week's phone conversation with a Cayman banker."

Another strategy, assuming that you're not facing audit, is to move your offshore holdings into legally non-reportable forms. This includes international insurance policies; property maintained in an offshore safety deposit box; or offshore real estate or other personal property from which you do not derive any income.

For More Information. As we've stated many times before, if you have unreported offshore accounts, you should contact an experienced tax attorney to help you deal with the problem. Two attorneys members may consult for assistance in IRS audits of unreported offshore holdings and/or income are:

Donald McPherson. **Tel.:** +1 (602) 866-9566. **Fax:** +1 (602) 866 3799. **WATS:** 1-(800) 232-8477. **Link:** www.beatirs.com.

Richard Duke. **Tel.:** +1 (205) 823-3900. **Fax:** +1 (205) 802-9066. **E-mail:** richard@assetlaw.com. **Link:** www.assetlaw.com.

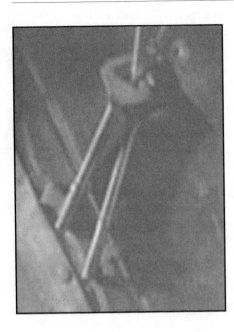

CHAPTER FIVE
Investments

In this chapter we get down to the nuts and bolts of the expansion, accumulation and protection of personal wealth. Each of these articles deals with an important aspect of offshore investing and financial strategies.

Some of this is very basic: how to recognize investment risk, how to spot a scam, how to avoid lending money. Other articles describe time-tested strategies proven to produce extraordinary profits.

Part One—Your Investments

Profits from the Global Economy

by Robert E. Bauman, JD, & David Melnik, QC, *The Offshore Money Manual 2000*

Modern global commerce began in the year 1571. So argues Dennis O. Flynn, head of the economics department at the University of the Pacific. In that year, the Spanish Empire founded the city of Manila in the Philippines. Manila was designed to receive the silver-laden galleons that traveled across the Pacific Ocean from the New World. This precious metal was bound not for Spain, but for the Imperial Court of China.

This was the first recorded period in which all the settled continents were actively trading with one another. The separate national economies of the world had become interdependent. Early proof of these global ties emerged when silver began to depreciate, resulting in worldwide inflation.

Globalization continued through war and famine for more than 300 years. Historians point to the period just prior to World War I as the apogee of international economic integration. In 1913, the British Empire was at its zenith. Foreign trade accounted for half of England's national product, and overseas investments equaled half of all domestic assets. British traders were everywhere, and British banks funded massive development around the world.

The "Great War" devastated this thriving international economy. The greater part of the twentieth century has been an era of strict protectionism, tariffs and disruptive military and political conflicts. This culture of confrontation ended only with the demise of both the Soviet Union and the Cold War in 1991. It has since been replaced by a new economic openness that offers investors some real opportunities for profit and growth. Recent setbacks in Asia have risen eyebrows, but investors the world over seem more willing than ever to go offshore.

The Rise of Global Investing

Cross-border investments are once again the rage. Even the 1994 Mexican economic meltdown could not slow demand for profitable offshore opportunities. At this writing, there are approximately 1,200 emerging-market investment funds managing over US$100 billion in equities. Add to that figure the billions in financial instruments and the total is overwhelming.

International and "emerging nation" mutual funds offer a simple way for American investors to profit from the growth of foreign companies. Such funds eliminate the inconvenience associated with direct ownership of foreign shares. American investors can also profit from American Depository Receipts, or ADRs. These are listed securities traded on U.S. stock exchanges. ADRs represent shares of a foreign stock and are issued by U.S. banks that take possession of the securities. The banks convert dividend payments into dollars and deduct any foreign withholding taxes. ADRs give investors a greater guarantee of safety, as participating foreign companies have to meet certain U.S. Securities and Exchange Commission (SEC) accounting and disclosure standards

Over the past 20 years, capital markets outside the U.S. have grown rapidly in size and importance. In 1970, non-US stocks accounted for 32 percent of the world's US$935 billion total market capitalization. By 1995, foreign stocks represented over 60 percent of the total world stock market capitalization of US$10 trillion plus.

While top U.S. stocks have performed exceptionally well over the years, international stock markets historically have outperformed Wall Street as a whole. In the decade ending in 1992, the U.S. stock market provided an annualized total return of 16 percent. This represents one of the best performances of any 10-year period in U.S. history. During that period 12 foreign equity markets performed better.

The rapid growth of capital markets around the world has also created abundant opportunities for fixed-income investors. Worldwide bond market capitalization now exceeds worldwide equity capitalization. Non-US bonds account for more than half of the world's bond market value.

Non-American investors have realized the enormous profit potential of cross-border investment. Rebounding from a 10-year low reached in 1992, foreign investment in the U.S. economy has sharply increased. In 1994, foreign investors spent US$47.2 billion acquiring or starting new U.S. businesses, up 83 percent from 1993. While direct investment from Japan has declined, western European investors have made up the difference.

Avoiding Roadblocks to Prosperity

This international economic integration continues despite U.S. laws designed to hinder such activity. One of the main obstacles remains restrictive securities legislation. Any "investment contract" for a security sold in the United States must be registered with the SEC and similar agencies in each of the states. This is a prohibitively expensive process. The U.S. also requires far more disclosure than most foreign countries, and burdens the process with different accounting practices.

International fund managers are practical people who look at the bottom line. Many correctly calculate that operating costs in the U.S. would wipe out any profit margin they could achieve. Ironically, several mutual funds and hedge funds with top performance records are run from the U.S. by U.S. residents, but do not accept investments from Americans. To avoid SEC red tape and registration costs, investment in these funds is available only to foreigners.

Fortunately, there are ways for U.S. citizens to get around these obstacles. Although you're a U.S. citizen, you can qualify under the law as an accredited investor. As such you will have a freer hand to buy non-SEC registered foreign stocks and mutual funds directly. An "accredited investor" is defined by SEC rules as an individual who has a net worth of US$1 million or more, or an annual income of at least US$250,000. In other words, you must have a lot of money.

You can also buy foreign securities through corporations or trusts you have created offshore. Properly structured foreign trusts and corporations—and we do mean properly structured—are not considered "U.S. residents, persons, or citizens." These entities therefore have the unrestricted right to buy non-SEC registered securities.

SEC "Regulation S" has actually made it easier to make such investments. It clearly defines the exemptions allowed by U.S. securities laws. These exemptions permit investment in non-SEC registered securities through a foreign trust and/or corporation. The most important restriction: the grantor who creates such entities must include income from these sources as personal income on annual tax returns.

Typically, the IRS has a web of rules and regulations that aim to wring maximum revenue from Americans who go offshore. These tax laws are extremely complex, so move cautiously and only with expert professional advice. At every step of the way, find out exactly what the U.S. tax consequences will be before you proceed

---

An Offshore Bill of Rights

by Vernon K. Jacobs, CPA, CLU, *The Sovereign Individual*, May 2001

The United States presents the largest obstacles of any country to its citizens living, doing business or investing offshore.

Indeed, the United States is guilty of the same practices it condemns in other countries by frustrating its citizens from living and working outside its borders and restricting access to financial markets in other countries.

I think it's time for Americans who want to live or invest overseas to demand fair treatment. And it's time for the United States to end its own discriminatory harmful tax practices. If I were writing an offshore "Bill of Rights" to deal with these grievances, here's what I'd include:

1. *No income taxation without permanent residency.* The biggest problem of all is that U.S. citizens are taxed on their worldwide income even when they are not permanent U.S. residents. The United States is the only major country imposing such a global tax dragnet.

2. *No tax penalty for an individual changing citizenship.* It should be a fundamental right of all persons to change their citizenship. The tax laws should not punish those who make that choice. This is not the case in the United States, which imposes an "exit tax" on persons giving up their citizenship. In addition, those who "renounce" their U.S. citizenship for tax reasons may be permanently excluded from the United States. The U.S. government has condemned exit taxes in other countries, and essentially prohibits the 50 states from imposing exit taxes on state residents who change their domicile. But when it comes to federal law, the same principles don't apply. If the government wants to impose an exit tax, it should not matter if the departure is for a tax-motivated purpose. At a minimum, all persons giving up U.S. citizenship should have the right to argue before an independent tribunal that they are leaving for non-tax reasons.

3. *No discriminatory tax treatment against offshore fixed annuities.* Another problem is that the United States imposes punitive and discriminatory taxes against many offshore investments. For instance, offshore fixed return annuities are discriminated against, tax-wise, versus domestic fixed return annuities. The effect of this rule is to subsidize U.S. insurance companies. This subsidy acts, in effect, as a protective tariff that could be challenged as an "unfair trade practice" before the World Trade Organization. These measures also could be considered "harmful tax competition," which the Organization for Economic Cooperation and Development (OECD) is trying to stamp out.

4. *No discrimination against offshore funds.* Another unfair trade practice is the draconian tax consequence when U.S. citizens, even those living outside the United States, purchase shares in almost any offshore mutual fund or unit trust. Unless the investment is sheltered in a qualified retirement plan or offshore insurance policy, the tax bill when they sell or are deemed to take an "excess distribution" can equal 100 percent of their initial investment. The IRS has issued two sets of regulations that allow investors in certain offshore funds to pay tax on their income or gains each year, including unrealized capital gains. Both sets of regulations are discriminatory—there is no tax on capital gains in U.S. funds until the shares are sold. But a bigger problem is that almost no offshore funds qualify for this treatment.

Instead, investors must rely on a "throwback" provision that permits tax deferral, but imposes an interest charge for that privilege, applied to each year the fund has been held. This charge, plus the fact that gains are taxed at the highest tax rate that applied for each year of deferral, can wipe out all income or gain, plus part or even all of the initial investment. It was not the intention of Congress to penalize U.S. investors in offshore funds. Yet the regulations the IRS has issued to interpret the law effectively do so. I believe the real reason for this complex set of rules is for the IRS to deter U.S. persons from investing offshore.

At the least, the law should permit a deferral of tax and the treatment of any distributions as ordinary income in the year received, plus a deductible interest charge on the deferral.

5. *No tax penalties on entrepreneurs with foreign businesses.* Any U.S. person who has ever operated a business abroad knows the potential pitfalls that can arise from the IRS characterizing foreign income as U.S. income. We need clear-cut rules to establish when a U.S. business has a nexus or

permanent establishment in another country.

6. *No micro-management.* Congress passes laws that encourage the IRS to intrude into the smallest and most insignificant transactions in order to prevent the slightest element of evasion of the tax laws. The concept of income is one of the most elusive that could have ever been used as the basis for a major tax system. Accountants and economists don't agree on fundamentals as to what income is or when it has been realized.

The Congress and the IRS should quit trying to force everyone to comply regardless of what it costs. Enforcement should be administered on a cost/benefit basis so that compliance for compliance sake is not the rule. This would require that Congress instruct the IRS to adopt a system of "materiality." This is a difficult concept to define, mainly because the government is not likely to specify what constitutes a "material" case. Whatever threshold they set would be an open invitation to cheat up to that level. The practical definition is that the government should not expend more to enforce the tax laws than the effort is worth in added tax collections. Enforcement for the sake of enforcement is a "power" issue of not wanting anyone to deviate from the rules.

7. *No shifting of costs to taxpayers.* We grossly understate the real cost of compliance with our tax system because we force the cost burden onto businesses and the taxpayers. Many small start-up ventures never occur because of the obstacle imposed by the cost of complying with a host of reporting requirements. The small business with one employee has to file substantially the same forms as a large business, at least in terms of federal tax law. There should be some kind of reasonable allowance for those who are required to serve as assistant tax collectors based on the time required to comply with the laws.

8. *No confiscatory tax rates.* Over the past 30 years, I've observed that there is a high correlation between the effective tax burden and the amount of time and effort taxpayers will exert to avoid or evade taxes. As tax rates increase, taxpayers begin searching for loopholes. After a few years, the IRS persuades Congress to pass laws that curtail these loopholes. But, lower effective tax rates would accomplish the same result. And, when tax rates are cut, the complex rules that were enacted to curtail the loopholes remain law.

The same principal applies with respect to offshore tax issues. If U.S. tax rates are effectively lower than in most other major countries, the IRS doesn't need complicated rules to prevent taxpayers from using foreign structures to avoid taxes. And if lower tax rates are available to foreign persons, the United States will attract capital from higher tax countries without maintaining one set of tax rules for U.S. taxpayers and another for non-resident aliens with U.S. source income, as we have now.

Uniform rules for U.S. residents and non-residents will also preclude the OECD and the EU from contending that the United States has a "ring-fenced" system that favors foreign persons over domestic persons.

It's time for the United States to end "Harmful Tax Competition" against its own citizens and the rest of the world. Enacting the reforms in this Offshore Bill of Rights would be a good start.

———◆———

Eight Myths About International Investing
By Mark Nestmann, *The Sovereign Individual*, October 2002

In the wake of the Enron scandal and the debate over U.S. corporations "expatriating" to Bermuda and other low-tax jurisdictions, the media bias against international investing has reached an all-time high.

An example of the breathtaking arrogance and ignorance of the mainstream media comes from a *Washington Post* editorial (Aug. 21, 2002). The *Post* questions the "patriotism" of U.S. companies reincorporating offshore. The *Post* completely ignores the fact that the U.S. Tax Code makes it difficult for U.S.-based companies to compete globally.

But the *Post* editorial is mild by comparison to those appearing elsewhere. For instance, the Superior, Wisconsin, *Daily Telegram* thunders: "It's Time to Eliminate Offshore Tax Havens."

To counter this massive disinformation campaign, this column highlights the most important myths and outright lies about international investments put forward by the mainstream media, along with our response.

Myth #1: "Many international investments are illegal."

The fact: There are no U.S. laws prohibiting any international investment, although most of them are taxable and must be reported to the IRS.

Myth #2: "It's not patriotic to invest internationally."

The fact: The United States is the world's largest tax haven and has attracted more than US$10 trillion in foreign investment. The U.S. government offers tax-free access to America, but only if you're not from the United States. When Americans invest overseas, they are only taking advantage of the same opportunities the U.S. government offers foreigners, but forbids its own citizens. Indeed, if tax havens were ever "abolished," the United States would suffer more than any other country.

Myth #3: "I'm not rich, so I can't benefit from international investments."

The fact: You can open an international bank account for as little as US$15,000 and have easy access to a wealth of investment opportunities, including foreign stocks, bonds and CDs.

Myth #4: "I'll be audited by the IRS if I invest internationally."

The fact: The overwhelming majority of IRS investigations of international investors are individuals who didn't report the existence of, or the profits from, these investments—not those who did.

Myth #5: "U.S. investments are safer than international investments."

The fact: Many international markets are safer than the United States. For instance, the Swiss insurance industry has never experienced a business failure in its 140-year history. By comparison, about 1% of U.S. insurance companies experience serious financial difficulties, including bankruptcy, each year.

Myth #6: "It's more expensive to invest internationally than in the U.S."

The fact: Many international investments are a better deal than their U.S. counterparts. For instance, if you purchase foreign currency CDs outside the United States, you'll almost always receive higher interest rates and pay lower fees.

Myth #7: "All the investments I want to make are in the United States."

The fact: More than 70% of global financial activity takes place outside the United States. Indeed, convenient access to international markets is one of the most important reasons to diversify internationally.

Myth# 8: "There are no longer any privacy advantages to international investing."

The fact: While you are required to report and pay taxes on most international investments, when you move assets outside the United States, those assets disappear from the domestic "radar screen." They are virtually invisible to business competitors, sue-happy lawyers and identity thieves, if not to the IRS.

The fact is that international investing is safer and more profitable than ever, and it's perfectly legal to participate. A good place to begin with is The Sovereign Society's Global Market Investor service, overseen by Council of Experts member Eric Roseman. GMI features international investment portfolios, ranging from very conservative to very aggressive. To learn more, see http://www.agorainc.com/reports/GMI/WGMIC901/.

Fortress U.S.A.: Overcoming Protectionist Roadblocks to Offshore Investments

By Robert Bauman, *The Sovereign Individual*, January 2004

President George W. Bush often bills himself in his public utterances as a "free trader" devoted to open world markets and unfettered global commerce.

In fact, Bush has been one of the most protectionist presidents since Herbert Hoover signed the disastrous Smoot-Hawley Tariff into law, helping to turn a recession in1929 into the Great Depression.

"Free trader" Bush has imposed highly protectionist measures supposedly to help American steel makers, textile workers, farmers, and numerous other special interest groups. These restrictive policies fly in the face of the theory behind truly free trade—that goods and services can be produced anywhere in the world, then sold at lower prices, thus benefitting sellers and consumers alike, regardless of where they reside.

Investment Protectionism

Slapping a high tariff on imported steel is a dramatic event, easily portrayed by the American news media in terms of prices, costs, tonnage and jobs. But for decades, there have been numerous U.S. government protectionist laws and polices in place that frustrate, impede and damage the ability of Americans to do business abroad—especially when it comes to investing in foreign stocks, bonds and other profitable ventures.

And it is obvious that, just like the more visible tariffs on imported goods, U.S. offshore investment restrictions provide a direct financial benefit to powerful business interests. These include domestic stockbrokers, insurance and annuity salespersons, bankers and investment interests—all of whom have powerful lobbies and make huge campaign contributions to both political parties.

More and Better Investments Offshore

I'll describe the specifics of these restrictions—and how you can overcome them—in a moment. But first, you should know exactly what it is that the government doesn't want you to know.

The fact is that some of the most profitable investments to be made anywhere can be found offshore. Over the past 20 years, capital markets outside the U.S. have grown rapidly in size and importance. In 1970, non-U.S. stocks accounted for 32% of the world's US$935 billion total market capitalization. By 2000, foreign stocks represented over 65% of the total world stock market capitalization of US$15 trillion plus. In 2000, mutual funds, pension funds and other institutional investors controlled US$25 trillion, 12 times the comparable 1980 figure. Where autos, steel and grain once dominated world trade, now trade in stocks, bonds nd currencies reign supreme.

While, with some notable exceptions, top U.S. stocks have performed well over many years, international stock markets historically have outperformed Wall Street as a whole. The rapid growth of capital markets around the world has also created abundant opportunities for fixed-income investors. Worldwide bond-market capitalization now exceeds worldwide equity capitalization. Non-U.S. bonds account for more than half of the world's bond market value.

Non-American investors have long realized the enormous profit potential of cross-border investment. And while it's taken years for U.S. investors to discover this potential, they are slowly but steadily increasing their participation in foreign markets. This trend has been particularly noticeable in pension funds. In 1980, less than 1% of U.S. pension-fund assets were invested abroad. By 2000 that figure had risen to 20%. More than pension funds, mutual funds and stock purchasers, banks have bought into emerging markets in a big way.

At the same time that investments have become more mobile, capital itself has as well. Finance and technology now dominate the economic scene. On a typical business day, the total amount of money moving in just the world's foreign exchange markets is US$2 trillion. That's ten times more than in 1986. It's also a sum equivalent to total current world trade for a full four-month period!

Wealth has become stateless, cash without a country, circulating wherever the owner finds the highest return and the greatest freedom.

From 1970 to 2000, spending by investors in industrialized nations on offshore stocks increased 197 times over, and national capital markets have merged into one fast-moving, global capital market. As stock markets close in London, they open in New York, and as U.S. exchanges end the day, markets in Hong Kong and Tokyo come to life.

Avoiding Roadblocks to Prosperity

International economic integration continues despite U.S. laws designed to hinder such activity.

One of the main U.S. obstacles remains highly restrictive securities legislation that blocks offshore investments. Under laws adopted during the 1930s, any "investment contract" for a security sold in the United States must be registered with the Securities & Exchange Commission and similar agencies in each of the 50 states. The SEC requires far more disclosure than most foreign countries, and adds more burdens to this process by using and insisting on different accounting practices than those used by most other nations.

International business managers are practical people who look at the bottom line. Many correctly calculate that the costs to comply with U.S. registration requirements would wipe out any profit margin they could achieve by making U.S. sales.

You might think that this restriction applies not only to investors, but also to managers. It doesn't. For instance, U.S. residents manage many top offshore hedge funds from the United States—yet these same funds do not accept investments from Americans.

About the only easy way that the government seems to approve of "offshore" investments is via American Depository Receipts, or ADRs. These are listed securities traded on U.S. stock exchanges. ADRs represent shares of a foreign stock and are issued by U.S. banks that take possession of the securities. The banks convert dividend payments into dollars and deduct any foreign withholding taxes. ADRs give investors a greater guarantee of safety, as participating foreign companies have to meet certain U.S. Securities and Exchange Commission (SEC) accounting and disclosure standards.

Chinks in the Protectionists' Armor

Fortunately, there are ways for U.S. citizens to get around these obstacles. One of the easiest ways, if you are wealthy enough, is to qualify as an accredited investor. As such you will have a freer hand to buy non-SEC registered foreign stocks and mutual funds directly. An accredited investor is defined by SEC rules as an individual who has a net worth of US$1 million or more, or an annual income of at least US$200,000 for two successive years.

You can also buy foreign securities through corporations or trusts you have created offshore. Properly structured foreign trusts and corporations—and I do mean properly structured—are not considered "U.S. residents, persons, or citizens." These entities therefore have the unrestricted right to buy non-SEC registered securities.

SEC "Regulation S" has actually made it easier to make such investments. It clearly defines the exemptions allowed by U.S. securities laws. These exemptions permit investment in non-SEC registered securities through a foreign trust and/or corporation. The most important restriction: the grantor who creates such entities must include income from these sources as personal income on annual tax returns.

Some Caveats

There are many other reasons, besides higher returns, for investing offshore. These include far greater financial privacy, stronger asset protection, and much wider investment diversification.

Unfortunately, tax savings are not generally available to offshore investors. The general rule for U.S. investors who invest outside the U.S. is that they are subject to income and capital gains taxes the same as with U.S. investments. However, this rule only applies to direct investments and not to investments made through a foreign trust, foreign corporation (or IBC) or a foreign partnership. In some cases, use of such legal entities allows deferral of taxes. There are also special tax rules for investments in foreign annuities or foreign life insurance companies and mutual funds or investment companies.

As you can imagine, the U.S. Tax Code imposes all sorts of complex tax rules on offshore investments that aim to wring maximum revenue from Americans who go offshore. These tax laws are extremely complex, so move cautiously and only with expert professional advice. At every step of the way, find out exactly what the U.S. tax consequences will be before you proceed. Also make sure you understand what you need to report to the IRS about your offshore investments.

Overcoming the Information Blackout

Some of the most draconian tax provisions relating to offshore investments are aimed at offshore mutual funds. Not coincidentally, these funds are some of the easiest and most profitable ways U.S. investors can participate in foreign markets. At this writing, there are approximately 1,500 emerging-market investment funds managing over US$200 billion in equities. These funds offer a simple way for American investors to profit from the growth of foreign companies by eliminating the inconvenience associated with direct ownership of foreign shares.

The IRS regulations relating to offshore funds are designed to prevent U.S. persons from deferring income in them, a privilege that is not accorded to U.S. funds. You might think the IRS would want to make it easy for U.S. taxpayers to simply pay taxes on their income or gain each year from the fund, in the same manner as for U.S. funds. Alas, that's not the case.

Indeed, the only way that the U.S. owner of shares in an offshore fund can recognize the gains each year is if the fund meets one of two sets of stringent IRS regulations. Unfortunately, this requires the fund managers to jump through many accounting and regulatory hoops. Most managers don't bother even trying to comply, and to make sure they're not asked, most offshore funds prohibit direct investment by U.S. persons.

As a result, U.S. taxpayers are forced to use the much less favorable fallback method of calculating gains on what the IRS calls a "passive foreign investment company" (PFIC). The PFIC regulations require investors to defer paying interest on tax until they sell the funds or are deemed to take an "excess distribution." This requires calculation of a punitive interest charge that, over a period of years, can not only eliminate all profits in the fund, but additionally eat into and, in extreme cases, exceed the principal amount of the investment.

Fortunately, there are a few exceptions to these rules. While most offshore funds are organized as corporations, an increasing number are organized as limited partnerships, limited liability companies or similar tax-neutral structures. U.S. shareholders in such funds simply pay tax on their pro-rata share of income or gain from the fund, bypassing the punitive PFIC rules.

Another option, which works for any kind of offshore fund, is to purchase them through a tax-sheltered investment, such as a retirement plan or offshore variable life insurance policy. However, make such investments cautiously, and only then with the assistance of a qualified international tax planner.

Conclusion

While the obstacles to offshore profits are many, they are not insurmountable. In spite of the roadblocks to prosperity the U.S. government imposes, there are many legal ways to achieve your investment objectives. And with the global return to a growing, greater prosperity, 2004 could be your offshore year.

Ways for Americans to Invest Offshore

by Mark Nestmann, *The Sovereign Individual*, April 2001

Unless you have no interest in offshore investing, or have been hiding under a rock, you know that the world's most powerful governments are engaged in a systematic campaign against low-tax offshore jurisdictions.

But despite the best efforts of the alphabet soup of global organizations such as the Organization for Economic Cooperation and Development, Financial Action Task Force, et al., offshore investing is by no means dead.

While it's become difficult-to-impossible to hide money from the tax man offshore, you can still take your domestic wealth off the radar screen to achieve practical, if not necessarily impenetrable, privacy. Offshore holdings also give you more flexibility trading foreign markets. And bank secrecy is still very useful for commercial purposes, even if it's hardly "absolute" in tax and (especially) criminal investigations. Finally, offshore insurance policies and trusts continue to provide significant benefits.

Practical Privacy and Lawsuit Protection

The single best reason in my view to move assets outside your own country is to protect yourself from the global litigation epidemic. Truly frivolous litigation is no longer a U.S.-only phenomenon. The U.K. and Canadian legal systems are also undergoing a quiet, yet revolutionary, transformation that dramatically increases the odds of being sued successfully.

Even something as simple as an offshore bank account provides substantial protection from frivolous lawsuits. This is one reason why The Sovereign Society developed its "Offshore Convenient Account" member benefit (see www.sovereignsociety.com/membersonly.html).

By transferring assets to a financial institution outside your own country, you gain a significant practical degree of financial privacy and asset protection. If you live in a country that taxes its residents' worldwide income, you won't generally obtain tax advantages, but the assets will disappear from the domestic "radar screen." Since lawyers size up targets for lawsuits by looking for their money, someone considering suing you may decide to find a target with more visible wealth.

If you live in an English-speaking country, it may also be much more difficult for a successful litigant to collect against assets in an offshore account. For instance, in Austria (where the Society maintains a Convenient Account relationship with Anglo Irish Bank) according to Austrian attorney Bert Ortner: "It is virtually impossible for a U.S. litigant to collect a judgment. It is possible only with a treaty and the United States has no treaties to collect judgments with any other country. This is true also in the realm of punitive damages, the enforcement of which is—punishment—which in Austria is reserved for the criminal courts. I have never seen a case where money was actually repatriated to the United States. It would also make no difference if the litigant were a government agency. There would still be no jurisdiction in Austria without more than a tourist simply making an investment in an Austrian bank. The only exception would be if the judgment comes under the authority of the U.S.-Austria Mutual Legal Assistance Treaty."

The situation for Canadian depositors in Austrian banks is almost as favorable as it is for U.S. depositors. According to Ortner, only arbitration awards and judgments from British Columbia are enforceable. Nor are Australian judgments, with the exception of arbitration awards, enforceable in Austria. On the other hand, Austria will enforce final judgments from Great Britain. But even then, the assets are still off the radar screen. The bottom line is that an offshore account provides practical asset protection and privacy.

State-of-the-Art Offshore Asset Protection

In recent years, courts in the United States and other countries have become frustrated by their seeming inability to enforce judgments against persons or companies with assets abroad. Especially where the creditor is a government agency, U.S. courts have ordered defendants to repatriate their offshore assets, or face contempt charges and, in a few exceptional cases, jail. If this concerns you, you may want to consider an offshore structure, such as a trust or limited liability company. And while it's true that many of asset protection structures that are available offshore are also available domestically, offshore structures are far more effective for asset protection.

The reason is that courts in many states have ruled that domestic structures may be invaded in various circumstances; e.g., to enforce claims for child or spousal support. And as an example of current trends, the Supreme Court of Mississippi has ruled, in effect, that if a beneficiary of an irrevocable spendthrift trust is a "bad person" (in this case, an alcoholic who caused a wrongful death), the courts may award payments from the trust to another party. The laws of popular offshore trust jurisdictions, such as Nevis, have no such exceptions.

But what if you don't have US$500,000 to place in an offshore trust, the minimum amount that most experts recommend for the structure to be cost-effective? Then you can use offshore structures such as a limited liability company (LLC). True, you can also form a domestic LLC, but for asset protection, one formed outside your own country will provide much greater asset protection. Similarly, U.S. life insurance and annuity contracts can sometimes provide asset protection, but better protection is available offshore.

Tax Benefits are Still Available

Nor is it true that you can no longer achieve tax benefits by investing, doing business or even living offshore. For U.S. persons, offshore life insurance policies or variable annuities remain a great way to defer income taxes on your gains.

In most countries, if you form a foreign corporation and go into business with someone outside your own country, you have the opportunity to defer taxes indefinitely on the profits. The price, though, is that you may not be able to own more than 50 percent of the business to avoid the "controlled foreign corporation" provisions of your country's domestic tax legislation. But if you are doing business with a foreign partner, this obstacle is easy to overcome.

Another opportunity is to leave your home country and move to a lower tax jurisdiction. In most countries, all you need to do to avoid income tax liability is to prove that you have given up permanent residency there. U.S. citizens must do more, however they must actually give up their U.S. citizenship. Yet even here, there's a silver lining. If you leave the United States to live elsewhere, and receive wages or salary from an offshore source, you can keep your citizenship and still be eligible to earn up to US$80,000/year without being subject to any U.S. income tax. If you are married, and your spouse is also overseas, the exemption doubles to US$160,000.

The bottom line is that despite a concerted disinformation campaign by governments and the media to discredit offshore investing and businesses, more than US$6 trillion has made its way into dozens of offshore centers worldwide. The overwhelming majority of this money represents legitimate investments made by individuals and businesses that are not trying to evade taxes or launder money.

And there's no reason why you shouldn't join them.

How to Choose Offshore Investments
By John Pugsley, *The Sovereign Individual*, January 2004

Sovereign Society members are generally above average in assets and in financial acumen. Yet member correspondence and interaction at our seminars tells us that many members are uncertain how to choose offshore investments. Part of the problem is confusion about what it means to invest offshore. A second and greater part comes from a failure to understand how to structure a rational financial plan.

There is little objective information on how you should design a long-term plan for the emulation and protection of wealth. This isn't hard to understand, since the investment industry profits by selling stocks, bonds and real estate, not by offering effective strategic advice.

Before choosing offshore investments, decide what type of assets meet your financial goals. Essentially, there are four types of assets: tangibles, money, businesses, and real estate. Tangibles are things that are useful, such as industrial commodities, gold, silver, precious gems, and collectibles. Money, the medium of exchange, takes the form of cash, or negotiable instruments (bank deposits, CDs, and bonds). Businesses can be wholly owned or partially owned through partnership interests or corporate shares (equities). Real estate can be owned as raw land or residential and commercial properties.

The following points provide a guideline of how to allocate your assets, depending on what you foresee for the overall economy: (1) Tangibles rise and fall in price as economic booms and recessions increase or decrease consumer demand. (2) Equities rise and fall depending on the skill of individual business managers, and general stock market cycles. (3) Bonds, even "risk-free" U.S. Treasuries, rise and fall with an inverse relationship to interest rates. (That is, as interest rates rise, bond prices fall, and vice versa.) (4) Since most real estate is mortgaged, property prices also have an inverse relationship to interest rates.

You should determine your portfolio balance by your evaluation of the economy and interest rates. However, there is another factor you must keep in mind—political risk.

Nowhere is political risk more pronounced, and less acknowledged, than in the U.S., where investors must consider: (1) Legal risks. Laws such as the USA PATRIOT Act give the government power to secretly confiscate property without a hearing. (2) Regulatory risks. Government regulations can devastate an industry or adversely affect property rights. For instance, environmental restrictions on developing property in "wetlands" have made millions of acres of U.S. property virtually worthless. (3) Tax risks. Changing the tax treatment of an investment can have devastating effects. For instance, when Congress decided to shut down "tax shelters" in the 1980s, real estate prices in some markets fell 50% or more. (4) Monetary risks. U.S. monetary policy overshadows all investments. Will the Federal Reserve increase interest rates and decimate bond values? Or will it expand the money supply, leading to inflation, and further favoring physical commodities as investments?

We believe monetary risks will have the most immediate impact on investors in 2004. Soaring federal budget deficits leave the Federal Reserve no choice but to continue to create money out of thin air, adding billions in new money to the banking system every month. As themoney supply expands, the unavoidable consequence will be a decline in the value of the dollar relative to other currencies and gold. It will also result in price inflation for goods and services priced in dollars.

As prices for goods and services rise, investors in dollar-denominated bonds and other monetary instruments will demand higher interest rates. As U.S. interest rates rise, dollar-denominated bonds will fall in value, as will U.S. real estate prices. Business activity will slow, resulting in declining stock prices.

This outlook leads us to make investment recommendations that we believe will perform well despite increasing U.S. monetary risks: (1) We recommend keeping the money portion of your portfolio in short-term bonds, preferably diversified among stronger currencies (e.g., the venerable Swiss franc). (2) In dollar terms, precious metals, and particularly gold and silver, will continue to rise, possibly entering an explosive bull-market phase. (3) The equities portion of all portfolios should include stocks outside the U.S. market. We also recommend a core position in securities such as the Prudent Bear Fund (NYSE-BEARX) that will profit from declining U.S. stock prices.

None of these investments need to be purchased offshore. Yet, the most obvious way to minimize political risk to your investments is to diversify your portfolio internationally, which is, of course, the raison d'être of The Sovereign Society.

However, don't choose an investment only because it is offshore. Choose it only after deciding if your portfolio needs that type of asset to give it the appropriate balance of risk and reward. You should also consider how a particular investment is likely to perform relative to all other assets in that category.

Assuming you decide to take the plunge "offshore," should you invest directly? Through an off-shore bank account? Through an offshore corporation, offshore insurance policy, annuity or offshore trust? These are the questions considered in this and other issues of TSI. Read the analyses we present carefully, determine if the recommendations we make fit into your long-term financial plan—and invest accordingly.

Change the Location of Your Assets
by Marshall J. Langer, *The Tax Exile Report*

Many countries impose estate or inheritance taxes on property situated in the country even if owned by nonresidents. Although you cannot move real estate, you may be able to change the situs of personal property.

The location of your assets may determine whether they are subject to capital transfer taxes such as the estate and gift taxes. A U.S. citizen or domiciliary is subject to these taxes on all transfers he makes no matter where the property is located. However, a non-domiciled alien is subject to these taxes only on property located in the U.S. With minor exceptions this rule extends to a tax-motivated expatriate.

For example, the stock of a foreign corporation that produces foreign-source dividends will normally be a foreign asset. However, a tax-motivated expatriate may be taxed on his share of the U.S. assets owned by a foreign corporation if certain ownership tests are met. Foreign bonds and foreign bank accounts are foreign assets. Foreign real estate is also a foreign asset for transfer tax purposes.

Own Only Foreign Assets

In general, you will find it advantageous to own only foreign assets. You should keep gold, jewelry, antiques, art and other personal property outside the U.S. You should not keep large amounts of U.S. dollars or foreign currency in the U.S. You should not keep U.S. tax-free municipal bonds because such bonds are tax-free only for income tax purposes, not for estate and gift tax purposes. You should not be partners in partnerships that own U.S. property nor should you do business in the U.S. You should be able to retain U.S. life insurance policies. When you are no longer at risk under the anti-expatriation rules, you can reacquire some U.S. bank accounts and bonds and own other U.S. assets, such as stock and real estate, through a foreign corporation that will then shield you from the estate tax.

Why You Should Own Non-U.S. Investments In Your Retirement Plan
by Larry Grossman, *The Sovereign Individual*, June 2003

Contrary to what you may have been told by your broker or banker, you can own almost any U.S. or non-U.S. investment in your retirement plan, including offshore mutual funds and virtually any kind of foreign real estate.

Imagine owning an exotic beachfront retirement home on a lush tropical island—purchased with the tax-deferred dollars you have been saving. Add to that the salary your retirement plan will pay you to manage the property. The icing on the cake is the freedom from the worries that plague most Americans when they think about their dwindling retirement plan assets.

Most of these opportunities are never made available to the average U.S. citizen—few people aside from the ultra-wealthy have ever even known of their existence. Trust me, your regular U.S. broker will never tell you these opportunities exist, probably because he's simply unaware of them himself.

Why Take Your Retirement Plan Offshore?

1. Investment diversification. Many of the world's best investments and money managers will not do business with U.S. citizens directly. They have simply made the choice that it is easier to do business with the rest of the world than to comply with the draconian U.S. rules.

2. Higher returns. There are opportunities in the traditional financial markets, such as offshore mutual funds and London-traded investment trusts with much higher returns then are generally available in U.S. markets. For example, the BFS Income and Growth Fund returned 75% over the last year; and the Jupiter Financial Fund has a one-year return of 57.1%! These "split capital" trusts aren't normally available to U.S. investors.

3. Currency diversification. Investors looking to stabilize their portfolios can protect their wealth against the falling U.S. dollar by simply holding other currencies (like Japanese yen or Swiss francs). And opportunities in foreign currencies are plentiful—like earning nearly 20% this year on the declining dollar versus the euro.

4. "Insurance" from closure of U.S. securities markets. We all learned the need to have part of our assets outside of the United States when our markets were shut down for five full trading days following the terrorist attacks of Sept. 11, 2001. But although U.S. markets were closed, individuals with foreign accounts were able to trade securities on foreign exchanges.

5. Asset protection. All types of retirement plans have come under attack in the courts. If a creditor gets a judgment against a "qualified plan" that's not properly administered, or a "non-qualified plan" in a state where such plans aren't protected, the judgment is easily enforced.14 In contrast, if you invest your retirement plan in a suitable jurisdiction—Switzerland, for instance—it can be configured to be essentially judgment-proof.

6. Financial privacy. Many people want protection from the prying eyes of business partners, estranged family members and identity thieves surfing the Internet. And financial privacy can be the best protection against frivolous lawsuits that end with big judgments—if you do not appear to have enough assets to justify the time and expense of an attack in an attorney's mind, he will not view you as a target.

Simply put, assets you place "offshore" are off the domestic asset tracking "radar screen."

What investments can your retirement plan make offshore? Almost anything! The only restrictions that apply are against most collectibles and some types of insurance. Amazingly, most investment restrictions people have run into are imposed not by legislation, but by the custodian or plan administrator.

For instance, are you interested in international real estate? Well, your IRA or pension plan can own raw land, condos, office buildings, single or multi-family homes, apartment buildings and improved land, so long as the real estate is not for your current personal use.

How about offshore funds? Most offshore funds won't sell directly to U.S. investors, and even if they did, the U.S. tax consequences of owning most offshore funds can be punitive—unless you purchase them through your IRA or pension plan.

For many investors, their retirement plans have become one of, if not, the largest asset they have. Clearly, it is vitally important to have these assets in a position where they can provide access to the global trading markets, the world's best investments and money managers and added asset protection. I urge you to act now while you are still able.

(About the author: Larry Grossman is a Certified Financial Planner, a Certified Investment

Management Analyst and a member of The Sovereign Society's Council of Experts. Grossman was one of, if not, the first financial advisor to develop a tax-compliant method for taking IRAs and pension funds offshore. He is Managing Director of Sovereign International Asset Management, LLC. Contact: Larry Grossman, 1312 Alt 19, Palm Harbor, Fla. 34683 U.S.A. WATS: (888) 609-7425. Fax: +1 (727) 784-6181. E-mail: lgrossman@worldwideplanning.com. Link: http://www.worldwideplanning.com.)

————— • —————

Choosing a U.S. or Offshore Investment Advisor
by Ron Holland, *The Sovereign Individual*, July 2000

The Internet is driving down the cost of investment advice and financial transactions. It is making insurance products and mutual funds with high front-end loads and full-commission stock-brokers obsolete. I believe that knowledgeable investors will in the future either use low commission (e-trade type) brokers or fee based investment advisors.

Internet based e-trade accounts are great when you know what you want to buy. But low commissions have an unfortunate corollary: excessive trading and increased investor losses. Expect this trend to persist as commissions and investment advisory fees continue to fall.

Nowhere is this trend more evident than in the world of day trading. According to *Worth* magazine: "a recent study of retail day traders by the North American Security Administrators Association found that only 11.5 percent of them do it profitably and want an acceptably low chance of ruin. Seventy percent of day traders are so bad that they are likely not just to lose money but to lose all of their money."

Fee-based advisors avoid a conflict of interest because they don't get paid for merely moving your money around in possibly losing trades. Rather, they are paid a flat fee and possibly a bonus if the portfolio grows in value as a result of the their investment management.

What should you look for in a fee-based advisor? Here are some recommendations based on my more than 30 years of experience as an investment advisor:

Choose an advisor with substantial money under management and experience. Find out in writing the amount of funds currently under management (not investments previously sold by commission). Choose one with at least five years in the money management business and US$50 million under management.

Expect to provide detailed information to the advisor. Advisors should ask for detailed information about your financial situation. Be prepared to answer questions about existing investments, net worth, tax returns and investment needs. An advisor who doesn't request and review this data is not someone you want to manage your portfolio.

Weigh the pros and cons of onshore verses offshore investment advisors. Offshore advisors generally have a wider range of potential investments available. They will also provide a degree of confidentiality and privacy not available from SEC-registered or U.S.-based advisors. But an offshore advisor will generally charge higher fees. And you may not receive the level of service, feedback and convenience of a domestic advisor. Also remember that most offshore managed investments are reportable as a "foreign financial account." Some experts believe acknowledging such an account can be a red flag on your tax return.

Ask a friend. Ask your friends who they recommend for good performance and service—then check them out. Also check out portfolio managers who your favorite newsletter editors or advisors recommend. One caveat: you need to determine if this is an objective recommendation or if they are a referral agent to a specific advisor. I recommend consulting with financial professionals who use a variety of advisors, not just one or two. You're likely to receive more objective advice.

Find an advisor with a compatible investment philosophy. Choose an advisor with whom you feel comfortable philosophically. For example, if you believe in Austrian economics or "hard money" investing, consider an advisor who shares your concerns and who knows how to apply these economic principles in investing. The same principle applies if your interest lies specifically in technology stocks, global investing or if you just want a balanced income or growth portfolio.

Avoid sales pressure. If you are paying for investment advice, why should you be subject to selling pressure? The answer is, you shouldn't. If the advisor doesn't spend most of your time together asking you questions and listening to your answers, he may not be doing his job. Beware of an advisor who brags about performance and doesn't explain the investment risks. Also watch out for any back end load or penalty charges if you change advisors. Most advisors charge a percentage of assets under management with little or no termination fees.

Consider a financial professional to help you pick the right investment advisor or advisors. Most major broker/dealers have access to a variety of money managers who they monitor for performance, client service and strategies. If an advisor makes mistakes and performance or service falters, then the financial professional can work with you to fire the advisor and choose one more appropriate for your needs. This is the service that I provide to clients throughout the United States.

———————•◆•———————

Investment Risks To Guard Against
By Marc-Andre Sola, October 2001

Mr. Sola is president and CEO of NMG International Ltd. in Zurich, Switzerland. Contact: Tel: +41 1 266 21 41 Fax: +41 1 266 21 49 e-mail: Web site: www.nmg-ifs.com

Inherently, any investment involves risk. Considered alone, "risk" sounds negative but considered in the overall investment picture, risk is much more manageable. The more risk is understood, the more you can turn risks into financial opportunities.

1. *Inflation risk* This is the danger that the cash you invest will buy less in the future because of rises in prices of consumer and other goods. When the rate of inflation rises, money loses purchasing power. This is especially true with fixed income investments. As long as investments produce returns at constant rates, they can be threatened by inflation. Inflation risk is tied to interest rate risk, because interest rates often rise to compensate for inflation. If your savings and investments are failing to outpace inflation, you may wish to consider investing in growth-oriented alternatives such as stocks, stock mutual funds, variable annuities, or other vehicles. Equity stocks, gold and other tangibles have proven to be the best hedge against inflation.

2. *Investment risk.* As noted, risk is an inherent, basic part of investing. For those nervous folks who worry a great deal, investments may not be suitable. Generally, investors must take greater risks to achieve greater returns. Those who do not tolerate risk very well have a relatively smaller chance of making high earnings than do those with a higher tolerance for risk.

3. *Interest Rate Risk.* Bonds and other fixed-income investments are sensitive to changes in interest rates. When interest rates rise, the value of your fixed interest income investments falls. After all, why would someone pay full price for a bond at 5 percent when new bonds are paying 7 percent? Of course, the opposite is also true. When interest rates fall, existing bonds with fixed higher rates increase in value. As an alternative, consider investing a part of your fixed income in deferred fixed annuities. These investments pay you a competitive interest and you avoid market risk.

4. *Exchange rate risk.* Exchange risk arises when a particular nation's currency loses value when exchanged for foreign currencies. As an investor it is important for you to understand currency fluctuations and know the value of the leading strong currencies such as the U.S. dollar, the euro (EUR) or the Swiss franc. Over many years the Swiss franc has continued to be one of the strongest of all national currencies. If your home currency is likely to lose value compared to these stronger

currencies, you should consider investing some of your money in one or more of these currencies. If, however, your home currency is strong, such as the British pound sterling, a diversification into other currencies has to be monitored carefully.

5. *Economic Risk.* When the economy experiences a downturn, the earnings capabilities of most businesses may be threatened. While some industries and companies adjust to downturns in the economy very well, others, particularly large industrial firms, take longer to react. In such situations risk is reduced by investments in those industries likely to prosper even in a downturn, but this requires knowledge on your part of the companies you choose.

6. *Market Risk.* When the market as a whole experiences a downturn, that tends to pull most equity shares down as well. Afterward, the affected stocks recover at rates closely related to their fundamental strength, regardless of overall market swings. Market risk affects almost all investments, including stocks, bonds, and real estate, but at different times. The key is to invest for long-term gains because over the long haul risk is reduced and averaged out. That strategy marks the serious investor compared to the day trader seeking fast profits.

7. *Liquidity risk.* Liquidity risk is the risk that an investment, when converted to cash, will experience loss in its value. To reduce the risk of being forced to sell at the wrong time, when the price of your investment is down, you should plan thoroughly your future needs for liquidity and select investments with varying time lines that allow you to liquidate when needed.

8. *Creditor risk.* This involves the risk that arises when the issuer of a stock or bond cannot meet his obligations when they come due. This may be an inability to pay periodic interest or return on principal on time. This risk can be reduced by diversifying investments within an asset class and by selecting investments with first class, "blue chip" companies. The credibility of a creditor can be predetermined by consulting one of the top rating companies such as Standard & Poor's or Moody's.

By understanding the different types of risk and keeping a constant eye on your investments, you will be able to manage your money far more effectively. Remember, strategic investing doesn't mean "taking chances" so much as "making sound decisions." Long-term investing and diversification are some of the most effective strategies you can use to minimize risk and increase potential return.

How to Recognize an Investment Scam
May 1996

The lure of a quick buck is all around us, and may seem irresistible, especially when money is tight and investment returns shaky. That alluring offer guaranteed to make you a millionaire can paint a very pretty picture indeed. However, in most cases, these pictures need some serious reviewing, and investors should be extremely wary.

In some cases, the pictures are simply gross exaggerations. Money can indeed be made—but it's not as easy or as quick as the promoters make it sound. Other deals are nothing but scams, underwritten by con artists intent on using your money to underwrite their retirement. An appeal to greed.

So, how do you spot—and avoid—these dangerous pictures? Here are some of the warning flags:

- *Promised investment returns that are substantially higher than average.* Every percentage point increase above the going treasury bond rate should be considered an increase in risk. When an offer promises risk-free returns to 10 percent above the treasury rate, you shouldn't only be seeing flags, you should be hearing sirens.

- *"Now-or-never" sales pitches, or "limited-time offers."* Promoters give you this special opportunity now, but can't guarantee they'll be able to "hold your spot"—even for an hour. Why? If you think about it too long, you might come to your senses, so they want your check or credit card number now.

- *Solicitations (usually phone pitches) from unlicensed companies.* Before handing over your money, you should know a lot about the company you're investing with. Check it out with the agency that registers or licenses businesses, like the Department of Corporations, the Department of Insurance, the Secretary of State or the Securities Commission. If you can't find the company through inquiries there, how easily do you think you'll find your money once it's gone?

- *Offshore companies.* Unfortunately, the many legitimate advantages offered through investing with offshore banks or corporations have sometimes been over-promoted by unscrupulous con artists, all too ready to relieve you of your assets and then hide behind the same blanket of financial privacy you wanted to enjoy for yourself. You should thoroughly investigate any agency or organization offering assistance with offshore investments. Deal only with long-established firms of proven reputation, and request references before entrusting your hard-earned money to anyone who claims to be an "expert" in the offshore investment field.

- *Glib responses.* You know the adage, "If it sounds too good to be true, it probably is." So ask, "If this is such a sure-fire deal, why are you offering it to me? Why won't the banks touch it?" Con artist response: "It's such a complex deal the banks don't understand." This is one of the great lies of investing. Banks understand only too well. It's their job. If they won't touch it, you probably shouldn't either.

Given those dangers, here are some steps you can take to ensure you don't wind up the victim of a scam artist:

- *Don't invest with someone who just calls over the phone.* Get a prospectus first, which should provide a detailed analysis of the deal and its risks. Never send money or give out a valid credit card number without it.

- *Check out the company and its officers.* Know whom you're investing with and what their history is in the business. Many scam artists go from one con to the next—and they leave a lengthy trail behind them. Check your wheeler-dealer out with governmental agencies or the courts before handing over your cash.

- *Don't let someone else do your reading for you.* You wouldn't walk blindfolded into a car dealership and say, "Give me a good one for $20,000," so don't do it with your investments. Don't rely on a friend to fill you in. Do the reading yourself—and talk to your accountant, financial planner, attorney or other adviser before taking the plunge.

As long as there are investments, there will be investment scams and swindlers seeking victims. However, with a little common sense and a few precautions, you should be able to avoid becoming one of the latter.

Fraud Alert—Six Scams to Avoid
By Mark Nestmann, *The Sovereign Individual*, September 2002

According to a recent Internet survey conducted among supposedly experienced investors by www.offshorebusiness.com, 22% of respondents expected offshore returns of 100% or higher per year; 32% of respondents expected returns of at least 50%; and 42% of respondents expected returns of at least 25%.

These unrealistic expectations are the main reason why so many people become victims of offshore frauds. In addition, offshore passport fraud and tax fraud is rampant. This column outlines how these frauds operate and how to avoid them.

1. Prime bank note/bank debenture schemes. These schemes generally promise monthly returns of 30% or more with "no risk." One scheme involves trading of so-called bank credit instruments (debentures). Promoters also use terms like "bank purchase orders" or "promissory bank notes" and claim to be operating under guidelines from the International Chamber of Commerce. But the ICC has issued a warning that no such investments exist. According to the ICC's Commercial Crime Bureau, this scam costs investors in North America alone more than US$10 million in daily losses.

2. Offshore promoters promising to assist in tax evasion. Promoters of "prime bank notes" and similar schemes often claim that their particular arrangement offers absolute secrecy and that profits from the scheme need not be reported on your tax return. The unspoken purpose of this promise is to reduce the risk that defrauded investors will ever sue or complain that they have been defrauded, since to do so would invite an investigation for tax evasion.

Remember: Taxpayers in the United States, Canada and some other OECD countries are required to pay taxes on their worldwide income. Also remember that there is a global crackdown against bank secrecy and that the implication that secrecy would apply in an investigation from "any source" is highly questionable.

3. The Nigerian fraud. In this scheme, which the FBI says has resulted in more than US$5 billion of losses in the United States alone, you receive an unsolicited e-mail or fax from Nigeria (and, with increasing frequency, other countries) asking you to allow the writer to deposit several million dollars into your bank account. You are promised a generous commission for doing so, which is necessary because the writer is engaged in activity which is implied to be illegal. As evidence of your good intentions, you are asked to send an advance fee to an offshore account. The fee, of course, promptly vanishes. In addition, the fraudsters may try to clean out the account from which you wrote the check.

4. "Pure trust" schemes. So-called "constitutional" or "pure" trusts are promoted as entities legally exempt from all taxes. But in fact, a U.S. grantor of a trust in which the grantor remains a possible beneficiary is taxed on an individual basis on the income from the trust. These schemes are at the center of the current IRS crackdown against "abusive trusts" that has resulted in several recent convictions of promoters. "Pure trusts" are also being promoted in Canada and Australia–with the same disastrous tax results for those persons relying on the promises of promoters.

5. "Brass plate" bank schemes. There are still offshore jurisdictions where it is easy to purchase a bank charter. Promoters claim that once you've set up an offshore bank, income it generates is tax-free. The truth is much more complex—a comprehensive tax analysis by a qualified practitioner is required to determine if you will obtain any tax benefits from such an arrangement. Even if you can, unless the offshore bank is a bona-fide commercial institution with a physical presence, it is prohibited from doing business in the United States. Such "shell banks" are a major target of the U.S. "war on terror," although there is little evidence that they have ever been used in terrorist financing.

6. Fraudulent passport offers. Only two nations currently sell legally authorized "instant" citizenship: St. Kitts/Nevis and the Commonwealth of Dominica. However, there are many other offers for "instant" citizenship in other countries promoted on the Internet and elsewhere. We have warned readers to avoid "instant" passports from an unnamed EU country being sold for US$8,000, and that these sales constituted criminal activity under domestic laws and international treaties. (That country, it was later revealed, was Greece.) We have now learned that our analysis was correct. In one case, a purchaser flew to Athens to supposedly meet someone from the law firm handling the passport sales. But instead, when he arrived, he was kidnapped. His kidnappers demanded an additional US$30,000 and told him that he had 24 hours to pay the money, or otherwise they would not be responsible for what happened. He was released after retrieving these funds, but never received the passport.

How to Avoid Being Defrauded

The best way to avoid offshore investment and tax frauds is to conduct your own "due diligence." One quick check you can do is in a search engine such as www.google.com. Enter in the name of the company promoting a scheme along with the word "scam" or "fraud" and peruse the results. If there are a lot of complaints–steer clear.

Two investigators who have compiled a database of offshore frauds are Matt Blackman (www.goldhaven.com) and David Marchant (www.offshorebusiness.com). Access to their databases is available for a nominal charge. Another good resource to avoid offshore fraud is www.quatloos.com. Beyond these resources, a professional investigator charging US$75/hour or so can uncover enough information in a few hours to give you a good idea of whether the investment being considered is a reputable one.

The best way to avoid offshore passport fraud is to deal only with reputable companies that offer strictly legitimate documents. One such firm is *Henley & Partners*, Kirchgasse 24 8001 Zurich Switzerland. **Tel.**: +(41) 1 267 60 90. **Fax**: +(41) 1 267 60 91. **E-mail**: chris.kalin@henleyglobal.com. **Link**: www.henleyglobal.com.

Due Diligence in Offshore Investing
by David Marchant, *The Sovereign Individual*, July 2000

Early in 2002, I was contacted by the Reverend Albert Jackson, head of the U.S.-based "Church of the Oversoul" (http://www.oversoul.org). Jackson claimed to have invested US$230,000 of church members' funds with The Harris Organization Financial Services Group of Panama in October 1999. When he requested a US$15,000 redemption two months later to support humanitarian projects, he was told that no money was available. Oversoul has unsuccessfully sought to redeem its investment ever since.

Jackson contacted me for assistance after learning that my company, Offshore Business News & Research Inc., and I had won a libel trial in Miami after The Harris Organization sued over an article we published in *Offshore Alert* newsletter making serious allegations against Harris.

What I found remarkable during my correspondence with Jackson was his admission that he had been aware that a judgment had been entered in favor of OBNR before he had invested the US$230,000. Nor did he obtain a copy of the judgment prior to investing.

If he had, he would have read Judge Michael Moore's comments that The Harris Organization's 1997 audited financial statement was "of questionable validity," that the group had prior involvement in "fraudulent and criminal activity" and that it had a "continuing association with persons and entities that had been involved in or advocated criminal activity." And that "from the time he published the initial article to the present, Marchant had evidence which provided persuasive support for the truth of each of the allegations at issue." These "allegations at issue" included one that Harris was insolvent.

Jackson told me that he had contacted my firm prior to investing with Harris, but did not obtain a copy of the judgment or supporting documents because he believed there was a charge involved. The expense of obtaining a copy of a judgment from the clerk of the court rendering it is usually quite modest, although in this case, Rev. Jackson could have downloaded the entire judgment from our web site at http://www.offshorebusiness.com without charge. To save at most a few hundred dollars (usually much less), or an hour or two of free Internet research, church members have potentially lost US$230,000.

Unfortunately, Jackson's story is typical of a chronic reluctance among unsophisticated investors to carry out any proper due diligence before parting with their funds. For many, the existence of a web site is all the proof they require that an offshore provider is legitimate. It is extra comfort if someone has posted a message on one of the many Internet bulletin boards devoted to offshore investing along the lines of "XYZ provider has been returning 10 per cent per month for five years without any complaints from investors, take my word for it." Who cares if the message was posted anonymously? After all, the poster couldn't possibly be lying because he professes to be religious. Interestingly, many of these same bulletin boards are swamped with messages from people claiming to have been defrauded, often by the same companies!

Basic due diligence need not cost a fortune. A professional investigator charging US$75/hour can uncover enough information in a few hours to give you a good idea of whether the investment being considered is a reputable one. Of course, some companies charge much more. New York-headquartered Kroll Associates charges $200 per hour, plus expenses. Their services might be worth considering if you're considering an investment in the hundreds of thousands of dollars, but might not otherwise be cost-effective.

One of the greatest strengths of offshore investing—secrecy—is also one of its biggest down sides when it comes to carrying out due diligence. However, everything has its price and, if you are prepared to spend the money, it is possible to obtain virtually any information you want, even offshore. I have a contact who can obtain balances, account signatories, details of money transfers and other information at most offshore banks. The price for such a service is in the US$5,000-US$7,500 range, depending on the bank and the jurisdiction.

Bank secrecy laws count for little if a bank employee decides to sell information for money or for their personal liberty. The latter occurred in the case of former banker John Mathewson, who gave U.S. authorities complete details of account-holders at Cayman-based Guardian Bank & Trust to escape a prison sentence for money laundering.

Citizens of the information-friendly United States own many offshore businesses. It is relatively easy to conduct a basic background check on their principals, once their identity is known. In less than an hour, I can perform a computer-assisted search of criminal and civil litigation in U.S. federal courts, civil checks in state courts and obtain details such as Social Security Number, current and prior addresses, professional licenses, property ownership, company involvement, etc. on anyone who has legally lived in the United States.

While many of you might consider this to be an unconscionable invasion of privacy, it nevertheless represents money and time well spent if it prevents you from being ripped off. There's no point setting up an offshore structure to avoid paying 30-40 percent tax if you're going to squander 100 percent of it by investing with a con artist.

Five Ways to Profit from Global Real Estate
By Lief Simon, *The Sovereign Individual*, January 2004

If you've made 10% a year on your U.S. investments in the last couple of years—which isn't bad—you've actually lost money if you count in the dollar depreciation.

Offshore real estate is an excellent hedge against the dollar, the U.S. economy, and U.S. stock markets. It's a hard asset. You can stand on it...and take enjoyment from it, while you watch the value appreciate.

How can you profit from offshore real estate? Specifically, in five ways:

1. Currency appreciation. You can still buy real estate in many parts of the world for much less in dollar terms than you could have only a few years ago. A real estate investment you make now with the euro, the New Zealand dollar, or even the lowly Czech koruna has the potential to net you extra profits as the U.S. dollar falls. But this is quickly changing. In fact, the dollar index is down 25% from its high two years ago.

2. Capital appreciation. Offshore real estate investments can appreciate faster than U.S. real estate. Because of the low price there is a higher ceiling for appreciation. That's driven by the fact

that with the Internet and e-mail, many people can work from anywhere on the planet. In the right real estate markets, it's possible for you to earn returns of 200%... 640%... or even 900%. While these returns are exceptional, real estate, as the investment adage goes, "can't go to zero." You can take enjoyment from it, and use it for vacations...while it's appreciating, year after year.

3. Leverage. With real estate, you can often get financing to make your investment, and use that leverage to invest a small amount and yet reap the gains on a large amount. While financing outside the United States is generally not as easy to find as inside the United States, it is becoming increasingly available.

4. Rental income. Properties that produce rental income that exceeds holding costs will make you money. For instance, the long-term rental market in Argentina is well developed and offers good potential, as does the market in France.

5. Asset protection. Offshore real estate is an easy way to move some of your assets offshore. There are few restrictions placed on Americans by the government regarding the purchase of property overseas. And once you own property abroad it's extremely difficult for the government, creditors, or anyone else to get at it.

There's a sixth advantage as well, but it's difficult to define in strictly financial terms. A dwelling in the right offshore jurisdiction offers you a safe alternative if things go bad at home. In the United States, for instance, many Americans fear for their constitutional rights. It seems as though those rights are fading quickly in this age of the USA PATRIOT Act and "homeland security." And although many governments around the world are even worse, others are muchless intrusive.

Where should you be looking right now? I'm interested in three destinations in particular:

1. The most undervalued raw land in the world. Nicaragua offers the best land deals in Latin America...and some of the most undervalued raw land in the world. The prospects for this country seem to get better every day. The economy is growing faster than that of any other country in the region. The president, Enrique Bolanos, is firmly committed to attracting foreign investment and is doing everything in his power to make his country as appealing as possible. We've seen steady appreciation in land values over the past seven or eight years. This appreciation will continue and accelerate in the coming years.

2. Government-backed guaranteed investment returns. The French Leaseback Program, a government-sponsored program, was created to attract foreign investors to build tourist accommodation in France. In a nutshell, when you buy an apartment, you get a heavy discount (19.6%) off the purchase price, you enjoy up to 95% financing, and get guaranteed minimum rental returns for nine years (up to 6% of the purchase price per year). Most people (including most French realtors) have never heard of this special program. But it's the easiest and safest way I know to invest in Europe.

3. A "Survivor's" Paradise. Contadora, the largest of Panama's Pearl Islands, has long attracted the attention of Panama's elite—because of its sheer natural beauty...and, mostly, because of the privacy it afforded. Until recently, few in the world even knew this island existed. But this is changing in a dramatic way. "Survivor," perhaps America's most popular reality TV show, is airing its current series as I write. The location? The Pearl Islands of Panama.

Remember what happened after "Temptation Island" aired its series filmed on Ambergris Cay, Belize? Real estate values rose 100% and more in six months. The real estate market on Contadora is small and limited. Not a lot of inventory. The spike in values here could be even greater.

For More Information

Lsimon@InternationalLiving.com. (Lief Simon manages Global Real Estate Investor, a small group of the world's savviest real estate investors. Members learn specifically how, where, when, and for what investment return to buy offshore real estate. To learn more, visit www.globalrealestate investor.com.)

Why Gold Is Money

by Michael Checkan, *The Sovereign Individual*, October 2003

With trillions of dollars, euros and yen circulating in paper and electronic forms, it is easy to forget that gold is and always has been money. For 5,000 years, it has been the only currency that is no one's liability.

Gold is money. Current practice is to translate its value into the denomination in which its price is quoted on international markets—the U.S. dollar. But gold is a currency in its own right and has been throughout recorded history.

Gold's role as money has been diminished by governments hijacking the right to issue money. Legal tender laws require citizens to accept fiat paper money as a "substitute" for gold. This monopoly money gives governments the power to tax the users of their money through inflation.

Globalization and the liberalization of financial markets have created choice in so many areas of our lives. So far privatization has not extended to the issuance of money.

Gold is No One's IOU

Gold as money remains in use today in both the public and private sector.

Central banks hold more than 33,000 tons of gold as part of their currency reserves; i.e. as money. Central banks hold gold because it has all the characteristics of money: it is a medium of exchange, a store of money and a unit of value.

Gold is no one's IOU. It is the asset of last resort. Had the government not sold off all of its gold a decade ago, there is a strong argument that Argentina may have been better off during its recent travails when it defaulted on US$132 billion of debt. Had the government retained some gold, it could have used it in the same way a motorist might use a reserve tank on a car, to tide it over in the short run. It could have also used gold to establish a new gold-backed currency.

In addition to the monetary reasons for holding gold, central bankers also accept the fact that people like their central bankers to hold gold. This was part of the motivation of the European Central bank in adopting gold as a reserve asset. The Chairman of the Federal Reserve, Alan Greenspan has an avowed affinity for gold and recently reminded us that fiat currencies have a history of mismanagement.

Gold as a Hedge Against Uncertainty

Unlike many asset classes, gold has maintained its purchasing power over decades and even centuries in the face of inflationary pressures. In addition, the price of gold typically moves inversely to the value of the dollar. These are two compelling reasons to use gold to diversify investment portfolios.

The demand for gold has continued to exceed the supply of newly mined gold by a large and widening margin for many years. Until recently, gold prices did not increase as a result because the shortfall in supply was made up by gold sales from central banks. Such sales have now slowed to a trickle.

The demand for gold has come primarily from the private sector. That some 80% of global gold demand is from the jewelry sector understates gold's monetary role. The use of gold as an adornment probably precedes its monetary use. But in many cases gold jewelry is held as much for its capacity as a store of value as for its cosmetic properties.

In a way, privately held gold continues to play a vital role as a parallel currency in countries where faith in the government's money remains tarnished by economic mismanagement, war or natural disasters. But in developing countries gold is not only held in bad times: it is used where the tradition of using gold as money stretches unbroken over the ages. No government dictate can change that.

The developed world is not immune from economic uncertainty and the demand for gold as a buffer against uncertainty is as real as ever.

The Best Ways to Own Gold

Investors hold gold in many different forms, some more convenient than others. In Vietnam, taels (pure sheet gold weighing 1.2 ounces) are used alongside the local currency, particularly when property is purchased. In Turkey, legal tender gold coins are used in day-to-day transactions.

Recent events in Japan have shown gold to be the asset of preference when concerns about continued recession, fragility of the banking system, low interest rates and equity prices prevail. In Japan, demand for gold rose 54% in 2001 and by February 2002 investors were buying gold at a rate of about a ton per day.

Private investors worldwide hold an estimated 22,000 tons of gold in a variety of forms ranging from jewelry to government guaranteed gold certificates. In some cases, they hold physical gold in the form of bullion coins. One ounce Australian Kangaroos, American Eagles and Canadian Maple Leafs, all of which are legal tender, are the most popular choices.

Clearly, gold is the only real money. The central bankers know it, and the average "man on the street" knows it as well!

It's Still as Good as Gold

by Robert E. Bauman, JD, November 1998

From September 1929 to April 1932, the Dow Jones Industrial Averages Index slid from 382 to 56, a drop in value of nearly 90 percent. Some 4,000 U.S. banks closed their doors and soon millions were unemployed. The Great Depression had arrived.

During that same bleak period the price of gold skyrocketed 70 percent. The value of gold producer stocks, like Homestake Mining, shot up almost 800 percent. After the market crashed, anyone holding 10 percent of an investment portfolio in gold and mining shares would have had all their other losses neutralized by their gold.

Gold also increased in value after "Black Monday," October 19, 1987, when the Morgan Stanley index of world shares fell 19 percent over 10 days. And during most all the mini-crashes of the stock markets since then, gold has held its value.

So why hasn't gold moved dramatically higher recently as Wall Street joined other world stock markets and currencies that have taken a nosedive? Is gold finally dead? Has faith in gold transferred to government-backed paper? Don't you believe it.

It's true that with the U.S. stock market at an all-time high in 1998, gold was near a 21-year low at US$278 per ounce in January 1988. It sank even lower to an early September price of about US$271, not far above production costs (averaging about $250 to $260 per ounce).

Several factors, all of them unusual, have kept gold down. The precious metal is denominated in the momentarily strong U.S. dollar, making it less affordable in traditional gold buying markets like India and much of faltering Asia. Until recently gold prices have been depressed by increased production in South Africa, Canada and Australia. But close observers see a supply deficit developing that can boost prices quickly.

If the U.S. Federal Reserve bends to pressures to cut interest rates as a stock market booster, the dollar could weaken fast, causing a flight to the gold backed Swiss franc and to gold itself.

Douglas M. Cohen, a Wall Street analyst, told the *New York Times*, "Gold has thousands of years of history on its side. That history is full of episodes when people insisted gold was dead, and sure enough, gold has tended to rally back very strongly."

Gold ownership has always defended against both inflation and deflation. That's because of its constant purchasing power. Compare gold today with the biblical times of the Old Testament during the reign of King Nebuchadnezzar. Then and now an ounce of gold buys about 350 loaves of bread. The same quantity of gold will buy a loaf of bread today under Tony Blair's New Labourites as it would have under an earlier, less decorous reign, that of King Henry VIII in the sixteenth century.

One gold mutual fund manager summed it up: "Gold is the only real money. Silver is only pocket change and everything else is really just a credit instrument taken on faith." That's sadly accurate when paper money, like the Indonesian rupiah and the South Korean won, declines in value hourly.

But as Asian currencies evaporate, gold remains solid. Every paper currency buys far less than it did at the turn of this century, but gold buys almost twice as much. That historic record demonstrates true insurance against economic swings.

Think about it. Gold cannot be inflated by printing more. It cannot be devalued by government decree. And, unlike paper currency or investments in stocks and bonds, gold is an asset which doesn't depend on anybody's promise to repay.

Although gold has been mined for more than 6,000 years, only about 120,000 metric tons have been produced. Lump that together and it's just enough for a cube measuring only 18 meters (about 55 feet) along each of its six sides. New gold mined each year totals less than 2,000 metric tons, about the size of the living room in a small modern house. Gold remains one of the scarcest, and most sought after metals on earth.

Time and again, gold has proven the successful hedge against devaluation of an investor's national currency. It's one of the few investments that survives, even thrives, during times of economic uncertainty.

With gold at record low prices and the world facing what could be a prolonged period of major economic turmoil, buying gold now may be the best bet. People who have known prolonged prosperity may not fully understand just yet the historic implications of gold and its role when bad times arrive. Once they do, it will be again the one investment that's still "good as gold."

Part Two—The World's Best Investment Strategies
Global Strategies That Work
by Eric Roseman, *The Sovereign Individual*, August 2000

What strategies are the most effective for global investors? For those with patience, the search for value remains the best strategy. Since 1995, however, growth-based investments have far outpaced value investing in the race for profits. But over time, no other long-term strategy has produced better results for investors than buying and holding undervalued stocks or countries. Here are some pointers:

1. *Buy undervalued country markets or indices representing those nations.* Research conducted by Michael Keppler of Keppler Asset Management in New York proves that, over time, value always wins. Keppler, the advisor to the State Street Global Advantage Funds (Luxembourg), uses a value-based methodology to scan for low price-to-earnings ratios, low price-to-book-value, low price-to-cash-flow ratios and dividends.

Today, some of the best bargains in a very overvalued market include Germany (low price-to-cash); Austria (cheapest of all Euro bourses); Thailand (low P/E); Indonesia (low P/E); Belgium (low P/E) and the Philippines (low price-to-book). Most of these bourses performed poorly in 1999, but I anticipate significant gains in the next 12-24 months.

To invest in these markets, you can choose among three different products. Actively managed open-ended funds tend to perform the best. Some of the best open-ended country funds are domiciled in Luxembourg (Fidelity) and Hong Kong (Jardine Fleming).

Closed-end funds are listed on the NYSE and London SE (investment trusts). These funds tend to trade at a discount to their net asset value—often 20 percent or more. If you can't find an open-ended fund for the country you're targeting, choose this route.

Index-linked products are my last choice—they simply don't perform as well in a bull market. For instance, the best funds in Japan in 1999 soared over 200 percent compared to only 59 percent for the World Equity Benchmark Series (WEBS).

2. Open-ended funds usually outperform closed-end funds. The reasons vary, but are tied to poor liquidity for the closed-end fund, a huge discount to net asset value deterring new investors and generally higher fees. Another factor is the "home market listing" phenomenon. A small decline in New York will affect your closed-end's price even though the international market it's representing has gone up. This isn't a frequent occurrence, but in 1994 resulted in losses for NYSE-listed Korean and Indian funds despite that both these markets moved up sharply.

3. Offshore country funds perform better than U.S. funds. One reason is that there are more than 15 times as many offshore country funds as there are U.S.-based equivalents. Another is that offshore country fund managers usually live in the market they target, giving them a better "feel" for investments there. My favorite offshore open-ended country fund organizations include Fidelity Investments (Luxembourg), Jardine Fleming (Hong Kong), Fleming's (Luxembourg), and INVESCO-LGT (Ireland & Luxembourg).

4. U.S.-based global and international funds outpace offshore rivals. According to Morningstar, U.S.-based international equity funds (excluding U.S.A.) have trounced the Morgan Stanley Europe, Australia, Far East Index (EAFE) by 57 percent since 1996, 57 percent since 1994, and 79 percent since 1989.

One reason why U.S.-based global funds perform better is lower fees. In the United States, the average total expense ratio for global funds is approximately 1.43 percent compared to 1.84 percent offshore. Front-end loads can also be avoided more easily in the U.S. market if you invest via Janus, Tweedy, Browne and fund supermarkets like Jack White and Charles Schwab.

Another reason is that the huge U.S.-based global investment houses manage billion-dollar funds that far surpass much smaller products offered offshore. A large fund benefits shareholders by providing lower fees, better liquidity and less possibility of going under due to their sheer asset size. Some of the best funds of the 1990s were multi-billion dollar vehicles such as Janus Worldwide, American Funds New Perspective and Tweedy, Browne Global Value.

Many international and Canadian residents can also buy these funds (ask for an IRS W-8 form).

5. Managed futures funds offer potential bear market protection. In severe corrections or bear markets, managed futures have made enormous profits for investors. The Turtles, or the trend-followers in the futures industry, remain the most reliable bear market tools, aside from put options.

Turtles are diversified managed futures funds sold in the United States and offshore to high net worth individuals. Unlike conventional futures funds, the Turtle traders are highly diversified in more than 125 global markets, including global commodities, interest rates, bonds, currencies and stock indices. They offer negative correlation to traditional investments (stocks and bonds), particularly during bear markets and crashes.

The world's oldest and best Turtle traders are Dunn Capital Management (Florida), Chesapeake Capital Corporation (Virginia), and John W. Henry & Company (Florida). Each earned stunning profits in the last global bear market of 1990, while Dunn and John Henry made fortunes in the

1987 crash. And in August 1998 when world bourses collapsed, all three advisors earned tremendous gains, offsetting losses for conventional portfolios in stocks. A little money invested in the Turtles can go a long way.

For an explanation of the Turtle trading system, see www.turtletrader.com.

6. *Low volatility hedge funds offer the lowest risk and most consistent returns.* These funds can deliver returns in the 12-15 percent range each year without being aggressive. The trick is finding a long-term winner in a sector that is still relatively new since 1995 and backed by good managers. Perhaps one of the best low volatility hedge funds in the industry remains the Momentum AllWeather Fund. This multi-manager product continues to earn top marks for its consistent returns and low volatility.

7. *Warrant funds only for the aggressive bull.* Only aggressive investors with an appetite for short-term risk and immense volatility should stake a (small) percentage of their assets in these gun-slingers. They should be used only to compliment an existing weighting. For example, if you're really bullish on Asia, buy a well-managed regional fund, two or three single- country funds, and a small position in a warrant fund. If you're right, you can earn over 100 percent in just months. If you're wrong—don't ask. In the current investment environment, I'm not recommending any warrant funds.

8. *Dogs of the Dow and the Dow Five-Stock Strategy.* You choose among the top ten highest yielding Dow 30 Industrial stocks on January 1, hold them for a year, and make the same determination the following January 1. This strategy has been a long-term winner, although it performed poorly in 1999.

Even more profitable is the Dow Five-Stock Strategy. You select the top ten highest yielding Dow stocks, then isolate those issues sporting the lowest share price. Since 1969, the Select Five has earned 18 percent per annum.

The Dogs and the Select Five were pioneered by Michael O'Higgins, author of *Beating the Dow with Bonds* (Harper Business, 2000). O'Higgins himself since 1998 has opted for bonds because of ultra-high stock prices. Of course, bonds suffered a big drop in 1999 and that didn't work, either.

Although both programs offer compelling long-term returns, this approach seems flawed in today's low dividend environment. The Dow 30 has no tech stocks with a dividend yield. And you barely get a dividend on the Dow at 1.3 percent. That won't help you in a bear market.

It is hard to argue against this proven strategy. But because it now contradicts its own philosophy of buying value stocks with high dividends, I'm not sure either program will work until we suffer another bear market. For more information on the Dogs, see http://www.dogsofthedow.com/dogytd.htm.

9. *Insider buying is a key signal.* A good contrarian strategy is to buy shares of companies in which the corporate executives are aggressively purchasing the stock. This is particularly true if more than one executive is buying. For companies listed on U.S. exchanges, it's easy to follow insider buying and selling because U.S. law requires a formal filing with the Securities and Exchange Commission within seven days following these purchases or sales.

Historical studies continue to document this time-tested approach. See, for example, Anthony Gallea and William Patolon, *Contrarian Investing* (Prentice Hall Press, 1999).

This is a value-based strategy because executives usually buy after a big drop in the stock price, when the stock has a single-digit P/E and a high dividend yield. A good rule of thumb is to buy shares after an insider has purchased at least US$120,000 worth of common stock and preferably, when several insiders buy stock worth at least US$1 million or more at the same intervals.

I still prefer a good mutual fund to stock picking. You really have to be on top of your stocks in today's highly erratic market. Of all the stock-picking strategies, though, I think the Insider approach makes the most sense, provided the company is a good name, under good management and a recipient of substantial net buying following a dramatic price decline. Today, this includes

Mattel (NYSE/MAT), and Tricon Global Restaurants (NYSE/YUM).

10. *Indexing is cheaper in the United States.* U.S. funds typically levy lower annual fees than their offshore counterparts. Only one fund company offshore has a very low fee structure: Vanguard Group in Dublin. Unfortunately, the minimum investment is US$100,000 for its index-linked products: Vanguard S&P 500 Index Fund Portfolio, Vanguard Europe Index Portfolio, and the world's only MSCI World Index clone, the Vanguard Global Index Fund. The management fee is only 0.50 percent per annum. But fees at Vanguard's U.S.-domiciled index funds are even lower: an average of 0.20 percent per annum.

Contacts for funds mentioned in this article

- *American Funds.* **WATS**: (800) 421-0180, ext. 23 (U.S.A.). **Tel.**: +1 (714) 671-7000
- *Chesapeake, LP.* **Tel.**: +1 (303) 572-1000. **Fax**: +1 (303) 832-9354 (US$25,000 minimum)
- *Chesapeake Select* (Caymans). **Tel.**: +1 (804) 285-5420. **Fax**: +1 (804) 285-5418
- *Dunn Capital Management Inc.* **Tel.**: +1 (561) 286-4777
- *Fidelity Investments Luxembourg S.A.* **Tel.**: +(352) 251-351-5555 **Fax**: +(352) 250 340. **Link**: www.fidelity.co.uk
- *First Chesapeake Capital Corporation.* **Tel.**: +1 (703) 883-8175
- *Fleming Fund Management* (Luxembourg) S.A. (Flemings & Jardine Fleming). **Tel.**: +(352) 3410-3020. **Fax** +(352) 3410-2221. **Link**: http://www.flemings.lu
- *Invesco/LGT.* **Tel.**: +(44) 1481-722-746. **Fax**: +(44) 1481-722-679. **Link**: http://www.invescogtoffshore.com
- *Janus.* **WATS**: (800) 975-9932 (U.S.A.). **Link**: http://ww4.janus.com
- *Momentum U.K. Limited.* **Tel.**: +(44) 20 7581 5841. **Fax**: +(44) 20 7581 5545 **E-mail**: info@momentumuk.com. **Link**: http://www.momentumuk.com
- *Tweedy, Browne.* **WATS**: (800) 432-4789 (U.S.A.)
- *Vanguard Group* (Ireland). **Tel.**: +(353) 1-612-3226

How to Build a Portfolio to Cope With Uncertainty
Interview With Harry Browne, *The Sovereign Individual*, August 2002

(Ed. Note: *"No one can reliably predict the future." That's the bedrock principal upon which author, investment advisor, and two-time Libertarian candidate for the U.S. president, Harry Browne, based his plan for a "permanent portfolio" when he began developing it in the 1970s. The portfolio is designed to grow in value regardless of current economic conditions).*

TSI: "Uncertainty" is certainly an appropriate term to label the times we live in. How does the "permanent portfolio" idea that you devised nearly 30 years ago deal with it?

Browne: You cannot eliminate uncertainty. In 30 years, I have found that no one can reliably predict future gold prices, stock valuations, the direction of the economy, or anything else that has to do with human action. Rather than trying eliminate or overcome uncertainty, we have to accept it and handle investments as though we have no idea what's coming next—even when you think you do. The goal is to devise a portfolio that will protect you whatever may happen. If you do, you should experience steady growth of an unspectacular, but reliable, kind. It isn't that you'll never have a losing year, but it will be rare when you do—and the loss will be mild when it does happen.

TSI: What investments comprise your permanent portfolio?

Browne: Anything that happens—war, peace, civil unrest, instability, good times, bad times, and so on—will translate itself into one of four economic environments: prosperity, inflation, recession, or deflation. Fortunately, each of these environments has an investment that does particularly well in it. Stocks and bonds both profit during prosperity; gold does well during inflation; bonds do well in a deflationary depression. And although nothing does well in a recession, cash helps to cushion the fall in other investments—and, unlike the other three environments, a recession (a period of tight money) by definition automatically ends within a year or so. Thus four investments—stocks, bonds, gold, and cash—cover all the bases. No matter what economic environment dominates the next year at any given time, you know that at least one investment will be taking care of you.

Your first reaction might be that you could have three losing investments and just one winning investment during a given period. That's definitely possible, but the winning investment almost always has a greater impact on a portfolio's performance than the losers. An investment can rise several hundred percent, but no investment can lose more than 100% of its value—and in real life a horrendous bear market might cause an investment category to lose 25-40%. For example, if someone had convinced you in 1970 to split $100 by putting $90 in stocks and $10 in gold, what would have happened over the next decade? In 1980, your stocks would have dropped in value to only about $40, but your $10 of gold would be worth close to $200.

TSI: Why place cash into the portfolio? And how do you define "cash?"

Browne: Cash will never be a big winner in any economic environment. But it will help cushion the impact of declines in other investments during a tight-money period. The year 1981 was a good example. Stocks, bonds, commodities, currencies, gold, and silver all fell in value the permanent portfolio's loss was only 6.7%, and it was more than offset when everything took off upward the following year.

"Cash" actually means short-term debt instruments denominated in the currency you depend upon—for U.S. residents, the U.S. dollar. The two safest and easiest ways to hold cash are with U.S. Treasury bills or a money market fund investing only in T-bills. You use Treasury securities to eliminate the need to evaluate credit. Commercial paper or other debt instruments require continually monitoring the credit standing of the issuers. But the U.S. Treasury will always pay its bills by either taxing or printing money.

The one basic objective of the permanent portfolio is to allow you to ignore your investments and focus on the things in life you do better and enjoy more. Thus an important criterion is that you shouldn't have to monitor the elements constantly to make sure someone's credit hasn't gone bad.

TSI: Why place gold into the portfolio? And how do you define "gold"?

Browne: Gold profits from inflation. It does so because it's the second most popular form of money in the world after the U.S. dollar. Gold is also accessible almost everywhere in the world and is accepted universally as a store of value, whereas currencies like the Swiss franc, euro, and yen are not. When inflation appears to threaten the dollar's value, some foreigners who are holding dollars become concerned and trade some part of them for gold.

Gold in the permanent portfolio consists of gold bullion or one-ounce gold coins that have no collector value. The link between dollar inflation and the price of gold doesn't necessarily exist between the dollar and numismatic coins or gold stocks.

TSI: Why place stocks in the portfolio? And how do you define "stocks?"

Browne: Stocks appreciate during times of prosperity. But no one can accurately predict when the market will take off or which sectors will perform the best. So it's best to split the stock portion between two or three funds that clone the S&P 500. They stay fully invested at all times, so that you aren't relying on someone's opinion as to when to be in stocks.

TSI: Why place bonds in the permanent portfolio? And what kind of bonds should you purchase?

Browne: Bonds are there so that you can profit when interest rates are dropping. This is likely in two of the economic scenarios. Interest rates usually drop during most of a period of prosperity. They also drop during a deflation. In the 1930s, interest rates on U.S. Treasury bonds dropped as low as 1%. If that were to happen today, you'd have a huge profit in bonds—more than offsetting your losses in stocks and gold. As with cash, you don't want to monitor the credit of the bond issuer. So U.S. investors can purchase U.S. Treasury bonds for this portion of the portfolio. A second qualification is that you want the bond to have a large impact on the portfolio when interest rates change. So you should hold 25-year Treasury bonds.

TSI: How has the permanent portfolio concept performed since you first originated it?

Browne: Very well. It has an overall return averaging about 10% annually, or about 5% above the underlying inflation rate. I've used this approach for over 20 years, and I've tracked it back to 1970—and there have been only three losing years. As I mentioned earlier, the worst year was 1981, when the portfolio lost almost 7%.

Even though the permanent portfolio concept has at times trailed stock investments—or, in fact, whatever is the hottest investment of the moment—in those 20 years I've never heard from a single person who regretted using this concept.

TSI: How do you divide the portfolio? And how do you reallocate your holdings as the market causes the values of the components to change?

Browne: Simply put 25% of the funds you wish to earmark as your "permanent portfolio" into each of the four investments. At least once a year you should check the values of the investments. If any investment has appreciated to represent 35% or more of the value of the overall portfolio or fallen in value to 15% or less, you should adjust the portfolio by selling enough of the "winners" and buying enough of the "losers" to bring the respective percentages back to 25%. Otherwise, you don't need to do anything.

Such an adjustment is necessary to preserve the concept of the portfolio. For example, gold soared in the 1970s, so without occasional readjustments, by 1980 you'd have 60% of the new value of the portfolio in gold alone—just before the gold price crashed. Your overall portfolio could have lost roughly 30% in 1980. But by adjusting when necessary, you know that no individual investment's fall can hurt you, and you'll know that each investment is big enough to carry the whole portfolio upward whenever it needs to.

TSI: What percentage of a person's wealth should be in a permanent portfolio?

Browne: For many people it should be 100%. I don't think there's anyone for whom it should be 0%. The permanent portfolio should consist of whatever funds you can't afford to lose. If you have assets beyond what you need to meet living expenses, retirement, or your children's education, you can set up a second portfolio—a "variable portfolio"—with which you can bet on future price trends in whatever way strikes your fancy. Just make sure you fund that second portfolio only with money you can afford to lose.

This points out the difference between investing and speculating. Investing is accepting the returns the market is offering to everyone. Speculating is believing you can beat those returns through superior knowledge, insights, or connections. Ironically, most people's returns fall short of what the market is offering, because they've tried to beat the market and wound up getting less than they could have by spending the time playing golf or listening to music.

TSI: Have you considered adding another category to the permanent portfolio—foreign currencies, for instance—that would help hedge against a decline in the dollar?

Browne: Other than the four investments I've included, no investment has a firm link to any of the four economic environments that the permanent portfolio is designed to cover. The Swiss franc, for instance, could go up or down in any environment. When the U.S. is inflating, we expect the dollar to fall against the franc. But this isn't automatic; the Swiss could be inflating as fast or faster at the same time, for instance.

However, if anyone could come up with an investment that profits automatically during a period of tight money or recession, I'd consider it carefully, because that's the one economic environment I don't know how to profit from. Fortunately, periods of tight money and recession are self-limiting. They always come to an end within a year or so. Either the economy adjusts to the new, slower level of money growth and things pick up, or the Federal Reserve quits fighting inflation and speeds up money growth, leading to prosperity in the short term and inflation in the long term.

(Harry Browne is the author of eleven books. His first book, How You Can Profit from the Coming Devaluation, *was published in 1970. Browne's warnings proved to be accurate when the dollar was devalued twice and his recommended investments rose many times over. Ten more books followed, and from 1974 to 1997 he published Harry Browne's Special Reports, a newsletter covering the economy, politics, and investments. His latest book,* Fail-Safe Investing, *explains in detail how set up a permanent portfolio. In the late 1990s, Browne was one of the few people who recognized from the outset that Y2K would not cause serious problems. He is now the Director of Public Policy at the American Liberty Foundation, a non-profit organization that puts libertarian ads on national television. His investment work is now limited to one-time consultations to help people set up a permanent portfolio. Link: www.HarryBrowne.org. E-mail: HarryBrowne@Harry Browne.org.)*

How to Buy Foreign Currencies for Two Cents on the Dollar
by Mark Nestmann, *The Sovereign Individual*, April 2001

Is it bedtime for the buck? The bursting dot.com bubble, bulging U.S. trade deficit and slowing economy are cracking the foundation of the dollar's global power.

Meanwhile, Europe, Asia and Latin American economies are growing stronger. The era of dollar domination appears to have ended. For Americans this means higher prices. For investors this could mean disaster—or rare opportunity.

For years, foreign capital inflows buoyed U.S. stocks, bonds and the dollar, and helped support America's credit-addicted economy. It was self-feeding; a stronger dollar meant greater confidence in U.S. investments and more buying.

More buying led to higher prices, which led to even greater confidence, and even higher prices. A falling dollar threatens foreign holders of U.S. investments as it reduces, or wipes out, returns when converted back into their home currency. For example, a 20 percent fall in the U.S. dollar against the British pound erases a 20 percent U.S. stock capital gain owned by English investors converting their "profit" back into pounds. This is exchange-rate risk.

Exchange rate risk, plus other bearish forces cited above, are primed to trigger dollar dumping. In turn, causing dollar-denominated investments to fall farther and faster than would otherwise be the case. So how do you best take advantage of this emerging opportunity?

Not on Wall Street

The smart way to cash-in on a falling dollar is to invest directly in the foreign currency exchange or "FX" market. This is the market in which transfers of one currency into the currency of another country take place. It is by far the largest global financial market, ranging from a tourist exchanging a few dollars at an airport to multi-billion dollar transactions between corporations and governments.

Unfortunately, most FX vehicles promoted by Wall Street are far from a pure play; so, even if you're right on the dollar, other factors can erase your profits, and even compound risks. This is especially true of foreign stocks and bonds, as their prices frequently have little or no reliable dollar correlation.

On the other hand, FX bank and checking accounts, and CDs often have prohibitive minimums of US$20,000 or more, require a physical switch out of dollars and, in the case of CDs, extended holding periods to avoid penalties. Also, FX "round lots" run US$5 to US$10 million, forcing most investors to go through layers of far more expensive "odd lot" middlemen banks or brokers.

But what if you could "rent" currencies for far less than their full value, without your money ever leaving home? And do it at round lot commissions, even if you have just a few thousand dollars to invest, rather than millions? The answer to those questions is a vital, but little known, way to profit from a falling dollar.

Foreign Currency Call Options

A call option is like buying insurance. Take your homeowner's policy for example. You pay a "premium" to the insurance company in exchange for the right to "sell" your house to the insurance company for its market value if it is destroyed. This right is good for a specified period of time.

FX call options are similar. When you buy an FX call you make a payment (known as a "premium" just like in insurance) for the right but not the obligation to buy a particular currency at specified price for a fixed period of time.

The key phrase is "not the obligation." Since call holders are not obligated to buy, all they have at risk is the cost of the option itself. Profit potential, on the other hand, is unlimited. Call options are "opportunity insurance" that you don't miss out on a move if it takes place.

Buy Swiss Francs For Two Cents On The Dollar

For shorter-term investment plays, FX futures and options on futures contracts are hard to beat, as you'll discover in the following simplified example: Swiss franc futures contracts for June delivery were recently selling for about US$0.61, with the June 62-cent call option on the underlying futures selling for 120 points. Both the option and underlying futures contracts are 125,000 Swiss francs, so each "point" (1/100) is worth US$12.50 (125,000 ~ 120 = US$12.50 per point.) This makes the June 62-cent calls worth US$1,500 each (US$12.50 x 120 points = US$1,500).

For US$1,500, you get the right but not the obligation to buy 125,000 Swiss francs at 62 cents each. This right is good until option expiration in June. Compare this with the outright purchase of 125,000 Swiss francs. At the going rate of 61 cents, it would cost you $76,250 (61 cents x Sfr125,000 = $76,250).

But buy the 62-cent call, and you "rent" the investment opportunity in the same US$76,250 worth of Swiss francs for only US$1,500—a mere 2 percent of the cost of buying them outright. Indeed, it is like getting Swiss francs for two cents on the dollar.

Now say the Swiss franc rallies to 64 cents, your 62-cent call will be worth at least the difference between the 62 cents you have a right to buy for, and the 64 cent market price or $2,500 (2 cents x Sfr125,000 = $2,500.) Should the franc rally to 66 cents, your option would be worth $5,000. At 70 it would be worth $10,000.

Swiss Franc Option Profit reveals the tremendous leverage built into FX options. Even a small percentage move in the exchange rate could mean big percentage gains in your call. A rally from the cash price of 61 cents to 64 cents is 5 percent, but your option gains US$1,000 or 66 percent. An 8.2 percent rally to 66 cents means a US$3,500 or 233 percent gain for your option. The leverage is even greater the higher the market climbs.

What's the downside? If the Swiss franc doesn't rally, you forfeit all or part of the $1,500 paid for the 62-cent call (plus a modest transaction cost)—but no more. The buyer of physical Swiss francs will still own them. Whether or not this is beneficial depends on the level of the franc when the option expires.

At 62 cents, the fully paid buyer comes out ahead. However, at prices below 59.8 cents you are better off having bought calls. For example, a decline back to old lows at 55 cents would give the franc buyer a paper loss of US$7,500; while the 62-cent call would have a maximum loss of only US$1,500.

Cut Already Low Costs in Half

You can make this strategy even more economical by taking the difference between the purchase price of the 62-cent call and 125,000 Swiss francs (or other amount) and putting it in a money market fund. Three months of interest on US$74,750 at 5 percent is about US$935. This covers more than half the cost of your call, lowering your risk to US$565. Meanwhile, the bulk of your money is still there for other opportunities, without the time, trouble, and added expense of converting it first back into dollars.

There are two final call option benefits. First, you do not need to exercise your option in order to take profits or cut losses; simply sell it before expiry, just like a stock option contract. Second, there are numerous strategies allowing you to customize your risk/reward, sometimes starting at just a few hundred dollars.

Of course, prices will have changed by the time you read this column, but you can take the lessons learned from this example and apply them to any currency option contract, including: the Australian dollar, Brazilian real, British pound, Canadian dollar, French franc, German mark, the Euro, Japanese yen, Mexican peso, New Zealand dollar, Russian ruble, South African rand, and U.S. Dollar Index.

How to Get Started

You can't trade these FX options through your stockbroker as they are listed on commodity futures exchanges. Therefore, you need a separate futures account. If you do not have a futures account, or experienced FX futures broker, one broker familiar with this strategy is Sue Rutsen at Fox Inc. in Chicago. U.S. WATS: 1 (800) 345-7026. Tel.: +1 (312) 341-7494. Sue and her team have been trading FX options since 1982. If you mention that you are a member of the Sovereign Society, Sue will send you the popular *IPS Short Course In Futures and Options* (a US$14.95 bookstore value) free.

No-Risk Deals

by Gary Scott, *Borrow Low—Deposit High*, 1998

A unique offshore investment in which a bank will link your deposit to one or more stock exchange indexes. If the index falls, you still get back your initial investment—if it rises, you can get up to 90 percent of the rise! All with zero risk!

Once you understand how to invest in many types of investments through your private bank, you can begin to increase safety and profit potential by using a "no-risk" discipline.

Many investors are not happy investing just in equities. Investors who find shares too volatile or lacking sufficient income may want to reduce their portfolio's risk (yet maintain the portfolio yield) by having a "barbell" portfolio, which combines equities and bonds or cash. This approach brings maximum return and lowers volatility. It is called a "barbell" approach because the cash or bonds and equities each represent the opposite ends of the risk-return factor in investing.

In a barbell, investors put one portion of their portfolio (usually a small part) in a portfolio they consider aggressive, volatile or high-risk, such as equities. They place the other part in a portfolio they consider extremely safe, such as interest-bearing deposits, money market funds, short-term bonds or managed currency funds.

A typical portfolio could have 70 percent cash or short-term bonds (for maximum safety), and 30 percent higher risk bonds and equities (for growth).

No-Risk Deals

A growing number of banks, such as Jyske Bank, are beginning to offer special barbell portfolios that they call "no-risk deals." These deals guarantee capital, usually over a two-year period, plus provide considerable capital gains potential as well.

What the bank does is invest a portion of the capital in discounted bonds, so in two years the full capital invested will be available. Then the bank invests the difference in options on the stock exchange index chosen. I tried investing in a no-risk British stock account at Jyske Bank and made 38 percent profit over two years! Yet the bank guaranteed I would not lose a penny of capital. My entire risk was the potential interest of my investment over two years.

I have since rolled my capital and profit (all of which is now guaranteed) into Jyske's next Stock Index Account which invested in the Japanese Stock Index. This deal guarantees the return of my initial investment and I get about 90 percent of any rise in the Japanese index. I am risking only the interest my investments otherwise earn. I concluded Japan was in a mess and shares were selling at really low prices. My bet was that Japan would sort out its mess within the next two years. If so, and if Japan's stock market responds accordingly, I'll profit again.

More important than these Jyske deals (or others I introduce here) is the principle involved! During the next 15 years, it makes sense for us to build our own portfolio using a no-risk strategy. We can do this through the safest investments of all—discounted bonds, treasury bills and banker's acceptances.

Discounted bonds, treasury bills and banker's acceptances are promises to pay a guaranteed amount of money at some time in the future. Purchased at a discount, these are generally favored debts in any instance of liquidation. These include zero coupon bonds, short-term government bonds and treasury bills, as well as banker's acceptances.

These are even safer investments if held at a safe overseas bank in a custodian account. Investments held in custodian accounts are not lost even if a bank goes broke! Thus holding investments in this way gives discipline, asset protection, and investment protection. And even if the bank where you held such investments went broke and the institution behind the investment went broke, you would still have a good chance of getting all your money back.

The way these investments work is simple. For example, a two-year, zero coupon bond yielding in the six percent range sells for about US$880. Invest US$880. In two years you get US$1,000.

A super-safe strategy to use in your private bank account for those who want to maximize safety and profit potential is to discipline yourself to investing only future earnings of capital on risky investments. For example, let's say you wanted to invest $10,000 for two years in a high-risk investment (such as South Korean equities). You would invest $90,000 in a two-year, zero coupon bond (AAA rated) which is guaranteed to be worth $100,000 in two years. Then invest $10,000 in the South Korean equities. Even if you lose your $10,000 in Korea, your discipline will assure in two years you still have your original capital.

This is an incredibly simple strategy which creates a tight self-imposed discipline. You allow yourself to invest in high-potential, high-risk deals, but also assure yourself you won't get wiped out. This type of discipline also gives you a great deal of emotional staying power.

You can use this strategy in the short or longer term by simply varying the length of maturity of the discounted bond or paper. Ranges vary from three months to years. To understand this better, ask your investment advisor or banker to tell you more about discount or zero coupon bonds, discounted bills and banker's acceptances.

More and more private banks will begin to offer this type of transaction. Listed below is another company (a subsidiary of a bank) with no-risk deals.

We should always consider the costs of opportunity, so no-risk deals are really just mental exercises. (Yet, so too are all investment disciplines!) For many, no-risk deals are really good disciplines.

They lock away money into good but high-risk investments we would otherwise skip if we had to buy them with a full-risk mentality.

Contacts

Midland Offshore, PO Box 26, 28-34 Hill Street, St. Helier, Jersey JE4 8NR, Channel Islands, U.K. **Tel:** +44 1534 616333. **Fax:** +44 1534 616222. This company (which should be checked closely) is not a bank, but advertises itself as a member of the Hong Kong Shanghai Bank Group, which is one of the largest banks in the world. This firm offers two no-risk deals:

1. *Anglo American Security Plus Plan* links your returns to the U.K. and U.S. stock market for three to five years. This investment guarantees the return of your capital plus potential to earn up to a flat rate of 12 percent per annum and includes a minimum flat rate of 3.6 percent per annum.

2. *European Growth Plan* links your investment for three and one-half years and could return up to 17 percent per annum, plus guarantees the return of your capital. The minimum investment in each plan is US$5,000.

Bond Mutual Funds

by Gary Scott, *Borrow Low—Deposit High*, 1998

Here you learn about the special offshore bond mutual funds that invest in multiple currencies and a variety of bond issues and maturities. Some of these ultra-safe funds have delivered up to 76 percent return in the past five years. Some may give you tax-deferral benefits, even if you are an American!

Another way to invest in bonds, especially for smaller accounts, is to use bond mutual funds. There are several types of funds your private bank can buy for you. The first type of fund is a closed-end fund traded on the New York Stock Exchange. Listed below is a sample of such funds.

		Performance		
Name	Fund Manager	1 Yr.	3 Yrs.	5 Yrs.
Aberdeen High Income Fund	Aberdeen Group	+54.5%	+83.7%	-
Shires Income Fund	Glasgow Group	+45.3%	+90.4%	+129.1%
Henderson High Income	Hendinvest	+35.8%	+65.6%	+103.6%
Glasgow Income	Glasgow Group	+33.3%	+69.2%	+114.8%
Investors Cap Pkg Fund	Ivory & Sime	+28.4%	+77.0%	+ 72.2%
Guinness Flight Fund	Guinness Flight	+27.3%	-	-
Fleming Income & Capital	Fleming Invest	+26.8%	+69.7%	+ 87.2%

Emerging Bond Funds

The above funds invest mainly in major markets, but there are also New York-traded emerging market bond funds. A few are listed below:

- *Templeton Emerging Market Fund*: Currently holds bonds issued by governments of Mexico, Venezuela, Ecuador, Brazil, Argentina and Russia. This fund returned 10.9 percent over the past year and 20.1 percent since inception in 1993.

- *Scudder High Income Fund*: Currently holds bonds of Venezuela, Argentina, Brazil, Panama and Jamaica and rose 22.2 percent last year and 71.4 percent since inception July 1992.

- *Morgan Stanley Emerging Market Fund*: Currently holds bonds from Argentina, Mexico, Ecuador, Brazil, Venezuela, Jamaica and Russia and rose 30.4 percent last year and 75.8 percent since July 1993.

These emerging market funds can put extra zip in your portfolio, but of course add risk.

There are also investment trusts, similar closed-end mutual funds that trade on the London Stock Exchange.

There are also numerous overseas open-end bond mutual funds which fall into several categories. General bond funds invest in one currency in a variety of issues and maturities. Global bond funds invest in a variety of issues and maturities in many currencies.

Listed below are just a few of many overseas bond funds. These examples show single currency funds, regional funds and global funds. You will gain much by contacting these funds to see what they offer, but before choosing any bond, managed currency, money market or equity fund, discuss with your banker which funds best suit your needs and which funds are available from your banker (if your banker will buy funds).

- *Aetna Australian Dollar Bond Fund*, 21 Ave Du La Liberte, L-1931, Luxembourg. **Tel.:** +352 29 54 94 355. **Fax:** +352 29 54 94 20. This is a single currency fund. Aetna offers many different bond funds.

- *SBC EM Ec Portfolio Latin America Bonds Fund*, SBC, PO Box 2, 26 Route d'Arlon, L-2012, Luxembourg. **Tel.:** +352 451211. This is a Latin American regional bond fund. SBC offers many different bond funds.

- *Guinness Flight Asian Currency Bond Fund*, Guinness Flight House, PO Box 250, La Plaiderie, St. Peter Port, Guernsey GY1 3QH, U.K. **Tel.:** +44 1481 712 176. **Fax.:** +44 1481 712 065.

- *Invesco PS Global Fund*, PO Box 271, Invesco House, Grenville Street, St. Helier, Jersey, JE4 8TD, U.K. **Tel.:** +44 1534 814 000. **Fax.:** +44 1534 814 100.

If you plan to buy mutual funds through your overseas bank there are many factors to consider and discuss with your banker and your other tax professionals.

First, check the tax consequences with your local tax professionals. Some mutual funds create different types of tax liability than others. For example, the Guinness Flight Currency Fund shown above is an offshore open-end fund. However, Guinness Flight also has a closed-end U.S.-registered fund traded on the New York Stock Exchange. An open-end Guernsey-managed fund could be considered a personal foreign investment company (PFIC) fund under U.S. tax law. This could create some tax deferrals in the short term, but extra tax and interest upon sale of the fund. However the New York-traded fund would not be considered a PFIC.

Generally you will have at least three types of funds to choose for any investment idea you might have, a New York- and London-traded closed-end, and an offshore open-end fund. Check with a professional in your tax jurisdiction to see which fund is best for you.

Second, check the fees. Some mutual funds are no load, others charge up to six percent initially when you buy. Some funds charge one percent per annum, others more. Remember your bank will also charge you a fee to hold the funds, plus may even charge you to buy the funds.

Third, ask about liquidity. Many funds trade only once per week and can be slow in liquidating. Overseas mutual funds generally cannot be bought or sold as quickly as closed end stock exchange mutual funds. I have seen examples of two week delays from the time of placing an order until monies are received from open-end funds.

Fourth, can and will your bank buy the fund? Some banks won't buy any mutual funds for clients (or for clients who live in certain countries). Other banks won't buy open-end offshore funds but will buy closed-end funds if they are traded on a stock exchange. Other banks have their own in-house funds, managed by a subsidiary of the bank, which they offer for their customers. Still other banks have a list of funds which they are prepared to buy for their customers.

Managed Currency Funds

by Gary Scott, *Borrow Low—Deposit High*, 1998

Here is the easiest and most cost-effective way to invest in a basket of currencies with very little risk—yet with great potential for high returns.

If your bank does not have an extensive currency management capability, you may instead gain the same results with managed currency funds. These funds invest in very safe, top quality, short-term monetary instruments, usually for the purpose of conserving and increasing capital. The managers of these funds try to pick currencies which pay high interest rates and are likely to rise in value.

There are three types of managed currency funds, some more conservative than others. There are highly leveraged funds which are speculative and not conservative at all. There are also lightly leveraged funds that are not as safe as those that do not use leverage. There are also diversified funds which focus on trying to attain diversification to reduce volatility, while other funds place emphasis on weighting the portfolio towards growth.

To give an example, let's compare three managed currency funds, the Guinness Flight IF Managed Currency Fund, JF Managed Currency Fund and Rothschild Five Arrows Managed International Currency Fund.

The JF Fund, which invests more for growth, can be lightly leveraged (10 percent of fund) and is slightly riskier than the other two funds. In one performance survey, this fund was up 12.63 percent (while the non-leveraged diversified type funds were up only three and four percent). This excellent performance was obtained because at the time of the survey, the fund held a large part of its portfolio in high-yielding, fast-rising British pounds. Sixty percent of the portfolio was in pounds sterling. The portfolio also had contained 20 percent yen.

The more conservative, broadly diversified Guinness Flight and Rothschild Funds rose 4.34 percent and 3.03 percent over the year, suffering in dollar-adjusted performance because of the U.S. dollar's appreciation. These funds were broadly diversified and hence all the non-dollar currencies which they held were dropping compared to the dollar.

Listed below are managed currency funds I recommend:

- *AIB US$ Managed Currency Fund*, Michael O'Hara, PO Box 2751, AIB International Center, IFSC, Dublin 1, Ireland. **Tel.:** +353 1 874 0777. **Fax:** +353 1 874 3050.

- *AIB Grofund ECU Managed Currency*, AIB Investment Managers, Percy Place, Dublin 4, Ireland. **Tel.:** +353 1 661 7077. **Fax:** +353 1 661 7038.

- *Century L Pound Sterling Managed Fund*, Century Life International, Albert House, South Esplanade, St. Peter Port, Guernsey GY1 1AP, U.K. **Tel.:** +44 1481 727066. **Fax:** +44 1481 724468.

- *Guinness Flight IF Managed Currency Fund*, Guinness Flight House, PO Box 250, La Plaiderie, St. Peter Port, Guernsey GY1 3QH, U.K. **Tel.:** +44 1481 712176. **Fax:** +44 1481 712065.

- *JF Managed Currency Fund*, Fleming Fund Management, 6 route de Treves, Senningerberg L-2633, R.C. Luxembourg B27900. **Tel.:** +352 3410 3050. **Fax:** +352 3410 2217.

- *Hambro Emma Continental European Fund*, PO Box 225, Barfield House, St. Julian's Avenue, St. Peter Port, Guernsey, GY1 3QL, U.K. **Tel.:** +44 1481 715454. **Fax:** +44 1481 710285.

- *Mercury MMT Sterling Managed*, Grenville Street, St. Helier, Jersey, JE4 8RL, U.K. **Tel.:** +44 1534 600600. **Fax:** +44 1534 600687.

- *Skaniford Dollar Currency*, Skandia SICAV, % BIL, 2 Boulevard Royal, L-2449, Luxembourg. **Tel.:** +352 45901. **Fax:**+352 4590 2010.

Because the investment priorities of managed currency funds vary to such a degree, be sure to review the charter and the portfolio of any such fund before you buy. If you want a conservative investment, choose a diversified, non-leveraged fund.

Many overseas mutual fund managers will not deal directly with residents of the U.S., Canada or U.K. because of securities laws in these countries. Buying such funds through overseas banks is a perfect way to hold them. Some banks will buy mutual funds for clients, others will not. The only way to know is to ask.

Borrow Low, Invest High

By Thomas Fischer, *The Sovereign Individual*, 2002

One way to profit from currency fluctuations is to borrow funds in a currency that is falling and invest the proceeds in an appreciating currency. This strategy is often referred to as a "multi-currency sandwich." Current conditions in the currency markets make two such trades attractive.

Overseas private banks commonly lend money in a choice of major currencies to clients who have assets held by the bank. Jyske Bank is one such institution. Jyske's Invest-Loan program offers the opportunity to leverage your deposit up to four times depending on the securities you purchase. You benefit from the difference between the higher returns on the leveraged investment and the lower cost of borrowing. Such leverage provides an opportunity for higher than normal investment returns. Switching between currencies and securities can occur with a single telephone call and you can exit from the program whenever you wish.

Borrow Low...

What are the appropriate currencies to use for such a trade?

Several factors indicate that the Japanese yen is an appropriate lending currency as it is expected to continue to weaken in the longer term: China's acceptance in the World Trade Organization and impressive growth threatens Japan's status as the regional economic superpower. Japan has accused China of pursuing a cheap currency policy to protect its exports and may "allow" the U.S. dollar-yen exchange rate to rise to 160.

Lower credit ratings of Japanese government bonds may encourage foreign investors to sell Japanese bonds, further weakening the yen. It is rumored that 70% of Japanese companies and financial institutions actually had a negative share capital if their assets were valued at market value. If proven true, 40 years of Japanese pension contributions have disappeared.

Japanese decision-makers hope that an upturn in the U.S. economy will help pull the economy out of the mire, strengthening the yen in the short and medium term. This situation could lead to losses in this recommended trade, so we would recommend unwinding it if sustained growth in the U.S. economy resumes. In the long term, an appreciating yen may make things worse, because necessary structural changes will then be canceled or postponed. It is therefore unlikely that the yen will continue to strengthen in the longer term.

Another appropriate lending currency may be the Swiss franc. While the franc has for decades been viewed as a "safe-haven" currency, the Swiss National Bank is now warning of a too strong franc, and recently reduced interest rates accordingly. We have seen a move towards the Norwegian kroner as a safe-haven currency as Norway is a politically stable and neutral country with huge oil income. This development and an increasingly shaky Swiss economy may lead to a decline in the Swiss franc.

We currently recommend a 50% position in Japanese yen and 50% in Swiss francs as lending currencies for multi-currency sandwich investments. When/if the yen or franc strengthens this should be a selling opportunity. Investors can, however, switch between any loan currency and split between currencies at any time.

...Invest High

What investments are attractive for the proceeds of yen or Swiss franc loans? Investors with the U.S. dollar as their base currency will benefit if they invest in euro denominated bonds. We recommend bonds with short-term duration such as Ericsson maturing in July 2004 (yielding 7.25%) and ABB maturing in December 2003 (yielding 7.40%).

Investors will obtain further gains if the dollar continues its slide against the euro, as is expected. A technical indicator that the dollar may weaken further is that its trading range after September 11, 2001 has been breached to the downside. The last defense for the dollar appears to be 115 in J. P. Morgans USD index. This index is currently above 117. If the 115 level is breached, it will render a further 10% weakening of the dollar likely.

Another attractive investment for loans in yen or Swiss franc are Australian bonds. Australia avoided the global economic slowdown thanks to swift monetary easings and to the weakness of the currency. Consumer confidence is robust and at its highest level for three years. However, inflation in Australia is above the Reserve Bank of Australia's (RBA's) inflation target of 2%-3%. RBA is therefore likely to raise interest rates in the near future. This will make the Australian dollar more attractive. The currency will also be buoyed up if the world economy should pick up, which will increase demand for Australia's commodities.

Due to the rising inflation, long bond yields have risen. We therefore recommend short-term Australian bonds, because such an investment will mainly be currency-driven. We recommend the Transco bond (maturing 2008) issued in Australian dollars and yielding 7.15%. Transco is a natural-gas transportation and storage business of Lattice group Plc (U.K.). The company has a monopoly on gas distribution in the United Kingdom. The rating is A2/A with a stable outlook from all rating agencies.

The cost of entering Jyske's Invest-Loan program is 1% of the loan (applicable for up to five years, and which can be extended for a further five years for a modest fee). Both brokerage and safe custody fees are highly competitive. Investors can open either personal, corporate or trust accounts with a minimum of US$30,000 and the necessary documentation. All advice from the investor's Jyske Bank personal investment adviser concerning possible market developments is free of charge and non-commissioned.

(For more information, contact Thomas Fischer, Manager, International Client Relations. Tel.: +(45) 33 787 812. Fax: +(45) 33 787 833. E-mail: fischer@jyskebank.dk Link: www.jbpb.com. **Ed. Note:** *The multi-currency sandwich strategy is only appropriate for aggressive investors, as the leveraged gains possible can become leveraged losses if the currency you have borrowed against begins to rise in value.)*

Gold Accumulation Accounts
by William T. McCord, *How to Use Swiss Banks for Safety, Privacy & Global Profit,* 1998

Here is the conservative, yet ingenious, Swiss way to speculate in gold. You can make a profit even when the price of gold doesn't move!

Many investors still feel it is important to hold gold in their portfolios, and for good reason. Unlike real estate, gold is immediately redeemable at current market prices. Unlike stocks, the price of gold cannot be mismanaged. Unlike bonds, gold cannot default. And unlike almost all of the world's currencies, the value of gold cannot be inflated away. Since the reign of the ancient Egyptian emperors, gold has always been highly valued as the perfect asset in times of uncertainty. During 1998, the price of gold per ounce fell to a 12-year low, so gold may be a bargain. And what better place to accumulate a position in gold than in Switzerland, the land of the gold-backed franc?

Those who speculate in gold, buying and selling it like any other security, engage in a dangerous game. The smart investor who buys gold, holds it as a hedge against unforeseen calamities. The real value of gold lies not in its speculative value, but in the long-term peace of mind it offers. Regardless of economic or political disaster, the worldwide purchasing power of gold has endured throughout the ages.

Many Swiss banks have gold accumulation programs which allow you to use a dollar cost averaging approach to make your purchases. These programs follow the same systematic buying technique used by investors to purchase mutual funds. You buy a fixed dollar amount of gold the same time every month or each quarter. You will make some of your purchases at market highs and some at market lows, but over time you will buy more gold at low prices than high ones. This is a wonderful way to systematically purchase gold without trying to beat the gold market. The chart below shows how purchasing gold through a dollar cost averaging program works.

Date of Quarterly Purchase	Investment	Price of Gold Per Ounce	# of Ounces Purchased
Jan. Yr 1	$5,000	$395.00	12.658
Apr. Yr 1	$5,000	$360.00	13.889
Jul. Yr 1	$5,000	$320.00	15.625
Oct. Yr 1	$5,000	$310.00	16.129
Jan. Yr 2	$5,000	$370.00	13.514
Apr. Yr 2	$5,000	$395.00	12.658
TOTALS:	**$ 30,000**	**$358.33 (avg. price)**	**84.473**

In this hypothetical example, you made six purchases of $5,000 each, exactly three months apart. Your final purchase at $395 per ounce in April of Year 2 was the same price as your initial purchase in January of Year 1. From the beginning of the 18-month purchase period to its end, the price of gold did not rise a penny. However, four of your purchases were made at prices below the $395 high. One purchase was made as low as $310 per ounce. Notice that the lower the price, the more ounces you purchased. You accumulated a total of 84.473 ounces of gold, which, valued at the last purchase price of $395, meant your gold was worth $33,367. Even though the price of gold did not rise over the 18-month period, you still made over $3,000 in profit, or a 7.5 percent average yearly rate of return. As you can see, dollar cost averaging can be a safe and effective way to buy a volatile security such as gold.

You can usually begin a gold accumulation program with as little as US$5,000 with US$2,500 in subsequent investments. You can increase, decrease, stop or re-start your systematic purchases any time you want. If you decide to liquidate your holdings, you can have the physical metal sent to you or you can redeem it in the currency of your choice. Your gold is completely liquid just like any other investment in your Swiss bank account. Most clients have their gold held in safe storage at their Swiss bank.

The Swiss live by a simple motto: "Be prudent, be patient, and be prepared." This is the role of gold in a well-diversified portfolio.

Swiss Franc Annuities

You can also own Swiss franc annuities in your bank account. Investors around the world seeking safety of capital, currency diversification and absolute privacy are buying Swiss franc annuities. Swiss annuities offer guaranteed interest rates and are usually denominated in Swiss francs although you can also own them in dollars and euros. Your annuity principal and interest are guaranteed by the insurance company which issues the annuity. Swiss insurance companies are among the oldest, largest and financially-sound insurers in the world.

In addition to the guarantee of principal and annual interest payments (approximately four percent at this time), Swiss annuities are tax-free in Switzerland. You never owe any Swiss tax on an annuity. Swiss annuities have rewarded American and British investors with stock market-like returns during the past 25 years, due to the strength of the Swiss franc against the dollar and the pound. For investors from both countries, a Swiss annuity has averaged approximately 10 percent per year since 1972 (four percent interest plus six percent currency appreciation). That's an unheard of return in a guaranteed investment.

Swiss annuities are the only investments expressly protected from creditors by Swiss statute. Under Swiss law, all life insurance policies including annuities are protected from the policy owner's creditors if the owner's spouse, children, grandchildren, or an irrevocable third party are named as the beneficiaries. The Swiss view life insurance proceeds as belonging to the owner's family, and as such protect the proceeds from claims by others. People in high liability professions, such as doctors, are the biggest purchasers of Swiss annuities because of the protection they offer from lawsuits.

A Swiss bank can arrange your purchase of a Swiss annuity. Most annuity owners keep the original annuity policy in safekeeping at the bank as added protection against potential lawsuits. You can request your bank to send you a copy. It's better to have the added safety of not being in possession of the policy, which you surrender to the insurance company upon liquidation. It may throw one more roadblock in the path of someone trying to sue you.

Low-Cost Asset Protection Through Swiss Annuities
By Marc-Andre Sola, *The Sovereign Individual*, June 2002

A Swiss insurance policy is one of the least costly ways to achieve almost instant asset protection. After only one year, no new claims may be made against the assets in the policy, and after five years, even existing creditors may not make a claim. What's more, you can name your spouse or descendants as revocable beneficiaries and still have asset protection. Even better, Swiss insurance policies designed as variable annuities can provide tax benefits for U.S. policyholders.

Other benefits of Swiss insurance policies include:

Swiss insurance contracts are covered by strict data and privacy protection rules. Except in the event of a criminal investigation as defined by Swiss law, neither the initial purchase of the policy, nor individual payments, nor interest or dividends earned, may be reported to anyone but the policyholder or beneficiaries.

Insurance companies in Switzerland do not report to any government–Swiss or foreign–if the policyholder is not resident in Switzerland.

Swiss insurance policies annuities are free from any Swiss tax. In particular, the 35% Swiss withholding tax on interest and dividends earned in Switzerland does not apply. The policyholder is obliged to report and pay taxes only if required under his or her domestic law.

Switzerland has the world's strongest insurance industry. There have been no failures of any Swiss insurance company in the 140-year history of the industry.

Opportunity for currency diversification. Swiss insurance policies may be denominated in various currencies, including the Swiss franc, euro and U.S. dollar.

Swiss insurance policies have additional benefits for U.S. policyholders. These include:

No excise tax. Unlike foreign insurance policies from most other countries. Swiss insurance policies are not subject to a 1 percent U.S. excise tax. This is a provision of the new U.S.-Swiss tax treaty and applies to premiums paid by a U.S. citizen to an insurance company domiciled in Switzerland.

Income on Swiss variable annuities can be tax deferred. Unlike most other offshore investments, some Swiss variable annuities are designed to meet IRS requirements for tax-deferred growth. With these annuities, the internal buildup inside the policy is tax-free until the income is received.

No 31% withholding tax. Offshore banks maintaining U.S. custodial accounts with U.S. correspondent banks or brokers must identify their U.S. customers to the IRS, or have all income and gross sales proceeds derived from securities transactions subjected to a 31% withholding tax. Swiss insurance policies are not subject to these requirements, even if their underlying investments include U.S. securities.

Qualified for U.S. pension plans. Swiss annuities and endowments can be placed in many tax-sheltered plans, including Individual Retirement Accounts or corporate plans. A U.S. custodian can hold the annuity contract.

Tax-free exchanges. You may exchange tax-free a domestic insurance policy for a foreign insurance policy or a foreign insurance policy for another foreign insurance policy.

Some tax advisors take the position that foreign annuities need not be reported to the U.S. Treasury as a "foreign bank, securities or other financial account." But check with a qualified advisor before you take this position.

Offshore Variable Annuities May Grow Tax-Free

The term "annuity" is often misunderstood because it is used in so many different ways. Most often, it denotes arrangements where an insurance company agrees to make a series of payments to someone for the rest of their life in exchange for a single, fixed premium. For example, if you give an insurance company US$100,000 at age 65, they might agree to pay you an income of about US$700 a month for the rest of your life. That's a typical life income annuity.

Prior to receiving income, investors may wish to let interest and dividends inside the annuity accumulate. During the accumulation or deferment period, Swiss fixed annuities are comparable to certificates of deposit. An annuity contract may be of any duration. It can be for the lifetime of the annuitant or the joint lifetime of two annuitants. The contract may also provide for a guarantee of enough payments to at least equal the amount that was paid for the contract.

A *fixed annuity* is one where the insurance company guarantees to make payments of a fixed amount for an agreed upon term of years or for the lifetime of the annuitant or joint annuitants. Implicit in this arrangement is an assumed rate of interest the insurance company will pay based on the deposits made by the policy owner.

Offshore fixed annuities no longer provide tax deferral for U.S. persons. Nor do they permit you to have any influence over the selection of the underlying investments. However, under Swiss law, they offer the same asset protection advantages as any other insurance contract. They also have the lowest investment minimums of any Swiss insurance product (approximately US$20,000).

The guaranteed minimum return depends on the type of policy, the company issuing it and the currency in which the policy is denominated. A typical guaranteed "technical" rate is 2.5% for a policy denominated in Swiss francs. To this figure, an insurance company will add a "bonus" of 1.5%-2.5%, depending on the performance of the company and the selected currency.

In a *variable annuity*, some or all of the funds on deposit are professionally managed portfolios of stock and bonds selected according to the objectives of the purchaser. The investment income will vary depending on how well the underlying investments perform. The benefits paid vary with the performance of the investments. For a minimum investment of approximately US$50,000, Swiss variable annuities offer a combination of asset protection, a choice of asset allocation strategies based on your tolerance for risk and (for U.S. investors) tax deferral.

Swiss Annuities: Rock-Solid Asset Protection

Under Swiss law, asset protection applies to all life insurance policies as well as life insurance policies linked to mutual funds and derivatives. Annuities, fixed or variable, are treated as life insurance policies under Swiss law.

Asset protection with a Swiss life insurance policy is tied to the choice of beneficiaries and whether the assignment of beneficiaries is irrevocable. When a foreign investor (the "policy owner") purchases a Swiss insurance policy and designates his or her spouse and/or descendants as beneficiaries, the policy is protected by Swiss law against any debt collection procedures instituted by the creditors of the policy owner and is not included in any Swiss bankruptcy procedure.

Even when a foreign judgment or court order expressly decrees the seizure of the policy or its inclusion in the estate in bankruptcy, the policy may not be seized in Switzerland or included in the bankruptcy estate.

Protection is guaranteed in the event of the policy owner's bankruptcy because ownership is automatically transferred to the beneficiaries. Only the beneficiaries, as the new owners, can give instructions to the insurance company. It is important to make sure that the insurer knows about the foreign bankruptcy decree and that the beneficiaries inform the insurer of their succession. This protection applies whether the designation of the policy owner's spouse or descendants as beneficiaries is revocable or irrevocable. The policy owner may therefore revoke this designation prior to the expiration of the policy if at such time there are no threats from creditors. The same protection is also available to individuals or legal entities (such as trusts) named as beneficiaries that are not the spouse or descendants of the policy owner. However, the beneficiary designation must be irrevocable for asset protection to exist.

The only exception to these rules is if the purchase of the policy or the designation of the beneficiaries is determined by a Swiss court to be a fraudulent conveyance under Swiss law. This condition is fulfilled under the following circumstances:

(1) If the policy owner designated the beneficiaries less than one year before debt collection proceedings were initiated that eventually led to the policy owner's bankruptcy or the seizure of the policy owner's assets; or

(2) If the beneficiary was designated with the clear intent to damage creditors or to treat some creditors more favorably than others within five years of the date debt collection proceedings resulting in a bankruptcy decree or in the seizure of assets were initiated against the policyholder.

The creditors must prove not only the policy owner's intent to defraud but also that the beneficiary had knowledge of such intent. Clearly, these requirements cannot be met when the beneficiaries were designated when the policy owner was solvent and no creditors asserted any claims that could render the policy owner insolvent.

These conditions apply even if the debt collection or bankruptcy laws in the country where the debtor's assets are located or where the bankruptcy order issued does not afford such protection. Only the Swiss rules on fraudulent conveyance apply. Creditors cannot void beneficiary designations without a ruling to that effect by a Swiss court.

At the expiration of the insurance contract, the policy owner may collect the proceeds pursuant to the policy, extend the policy, or roll the proceeds over into a new policy. If at expiration, a creditor appears or the owner becomes insolvent, a new policy would not be protected whereas an extended policy would.

The asset protection features of a Swiss annuity are most effective if the Swiss insurance company maintains possession of the policy. Otherwise, a creditor could seize the policy in accordance with local collection and bankruptcy rules.

Anti-Duress Provisions of Swiss Insurance Contracts

A foreign court may order a policy owner under its jurisdiction to revoke a beneficiary designation and include assets in a Swiss insurance policy in a foreign bankruptcy estate. To comply with such an order, the policy owner must inform the insurer that he or she revokes the prior beneficiary designation. In this situation, a Swiss insurance company is under no obligation to comply with the policy owner's request:

(1) in an irrevocable designation of a beneficiary third party, as this would contradict the irrevocability of the designation;

(2) in a revocable designation of the spouse or descendants as beneficiaries, as such beneficiaries automatically succeed into the rights and obligations arising from the insurance contract the moment the policy owner is declared bankrupt. (The spouse or descendants must inform the insurer accordingly.) The only exception is if these individuals expressly object to such succession; or

(3) if the insurance company concludes that the instruction received does not express the policy owner's true intent and was forced upon him or her by a foreign court.

These anti-duress provisions are similar to those found in some offshore trusts, and are available in all Swiss insurance policies.

Swiss annuities offer a plethora of benefits, including strong asset protection. However, to obtain asset protection from them, you must purchase them before a creditor makes a claim against you. You can't buy fire insurance when you smell smoke!

Swiss & Liechtenstein Insurance Investments:
Privacy, Asset Protection, Tax Deferral & More!
By Mark Sola, *The Sovereign Individual*, January 2004

Swiss and Liechtenstein insurance investments are unique in the offshore world. They offer near-ultimate privacy, safety and asset protection in a very non-controversial investment.

Privacy and discretion is the backbone of the Swiss financial industry. It is a criminal offense to divulge information on bank account and insurance policy holders, punishable by fines and in aggravated cases, by imprisonment. The only exceptions are in a criminal investigation.

Liechtenstein's secrecy laws are even stricter.

Swiss and Liechtenstein insurance investments are also safe. There has never been a failure of an insurance company in Switzerland or Liechtenstein in the 140-year history of the industry. Asset protection in a Swiss or Liechtenstein insurance policy is guaranteed, without expensive and complex structures. When you purchase an insurance policy in either jurisdiction and designate your spouse as the beneficiary, or another person as an irrevocable beneficiary, the policy is protected against any debt collection procedures instituted by your creditors.

It is important you establish the policy before bankruptcy or other collection procedures have commenced. Swiss or Liechtenstein fraudulent conveyance laws may apply if the policy was established within one year before bankruptcy or seizure, or if the policy was established with the intent to damage creditors.

The asset protection provisions of these laws don't apply in the event of fraudulent conveyance, or if beneficiaries aren't specified in the way I just described. In that case, a foreign judgment can be enforced against the contract. However, creditors must file a claim in a Swiss court, following Swiss legal procedures. This is an expensive undertaking for any litigant. Making a claim against a Liechtenstein insurance contract is even more difficult because Liechtenstein does not enforce foreign judgments. In both countries, the courts generally enforce only actual damages, not punitive damages.

Another advantage of Swiss and Liechtenstein insurance policies is that they are non-controversial. Purchasing a foreign insurance policy doesn't raise the same level of scrutiny as, e.g., forming an offshore trust. Plus, the reporting requirements for U.S. persons who purchase foreign insurance policies are practically non-existent.

An Insurance Policy for Almost Everyone

Three primary types of Swiss and Liechtenstein insurance policies are available to non-residents: fixed annuities; variable annuities; and portfolio bonds.

Fixed annuities are available for a minimum US$20,000 investment and may be purchased in U.S. dollars, euros or the Swiss franc. With some policies, you can also switch currencies after you buy. The policy earns guaranteed interest of approximately 2.5% per annum, plus dividends. In recent years, total returns have averaged about 3.5% per year, plus (in the case of the euro and Swiss franc) some impressive foreign currency gains versus the U.S. dollar.

Variable annuities. Swiss variable annuities, with a minimum investment of US$50,000, allow you to hold mutual funds within your insurance policy. You can choose conservative, balanced or aggressive management of your portfolio. Unlike a fixed annuity, the value of a variable annuity is not guaranteed.

Portfolio bonds. The Liechtenstein portfolio bond, with a minimum investment of US$200,000, provides an insurance "wrapper" around nearly any investment, giving you near-instant asset protection for those funds. The Liechtenstein insurance company opens an account in its name with a bank of your choice. You maintain full control of your assets or you may designate a financial adviser to manage the investments within the bond.

For More Information

For more information on Swiss and Liechtenstein insurance policies, contact me c/o NMG International Financial Services, Ltd., Goethestrasse 228001 Zürich, Switzerland. Tel.: +(41) 1 266 21 41. Fax: +(41) 1 266 21 49. E-mail: marcsola@nmg-ifs.com. Link: www.nmg-ifs.com.

(Marc-André Sola is an attorney and a member of The Sovereign Society Council of Experts. An expert on the insurance laws of Switzerland and Liechtenstein, Mr. Sola is a managing partner of NMG International Financial Services, Ltd., a subsidiary of the worldwide NMG Group.)

You Don't Need to Be Rich to Invest Offshore: Here's Proof!

By Mark Nestmann, *The Sovereign Individual*, April 2004

One of the most common questions we receive from Sovereign Society members is, "I'm a small investor…can I legally buy the types of offshore investments you recommend?"

The answer is a resounding yes. Here are a few ideas:

1. Offshore funds. There are over 100,000 offshore funds, some with investment minimums as low as US$5,000. A great example is GAM Diversity, a low-risk hedge fund that has gained an average of 13% per annum since 1989, with 50% less standard deviation, or risk, than its benchmark index (MSCI World Index). While GAM Diversity is now closed to new investment, GAM Diversity III), managed in the same manner, is still available. Link: www.gam.com.

(Note U.S. citizens or residents generally can't purchase offshore funds directly. We recommend that you buy them through an offshore bank, such as The Sovereign Society's Offshore Convenient Account partners in Denmark or Austria. Due to tax considerations, we also recommend that you purchase them through a tax-deferred vehicle such as a retirement plan.)

* Jyske Bank, Copenhagen, Denmark. Contact: Thomas Fischer. Tel.: +45 (33) 787-812. Fax: +45 (33) 787-833. E-mail: fischer@jyskebank.dk. Link: www.jbpb.com (minimum account size for offshore funds: US$14,000).

* Anglo Irish Bank (Austria) AG, Vienna, Austria. Tel.: +(43) 1 406-6161. Fax: +(43) 1 405-8142. E-mail: welcome.desk@angloirishbank.at. Link: www.angloirishbank.at (minimum account size for offshore funds: US$100,000).

2. Foreign currency CDs. You can also use your Offshore Convenient Account to purchase

CDs in nearly a dozen different currencies for a minimum investment of only US$5,000. And foreign currency diversification can be a very smart investment. For instance, if you purchased a US$5,000 British pound CD in on Jan. 1, 2003, one year later, it was worth US$5,700, including interest. If you purchased a euro CD, you did even better, with your CD worth US$6,100, for a total return of 22%. (Note: The Sovereign Society no longer recommends euro CDs, although we still like the British pound and Canadian and Australian dollars.)

Foreign currency CDs are available from Anglo Irish Bank (Austria) for a minimum investment of US$5,000 (minimum account size for CDs: US$25,000). They are available from Jyske Bank for a minimum investment of $14,000 (US$17,600) (minimum account size for CDs: $14,000).

3. Swiss annuities. For only US$20,000, you can purchase one of the safest annuities in the world—one from Switzerland. You obtain a modest income, but the real attraction of a Swiss annuity is virtually ironclad protection from creditors. If you're looking to create an offshore "nest egg" that no one can touch, a Swiss annuity is one of the best investments you can consider.

Swiss annuities are available through Sovereign Society Council of Experts member Marc-André Sola. Contact: NMG International Financial Services, Ltd. Tel.: +(41) 1 266-2141. Fax: +(41) 1 266-2149. E-mail: marcsola@nmg-ifs.com. Link: www.nmg-ifs.com. They are also available through Council of Experts member Dr. Erich Stoeger's company, Euraxxess AG in Ebmatingen/Zurich, Switzerland. Contact: Mrs. Bernarda Pesantez. Tel. +(41) 1 980-4281. Fax: +(41) 1 980 4255. E-mail: info@euraxxess.com. Link: www.euraxxess.com.

4. Offshore precious metals ownership. For only US$10,000, you can purchase a Perth Mint Certificate (PMC), a depository receipt acknowledging your ownership of gold, silver, platinum or palladium bars or coins stored in a government-guaranteed depository in Western Australia. This is the only government guaranteed precious metals accumulation program in the world.

Like foreign currencies, precious metals have been smart investments in recent years. For instance, if you purchased a US$10,000 gold PMC on Jan. 1, 2003, it would have been worth US$12,100 by year-end—a 21.1% gain.

For more information on PMCs, see www.perthmint.com.au/gc/depository/depository_layout2.asp?url=1. Two members of The Sovereign Society's Council of Experts are approved dealers for PMCs. Michael Checkan is president of Asset Strategies International, Inc., in Rockville, Md. Link: www.assetstrategies.com. Dr. Erich Stoeger is Chairman of EurAxxess, AG, in Switzerland. Link: www.euraxxess.com.

Of course, if you have more than US$20,000 to invest offshore, you can enjoy a larger number of investment options, including tax deferred variable annuities (minimum US$50,000), portfolio management (minimum US$250,000 and up), etc. But you don't need this much to get started…so what are you waiting for?

Part Three—The Six Best Countries to Do Business

Barbados: A Tropical Island Where Government Pays Your Rent

The Business Havens Report, 1998

Here you learn how to set up a tax-free business on a tropical island where labor is cheap—60 percent less costly than in the U.S.—and where the government will pay your rent!

Barbados is a beautiful Caribbean island, a tropical paradise. It is the most easterly of the Caribbean islands, enjoying warm weather all year round. A popular tourist destination, the island attracts many thousands of tourists every year.

The local economy is based on sugar, tourism, light manufacturing, data processing, and offshore business. The population of 252,000 speaks English and is 98 percent literate. A significant portion of the workforce is trained in the use of computers, data processing and various types of factory machinery. It is an excellent business haven, offering especially strong incentives for the establishment of new business operations that include information and financial services or manufacturing.

The island, independent since 1966, has a stable, pro-private enterprise government committed to foreign investment. Barbados offers employers a skilled, English-speaking workforce with significantly lower wages than in the United States and Canada.

Barbados is a modern nation, with satellite communications, strong international air and sea connections to major cities across the world and an extremely attractive package of business incentives. The government especially seeks those considering corporate relocation or establishing new enterprises on the island. Doing business in Barbados can be both enjoyable and profitable. Bureaucratic red tape and government intervention in the economy are minimal.

During the past 40 years, the Barbadian economy has diversified, and attained an impressive per capita income, while maintaining low inflation and low debt. For three centuries British colonial administrators governed, building traditions that produced a vigorous, cultured society and a committed democratic form of government. The people of Barbados, the Bajans, are well educated, confident, and sophisticated.

Barbados has an established reputation as peaceful and politically stable. It is a member of the United Nations, the Organization of American States, and the Caribbean Community (CARICOM). It has double taxation treaties with the U.S., Canada, the U.K., Finland, Sweden, Norway, and Switzerland.

The island is served by major international banks including the Royal Bank of Canada, Bank of Nova Scotia, Canadian Imperial Bank of Commerce, and Barclays Bank. Major local banks include Barbados National Bank, Caribbean Commercial Bank, and the Mutual Bank of the Caribbean.

Direct air services to North America and Europe are provided by British West Indian Airways (BWIA), American Airlines, Air Canada, and British Airways, among others. The modern harbor serves both passenger and cargo ships.

The legal system is basically English common law augmented by its own statutory modifications. Business incorporation generally follows the typical British pattern, but words that designate corporate status include "limited," "corporation," or "incorporated" (or their abbreviations). In that respect, they follow the U.S. model. Shares may be divided into classes with no par value, and with either unlimited or stated maximum capital. The number of directors is unrestricted, although companies frequently use one or more Barbadian directors to show management and control in Barbados.

Very Pro-Business

One of the major attractive features of Barbados is its liberal attitude towards the formation of international business companies (IBCs). The Ministry of Finance issues IBC licenses. IBCs incorporated in other nations can receive resident status in Barbados, provided they have no more than 10 percent ownership of assets or capital by residents of the CARICOM region. IBCs here tend to be international trading operations.

An IBC, shares of which form all or part of the assets of a foreign trust under the management of an offshore bank, is exempt from tax on its profits and gains. But its activities must be restricted exclusively to buying, selling, holding or managing securities. Otherwise, IBC tax rates vary from two and one-half percent on profits and gains up to US$5 million, to one percent of profits and gains exceeding US$15 million. Normal business deductions are taken into account in determining the net income on which the tax is assessed. IBCs are not subject to restrictions of the exchange control act.

The usual forms of trusts are also available in Barbados. Special provisions also exist for captive insurance companies, offshore banks, and offshore trust companies, all of which are subject to various licensing and supervision requirements.

The primary value in locating a business in Barbados, as compared to other nations with friendly IBC statutes, is a company's ability to qualify under the double taxation agreements Barbados has with many nations.

Business Incentives

Barbados has adopted significant laws to attract businesses. These laws guarantee tax freedom, exemptions, subsidies or even cash grants. The incentives listed below apply to certain businesses, but many other companies, because of the nature of their operations, may be eligible for incentives under several categories.

Corporate information services incentives:

- A low tax rate of 2.5 percent for data entry operations operating as international business companies.

- Exemptions from import tariffs on production-related equipment, such as computers.

- Cash grants for training.

- Subsidized space in 10 industrial parks.

- Possibility of accelerated depreciation allowance.

Manufacturing and export industry incentives:

- Full tax exemption on corporate profits for up to 10 years.

- After 10 years, a low tax rate of 2.5 percent thereafter.

- Full exemption from import duties on equipment parts, raw materials, and production machinery.

- Simplified customs procedures.

- Factory space in modern industrial parks available at significant subsidies.

- A worker training grant program that reimburses employers a maximum of 75 percent of wages paid to trainees during the first six months of a startup business's operation. Reimbursement is paid by the Barbados Investment & Development Corporation.

- Free coordination and speedy investment approval procedures. The Investment & Development Corporation offers liaison services with all other government agencies.

Incentives for international service companies with offshore operations:

- Full tax exemption for U.S. foreign sales corporations.

- Full tax exemption for captive insurance companies.

- A tax rate of one to 2.5 percent on profits of investment companies.

- A tax rate of 2.5 percent on international business firms and information technology service companies.

Incentives for foreign investors:

- A low maximum tax rate of 2.5 percent on profits.

- Exemptions from all local taxes on dividends, interest, fees, royalties, management fees, or other incomes paid to non-residents.

- Exemptions from local taxes on transfers of securities or assets, with the exception of real property located in Barbados or equipment used on the island.

- Exemptions from taxes and duties on machinery, computer equipment, raw materials, goods, and other articles imported into Barbados.

- Exemption from exchange controls.

- Exemption from public filing of financial statements.
- A guarantee of all the above benefits for a period of 15 years.

Contacts

- *Barbados Government*: www.bgis.gov.bb/.
- *Barbados Investment and Development Corp. Offices*:
    - 800 Second Ave, 17th Floor, New York, NY 10017-4709, U.S.A. **Tel.**: +1 212 867 6420. **Fax**: +1 212 682 5496.
    - 5160 Yonge St, Suite 1800, North York, Ontario, Canada M2N 6L9. **Tel.**: +1 416 512 0700, **Fax**: +1 416 512 6580.
    - Princess Alice Highway, Bridgetown, Barbados, West Indies. **Tel.**: +1 809 427 5350. **Fax**: +1 809 426 7802.
- *Barbados Government Information Service*, Bay Street, St. Michael, Barbados, West Indies. **Tel.**: +1 246 426 2232. **Fax:** +1 246 436 1317.
- *Chancery of Barbados*, 2144 Wyoming Avenue NW, Washington, DC 20008, U.S.A. **Tel.**: +1 202 939 9218 or 939 9219. **Fax**: +1 202 332 7467. Consulates: Miami, New York, Los Angeles.

Chile: Government Pays 75 Percent of Your Business Expenses
The Business Havens Report, 1998

Chile is a stable nation with the second oldest constitution in the western hemisphere (1833), where industrial growth is set to double in the next few years, and where the government welcomes foreign investors with inducements seen nowhere else.

Chile is a country where the future means economic opportunity. Already well known among international investors for its open trade policies, encouragement of investment and pro-business outlook, Chile is on the rise. The country's leaders see a growing economy as fundamental to better living standards and prosperity for all Chileans.

Outstanding investment opportunities abound in many sectors including: manufacturing, forestry products, software design and production, fisheries, farming, mining, paper production, infrastructure expansion, and energy production.

To encourage investment, Chile has a Foreign Investment Committee, the purpose of which is to simplify the process for interested investors and to provide information on financing, insurance and legal requirements. Government red tape has been cut to a minimum.

In an environment of certainty and ample guarantees, foreign investment has made a significant contribution to economic development. With an annual GDP growth rate of six percent in recent years (one of the world's highest rates), direct foreign investment accounted for an average of 20 percent of GDP. Exports generated by foreign investment projects currently represent 25 percent of the total. During 1993-1997, foreign investment contributed more than 7 percent of total new employment.

The success of the Chilean economy has greatly increased its competitiveness in world markets. The prestigious World Economic Forum ranked Chile fifth among emerging economies, ahead of South Korea. Given Chile's low risk (an A-rating from Standard & Poors), many local firms have issued significant amounts of financial instruments abroad, principally American Depository Receipts.

But Chile is much more—a stable, democratic country whose constitution of 1833 is the second oldest in the Americas. It is a land of spectacular scenery and vast natural resources, populated by an energetic people of various European, Asian and Indian ethnic groups, all of them proud to live in one of the world's most beautiful countries.

Geography

Chile is located in southwest South America. It shares a common border with Peru to the north, Bolivia and Argentina to the east. Its west coast meets the Pacific Ocean, and its southern-most point ends at the tip of the South American continent. Several islands and archipelagos are included in the country's overall area of 292,258 square miles (756,945 square kilometers). Chile is a narrow country, extending north and south along the west coast of South America. Its length is about 2,650 miles (4,270 kilometers) and its width is less than 110 miles (180 kilometers).

Economy

From half a century after 1900, Chile's economy centered on the mining and export of copper. In the late 1940s, government finally began to encourage industrial growth and diversification. Today Chile is one of the leading industrial nations in Latin America, and still remains one of the continents largest mineral producers.

Chile is absolutely committed to free trade. The country's leaders see economic success as dependent on international trade, and exports to more than 150 nations form a vital sector of Chile's economy. Along with raw materials such as mining and forest products, Chile's major exports include fresh fruits and juices, fish, delightful wines, soft drinks, liqueurs, vegetables, leather goods, furniture, clothing, footwear and textiles. Chile also exports various services, including engineering, advertising, design, printing and film animation as well as high-tech products such as computer software.

Below are economic sectors deserving of special mention.

- *Mining.* Deposits of copper are among the world's largest and Chile is one of the world's leading copper producers. Copper accounts for nearly 50 percent of total annual exports. Extensive oil and natural gas deposits, located in the Strait of Magellan and Tierra del Fuego, make natural energy production an important industry. Chile also has major deposits of iron ore, coal, sulfur, silver, gold, manganese, molybdenum, nitrates and iodine.

- *Manufacturing.* Much industry is related to refining and processing of minerals, forestry products and agricultural products, but Chile also is a leading producer of steel in South America. Other important products include cement, textiles, glass, chemicals, pulp and paper, electronic equipment and automobile assembly. Many manufacturing companies are investing in high-tech production methods to increase productivity.

- *Forestry.* With forests covering about 12 percent of the total land area, forestry products are a big part of Chile's economy. Lumber, wood pulp and paper are the mainstays, and the forestry industry is expected to double in size in the next decade.

- *Fishing.* Taking advantage of the rich waters of the Pacific, Chile's fishing industry is one of the most productive in South America. Sardines, salmon, swordfish, sea bass, mackerel, hake, lobster and anchovy are the species most sought. The catch is processed in Chilean plants for world-wide distribution. Chile is the world's second largest exporter of salmon, and its salmon, swordfish and sea bass appear on tables as far away as the US, Europe and Asia.

- *Agriculture.* Chile produces wheat, potatoes, corn, rice, sugar, beets, tomatoes and oats. Fruits and vegetables are exported worldwide. Fine wines, which have gained an excellent reputation, are produced in the Central Valley. Overall, farm products account for about 10 percent of Chile's GDP.

While these sectors offer superior investment opportunities, in recent years foreign funds have flowed into new infrastructure projects, especially electric generation and energy and the development of the natural gas deposits in Chile's southern cone.

Infrastructure

While Chile's infrastructure is considered to be adequate for the country, the government has encouraged infrastructure development and modernization. In 1994, for example, communication and transportation systems showed the highest rate of growth in the country's economy after the fishing industry.

Chile's telecommunications system is able to handle the needs of any modern company. Reliable telephone, computer data links, and facsimile lines are available to businesses located in any of the major cities. Remote areas in the far south and north, of course, offer more limited services. The country has a variety of communications media, including numerous periodicals, over 80 newspapers, over 350 radio stations, and several independent TV stations. Cable TV is available in some areas, particularly around Santiago.

During the last few years, Chile's roadways have been extended and improved substantially. The country has over 50,000 miles of roads (about 80,000 km). The investment in roadways has been in response to the significant overland cargo shipped to nearby trading partners, including Peru, Argentina, Brazil, Bolivia, Paraguay and Uruguay. With continued growth of the economy, it can be expected that further improvements in the country's roadways will be undertaken.

Like the roadways, both air and sea traffic have responded to the country's growing economy. Chile has several airports. The major international airport is located in Santiago, and several airports offer regular domestic service. Several American, European and Latin American airlines maintain direct flights from the U.S., Europe and Latin America cites. While some goods are transported by air, over 90 percent of exports are shipped by sea. To adequately handle this demand, shipping companies are investing in new ships and equipment and many seaports are modernizing their facilities and operations. Chile has numerous seaports, Valparaiso, Talcahuano, Tome, Antofagasta, San Antonio and Punta Arenas are the principal ones, from which businesses may ship their products.

Financial System

Chile's financial system is fully equipped with services investors and entrepreneurs require to establish a business. The Central Bank of Chile has extensive powers to regulate monetary policy. The country also has a state bank, commercial and development banks and financial services companies. The system is solid and dependable. During the recent Asian crisis and its continuing aftermath, skillful actions by the Central Bank prevented a run on short-term capital investments. These policies keep Chile free of the monetary troubles that have engulfed nations like Brazil, South Korea and Indonesia.

Incentives for Investment

Chile has put in place a stable legal framework based on principles such as non-discrimination, neutrality, openness and equal treatment of foreign investment. Investors have flocked to a nation where an environment of safety and certainty prevails.

Since 1974, the Foreign Investment Statute has been a principal attraction for foreign capital. This law created a framework of confidence and credibility in the international economic community so that today more than 60 countries have investments in Chile.

The Foreign Investment Statute offers a framework of special guarantees. The investor signs a legally binding investment contract with the government which cannot be changed except by mutual consent. This is a most important guarantee for the investor because the Government, even by a new law, cannot unilaterally modify the terms of the contract.

Free Zones

There has been increased emphasis on exports, plus the signing of a series of bilateral economic agreements, including trade and the promotion and protection of investments. Currently Chile has signed a total of 33 Investment Promotion and Protection Agreements, and others are being negotiated.

Despite Chile's robust economy, the government maintains various incentives to encourage foreign investment. The primary objective is attracting investment that will sustain economic growth. These incentives fall into three broad categories: Free Zones, Regional Incentives and Forestry Sector Incentives.

Free Zones: The towns of Iquique and Punta Arenas have operated as free zones since 1975. Free zone businesses include manufacturing, assembling, packing, display or deposit for transshipment. Imported goods remaining within a zone are not subject to any value added tax (VAT) or custom duties and zone companies are exempt from VAT on sales and services that occur within the zones.

Regional Incentives: Companies or investors with commercial operations in Chile's remote areas are eligible for exemptions on income tax, VAT, custom duties and similar charges. Special subsidies and fiscal bonuses may also be available.

Forestry Sector Incentives: Investors and companies with commercial activity within the forestry sector, and those that own land deemed suitable for forestry, may be eligible to benefit from specific incentives, including:

- A 75 percent subsidy of costs related to the planting of forests.
- Specific properties deemed suitable for forestry are exempt from real estate taxes.
- A 50 percent reduction in personal progressive income taxes on income gained from commercial forestry activities.

It should be noted that companies that contract with the state to exploit oil reserves and atomic materials also may be eligible for tax reductions and exemptions. The authority to grant such reductions or exemptions resides with Chile's president. Normally, the determination of any reductions or exemptions is done on an individual basis.

Living in Chile Today

In and around urban areas, Chile's culture is quite cosmopolitan. Santiago is a modern city by any standards, and its residents have access to all the wonders of our technological age. The city is filled with parks and wide streets, excellent hotels and fine restaurants that offer world class menus. During Chile's winter, from June to September, Santiago's people may wish to ski in the mountains to the east, or, throughout the year, they may visit marvelous beaches that lie an hour and a half to the west.

In the more isolated areas, the culture is dominated by a mixture of Spanish and Indian heritage. Life here is slower and centers around the land. It may be said that Chile has something to offer everyone. Indeed, many investors find that to be true in the country that has been called South America's land of opportunity.

Contacts

Chile is committed to attracting investment, and the country maintains several agencies whose purpose is to assist investors who may wish to learn more about the country's business opportunities.

- *ProChile* is the Chilean Trade Commission within the Ministry of Foreign Affairs, and has 35 commercial offices worldwide. The organization's role is to support and advance business by assisting development of exports, establishing international business relationships, fostering the exchange of goods and services, attracting foreign investments and forging strategic alliances.

  ProChile New York, 866 United Nations Plaza, Suite 302, New York, NY 10017, USA. **Tel.:** +1 212 207 3266. **Fax:** +1 212 207 3649.

- *National Chamber of Commerce of Chile*, Santa Lucia 302, Piso 4, Santiago, Chile. **Tel.:** +562 639 6639 or 639 7694. **Fax:** +562 638 0234.

- *U.S. Embassy Commercial Bureau*, Av Andres Bello 2800, Santiago, Chile. **Tel.:** +562 232

2600. **Fax:** +562 330 3710.

- *AMCHAM-Chilean-American Chamber of Commerce*, Av Americo Vespucio Sur 80, Piso 9, P O Box 82, Santiago 34, Chile. **Tel.:** +562 208 4140. **Fax:** +562 206 0911.

- *Consul General of Chile*, 801-2 Bloor St. West, Toronto, Ontario, Canada, M4W 3E2. **Tel.:** +1 (416) 924 0176. **Fax** +1 (416) 924 2627. **E-mail:** mskoknic@prochile.org.

United Arab Emirates: Tax-Free Business/Residency

By Mark Nestmann, *The Sovereign Individual*, January 2003

Continued pressure by high-tax countries and organizations such as the FATF/OECD against "traditional" tax havens has in many cases made them less attractive as bases for international business. But a few haven countries have successfully resisted these pressures.

One such jurisdiction is the United Arab Emirates (UAE). Due to its immense oil wealth, strategic location and substantial industrial and financial infrastructure, the UAE has successfully withstood the pressures imposed on haven countries to dismantle their tax advantages and eliminate financial secrecy.

The UAE imposes no taxes on sales, profits, incomes or capital gains on onshore or offshore companies. It has zero taxes because it does not need tax revenues. Oil royalties are more than sufficient to fund the country's budget.

There are no foreign exchange controls, quotas or trade barriers. The UAE dirham is freely convertible and is linked to the U.S. dollar. No revaluation has occurred since 1977. Tax-advantaged residency programs for foreigners and their families are also available. Foreigners may own 100% of UAE companies, which are ideal vehicles through which to pursue international business and commerce in a tax-free environment. And while anti-laundering laws are now in place, they have not ended the UAE's longstanding tradition of bank secrecy.

The UAE borders the Gulf of Oman and the Persian Gulf, between Oman and Saudi Arabia. Strategically placed, the UAE is of vital importance to Western countries. It is also a gateway to over 1.5 billion consumers in countries surrounding the Red Sea and the Persian Gulf.

According to Ken Irving, a UAE offshore services provider: "The UAE has a sophisticated and wealthy indigenous and expatriate population that demands the highest level of financial and commercial confidentiality. A long tradition of commercial secrecy exists. Since there are no personal or corporate taxes (except on foreign banks and oil producing companies) the government takes no interest in the pursuit of legitimate business.

The government has no tax information exchange agreements or mutual legal assistance treaties in effect with any other country. In the post OECD/FATF world, the UAE offers significant tax advantages along with substantial banking and commercial confidentiality. These advantages are not being challenged due to the geopolitical importance of the UAE to the West. The UAE is as good an ally as the West has in this region (U.S. aircraft carriers and warplanes are based here). Therefore the West leaves offshore activities alone. In contrast, few of the offshore jurisdictions under assault by the OECD/FATF have any strategic importance.

Substantial Infrastructure, Generous Incentives

Comprised of seven emirates, the most commercially developed of which is Dubai, the UAE is politically stable and staunchly pro-Western with a liberal and tolerant lifestyle. However, the UAE is not a democracy. It is ruled by powerful families and has neither elections nor political parties.

Many multinational companies, from Microsoft to CNN to Cisco have established tax-free operations in one of the UAE's 10 free trade zones (FTZs). In a survey by *Euromoney* magazine, the UAE was found by business executives to have the least political or economic risk of any Middle

Eastern nation. Indeed, the UAE has been so successful in demonstrating its international stability that the government of land-starved Jersey is considering moving some of its offices to the UAE.

Many smaller offshore centers have little to offer in the way of a financial infrastructure consisting of a substantial network of banks, trust companies, fund managers with laws and courts set up to enforce property rights and contracts. The UAE, and in particular, Dubai, is practically unique in having such a network along with an extensive industrial infrastructure (state-of-the-art port facilities, telecommunications, etc.).

Dubai's Jebel Ali, home to more than 1,400 companies, is the largest FTZ in the Persian Gulf. Its harbor is the most important port in the Middle East and is ranked among the world's top 15 in terms of container throughput.

Dubai's international airport, itself a FTZ, is the second busiest in the world (next to Tokyo) in terms of passenger volume and second only to Seattle as a sea-air hub. E-commerce is rapidly developing in Dubai. In 2002, the first phase of the government-funded Dubai Internet City was completed. Hundreds of companies have already taken out licenses to locate in this FTZ due to its highly developed technical infrastructure.

Investors can use FTZs as jurisdictions from which to conduct tax-free business in a secure and confidential environment. FTZs are administratively separate from the UAE and are governed by regulations set out by their individual boards of directors. All FTZs offer a guaranteed tax-free period ranging from 10-20 years as well as exemption from import duties (as long as products are not imported into the UAE). Within the FTZs two types of entity may be established. A Free Zone Entity/Establishment (FZE) is a limited liability company, which can be owned 100% by non-residents. It must be re-licensed each year. Alternatively, a branch of a company from any jurisdiction may be registered in the FTZs. Both FZEs and branches may conduct business internationally. The licensing process can be completed in three to five working days including bank account opening. FTZs and branches must appoint a local manager (agent) who is responsible for the conduct of the business. The local manager may act as nominee for the beneficial owner. FZEs and branches registered in the free zones may conduct any and all activities undertaken by international business companies in other offshore jurisdictions, including trading, financing, holding interests in subsidiaries, owning property outside the UAE, professional services, etc.

Dubai's Beneficial Tax Treaties

Despite being a zero-tax jurisdiction, Dubai has a substantial network of tax-treaties, in no small part due to its strategic location and economic clout. Tax treaties are in effect with Jordan, Sudan, Syria, Kuwait, Yemen, Egypt, Finland, France, India, Pakistan, Poland, China, Germany, India, Indonesia, Italy, Malaysia, Romania, Singapore, Algeria and Turkey. Tax accords were signed by the United Arab Emirates and Sudan in 2002. Since Dubai does not impose taxes, its tax treaties are designed to reduce any tax levied in a foreign jurisdiction on profits remitted from Dubai to that jurisdiction. Under these treaties profits derived from shares, dividends, interest, royalties and fees are taxable only in the contracting state where the income is earned.

In principal, this means that such profits generated in Dubai can be remitted tax-free to treaty countries. Therefore, dividend income paid by a Dubai company to its corporate parent in a country that has a tax treaty with Dubai may potentially be received tax-free.

However, many countries have inserted "anti-avoidance" provisions in tax treaties that require that companies seeking to benefit from a tax treaty pay some minimum amount of tax. Review both relevant tax law and the treaties themselves before assuming that such income is tax-free.

Dubai: "Epicenter of Terrorist Financing?"

In 2002, Dubai gained a degree of international notoriety after being labeled by the U.S. Treasury Department as the "epicenter of terrorist financing." The justification for this designation appears to be the fact that informal money transfer networks, or hawalas, are prevalent in Dubai.

At least some funds wired to those persons who carried out the September 11, 2001, attacks on the United States appear to have originated in Dubai hawalas.

Dubai is also an important center for gold trading and terrorist money is allegedly converted to gold through local merchants. Indeed, a "gold and diamond park" exists within the Jebel Ali FTZ (www.uaefreezones.com/fz_gold.asp).

However, despite these allegations, neither Dubai nor the UAE have been placed on the FATF money laundering "blacklist." This is no doubt is due to their economic and strategic importance, but the UAE also made money laundering a crime in 2002. UAE financial service providers are also required to report "suspicious transactions" to a newly formed Anti-Money Laundering and Suspicious Cases Unit. In addition, the UAE Central Bank has begun a mandatory registration of hawalas operations in the UAE. All international money transfers carried out through Hawalas must now be reported to the Central Bank.

Local sources tell us the government is serious about enforcing the new laundering law, but determined that it not hinder legitimate international business or the long tradition of confidentiality prevailing in financial services.

Tax Advantaged Residency in Dubai

A significant percentage of Dubai's population is comprised of foreigners working in its rapidly expanding economy. The emirate also welcomes investors, entrepreneurs and wealthy retirees, all of whom are invited to benefit from the tax incentives offered in the Jebel Ali Free Zone. Dubai imposes no personal taxes other than import duties (mostly at rates up to 10%), a 5% residential tax assessed on rental value and a 5% tax on hotel services and entertainment.

The emirate offers an excellent lifestyle with year-round swimming, sailing, waterskiing, scuba diving, golf, soccer, cricket, tennis, and horse racing. Superior hotels, restaurants, and nightclubs are available. The quality of health care in Dubai is among the best in the Gulf.

The ethnic makeup of Dubai's foreign residents varies, but most come from India, Iran, Europe and other Arab countries and reside in the cities. Nationals from any member of the Gulf Cooperation Council (Saudi Arabia, Kuwait, Bahrain, Qatar and the Sultanate of Oman) and British nationals with the right to reside in the United Kingdom do not need visas to enter the UAE. GCC nationals can generally stay permanently. Britons can stay for a month and can then apply for a visa for a further two months.

For More Information:

- *FTZs:* **Link**: www.uaefreezones.com/fz_ad.asp.
- *Dubai free trade zones.* **Link**: www.dubai.ae. Information on Dubai residency is also available from this web site.
- *Doing business in the UAE.* **Link**: www.mideastlaw.com/uae.html.
- *Dubai financial services providers.* **Link**: www.lowtax.net/lowtax/html/dubai/jdbsdircfsr.html.

A Dubai corporate services company familiar with the work of The Sovereign Society is *Connaught Asset Management*. Contact: Ken Irving, Connaught Asset Management FZE, 41st Floor Emirates Towers, P.O. Box 31303, Dubai, UAE. **Tel.**: +(9714) 319-9328. **Fax**: +(9714) 330-3365. **E-mail**: kenirving@connaughtasset.com. **Link**: www.taxhavenco.com/uae.htm.

———◆———

Malta: Crossroads for Government-Business Partnership
The Business Havens Report, 1998

Here's a Mediterranean island where business is welcome, business loans are available at only 3 percent interest, and you won't have to pay any corporate taxes for 10 years. The government will even pay to train your staff!

In the center of the Mediterranean Sea, with Italy to the north and Africa to south, lie the Maltese Islands, the crossroads of East-West sea trade. Malta is an ancient nation, but one with a thoroughly modern outlook.

In recent years the Maltese government has actively courted foreign capital with an attractive program of incentives aimed at investors and entrepreneurs. It includes generous tax incentives and inducements such as soft loans, training grants and customized facilities at subsidized costs.

This pro-business policy seeks to build on Malta's many existing strengths: favorable trade relations with countries around the world; a strategic location on world shipping lanes; a high quality, productive, English-speaking workforce; an excellent climate and quality of life; and modern health care and educational systems.

Economy

In the last decade, Malta's economy has averaged an annual growth rate of over 7 percent. The nation has maintained a surplus balance of payments, stable currency and low inflation (less than one percent), all impressive numbers. They reflect the overall strength and diversity of the Maltese economy.

Traditionally agriculture was important, but the economy has undergone significant change. Manufacturing, especially high-tech industries, now accounts for over a quarter of Malta's GDP. About 26 percent of the labor force works in services, 22 percent in manufacturing, 37 percent in government and 2 percent in agriculture. Major industries now include textiles, machinery, food and beverages and high-tech products, especially electronics. Tourism is also a growing and increasingly important sector. Key sectors that provide exceptional investment opportunities include trade, tourism, manufacturing, maintenance services and international financial services.

The Maltese government favors expansion in the following areas: high technology products that require sophisticated production skills; expertise in the areas of marketing and exporting; manufacturers requiring a high degree of quality control or specialized production processes; and re-engineering services.

The Maltese government has enacted legislation to increase the islands' role as a leader in international finance services. These laws provide a variety of tax and financial incentives to banks, insurance companies, fund management firms, trading companies, trusts and investment companies.

As an historic trading center throughout history, Malta has favorable trade relationships with many countries. Maltese-produced goods are exempt from customs duty or restrictions with the countries of the European Community. Special access has also been obtained with markets as far ranging as the U.S., Canada, Japan and Australia.

Malta's open and free business environment promotes growth and enterprise. The official attitude toward business is progressive. Red tape is minimized, capital for most companies is readily available, and foreign investment is welcomed.

Incentives

Official Maltese incentives for investors, include:

- A 10-year tax holiday for industries that are at least 95 percent export-oriented.
- An exemption from local and municipal taxes.
- Special three percent interest loans for investment in new factories, machinery and fixed assets.
- Investment tax credits, accelerated depreciation allowances, reduced rates for reinvested profits.
- Special allowances for costs associated with research and development and for costs of export promotion.

- Training grants provided by the Employment Training Corporation to employers for one-half the minimum wage for up to 48 weeks for training new employees; also training for existing employees can be eligible for a tax deduction equal to 120 percent of the training cost.

In addition, Malta offers investors and businesses several other important advantages, including:

- Duty-free importation of materials or parts when used in export products.
- Duty-free shipment on various products shipped to the EU.
- Reduced tariffs on products exported to the U.S.
- Free repatriation in any currency and to any country of profits, capital and dividends.
- Modern production facilities from the Malta Development Corporation including made-to-order factories based on needs.
- Low-cost development land.
- Work permits for expatriates get quick approval, allowing businesses with special needs to bring in required expertise.

Taxes

Malta has three types of taxes: income, corporate and estate taxes. There are no property or real estate taxes in Malta. Income tax rates for expatriates range from two to 30 percent and expatriates do not pay capital gains tax.

Though the corporate tax rate is 35 percent, tax incentives and tax holidays reduce that rate significantly. Companies may also be eligible for exemptions from local and municipal taxes. Transfers of interests in a Maltese company from one expatriate to another who is not domiciled in Malta are exempt from estate taxes.

Contacts

- *Malta Development Corporation*, Malta Development Corporation, P.O. Box 141 GPO 01, Marsa, Malta. **Tel.**: +356 441888. **Fax**: +356 441887. In the U.S., contact Ms Paula Calamatta, 1 202 462-7991. **Fax**: 1 202-462 0927. **E-mail**: paulamdc@yahoo.com. **Website**: http://www.investinmalta.com.
- *Embassy of Malta*, 2017 Connecticut Ave. NW, Washington, DC 20008, U.S.A. **Tel.**: +1 202 462 3611. **Fax**: +1 202 387 5470.

———————•◆•———————

Portugal: Foreign Business Always Welcome
The Business Havens Report, 1998

Portugal is a beautiful land with an official welcome mat out for all kinds of business investment. They'll give you substantial cash grants, just to help you get started!

Portugal is one of the world's oldest countries. It became an independent nation in 1143, and has maintained its independence and national boundaries from the thirteenth century to this day, save for a brief period under Spanish domination between 1580 and 1640. Portugal became a republic on October 5, 1910, and today is a strong democracy.

Portugal's geographic location at the southwest corner of continental Europe assures quick and easy access not only to the European market but also to the eastern seaboard of the United States and the African continent.

Nearly half of the 10 million population is economically active. Population density is highest in the Lisbon area, in the northern city of Porto and other coastal cities. Portugal's territory is twice the size of Switzerland and about the same as the State of Indiana in the United States.

The new era for Portugal began in 1986. It was then the country entered the European Union

(EU) and launched a series of bold business reform initiatives that opened up the economy to the world. The results are significant. Many international experts view Portugal as one of the best investment choices in all of Europe.

Today's Portugal courts foreign and domestic capital, provides alluring financial and tax incentives and encourages investment in all sectors of the economy. The fact that global companies, including Ford, Siemens, Pepsico, Texas Instruments, Samsung, Microsoft, General Motors and Volkswagen, have invested heavily in the country, and others have expressed genuine interest in establishing operations, indicates Portugal has arrived as a business haven.

It may be just the place for your business or investments. Portugal wholeheartedly welcomes investors and entrepreneurs.

Fast Growth, Low Inflation

Portugal is one of Europe's fastest growing economies, with one of the highest GDP growth rates among all industrialized countries. Direct foreign investment has also increased from US$164 million to US$4.4 billion in less than a decade, an enormous sum. No less important, inflation has stayed under control and the unemployment rate is one of the lowest in the EU. Economic growth rates are expected to average between three and four percent through the end of the decade and beyond.

Portugal has made great strides in positioning itself as one of the world's best business havens. The country invested substantially in infrastructure, transport and telecommunications systems. The service sector has grown, the financial system is modern and the manufacturing sector has responded with its own expansion and modernization.

With all this, Portugal also offers investors political and social stability, an industrious people, and an interesting culture and heritage.

A Modern Economy

Portugal's opportunities for business are virtually boundless. As an EU member since 1986, Portugal has adopted laws and policies that have restructured its economy, opening its domestic markets and encouraging foreign investment. One of the first European colonial nations 500 years ago, Portugal pioneered trade throughout the world and still has strong ties to the rich markets of Europe, South America, Asia and Africa.

The country's sound economic policy is built on four guidelines:

1. Governmental budgetary discipline and spending controls.

2. Maintaining stable exchange rates while restraining the rate of inflation.

3. Promoting structural economic reforms to increase productivity and competitiveness.

4. Creation of a favorable environment for investment and competition.

The results are noteworthy. The inflation rate decreased from 12.6 percent to 5.4 percent, the best reduction of any other European country during the same period in the early 1990s. The economy has expanded and diversified, foreign investment has increased dramatically and the process for foreigners establishing a business has been streamlined.

While Portugal favors any new business enterprise, its privatization program and investment policies created exceptional opportunities in the key sectors of banking, financial services, telecommunications, petroleum, petrochemicals and steelmaking.

No Comparison

When investors compare Portugal's pro-business advantages and benefits with those offered by other nations, Portugal wins. Here's why:

- Extremely competitive tax and financial incentives.

- An open economy that permits companies to establish operations in all private sectors.

- Guaranteed protection for international transfers of dividends, capital gains, and proceeds from sales of investments.

As Portugal's economy has grown, the mix has changed considerably. In the past, agriculture played the major role. Currently, agriculture accounts for about nine percent of the GDP, with industry at 30 percent, and the service sector 61 percent. The work force has also been transformed. From 1982 to 1992, the proportion of labor in agriculture dropped from 25.2 percent to 11.6 percent, while workers employed in industry rose from 21 percent to 32 percent. Service sector workers increased from 37.3 percent to 55.2 percent. The service sector has boomed. Financial and retail services have increased steadily and tourism is now a major part of the economy.

Portugal's manufacturing sector includes chemicals, plastics and rubber, which account for 20 percent of total industrial output. Other important industries include clothing, footwear, textiles, foodstuffs and beverages, most notably wine. Foreign investment has been particularly heavy in the automotive and paper sectors, but also construction, especially in infrastructure improvement. Overall, much of Portuguese industry is characterized by small- and medium-sized firms keenly aware of the need to remain competitive.

Although Portugal's imports exceed its exports, the latter is growing, with about 75 percent going to other EU countries. Many products are manufactured or assembled by multinational companies with facilities in Portugal. Beyond the EU, Portugal has trade ties to countries around the world.

Investor Guarantees

Portugal's expanding economy is impressive, but what attracts foreign investors and new business is a host of government incentives guaranteed by law. These include:

- A non-discriminatory policy that treats domestic and foreign investors on an equal footing.
- Asset protection and security for both foreign and domestic owned companies.
- Financial and fiscal incentives with statutory guarantees.
- An unrestricted right to transfer abroad dividends and profits on sales or investments.
- The right to organize a corporation entirely with foreign capital, control and management.

Financial Incentives

Portugal's financial system has expanded in response to demand for services. The Bank of Portugal (BOP) and Ministry of Finance are the operating agencies in this sector. The BOP, the central bank, regulates the banking system by controlling financial policy and foreign exchange. Portugal has a host of commercial banks, savings banks, investment companies, brokerage houses, investment advisors, venture capital companies, investment fund management companies and finance companies.

Foreign investment is encouraged, especially in the following sectors: tourism, manufacturing of electrical and electronic components, agricultural and food processing, motor vehicle production, mining, fisheries and fish farming, and projects deemed to contribute to industrial development of a region or the nation as a whole.

The two broad categories of incentives are tax breaks and investment guarantees. Major tax incentives include:

1. An eligible entrepreneurial or venture capital company incorporated is exempt from corporate income tax for the first eight years of operation. Bank deposit interest, however, is subject to a 20 percent withholding tax.

2. An eligible real estate holding company enjoys a reduced corporate tax rate of 25 percent for a period of from seven and ten years.

3. Fifty percent of dividends on shares purchased from the government in a privatized business are tax-free for five years after the date of acquisition.

4. Large investment projects designed to increase exports may be eligible for tax incentives. Projects are evaluated on an individual basis.

The Portuguese Foreign Trade Institute (ICEP) administers the comprehensive program of fiscal and financial incentives. It provides expertise and information about the economy, laws and regulations, guiding companies as they establish operations and functioning as investment consultants.

Major incentive programs include:

PEDIP II (The Strategic Program for the Improvement of the Internationalization of Portuguese Industry)

Purpose: increase competitiveness by fostering technology and diversification in the industrial sector. Primary focus on investment in manufacturing and mining.

1. Cash grants for 30-70 percent of the cost of initiatives to modernize, implement new technologies, conduct research and development, train staff in new methods or processes or conduct strategic or feasibility studies.

2. Loan rates reduced 40-80 percent for new machinery, construction and start-up capital.

3. Cash grants to small investment projects by companies employing fewer than 250 people.

SIR (Regional Incentive System)

Purpose: Encourage job creation in designated underdeveloped areas. Cash grants and reduced rate loans for companies investing in manufacturing, mining, tourism and trade.

RETEX (Program for Regions Dependent on the Textile and Clothing Industries)

Purpose: This EU associated program promotes industrial modernization in regions strongly impacted by changes in the textile and clothing industries.

1. Subsidies for 40-60 percent of total investment costs for increasing productivity by modernizing processes in established companies.

2. Subsidies for 40-60 percent of total investment costs of programs aimed at increasing global competitiveness, participating in international trade fairs and promotion of Portuguese products.

3. Reduced loan rates for establishing Portuguese-owned companies in other countries.

Other programs aimed at specific companies and projects include:

FRIEs—investment capital for companies or their foreign branches that implement restructuring or internationalization.

SIFIT II—reduced-rate loans to support and stimulate projects in the tourism sector.

SIFIT III—also finances tourism projects, with long-term, interest-free repayable subsidies including investments in new building, installation, extensions, remodeling, and re-conversions of hotels, restaurants and other tourist attractions.

PAMAF—loans and grants for investment in Portuguese agriculture.

PROCOM—reduced rate loans for retail, wholesale and distribution companies, with subsidies of from 35-70 percent of total investment costs, based upon pre-approved specific projects.

There are also special credit lines for small- and medium-sized companies provided by the European Investment Bank, with reduced interest rates and extended grace periods.

While these incentives primarily are for mainland Portugal, other specific incentives are available for the Portuguese islands of the Azores and Madeira.

Portuguese Lifestyle

Portugal offers a mix of modern cities, delightful countryside and a fine climate. The country combines mountains, grasslands and beaches with both new and ancient cities connected by modern highways. Lisbon, the capital, a charming city of old world beauty and modern facilities, is also a city of business that welcomes investors, entrepreneurs and corporations.

The country's southern coast, the Algarve, has a Mediterranean culture with Moorish influences, and is one of the favorite vacation retreats for Europeans.

Contacts

- Official government website: www.portugal.org.

- *Portuguese Foreign Trade Institute* (ICEP), Avenida 5 de Outubro 101, 1016 Lisboa Codex, Portugal. **Tel.:** +351 1 793 0103. **Fax:** +351 1 793 5028.

- *Portuguese Trade & Tourism Office*, 4th Floor, 22-25A Sackville Street, London W1X 1 DE, England, Trade and Investment Office. **Tel.:** +44 171 494 15 17. **Fax** +44 171 494 15 08. **E-mail:** iceplond@dircon.co.uk.

- *Portuguese Trade Commission*, 590 Fifth Avenue, 3rd Floor, New York, NY 10036-4702, USA. **Tel.:** +1 212 354 4610. **Fax:** +1 212 575 4737. **E-mail:** erodrigues@portugal.org.

- *Portuguese National Tourist Office*, 590 Fifth Avenue, 4th Floor, New York, NY 10036-4704, USA. **Tel.:** +1 212 354 4403 or 354 4404. **Fax** +1 212 764 6137. **E-mail:** fcosta@portugal.org

Portuguese Trade & Tourism Offices

- 1900 L Street NW, Suite 310, Washington DC 20036, USA. **Tel.:** +1 202 331 8222. **Fax:** +1 202 331 8236. **E-mail:** mgarcia@portugal.org.

- 88 Kearny St., Suite 1770, San Francisco, CA 94108, USA. **Tel.:** +1 415 391 7080. **Fax** +1 415 391 7147. **E-mail:** jfdias@portugal.org.

- 60 Bloor Street West, Suite, 1005, Toronto, Ontario M4W 3B8, Canada. Trade & Investment Office: **Tel.:** +1 416 921 4925. **Fax:** +1 416 921 1354. Tourist Office: **Tel.:** +1 416 921 7376. **E-mail:** iceptor@idirect.com.

- *Delegation Commerciale et du Tourisme du Portugal*, 500 Sherbrook Street West, Suite 940, Montreal, Quebec H3A 3C6 Canada. **Tel.:** +1 514 282 1264. **Fax:** +1 514 499 1450. **E-mail:** icepmtl@netcom.ca.

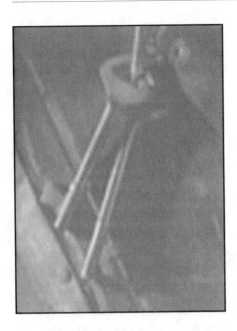

CHAPTER SIX
Your Finances & Estate Planning

This chapter describes the available legal mechanisms you can use to protect your wealth, such as the offshore trust and other trusts, the international business corporation and the limited liability company.

Most important, we present the philosophy and mind set of people of wealth, the tycoons who have made it and who "have it made." And we tell you who the experts are and how to contact them.

Part One—Financial Philosophy

The Tycoon Mentality
from *Think Like a Tycoon, 1997*

What makes people of great wealth "tick"? How do they differ from their fellow man? What special talents and thinking characterize the successful entrepreneur? Here the philosophy of wealth is explained.

If you sincerely want to become a tycoon, you must think like a tycoon. You can learn to think like a tycoon by reading this very carefully. The principles covered here apply to all forms of managing your money. Living a good life or being exceptionally successful in business requires more than a can of beer, a TV set and wishing for a winning lottery ticket.

Tycoon is a Japanese word meaning *ty* - great and *coon* - *shogun*, a military leader. A tycoon is someone with ambition and drive who has placed himself in a position of importance. In the case of a great general like Patton or a great politician like Winston Churchill—or anyone great—one characteristic is universal: Great people thoroughly enjoy what they do. To be great at what you do, you must believe that what you do is fun.

An episode of the "Peanuts" cartoon strip once showed Charlie Brown playing with half a yo-yo. It was broken. But he was having a good time dangling it, bouncing it up and down the wall and playing "fetch" with Snoopy. Suddenly Lucy comes along. "You stupid dummy," she says, "you can't have a good time with half a yo-yo. Everybody knows that." Dejected, Charlie Brown throws his toy on the ground: he hadn't known that.

This story has a moral for prospective tycoons. Fuzzy-thinking leftists and other depressing types like Lucy have convinced many people that doing something that makes a lot of money is abnormal, immoral or, at best, dull. They would like to make U.S. capitalists feel guilty for becoming rich and—shudder—actually having fun making it. Albert Einstein, when asked on his last birthday what he'd do to benefit the world if he could live his life over again said, "I'd like to go into business and make some serious money."

So ignore the socialist do-gooders. They don't produce products or services. All they want to do is make us feel guilty. Fuzzy-thinking leftists fail to realize that capitalists don't just rake in money and count it—bank clerks do that. A tycoon is involved in something creative and beautiful. He (or she) must invariably bring forth upon the world a product or service that people want. A "something" that people willingly part with their earnings or savings for. He's not ashamed to take their money because (unlike forcibly extracted tax money, which pays for dubious social services or more tax collectors that nobody wants) a capitalist exists for the people. He works for the people. He serves them only so long as his products or services meet their needs. A tycoon needs the people as much as they need him. However, being creative—like an artist, musician or new mother—a tycoon has far more fun at living than the wage-slave at his routine job. Tycoons enjoy doing what they can be great at, providing an abundance of goods and services that people want and can afford. Every tycoon has an invisible directive flashing like a neon sign in his brain: Find a need and fill it.

Find A Need And Fill It

A tycoon doesn't count his money every day to measure his success. Dollars or pounds are just evidence of votes from the previous day, votes of confidence in the particular goods or services that the tycoon is providing. A tycoon gets his confidence from within himself, not through these monetary votes. Any businessman who wants to keep on being successful, however, must continue to deliver needed goods and services or the people will vote their money for a new tycoon.

Some individuals, of course, can never become tycoons. They thwart themselves right from the beginning. They make excuses: "I'm not smart enough." "I don't have enough money to start." "I have no business sense." These are all cop-outs. With the right attitude, anyone, including you, can become a tycoon. If you think you're dumb—relax. Most tycoons have average IQs. The straight-A students are too busy getting PhDs and looking for teaching jobs to make it in business. You can begin with little or no money and become a multi-millionaire. Most of today's industrialists were poor a few years ago. So not having any money to start with, the second excuse, doesn't wash either. As for having no business sense—well, you're reading this report. That's pretty sensible. Whatever acumen you lacked before today, you'll have by tomorrow.

Other individuals wait until they are already tycoons before they thwart themselves. All people should learn from their own mistakes, but you can benefit more cheaply from other people's mistakes. It helps to look at what some successful tycoons who failed have in common. Businessmen who have made it big once and then went downhill have frequently over-expanded. They got careless and didn't attend to emergencies or details. They didn't have time anymore. In contrast, a successful tycoon leaves nothing to chance. He makes time to watch over his investments or hires competent help to do it for him. It's much easier to be extremely successful on a small scale when you're starting out in familiar territory than it is when you have the riches of a Howard Hughes. Does that surprise you? Allow me to illustrate.

Once a business deal was proposed to me in Reno, Nevada. The big selling point was that one of the richest men in the world, Donald Trump (who made his fortune in real estate), had taken 25 percent interest in it. Therefore (I was told) I should be willing to take 10 percent (ten "points" in tycoon-talk), because Trump was pretty smart and wouldn't have had a 25 percent interest in a deal if it wasn't any good. The deal went sour shortly after that. I should have known it would! Now when I hear that extremely rich people have an interest in a project, I run the other way.

A "red ribbon" deal usually won't make money for anyone but the promoters. Super-rich people seldom have time to investigate new ventures; they are too busy keeping what they have to be effective in fields outside their immediate area of expertise. I am sure that if Trump had a good deal that he investigated and put together personally, he would have taken all of it for himself and not sold any points to outside investors. But the fact that Trump, a super-rich New Yorker, was investing in a Nevada property deal, probably meant that he relied on someone else's judgment. That "someone else" would not have sought me out as an investor if it had been a super deal.

Tycoons who have been very successful often make bad investments. They don't attend to the details of investigating a situation as thoroughly as they would have done when they were starting out. The best deals are the deals that you go out and find yourself. They are not prepackaged "no work, no worry" deals all wrapped up with a red ribbon, where all you do is write a check. The red ribbon deal will only tie you in financial knots. The Red Ribbon Rule: If a deal sounds too good to be true, it is too good to be true!

Another common characteristic of a tycoon destined to go downhill is that he feels "too important" to attend to humble work. He passes by one of his properties, for example. In the old days, he would have taken time to pick up junk spilled by the rubbish collectors and put it in proper cans. At the very least, he'd have given the janitor or the tenants a gentle reminder to clean up their act. But now, looking at the mess, he doesn't notice. He's too busy whizzing off to negotiate a pie-in-the-sky deal or fighting his wife in a divorce case. A lack of pride in ownership means the start of decline—the beginning of the end. When you're no longer concerned with detail (and willing to see to it yourself), you're heading for trouble. If an owner doesn't care anymore, his business goes to pot.

Another characteristic of aging tycoons is a sudden fear of competition. When new at the game, competition is a challenge. The embryo tycoon steals his competitors' best ideas and avoids their mistakes. Determined to beat the competition one way or another, the upstart comes up with innovative methods. He works at it all day and Christmas too. However, once on top, some tycoons start to worry about all the young upstarts moving into "their backyards" as if it were an exclusive preserve. In the case of manufacturers it is "cheap foreign goods." "Why," they worry, "are those Sayonara Sleeping Pills becoming more popular than my Yankee Doodle Doze?"

Instead of trying to produce a new or better product, some old tycoons retreat into deep leather chairs at the Old Fogy Club. Old, has-been tycoons never die, they just become ineffectual aristocrats. At worst, a formerly successful tycoon these days becomes a "gold bug." A "gold bug" is someone who buries or stashes most of his assets in a Swiss bank in gold. Of course in a nation run by irresponsible politicians who print and spend money like toilet paper, building one's personal gold reserves, to a reasonable level, is only prudent. But when you start concentrating on reducing the size of your business operations and finding ways of becoming 100 percent liquid, then you can produce no products, no progress and no profits.

The entire French nation nearly collapsed economically in the pre-de Gaulle era because a large number of French people (perhaps for good reasons) chose to take their wealth, convert it into gold coins and bury them in their gardens. Buried gold coins (while providing some degree of safety and security in times of political turmoil or revolution) will not make you rich. A business operation is like a vine. Once it stops growing, it dies.

What are the characteristics that help a tycoon succeed? A tycoon on the way up is always able to motivate his staff, partners and the people who work for him. When he makes it big, an enthusiastic, loyal staff will be needed more than ever. But sometimes a tycoon forgets his staff. Don't forget—when you become valuable in terms of dollars, your staff becomes equally so in terms of support. Some employees respond best to praise and titles, others, to money. Imaginative gifts or bonuses can score you more points than money! How about a round-trip ticket to Hawaii for your secretary or property manager? The successful tycoon always keeps thinking of ways to put a smile on the faces of his team.

Some tycoons believe that inspiring fear in their associates is an effective method of getting them to work. I strongly disagree. Fear is good only for incompetents, because only incompetents are afraid of getting fired. If an employee or business associate is good enough, he can always find work with the tycoon down the road. Thus, if you can't make the work situation pleasant for those who contribute to your success, something is wrong. You can never get the best out of employees through fear. Remember: Motivation is better accomplished by carrots than the stick.

On the home front, the same rule applies. Keep the peace. Give recognition and daily compliments to the people around you - your children, your spouse, your friends. Make the people you know feel good about themselves. Act like a loving, concerned human being—even if you are really a selfish slob. Donald Trump took his wife for granted and is said to have ordered her to "go and fetch" things like a dog. His inconsiderate behavior cost him half his fortune—besides breaking up his once happy family. If your staff and family feel good about themselves, they'll work harder and feel better about you.

If you're making a compliment, don't make the mistake of taking it back. I've heard people say things like, "Gee, you look younger. Are you dyeing your hair?" Say it and mean it. If you personally get a compliment, don't argue. Accept it graciously, a simple "thank you" will do. Make the people in your family or organization feel secure. If you feel it, say, "I love you." Give praise and recognition generously! Tell them, "I really like being with you." Or, "I like working with you." Give the reasons. Your own life will be better if those you live and work with know that you like them. Tell them often. If you have to be critical, try to be positive in your criticism. When the toast is served burned to a crisp, say, "I really enjoyed the breakfast, honey, but next time around could you set the toaster a bit lighter?" For business associates just substitute different words. Try it—it works.

The Tycoon's 10 Point Credo
Think Like a Tycoon, 1997

A tycoon is:

1. *Organized*: I will schedule a written program of my activities and objectives and stick to it the entire day.

2. *Dedicated*: I will do at least one thing I should have done, but have been putting off.

3. *Confident*: I will feel as good as possible and achieve a sense of well-being by meditating 15 minutes every day. I will exercise or jog another 15 minutes.

4. *Appreciative*: I will tell my family, friends and business associates "I like you" and mean it. I will be generous with praise and compliments.

5. *Optimistic*: I will not dwell on past failures but will think positively about the present and the future.

6. *Educated*: I will read something to improve my mind each day and will keep away from non-productive and time consuming people and activities.

7. *Thrifty*: I will not be a consumer or a taxpayer any more than is absolutely necessary.

8. *Sociable*: I will be charming and agreeable to everyone and speak badly of no one.

9. *Alert*: I will be open to new ideas, experiences and people who might teach me something new. I will not let myself fall into a rut or routine.

10. *Dependable*: I will meet all my business, social and moral obligations punctually, honestly, and honorably.

Kinds of Assets & Their Relative Immunity
PT, 1996

Assets that are easily located, subject to court judgments, attachment, seizure or a lien:

The simple title to property. Where you actually live is your most easily discoverable asset. It can be discovered by questioning neighbors or searching public records. Many town directories have a symbol that indicates whether a property is owner occupied or tenant occupied. Trying to hide ownership through a third party will usually offer no protection, as a creditor will have the right to all details of ownership. Similarly, properties held in company names or through other cover stories may not hold up. Accordingly for the true PT, home should always be just a rental.

Leaseholds. In all common law countries, in order for a leasehold or other interest in property of more than one year to be valid, it must be publicly recorded. Public records are indexed in various ways, such as through name of party, date of transaction, location of property and category of property. A search through public documents, now usually carried out by computers, will turn up any recorded transactions in your name. Any lease at below market value rents can be taken over by a creditor.

Any interests in real property including mortgages owned. These are recorded and thus discoverable and can be seized, as above.

Partnership interests, automobiles, yachts, aircraft, dogs, horses or any property that requires a license. Owner lists, as above, are public or quasi-public records. Normally, only local records are searched. If no one knows that you have a home and yacht in a remote place, it will probably be safe.

Bank accounts, savings accounts, certificates of deposit, corporate stocks or bonds or assets held in partnerships. In many countries, each individual is required to have an identifying number for financial transactions. Normally this number or the name of the holder is circulated to banks, insurance companies and financial institutions. Any accounts can then be frozen pending legal action. Even accounts abroad can be tied up if they either are or become known to creditors.

Assets more difficult to locate, but not immune from legal discovery or judicial seizure, include cash, gold, travelers checks, bearer bonds, paintings, stamps, coins, beneficial interests in trusts, out of town property and property owned in company names, alternate identity names or straw names.

This type of property can be located in several ways. The most common is by obtaining copies of all financial statements ever made in connection with bank loans, credit card applications or income tax returns. Newspaper articles are also checked for clues as to assets and known haunts abroad. Once the location of an asset is known, a creditor may physically seize property by court order, even if it is in a safe deposit box or outside the country.

Assets immune from judicial seizure or legal discovery:

Assets in foreign countries that are forgotten or overlooked. Do I have to spell it out? Consider the wondrous benefits of bank accounts or the contents of safe deposit boxes in a country with true bank secrecy.

Assets controlled by others for your benefit, i.e., various types of trusts. For instance, a wealthy person can donate his money to a Liechtenstein trust. In doing so, he would give up control of certain assets to trustees whose duty it would then be to manage the money or property and dole out, for instance, a monthly allowance to your favorite grandchild, or to you.

If the amount of the allowance is at the sole discretion of the trustee, a creditor will not be allowed to seize the assets of the foundation if it is established properly. Once again, there are a few exceptions, such as if the assets in a trust were gained by bank robbery, criminal dealings or fraud.

Other assets not subject to seizure because they are in the sole discretionary control of others include annuities, pension plan assets, entailed life estate or homestead property, the cash value of life insurance policies and the beneficial interests in irrevocable trusts. However, once a check is issued to a debtor or any payments are out of the control of the trustee, such assets are fair game and may be seized.

Depending on local laws, certain small amounts of property may be exempt from seizure by creditors. For example, in Texas, the law makes "tools of the trade, forty acres and a mule" traditionally exempt from creditor claims. In Florida, a person's homestead (the place he actually lives) is exempt from seizure, no matter how great its value may be. Normally, an individual is protected from being stripped bare. However, the rules differ widely. In Switzerland, there is no such thing as bankruptcy as it is simply illegal for a Swiss not to pay a court award (judgment debt) to another Swiss.

New Age Planning: The European Way to Protect Your Assets

By Marc-Andre Sola, *The Sovereign Individual*, October 2001

Rather unfamiliar to many offshore investors is an investment structure called a "Portfolio Bond." This type of investment combines the best of two worlds, banking and insurance, and can be located in a safe offshore jurisdiction.

How It Works

The Portfolio Bond can be considered as a simple holding structure through which the investor (or his/her adviser) can direct the insurance company to invest in a wide range of investment vehicles such as stocks, bonds, mutual funds, or cash deposits. The underlying investments can be selected freely.

Specifically, the investor signs a contract in his name with an insurance company, usually domiciled in an offshore tax haven. The insurance company opens an account with a bank selected by the investor, who in turn receives a policy from the insurance company. From a legal standpoint, the investor is the client of the insurance company and the insurance company is a client of the bank.

The policy value consists precisely of the value of the assets placed there by the insurance company on the investor's behalf and that amount grows as investments are managed properly. Legal entities and/or natural persons can be designated as beneficiaries.

With certain annuities and insurance companies, the policy owner also may be a legal entity, such as a trust or corporation. The person insured, however, must in all cases be a natural person.

Overview of Benefits

Asset Protection: Properly structured and established in Switzerland or Liechtenstein, for example, insurance policies enjoy legal protection from creditors. This protection is very strict. Even where a foreign judgment or court order decrees the seizure of such policy, or its inclusion in an estate in bankruptcy, the insurance policy may not be seized under the laws of Switzerland or

Liechtenstein or included in a bankruptcy, unless the policy is proven to be a fraudulent conveyance. In case of bankruptcy of the owner of the policy, protection is also guaranteed since the ownership is transferred to the beneficiaries automatically when the bankruptcy is filed. Any instructions from the original policy owner attempted to be imposed by a bankruptcy court will be ignored by a Swiss or Liechtenstein court.

Separate, Simple Estate Planning Device: A Portfolio Bond is also well-suited for making distributions separate from the policy owner's personal estate. Neither power-of-attorney, nor last will nor certificate of inheritance is required for payments to be made upon the owner's death. Beneficiaries get immediate access to the funds according to the payment method chosen by the policy owner.

Confidentiality and Privacy: In Liechtenstein, for example, a separate insurance secrecy law protects the privacy of policy owners. With the recent introduction of U.S. withholding taxes on U.S. assets held in foreign accounts and with the tough reporting requirements for investments made through offshore trusts, offshore insurance vehicles, if correctly structured and located in the right jurisdiction, can add strong privacy to your existing investments made through an offshore trust or a bank account.

Tax Advantages: Unlike many offshore investments and structures, Portfolio Bonds are, in certain jurisdictions, completely free of local taxes. As far as income, capital gains, estate or withholding taxes are concerned, the law of the investor's tax domicile is decisive. In many countries insurance policies enjoy substantial tax benefits if correctly structured, i.e., the Portfolio Bond can be tailor-made to fit the U.S. legal requirements for privileged and deferred tax treatment.

Conclusion

Either in combination with offshore or domestic planning structures or alone, a Portfolio Bond is a useful and cost effective tool to upgrade an existing portfolio of investments. A portfolio's features can be expanded or improved with regard to asset protection, confidentiality, reporting burden, insurance coverage and flexibility, reducing costs and taxes, including transfer and estate taxes as wealth passes from one generation to another.

Whether concerned with taxes or the threat of litigation or looking to diversify assets globally, with the Portfolio Bond, high net worth individuals can address those concerns, as well as have access to leading investment managers and to investments otherwise not available to the public.

How to Avoid Lending Money
Think Like a Tycoon, 1996

If someone approaches you with a request to borrow money, always assume that one or more of the following will happen:

1. The person pushing the deal is involved in something illegal and soon will be in jail.

2. Within 10 minutes of getting your money, your new partner or debtor will:

a) Be abandoned by a lover. He'll decide life isn't worth living and will split the scene (with your cash) for Brazil. Or perhaps he'll go to an even more celestial region by jumping from the top of a skyscraper.

b) Have his mother, father, sister, brother, spouse, and children simultaneously afflicted with terminal leukemia or another fatal disease and meeting their medical bills will become far more important than returning your money.

c) Turn into a certified lunatic or have an accident that will make him a vegetable.

d) Be murdered or fatally injured.

e) Learn that a person he trusted with the investment will turn out to be a thief and will disappear not only with your money, but with your partner's or debtor's alleged life savings, those of his widowed mother and so on.

f) Tell you that the business deal that was so highly touted in the initial meeting just "didn't work out."

After hearing those stories in at least 50 deals, I vowed never again to invest in a red ribbon deal or lend out money without being physically in possession of the security for the loan.

A basic rule to remember in dealing with other people is, if anything can possibly go wrong, it will! Assume that all of the above (and more) will really happen in every deal, loan or investment. Protect yourself in advance. With a little bit of luck, you'll do a lot better than I did, particularly if you meet an inventor.

The most dangerous person you'll ever meet in your business career is not a robber, murderer or even the infamous tax man. The most dangerous person you'll have the misfortune to encounter will be an inventor. Once an inventor has you believing in his new product or process, your entire fortune and all your prospects will go down the tubes. The time demanded of you to promote the invention and attract further investors will become an endless treadmill. Your money will go into a bottomless pit!

I want to repress all memories of the time I became involved with the inventor of a solar panel. The small-scale prototype was convincing. It produced useable heat and energy in arctic climates with only a few hours of sunlight per week. Once installed, fuel and operating costs were almost nil. Because of tax credits and a financing package available to the buyer, any user of these panels would actually make money from day one. Nothing could possibly go wrong. Wealthy Arabs (he said) had already been after the patents for US$3 million, but the inventor didn't want them shelving his project in order to sell the world more of their oil. That was his story anyway.

It seemed like the opportunity of a lifetime. The inventor's projections showed that my US$10,000 investment would return a million a year. At least! Of course once production began, there were a few "minor bugs" to be worked out. Three more US$10,000 contributions were required, each one to "turn the corner." To my sorrow, the corner never was turned and probably never will be turned. I kissed my US$40,000 goodbye.

What went wrong? In my case, the invention in large size just never worked nearly as well as the doll-house sized prototype. But with your inventor friend, it might be anything. Go over my points on "How to Avoid Lending Money" on the previous page. These are only a few of the things that can go wrong. Dealing with a product that works is tough enough, but backing an unproven item—a new invention—will give you what I got from my solar panel: a lot of useless hot air.

DuPont or IBM can afford research and development. They can afford a dead loss on 99 out of a 100 ideas because of the one product that makes it big. You are not in that league. Don't be a pioneer!

A sound rule to follow is that if someone wants your money (inventor or otherwise) ask the magic question. If you can't be placed in a 100 percent secured position, run like hell in the opposite direction! The sad truth is that most inventions, like most movies, most oil wells, most property syndicates, most new products, and most commodity options never make the novice investor a penny. The only "sure thing" in an investment is probably in your backyard. Or your neighbor's backyard. Something that you think up, promote and control 100 percent.

No-Money-Down Deals
Think Like a Tycoon, 1997

My definition of a "no-money-down deal" is any acquisition of property or a business where you don't put up significant sums of your own money. That includes buying property for cash with an unsecured loan, then after the closing settlement, arranging for a combination of first, second and possibly third loans on the property so that none of your own money remains tied up in the deal.

Many deals require several steps until you get your money out by refinancing. Others require little or no cash to begin with. Let's look at them in the order I regard as most preferable to the buyer:

1. Seller gives buyer option to purchase at a reasonable price for a lengthy period of time. The contract provides that buyer gets possession at a low rent during the option period.

2. Outright sale with seller carrying back a loan for the entire purchase price. Often sellers will insist that this be done with a contract of sale by which the seller retains title as security for buyer's meeting his obligations.

3. Sale with seller taking as down payment the buyer's personal or secured note—or a legitimate property in trade. The balance of financing (usually 70 to 95 percent) comes from a lending institution.

4. Down payment borrowed from an outside lender by seller who refinances the property. Buyer assumes loan and seller carries balance due him in the form of another note or IOU.

5. Down payment borrowed from outside lender either on an unsecured note or secured by the property buyer already owns.

6. Property is 100 percent (or more) financed by an institutional lender. The most common ways of obtaining such a loan are:

   a) Outright fraud by manufacturing phony documents, which establish a higher-than-actual sale price. This practice is emphatically not recommended, although you will probably find it to be quite common.

   b) Over-valuation of property or oddball assets used to put together a trade.

   c) Rebate for repairs from the seller or other imaginative schemes to transfer part of purchase price back to buyer at or shortly after closing.

   d) Drastically increasing value of property by some action taken by buyer between time of contract and closing, for example: favorable re-zoning, lot split, or issuance of building or planning permits; evicting undesirable tenants or establishing new and favorable leases; sub-dividing; establishing higher and better use for property. I personally prefer this option.

7. Property bought with substantial down payment (or all cash) with this cash recouped shortly after purchase by refinancing.

8. You use investor-partners for cash. They get half the profits on the deal for putting up all the money.

Why should you try to make no-money-down deals? The answer is that with this method it is possible to acquire a large number of properties having a high dollar value in a relatively short time.

In the western U.S., the laws of many states make purchase-money loans non-recourse, meaning that if the deal goes sour you can walk away. There is no downside risk. No one can claim your other assets. In eastern states, Great Britain and other countries, the same risk-free status can be obtained using land trusts, straw men, corporations and other legal entities to insulate you as the buyer from personal liability.

By acquiring large amounts of property over a short period of time, you will quickly become a millionaire. All you have to do is buy lots of carefully selected property, sit back and wait. Your debts, reduced by the declining value of paper money, will become insignificant. Rents and property prices will go up. Your equity will soon grow to a million or more.

The Beauty of Back-to-Back Financing
Banking in Silence, 1997

Here you learn about a unique way to bring offshore funds home without having to pay a cent in taxes on your money. You may even be able to claim part of the money as a tax-deductible expense!

There are a number of advanced offshore strategies that may help you in your search for financial privacy. Some require working through an offshore corporation or trust. Others avoid the expense and hassle of such legal entities. Still others are the pet projects of certain offshore "expert advisers" who discovered they can earn a tidy living offering bogus advice about the "virtues" of a particular privacy strategy.

What follows is not bogus. It's a unique way to bring offshore funds home without having to pay a cent in taxes on the money. In fact, using this method, you can even claim part of the money as a tax deductible expense.

Back-To-Back Loans

Lynden Oscar Pindling, the late prime minister of The Bahamas, for years lived mainly on such loans. Most come from foreigners seeking government favors. Records show the prime minister and his wife received nearly US$17 million in gifts and loans from foreigners in the years 1977 to 1989. In his case, the difference between a loan and a gift seemed unclear. Pindling kept scant financial records and although he did keep up interest payments on some loans, most lenders never expected repayment. All loans were unsecured, poorly documented and usually did not require the payment of interest.

Sir Lynden, knighted by Queen Elizabeth in 1983, passed away in 2000, but he lived in Lakeview in a property best described as combination villa and a palace. His mortgage payment was US$4,500 a month, plus interest payments on bank loans ranging from US$7,000 to US$8,000 per month. As Bahamian PM, his annual salary was a relatively modest US$100,000. So constantly obtaining new loans was essential to keep his head above water. For a former prime minister of The Bahamas, however, loans were not hard to come by.

A few years ago the *Miami Herald* chronicled the state of The Bahamas in an article titled "A Nation for Sale." One conclusion: "You can buy an airstrip, or an island. You can buy citizenship. You can buy protection. You can buy justice. And should your drug cargo get seized by police, you can even buy it back."

For those of us with less influence to peddle, loans don't come easy. However, what I call "back-to-back loans" are always a sure thing.

Back-to-back loans—borrowing against your own funds held on deposit—is also low cost. Instead of the usual full interest rate, you pay a "spread" to the lending bank or financial institution. That's the difference between the highest deposit interest rate and the lowest rate at which the bank lends to its most solid customers.

The major selling point of a back-to-back loan is that it is tax neutral. You can bring home these offshore loan proceeds in privacy, without paying a penny in tax for the privilege. But be sure to meet any applicable cash reporting requirements.

Back-to-back loans, also called "arms length" loans, are a preferred way of moving cash back to your home country while legally avoiding taxes. It's rumored some people who earn "black money" from moonlighting or selling goods abroad in the informal economy put their cash into offshore accounts held in the name of an offshore corporation. The bank then obliges them by loans, not to the corporation, but to the one who controls it. The loan may be from the offshore bank itself, or from one of its correspondent banks in a home country.

Back-to-back loans are used to borrow for personal or business reasons. If you are like ex-Prime

Minister Pindling, living off your loans, you don't have any personal property eligible to be seized or attached in court proceedings. That's strong protection from creditors, ex-wives, bankruptcy, foreclosure, IRS liens and other ills of the world.

How It Works

Back-to-back loans usually are rather low cost. If you make the right arrangements, when you send US$100,000 of untaxed money abroad, $99,000 will come back as a loan. Of $10,000 paid in interest, $9,900 is for interest on the offshore loan. In a normal case, business loan interest is tax deductible. Thus even though a back-to-back loan appears to cost about one percent interest, you might make money on the deal because of a tax deductible expense.

Because the loser is your government, which always thinks you never pay enough taxes, keep your loan activity strictly quiet. The IRS bureaucrats view back-to-back loans as a gray area of finance so don't flaunt your good fortune.

When negotiating loan terms, which you can pretty well dictate, don't become too outlandish or exotic. That draws unwanted attention to yourself. Back-to-back loans are best negotiated directly with a reputable offshore bank, one with an established name that lends substance and credibility to the arrangement. What you want is a personal loan secured by funds in a blocked deposit in the bank. That the blocked funds belong to a company you personally control should not be an obstacle.

Creating the loan package is uncomplicated, but don't expect the bank to have a standard loan form ready. You must tell them what you want and how you want it done. And don't swallow fee costs from a set list. You should negotiate fees individually.

In an optimum arrangement, your offshore company's funds are on deposit earning tax-free interest. This is the money that secures your loan. A taxpayer can usually deduct interest payments to a bank, depending on the exact local rules and the loan provisions. Most foreign banks constantly deal with the private international community and thus are familiar with back-to-back loans. But never expect tailor-made solutions. Depending on local customs, it may take some time.

Reduce as little as possible to writing, at least concerning the exact mechanics of the deal. If you are a resident of a high-tax country where stamp duties on loan contracts are the norm, be sure your loan agreement is signed in the offshore bank's offices to avoid that tax. It is always best to work exclusively with banks located in foreign jurisdictions, rather than an offshore bank's branch offices or correspondent banks located in your home nation.

For added financial privacy, have your local resident agent make the loan arrangements with the offshore bank. You might even have your offshore corporation formally authorize deposit funds to be pledged for a bank loan to a third party associated with the company, rather than in your own name. That person can then convey the funds to you. It may require a little extra paper work, but it can be well worth the trouble.

Protect Your Assets with Alternative Investments
By Dr. Erich Stoeger, *The Sovereign Individual*, December, 2002

Do you believe that the current financial turmoil is just a short-term phenomenon? If you do, I have a bridge that crosses over the Limmat River in downtown Zurich to sell you!

In this, the worst bear market since the Great Depression, US$7.7 trillion in value has disappeared from global equity markets. It is not hard to see why: double dip recession in the world's largest economy, the United States. Impending war in the Mideast. A 10% drop in the value of the U.S. dollar on the world currency markets.

The view of America from Switzerland is that these uncertain times will be around for some time to come. So, turn off your radio! Tune out CNBC! Forget your stockbroker! Listen to what the market is telling you. The writing is on the wall.

We are in the midst of a once or twice-in-a-lifetime bear market, the worst since the 1930s. The global economy is in dire straits, and unlike past recessions, America is in no condition to rescue it.

Here's the mainstream tenor from a recent edition of the *Wall Street Journal*: "Stocks narrowly escaped a four day rout as enticing prices helped investors shake off another accounting-related setback that had sent the Dow Industrials tumbling more than 200 points earlier in the session...."

Admittedly, corporate ethics—or lack thereof—are important factors. Trust in the underlying rules of the markets is a prerequisite for those markets to properly function. And surely, that trust has been injured severely. However, accounting scandals are but another symptom of deeper, more fundamental issues and problems.

The worst problem for America—and for the global economy—is its horrendous balance-of-payments deficit, which in 2002 is likely to exceed US$400 billion. The United States is now the world's largest debtor nation, with more than US$4 trillion owed by the United States to other countries. This situation will eventually be resolved, most likely by a progressive devaluation of the U.S. dollar. Yet if this occurs, U.S. investments will be even less attractive than they are now.

We recommend the following *urgent* steps towards an improved and "crisis-compliant" personal asset strategy.

1. *Get liquid.* We mean readily available *cash* for transactional everyday purposes. This goes for *all* readers everywhere.

2. *Get out of debt* that you are not *sure* you can handle, and do it *now*.

3. *Get out of stocks* if you can. For stocks that you cannot sell, consider employing put option hedges for at least one year.

4. *Get some real money*, e.g., physical gold, and store it in a safe location.

5. *Create a wealth preservation plan* that ensures asset protection of the highest possible grade, supreme institutional safety, *and* continuous investment flexibility that will allow you to reallocate your assets, possibly back into the stock markets, when the market is right for that.

6. *Adjust your allocation towards safety.* This will dramatically reduce the risk of loss.

7. *Decide and then take action.* This is not a time to think in national or patriotic terms. Think for yourself and think of your family.

Here are five strategies that you can implement immediately:

1. *The Perth Mint Certificate* (PMC). This is the world's only government guaranteed precious metals certificate program. EurAxxess is the first approved dealer of the Perth Mint Certificate Program in Europe. The PMC is an excellent vehicle to own and store gold, silver, platinum and palladium abroad. It is guaranteed by the government of Western Australia, which holds a AAA rating from Standard & Poors. While achieving geographical diversification, your overseas relationship is with a non-bank vault and under U.S. law, is not considered a foreign bank account. The PMC is evidence to your legal title to a specified amount of precious metals physically stored in Australia in your name. It can be bought and sold through a worldwide network of approved dealers. You can arrange for physical delivery any time. The metals price through the Perth Mint is very competitive and the minimum transaction is only US$10,000 initially and US$5,000 thereafter.

2. *Swiss annuities, endowments and insurance wrappers.* These investments offer solid asset protection, are offered in a variety of currencies, provide multi-currency capabilities, flexible estate planning features, tax deferment and more.

3. *Bear market annuity policies.* These include a personally tailored and professionally managed mix of bear market oriented assets in the currency of your choice such as the euro, Swiss franc or Norwegian kroner.

4. Bear market asset allocation and management. Unlike many other advisors, EurAxxess does not manage portfolios based on obsolete asset allocation models that assume equities are the unquestioned investment of choice. Our investment choices are based on dynamic investment models based on evidence that the global economy is entering a long-term bear market in equities.

5. Global services for U.S. retirement accounts. It remains perfectly legal for Americans to invest their IRA in foreign currencies and other types of non-U.S. investments without giving up tax deferral. Things might get worse before they get better. Be prepared and contact your Swiss connection for long-term wealth protection.

Part Two—Your Estate Plan
Grave Consequences: Offshore Estate Planning
by Derek R. Sambrook, *The Sovereign Individual*, August 2000

"We have left undone those things which we ought to have done; and we have done things which we ought not to have done." —Book of Common Prayer

This mournful reflection introduces a subject which most of us instinctively wish to avoid: death. There are many ways of expressing it—demise, departure, expiration, passing on, and the more pithy, bite the dust or kick the bucket (more about this receptacle later). But there is only one way of describing the condition when someone dies without leaving a will: intestate. This is best avoided for the sake of those left behind. If any of your assets (estate) are offshore, the problems are usually compounded.

Let's take a simple example, for which the names have been changed to protect the innocent and, in this case, also the foolish. The bank in the Cayman Island only knew that their client was dead when his widow arrived at the offices. Mr. Schubert had established the account only two years ago. Mrs. Schubert showed the last account statement and produced her late husband's canceled passport. She wished to close the account and transfer the US$600,000 in it back to Europe. Although her husband had left her a house and movable property, there was little cash available once all debts had been cleared.

The bank manager recalled Mr. Schubert's visit, remembering how the bank's trust officer had advised him to establish a trust to cover the contingency of death. Mr. Schubert had said that he would be doing something, perhaps on his next trip.

The banker conferred with the trust officer. Wouldn't it be all right to give the money to the widow? The response was an emphatic "No!" Only the executor of the estate could give proper instruction to the bank. Otherwise, the bank would be at risk. There are many legal precedents that have found non-executors liable for creditors, tax and beneficiaries' claims.

I could relate many similar tales of woe drawn from my 25 years of experience as a trustee and an executor. In any estate—even if it's insolvent—someone has to settle, at least, with the creditors. A will is a fundamental necessity, after which the need for a trust can be considered in the light of the nature and location of assets.

Trusts and wills can be domestic or offshore and there can be more than one. It is often wise to have either a will or trust dedicated to your offshore assets. But most people never execute even a domestic will. Of those who do, a good 50 percent rarely review them on a regular basis. The greatest neglect, however, seems to be reserved for our offshore estate. It is an irony that assets cultivated and protected like orchids in a hothouse during life are abandoned and neglected at our demise.

With offshore assets, an executor will need to appoint agents in each country. Until the foreign courts have accepted the executor's authority, the foreign assets will be frozen. It is not uncommon for several months to pass before an executor's authority is confirmed—especially where all supporting documentation must be officially translated into another language. If there is no will, the delay before an executor is appointed will have a domino effect offshore. All this adds significantly to the costs of winding up the estate.

Most sophisticated offshore investors manage their assets through an offshore company. These companies are like buckets into which assets are poured—real estate, investments, business agreements, bank accounts, etc. The trick is to keep everything in this metaphorical bucket without having it kicked over and spilling the assets.

This is best provided for by living trust. The holding company shares are transferred to a trust established and active during a person's lifetime and managed by a trustee. A properly drafted trust deed will guarantee a smooth transition of ownership, whoever dies and when.

I hope that some readers who fall into the category of will-evaders are provoked into action. They should get advice from a qualified practitioner experienced in the administration of estates and trusts so that the only tears shed at the grave side are ones of sadness, rather than anguish and frustration.

Incidentally, Mrs. Schubert left the Cayman Islands empty-handed. Her late husband had died intestate which produced a line of succession that reduced her inheritance significantly. It was only after two years of family squabbling that the funds in the Cayman account were finally released.

Since then, the bank has identified a few foreign inactive accounts with hold-mail instructions and no contact details. Will someone eventually claim them if the account-holder is dead? What if the customer told no one about the account? Depending on the jurisdiction, unclaimed monies in most cases eventually pass to the Treasury. Sad.

This article started with a somber preamble, so let me end with a personal maxim, which conveys the same message, but without the gravity: Ashes to ashes, dust to dust; Wherever the cash is, have a will or trust.

Offshore Variable Annuities: Asset Protection & Tax Avoidance

by Robert E. Bauman, JD, *The Sovereign Individual*, June 1999

As the United States, the United Kingdom and the European Union continue to tighten the tax and financial reporting screws on wealth, a worldwide search is on for private, profitable, yet strictly legal ways to protect and invest assets. Here's a financial product that fits the bill.

The offshore trust is the oldest and arguably the most effective means of preserving assets. But offshore trusts are becoming more controversial and the reporting requirements connected with their formation and operation are becoming increasingly onerous.

Concurrently, many of the world's best investments are denied to U.S. persons caught in a tangled net of government regulations that repulse foreign brokers and securities dealers. For instance, a recent survey shows that U.S. investors are effectively locked out of 80 of the world's top 100 most profitable mutual funds.

An Old Alternative Made New

An offshore variable annuity is one of the easiest, least expensive methods to invest in these otherwise unavailable offshore funds. Moreover, you obtain complete tax deferral until funds are actually withdrawn and your investments can be transferred from one fund manager to another with no tax consequences. Plus you achieve significant asset protection.

According to the *Wall Street Journal*, "Offshore annuities are becoming an investment vehicle of choice for those who have oodles of money they want to shelter from taxes." Offshore variable annuity investments typically start at a minimum of US$250,000, commonly exceeding US$1 million or more. (In contrast, the average domestic U.S. annuity buyer's initial investment is US$25,000 or less.)

Hywel Jones, an insurance service advisor in The Bahamas summarizes what investors are seeking: "The primary objectives in purchasing insurance offshore are asset protection, greater wealth accumulation and access to international investment opportunities."

Because they are offshore, away from restrictive U.S. laws, foreign insurance companies can be flexible in negotiating fees. Typical annual fees range from 0.65 percent to 1.25 percent of the net assets in the annuity account. For large accounts, fees of less than 0.65 percent are negotiable.

In addition, unless eliminated by a tax treaty, a one-time one percent federal excise tax is levied on all life insurance and annuity contracts issued to U.S. persons by foreign insurers.

Defer Taxes With an Offshore Variable Annuity

Foreign or domestic, a variable annuity is a contract, usually denominated in U.S. dollars, between you and an insurance company that provides tax deferred savings. It can serve as a savings or retirement vehicle using investment structures much like mutual funds, sometimes called "sub-accounts."

Here is how it works: you buy a variable annuity contract (policy) for an agreed upon sum, often referred to as a "single premium." These monies are invested by the insurance company in one or more investments that you approve, such as an offshore hedge fund.

The annuity contract requires periodic payments by the insurance company to you representing the increased value of investments on which the annuity is based. The money compounds, tax-deferred, until you withdraw part or all of it, at which time it is taxed as regular income.

This tax deferred accumulation can continue until the contract's maturity date, usually when you are 85 or older—usually a time when total income is lower. An annuity is not "life insurance," so you need not take a medical examination to determine "insurability."

In most cases when the annuity matures, it either must be surrendered or converted to a life annuity that pays out a specified sum, at least annually, for rest of your life, or for some other agreed period of time. Because most investors buy variable annuities for their tax deferred savings features, withdrawing funds as needed, most variable annuities never convert to a life annuity.

Strong Asset Protection

Variable insurance annuities offer significant asset protection, shielding the cash invested and the annuity income from creditors and other claimants. Practical asset protection exists since 1) the policies are issued by offshore insurance companies with no affiliates in the United States; 2) the policy's underlying assets are held entirely outside your home jurisdiction. Any domestic investments are made in the name of the insurance company, not your name.

Statutory asset protection exists in many jurisdictions for annuity contracts as well. In the Isle of Man (a jurisdiction that is home to 192 insurance companies), claims by creditors only can be made through the local courts. The Bahamas recently adopted legislation that exempts the proceeds of any annuity or insurance policy from claims by your creditors or claims against your estate or any beneficiary under the policy, including an associated trust. The law blocks attachment, garnishment or any legal process. A special clause forbids annuity redemption or cancellation "during any period where the owner is acting under duress imposed by any lawful authority or otherwise, other than lawful authority in The Bahamas."

The Bahamian law also protects annuity investors from claims against the offshore insurance company itself. It requires companies to establish "segregated accounts" on their books in which individual policy owner premiums must be held separate and apart from other insurance company assets, and from assets of other policy owners.

When a variable annuity is issued, the investment assets must be placed in this account and used only to satisfy the variable annuity obligation. If the company has financial problems, these segregated assets cannot be reached by insurance company creditors or creditors of other policy-holders.

The Cayman Islands, home to many leading offshore insurance companies, has a similar "segregated accounts" law.

In Switzerland, according to Swiss attorney Urs Schenker, "A life insurance policy... is protected from the policy owner's creditors if the policy owner has irrevocably designated a third party as beneficiary or if the policy owner has irrevocably or revocably designated his spouse and/or his descendants beneficiaries."

The Swiss Insurance Act prevents a properly structured insurance contract from being included in a Swiss bankruptcy procedure. The law also protects the contract from foreign seizure orders or orders including them as part of foreign estate proceedings. Under Swiss law, if you are unable to pay your debts or file bankruptcy, all rights under the contract are assigned to the beneficiaries. Other offshore jurisdictions with a well-developed insurance sector provide statutory protection against creditor claims for insurance policies.

Offshore Variable Annuities & Taxes

Section 72 of the U.S. Internal Revenue Code treats both foreign and domestic variable annuities the same. But the IRS rules must be followed by an insurance company in order for accumulations to qualify for tax deferral. Always obtain a copy of legal opinions an insurance company has concerning U.S. tax treatment of annuities issued by that company. Check with your tax advisors if in doubt.

To the extent that the funds you withdraw from a variable annuity represent deferred income, they are taxed at ordinary U.S. income tax rates.

A loan against a variable annuity from the issuing insurance company to the owner, or a third party loan secured by a pledge of the annuity, is a taxable distribution. Certain unsecured loans, however, may be tax-free. Also, borrowing against an annuity when it is purchased is not taxable since no deferred income has accumulated.

Thus you can acquire a US$2 million annuity contract and borrow up to US$1 million of the purchase price, pledging the annuity to secure the loan, with no adverse tax consequences. Under U.K. tax laws, up to five percent of a "bond" (annuity) value can be withdrawn annually as income and taxes are not payable until the bond is finally "encashed" upon termination.

However, the Inland Revenue apparently believes that these requirements are not always adhered to. In 1998, the National Irish Bank was placed under investigation by the Inland Revenue for allegedly assisting more than 200 investors to conceal £30 million (US$48 million) of income using offshore annuities. The bulk of the funds were invested in annuities sold by the Isle of Man based company, Clerical Medical International (CMI) and promoted in Ireland by NIB.

Structuring an Annuity with an Offshore Trust

Variable annuities can be used alone to hold assets or in conjunction with a trust. The trust can provide significant estate planning opportunities.

An insurance contract that you hold in your name will at your death have its cash value paid to one or more named beneficiaries. Your estate will be liable for both estate taxes and income taxes on any deferred income at death. But if you place ownership in a trust, the value of the annuity at death can be excluded from your estate.

Another tactic to reduce U.S. taxes is to name a charitable remainder trust (CRT) as the beneficiary of an annuity. This strategy avoids taxes on the increased value of the annuity at the owner's death and allows an estate tax deduction for part of the annuity value. The CRT can invest tax-free and make annual annuity payments to its life beneficiaries who pay income taxes on these distributions. When the CRT is dissolved, the remainder must go to a qualified charity, which can include a family-controlled private foundation.

Another possibility is to use a "defective" grantor trust in conjunction with the annuity, thereby allowing the annuity to be treated as an immediate gift to the beneficiaries. That eliminates the annuity's value from your estate. Long-term tax benefits also are possible by electing the US$1 million "generation skipping tax exemption" when the trust is created. This election means the annuity proceeds can serve as the asset base for producing benefits for several generations free of estate taxes. Consultation with a qualified professional is essential to achieve these results.

Information on Offshore Variable Annuities

Federal securities laws and state insurance laws prohibit companies offering offshore variable annuities from soliciting U.S. investors. These laws do not, however, prevent U.S. tax advisors, attorneys, estate planners or accountants from explaining the potential benefits of offshore annuities to their clients. Nor do they prohibit you from making your own inquiries.

Many offshore insurance companies require that you sign the annuity contract outside the U.S. If you don't wish to travel, you can designate an agent with a power of attorney who can sign for you.

Watch Your Step

Before you purchase an offshore variable annuity, carry out your own personal "due diligence" concerning the insurance company, the laws of the jurisdiction and the proposed insurance contract itself.

Reportable or Non-Reportable?

Although the U.S. requires citizens and residents to disclose an interest in offshore financial and bank accounts that in aggregate exceed US$10,000, there is controversy about whether annuity contracts fall within either classification and therefore need to be reported.

Most companies that offer offshore variable annuities claim that they are non-reportable. However, an opinion letter from the U.S. Treasury Department and a widely cited book on the Bank Secrecy Act quoting the letter claims that annuity contracts are reportable.

According to an attorney in the Financial Crimes Enforcement Network's Office of Legal Counsel, the letter remains a "valid" statement of Treasury policy on this matter. However, the opinion letter does not have the force of law and there are no official Treasury regulations with the force of law published on this matter.

Further, there appears to be only one reported case where a person was prosecuted for not reporting a foreign account that was clearly not a bank account. A key operative in the Iran-Contra affair had an offshore company set up for him by U.S. intelligence. A Swiss firm that provided "a broad range of financial and investment management services," but that was not a bank under Swiss law managed the company.

However, the firm made disbursements from the account at the defendant's direction. The court concluded that it would not be bound by the definition of "financial institution" in the Treasury regulations since the defendant used the firm to make transactions typically made through a bank. The conviction was upheld on appeal.

In contrast, there is no practical way to use a variable annuity to make transactions "typically made through a bank." In light of the failure of the U.S. Treasury to issue a definitive official pronouncement on the reporting status of offshore variable annuities, it seems relatively safe to merely report and pay tax on taxable distributions you receive and not separately report the existence of the contract itself. Consult with your own tax advisor for further guidance.

For more information on offshore variable annuities, contact:

Vernon K. Jacobs, CPA, CLU, Research Press, Inc., Box 8194, Prairie Village, Kansas 66208, U.S.A. **Tel.**: +1 913 362 9667. **E-mail**: jacobs@offshorepress.com. **Website**: www.offshorepress.com. (Jacobs is a certified life underwriter and offshore insurance advisor, and a member of the Sovereign Society's Council of Experts).

Offshore Life Insurance: Four Key Tax Advantages

By Selwyn Gerber, CPA, *The Sovereign Individual*, January 2002

The combination of income tax and estate tax, can, upon the death of U.S. citizens or residents, consume 50% or more of their estate. Avoiding these ruinous tax consequences is a key consideration in U.S. estate planning. To this end, offshore life insurance offers several key benefits when optimally structured: Tax-free build-up of cash values, including dividends, interest and capital gains.

Tax free borrowing against cash value. Policyholders have easy and tax-free access to as much as 90% of invested funds (including appreciation) through policy loans. These loans need not be serviced with interest payments and are deducted from the proceeds at death. Used in conjunction with an irrevocable life insurance trust, tax-free distributions (in the amount of the loans) to beneficiaries are possible.

Tax-free receipt of the death benefit. Freedom from estate and generation-skipping taxes. If structured properly, taxes on the investment appreciation within the insurance framework are eliminated since beneficiaries are not taxed upon receipt of the death benefit.

Only life insurance can claim these four advantages. Essentially, the investor saves the costs of income taxes on portfolio income and transactions (depending on portfolio turnover, anywhere from 20% to 50% of the annual pre-tax returns) in exchange for the cost of insurance; approximately 1-3% per year.

An all-domestic solution is sufficient in some circumstances. However, for larger estates, a foreign insurance company and possibly, a foreign trust, are often employed. Benefits include:

- *Increased asset protection.* Many offshore jurisdictions provide statutory asset protection for the death benefit and investments held by an insurance policy. In the United States, such protection exists only at the state level with coverage varying significantly between states. And, as a practical matter, it is much more expensive for a creditor to bring a claim before a foreign court than a domestic court.

- *Decreased opportunity for the estate to be contested.* It is far more difficult for a family member or other claimant to challenge estate arrangements made offshore, rather than domestically.

- *Access to international investments.* Offshore insurance policies provide tax-advantaged access to international asset managers and to offshore funds that are otherwise not easily accessible to U.S. investors.

- *Increased privacy.* The confidentiality statutes of some jurisdictions (e.g., Switzerland) give insurance policies the same protection against disclosure as bank accounts. Even where no secrecy statutes exist (e.g., Bermuda, the Channel Islands, the Isle of Man), confidentiality still applies. This protection can be an important shield to frivolous claims and investigations. What's more, assets held offshore are off the domestic "radar screen" and cannot easily be identified in a routine asset search.

- *Non-existent disclosure requirements.* Neither the acquisition of an offshore life insurance policy nor income or gain within it is reportable to the IRS.

Although these advantages apply to all offshore life insurance policies, the most flexible form is "private placement variable universal life insurance" (PPVUL). This form permits complete customization to ensure that individual needs are met. Underlying investments can take virtually any form, including offshore funds that, without the use of an insurance framework, would be exposed to unfavorable U.S. tax treatment. Investors can nominate trustees, custodians and asset managers.

In addition, the underlying investments are not part of the insurance carrier's general account. Rather, the assets are placed in separate accounts that are legally segregated from claims of the insurance carrier's creditors. There is no risk to these assets in the event of carrier bankruptcy or reorganization.

As PPVUL structures represent a customized solution to international tax planning, there are many possible applications. In the case of a U.S. person who both funds the structure and is the individual insured, a U.S. or foreign trust could be set up to hold the life insurance policy. For larger estates, this trust is set up outside the grantor's estate. This means that distributions from this trust after the grantor's death will not be subject to estate tax. Properly structured and funded, there could be no income or estate tax levied for 100 years or even longer.

It is also possible to provide tax-free income to a U.S. beneficiary using a non-U.S. donor/insured person. However, this structure faces onerous IRS compliance requirements and is suitable only if a bona-fide offshore donor is available. Other variations are also possible; e.g., to provide tax-free income to non-U.S. beneficiaries using a U.S. or non-U.S. donor/insured person.

To preserve tax benefits, there must be a minimum level of insurance and investments must be made in a series of annual installments. While policy owners can choose among investment managers, they cannot direct a manager into a particular investment or strategy. If these guidelines are not followed, the IRS taxes any withdrawal or borrowing as ordinary income.

Initial fees for this structure include set-up fees of 2% to 3% of premium dollars contributed. Recurring fees include investment management fees, insurance company administration and overhead charges and the cost of insurance cover. Total annual costs exclusive of asset management fees are typically 1-3%.

Contrary to widespread belief, the costs relating to the establishment and maintenance of a PPVUL strategy are surprisingly inexpensive. This approach is therefore an important option for those seeking a flexible tax advantaged comprehensive estate plan providing tax efficiency and access to a wide selection of international asset management options. However, the strategy is most cost effective for estates that can invest US$500,000 or more in the offshore insurance policy.

Foreign Trusts—Ultimate Offshore Asset Protection
by Robert E. Bauman, JD, & David Melnik, QC, *The Offshore Money Manual*

Offshore trusts—especially the asset protection trust—can place your wealth beyond the reach of claimants, creditors, irate ex-spouses and even the government of your home country.

If you ever ask a lawyer to define a "trust," your eyes may glaze over as you listen to something like this: A trust is a legal device resulting when a person who creates the trust (variously called the "grantor," "donor," "trustor," or "settlor") conveys all and every legal and equitable right, title and interest that he or she holds in certain real property (the "corpus") to a second party (the "trustee"), perhaps a faithful friend, professional financial manager or a bank trust department, who holds the assets for the benefit of one or more named persons or entities known as "beneficiaries," according to the terms of the grantor's basic trust contract, called a trust "declaration."

Impressive. Overwhelming. At least it wasn't in Latin.

Simply put, a trust is a three-way legal device. It allows one person (the trustee) to take title and possession of any kind of property to be held, used, and/or managed for the benefit of one or more other persons (the beneficiaries). The person who creates the trust (the grantor) decides what it will do and donates property to fund it. More simply: the grantor gives money to the trustee to administer for the benefit of a stated beneficiary, being careful all the time not to attract gift and capital gains taxes.

The possible variations on this basic theme are endless. There can be any number of grantors, trustees and beneficiaries. Two parents can entrust four people with money intended to benefit their six children. The assets placed in the trust can also be varied. You can choose cash, stocks, or any other vehicle you possess.

Whatever the arrangement, the trust must have a reason for being. To create a trust, the grantor signs a lengthy written declaration or indenture describing what he or she has in mind. This document spells out specific details of trust operation including income distribution and trustee powers. These instructions are binding both during and after the grantor's lifetime.

Thousands of court rulings have given unique definition to almost every word and phrase used in a trust declaration. Drafting one correctly requires expert legal advice. Before creating a trust, all estate planning must be coordinated and reviewed; the right hand must know what the left hand is doing.

What a Trust Can Do

A trust may be created for any legal purpose that does not run counter to public policy. That is a broad spectrum by any standard. The government constantly attempts to narrow the choices, but the fact remains: you can create a trust for almost any purpose.

A trust can conduct a business. It can hold title to and invest in real estate, cash, stocks, bonds, negotiable instruments, and any other kind of property. Trusts are often created to care for minor children or the elderly. Others are established to pay medical, educational or legal expenses. Again, the possibilities are endless.

For our purposes, there is one very important role a trust can serve, especially an offshore trust. In carefully arranged circumstances, trusts can serve as excellent wealth and asset protection devices.

Trusts Go Way Back

Before explaining how you can benefit from a trust, let's take a look at the history and progression of this all-important investment device.

Trust arrangements stretch all the way back to ancient Egypt. Ancient Germanic and French law recognized the trust as well. From the time of Mohammed, it was a fundamental principle of Islamic law. In the Middle Ages, the quasi-religious order of the Knights Templar acted as international financiers. They used trusts to help royal and ecclesiastical investors shield their financial activity from the public and one another. Citizens of sixteenth-century England used them to avoid feudal taxes on property inheritances and restrictions on land transfers. In fact, the trust is probably the world's oldest tax shelter.

Over centuries, the trust has been refined repeatedly by practical use and development, especially in England. This process was later carried on in the British Commonwealth nations and in the United States. American judges have played a large role in perfecting modern domestic trusts, producing significant beneficial legal and tax consequences for U.S. citizens.

Trusts are now used most often in personal estate planning. They allow you to pass property title to heirs while minimizing probate court costs, legal fees, and inheritance taxes. Nationally, probate fees (exclusive of taxes) average from one percent to 15 percent of estate value, a substantial chunk. Probate in some states like California can drag on for years while legal fees pile up and beneficiaries are left in limbo.

The Foreign Asset Protection Trust

In recent years, an asset-protection device in trust form has gained worldwide popularity. The foreign asset protection trust (APT) is a personal trust created and based in a foreign nation. It will shield your assets better than any domestic trust ever can, simply because it is located outside the United States. Distance makes the trust grow stronger. This trust shields business and personal assets against demanding creditors, litigation and other unpleasant financial liabilities.

The key to creating such a trust is simple: planning. The APT must be planned and created long before you really need it, at a time of personal financial calm. As a belated response to a imminent financial crisis, it will achieve little. Last minute attempts to create an offshore trust can lead to civil liability for concealing assets or fraud under the "Fraudulent Conveyers" legislation found in American bankruptcy law. In litigation-crazed America, you should not wait for trouble before taking offshore precautionary measures.

As a practical matter, placing title to property in the name of an offshore APT cannot really protect any assets that physically remain within an American court's jurisdiction. Assets actually transferred to the APT's foreign jurisdiction, like funds moved to an offshore bank account, are usually safe from a U.S. creditor, even if he knows the account exists.

Locating Your APT

Certain countries tailor their laws to welcome foreign-owned APTs. Although these nations may be diminutive in geographic size and total population, their capital cities have well-developed, efficient banking and legal communities. Banking and legal officials understand APT law and finance. More importantly, they want your business and are eager to please.

There are established APT havens all over the world. From the Cayman Islands to the Isle of Man, investors looking for the perfect investment location have a wide variety of options.

Strong Creditor Deterrent

While the APT concept may be new to you, thousands of American citizens have successfully followed this international road to wealth protection. Here's what makes an offshore APT so attractive:

- *Start Over*: Courts in asset-haven nations usually don't honor or even recognize the validity of U.S. court orders. A foreign creditor trying to collect must re-litigate the claim in a local court, use local lawyers and obtain another judgment. Sheer legal complexity and cost are likely to produce a quick and satisfactory compromise with all but the most determined adversaries.

- *Minimal Needs*: To operate your APT, you'll need little more than a trust account in a local or multinational branch bank. The bank can provide trustees and working staff experienced in trust matters. With modem communications, conducting business will be much like having an account in another American city. Most banks offer US dollar-denominated accounts, often with better interest rates than American financial institutions offer.

- *More Control*: As grantor of a foreign asset-protection trust, you can exercise far greater control over assets and income than American trust law permits. U.S. rules that discourage you from creating a trust for your own benefit do not apply in these countries. In all 50 states and the District of Columbia, a trust with the grantor as beneficiary won't protect against creditors. It will in these foreign jurisdictions.

- *Fast Acting*: Foreign law usually does not support strict application of U.S. fraudulent conveyance and bankruptcy laws. Some countries have a strict statute of limitations on creditor suits; a claim must be filed within two years from the date the APT was established. The Cook Islands has a one-year limit. It may take a creditor longer than that just to discover the existence of an offshore APT.

- *Investments*: An offshore APT is great for diversified international investments. Your trustee handles the paper work, while you give long-distance directions. You can take advantage of the world's best investment opportunities without worrying about restrictive U.S. securities laws.

- *Flexible*: An APT provides added flexibility in the case of personal disability, when transferring assets, or avoiding domestic currency controls. Your foreign APT trustee can even make your mortgage payments and other personal bills on a regular basis.

- *No Insurance*: An APT is a good substitute for, or supplement to, costly professional liability insurance. Such a trust can even be used as an integral part of a prenuptial agreement.

- *Quick Change*: Often the trust declaration contains a *force majeure* clause that allows the situs, or location, of the APT to be changed at any time. Originally meant to be used in time of war, civil unrest or major natural disasters, this clause can also be activated if the offshore haven decides to change its APT-friendly laws. A complimentary feature in many APT-haven countries is a provision that allows instant acceptance of a transfer of an existing APT from one country to another with no break in legal operation. This can be done merely by filing a registration form and paying a filing fee.

Creating an APT

The legal structure of a foreign APT differs little from an American trust. You, as grantor, create the APT, transferring title to assets that are administered by an offshore trustee according to the trust declaration for the named beneficiaries. In some nations the law requires the naming of three trustees, two located in the grantor's home country, and one independent managing trustee located in the offshore country. Most countries do not permit the grantor to serve as a trustee, but they do allow a grantor to retain an unrestricted right to remove the trustees at will. This assures that trust administration reflects your wishes.

Foreign trust law, unlike strict American "arm's length" requirements, allows you to be a beneficiary while maintaining effective control over the investment and distribution of the trust principal. The trust declaration can give the grantor a large measure of control, including the right of prior approval of investments or distributions.

Many of these nations require appointment of a local "trust protector." This individual acts as a neutral party who ensures trust objectives are met and the law is followed. A protector does not manage the trust, but can veto trustee actions in some cases.

Privacy is Paramount

Most of these countries require very little information about an APT at the time it is registered with the government. The terms of the trust agreement and the parties involved need not be disclosed, and any information filed is not available as part of a public record. The only public record is a registry of the APT by name, date of creation and the name of the local trustee. In these privacy-conscious countries, a trustee is allowed to reveal information only in very limited circumstances, and then usually only by local court order. This offers a distinct privacy advantage over offshore corporations (usually called international business corporations, or IBCs). At least one person involved in organizing a corporation must be listed on the public record. So must the corporate name and address. Some countries require corporate directors to be listed as well. This gives privacy invaders a starting point.

Another issue that worries most people is physical distance. How can you rest easy when your money is thousands of miles away, in a foreign nation, controlled by an unrelated trustee? This concern is justified, but can be easily overcome. The trick is to choose reliable people to manage your trust. The experts in the legal and banking industries in these nations have extensive experience with APTs. References are in order, and each one should be checked carefully. We suggest a few reliable contacts below. Call them, and they will be able to set you on the right path.

One thing is certain: your offshore trustee should have no connections that might subject him to pressure from U.S. courts. If you are considering an international bank trust department as your trustee, ask them bluntly what their policy is in such situations. It is better to go with a local, in-country bank or trust company. These will be less likely to buckle under pressure from a U.S. court.

What Do You Put into Your Foreign APT

While you need not physically transfer your assets offshore, it is wise to do so. If you don't, it will be easy for U.S. courts to seize them. The best vehicles for trust investment are cash and evidence of intangible assets. Easily portable assets, such as precious metals, coins, jewelry or gem stones also can be transferred offshore for storage in the APT's name. But remember, if you transfer something other than cash, and you are not the beneficiary, you run the risk of attracting substantial gift and capital gains taxes. Be sure to consult with a professional before moving your assets.

We repeat: simply transferring title to real estate or a business located in the United States to an offshore trust does not remove those assets from the reach of American creditors and courts.

APT Combined With a Limited Partnership

One popular option is to combine an offshore APT with an American-based family limited partnership. Because limited partnerships give maximum asset protection and management control guaranteed by law, they are one of the most effective asset protection devices in the U.S. today.

In a family limited partnership, husband and wife might control one percent of the partnership as managing general partners, with title to 99 percent of the shares transferred to your children as limited partners. You can continue transferring property to your children a number of years after the partnership is established. Each parent can give up to US$10,000 per child exempt from U.S. gift taxes when counting partnership value transfers. Part of the combined US$1.2 million estate-tax exemption can be used as well. (Again, this will increase to US$2 million by 2006.)

This is not a drastic surrender of wealth to your children. As limited partners, your children have no control over the assets. You and your spouse, the managing general partners, have all the control. You decide how the money is invested and how the cash is distributed. Although limited partners do own the assets, they are considered inactive owners.

An extra-tough layer of asset protection is achieved when title to the 99 percent limited partnership interest is transferred to an offshore APT. That extra layer of legal distance will make potential creditors think twice before pursuit. To get to your assets they would not only have to show the partnership formation was somehow illegal, but also crack the APT title in the foreign court. An excellent place to utilize this strategy is Scotland, which charges no income taxes on foreign owned limited partnerships.

Unique Benefits of Offshore Asset Protection Trusts:
An Interview With Gideon Rothschild
The Sovereign Individual, October 2002

[**Ed. Note**: Of all domestic asset protection structures and techniques available for U.S. persons, the "spendthrift trust" offers the greatest asset protection. However, a person forming a domestic spendthrift trust generally cannot be a beneficiary of that trust and still have asset protection. With a foreign trust, you can obtain both asset protection and benefit from the trust. New York attorney Gideon Rothschild, a member of The Sovereign Society's Council of Experts, explains. TSI interviewed him on August 23, 2002.]

TSI: Could you briefly summarize the options that a U.S. person has to protect their assets in the event of judgment or bankruptcy?

Rothschild: There are many types of assets protected under either state or federal law. State homestead statutes, for instance, may protect some or all of the value of a person's residence from creditors. Texas and Florida are well known for such statutes.

The federal ERISA statute protects qualified retirement plans. Individual Retirement Accounts (IRAs) are not included under this statute, but many state statutes protect IRAs from creditors. My web site contains two articles that discuss state exemptions for retirement plans, insurance and annuities, along with a state-by-state chart for each separate set of rules. The articles are posted at www.mosessinger.com/resources.

Unfortunately, exemptions at the state level generally protect only individuals living in that state. For instance, to benefit from the Florida homestead law, you must live in Florida for at least six months and physically reside in the residence you wish to protect. A new federal bankruptcy law now pending in Congress may extend this period to 40 months.

TSI: What about domestic trusts?

Rothschild: Trusts have been around for hundreds of years, and every state recognizes the "spendthrift trust" rule. They provide highly effective asset protection. So long as the assets remain in trust, the beneficiary's creditors can't reach them. To qualify for this protection, the trustee must not be required to distribute the assets to the beneficiary at any particular time. Nor can the beneficiary have the right to withdraw the assets.

Retaining property in trust for the entire lifetime of a beneficiary is much more effective to protect that beneficiary from creditors than outright bequests. Parents often worry that their children will have to beg for distributions from the trustee. But there are many ways of providing the children some degree of control without giving up asset protection benefits, although the more control the beneficiaries have, the less protection there will be. A middle ground may be to give the children half the estate outright and keep half in trust

The Limitations of Domestic Trusts

TSI: What limitations exist to the protection provided by a domestic spendthrift trust?

Rothschild: There are cases where domestic courts have ordered that a distribution be made from trust for the benefit of certain preferred classes of creditors. However, even this result could be avoided with proper drafting.

Apart from poor drafting, the primary limitation of domestic trusts is that you must give up all rights to the assets you place in trust to obtain asset protection. Otherwise, you have what is called a "self-settled trust." A long line of case law stipulates that such trusts can be invaded for the benefit of your creditors.

There are other potential problems with domestic trusts. What happens if you set up a trust for your spouse, and he or she dies before you do? What happens if you and your spouse become divorced? The only effective way that you can both benefit from a trust and protect the assets you place into it is to use an offshore asset protection trust (APT) structure.

The Cook Islands was the first jurisdiction to enact such laws, followed by Nevis, the Turks & Caicos Islands, St. Lucia, Gibraltar, etc. Each statute differs slightly. Some jurisdictions stipulate that they won't recognize foreign judgments. If a U.S. creditor tries to enforce a U.S. judgment against a foreign APT, the creditor will have to start an action all over again under the foreign jurisdiction's laws, which are generally less sympathetic to expansive theories of liability than U.S. courts. Most offshore APT statutes stipulate that if the creditor loses, it must generally pay the defendant's legal fees. The creditor may even be required to post a bond for this purpose, before litigation begins.

I should emphasize that there are no tax benefits to APTs, although there are many promoters who claim that if you purchase one of "their" offshore trusts, you'll never have to pay taxes again, etc. Falling prey to such promoters can get you into a lot of trouble—avoid them. (See www.ustreas.gov/irs/ci/tax_fraud/index.htm.)

TSI: In recent years, APTs have come under attack in the courts. Some attorneys now say that such trusts are ineffective. How do you react to this criticism?

Rothschild: What the courts have criticized isn't the APT concept so much as the way it has been misused. APTs (and all asset protection planning) should be employed to protect wealth against claims by unknown future creditors, not against claims by persons to whom you currently or foreseeably owe money. If you try to avoid current creditors there are remedies available under state and federal fraudulent conveyance statutes. In some cases that have reached the courts, the person forming the offshore trust (the "grantor") made fraudulent transfers. In others, the grantor retained too much control over the trust assets. But even here, the creditors still haven't been able to get the assets, although in the Lawrence case, the grantor has been in jail for more than two years for contempt of court.

If you move assets into an offshore APT when there are no claims pending, I don't believe you will be exposed to a contempt of court situation. Indeed, I've had judges on several seminar panels indicate that if you create an offshore trust before a creditor has a claim, they would be unlikely to hold you in contempt.

Now, it's not impossible that another judge might feel that the only way to get even with you for making your assets unavailable to future creditors is to throw you in jail. However, the vast majority of cases involving offshore trusts never reach a judge. They are almost always settled out of court because the creditor realizes that most any judgment won't be collectable. Lawyers working on a contingency basis don't want to waste their time going after someone who is judgment-proof.

Are State APT Statutes Effective?

TSI: In the last few years, several U.S. states have enacted so-called APT legislation. What is your view of these statutes?

Rothschild: Nevada, Alaska, Delaware and Rhode Island have adopted statutes intended to provide the same protection as those in the Cook Islands, etc. However, these laws are untested. If you live in one of these states and form such a trust, and a claim against you originates in that state, the trust might survive. But if you live in Florida, form a Delaware APT, and are sued in Florida, a Florida court might well rule that since the trust is "self-settled," the assets are available to creditors under Florida law. Then the creditors could seek to have the judgment enforced in Delaware, under the U.S. Constitution's "full faith and credit" clause. Why take that risk?

TSI: What percentage of a person's wealth should be placed in a foreign trust?

Rothschild: This isn't something that can be expressed in percentages. In general, the most conservative approach is the "nest-egg" strategy; keeping sufficient assets in an offshore trust so that in the event of financial catastrophe, you aren't wiped out. Transferring all your assets to an offshore trust might be viewed with skepticism by a court.

TSI: You've discussed primarily offshore trusts so far. Some attorneys are now recommending that U.S. persons use offshore insurance structures for asset protection instead of a foreign trust. What is your opinion of this suggestion?

Rothschild: For individuals with smaller estates, foreign single premium fixed annuities or variable annuities may be appropriate, although U.S. persons aren't permitted to purchase such contracts in most countries. Usually, you'll have to form a foreign entity such as an international business company (IBC), and doing so creates its own tax problems. (**Ed. Note**: Switzerland is an exception—individuals can purchase insurance contracts there).

In larger estates, we may recommend the purchase of a foreign life insurance policy through an offshore trust. This provides asset protection and with proper planning, the income earned within the policy is income tax free. The client can designate his own investment manager and depending on how the trust is structured, the death benefit may even be estate tax free.

TSI: Can you provide a few examples of individuals who may be able to benefit from offshore trusts?

Rothschild: My clients have a net worth ranging from US$1 million to over US$1 billion. They include doctors who can no longer purchase malpractice insurance because it's no longer offered in their state or because it's become so expensive. Or their carriers have gone bankrupt and they're going "bare." This has become a serious problem in many states.

With the post-Enron scandals, persons who serve on the board of directors of a public company are at risk of becoming targets of class action lawsuits. With stock prices dropping, it's not a question of fault, but of "where is the deep pocket?"

Also, and this is a point that The Sovereign Society has made for years, an offshore trust is an easy way to diversify investments internationally. An offshore trust can purchase foreign currencies, foreign securities, etc.

Nor should one forget history. It was only 60 years ago that Hitler was expropriating assets of wealthy Jews. Today in Zimbabwe, Mugabe is confiscating property from whites. In Great Britain, it was against the law to move assets outside the country until the 1980s. In many Latin American countries, persons perceived as wealthy are at a much higher risk for kidnapping. If the United States ever experiences a significant financial crisis, with the stroke of a pen, the President can prohibit the movement of funds abroad. If you don't have assets offshore in some form, you're defenseless.

You also have greater privacy. Yes, you have to comply with tax laws, but the assets are "off the radar screen" to ordinary creditors.

I think the best testimony as to whether APTs are effective came from a bankruptcy attorney with whom I served on a panel at a legal conference. This attorney is an outspoken advocate of "creditor's rights" and finds the entire concept of APTs abhorrent. However, even he admitted that they are basically inviolable!

(**Gideon Rothschild** *is a partner in the law firm Moses & Singer, LLP. He specializes in domestic and international estate planning and asset protection for high net worth individuals. The immediate past Chair of the Committee on Asset Protection of the American Bar Association, Rothschild is a nationally recognized authority on the use of offshore trusts and other planning techniques for wealth preservation. Contact Rothschild c/o Moses & Singer LLP.* **Tel.**: *+1 (212) 554-7806.* **Fax**: *+1 (212) 554-7700.* **E-mail**: *grothschild@mosessinger.com.* **Website**: *www.mosessinger.com.*)

Liechtenstein's Unique Trusts
by Reinhard Stern, *Austria & Liechtenstein Report*, 1997

The Principality of Liechtenstein (in German, *Fuerstentum Liechtenstein*, thus the FL stickers on its cars) is one of the world's smallest countries. Investors often call it the "mini-Switzerland within Switzerland." Liechtenstein's fiscal fame is based on bank secrecy laws even stricter than those of Switzerland and on the vast number of letter box firms and holding corporations administered by Liechtenstein attorneys. Because the country is so small, it depends heavily on outside investment, a situation which works to the advantage of international investors and foreigners with accounts there. Relative to its size and population, Liechtenstein is the world's most highly industrialized country, with concentration in the metal, chemicals, pharmaceutical, textile and food sectors.

Liechtenstein lies nestled between Switzerland to the west and Austria to the east, slightly off the most heavily traveled highways. It is easily accessible by both autobahn and the main train line between Zurich and Chur, which lie just to the south. It's also on the main route to the most popular destinations in the Alps, including St. Moritz in the Engadin area. For travelers on their way to Austria's Arlberg region, for example to St. Anton in Tirol, Vaduz is just a short detour. Liechtenstein's total land area is only 157 square kilometers (62 square miles), the same size as Washington, D.C. The Rhine Valley occupies one third of the country, and the Alps cover most of the rest, leaving only one quarter of the land arable.

Bank Secrecy

Bank secrecy is the same as in Switzerland. There is no sharp delineation between simple failure to pay full taxes and tax evasion, and non-compliance with foreign tax regulations is not punishable by law. According to a European treaty governing legal obligations in criminal matters, Liechtenstein authorities are only obliged to provide information normally protected by bank secrecy laws if a criminal offense, including tax fraud, is being prosecuted in a foreign court of law, but not if the prosecutors are tax or fiscal authorities.

As in Austria and Switzerland, violations of bank secrecy are punishable by law in Liechtenstein. Foreign tax investigators who try to circumvent bank or tax secrecy laws while within Liechtenstein territory take a great risk.

[**Ed. Note**: Under pressure from the Financial Action Task Force of the G-8 major nations, Liechtenstein adopted a stringent anti-money laundering law in 2000 and began enforcement in 2001. The law allows the government to freeze assets and conduct investigations based on allegations of criminal financial conduct made by foreign governments. It also allows limited information sharing in such cases.]

The Trust (*Stiftung*)

One of the most attractive financial options for managing and protecting your funds is the famous Liechtenstein *Stiftung* or trust. Under the law, a trust is looked upon as a person with all the rights and the responsibilities of an individual to whom you give your assets as a gift. The emphasis is on the word gift.

The trust statutes include a ruling covering the succession of heirs or beneficiaries. As the founder of the trust, you can designate your heirs in a by-statute of your will and later make any changes you want at no further cost. Your corporate statutes must include a clause stipulating your right to cancel the trust at any time. Without this stipulation, the trust could revert to the Principality of Liechtenstein in the event of your death. Liechtenstein levies an annual capital tax of one pro mille on trust funds. In other words, a trust worth one million Swiss francs— US$820,000, a financially workable figure—pays Sfr.1,000 or US$820 per year in taxes. A minimum initial investment of roughly US$500,000-600,000 is advisable; the breakeven point of a trust is US$410,000.

The Commercial Trust (*Anstalt*)

While a *Stiftung*-type trust can only administer your funds, an alternative form called the *Anstalt* or commercial trust functions like a company and can both manage your money and conduct business. A commercial trust requires a minimum base capital of Sfr50,000 and must produce a yearly balance sheet. At the end of the fiscal year, it also has to pay one pro mille capital tax. Although Austria and Liechtenstein have a double taxation agreement, authorities of the two countries do not exchange information on business activities.

As the owner of a Liechtenstein commercial trust, you can enjoy tax-free resident status in Austria because as long as you don't work in the country, you are not liable to Austrian taxation. Your firm, however, is located in Liechtenstein, and all your commercial transactions are done there. You can live on the funds you funnel to Austria, and Austrian fiscal authorities have no access to information on your business activities.

Here's an example of how the commercial trust can work. A couple named Kramer owned and resided in a villa located on a desirable 25,000-square-meter piece of property on the Attersee, a lake in Austria. They hired a lawyer in Liechtenstein to register the Kurt Commercial Trust there. Two years later, the foundation bought the Kramers' estate for one million schillings, about one tenth of its real value.

The significance of the transaction between the Kramers and the Kurt Commercial Trust is that it was completely anonymous. No one knew that the Kramer family was behind the trust. By selling their property to the trust, the Kramers protected it and kept it away from their heirs. They also saved a great deal of money, because the trust bought their estate at a very low appraised value. It was exempt from normal taxes on the income from a sale which would have automatically moved the Kramers into a much higher tax bracket. In short, commercial trusts are very advantageous in real estate dealings, for example buying property in Austria.

Obviously, then, a commercial trust offers you several advantages when it comes to managing funds, buying real estate and saving on taxes. First, by naming a Liechtenstein lawyer as a trustee and yourself as a beneficiary, you establish anonymity. The only visible documentation is the certificate of ownership (*Inhaberpapier*). You also eliminate the need to report this inheritance to the fiscal authorities later; consequently you will pay no gift tax on it. If the beneficiary of a commercial trust is a trust rather than a person, there is no way to trace the owner. Fiscal authorities are satisfied with the explanation above.

Second, your investment grows at a much faster rate because capital taxes are so low in Liechtenstein. An important note: as founder of the trust, you should not have any further influence on the management of the money you have "given away." This is a point Austrian tax authorities have been checking very closely.

Third, as the owner of the trust, you should stipulate in the statutes that dividends are always to be reinvested in the trust rather than paid out. This way there is no income tax to be paid on the money you funnel to Austria. Naturally the beneficiaries only have to pay taxes on this money if it is brought to Austria.

Fourth, in Austria nobody owns or has to pay taxes on this money, so it is not subject to estate taxes.

Another very important and widely used arrangement is the family trust. If your wife or children can be named as the second, third or fourth beneficiaries, you don't have to pay a gift tax when their money is transferred.

What does a trust cost? Instead of high taxes, you have to pay certain costs in Liechtenstein, including the expense of setting up the trust and the lawyer's fee. These costs are not dependent on the amount of money invested in the trust and usually amount to around Sfr4,000 or US$3,000. Yearly costs for trust administration run between Sfr3,000-3,500, or roughly US$2,000-3,000. The capital tax in Liechtenstein is one pro mille of the capital of the trust, and there is a four percent tax on returns. Total costs can thus amount to US$5,000. There are no inheritance taxes to be paid if there is a stipulation that the trust is to be dissolved upon the death of the founder.

The cost is the same for a commercial trust. However, you have to invest Sfr.30,000 as the founding capital and pay an annual one pro mille capital tax for trust administration. Since it is a commercial business, you also have to pay the fee for the fiscal report at the end of the year.

The Trustee

To found a trust, you must retain the services of a trustee, called a *Treuhaender*. Liechtenstein lawyers can have power of attorney to conduct business in their client's name, while Swiss lawyers cannot. The most important aspect of such an arrangement is for you to remain completely anonymous. That's why you need a person the bank officials know and respect to manage your assets.

The trustee will handle all the initial legal arrangements, including helping you with the wording of your trust statutes and delivering your money and securities such as deeds, stock certificates, etc. to the bank. He then manages your trust funds according to your wishes as stipulated in the trust, collects the interest from the bank in cash, and turns it over to you in the privacy of his office. In other words, the lawyer or trustee acts as a middleman, ensuring the complete anonymity of the trust's founder.

The first step, of course, is to locate and hire a lawyer. One possibility is to find an Austrian lawyer who agrees to act in your name. There are several competent, experienced lawyers in Vienna who offer this service, but their fees are high because they have to work through a colleague in Liechtenstein. The second, more viable option is to retain the services of a lawyer right in Liechtenstein—someone who is thoroughly familiar with the procedure and knows the right people. Liechtenstein has over 90,000 registered accommodation addresses, and more than 400 of them are administered by a single lawyer.

It is vital for you to know that when you set up a trust, you are in effect turning all your money over to the trustee. You have no legal recourse if he should mismanage or misappropriate your funds; you cannot take him to court or sue him. You must therefore be extremely careful in your choice of a trustee.

Considerations

Before you decide to go to a Liechtenstein trust office to start a trust or commercial trust, you should know the answers to the following questions:

1. Should you have only one beneficiary—yourself—or should your spouse or your children be included?

2. Who will succeed you as the first beneficiary in the event of your death?

3. Who will be the final heir if all the other beneficiaries die at the same time?

4. Should the profits be reinvested or paid out annually?

5. Should interest be paid to each beneficiary or only to you?

6. Should the funds be recoverable only after a certain date, for example your child's thirtieth birthday? (This applies only to the trust.)

7. Have you made provisions for a cancellation clause in your trust? Without it, the trust will be perpetual and your money inaccessible.

The Accommodation Address

Now let's discuss the institution called a *Briefkastenfirma*. This German term translates literally as "letter box firm" but is sometimes called an accommodation address. It is an entity geared to the specific needs of the client. It allows the owner of the company to enjoy problem-free capital growth in a foreign country and funnel his money back to the country where he currently resides. The accommodation address receives commissions, a percentage of the profits, license fees and patents - all income which is usually taxed by the fiscal authorities. It also charges fees for all kinds of services, for example consulting, inspections, audits and mediation, and can set the prices on the invoices. In short, the services of a company which has its seat in a fiscal paradise exist only on paper.

Although the accommodation address is a very old practice, it is still forbidden. That's why all these fees are moved back to Austria as loans. If the capital gains and profits in Liechtenstein are too high, they are funneled to Panama by means of a document called a "profit-transfer contract" and your primary investment stays in Liechtenstein accounts. Naturally, issuing falsified statements and bills is both unethical and illegal.

———— •◆• ————

Hybrid Trusts

by Robert E. Bauman, JD, & David Melnik, QC, *The Offshore Money Manual*

You can use a Liechtenstein trust to control a family fortune, with the trust assets represented as shares in holding companies that control the relevant businesses.

Liechtenstein's trust laws are very practical and theoretically interesting. This is due to the country's unusual combination of civil law and common law concepts. Enacted in 1926, the Liechtenstein Diet adopted a fairly faithful reproduction of the English-American trust system. They even allow the trust grantors to choose governing law from any common-law country. This places the Liechtenstein judiciary in the unique position of applying trust law from England, Bermuda or Delaware when addressing a controversy regarding a particular trust instrument.

Even though it is a civil law nation, a trust located in Liechtenstein can be useful in lowering taxes, sheltering foreign income, and safeguarding assets from American estate taxes. The law allows quick portability of trusts to another jurisdiction and accepts foreign trusts that wish to re-register as a local entity.

The trust instrument must be deposited with the Commercial Registry, but is not subject to public examination. (A trust has the option of requesting full commercial registration, in which case the document is open to inspection).

Trust, Anstalt & Foundation Services

- *Administrust Services Reg*, J. Rheinbergerstrasse 6, PO Box 634, FL 9490 Vaduz, Liechtenstein. **Tel.:** +41 75 2323021. **Fax:** +41 75 2325040.

- *Asphaleia Truhand Aktiengesellschaft*, PO Box 1130, FL 9490 Vaduz, Leichtenstein. **Tel.:** +41 75 2323878. **Fax:** +41 75 2323882.

- *Agentia Truunternehmen Reg*, Landstrasse 36, Postfach 1608, FL 9490, Vaduz, Leichtenstein. **Tel.:** +41 75 2328332. **Fax:** +41 75 2320064.

- *Industrie und Finanzkontor* (founded 1948), Altenbach 8, PO Box 339, FL 9490, Vaduz, Liechtenstein. **Tel.:** +41 75 2322135. **Fax:** +41 75 2375859.

- *PrasidiaiAnstalt* (founded 1931), Aeulestrasse 38, PO Box 583. FL 9490 Vaduz, Liechtenstein. **Tel.:** +41 75 2365555. **Fax:** +41 75 2365266. **Telex** 889 277.

- *Government Official Registrar's Office*, House of Parliament, F1 9490, Vaduz, Liechtenstein. **Tel.:** +41 75 2366111 (for all registrations except banks). **Fax:** +41 75 2365266.

Choosing an Offshore Trustee

By Derek Sambrook, *The Sovereign Individual*, March 2003

The alarming increase in litigation and jury awards, particularly in the United States, has fueled interest in offshore trusts. Dozens of competing offshore centers have drafted trust legislation purporting to provide "asset protection."

The popularity of offshore trusts has led to a proliferation of companies promoting offshore trusts. Indeed, advertisements in leading financial magazines offer for sale offshore trust companies that are "legal, legitimate and affordable."

That tag can apply equally to firearms, which, like trust companies, are potentially hazardous in the wrong hands. Amateurs managing trusts can be like children playing with guns, unable to perceive the dangers present.

These include not only errors in drafting or administering a trust, but the improper use of other structures that may be connected to the trust. We live in a complex world of elaborate strategies and exotic products, the use of which is dangerous in the hands of the novice trustee. The glossy advertisements for offshore trust companies neglect to inform prospective trustees of these dangers.

Critical errors can be made even before the administration of a trust begins. Trustees may cut corners by cannibalizing pre-existing trust deeds and presenting a defective document to the client. Concealed defects often have a long incubation period and may not become apparent for years, by which time the problems may have compounded.

A "boilerplate" deed prepared by an offshore trust promoter will not necessarily provide for your special needs. Such a deed will, however, remain a convenient option for the novice trustee who, more often than not, is also involved in the marketing of the product.

In seeking protection offshore, you do not want to go from the frying pan into the fire. You need the help of specialists and not salesmen. A qualified and seasoned trustee can serve as a safety net by attempting to provide remedies or divert disasters resulting from zealous marketing.

In my 30 years as a trust and estate practitioner, I have seen many such disasters. In one case, inexperienced trustees tampered with a boilerplate trust deed and in doing so, omitted a crucial clause that covered the "rule against perpetuities." This rule, in those jurisdictions where it is observed, does not allow a trust to exist in perpetuity, and if the deed omits the vital provisions, the trust will be void from its inception.

The error only came to light several years after execution of the trust deed and the resulting tax consequences for the trust settlor turned out to be extremely costly. The corporate trustee was faced with a resulting lawsuit, which practically put it out of business.

In another case, a trust deed provided for a discretionary class of beneficiaries, any one of which could be chosen by the trustees to receive assets from the trust. Crucially, the list of beneficiaries could not be altered: no new names could be added and no existing names could be removed.

By misinterpreting the straightforward provisions of the deed, the trustee created a new trust, but only included two instead of five of the names in the class of beneficiaries recorded in the original trust deed.

Practically all the assets, which were substantial, were transferred to this new trust. The trustee had never made any distributions in the past, but now did so from the new trust. In exercising its discretion, but excluding some of the original beneficiaries from the process, a breach of trust resulted, and the bank trustee found itself in court.

The lesson from these experiences is that just as you should weigh the virtues of an offshore jurisdiction against the level of regulatory competence it offers, so should you select the trustee in a jurisdiction by first judging his ability.

It is, in my opinion, more important to choose the right trustee than it is the jurisdiction. After all, this is the age of electronic wizardry where, with qualification, the physical location of the trustee becomes more and more academic.

So, if you are confronted by a trustee who believes that a bare trust is associated with nudity, that an express trust is somehow quicker to manage than a normal one and that the legal definition of the three essential elements of a trust is a client, his checkbook and a pen, I suggest a hasty departure.

I subscribe to the observation made by Ralph Waldo Emerson: "If a man write a better book, preach a better sermon, or make a better mouse-trap than his neighbor, 'though he build his house in the woods, the world will make a beaten path to his door.'"

If you find yourself either on an arduous journey into Tibet or slashing your way through the Central American jungle, but sure of finding the right trustee, console yourself with the thought that it will be well worth it.

I also think that the choice of trustee should be made after a personal visit to a short-list of practitioners. The initial meetings themselves will normally send you positive or negative signals, although it is very important to see through the fog of pleasing personalities and smiles when trying to determine the quality of management.

"What are your trustee qualifications and what is your experience?" These are the two most important questions to ask when choosing an offshore trustee because all other considerations or concerns should be secondary in importance. The Watergate moment, as I describe this interrogative approach, has been known to make some offshore trustees very uncomfortable when providing the answers.

All About Foreign Corporations
January 1998

As our world becomes smaller, we think, plan and work with an eye toward expanding our horizons both at home and abroad. The use of a corporate vehicle as a means of this expansion is nothing new. What is new and what must become second nature to PTs of all types is the idea of "foreign" corporations.

No longer will a domestic corporation satisfy one's needs. The average business person today is far more sophisticated than the business person of even 10 to 15 years ago. Corporate structuring and planning have achieved higher levels of complexity than ever before, while the need for anonymity remains strong.

Professionals must keep pace and be constantly on the look out for new ways to assist clients. One way is to have a clear understanding of the characteristics of foreign corporations and how they may be put to advantageous use.

Foreign corporations are used outside of the place of incorporation for a variety of activities including trading, trade financing, holding assets, manufacturing and tax minimization. They are often used for trading with or in countries where satisfactory local commercial or corporate law is deficient or absent. Joint ventures often use foreign corporations when the participants are from different countries and prefer to incorporate in a jurisdiction neutral to all of the parties.

Foreign corporations can also serve to isolate or separate activities, assets or profit centers for tax, accounting or liability reasons. Where assets are cumbersome or expensive to transfer, like patents, copyrights or trademarks, it is sometimes feasible to have such assets held by separate corporations allowing the individual to transfer the shares in the corporation rather than the asset itself.

In some cases, a foreign corporation, recognized as a citizen or national of the place of incorporation, may confer a trade advantage or may help avoid a disadvantage. It may also be used as an integral part of a trust structure.

Certain countries, moreover, seek to make it attractive to incorporate in their jurisdiction, even when activities are to be conducted elsewhere. In fact, there are so many "tax efficient" jurisdictions that an initial problem for most users is how to select from the available options.

When selecting a place to incorporate, most professionals emphasize the following criteria:

- the legal and political attitude of the jurisdiction toward commercial activities;
- features of the corporate law that facilitate incorporation and continuing management;
- the level and speed of service obtainable in and from the jurisdiction; and,
- cost.

Generally, a desirable jurisdiction should be politically neutral, follow a policy of free trade, not interfere with the commercial activities of corporations established there, and be politically acceptable to other countries and places in which the corporation may be trading. Formal diplomatic recognition as well as commercial recognition and acceptability are important. Commercial recognition is a feature of an offshore jurisdiction that is earned. Use of a jurisdiction in financial transactions allows banks to become familiar and more comfortable with its legal system and forms of corporate documentation.

Most popular jurisdictions have a legal system derived from a major western country and greatly favor corporations which are non-resident in nature. Professionals prefer their western style legislation since it provides a familiar basis for legal interpretation and facilitates understanding of their laws in international practice, particularly in developed countries. In addition, there is inherent in the western tradition the protection of private property and the promotion of international trade.

In order to be successful, a corporate law must provide those entities under which it is formed with the legal capacity to conduct all forms of commercial activity anywhere in the world, allow for a simple management structure and provide the corporation with broad financial powers. In addition, they should be highly confidential and have minimal requirements for maintaining the legal existence of the corporation in compliance with the laws of the place of incorporation.

All jurisdictions have at least two maintenance requirements: 1) maintaining an agent for the service of process; and 2) paying an annual franchise fee or tax. In jurisdictions patterned on United States law, there are generally no further requirements. This should be considered when choosing between a United States or a United Kingdom style jurisdiction.

U.K.-style jurisdictions usually require annual filings regarding directors end officers and at a minimum will request that the annual accounts of the corporation be maintained in the jurisdiction. Such accounts may be subject to review by the Registrar but in some cases need not be filed. This is one major advantage of the U.S.-style jurisdictions over those following the U.K. model.

Finally, formation services should be easy to obtain and should guarantee corporate existence in one or two working days. The level of service between jurisdictions varies. There can be variation within the jurisdiction in a situation where there is competition between rival franchises engaging in the business of incorporating "offshore" companies.

An organization able to offer a wide range of services is undoubtedly able to provide the best service; one that is most adequately equipped with trained personnel to handle questions informally, and that has a larger base of experience upon which to draw when answering these questions.

Costs may vary considerably, with incorporation fees varying from US$575 to US$3,500. Minimum annual fees vary from US$350 to over US$1,000, depending on the jurisdiction and the local maintenance requirements. There should be no other mandatory fees or charges either upon incorporation or for the maintenance of the corporation.

The Limited Liability Company
March 1996

The limited liability company (also called LLC) is a form of business entity increasingly popular in the United States and some tax haven jurisdictions, although a similar entity has been available in Germany, France, and many other countries for decades. Until its recent acceptance by a number of U.S. states, the business executive had three common choices when forming a business: the sole proprietorship, the corporation, or the partnership.

The LLC is a hybrid between the partnership and the corporation. It has all the flexibility of a partnership to define its own management structure, rules of procedure, voting rights, distribution of profits and a myriad of other details. The structure is created by a contract among all the parties. At the same time, if structured properly all the members and the management will enjoy limited liability typical of a corporation.

It is generally assumed that the combination of these two elements will be the reason most LLCs are formed, although there is a great deal of latitude with regard to the structure. Because it has partnership elements, in most jurisdictions that do not tax partnerships as entities but pass the tax liability through to the partners, the LLC is an attractive option.

The origin of the modern LLC laws allowing limited liability companies is in the German law of 1892 which created the GmbH (*Gesellschaft mit beschranker Hafiung*). In the 60 years which followed, almost 20 countries adopted similar laws. In France, for example, the same type of company is known as the SARL (*Societes de Responsabilite Limitee*). In Central and South America it is known as the *limitada*.

In the U.S., the first state to adopt a modern limited liability company statute was Wyoming, on March 4, 1977. Florida followed in 1982. Legislation was passed in Delaware in July 1993 that now provides for Delaware corporations to convert their status to LLC by merging the old corporation into a new LLC. The LLC may take the same name as the corporation.

The IRS gave assurance the entity could qualify to be treated as a partnership on September 2,

1988, in Revenue Ruling 88-76. In February 1993, the IRS issued four revenue rulings describing the classification standards that apply to LLCs that desire partnership tax treatment.

As the LLC steadily gains popularity as people learn its benefits, it could replace the partnership and the corporation as the preferred entity. Now the LLC is being adopted by various tax haven jurisdictions, including the Turks & Caicos Islands, Nevis, the Cayman Islands, the Channel Islands, and the Isle of Man.

An LLC is taxed in substantially the same manner as a limited partnership in most jurisdictions that have both limited partnerships and LLCs, without the disadvantages that limited partnerships have with regard to liability. A limited partnership must have at least one general partner who is liable for debts of the partnership, while all of the members of an LLC may be protected from such liability. The participation of limited partners in the management of a limited partnership can result in a loss of limited liability protection, while such participation by members of an LLC will not have such effect, provided such management does not violate the applicable LLC statute.

Generally, each party to an LLC must agree to a contract with all the other members that will become the "constitution" of the company. This document may be called a company agreement, articles of organization, or even minutes of the first meeting of members, depending upon the jurisdiction. Companies planning to operate their business in a jurisdiction that does not currently recognize LLCs should seriously consider the consequences of possibly losing their limitation on liability in that jurisdiction, before forming an LLC.

The corollary of this is that since the form is well recognized in a number of civil law countries, foreign investors may find it a useful vehicle for making investments in those countries, since the legal and tax status will be relatively clear. It is important to remember that in those countries to which the entity is new, this is a rapidly evolving area of law and it may be a while before matters are fully settled. Sole owner companies cannot be LLCs (except in Texas, which permits one member, but it is not known yet if that will be recognized for federal tax purposes). An LLC must have two members, by definition, or it automatically dissolves. (Of course, the second owner could be a children's trust or a family limited partnership holding one percent.) And most jurisdictions have allowed two corporations, both owned by a single parent, to be the members of an LLC. Keep in mind the laws of individual jurisdictions are still evolving, as is the treatment by the tax authorities that deal with LLC entities.

Charitable Giving: Tax Avoidance, Asset Protection and Dynastic Wealth Control

by Mark Nestmann and Robert E. Bauman

The old saying, "you can't take it with you," is true. Yet, using both domestic and international charitable structures, you can do the next best thing: set up a pool of wealth that will not only survive your death, but support whatever lawful cause in which you believe passionately.

Many of the world's wealthiest people already know this. For instance, Microsoft founder Bill Gates has already transferred a staggering US$40 billion to the Bill and Melinda Gates Foundation. Depending on where you live, charitable giving can generate huge tax savings. Charitable giving can also provide you and your loved ones a lifetime income virtually immune to attack by creditors.

Larger estates can form their own charitable structures so that after death, families have the opportunity to control the disposition of wealth over generations, while minimizing ongoing tax liabilities. The use of a charitable structure doesn't necessarily mean that your heirs will receive a smaller inheritance. Combining the charity with a life insurance structure can replace what was "lost" in making the original charitable contribution.

In most countries, the social function of charities makes them relatively non-controversial to tax authorities, an important virtue when tax collectors are aggressively seeking new sources of revenue to fund the soaring cost of the welfare state. The United States, reflecting its long tradition of private responsibility, is particularly generous in the tax breaks it provides to charitable giving.

The law allows income tax deductions for cash donations up to 50% of your adjusted gross income (AGI). Generally, a deduction for full fair market value of property, such as stock, with no capital gains tax paid, allows a deduction of up to 30% of adjusted gross income. Nationwide, there are about 700,000 "qualified" nonprofit charitable groups. Charitable gifts also reduce the size of your estate for estate and gift tax purposes.

A Blockbuster Charitable Trust

Trusts offer an efficient means of passing property title to your spouse, heirs or your favorite charity. At death, a trust avoids lengthy and complicated probate court procedures required when the estate must be administered under a will. A properly written trust declaration can avoid payment of most estate, gift or inheritance taxes.

One of the most useful charitable trusts is a charitable remainder trust (CRT). The trust takes its name from the fact that the charitable entity (called the "remainderman") eventually gets title to the trust property when the trust ends.

The CRT is also called a "life income" or "wealth accumulation" trust, because the grantor who creates the CRT (as well as other possible beneficiaries) receives continuing lifetime payments from this trust.

Here are some of the benefits a CRT gives back to its creator:

* Achieve personal philanthropic goals.

* Take a large charitable deduction (for the value of the donated assets) against your current year income tax liability.

* Avoid all capital gains taxes on donated appreciated property, regardless of the original cost basis.

* Guaranteed retirement income for life (your choice, immediate or deferred). For instance, you can convert your low-yield real property into a high-income investment guaranteed to provide you and your spouse (the "non-charitable beneficiaries") financial security. You can also have your CRT serve as a legal recipient for "roll-over" of your qualified pension plan or individual retirement account, which will boost both your retirement income and tax savings.

Nor is there any need to deplete the size of the estate that you leave your heirs. For instance, your estate can purchase life insurance coverage for your life or for you and your spouse's joint lives to replace the monies going to your favorite charities. The one CRT drawback is its complexity; in order to be certain your structure qualifies under tax laws an expert should draft it. Our experts say that the donated CRT start-up assets should be valued at least at about US$50,000 to make the plan feasible.

A CRT trust is an irrevocable living trust. The "living" refers to the time when it is created-while the grantor is alive (as compared to a testamentary trust created in a will). It is "irrevocable" because your control over the donated assets ends once the trust is created and the assets are formally transferred.

As in any irrevocable trust, the CRT also serves as an ironclad asset protection device. Once the trust gets the assets, the grantor no longer has title to nor any ability to reacquire those assets. A timely placement of assets into a CRT, well in advance of any claims against you, is an absolute defense against claims from future unknown creditors.

Once you have created your CRT, the institutions or groups lucky enough to be the objects of your generosity might want to reward their benefactor with a seat on their board of trustees. The CRT possibilities of immortality carved into stone are endless: libraries, hospitals, the arts, museums, symphony halls, campus buildings, etc. Here's a real-world example of how a CRT can benefit you: Suppose you own a building worth US$1 million currently, with a fully depreciated basis of US$40,000-meaning a taxable capital gain of US$960,000 when you sell it. This means a federal-state capital gains tax (CGT) liability (if you live in California) of US$344,832! Still, your net is US$655,168-not bad for an original US$40,000 investment. If you reinvest your profit and earn a 10% return in the first year, you would get US$65,517 in income, fully taxable at current federal and state income tax levels. If you don't reinvest, the full US$655,168 becomes personal income.

But if you create a charitable remainder trust, then donate the building to the tax-exempt CRT, you pay no capital gains tax. Nor does the CRT trustee who later sells the building pay any CGT because the entire sale proceeds go into the trust for reinvestment-US$1 million, tax free.

Nor have you received any of this money as personal income. In addition, as grantor of CRT property you receive an immediate charitable tax deduction for the total value of the donated property, applicable to the income tax year in which the transfer occurs. The total income tax deduction, to the allowable maximums discussed earlier, is measured by a complex IRS formula, including present appraised fair market value of the projected remainder interest.

Get An Immediate Tax Deduction Using a Charitable Lead Trust

With interest rates near historical lows, some experts recommend the use of a charitable lead trust (CLT) rather than a CRT. One is Sovereign Society Council of Experts member Gideon Rothschild. A CLT produces an immediate tax deduction and helps the charity of your choice for an extended period. It eventually passes assets to family members with a minimum payment of estate and gift taxes. Because the present value of the charitable interest at the time of the donation is deductible, gift or estate taxes are significantly reduced.

The resulting income or estate tax savings depend on when this technique is used:

1) An immediate income tax deduction is available to a grantor who establishes a CLT during his or her lifetime, the deductible amount being measured by the present value of the income stream going to the charity for the stated period.

2) If the CLT takes effect at the grantor's death, his or her estate receives a charitable deduction for the present value of the future income that will go to the charity.

The CLT is established when a donor transfers income-producing property to a trust. The trust, in turn, will provide the charity with a guaranteed annuity or annual payments equal to a fixed percentage of the fair market value of the trust property that is computed each year. When the specified period ends, the remaining property is returned to the donor, or it goes to a non-charitable beneficiary of the donor's choice, often an heir or other younger family member.

Charities as Part of an International Estate Plan

As with many other aspects of long term financial planning, setting up an offshore charitable structure can provide additional benefits. The primary benefit is that an offshore configuration provides greatly improved prospects for setting up a dynastic structure that can control the disposition of wealth over generations, in contrast, e.g., to the laws of the United States.

Wealthy individuals usually have more assets and income than they need. However charitably minded they are, they may not wish to give up family control over the assets, both in life and after death. This may be true, e.g., when the assets being donated are shares in a private company owned by the donor.

In the U.S. context, a domestic irrevocable trust such as a CRT generally will not permit such a degree of control to be exercised. Additionally, in the many U.S. states and foreign jurisdictions with an English common law background that have not eliminated the "rule against perpetuities," dynastic control through a trust may not be possible, as the trust will eventually be required to dissolve. In contrast, by using an offshore charity, the stock can be donated to the charity-perhaps one established by the donor. The charity is so structured as to ensure that, in perpetuity, the control of the charity remains in the hands of the donor and his descendants. Not only can the charity (which is not subject to any rule against perpetuities) be used to perpetuate control, but it will also take the assets concerned outside the tax net.

According to Charles Cain, who heads up Skyefid Limited, an Isle of Man based international financial consultancy, "For a U.S. person to create a dynastic structure, an overseas charity is more effective than a U.S. charity. This is particularly true if the U.S. person wishes to avoid the very tight U.S. rules that effectively prevent the donor of assets into a charity from controlling that charity, or deriving benefit for his family from that charity. Nobody else has such strict rules."

Along with the benefit of greater control, there are potential drawbacks to an international charitable structure, the most significant one being that most greater complexity and higher costs. One source of complexity is the need, often using some rather esoteric mechanisms, to create a structure where a U.S. donor can both obtain a charitable deduction and shift the assets into an overseas charity.

Obviously, structures of this type require sophisticated planning by experienced international tax practitioners. This is not a job for an amateur.

For More Information

If you plan to name a domestic charity as a beneficiary of your estate, that charity may be able to provide assistance. Most major charities have "planned giving" departments eager to provide extensive help to your lawyer or CPA. The National Committee on Planned Giving is an association of varied professionals active in planned gifting advice with 78 local chapters. **Tel:** + 1 (317) 269-6274. **Fax:** +1 (317) 269-6276. **E-mail:** ncpg@iupui.edu. **Link:** www.ncpg.org. Two attorneys, both members of The Sovereign Society's Council of Experts, who have extensive experience setting up the charitable remainder trusts described in this column are:

Michael Chatzky, Chatzky & Associates, 6540 Lusk Boulevard Suite C121 San Diego, CA 92121 **Tel:** 858.457.1000 **Fax:** 858.457.1007 **E-mail:** MGChatzky@aol.com.

Gideon Rothschild, Moses & Singer LLP, 1301 Avenue of the Americas, New York, N.Y. 10019. **Tel.:** (212) 554-7806. **Fax:** (212) 554-7700. **E-mail:** grothschild@mosessinger.com

If you are interested in setting up the type of international dynastic structure discussed in this article, an expert in this area is: Charles Cain, Skye Fiduciary Services, Two Water St., 1M8 1JP Ramsey, Isle of Man. **Tel.:** +(44) 1624 816117. **Fax:** +(44) 1624 816645. **E-mail:** mail@skyefid.com. Link: www.mcb.net/skye.

Saving U.S. Taxes with Trusts

Vernon Jacobs, CPA, CLU, *Offshore Tax Strategies*, June 2001

Once upon a time, before Congress changed the law in 1986, wealthy families established multiple irrevocable trusts that were designed to accumulate income at low tax rates. Each trust was treated by the IRS as a separate taxpayer and the trust tax brackets were similar to the brackets for individual taxpayers. Today the tax brackets for trusts are very compressed. The first $1,750 of annual trust income is taxed at a rate of 15 percent. Any income in excess of $8,450 is taxed at the top rate of 39.6 percent. As a result, trusts are no longer used as devices to accumulate income.

Income Splitting

However, trusts can be used to divide income among family members, each of whom may be eligible for a separate set of lower tax rates. Unlike a partnership, the income of a trust is not taxable to the beneficiaries until it is distributed. At that time, the trust treats the distribution as a deduction, the beneficiary treats it as taxable income. Because of the compression of trust tax rates, most trusts now provide for current, rather than deferred, distributions of trust income to beneficiaries.

Other Tax Saving Methods

Additional tax savings for income from a trust will depend on the nature of that income. If some of the income is an allocation of interest or dividends, there are tactics that may be useful in minimizing some taxes on that income. The major factor in determining the amount of trust income is the manner in which the trust assets are invested. The trustee can choose between interest bearing investments and high dividend yield stocks, or various capital growth investments. In some limited cases, a trust can defer income by investing trust assets in a tax deferred annuity, something that definitely should be considered.

Foreign Grantor Trust

In the case of a foreign grantor trust, the U.S. grantor (settlor) of the trust is subject to tax on all the income of the trust, whether it is distributed to the beneficiaries or not. Generally, distributions to the U.S. beneficiaries will be treated as gifts by the trust grantor. Gifts are not taxable to the recipient but may be subject to a gift tax by the donor. When and if the estate and gift tax are actually repealed, this strategy may require reconsideration. Until then, it's an effective way to transfer assets to your heirs at a minimum estate and gift tax cost.

Foreign Trust Accumulation Distributions

If a foreign trust does not have a living U.S. beneficiary, then distributions of current income to the beneficiaries will be treated as the income of the beneficiaries. If distributions exceed 125 percent of the current income of the trust, then there is a complicated "throw-back" tax computation in which the excess income is allocated to the years in which the income was accumulated as a non-grantor trust. There is an "additional tax" on such distributions that is like an interest charge on the deferred income of the trust. This tax can be minimized by making distributions equal to 125 percent of the current year's income of the trust.

[**Ed. Note**: In every case, detailed tax advice from a seasoned professional should be obtained in advance. This is especially true because of the 2001 U.S. estate tax repeal law and related revisions which contains phase in provisions for various tax estate tax exemptions and reductions.]

Recommended Attorneys

- *Graeme W. P. Aarons*, Solicitor, FM Trust S.A., rue du Pommier 12, Case Postale 406, 2001 Neuchatel, Switzerland. **Tel.**: +41 38 247979. **Fax**: +41 38 254664.

- *Michael Chatzky*, JD, Chatzky & Associates, a Law Corporation, 4250 Executive Square, Suite 660, La Jolla, California 92037, U.S.A. **Tel.**: +1 858 638 4530. **Fax**: +1 858 638 4535, **E-mail**: mchatzky@chatzkyandassociates.com. **Web**: www.chatzkyandassociates.com.

- *Alan Jahde*, LL.M., Anderson & Jahde PC, Suite 1000, 950 S. Cherry Street, Denver, CO 80222, U.S.A. **Tel.**: +1 303 782 0003. **Fax**: +1 303 691 9719.

- *Rainelda Mata-Kelly LLM*, Suite 305-307, 3rd Floor, Balboa Plaza, Balboa Avenue, Panama City, Republic of Panama, P.O. Box 0818-9012, Panama 6 (Bethania), Republic of Panama. **Tel.**: (Int. access code+507) 263-4305. **Fax**: (507) 264-2868. **Cell**: (%07) 612-5139. **E-mail**: rmk@mata-kelly.com. **Website**: www.mata-kelly.com.

- *Samuel M. Lohman*, JD, Lohman, Schwab, Flaherty & Associes, 11 rue Verdaine, CP 3377 Geneva 3, Switzerland. **Tel.**: + 41.22.317.8020. **Fax**: +41.22.317.8030. **Mbl**: 41.79.409.3841. **E-mail**: lohman@lsfa-law.com. **Web**: www.lsfa-law.com.

- *James McNeile, Solicitor*, Farrer & Co., 66 Lincoln's Inn Fields, London WC2A 3KG, U.K. **Tel.**: +44 171 242 2022. **Fax**: +44 171 917 7431.

- *David Melnik*, QC, Suite 311, 350 Lonsdale Road, Toronto, ON M5P 1R6, Canada. **Tel.**: +1 416 488 7918. **Fax**: +1 905 877 7751. **E-mail**: dm1976cp@netcom.ca.

- *Marcell Felipe*, JD, Goldstein & Felipe, LLP 888 Brickell Ave., 5 Floor Miami, FL 33133. **Tel.**: (305) 381-8500. **Fax**: (305) 381-6225. **E-mail**: mfelipe@marcellfelipe.com.

- *Jeffrey J. Radowich, JD*, Veneable, Baetjer & Howard, Suite 800, 2 Hopkins Plaza, Baltimore, MD 21202, U.S.A. **Tel.:** +1 410 244 7516. **Fax:** +1 410 244 7742.

- *Rothschild, JD, CFP*, Moses & Singer, LLP, 1301 Avenue of the Americas, New York, NY 10019, U.S.A. **Tel.:** +1 212 554 7806. **Fax:** +1 212 554 7700.

- *Timothy D. Scrantom, JD*, 180 East Bay St., Charleston, SC 29401, U.S.A. **Tel.:** +1 843 937 0110. **Fax:** +1 843 937 4310. **E-mail:** tenstate@aol.com.

Do You Need a Lawyer? How an Attorney Can Help in Offshore Planning

By Robert E. Bauman, JD, *The Sovereign Individual*, April 2004

In 1592 William Shakespeare wrote that oft-quoted line: "The first thing we do; let's kill all the lawyers." And of course, lawyer jokes are a favorite American past time.

But it's no joke when you need a lawyer. And if ever there is a time that legal advice can be helpful, it's when you're considering creation of offshore entities, such as a trust, family foundation or an international business corporation.

Here I'll show what offshore transactions you can safely conduct without a lawyer; which transactions you may be able to conduct without one; and when you should definitely hire a lawyer, or even two lawyers—one domestically, one offshore. Plus, I'll suggest how to find that most elusive of lawyers—one that is both competent and honest.

When Do You Need a Lawyer?

For relatively simple offshore matters, such as opening a bank or investment account, you really don't need an attorney. The paperwork is minimal and usually can be completed without professional assistance. And you can look to The Sovereign Society to explain the U.S. reporting rules, although we recommend that you verify our interpretation with your tax preparer.

Moving slightly higher in complexity is purchasing an offshore insurance policy, such as a Swiss variable annuity. Again, the paperwork involved is minimal. However, if the policy claims to legally defer U.S. income taxes, you may wish to have an attorney check out the wording of the policy to make sure it is U.S. tax compliant.

You should definitely hire an attorney if your proposed structure involves offshore entities such as a family foundation, or an asset protection trust (APT), or if you are considering acquiring a second citizenship or living abroad. In fact, in these circumstances, you may wish to use two attorneys—one domestic, and one offshore. (I'll explain why in a moment.)

Step #1 is to hire a domestic attorney to integrate any offshore components or structures into an overall estate plan. That means you need an American lawyer well versed in estate planning, federal and state taxes, trust concepts, wills and testamentary law.

Unfortunately, there are only a limited number of domestic attorneys who specialize in offshore asset protection and estate planning. One of the best ways to find one is to ask for referrals from friends. Ask associates for recommendations based on their personal experience. This input is valuable because friends have nothing to gain by steering you towards or away from any particular lawyer.

Another source of information is your U.S. state bar association. Ask if there is a special designation for estate planners in your home state. If so, make sure that any lawyer you consider has this certification.

Keep in mind names that come up repeatedly. These may be people who deserve a closer look, or they may be ones to avoid, since reputation counts for a lot, whether good or bad.

When you find an attorney, conduct an interview before you pay any fees. And make sure you obtain a detailed cost estimate of what your proposed offshore structure (including any offshore components) is likely to cost.

When to Use an Offshore Attorney

Often it is best to have your domestic tax attorney hire an offshore attorney to handle matters in a foreign nation. The strategy is to consult with your local attorney on general matters but when dealing offshore, use the offshore attorney to enhance attorney-client privilege. Using this technique, all communications, both written and oral, and subsequent attorney work-product, enjoy enhanced protection from any future disclosure orders of a U.S. court.

However, attorney-client privilege is not absolute. It has always been a requirement that attorneys report a client's pending or planned future criminal acts, if the lawyer is aware of them. Nor can an attorney cannot knowingly assist a client in committing fraud or a criminal act. More recent anti-money laundering and anti-terrorism laws now force lawyers to report "suspicious activities" of clients. (Such rules are now mandatory in the United Kingdom, although not in the United States.)

Increasingly, prosecutors offer individuals who are accused of criminal misconduct the "opportunity" to incriminate their attorneys in exchange for a lighter penalty. This has made many attorneys, particularly those engaged in international tax and estate planning, extremely wary. "Know your client" is therefore a modern attorney's watchword and guide.

Never discuss confidential information with an attorney unless and until you conclude a representation agreement in writing. This serves as the benchmark when privilege "attaches" and your communications are protected.

Your domestic attorney may be able to recommend a competent offshore attorney. Another source of information may be your offshore bank. You're likely to get a reliable recommendation since the bank wants to keep your business and they will know attorneys with investment experience.

Another source of offshore legal expertise is The Society of Trust and Estate Practitioners (STEP), the professional body for the trust and estate profession worldwide. Link: www.step.org.

The Sovereign Society can also be of assistance in helping you locate competent domestic or international legal practitioners. Many members of our Council of Experts are lawyers (see list at www.sovereignsociety.com/vmembers.php?sec=whoarewe). These experts regularly deal with offshore matters including banking, investment, asset protection, dual citizenship and international tax planning.

The English political philosopher John Locke said, "The end of the law is not to abolish or restrain, but to preserve and enlarge freedom." You can certainly do just that by "going offshore"—but only if you're armed with the best legal advice.

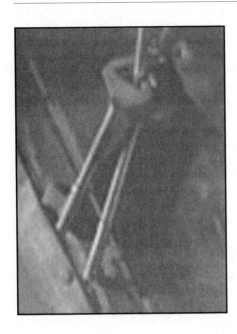

CHAPTER SEVEN
Taxes & How to Avoid Them Legally

No one needs to be reminded what a burden taxes have become. "Soak the rich" has been a popular slogan for political demagogues at least since the French Revolution. Today the tumbrel and guillotine have been replaced with the tax audit and grim tax collectors who slice off half of your income to finance their nanny state.

Citizens complain about high taxes but few do anything about them. Whether out of ignorance or fear, sheep-like taxpayers allow themselves to be herded through government shearing programs that strip them of most of their hard-earned wealth.

Here we give you firm examples of how bad taxation has become, what can be done to change this official robbery and specific, legal steps you can take to cut your losses, perhaps even down to zero.

Part One—Taxes

How Government Steals From You

PT2, 1997

Taxes can be considered straightforward theft by government. The tax-and-spend growth rate of most western governments during the past 60 years has been phenomenal. From a base of nearly zero, close to two-thirds of all wealth generated in western democracies is now spent by politicians, not by the people who create or earn such wealth.

Worse still, the percentage of wealth being confiscated continues to grow. At present, government spending grows faster than national income, personal income and per capita income when adjusted for inflation or taken as a percentage of gross national product. In grossly overtaxed Europe, it seems clear that the new bureaucracy of the EU will only succeed in adding yet another layer of parasitic new taxes.

The growth of government budgets diminishes your personal freedom. If more and more of your earnings and assets are taken, your liberty is limited by just that much.

In most industrialized countries citizens can no longer choose how to spend, invest or bequeath their own money. If any other institution practiced such profligacy while offering such inferior services, it would collapse. Because governments command the police and control the jails, they get away with this continued fraud.

You must take tax avoidance action, first by understanding the various forms of taxation employed by Big Brother, many hidden from the people who must pay the bills.

Income Taxes and Hidden Taxes

Hidden taxes, such as sales taxes, import duties and Value-Added Taxes (VAT), are reflected in raised prices. Sales taxes are generally believed to have a greater impact upon the poor since wage-earners and state-supported individuals tend to spend more of their earnings on consumer items. In France, much more money is raised from sales taxes than from income tax, most likely because wealthy Frenchmen hardest hit by income taxes now live abroad.

Borrowing

This is a deferred tax, and it is unclear who will eventually have to foot the bill. In an expanding economy with moderate inflation, an increase in national debt can be healthy, if the debt is used to pay for infrastructure like highways and communications systems that facilitate commerce and generate funds to retire the debt. In an ideal world, users of improved facilities would pay for them.

However, more typically, funds raised by government borrowing are squandered. They end up being exported. The poor buy imported consumer goods. The wealthy invest abroad. The country ends up impoverished, and living standards drop. Who then must pay the debt? No one and everyone! With a debt that becomes too large to service with taxes, the country can no longer simply roll the debt over by issuing more paper to pay off the interest and capital on bonds which have matured.

In such a situation, the government is faced with a hard choice. It can end the game with a default, as many third world countries are allowed to do from time to time; or, more likely, it can issue ever-more worthless currency to cover its debts. Russia has taken this rampant inflation route. In this scenario, the burden of both the borrowing and default falls on those who did not have the financial ability or good sense to ship their assets abroad.

How much money has been sent abroad to offshore money and tax havens? Recent figures indicate that more American dollars have been deposited abroad in secret accounts during the past 30 years than the total amount now on deposit in all banks in the United States.

This amazing situation means that more than half the U.S. national wealth has been exported. That's the obvious response of smart money to the growth of a rapacious government. The U.S. situation is not unique and many Europeans engage in the same practices. Most liquid wealth in the industrial countries is now beyond the reach of the tax collectors, regulators and planners.

Printing Worthless Paper Currency

This is historically the most common form of taxation. New currency by law must be accepted in payment of all debts, public and private. This running of the printing presses results in inflation and the erosion of the value of creditors' holdings, thereby reducing or eliminating government debt. It also raises general price levels.

This imposes a tax on those with assets in the form of cash, bonds or secured or unsecured debts due from others. Inflation shifts wealth from the creditor class who are owed money to the debtor class who owe money. It eventually erodes all wealth and brings about instability in the overall economy.

In times of inflation, no one can make long-term plans or invest in plant or equipment, even a farmer can't safely raise a crop of cattle or pigs. The creation of real wealth, economic growth, always declines when there is double-digit inflation.

———————◆———————

U.S. Taxes Are Higher Than You Think
by Marshall J. Langer, *The Tax Exile Report*, 1997

Tax rates of 50 percent or more are now common in many major industrial nations. As a result of clever schemes disguised as tax reform, some high-tax countries, led by the U.S., have diabolically reduced tax rates while simultaneously increasing the amount of taxes they actually collect.

A medical doctor living and working in America recently told me that he pays at least one-third of everything he earns as federal income taxes and that, when he dies, the federal government will take the other two-thirds of everything he expects to earn during the rest of his life. He added that he felt he was lucky that he lives in Florida which has no state income tax on individuals and, for practical purposes, no state tax at death. If he lived in California or New York, for example, his taxes would be even higher.

During the Second World War, the highest U.S. individual income tax rate reached 91 percent. The maximum rate was brought down to 70 percent and then to 50 percent. In those days, most taxpayers paid a much lower rate on a substantial part of their income, and a much lower effective rate on their total income.

Presidents Ronald Reagan and George H. W. Bush brought tax rates down. Until 1993, the highest U.S. federal income tax rate on individuals was theoretically only 31 percent, but deductions were eliminated and tax shelters were gone. For most high income earners the maximum tax rate effactually became a flat tax rate applied to all their taxable income. U.S. accountants showed that the way the tax was, the claimed maximum 31 percent rate was actually nearly 34 percent. For some people federal and state taxes combined to a rate of more than 40 percent.

[*Ed. Note:* U.S. income taxes were reduced by law from a maximum of 39.6 percent in 2001 to an eventual 34 percent maximum, with reductions phased in over a period of years.]

Alternative Minimum Tax

The U.S. now has two distinct tax systems; one that applies to most taxpayers and a separate one that prevents many high-bracket people from escaping high taxes. Regular income tax is computed under one set of rules, then an alternative minimum tax (AMT) is calculated on certain income under AMT rules. The wealthy pay whichever tax is higher. The AMT rate has crept up over recent years to a new high of 28 percent.

Double Taxes on Business

The U.S. is one of the few major industrial nations that still taxes most corporate earnings twice, first at the corporate level, then at the shareholder level. A corporation that earns $1 million pays about $400,000 in federal, state and city corporate income taxes. When the corporation distributes the remaining $600,000 as a dividend, its shareholders pay another 40 percent of that amount in federal, state and city taxes. About $640,000 of the $1 million earned by the corporation goes to the payment of income taxes. That is hardly a low tax rate. Nor is that all.

Capital Gains Taxes

Many countries do not impose any tax on capital gains. Some European countries levy a capital gains tax only on gains from real estate sales, or sale of shares by a shareholder who owns 25 percent or more of a company. The U.S. taxes its citizens on virtually all capital gains.

In the past, the U.S. taxed capital gains at a lower rate than ordinary income. There was a much lower rate on long-term capital gains from sales of capital assets held for more than six months or a year. In the 1980s, the highest CGT rate was 28 percent. [**Ed. Note**: In 1998 the CGT was reduced by Congress to 20 percent for most gains on property held for 12 months or more. In 2001 estate tax exemptions were increased annually to $1 million and beyond, with repeal of all estate taxes scheduled for 2010, assuming the law is not changed again. Unless Congress acts, in 2010, federal estate taxes will revert to their 2001 levels.]

If you now live or plan to live in a country that does levy a net wealth tax (the U.S. does not), consider two points: 1) Such a tax can eat up a substantial portion of your investment income. Even a one percent annual tax hurts. With a three percent annual wealth tax, as Uruguay imposes on local assets, your entire capital is gone in 30 years. 2) An annual net wealth tax gives the government a check on the accuracy of your income tax return. They can compare your wealth tax return from year to year for consistency with your income tax return.

Estate Taxes

Most high-tax countries impose death taxes on the value of all estate property that passes at death to heirs or other beneficiaries if the decedent was domiciled or living permanently within that country at his death. Some countries impose estate taxes on everything regardless to whom the assets go. Other countries levy inheritance taxes at a rate much lower on assets left to close family members, higher for assets going to distant relatives and strangers. Generally, these death duties cover all property wherever in the world located.

The U.S. imposes a federal estate tax on the fair market value of the worldwide assets of its citizens and domiciled resident aliens and on the U.S. property of foreigners who are not U.S. citizens. There is a marital deduction for all property passing from one spouse to the other, but only if the recipient is a U.S. citizen or a non-U.S. citizen who locks the assets into a special U.S. trust called a QDOT. The first $600,000 given by a U.S. person during his lifetime or at death is tax exempt. Everything above that is taxed at rates from 37 to 55 percent.

Although the maximum possible federal estate tax is 55 percent, there is a five percent extra tax on each dollar of fair market value between $10 million and about $21 million. As a result, if your estate reaches $21 million you pay a flat tax of 55 percent on each and every dollar and the original $600,000 exemption disappears.

The U.S. collects about $8 billion a year in estate and gift taxes, only about one percent of total tax receipts. Americans with net assets of $1 million or more are targeted by the federal estate tax. Anyone with less can generally avoid the tax with proper planning. Thus, only a tiny fraction of Americans are subject to the estate tax. Even fewer are really clobbered by the it. An estimated 80,000 Americans have a net estate of $5 million or more. These folks stand to lose half or more of their estates to federal and state taxes when they die. The IRS normally requires the estate tax to be paid in cash nine months after the date of death. Selling sufficient property to pay the tax during a declining market is a problem for those handling the estate, not for the government.

The worst part of the estate tax as it applies to wealthy individuals is that the taxpayer has the burden of proving the fair market value of the property subject to tax. It should not surprise you to learn that the IRS sometimes takes a rather aggressive view as to what real estate or the shares of a closely-held business is worth. If you have a large estate that is liquid with readily-valued assets, the federal and state taxes on the estate should not exceed about 60 percent of its real value. If you have assets that are hard to value, you may be assessed taxes that exceed 100 percent of the real value.

To prevent avoidance of death taxes, most high-tax countries also use similar criteria to impose gift taxes on lifetime gifts. They assess the value of all worldwide property given to anyone if you were domiciled or living permanently in the high-tax country at the time you made the gift.

Some countries tax all gifts made at any time during life. Others, only those gifts made within a few years before death, on the theory these were made in contemplation of death. Once again, some countries also impose their gift taxes based on one or more other criteria such as:

- The citizenship of the donor;
- The domicile, residence or citizenship of the persons receiving the gifts;
- The fact that the donor or recipient was, at some prior time, domiciled or resident in the high-tax country, or a citizen of that country.

Most high-tax countries also impose death duties and gift taxes on all gratuitous transfers of property located in that country without regard to the residence, domicile or citizenship of any of the persons involved. This is especially true in the case of real estate located in the high-tax country, but it may also cover other property.

The U.S. federal gift tax is now unified with the federal estate tax. An American gets the equivalent of a $600,000 exemption on his total transfers. It covers those transfers made by gift while he is alive and anything left over can be used for transfers at death.

Some other countries—even those with relatively high estate or inheritance taxes such as the U.K.—do not impose any gift taxes or exclude lifetime gifts if you live a given number of years after making the gift. Several countries normally thought of as being high-tax countries, such as Australia, Canada, New Zealand and Israel, do not now have any estate, inheritance or gift taxes.

The Eight-Way Tax Grab
by Marshall J. Langer, *The Tax Exile Report*, 1997

The octopus is a fearsome sea monster that uses eight uncoordinated tentacles to reach out and ensnare its hapless victims. Swimmers grabbed by any one of this beast's tentacles have a serious problem. Only if the victim has a knife sharp enough to cut all eight tentacles, does he win.

Similarly, any of eight different criteria can subject you to tax liability in your present home nation. Each test is used by some countries, most apply a few and the U.S. uses all eight. To avoid these taxes legally, you must eliminate each of these tax tentacles, one by one. They are: residence, domicile, citizenship, marital status, source of income, location of assets, timing and status of beneficiaries.

Residence

In many countries you are counted as a resident for tax purposes if you actually are present within the country for more than 182 days in any tax year. However, you are not necessarily a non-resident for tax purposes just because you spend less than half the year in that country. In the latter case you may still be taxed depending on factors other than time. In such countries, there is always a risk government will claim you are a taxable resident.

Many countries impose income tax on worldwide income based upon the residence of the taxpayer. In some, mere residence is sufficient to tax an individual on both his domestic and foreign-source income. In others, taxation of worldwide income is imposed only on taxpayers who are permanently resident (or domiciled) in the country.

You may be able to escape your present country's taxes by changing your residence to a country that does not tax its residents on their worldwide income. You may even be able to escape residence anywhere by moving around from place to place as a perpetual tourist (PT).

Domicile

The concept of domicile is significant in English common law nations. Domicile is not necessarily the same as residence. Your residence for tax purposes is usually determined each tax year, while your domicile is generally more permanent—the place to which you intend to return and where you have your roots.

Under British and American law everyone begins life with a domicile of origin. This can be changed to a domicile of choice, but not easily. Merely moving to a new place does not automatically change your domicile. The domicile concept made better sense 100 years ago than it does now. Picture a 20-year old Englishman in the days of Queen Victoria. He might take a job in India and live and work there for 40 years before returning to retire and die in England. While in India he was clearly resident there. But in the eyes of the law he remained domiciled in England because he always intended to return there.

It is often difficult to determine an individual's domicile in today's jet-set era. One major problem is that the taxpayer always has the burden of proof. Each government is likely to claim you are domiciled there if that means you or your heirs have to pay them taxes.

In the U.S., your place of domicile is determined by state law rather than federal law, so there are over 50 different sets of rules. Your domicile for federal tax purposes depends on the law of the state where you are domiciled. There have been a number of cases in which more than one state has claimed to be a particular taxpayer's domicile. Similar rules apply in other countries such as the U.K. where a person is domiciled in England, Scotland or Wales.

Domicile is very significant in determining U.K. tax liability. Those who are both resident and domiciled in the U.K. are taxed on all their worldwide income. A U.K. resident not domiciled in the U.K. need not pay income taxes on foreign-source income unless it is remitted to the U.K.

In most civil-law countries, there is little or no difference between residence and fiscal domicile. Domicile rules can be very erratic. A government may claim you or your heirs owe taxes even though you abandoned living there years before. Under U.S. rules, domicile can't be abandoned without establishing a new one somewhere else. One who tries to live as a PT may find themselves still domiciled in some U.S. state many years later. Under U.K. rules, if you abandon your domicile of choice without establishing a new one, your domicile will revert to that of your domicile of origin.

Citizenship

The U.S. is the only major country in the world that imposes income tax solely due to citizenship, but a few others levy estate taxes based on citizenship. The U.S. also imposes its gift and estate taxes on American citizens regardless of where they live or where they are domiciled. A U.S. citizen cannot escape U.S. income taxes merely by moving abroad. An American citizen does get some income tax benefits when living and working abroad, but these are of relatively little value to U.S. taxpayers with substantial annual income.

An American who wants to become a tax exile must not only change his residence and domicile but also must surrender U.S. citizenship. Since no one wants to become a stateless refugee, another nationality in a suitable country that does not impose taxes based on citizenship must be acquired first.

Some Americans qualify as "dual nationals." They already have the legal status as citizens of one or more other nations. That is no help tax-wise since a dual national is still an American citizen for all U.S. tax purposes.

Like most Americans, you probably do not have a second nationality. The first step towards tax exile is to acquire a second citizenship. The U.S. officially concedes that a U.S. citizen may voluntarily acquire another citizenship and the second passport that goes with it, without automatically losing U.S. citizenship.

The second, more traumatic step is giving up U.S. citizenship. An American who relinquishes U.S. citizenship may be able to obtain a multiple entry visa permitting visits to the U.S. the same as any other foreigner. However, a so far unenforced 1996 law authorizes the U.S. Attorney General to exclude from re-entry into the United States any individual who renounces U.S. citizenship to avoid taxes.

A person determined to have relinquished U.S. citizenship to avoid taxes remains subject to U.S. anti-expatriation tax rules for 10 years. Until recently, these rules had more bark than bite. With proper planning, former Americans could avoid these rules until the 10 years ran out. However, revised expatriation tax rules enacted in 1996 impose much tougher rules on citizens who have expatriated since February 1995.

Marital Status

Your marital status may affect tax liability. Not only whether you are married or single, but also where and how you were married and where you and your spouse have lived since marriage.

Many countries have community property rules under which each spouse is entitled to a half interest in all property acquired by the other spouse during the marriage. These rules apply in virtually all civil-law countries and in some common-law jurisdictions, including nine states in the U.S. Places as diverse as California, Texas, Quebec, the Channel Islands, Italy and Argentina all apply community property rules. For anyone married in, or with a marital home in, a community property jurisdiction, special planning to become a tax exile is needed.

Your marital status may also be significant even if you have not lived in a community property country. Example: a married woman's domicile may be the same as that of her husband, whatever her wishes may be. The U.K. permits a married woman to adopt a domicile separate from her husband. Less clear U.S. rules permit a married woman's separate domicile for some designated purposes, such as filing an action for divorce, but not for more mundane activities such as taxes.

Source of Income

Most countries apply a source test that imposes income taxes on all income derived within that country whether the person earning it resides within the country or not. Income paid to non-residents may be subject to a withholding tax, and the entity paying the nonresident must pay the tax directly to the government. Withholding taxes are generally imposed at a fiat rate on gross income derived by foreigners from domestic sources. The withholding tax rate is set by law but is often reduced by treaty. For example, the statutory U.S. withholding tax rate on dividends paid to non-residents is 30 percent, but portfolio dividends paid to a Canadian resident are subject to only 15 percent U.S. withholding tax under the income tax treaty between the U.S. and Canada.

Some countries, including many in Latin American, impose taxes only on a territorial basis. Applying a source test, they tax all income derived from domestic sources and exempt all foreign-source income.

Location of Assets

Most countries impose property taxes on real estate and other assets physically situated within their borders. Many nations impose capital transfer taxes on the disposition of property by a lifetime gift or at death because the property is located in that country. Taxes may be assessed on your worldwide assets because the government deems you to be a resident or domiciled there or because you are a citizen.

A tax exile must remove as much taxable property as possible from his high-tax home country to chosen places that do not tax assets merely because of their location. Personal property can be moved from one country to another. Real property cannot be moved but it can be sold or mortgaged and the proceeds can be moved abroad.

Timing

The taxation of income may depend on when it is considered to have been earned. Thus timing can be significant when moving from one country to another. A tax exile should postpone receiving income until after he leaves his high-tax country. In the U.S., for example, large tax-free gifts can be made between spouses only if the recipient spouse is a U.S. citizen when the gift is made.

It may be possible for a resident of a country to exchange domestic real estate for foreign real estate in a tax-free transaction while he is still resident. Or a former resident may be able to transfer domestic assets to a foreign corporation or sell foreign assets without tax liability after he ceases to be a resident.

Status of Beneficiaries

Not all members of one family usually become tax exiles. Frequently, one or both parents leave a country but their adult children and their grandchildren remain. Knowing this, a high-tax country may seek to impose taxes, interest and even penalties when assets are eventually distributed to remaining relatives. Careful planning at the outset can avoid these tax problems. Obviously, the planning is much easier when the children leave with their parents.

All of the Above

The U.S. uses all of the foregoing criteria to impose its federal taxes. Both U.S. citizens and resident aliens are taxed on worldwide income as citizens or as residents. Domicile is not necessary but if they are domiciled in the U.S. they are subject to U.S. gift and estate taxes on their worldwide assets and residence is immaterial. In cases where spouses have been married in a community property jurisdiction and one spouse is a U.S. citizen and the other is a non-resident alien, the U.S. may apply community property rules to tax the citizen spouse on half of the income earned by the non-resident alien spouse.

The U.S. taxes non-resident aliens on their U.S.-source income. It taxes non-domiciled aliens when they give U.S.-situs property by lifetime gifts or by transfers at death. If all other attacks fail, the IRS may demand taxes by claiming the income was earned before the tax exile left the country. The IRS also may impose transferee liability on beneficiaries over whom it retains jurisdiction.

The answer to all these attacks is careful planning. If you plan to become a tax exile, do it right or don't do it at all.

How U.S. Citizens and Residents Are Taxed

by Marshall J. Langer, *The Tax Exile Report*, 1997

Whether an alien is resident or non-resident is a critical issue of tax law. If you are either a U.S. citizen or an alien who is resident for income tax purposes, the following rules apply:

1. You pay federal income tax at rates up to 39.6 percent on all of your U.S.-source income except for tax-free interest from U.S. municipal bonds. [**Ed. Note:** U.S. income taxes were reduced from a maximum of 39.6 percent in 2001 to an eventual 34 percent maximum, with reductions phased in over a period of years.]

2. You are also subject to U.S. income tax on all of your foreign-source income, but you may generally take a foreign tax credit for foreign taxes paid.

3. Shares you own in a foreign corporation may subject you to current U.S. tax on your pro rata share of its undistributed earnings if the foreign corporation is either a foreign personal holding company (FPHC) or a controlled foreign corporation (CFC).

4. Your shares in foreign corporations may be subject to the passive foreign investment company (PFIC) rules.

5. Transfers of appreciated property to a foreign corporation or a foreign trust are subject to a 35 percent excise tax.

6. You pay U.S. tax at regular rates up to a maximum of 28 percent on capital gains derived from both U.S. and foreign sources. Gain is determined by reference to your historic cost, even if you acquired the property many years before you moved into the U.S. [**Ed. Note**: Since this was written, federal capital gains taxes have been reduced to 20 percent.]

How a U.S. Non-resident Alien is Taxed

If you are a non-resident alien for income tax purposes, you are subject to a substantially different taxing system. If you are a non-resident alien but you were a U.S. citizen or a long-term U.S. resident alien with a green card at any time during the past 10 years and you are treated as having expatriated for tax-avoidance reasons, you are taxed under a special system which denies you some of the beneficial tax treatment accorded to non-resident aliens generally, but only with respect to U.S.-source income.

Listed on the next page is the treatment accorded to you if you are a non-resident alien. The special rules that apply for 10 years if you are a former American citizen or long-term resident who has expatriated to avoid taxes are shown in italics.

1. You pay U.S. income tax at regular rates up to 34 percent on any income that is effectively connected with the conduct of a U.S. trade or business.

2. You are subject to a maximum 30 percent U.S. withholding tax on dividends, interest, and other investment income that you derive from U.S. sources; the 30 percent tax rate may be reduced or eliminated by favorable income tax treaty provisions. *If you are treated as a tax-motivated expatriate you might have to pay the higher regular income tax rate, up to 34 percent; you would not be entitled to benefits under any U.S. income tax treaties.*

3. Your interest income derived from some U.S. bonds and from U.S. banks and savings institutions would be completely tax free. *A tax-motivated expatriate would be taxable on this income.*

4. You are not subject to any U.S. income tax on your foreign-source income except under a few very limited circumstances.

5. You are not subject to the FPHC, CFC or PFIC rules. Thus, you are not subject to any U.S. tax on your share of undistributed earnings of a foreign corporation. *A tax-motivated expatriate remains taxable on dividends and gains derived from shares of his former CFC.*

6. Your transfers of appreciated property to a foreign corporation or a foreign trust are not subject to excise tax.

7. You are not ordinarily subject to any U.S. tax on your capital gains derived from foreign sources. Moreover, you do not ordinarily pay any U.S. tax on your capital gains from U.S. sources unless they relate to U.S. real estate or a U.S. business. *If you are a tax-motivated expatriate, you may have to pay a maximum 28 percent tax on your capital gains from U.S. sources.* This treatment would also apply to foreign property and securities that you acquired through tax-free exchanges of U.S. property for foreign property.

U.S. Withholding Tax Could Drain Foreign Funds From the U.S.

by Marshall J. Langer, *The Sovereign Individual*, April 2001

Just four days before the end of the Clinton Administration in January 2001, the IRS issued proposed regulations (with the apparent approval of the outgoing Treasury Department) that would, if made final, collect zero taxes for the U.S. Government, but could have a destructive effect on the U.S. banking system.

Since 1921, interest on bank deposits paid to nonresident alien individuals (and foreign corporations) has been tax-free unless the interest was effectively connected with the conduct of a U.S. trade or business. The proposed regulations would not change this status, but would require every bank operating in the United States to report to the IRS all interest paid to nonresident alien individuals so that the IRS could pass such information on to its tax treaty partners. The United States has no tax interest in collecting this information since it will not result in the collection of any U.S. tax.

Congress debated the wisdom of retaining the tax exemption on bank deposit interest on several occasions during the 1960s and 1970s. President Kennedy's Alliance for Progress was supposed to encourage Latin Americans to repatriate their flight capital and reinvest it in their own countries. Latin American governments complained that U.S. tax law encouraged taxpayers in those countries to invest in the United States.

In 1966, Congress decided to impose tax on bank deposit interest paid to foreign persons but, for balance of payments reasons, Congress postponed the effective date of such tax until the end of 1972. The effective date was postponed on two other occasions, the last of which was due to expire at the end of 1976.

During 1975 and 1976, Congress debated whether to extend the deposit exemption for three more years or make it permanent. The House of Representatives voted to make the deposit interest exemption permanent. The bill was debated on the floor of the Senate in July 1976. The Senate voted to extend the exemption for three years, but the conference report followed the House bill and the 1976 Tax Reform Act made the exemption permanent. No one in Congress seems to have even looked at the provision since 1976.

The 1976 Senate hearings clearly indicated that many senators felt that taxing such deposits could result in a substantial outflow of funds from U.S. banks to foreign competitors. During the debate, Senator Dick Stone of Florida stated that in gateway cities like Miami deposits from Latin Americans amount to as much as one-third of all bank deposits.

Most other countries, including major U.S. trading partners, similarly exempt bank deposit interest paid to foreign persons. Collecting information concerning such deposit interest and passing it on to other countries will almost certainly have the same effect as imposing tax on the interest. If these regulations are adopted in final form, there will be a massive outflow of funds from U.S. banks. Most of these funds will go to banks in major countries that do not collect taxes on such interest and have no rules to collect information with respect to such accounts.

Some EU members have tried in recent years to enact a directive that would compel all 15 EU countries to exchange tax information concerning savings by EU residents in other EU countries. Although they reached a compromise agreement on this issue last year, that "agreement" has more holes than Swiss cheese and it is highly doubtful that any EU directive requiring the compulsory exchange of information concerning bank deposit savings interest will ever enter into force.

Austria and Luxembourg have said that the directive will be nullified unless the information exchange system is also agreed to by certain third countries including the United States, Switzerland, Liechtenstein, Andorra, Monaco, the Channel Islands and the Isle of Man. Switzerland has since stated that it will not lift its bank secrecy under any circumstances but that it might consider taxing savings income of foreigners with Swiss bank accounts. Switzerland has also demanded that any agreement also be accepted by all of the major Asian financial centers. In the absence of a deal with Switzerland and other third countries, the directive will never take effect and some major European financial centers will continue to welcome bank deposits from foreign persons and pay them unreported tax-free bank deposit interest.

When and if all of the world's major financial centers can reach agreement and simultaneously begin to exchange information on savings deposits or simultaneously begin to withhold an agreed rate of tax on such bank deposits, it might make good sense for the United States to participate in that agreement. In the absence of such an agreement it would be financial suicide for the United States to take measures unilaterally either to exchange information concerning such deposits or impose its statutory 30 percent withholding tax on bank deposit interest paid to foreign persons.

I have spoken to a number of bank officers about these regulations. Many of them fear that there will be a massive outflow of funds from U.S. banks if these regulations are not withdrawn. Congress should request a General Accounting Office (GAO) study of the impact these proposed regulations would have on banks, especially those located in major money centers. At the very least, the IRS should be requested to postpone any hearing on these proposed regulations until after the GAO can complete such a report. If the GAO report confirms that these regulations would result in a serious outflow of funds from U.S. banks, the IRS should withdraw its proposed regulations and, if it fails to do so, Congress should require it to do so.

[**Ed. Note**: On February 16, 2001, the U.K. Inland Revenue adopted similar rules. As in the case of the proposed U.S. rules, the U.K. rules apply only to bank deposit interest paid to nonresident individuals, not to foreign corporations or other entities.]

Dealing with the IRS Pressure Against Offshore Privacy
By Dr. Erich Stoeger & Mark Nestmann, *The Sovereign Individual*, May 2002

The U.S. Internal Revenue Service has quietly embarked upon a new policy that, if unchecked, will make it impossible for privacy-seeking U.S. citizens or permanent residents to deal directly with offshore banks.

This policy is an offshoot of IRS regulations that require offshore banks maintaining U.S. custodial accounts with U.S. correspondent banks or brokers to adhere to various customer identification and disclosure requirements on their U.S. securities transactions, or have all income and gross sales proceeds derived from such transactions subjected to a 31% withholding tax. Such custodial accounts are generally used to purchase U.S. securities for the offshore bank's customers.

The regulations came into effect on January 1, 2001 and were purportedly issued to make it more difficult for U.S. persons investing in U.S. securities through offshore banks to evade U.S. taxes.

To avoid the 31% withholding tax, many offshore banks opted to become "qualified intermediaries" (QI) under the new requirements. This step required that the country in which the offshore bank is domiciled, qualify under IRS "know-your-customer" regulations and that individual banks in that country with U.S. correspondent accounts sign QI agreements with the IRS.

Offshore banks that signed QI agreements were obliged to provide the IRS with client details (such as Social Security numbers) on transactions in which U.S. persons (U.S. citizens, wherever they reside, and permanent U.S. residents, irrespective of their citizenship) made U.S. securities transactions.

To comply with these requirements, the offshore banks asked all of their clients to establish their tax status. From U.S. persons, the banks requested a completed IRS Form W-9 (identifying these individuals to the IRS). Banks operating in bank secrecy jurisdictions such as Switzerland,

Austria and Luxembourg were also required by their domestic law to obtain authorization from their U.S. clients to divulge their identity and transactions to the IRS.

In return, U.S. clients could continue to purchase U.S. (and non-U.S.) securities through an offshore account, while continuing to be protected by bank secrecy in all matters other than taxes. Non-U.S. depositors in offshore banks (which generally make up the majority of customers) were not required to complete Form W-9. Offshore banks could continue to purchase U.S. securities for such customers while maintaining bank secrecy.

Many U.S. clients were not willing to complete Form W-9. To protect their privacy, and to avoid the 31% tax, these clients sold their U.S. securities. From that point forward, they were effectively barred from dealing in U.S. securities through their offshore account.

As a consequence, those clients only had access to the two-thirds of world capital markets outside the United States. But for many U.S. investors, this was not a serious problem, as the purpose of their offshore account was to gain access to non-U.S. investments and for currency diversification, privacy and asset protection.

IRS Wants to Know Non-U.S. Securities Transactions

Access by U.S. persons who have not signed Form W-9 to non-U.S. securities through offshore bank accounts is now under attack by the IRS, due to a new interpretation of the QI agreements between the IRS and offshore banks.

The agreements stipulate that signatory offshore banks must submit to periodic audits by independent auditors to demonstrate their compliance with "know your customer" and other QI regulations. The IRS receives a copy of the audit report. It is now clear that these audits are leading to a dramatic deterioration in the quality of services available from offshore banks to U.S. persons and the manner in which their account relationships can be managed.

The first audit was of one of the world's largest offshore banks—Swiss giant UBS. During this audit, a seemingly trivial term in the agreement–"deemed sales"–was reevaluated and renegotiated.

The outcome, however, is anything but trivial: all securities transactions, both U.S. and non-U.S., by a U.S. person who has signed Form W-9, must now be reported by UBS to the IRS. This is because the transaction is "deemed" to have initiated from within U.S. geographical boundaries.

In February 2002, UBS began informing their U.S. clients of the new situation. The letters also set out new procedures that would henceforth apply to the relationship between UBS and its U.S. clients who did not complete IRS Form W-9, apparently in an effort to comply with both the terms of the audit and Swiss bank secrecy rules.

Quoting From The Letter: "We [UBS] will no longer be in a position to accept orders for transactions in securities ... we suggest that you give UBS a mandate to manage your account ... The reason for this sudden change of policy is the 'U.S. Tax Law' and especially the so-called 'Deemed sales in the United States.' This rule says that each transaction, which is potentially taxable in the United States, must be reported to the U.S. Authorities, regardless of the marketplace and the securities involved ...This reporting obligation is no longer limited on U.S. securities only, but includes all securities worldwide."

UBS no longer accepts any orders for U.S. or non-U.S. securities from U.S. persons who have not completed Form W-9 when the instructions are deemed to originate in the United States. This includes orders by telephone, fax, mail, e-mail or the Internet.

UBS can accept securities trading instructions from such customers only if the instructions originate outside the United States or if the client delivers them in person at a non-U.S. branch of the bank. No instructions may be accepted, or strategies discussed, in any U.S. location. The only instructions with a U.S. origin that will be accepted are payment instructions to the bank by whatever means was originally stipulated when the account was set up; i.e. by mail, fax, telephone or otherwise.

Finally, UBS will no longer mail any correspondence or account statements into the United States to U.S. customers who have not completed Form W-9. Consequently, such individuals who wish to receive account statements by mail will need to designate a foreign address for this purpose (such as a foreign mail drop).

Why was UBS the first target of the IRS? Most likely because of its huge size and extensive U.S. interests. Another factor may have been an agreement UBS signed in 1998 agreeing to provide U.S. regulators with all information "necessary to determine and enforce compliance with ...[U.S.] federal law." UBS signed the agreement as a condition for U.S. approval of its merger with Swiss Bank Corp. (SBC), which included SBC's U.S. subsidiaries and the U.S. branches of UBS, and was therefore subject to U.S. regulatory scrutiny. The agreement granted no exception for U.S. tax laws. Rather than defend their clients' privacy rights, UBS compromised and is now paying the price.

For the moment, most other offshore banks continue to take the position that transactions in non-U.S. securities by U.S. persons do not fall under the QI requirements. However, as the audits continue, sources within the offshore banking community predict that all offshore banks that have signed QI agreements with the IRS will be forced to severely restrict contacts with U.S. persons who have not completed Form W-9.

Privacy Options for U.S. Persons

Many U.S. clients of UBS, or other offshore banks subsequently subjected to the "reinterpretation" of QI agreements, will agree to have all their securities transactions, both U.S. and non-U.S., reported to the IRS. However, other U.S. clients will wish to have their offshore portfolio administered privately. What options remain for such individuals?

1) *They can set up a discretionary management mandate for their portfolio with the bank.* After an initial meeting (most likely outside the United States), the bank can manage funds, reinvest maturing investments and buy and sell non-U.S. securities according to a mutually agreed upon management strategy.

2) *They can set up a management mandate with an independent offshore portfolio manager.* Such a manager residing outside the United States is not bound by any restrictions deriving from the QI agreement between the IRS and the bank. After the appropriate agreements are signed, the bank can freely discuss the portfolio of a U.S. person with the independent advisor. In turn, the independent advisor can talk freely to his or her U.S. client and place investment instructions with the bank on a discretionary basis or in ongoing dialogue with the client. The manager can also receive statements from the bank and forward them on to such individuals. The investor may also receive in this manner more personalized private banking services and have an additional layer of control over the bank.

3) *They can employ an offshore representative and grant that individual a limited power of attorney for the relationship with the bank.* This allows the representative to initiate, terminate and monitor investments with the bank based on the account owner's instructions and to receive information and statements from the offshore bank to share it with the account owner. The limited power of attorney does not allow the representative to withdraw any funds from the account. The representative retains an independent position similar to an attorney or notary public, but should be specialized in financial services and global investing. The offshore representative is not subject to QI rules and does not have any QI restrictions to represent the account owner at the bank. This option should be less expensive than option #2 if the account owner wishes to make his or her own investment decisions.

4) *They can place the portfolio into an offshore entity, such as an offshore trust or "trust-like" structure* (e.g., a Liechtenstein establishment or Stiftung). The portfolio is managed by a professional trust company outside the United States. Due to the cost involved this is only advisable for large portfolios. In this context, the account holder at the offshore bank is the offshore enti-

ty and the bank does not deal with a U.S. person. The manager of the offshore entity is bound by the terms of the trust or other offshore structure to manage the portfolio in accordance with those terms. The offshore entity may also delegate the investment management to an independent professional money manager via a limited power of attorney or allow the bank to manage the funds on a discretionary basis. This approach also offers substantially greater asset protection than the first three options.

5) They can place the portfolio into an investment management vehicle through an insurance wrapper. The greatest flexibility is afforded by an offshore life insurance policy. Legally the investor is the client of the insurance company and the insurance company is the client of the bank. The funds will be managed by the bank or by an independent asset manager. In the latter case the investor indirectly has an option to influence the investment strategy. This approach, unlike the first four options, may offer tax deferral on income generated within the insurance policy. The insurance company will provide quarterly statements directly to the U.S. investor.

[**Ed. Note**: U.S. persons are legally obligated to pay taxes on their worldwide taxable income. This responsibility is not negated by the fact that they may manage their offshore portfolio in such a way as to avoid having such investments and the income or gain accruing from them automatically reported to the IRS by third parties. Warning: If you are subject to U.S. taxation, these strategies do not eliminate your obligation to pay tax on income or gains worldwide. In addition, you may be subject to additional disclosures, such as Form TD F 90-22.1—Report of Foreign Bank and Financial Accounts. Form 5471—Information Return of U.S. Persons With Respect to Certain Foreign Corporations. Form 8621—Return by a Shareholder of a Passive Foreign Investment Company or Qualified Electing Fund.]

How to Recognize a Tax Fraud

By Vernon Jacobs, CPA, and Richard Duke, JD, *The Sovereign Individual*, March 2003

Citizens or permanent residents of high tax countries naturally seek ways to reduce their tax burden. Every high tax country has an assortment of deductions, exemptions and exclusions by which you may legally reduce your tax burden. But there are always opportunists who seek to take advantage of those who want to reduce their taxes, but are not tax experts. This column reviews some of the most common schemes and tells you how to avoid them

Tax Myth: A U.S. Person Can Become a "Non-Resident Alien"

The United States is the world's largest tax haven. Bona-fide foreign persons can invest in U.S. government bonds or in the accounts of U.S. banks tax free. Income or gain from the securities of U.S. corporations are also tax-free to foreign investors.

It's completely understandable why many U.S. taxpayers want to use the tax breaks available to non-resident aliens. The trouble is, Congress doesn't want U.S. citizens and permanent residents to do that. They have passed an assortment of laws that make it nearly impossible for U.S. persons to enjoy these benefits.

This hasn't stopped promoters from coming up with various schemes that purport to convert a taxable U.S. person into a potentially non-taxable, non-resident alien. One popular scheme is to have a U.S. person form a foreign corporation (usually called an international business company or IBC) with bearer shares or with some kind of unsigned agreement with the promoter.

The problem with this approach is that if someone else is acting as your agent, nominee or intermediary, you will still be treated as the owner of that entity for tax purposes. The IRS and the courts have the power to disregard the legal formalities of an ownership arrangement and to look at the substance of the arrangement.

That's just one trap. There are many others. Almost without exception, your IBC will be deemed to fit into one or more of the following designations: (1) a "controlled foreign corporation" (CFC); (2) a "passive foreign investment company" (PFIC); or (3) "foreign personal holding company" (FPHC). All of these designations require significant disclosures and generally require shareholders to pay taxes on the IBC's current income. There are severe penalties for not filing these forms and paying the relevant taxes.

Of course, the promoters won't tell you this. Instead, they'll urge you to create a "secret" IBC. To maintain secrecy, they'll recommend that you give them signature authority over the IBC's bank accounts. That means the promoter can take the money from your accounts and then defy you to sue them. If you do, they will threaten to notify the IRS.

Once you settle with the IRS, to recover your money, you will still have to sue in a foreign country, with foreign lawyers, under foreign laws and subject to foreign judges. How much are you willing to trust someone in a foreign country who promises to help you break the law in the United States?

Scam: Create A Foreign Trust Without A U.S. Grantor

A foreign trust that does not have any U.S. beneficiaries or that is not funded by a U.S. person is treated as a non-resident alien for U.S. tax purposes, with the same tax advantages we've already summarized, in addition to potential estate tax advantages. It's called a "foreign non-grantor trust." A lot of U.S. taxpayers would like to have one of these trusts. However, since 1977, the U.S. Tax Code has treated a foreign trust with a U.S. grantor and any U.S. beneficiary as a "grantor" trust.

This means the person who creates and funds the trust (the "grantor") is treated as the owner of its assets and is taxed on any income earned by those assets, as if the trust did not exist.

Lots of promoters claim they have found ways to create a foreign trust through nominees, agents, foreign corporations or other deceptive arrangements, therefore making trust income purportedly tax-free. Most of these arrangements fail because the tax law looks through these intermediate parties to the person who has the real influence. If you are the person with the money, the IRS will treat you as the grantor no matter how many intermediaries you interject in the arrangement.

Scam: Transfer Gains Offshore With A Private Annuity

Private annuities are legitimate arrangements generally used as devices to transfer assets to one's heirs without first being subject to federal estate tax. However, they are often promoted as a method of getting funds transferred into a foreign corporation or foreign trust on a tax-favored basis.

A private annuity must be an unsecured contract entered into by the annuitant (e.g., the person receiving annuity payments) and someone NOT in the business of issuing annuity contracts. Thus, you can't enter into a private annuity with an insurance company.

This makes private annuities prime targets for con artists. Since the annuity is unsecured, if the person or entity from whom you purchased it defaults, you can't take back your property. You must pursue payment in the courts. And collecting from a con artist in a foreign jurisdiction isn't easy.

Some promoters pitch the idea of transferring property to an IBC in exchange for a private annuity. Both promoters and clients assume that the IBC is not a CFC, PFIC or FPHC. But in most cases, the corporation is in one or more of these categories. Then, the annuitant is in the position of being on both ends of the annuity transaction and "doing business with himself." This negates any tax advantages. Several other widely promoted structures don't work much better.

About the only way a private annuity arrangement is effective is when a foreign person is an heir of the U.S. person, in which case there is no need for the IBC. The foreign heir could simply enter into a direct annuity contract with the U.S. person.

Tax Myth: Diverting Profits To a Foreign Corporation

If you manage to create a foreign corporation that isn't a CFC, PFIC or FPHC, it might seem like a good idea to divert profits from a U.S. business into it. Indeed, this scheme is popular with hustlers who aren't familiar, or ignore, the U.S. tax laws relating to the "allocation of income" rules between related parties.

The IRS and many other tax agencies are permitted to re-allocate the profits of multinational enterprises back to the country where the profits were actually earned. Multi-national corporations have been trying to manipulate these highly complex rules for their benefit for decades. As their tax lawyers and accountants devise various schemes to do that, Congress amends the law to prevent this type of tax avoidance.

Tax Myth: Non-Taxable Employee Benefits From a Foreign Corporation

Some U.S. people believe that if a foreign corporation pays their foreign travel, lodging and other expenses, they are not required to pay any taxes on that income. If these expenses are paid directly by a bona-fide foreign company, there would be no reporting obligations from the foreign company to the IRS. However, you would have to show that the expenses, had they been made by a domestic corporation, would have been a tax-free reimbursement. And, if the person whose expenses are reimbursed is not an employee, sub-contractor, officer or director of the company, what business reason would the company have for paying them?

It appears that most people conveniently forget that the U.S. imposes its taxes on its citizens on their worldwide income. Barring any specific exception because of a foreign transaction, the tax treatment of any transaction outside of the U.S. is the same as the identical transaction in the United States. If it's legal in the United States, it's probably legal overseas. Otherwise, you are gambling on the IRS audit lottery.

Tax Myth: The Permanent Tourist Is Tax-Free

A group of people who call themselves "PTs" are advocates of the ideas of a writer who calls himself W. G. Hill. After reading an article by Harry Schultz advocating the concept of becoming a "previous taxpayer" or "perpetual traveler" and not having any permanent residence, Hill expounded on this idea with a series of books published in the early 1990s.

While the PT theory might have some validity with respect to those who are citizens of countries that tax on the basis of residence, it isn't valid for U.S. persons who are taxed on the basis of their citizenship. U.S. citizens are subject to U.S. taxes on their worldwide income regardless of where they live.

For U.S. persons to legally benefit from this idea, they must first acquire citizenship in a country that taxes on the basis of residence (such as Canada), then lose their U.S. citizenship and cease being a U.S. resident. And, losing your citizenship doesn't always result in total freedom from the U.S. tax laws and the IRS. For instance, if you are a non-resident alien working in the United States, you will still owe U.S. income taxes.

"Due Diligence" for Offshore Investing

Congress and the IRS have in recent years made a significant effort to crack down on offshore tax evasion. A major part of this effort has been to vigorously pursue promoters of the schemes discussed in this column.

That means if you decide to invest or do business offshore, it's more important than ever to do it right. And there are still completely legal and above-board methods to reduce, defer or even eliminate taxes on offshore investments. Offshore life insurance and deferred annuities, for instance, can be configured to provide these benefits.

Promoters, however, often don't know about these laws, or more frequently, don't want to take the time to become familiar with them. Even after our more than 40 combined years of professional practice, we're still amazed by the creativity of promoters hustling offshore tax and investment scams.

You can avoid being taken in by nearly every kind of offshore tax fraud by insisting that the promoter put its plans in writing to be reviewed by a competent international tax advisor. The mere suggestion of using your own advisor will probably generate a host of reasons why there isn't enough time, why the deal must be kept a secret, why it will save time and money to use their lawyer who is already familiar with the deal, etc. That claim should speak volumes.

Part Two—And How to Avoid Them

Tax Reduction: Is It Legal?
by Marshall J. Langer, *The Tax Exile Report*, 1997

Tax lawyers and accountants usually like to stress the distinction between two seemingly similar methods of tax reduction: tax avoidance and tax evasion. It is important to understand this distinction, as well as to realize the limitations of its applicability.

At first glance, the distinction seems quite obvious. Tax avoidance is using whatever legal means are available to minimize a tax burden; tax evasion is the use of illegal means to the same end.

Using the services of an accountant and classifying certain verifiable expenses as "business expenses" with a seemingly acceptable justification to reduce the taxable net income from one's business or profession is legal. Even if the tax collector does not accept the validity of these deductions and compromise fails, the businessman doesn't fear being indicted for a criminal offense. The worst that can happen is that he must pay more tax than he believes he should have to pay. This is tax avoidance.

On the other hand, willfully failing to report all or part of income on a tax return or failing to comply with other reporting requirements is acting illegally. This is tax evasion. Lawyers and accountants explain sternly that, while to the best of their abilities they can help a taxpayer avoid taxes legally, using all possible accounting tricks and legal loopholes, they will have nothing to do with tax evasion schemes. They cannot be accomplices to a crime; it could destroy them professionally and send them to prison.

As you can see, the distinction between avoidance and evasion is real and very important. However, look into the matter and one discovers the distinction is far from clear-cut. Vagueness, ambiguity and holes in the law make a muddle of just what is income and how one is legally obliged to report it if it is.

The law, personal tax strategy and a host of factors may produce so much uncertainty that a harsh legal decision against a would-be tax avoider is unlikely. The defendant's lawyer may see his client as a genuine tax avoider. The IRS lawyer may claim he is an evader; the judge may reach an in-between verdict; the appeals courts may reverse. The government may decide the dispute will cost more to prosecute than the government stands to gain, so they compromise or even drop the matter. Or the IRS may make an example of the avoider/evader, trying to force a new precedent and cow other potential tax dodgers. But even a clear-cut, legal tax avoidance attempt can be fought in court and end up as tax evasion.

Bear in mind there is a continuum between easy-to-discover tax avoidance, provable tax avoidance and punishable tax avoidance. One faces a set of probabilities, not hard and fast rules and facts, but on circumstantially determined chance.

While, for obvious reasons, it would be most unwise to tell a legal counselor or accountant flat out that one plans tax evasion, this does not mean that it is not possible to discuss with them possibilities that are legally dubious. Tax avoidance terminology must be used, a language in which everything involved can be fully understood by all parties but that in no way smacks of criminal intent. The most important distinction is to be made between tax reduction methods that can lead to prison, and those that protect you and your money from the tax man.

The legal distinction between avoidance and evasion is the key here. If pushed, one may admit being involved in tax planning for tax avoidance purposes—strictly within the letter of the law—

and that one abhors tax evasion as much as the next guy. There is no simple legal classification applicable to most approaches.

———◆———

Tax Avoidance Versus Tax Evasion

Mark Nestmann, *The Sovereign Individual*, July 2001

Every taxpayer has a right to try to avoid taxes. But when does complete legal tax avoidance turn into illegal tax evasion?

The answer seems intuitive: evasion is driving around a tollbooth to enter a toll road without paying. Avoidance is taking an alternate free route.

This fundamental difference couldn't be clearer. And courts in many countries have repeatedly stated: Tax avoidance is legal. Tax evasion is not. Justice Felix Frankfurter of the U.S. Supreme Court wrote: "As to the astuteness of taxpayers in ordering their affairs as to minimize taxes, we have said that, 'The very meaning of a line in the law is that you intentionally may go as close to it as you can if you do not pass it.' This is so because nobody owes any public duty to pay more than the law demands. Taxes are enforced extractions, not voluntary contributions."

In the House of Lords, the highest court of the United Kingdom and many other countries, Lord Clyde stated: "No man in this country is under the smallest obligation, moral or other, so as to arrange his legal relations to his business or to his property as to enable the Inland Revenue to put the largest possible shovel in his stores. And the taxpayer is entitled to be astute to prevent, so far as he honestly can, the depletion of his means by the Revenue."

Yet despite this ringing legal affirmation of tax avoidance, in practice, it's not always easy to tell the difference between evasion and avoidance. The line changes with amendments to tax laws, so that yesterday's legal avoidance easily converts to today's tax evasion.

Not knowing the difference can cost you dearly. For instance, non-domiciled residents of the United Kingdom can arrange their affairs so that virtually all their offshore income is tax-free, except for that repatriated for living expenses. This scheme is perfectly acceptable from a U.K. perspective.

But residents of most other members of the Organization of Economic Cooperation and Development (OECD) are liable to tax on their worldwide income—whether generated personally, or through a partnership, trust or as a shareholder in a corporation. There are narrow exceptions to these rules, but by and large—this is the law. Persons who fail to report their worldwide income, and pay tax on it, risk prosecution for tax evasion. And under U.S. law, if efforts are made to conceal the income, tax fraud or even money laundering charges are possible.

It is true that audit rates are relatively low, so many tax evaders are never caught. But no matter what the odds, the penalties for non-compliance are unforgiving.

Many offshore promoters ignore the law, or don't realize it has changed, and continue to promote tax-defective schemes:

- "Abusive trusts" in which the individuals forming and funding the trust are told by the promoter that the trust is "non-taxable" and "non-reportable."
- "Secret" and supposedly non-reportable offshore bank accounts.
- High-yield investment programs in many cases with your "profits" diverted into a supposedly "secret" offshore account.
- "Untax" schemes that claim by declaring yourself a "sovereign citizen," you are no longer subject to federal, provincial or state legislation, courts or taxes.

Hundreds of similar scams exist. Robert Bauman, the Sovereign Society's legal counsel and editor of the *Sovereign Society Offshore A-Letter*, reports: "Recently I saw an advertisement in major airline magazine touting purchase of an offshore "how to" investment book. A bit of checking turned up the fact that the author is accused in an SEC lawsuit of masterminding a $14 million stock fraud using a U.S. firm he founded."

Does It Pass the Common Sense Test?

The common element in these schemes is that they promise something that defies common sense—that is too good to be true.

Common sense dictates that if you live in a country that imposes an income tax on your worldwide income, you can't eliminate your liability to that tax by signing a piece of paper purportedly revoking your Social Security number, Social Insurance number or driver's license number.

Common sense dictates that it's not possible to generate "risk-free" returns of 500 percent or more each year on any investment, offshore or otherwise.

Common sense dictates that an offshore banker or trust promoter is not going to give you unbiased or knowledgeable advice about tax liabilities in your own country relative to their proposed structure.

In short, a simple benchmark to determine the difference between legal tax avoidance and illegal tax evasion is: "If I were to read about this technique or instrument in the newspaper, or hear about it from a friend, would I be skeptical, or not?"

We counsel members to stay away from tax schemes that fail the common sense test or that otherwise promise benefits that appear "unreal."

Many Legal Ways to Save Taxes

Fortunately, there are many completely legal tax avoidance strategies of which you can still take advantage. If you are a U.S. citizen, for instance, Sovereign Society Tax Advisor Vernon Jacobs (www.offshorepress.com) points out the following completely legal tax avoidance strategies:

1. U.S. persons who live and work outside the United States for at least 330 days in any consecutive 12 months can exclude up to US$80,000 in foreign source earned income from their U.S. income taxes.

2. U.S. companies engaged in export sales may be able to save some taxes (although the law relating to this issue is being changed).

3. The foreign source income of a foreign trust after the death of the grantor (settlor) of the trust (and his or her spouse) is exempt from U.S. taxes until distributions are made to a U.S. beneficiary. This provides estate tax benefits for your heirs but no income tax benefits for yourself.

4. A small amount of currency gains from non-investment and non-business purposes is excluded from tax.

5. Tax deferral is available for profits from a foreign corporation owned by U.S. persons if it has no significant investment income and if most of its income and assets are utilized in earning profits from a foreign based corporation conducting a trade or business located outside the United States. However, there are numerous complicated restrictions on this principle and it must be pursued with qualified advice.

6. When a U.S. citizen expatriates by giving up his or her citizenship, future income from sources outside the United States is not subject to U.S. taxation and non U.S. source assets are not subject to U.S. estate and gift taxes.

Jacobs lists more than a dozen additional legitimate tax avoidance techniques.

Why pursue exotic and potentially illegal tax cutting strategies when there are so many legitimate ones to choose from?

These legitimate tax avoidance strategies get a bad rap in the mainstream media. Witness the comments of self-proclaimed offshore expert, Jack Blum, to a *New York Times* reporter: "There is no legitimate reason for an American citizen to have an offshore account. When you go offshore, you are doing so to evade rules, regulations, laws or taxes."

Blum takes his mistaken cue from government policies that deliberately blur the distinction between tax avoidance and tax evasion. Charles A. Cain, editor of *Offshore Investment* magazine, charged in a 1998 editorial that "the line between tax avoidance and tax evasion" is purposely being blurred by governments, with honest people (and their tax advisors) being jailed for "failed attempts at tax avoidance" while "tax evasion is put down on a moral level with heroine and cocaine pushing."

The blurring of these lines makes it all the more important for you to follow proven and prudent tax avoidance strategies, and not cross the line into illegal, and potentially dangerous, tax evasion.

———————————◆———————————

Never Pay U.S. Taxes Again—Legally
By Robert E. Bauman, JD, *The Sovereign Individual*, October 2003

Expatriation: It's been called "the ultimate estate plan" and it's a legal, step-by-step process that can lead to the legal right for you to stop paying U.S. or other national income taxes—forever.

In sum, it requires professional consultations, careful planning, movement of assets offshore and acquisition of a second nationality. When all that's done (and done exactly right), you must leave behind your home country and become a "tax exile" with an established domicile in a low or no-tax jurisdiction. And, for U.S. citizens, this unusual plan requires, as a final step toward tax freedom, the formal relinquishment of citizenship.

A drastic plan? You bet. And in truth, there are many other perfectly suitable offshore strategies that The Sovereign Society recommends that can result in significant tax savings. These include international life insurance policies and offshore investments made through retirement plans. But for U.S. citizens and long-term residents who seek a permanent and completely legal way to stop paying all U.S. taxes, expatriation is the only option.

Blueprint to Ultimate Tax Avoidance

Individuals have been leaving their own land to seek opportunities elsewhere since the dawn of mankind. But it has only been since the development of the modern nation-state, and its taxation of the worldwide income of its citizen-residents, that expatriation has taken on significant tax consequences.

One of the first tax advisors to appreciate the potential tax savings of expatriation was my friend and colleague, Marshall Langer J.D., a valued former member of The Sovereign Society Council of Experts, now retired. Langer is an international tax attorney and the respected author of several major international tax treatises. He is also the daring creator of a now out-of-print book, The Tax Exile Report. This title gained international notoriety when the late U.S. Senator Daniel Patrick Moynihan (D-N.Y.), red-faced and angry, waived a copy of the book at a televised Senate hearing, denouncing it as "a legal income tax avoidance plan."

In explaining why "expatriation" is so attractive to wealthy Americans (and others), a few years ago a Forbes magazine article gave the compelling arithmetic: "A very rich Bahamian citizen pays zero estate taxes; rich Americans—anyone with an estate worth US$3 million or more—pay 55%. A fairly stiff 37% marginal rate kicks in for Americans leaving as little as $600,000 to their children." Even though U.S. estate taxes have been reduced since then, an even more impressive part of the Langer plan is the ability to escape American income, capital gains and other taxes.

When it comes to expatriation, however, Americans face a nearly unique burden. Unlike almost every other nation, with one or two minor exceptions, U.S. citizens and long-term residents cannot escape home country taxes by moving their residence to another nation. The only way to leave U.S. taxes behind is to give up their citizenship.

Toothless Penalties

Becoming a tax exile is not without problems, but, so far, they are more political than legal. The source of the current controversy over expatriation was a sensational article in the Nov. 24, 1994 issue of *Forbes* magazine, entitled "The New Refugees." Filled with juicy details (famous names, luxury addresses, big dollar tax savings), the story described how clever ex-Americans who became citizens of certain foreign nations, paid little or no U.S. federal and state income, estate and capital gains taxes.

Ever since, expatriation has been a favorite "hot button" issue kicked around by the American news media and "soak-the-rich" politicians. While current anti-expat provisions in the U.S. Tax Code are relatively toothless, various proposals would impose an immediate tax on unrealized capital gains on anyone who ends their U.S. citizenship. These use an arbitrary test of net worth and/or income tax paid over a period of years to assume an ex-citizen is trying to escape income taxes. Similar net worth/income tax provisions have been the law since 1996, which I'll explain in a moment.

It's understandable why politicians keep this political football in play. To the average uninformed U.S. taxpayer, expatriation seems like just another rich man's tax loophole. Before *Forbes* raised the issue, few people had even heard of the concept of formal surrender or loss of U.S. citizenship.

Taken together with the recent controversy over U.S. companies re-incorporating offshore to avoid U.S. corporate taxes (which is fully legal), candidates for federal office have in expatriation a convenient straw man that they can beat unmercifully. Former U.S. Treasury Secretary Lawrence Summers (now president of Harvard University) went so far as to call tax expatriates "traitors" to America. He later was forced to apologize.

Your Right to Give Up U.S. Citizenship

As a national political issue, expatriation is hardly new.

In the bitter aftermath of the War Between the States (1860-65), Congress hotly debated the status of people in the southern states that formed the Confederacy. Ultimately, Congress decided "rebels" who swore allegiance could again become U.S. citizens. The "Expatriation Act of 1868" formally recognized that all Americans do have a right to give up their citizenship, if they so choose. A century later, in the Foreign Investors Tax Act of 1966, Congress again decided to make an issue of expatriation. In that Act, lawmakers tried to impose onerous taxes on exiting wealthy Americans who relinquished their U.S. citizenship "with the principal purpose of avoiding" U.S. taxes, a highly subjective intention that was virtually impossible to prove. The IRS couldn't prove such "intent" and very rarely even tried.

A 1996 anti-expatriation law inspired by the *Forbes* article asserts limited U.S. tax jurisdiction for a period of 10 years over persons who renounce their U.S. citizenship "with the principal purpose of avoiding U.S. taxes." Also covered by this law are permanent resident aliens ("green card" holders) or anyone else who has resided in the United States for any eight of the preceding 15 years.

For the purposes of this law, tax avoidance is presumed to be the true purpose if, at the time of expatriation, an expatriate's net worth exceeds US$552,000 or he or she pays an annual tax bill exceeding US$110,000, figures that are indexed for inflation annually. However, with proper planning, it is relatively easy to avoid U.S. taxes during this 10-year period.

The lengths to which politicians will go to penalize expatriates is demonstrated by a never-enforced provision of U.S. law, also enacted in 1996, that permits the Attorney General to bar from returning to the United States anyone who renounces their U.S. citizenship to avoid U.S. taxes. In this manner, Congress lumped individuals exercising their legal right to avoid taxes with narcotics traffickers and terrorists.

Amidst the furor, thoughtful experts criticize what they see as a much broader and dangerous U.S. anti-expatriation precedent. They point out these laws involve not only retaliatory government acts against resistance to high taxes, but pose possible violations of human rights guaranteed by other laws and even the Human Rights Charter of the United Nations. It is worth noting that the U.S. Supreme Court has repeatedly affirmed the right of U.S. citizens to end their citizenship as well as the right to enjoy dual citizenship.

In reality, this political frenzy probably reflects collective envy more than any sense of patriotism by Americans or their congressional representatives. Expatriation is not as serious a problem as some pretend: fewer than 800 Americans, rich or poor, have formally given up their citizenship in recent years. Most expatriates give up their U.S. citizenship because they are returning to their native lands or marrying non-U.S. citizens.

Save Millions of Dollars, Legally

Despite the controversy, there remain very substantial tax savings for wealthy U.S. citizens who are prepared to give up their citizenship. While only a handful of very rich Americans have legally expatriated, these individuals include some prominent names: In 1962, John Templeton, respected international investor, businessman and philanthropist, surrendered his U.S. citizenship to become a citizen of the Bahamas. This move saved him more than US$100 million when he sold the well-known international investment fund that still bears his name.

Other wealthy ex-Americans who have taken their formal leave include billionaire Campbell Soup heir John ("Ippy") Dorrance III (Ireland); Michael Dingman (The Bahamas), chairman of Abex and a Ford Motor director; J. Mark Mobious (Germany), one of the leading emerging market investment fund managers; Kenneth Dart (Belize), heir to the billion dollar Dart container fortune; Ted Arison (Israel), head of Carnival Cruise Lines; and millionaire head of Locktite Corp., Fred Kreible (Turks and Caicos Islands).

How It Should Be Done

Long before you formally give up your U.S. citizenship, you should reorder your financial affairs in such a way as to remove from possible government control and taxation most, if not all, of your assets.

Here are the steps you must take:

- Move abroad and make your new home in a no-tax foreign nation so you are no longer a "resident' for U.S. income taxes;

- Obtain alternative citizenship and passport;

- Give up U.S. citizenship and change your legal "domicile" to avoid U.S. estate taxes;

- Arrange your affairs so that most or all of your income is derived from non-U.S. sources; and

- Title your property ownership so that any assets that remain in the United States are exempt from U.S. estate and gift taxes.

The following chart provides a planning timetable:

Year	Action Plan
0	Decide to expatriate
1-2	Strategize with expert advisors
3-4	Liquidate U.S. assets
5-6	Choose new jurisdiction
7-8	Move to your chosen residency haven
9-10	Give up U.S. citizenship

One of the most important decisions is the choice of a second nationality. Millions of Americans already hold a second nationality; millions more qualify almost instantly for one by reason of birth, ancestry or marriage. For instance, in many countries (Ireland is one), having a parent or grandparent born in that country will qualify children or grandchildren for immediate citizenship and passports after presenting the appropriate documentation.

Otherwise, you will need to qualify for alternative citizenship through prolonged residency (2-10 years) in a country in which you are eligible for residency based on your economic status or investments you make there. For instance, both Panama and Belize have formal tax-advantaged residency plans for foreign nationals who wish to make their home there. After five years, sometimes less, you can apply for citizenship.

Alternatively, you may choose to purchase economic citizenship, which can be obtained in a matter of months, but only at significant cost (minimum outlay of approximately US$100,000). The only two legitimate economic citizenship programs still in existence are from the Commonwealth of Dominica and St. Kitts & Nevis. For more information on these programs, see the Henley & Partners web site at http://www.henleyglobal.com/ec. Based on an exclusive arrangement with Henley & Partners, Sovereign Society members are eligible for a significant reduction of the applicable professional fees. Before making any move, it's absolutely essential to consult qualified professionals. We are pleased to provide the names of qualified professional advisors if you contact us at info@thesovereignsociety.com.

————◆•◆————

Don't Be Afraid to Fight the IRS
January 1994

Guilty until proved innocent is the maxim of the U.S. Tax Court when it issues a deficiency notice, claiming non-payment of tax. Since 1986, taxpayers have won only 10 percent of cases brought to the courts and 37 percent of the decisions were split.

It isn't easy to prove the IRS is wrong, but the courts are independent and you can go to Tax Court without paying the disputed amount in advance, unlike cases brought to the U.S. District Court or Court of Claims. Last year, the IRS issued more than 1.6 million deficiency notices where the results of an audit or a computer-generated demand for taxes were not agreed. There are 41 Tax Court judges who hold hearings throughout the country to decide if your tax assessment is correct. Don't be afraid of the IRS. Here are some tips to give you a better chance of upsetting the tax man's success rate.

The deficiency notice outlines the back taxes and penalties the IRS says you owe but it also tells you how to put forward a case to the Tax Court. You have 90 days to contest the deficiency notice, so file the petition quickly by registered mail and keep the receipt. It costs $60 to file the petition and send it to the office directed on the deficiency notice. Get a second opinion from a professional adviser on the merits of your case. This will cost $100-$225 for an hour's consultation.

A tax lawyer's time is expensive but if the amount at stake is $10,000 or less, you can represent yourself at a small-cases tax court, where about one-third of cases end up. These more informal courts are okay if you can simply explain the point at issue. The judge will accept almost any documents or testimony you think are relevant and will ask helpful questions. But if a complicated point of law is involved, or the amount concerned is more than $10,000, a tax lawyer's services, or those of a certified public accountant or an enrolled agent admitted to practice in Tax Court, will be needed, at a cost of at least $15,000 and a great deal more formality. There are 14 Tax Court-approved legal clinics where you can get free advice from supervised law students if you can't afford the fees.

Try for a settlement before the case reaches court. About 80 percent of cases are settled and the tax reduced. Your petition to the Tax Court automatically goes back to an IRS appeals officer who will set up a case discussion, which you or your agent can attend to discuss a settlement. It may be a good idea for your professional adviser to be present. Surprisingly, IRS appeals officers consider the merits of the legal case before deciding whether to proceed to court. Before your case is heard, you will have to swap evidence with the IRS attorney and agree to as many facts as possible. Do this and don't risk upsetting the judge which could mean restrictions on the evidence you can present.

Present all records you can with as much information as possible and, if there is a reason for bookkeeping problems, such as illness, back up the argument with a doctor's letter. Make your verbal testimony credible.

Why the IRS's Free Advice Is Often Worth Just What It Costs

By Dan Pilla. *The Sovereign Individual*, April 2004

Are you among the millions of citizens who seek free tax advice from the IRS? If so, it's worth remembering the wisdom of the old proverb, "You get what you pay for."

While the IRS's advice comes at no up front charge, it often bears a substantial cost in the long run because the agency makes so many mistakes. Worse, when the IRS gives you the wrong answer, it often penalizes you when you follow its incorrect advice! Fortunately, it's possible to eliminate penalties and interest the IRS imposes in these circumstances. This will show you how.

20% of IRS Answers "Flatly Incorrect"

The latest report of the Treasury Inspector General for Tax Administration confirms that the IRS's error rate in the advice it gives citizens through its walk in Taxpayer Assistance Centers (TACs) remains unacceptably high.

The latest study, released in January 2004, indicates that the IRS provided flatly incorrect answers 20% of the time. In another 15% of the cases, the IRS provided a "correct" answer without first obtaining all the background information necessary to respond. When this kind of incomplete advice is factored in, the total inaccuracy rate rises to a troubling 35%.

The problem here is that most citizens just don't know all the rules. The tax laws are simply so complex that most people don't know what background information they should provide to the IRS and have no idea whether the IRS asked sufficient questions to obtain the background facts.

Questions asked by the Treasury investigators were not esoteric tax law inquiries. All the questions dealt with narrow, relatively simple areas of law that TAC employees are trained in and are expected to know. It is obvious that TAC employees are simply not being trained adequately.

This brings up another disturbing aspect of the investigation. When the IRS's TAC employees are asked a question that is outside the scope of their training, they are required by operating guidelines to refer the questions to other, more qualified IRS personnel. In 31% of the cases, TAC employees answered questions that were outside the scope of their training, in violation of the referral regulations. We can only guess what the error rate is for those answers.

YOU Are Responsible for Incorrect Advice From the IRS

Don't let this shock you. The real question is, can you defeat the penalties and interest attributable to the IRS's incorrect advice? The answer is yes.

You are not subject to "any penalty" if it is attributable to "erroneous advice" provided "in writing" by the IRS. The defense is available when:

* The written advice was reasonably relied upon,

* Was in response to a specific written request, and

* You provided adequate or accurate information upon which to base the advice.

To prove this, you must file a written request seeking abatement of the penalty. Explain the facts in detail and present a copy of the IRS's letter containing the advice you relied on. You must also demonstrate that you provided all necessary and accurate background information upon which to base the advice. This is proven by providing a copy of the letter you mailed seeking the advice. Submit your request to the service center where you filed the return.

Unfortunately, most IRS advice is not written. And the IRS is required to abate penalties only when they are based upon erroneous "written" advice. However, the IRS's Penalty Handbook declares that the agency has "extended this relief to include erroneous oral advice when appropriate."

If you seek oral advice from the IRS, make sure you have records to prove your conversation. This should take the form of a written memo that sets forth the following:

* The date you phoned or walked into a TAC office;

* The person you spoke with, including their employee ID number (IRS personnel are required to provide this when asked);

* The specific office you phoned and the phone number called, or the address of the office you walked into;

* The questions asked and the background information you provided; and

* As completely as possible, the answers you received.

Keep this information in your permanent tax file for the year in question, together with your tax return photocopy and financial records. My latest book, The IRS Problem Solver, contains more details on this process.

What about canceling interest attributable to erroneous IRS advice? The tax law provides for the abatement of interest when it is attributable to erroneous IRS advice, but there is no authority to cancel interest in connection with verbal IRS advice.

Using a Tax Professional

Another option is to consult a tax professional. To save money, rather than ask a professional to prepare your entire return, you have the option of engaging that individual on an hourly basis. That way, you can get the advice you need about the specific problem you face without incurring the full costs of return preparation.

The Tax Freedom Institute is an association of tax professionals capable of helping you with all your tax preparation needs. Check out the TFI web site at www.taxhelponline.com. Or, call (800) 346-6829 for more information.

(Nationally regarded as an expert in IRS procedures, Dan Pilla is the author of more than a dozen books outlining solutions to tax-related financial difficulties, including his most recent book, The IRS Problem Solver (Harper Collins Publishers). Pilla is also the editor of the monthly newsletter Dan Pilla's Confidential Tax Bulletin and creator of the www.taxhelponline.com Web site.)

———————◆•◆———————

U.S. Citizens Can Earn Annual $80,000 Offshore Tax-Free
by Mark Nestmann, *The Sovereign Individual*, July 2001

If you are a U.S. citizen, you must pay taxes on your worldwide income. This isn't an uncommon requirement as most other OECD countries have similar laws. But you are subject to U.S. income tax even if you live outside the United States. The United States is the world's only major country that taxes its citizens and not just its permanent residents.

Fortunately, there's a silver lining. The Internal Revenue Code 6 contains an escape clause that allows you to earn up to US$80,000/year tax-free if you're working offshore. If your spouse accompanies you overseas, you can jointly earn up to $160,000/year, tax-free. You can obtain additional tax credits for your housing expenses.

If you've ever thought about living overseas, but didn't think you could afford to pay U.S. taxes on your earnings, or you are considering giving up your U.S. citizenship to permanently disconnect from U.S. taxation, this provision allows you to "test the waters."

The exemption applies only to earned income, not to investment income. But even then, there's a benefit: the tax bracket on which you pay taxes on unearned income may drop.

The requirements to qualify for this Foreign Earned Income Exclusion (FEIE) are fairly straightforward. You must qualify under one of two tests to be eligible: the "bona fide residence test" or the "physical presence test":

- *Bona fide residence test.* If you have established legal residency in another country for an uninterrupted period of at least one year, you qualify under this test. But if you file a statement with the tax authorities of a foreign country stating that you are a non-resident for tax purposes, you will be ineligible.

- *Physical presence test.* You qualify under this test if you are physically present in a foreign country (or countries) for at least 330 full days during any period of 12 consecutive months.

Under either test, you must prove that you have a new "tax home" outside the United States. There is no requirement that you live in a country that imposes an income tax. Finally, you must file IRS Form 2555 each year with your U.S. tax return.

Example: On January 15, 2003, John and Mary Johnson relocate from the United States to Belize, a country that taxes only income earned within Belize. The Johnsons lease a beachfront home for US$1,000/month.

The Johnsons could receive salaries of up to US$160,000, as employees, without being subject to U.S. income tax. They could receive an additional US$10,171 credit against the rent on their home.

In addition, fringe benefits that are non-taxable to a U.S.-based employee are also non-taxable overseas. For instance, the Johnsons' employer(s) could pay for their health and disability insurance, or issue stock options to them, with no additional tax liability.

To receive these benefits, you must file a U.S. tax return every year you are abroad. The FEIE election may not be taken retroactively.

Some additional precautions, according to Rufus Rhoades and Marshall Langer, co-authors of *U.S. International Taxation and Tax Treaties*: Don't work for a foreign partnership in which you have an equity position. All income from services, such as consulting, is considered earned income if your capital is not used in the business. But if your capital is a "material factor in the partnerships' income," no more than 30 percent of your net income qualifies for the FEIE. Corporations are not subject to this rule.

Social Security tax may not be exempt on your offshore earnings. In general, U.S. Social Security and Medicare taxes do not apply to wages for services you perform outside of the United States. However, if you are self-employed or work for an "American employer," or you are working in a country in which the United States has signed a "binational social security agreement," you will be subject to Social Security tax on compensation up to US$80,400 annually and Medicare tax on 100 percent of your earned income.

You can take either a tax credit or a deduction for income taxes imposed on you by a foreign country. However, you cannot take a credit or deduction for foreign income taxes paid on income that is exempt from tax under the FEIE or the foreign housing exclusion.

Persons who wander from country to country aren't eligible for the FEIE. Nor does living on a yacht qualify you for the exclusion. You must have a foreign "tax home."

Unless it is your legal residence in a particular jurisdiction you may not claim the FEIE to the extent that you derive income from a "restricted country." These countries are currently Cuba, Iraq and Libya.

The FEIE also has important limitations. The most fundamental one is that there is no exclusion for unearned income, rents, royalties, interest, dividends. You also remain subject to capital gains tax and estate tax.

How to Completely Avoid U.S. Tax Liability

For these reasons, if you wish to live outside the United States permanently, you might want to consider giving up your U.S. citizenship. This has its own complications, the most serious being that if the IRS considers your expatriation to be "tax motivated," there is a remote possibility that legislation enacted in 1996 will permanently exclude you from the United States, even to visit friends or family members. While Sovereign Society Board of Advisors member Marshall Langer says this provision is not currently being enforced, there is no assurance that it won't be in the future, although many legal scholars have declared it to be unconstitutional, saying it would never hold up in court.

For more details about the FEIE, see www.irs.gov/.

Five Legal Ways You Can Save Taxes Offshore
By Mark Nestmann, *The Sovereign Individual*, March 2004

You can own a Swiss chalet, tax-free. Earn up to US$80,000/year offshore...again, without paying a dime in U.S. income tax. Even purchase offshore mutual funds...without tax liability.

The U.S. imposes taxes on its citizens and permanent residents on their worldwide income. Yet, the tax laws have hundreds of "loopholes" you can use to reduce your taxes. And nearly every one of these tax breaks is available offshore—where you'll also find greater privacy and protection from the threat of lawsuits.

Plus, there are a handful of tax savings opportunities available ONLY if you work, invest or do business offshore.

Here I'll highlight one of the very best opportunities that you can take advantage of, right now, to begin saving taxes, safely and securely offshore. Plus, I'll give you capsule descriptions of several other little-known tax loopholes and show you how you can learn more about them.

Buy A Swiss Chalet With Your IRA

You can own almost any non-U.S. investment in your retirement plan, including offshore mutual funds and virtually any kind of foreign real estate. You can even have your IRA pay you a salary to manage your offshore real estate portfolio!

And that's just the beginning.

Want to purchase some of the lucrative offshore funds we've highlighted in past issues, such as Man-AHL Diversified PLC (up an average of 22.3% over the last 10 years)? One of the only ways to do so without suffering ruinous tax consequences is to buy it through your retirement plan.

Another benefit is asset protection. All types of retirement plans have come under attack in the courts. In contrast, if you invest your retirement plan in a suitable jurisdiction, Switzerland, for instance, it can be configured to be essentially judgment-proof.

If you'd like to unlock the hidden potential in your IRA, 401K or other retirement plan, check out the supplement enclosed with this issue.

More Offshore Tax Breaks

That's just the tip of the iceberg when it comes to tax breaks Congress provides U.S. persons who invest, work or do business overseas.

Here's a small sampling of some others:

* Earn US$160,000/year tax-free, courtesy of Uncle Sam. U.S. persons who live and work outside the United States can exclude up to US$80,000 per year in foreign earned income from their U.S. income taxes. Your spouse is eligible for another US$80,000 earned income exemption for a total US$160,000 exemption for a married couple.

* Defer tax on business income. If you form a foreign corporation that generates "active" income from foreign trade or business (not passive income from investments), and the business is also managed offshore, you don't need to pay taxes on the profits until you repatriate them.

* Defer tax on investment income. If you purchase an offshore variable annuity that meets IRS requirements, income from its underlying investments is legally tax deferred until you begin taking income from it.

* Tax-free bequests and better returns. Offshore life insurance offers the same tax benefits as domestic life insurance, namely, you can multiply a small premium amount into a large death benefit that is tax free to your heirs.

To receive these benefits, particularly in the case of doing business offshore or forming an insurance company. it's necessary to obtain expert tax advice. And of course, they're not for everyone—e.g., you may not want to get into the insurance business.

This is just a brief sampling of the literally dozens of tax saving strategies available offshore.

Part Three—International Taxation Schemes

United Nations Seeks Global Tax Authority

by Daniel J. Mitchell, Ph.D., The Heritage Foundation, *The Sovereign Individual*, July 2001

The United Nations recently issued a report attacking international tax competition and national fiscal sovereignty. There are four main recommendations in the report: an international tax organization, global taxes, emigrant taxation and a back door form of tax harmonization or information exchange. Every one of these initiatives would undermine individual liberty and encourage statist economic policy. Like the Organization for Economic Cooperation and Development and the European Union, both of which are pursuing similar agendas, the UN seeks to prop up inefficient, high-tax welfare nations by making it difficult for taxpayers to escape oppressive tax systems. Leaders of all low-tax nations, particularly the United States, should block the UN's radical scheme.

A key United Nations panel recently put forth a series of initiatives that would radically change national and international tax policy. Chaired by Ernesto Zedillo, former President of Mexico, the "High-level Panel on Financing for Development" endorsed the creation of an international tax organization, recommended the imposition of global taxes, and called for a form of tax harmonization known as information exchange. All governments would be expected to acquiesce to this scheme, which will be part of the agenda at the International Conference on Financing for Development, scheduled to take place in Mexico next March.

If implemented, the proposed changes would undermine the right of sovereign nations to determine their own tax policies. Yet the attack on sovereignty is minor compared to the likely effect on global economic performance. The report seems designed to prop up inefficient welfare states and promote more government spending. The report openly condemns tax competition, for instance, and repeatedly endorses expanded efforts to redistribute wealth and income.

But contrary to what is asserted in the UN report, tax competition is a desirable force in the world economy. Because it is increasingly easy for resources to cross national borders, politicians must exercise at least a modest degree of fiscal discipline in order to attract jobs, capital, and entrepreneurship. The UN proposals would undercut this liberalizing process and therefore erode the economic advantage of all low-tax nations, including America. The President and Congress should reject this extremist agenda, and this rejection should be echoed by all nations that believe in freedom and prosperity.

The UN report contains four major initiatives. Each one of these proposals is bad tax policy. All of the proposals undermine national sovereignty, and most of them represent an assault on the right to privacy. The unambiguous result of these policies is that governments around the world would be shielded from competition and politicians would have much less incentive to be fiscally responsible.

Creation of an International Tax Organization

The UN report endorses the creation of an International Tax Organization. This new body would have some relatively mundane responsibilities, such as collecting statistics and monitoring developments in tax policy, but facilitating bad tax policy seems to be the number one objective. The Zedillo report explicitly states that the International Tax Organization should help countries tax income earned outside their borders, and it also argues that such a body could "take a lead role in restraining tax competition."

At no point, however, does the report demonstrate any harm caused by fiscal rivalry between nations. Instead, readers are supposed to blindly accept the assertion that this competitive process is bad. But if competition is good for banks, pet stores, and car companies, then how can competition be bad for governments? The answer, of course, is that competition is good, but it is good for taxpayers and national economies rather than politicians. A global bureaucracy, by contrast, almost certainly would represent the interests of politicians. Like parallel efforts by the Organization for Economic Cooperation and Development (OECD) and the European Union (EU), it would create a cartel-like environment for purposes of undermining competition. Governments should not conspire to keep taxes high, and they certainly should not set up a supra-national institution to pursue a statist agenda.

An International Tax Organization is a threat to the best interests of all low-tax nations, including the United States. It also is bad news for taxpayers in high tax jurisdictions like France. Without tax competition, it is quite likely that many nations would impose even heavier burdens on their people. As such, any effort to restrict the tax-motivated flow of global capital would undercut the ability of all taxpayers to climb the ladder of economic opportunity.

The Imposition of Global Taxes

A major part of the report is a proposal to have global taxes, levies that would be imposed on the entire world. The revenues generated by these taxes would be made available for income redistribution and other purposes.

The report refers to this as "Innovative Sources of Finance, and highlights two options. The first is a levy on all international currency transactions, the so-called Tobin tax. The appeal of this tax, at least to the report's authors, is that it would generate a huge amount of money, up to $400 billion each year. That is the bad news. The good news is that the tax is so impractical that the report acknowledges the difficulty of implementing such a scheme. In short, currency traders would either avoid the tax, which the report admits could amount to 1,000 percent of profit margins, or develop derivative instruments that would be harder to tax. Combined with the fact that a currency transaction tax would throw a monkey wrench in the world trading system and impose a disproportionate burden on America's efficient financial markets, it appears a Tobin tax is not an immediate threat.

Unfortunately, the same cannot be said about the second option, a worldwide energy tax. The UN report is very enthusiastic about a tax on fossil fuel consumption, supposedly pegged so that each type of fuel (oil, gas, coal, etc.) would be taxed in accordance with its contribution to greenhouse gases. No mention is made of the tax rates that might be imposed or the amount of tax revenue desired, but the report does state that the tax should be high enough to discourage consumption. Interestingly, the authors seem oblivious to the fact that there is a tradeoff between raising revenue and discouraging consumption. In any event, a comprehensive global energy tax would dramatically hinder world economic growth. It would mean higher gas prices, higher electricity prices, and higher heating oil prices, and developing nations would be especially hard hit.

And if this agenda is not sufficiently frightening, the report also talks about global taxes on seabed mining, ocean fishing, and satellite launches. The drawback of these initiatives—from the UN perspective—is that they might not raise a large amount of money. The report also mentions taxes on trade, air travel, and arms exports, but concludes that these might not be politically feasible.

Turning People into Government Property

Perhaps the most radical proposal in the report is an initiative to give governments permanent taxing rights over their people. This taxation of emigrants is supposedly necessary to protect nations from economic loss when productive citizens emigrate. The report states that the enforcement of such a scheme could be one of the responsibilities of the new International Tax Organization.

This idea implicitly assumes that people are a form of chattel, the property of a government even if they seek opportunity elsewhere. To be sure, there are jurisdictions that suffer from "brain drain." French citizens have been fleeing to England in record numbers and Canadians often make their way to the United States. In a world that values individual sovereignty and personal liberty, this would not be an issue. And even if some governments think emigration is a problem, perhaps they should put their own houses in order before seeking to make their citizens perpetual tax slaves. After all, France's brain drain is mostly a reflection of that country's oppressive tax system. England merely happens to be the unintended beneficiary of France's fiscal policy mistakes.

The United States should be the strongest opponent of this scheme. Because America's free market economy promotes high levels of job creation and economic opportunity, the U.S. is a magnet for the world's entrepreneurs and other ambitious people. As such, it seems unlikely that the U.S. would support a policy that allows other nations to tax income earned in America. Critics may argue that this view is inconsistent and hypocritical (the U.S., after all, is one of the few nations to impose taxes on its citizens' overseas labor income), but self-interest is a powerful force. Foreign born workers in America, including both citizens and resident aliens, earn over $500 billion of labor income each year—nearly $600 billion including other types of income. Allowing other governments to tax that income, even at rates as low as 10 percent, could drain $60 billion out of the U.S. economy.

Back-door Tax Harmonization

Not only does the UN want to impose taxes on a global basis, it also wants to help individual governments tax income on a global basis. This is why the report endorses "information exchange," which means every government would be expected to collect private financial data on individual taxpayers and then share that information with other governments. High tax nations would then use this information to tax any income their residents earn in other countries. This initiative is very similar to the information exchange schemes being pushed by the OECD and the EU.

Information exchange makes sense, but only for jurisdictions with oppressive tax systems. Politicians from high-tax nations like France, for instance, get upset when taxpayers shift their savings and investment to jurisdictions with lower tax burdens and they desperately want the ability to continue taxing any income these assets generate. But this should be a matter for the French government and French taxpayers. Low tax nations should not be forced to suspend their financial privacy laws and act as vassal tax collectors for Europe's welfare states. Indeed, information exchange violates an important principle of international law, dual criminality, by seeking to force low-tax countries to put the laws of other nations above their own.

While this proposal will probably get the least attention of the report's four major recommendations, it could be the most dangerous. Information exchange is a back door form of tax harmonization since individuals would be taxed at the same rate regardless of where they earn their income. This initiative is a dagger aimed at the heart of U.S. financial markets since people from all around the world invest in the U.S. economy, but many would withdraw their funds if financial institutions were forced to act as informers for foreign tax collectors.

Conclusion

In addition to the specific proposals discussed above, the report calls for a doubling of foreign aid, more social welfare spending, higher taxes, and international bureaucracies that would interfere with the ability of sovereign nations to determine their own labor and environmental policies. Combined with the UN's recent pro-gun control meeting, it seems the organization is still wedded to an anti-American, anti-freedom agenda.

In the final analysis, motives do not matter. Regardless of whether the UN's behavior is driven by knee-jerk anti-Americanism or by hard-core socialist ideology, the organization's tax agenda would cripple the global economy. Low tax nations like America, the U.K., Switzerland and the so-called tax havens would suffer the most.

The good news is that the UN cannot move forward with its radical proposal without full support from the world's major governments. This means that the United States has effective veto power. To protect the interests of American taxpayers and to preserve prosperity and opportunity around the globe, Congress and the President should tell the bureaucrats at the U.N. to take a long walk off a short pier.

For more information: The UN Report is online at www.un.org/esa/ffd/a55-1000.pdf. The Center for Freedom and Prosperity Foundation is a public policy, research, and educational organization operating under Section 501©(3). It is privately supported, and receives no funds from any government at any level, nor does it perform any government or other contract work. It is the research and educational affiliate of the Center for Freedom and Prosperity (CFP), tel: 202-285-0244, website: www.freedomandprosperity.org.

Information Exchange Undermines U.S. Competitive Advantage
by Daniel J. Mitchell, Ph.D., The Heritage Foundation, July 2001

A specter haunts the world's governments. They fear that the combination of economic liberalization with modern information technology poses a threat to their capacity to raise taxes.
—Financial Times, *July 19, 2000*

When tax competition exists, politicians face pressure to keep tax rates reasonable in order to dissuade workers, investors and entrepreneurs from shifting their productive activities to a lower tax environment. As might be expected, politicians from high-tax countries dislike tax competition, and they have directed the Paris-based Organization for Economic Cooperation and Development (OECD) to eliminate tax competition between nations. The OECD is attempting to achieve this misguided goal by forcing all countries to participate in a system of global information exchange through which governments would collect and share private financial data. This would allow them to tax income on the basis of where investors and entrepreneurs live rather than where income is earned.

The OECD proposal is bad tax policy, bad privacy policy, bad sovereignty policy, and bad foreign policy. Under this type of scheme, residents of high-tax nations would be unable to reduce their tax burdens by shifting economic activity to a lower-tax jurisdiction. This would insulate politicians from having to compete for business, investment and entrepreneurial talent. The result almost surely would be higher tax rates.

Moreover, a worldwide system of information exchange would jeopardize financial privacy, since governments would be expected to collect detailed information about the income and assets of taxpayers and exchange that information with other governments. In addition, the OECD initiative is an assault on fiscal sovereignty, since the Paris-based bureaucracy is demanding that all nations participate in this system. Indeed, the OECD goes so far as to propose that low-tax jurisdictions (so-called tax havens) that do not participate in this cartel be subjected to sweeping financial protectionism. This radical step would hinder cross-border investment and economic development.

The OECD proposal is also a threat to fundamental tax reform. All major plans to fix the tax code (such as the flat tax) call for the elimination of double-taxation of savings and investment and a shift to a territorial tax regime—a system in which governments tax only income that is earned within their borders. The OECD plan, by contrast, is driven largely by a desire to double tax capital income earned in other nations.

Supporters of the OECD proposal claim that the assault on tax competition is necessary to stop tax evasion and money laundering. Both these issues are red herrings. The information presented below describes tax competition, discusses the OECD proposal, analyzes its likely consequences, and explains why the proposal is misguided.

What is tax competition?

Tax competition occurs when individuals can choose among jurisdictions with different levels of taxation when deciding where to work, save, and invest. This ability to avoid high-tax nations makes it more difficult for governments to enforce confiscatory tax burdens. In effect, tax competition pressures politicians to be fiscally responsible in order to attract economic activity (or to keep economic activity from fleeing to a lower-tax environment).

Tax competition can occur between countries or between state and local governments. Like other forms of competition, tax competition protects against abuses. For example, when there is only one gas station in a town, consumers have no options and likely will be charged high prices and given inferior service. But when there are several gas stations, their owners must pay attention to the needs of consumers in order to stay in business.

Why is tax competition desirable?

Tax competition promotes responsible tax policies. Lower tax rates reduce the burden of government on businesses and create an environment more conducive to entrepreneurship and economic growth. Without competition, politicians can act like monopolists, free to impose excessive tax rates without fear of consequences.

Competition between jurisdictions creates a check on this behavior. Whether this is desirable, of course, depends on one's perspective. Those who want lower tax rates and tax reform favor competition between countries. Those who want more power for the government and higher tax rates do not like such competition.

Is there real-world evidence of the impact of tax competition?

Almost every industrial economy in the world was forced to lower tax rates after Ronald Reagan implemented sweeping tax rate reductions in the 1980s. This did not occur because policy makers in other nations suddenly became pro-market, but rather because investors and entrepreneurs were shifting their activity to the U.S. economy and foreign politicians had no choice but to lower their personal and corporate tax rates in order to remain economically attractive. Tax competition is even more powerful today because it is increasingly easy for taxpayers to shift their resources to lower-tax environments.

Why is the OECD against tax competition?

The OECD is comprised of 30 industrialized economies, most of which are high-tax European nations. Many of the politicians from these nations resent low-tax countries for luring away savings, investment, and entrepreneurship. In an effort to eliminate the pressure of having to compete, they have directed the OECD to undermine the process of tax competition. This situation is similar to one in which a group of high-price, bad-service gas stations create a cartel to prevent new gas stations from opening.

What is the OECD trying to do?

The OECD has identified 41 jurisdictions around the world as "tax havens." These are jurisdictions that have both strong financial privacy laws and low or zero rates of tax. The OECD wants its member nations to be able to tax income that is earned by their residents in these low tax countries, so it is demanding that the so-called "tax havens" change their laws to help foreign governments identify those earnings.

Specifically, these low-tax jurisdictions are being asked to provide private financial data to OECD member nations (the OECD calls this "information exchange" even though low-tax nations get nothing from the deal). If the low-tax countries do not agree to become informers, the OECD will declare that they are "uncooperative" and ask member nations to subject these countries to financial protectionism.

What is the OECD's ultimate goal?

The OECD thinks it is wrong for taxes to influence decisions regarding where to work, save, and invest. The only way to keep taxes from influencing economic choices, however, is for all countries to "harmonize" their tax systems.

What is tax harmonization and why is it wrong?

Tax harmonization can be achieved in two different ways. Explicit tax harmonization occurs when nations agree to set minimum tax rates or even decide to tax at the same rate. In the European Union, for instance, member nations must have a value-added tax (VAT) of at least 15 percent. If tax rates in all countries are explicitly harmonized, a taxpayer's only option is the underground economy—which already accounts for one-fourth to one-third of GDP in many of Europe's welfare states.

The other way to stop tax competition is implicit harmonization. This occurs when nations are able to tax their residents on the basis of worldwide income so that it becomes impossible to reduce taxes by shifting activity to a lower-tax jurisdiction. In order to tax worldwide income, however, a country's tax collectors must find out how much income residents earn in other nations. This is why "information exchange" is such an important part of the OECD agenda.

Either type of tax harmonization would have grave consequences. Specifically, the OECD tax harmonization proposal:

- *Will lead to higher taxes.* Without the pressure of competition, politicians will be likely to impose higher tax rates and heavier tax burdens.

- *Will result in slower growth.* As fiscal burdens climb, the most likely impact will be higher taxes on savings and investment. This will reduce capital formation, leading to less productivity growth and lower wages.

- *Will undermine tax reform.* Simple and fair systems like the flat tax are based on the premise that income should be taxed only once and that governments should not seek to tax income earned in other countries (in other words, that the tax system should be territorial). The OECD initiative is diametrically opposed to these principles. It is based on the premise that savings and investment income should be double-taxed and that governments should be allowed to tax income earned outside their borders (what is known as a worldwide tax system).

- *Is a threat to free trade.* The OECD is trying to coerce low-tax countries to change their laws by threatening them with a wide range of taxes, fees, penalties, restrictions, and other trade barriers if they do not cooperate. This attack on global commerce could destabilize world markets and initiate a dangerous spiral of protectionism.

- *Violates national sovereignty.* Countries should be free to determine their own laws. Rather than bullying and threatening low-tax countries that are attracting "too many" investors and entrepreneurs, high-tax countries should take this as a signal that they should lower their own tax rates.

- *Is an attack on privacy.* An inherent feature of the OECD initiative is "information exchange," which means that foreign tax collectors would be allowed to rummage through financial institutions in low-tax countries for private financial information. Information exchange is a back-door form of tax harmonization.

- *Is a threat to American interests.* America is a low tax country by industrial world standards. Indeed, because we impose low or no taxes on foreign investors who purchase financial assets, we are a tax haven according to the OECD's definition. This has enabled us to attract trillions of dollars of investment from overseas, thus boosting our capital stock, increasing wages, and stimulating stronger growth. Undermining tax competition will harm our economy since it is quite likely that the OECD eventually will seek to compel the United States to change its desirable tax and privacy laws.

- *Is bad for the developing world.* As part of a market-based economic development strategy, countries should be encouraged to lower their tax rates. But if OECD countries impose their tax rates on the income that investors and entrepreneurs earn in other countries, tax competition is essentially eliminated. This will make it harder for poor countries to grow.

- *Is a threat to the Western Hemisphere.* Many of the so-called tax havens are Caribbean islands. These nations and territories depend heavily on their financial services industries to generate good jobs and enhance overall economic performance. If the OECD proposal succeeds, the impact on the region could be devastating. Potential consequences include political instability, increased crime, and widespread emigration.

How does the OECD justify its attack on tax competition?

In its two major reports, "Harmful Tax Competition: An Emerging Global Issue" (1998) and "Towards Global Tax Cooperation" (2000), the OECD argued that tax competition is not fair to high-tax countries because taxpayers shift their activity to low-tax jurisdictions. Recognizing that this is not the most persuasive argument, the OECD is now asserting that its anti-tax-competition proposal is needed to stop tax evasion and money laundering.

Should low-tax jurisdictions help enforce the tax codes of high-tax nations?

Countries with heavy tax burdens and high tax rates drive economic activity to other nations or into the underground economy. Assuming that taxpayers do not report the income from these activities, this is what is known as tax evasion. The OECD initiative, particularly the information exchange proposal, seeks to make it harder for taxpayers to "evade" taxes by shifting economic activity to lower-tax jurisdictions. (The organization does not address the other form of tax evasion, probably because it realizes that the underground economy will grow if the OECD succeeds in creating a global tax cartel.)

This approach is controversial because it assumes that governments have the right to tax income earned outside their borders. Perhaps even more disturbing, it assumes that low-tax nations are obliged to put the laws of other nations above their own, which violates a long-standing principle of international law known as "dual criminality." Dual criminality ensures that nations are not obliged to help enforce the laws of other nations unless the alleged offense is a crime in both jurisdictions. The United States, for instance, presumably would not help China investigate and prosecute pro-democracy protesters because supporting freedom is not a crime in America. This explains why most low-tax countries do not help high-tax countries enforce their tax laws, particularly when the high-tax country is trying to tax income that is being earned in the low-tax country.

Is tax evasion a major problem?

Given that even the OECD admits that tax revenues in its member nations are consuming a record share (more than 37 percent) of economic output, it is hard to make the case that tax evasion is widespread. Nonetheless, the fact that any tax evasion exists is troubling for those who believe that the laws should apply equally. This is true for both supporters and opponents of tax competition. The conflict is over how to deal with the issue.

What is the best way to reduce tax evasion?

Assuming that tax burdens are reasonable and governments are behaving justly (few people, of course, would condemn those who evade taxes that are confiscatory or those who refuse to pay taxes that are used to support corrupt and/or dictatorial regimes), there is a societal interest in minimizing tax evasion. The key question is how this goal can be achieved, particularly when dealing with cross-border economic activity.

The OECD assumes that tax evasion is rampant and presents its proposal as the only way to address the presumed crisis. This is a clever strategy, but it is also very misleading. An alternative, and far more effective, approach to reducing tax evasion incorporates territorial taxation and tax reform. The OECD's anti-tax evasion rhetoric is in fact a red herring: a tactic designed to draw attention away from the more critical debate between proponents of territorial taxation and advocates of worldwide taxation.

Which approach is better: worldwide taxation or territorial taxation?

High-tax countries that dominate the OECD's membership strongly prefer worldwide taxation, especially because it permits the double-taxation of income that is saved and invested elsewhere. This is why they are such ardent advocates of "information exchange," whereby financial privacy is sacrificed to allow governments access to the information they need to collect tax on any income their residents earn in other nations. Territorial taxation, by contrast, is based on the common-sense notion that governments should tax only income earned inside their borders.

Both approaches presumably would reduce tax evasion, but as the following discussion indicates, a territorial system does not cause the damage that is associated with worldwide taxation.

- *Tax competition.* A territorial system promotes competition since investors and entrepreneurs can take advantage of lower tax rates by doing business in jurisdictions with pro-market tax systems. A worldwide system, by contrast, essentially destroys competition since high-tax governments would have the right to impose their tax burdens around the world. Recalling the gas station analogy, this is similar to what would happen if a gas station charging $2.00 per gallon asserted the right to charge its customers a 50-cent surcharge if they switched to a gas station that charged only $1.50 per gallon.

- *Financial privacy.* A territorial system is much more protective of financial privacy, especially if capital income is taxed at the source (i.e., companies would pre-pay taxes on behalf of stockholders and bondholders, regardless of where they lived). Under this system, people would not be forced to divulge their personal financial information to the government every year. By contrast, a system of information exchange necessarily requires that at least two governments have access to wide-ranging details of a taxpayer's financial activity.

- *Fiscal sovereignty.* By definition, a territorial system does not create conflicts among nations regarding claims for the right to tax a particular flow of income. Each country has the right to impose any and all taxes on any and all income earned inside its borders. Any income earned in other countries, however, is off limits.

- *Tax reform.* A territorial system is consistent with fundamental tax reform. A flat tax, for instance, taxes only income earned inside national borders. A worldwide tax system, by contrast, is an impediment to tax reform, particularly since many high-tax countries favor information exchange because it allows them to double-tax income that is saved and invested. All major tax reform plans, including the flat tax, are based on taxing income only one time.

Why does the OECD highlight money laundering?

Accusations of money laundering provide a vehicle through which the OECD hopes to undermine financial privacy, paving the way for a worldwide system of information exchange. In reality, money laundering is not a problem that is typically associated with low-tax nations. In fact, reports indicate that most criminal proceeds are both earned and laundered in OECD nations. And a 1998 United Nations report acknowledged that money launderers tend to avoid so-called tax havens since they are viewed as a "red flag" by investigators.

How should countries deal with money laundering?

Assuming that basic civil liberties are respected and constitutional freedoms are protected, illegal activities should be vigorously prosecuted and criminal proceeds subject to forfeit. In the international arena, all countries should cooperate in the investigation and prosecution of universally recognized crimes. If a nation fails to assist in criminal investigations-for example, by acting as a safe harbor for terrorists—then coordinated international pressure is warranted.

Can the OECD's assault on tax competition be stopped?

The OECD has no rule-making authority. It has neither the power to impose sanctions nor the power to order its member nations to implement financial protectionism against low-tax countries. At most, it can ask its member nations to impose those barriers, and this is the Achilles' heel of the OECD agenda. For the OECD to succeed, it must convince all of its member nations to participate in a coordinated attack on low-tax countries.

Most important, the OECD needs the active support of the world's largest economy: the United States of America. This is why U.S. lawmakers control the outcome of this debate. If America chooses not to participate in the financial attack on low-tax countries, the OECD initiative will collapse.

Should America support the OECD agenda?

The OECD agenda is contrary to America's interests. The United States is a low tax country and a tax haven for foreign investment. Millions of jobs depend on the economic activity generated by our attractive tax and privacy laws. And if President Bush continues his efforts to reduce tax rates and eliminate the death tax, America is going to become an even more effective competitor in the world economy. It would therefore be self-defeating for the United States to support the OECD's attack on tax competition.

International Tax Treaties
Banking in Silence, 1998

One of the more civilized approaches governments take in their international war on financial privacy makes use of bilateral (between two nations) tax treaties. Currently the U.S. maintains such treaties with over 50 countries around the world.

Governments claim such treaties are aimed at eliminating double taxation of individuals who divide their time between or do business in two or more different nations. They don't mention that such treaties facilitate the exchange of tax and other information between the countries involved. This is used to ferret out those suspected of being tax evaders, those wise folks who have stashed their assets offshore.

For example, if a U.S. citizen invested money in Switzerland, the bilateral U.S.-Swiss tax treaty allowed a refund of most of the 35 percent withholding tax the Swiss government imposed on earned interest income paid within its borders. This required filing the appropriate form with the Swiss government, but information regarding the interest income was later forwarded to IRS. The IRS then cross checked to make certain the income was reported on the U.S. taxpayer's tax return and taxes paid.

In spite of themselves, governments sometimes inadvertently construct tax treaties that offer an unexpected bonus to the suffering taxpayer. But you have to know where tax treaty savings are hidden. Searching for these tax breaks is known as "treaty shopping." It means investing money in an offshore nation where domestic taxes are low or non-existent. But it must be in a nation that has a bilateral tax treaty with your home country, the provisions of which mean your tax liability at home will be cut also. Thus, treaty shopping is a perfectly legal way to reduce your tax burden. These loopholes infuriate IRS bureaucrats, so the U.S. government constantly renegotiates tax treaties with many nations in an attempt to close off such benefits. A few loopholes do manage to survive.

The free exchange of information under tax treaty provisions is usually limited to routine areas. If a specific request for information about a U.S. taxpayer is allowed by a foreign government, it must be pursuant to an on-going U.S. criminal investigation in which an indictment has already been issued. Foreign governments guard their sovereignty and don't want to be seen by their citizens as bowing to Uncle Sam. However, the U.S. government constantly tinkers with these agreements hoping to get the same free and easy access to foreign bank and financial records that it enjoys at home.

Tax Information Exchange Agreements Erode Offshore Secrecy

By Robert Bauman, JD, *The Sovereign Individual*, April 2002

Last July, in testimony before the U.S. Senate Permanent Subcommittee on Investigations, U.S. Treasury Secretary Paul O'Neill promised that to combat alleged offshore tax evasion, the Bush administration would negotiate tax information exchange agreements with at least half of the major offshore tax havens within one year.

O'Neill's surprise pledge followed months of the Republican administration's backing away from the Organization for Economic Cooperation and Development's blacklisting of 35 tax havens alleged to be engaged in "harmful tax competition." "We ought to pursue every tax cheat to the ends of the earth," O'Neill told the senators, but added emphatically: "I do not think it is appropriate for the United States or OECD to tell another sovereign nation what the structure of their tax system should be, period."

Uncomfortable with the OECD's high tax policies, which the Clinton administration had so lovingly embraced, O'Neill argued that bilateral tax treaties are a far better enforcement weapon against U.S. tax evaders who go offshore. The OECD's economic sanctions, he said, are "a last resort."

Important Distinctions

Tax information exchange agreements (TIEAs) are distinguished from both ordinary tax treaties and from mutual legal assistance treaties (MLATs).

"Ordinary" tax treaties are principally designed to provide relief from double taxation, with the secondary purpose of exchanging sufficient information so that taxpayers using them (primarily multinational corporations) do not abuse their provisions. The United States now has a network of more than 60 such treaties. Very few of them are with "tax havens," since most haven nations don't impose income or withholding taxes—the levies for which tax treaties are generally designed to provide relief.

MLATs are bilateral agreements to exchange information and evidence in investigations involving crimes such as drug smuggling, money laundering, etc., but not including tax evasion. The U.S. now has a network of more than 40 MLATs, including most "tax haven" nations.

By contrast, TIEAs obligate signatories to assist one another in their respective domestic tax investigations. They provide no benefits to private parties other than the somewhat nebulous advantage of permitting U.S. corporations to deduct expenses for conventions held in signatory nations.

The U.S. government and the IRS had tried without success for decades to obtain TIEAs with various tax haven nations. A principal reason was that tax havens impose no taxes and, applying the traditional test of dual criminality, they did not treat foreign tax evasion as a criminal matter. Financial secrecy laws were (and are) one of the major reasons for their economic success. For those reasons, few observers believed O'Neill would be able to carry through on his pledge, any more than had his frustrated predecessors.

A Big Domino Falls: The Cayman Islands

Nevertheless, under heavy pressure from the British Foreign Office, on November 27, 2001, the U.K. overseas territory of the Cayman Islands, the world's fifth largest financial center, signed a TIEA with the United States. The agreement gives the United States access to all banking and other records for U.S. criminal, civil and administrative tax investigations relating to U.S. income taxes. The new accord also requires disclosure of beneficial ownership of bank accounts, trusts, international business corporations and other entities.

However, treaty effective dates are delayed, for criminal tax evasion until January 1, 2004, and for all other tax matters, until January 1, 2006. Observers predict capital outflow from the Cayman Islands, which has already begun, will become a torrent well before the effective dates.

More Dominoes: Antigua & Barbuda, The Bahamas

Almost unnoticed, on December 6, 2001, Secretary O'Neill signed a similar agreement with Antigua & Barbuda. That pact followed the same pattern as the U.S.-Cayman TIEA.

Much better publicized was a TIEA with The Bahamas announced January 25, 2002. As with the Cayman Islands, the U.S.-Bahamas agreement effectively makes the Bahamian government an enforcement arm of the IRS. The effective dates are the same as for the Cayman agreement. Bahamas negotiators did manage a small escape clause: there is a three-month notice termination clause in the treaty. With a parliamentary election in The Bahamas this year and the possibility of a change of control, anything is possible.

Which country will be the next domino? Speculation has centered on one of the Society's top-rated asset havens—Panama—based on a Treasury Department announcement that it was negotiating a TIEA with that country. Our sources in Panama say any agreement will be far less expansive than the recent U.S.-Caymans or Bahamas treaties.

Honest Taxpayers to Benefit?

At first glance these developments may look like a dark cloud has engulfed tax havens. But it's a cloud with its own silver lining.

For those persons who feared "going offshore" because of unwanted suspicion of tax evasion, these treaties can provide assurance that signatory nations are open and above board when it comes to taxes. What's more, established haven nations have well-developed financial and banking systems that specialize in asset protection, trusts and international business corporations. Asset protection and streamlined, predictable regulation are still major advantages of offshore investing, even though, for honest taxpayers who meet U.S. reporting requirements, tax savings are often minimal.

Now, more than ever, there's good reason to "go offshore!"

Slippery Stepping Stones

by Robert E. Bauman, JD, November 1998

Do what the big boys do: use a multi-layered set-up of offshore corporations to legally reduce your corporate tax burden.

Smart offshore business operators, large and small, often avail themselves of a multinational tax break allowed under U.S. tax law. It's called "stepping stones" by international tax experts, "treaty shopping" by a disdainful IRS.

This generous tax break, for which most Americans can't qualify, proves that the U.S. can be a tax haven for foreigners, if they play their cards very carefully.

The creative tax strategy takes advantage of international bilateral tax treaties. It requires at least minimal business operations in two or more countries. You simply base a defined part of your business where taxes are lowest for just such operations. The total business gross volume need not be large, but the net should be big enough to justify the accounting and legal expenses. But the tax savings can be enormous.

Because it has a worldwide network of tax treaties, the Netherlands is a favorite base for stepping stone business operations by companies from all over the world. Low taxes make Holland ideal for passive interest or royalty income and for financing operations.

Once incorporated in Holland you're covered by the U.S.-Dutch tax treaty that requires no U.S. withholding taxes on interest and dividends paid from the U.S. to a Dutch company. A Dutch company in turn can make payments without tax withholding to a German, Canadian or other nation's firm.

The IRS hates such arrangements. To them it's tax evasion using phony affiliates of businesses operating within the U.S. Fortunately for astute taxpayers, if it's done right this system is legal and it works. The one key requirement is strict adherence to proper form and no corner-cutting.

That's where Laidlaw, Inc., an Ontario, Canada-based school bus and emergency vehicle provider, got caught by the IRS. The Canadian company, a US$3 billion operation, provides over 37,000 leased school buses in the U.S. and had US$617 million in 1997 operating income.

According to *Business Week* (September 14, 1998), in order to buy up competing U.S. bus operators, beginning in the 1980s a Laidlaw-established Dutch affiliate financing company (Laidlaw International Investments) provided it with hundreds of millions of dollars in low-cost loans. U.S. Laidlaw claimed that interest paid on the inter-company loans from their Dutch affiliate was a deductible U.S. business income expense. But as the loan interest was paid by the U.S. affiliates, it was immediately refunded to them by their Dutch cousins. Loans that came due were rolled over into new loans and never paid off.

The IRS says that Laidlaw never intended these arrangements to be bona fide loans; that they were simply cash flows from the Canadian parent company to its U.S. affiliates, passed through the Netherlands as a tax-cutting smoke screen. Thus no business interest deductions allowed. The belated tax bill for Laidlaw could reach more then $500 million dating back to 1989.

What's the big deal? More then half of all Canadian companies with U.S. subsidiaries use similar Dutch-based financing operations, as do many European-based business firms with U.S. operations. The tax experts are working overtime to make sure they too don't get Laidlawed by the IRS.

The moral: There are ways to save taxes offshore, but do it right and be damned sure you know what you can and cannot do.

Negotiate Your Own Tax Bill in Switzerland
by Marshall J. Langer, *The Tax Exile Report*, 1997

Did you know that Switzerland, widely known as a banking and tax haven, is also a place where a resident foreigner can negotiate with government officials the amount of tax he would like to pay?

Despite its fairly high taxes, Switzerland is an attractive destination for many tax exiles. You may be able to obtain both a residence permit, and a lump-sum tax arrangement, especially if you are retired. Obtaining a work permit is more difficult, but not impossible.

Switzerland has long been a favorite haven for rich and famous tax exiles from all over the world. It is not the easiest country in which to acquire residence, but if you are retired and have sufficient income, resident status in Switzerland is possible.

Foreigners living in Switzerland pay fairly high income taxes on their worldwide income. Federal, cantonal and local income taxes are levied on all income, except that derived from foreign real estate or a personally-owned foreign business. There are also cantonal and local wealth taxes on capital. Despite this, Switzerland is an attractive destination for tax exiles, primarily because it is one of the world's safest and most stable countries.

Switzerland may be suitable for you if:

1. You already have a satisfactory citizenship and passport, since it takes from 12 to 15 years to obtain either in Switzerland.

2. You are a wealthy retiree over 60 years of age who has never worked in Switzerland.

3. You want a new permanent residence and are willing to reside in Switzerland at least part of each year.

4. You are prepared to pay a prearranged lump-sum tax to the Swiss each year.

A Negotiable Lump Sum Tax Deal

Wealthy foreigners of retirement age can negotiate a lump-sum tax arrangement, called a *forfait*, with local cantonal tax administrators. The tax amount varies considerably depending on where in Switzerland you choose to live. Appenzell (Inner Rhodes), Switzerland's smallest canton, offers an attractive tax deal of at least Sfr65,000 (about US$45,000) per year. The smaller cantons will ask less, and you will pay considerably more in the larger, better-known cantons. Although one can apply for residency status at any Swiss embassy, I urge you to negotiate directly, and in person, with the authorities in the canton where you want to live. In any event, they are the ones who decide whom to admit as residents, and how much tax will be paid. Employ a competent local professional to work out the best deal.

Visit Annually

Despite recent changes, you can still visit Switzerland for up to three months each year without obtaining a residence permit and without having to pay Swiss taxes. As a visitor, you must observe the time rules faithfully. Swiss authorities keep records of exactly how much time each foreigner spends in the country.

Under tax rules, one is treated as a Swiss resident for tax purposes if 1) a person stays in Switzerland without working for more than 90 days in any year; or, 2) a person works in Switzerland for more than 30 days in any year.

In either case, you are deemed to have been resident from the first day of your stay in Switzerland. It doesn't matter whether you stay in one place or in several different places. Moreover, brief absences from Switzerland do not suspend your residence.

It used to be possible for a foreigner to "visit" Switzerland twice each year, for up to three months each time. That is no longer possible. A suggested program under the new rules: You can visit one of Switzerland's excellent winter resorts for about a month each February or March and one of its equally marvelous summer resorts for about a month each July or August. You can also spend a few days visiting your bankers at the beginning and end of each stay. It's a great life, if you can afford it.

An alternative is to obtain a "B permit" authorizing you to live and work in Switzerland. About 17,000 renewable B permits are available each year, most issued by cantonal authorities. Each canton has a small annual quota of permits allocated to it. Annual renewals are routinely approved. I have had success in obtaining permits for clients from the Canton of Neuchatel under its program to attract new business. Neuchatel offers special tax programs on an individual case basis for new residents.

Pros and Cons

Switzerland is clean, orderly, safe, stable and prosperous. Everything works and most things work well.

Everything in Switzerland is expensive. If you become a Swiss canton resident, you will be liable for Swiss inheritance and gift tax purposes. These taxes vary considerably from canton to canton but are not imposed by the federal government. Switzerland now has a value-added tax (VAT), but at a rate much lower than most other European countries.

Canadian Expatriates: The Tax-Man is After You

By David Lesperance, *The Sovereign Individual*, January 2003

While this article is of immediate interest to Canadians, non-Canadians considering expatriation should read it to understand how innocent sounding initiatives such as "fraud proof permanent residency cards" or "treaties to prevent double taxation" can be used to trip up expatriates from any country whose tax affairs may not be in proper order!

If you are a Canadian permanent resident temporarily working abroad, you have less than a year to reorganize your financial and legal affairs, or risk substantial financial loss and even possible criminal tax sanctions.

The newly introduced Permanent Resident card ("PR card") is a wallet-sized document that now proves permanent resident status when you re-enter Canada. The high-tech PR card is said to have substantial security benefits, but the process by which it is issued poses considerable challenges for permanent residents whose tax situation is not 100% in compliance with Canadian law.

All Canadian permanent residents must obtain a PR card. The application requires you to be physically present in Canada and must be submitted in time for processing and delivery before the deadline of December 31, 2003. After this date, only the PR card will be acceptable evidence of permanent residence status at Canadian border crossings.

The application requires a variety of support documentation to satisfy immigration officials that you have established a presence in Canada. Among other requirements, you must provide a certified copy of your most recent Canadian tax return. Failure to satisfy immigration officials of satisfactory presence in Canada will result in loss of your permanent resident status.

Canadian immigration officials are working with Canadian tax authorities to identify applicants who haven't filed tax returns. Failure to file tax returns by a permanent resident for three or more years is now considered tax evasion, a criminal offence with penalties including up to two years in prison and seizure of assets to satisfy the taxes.

Some non-filing or under-filing permanent residents may simply conclude: "Instead of jumping through these financial hoops, maybe I should relinquish PR status. My family is securely living in Canada and it makes sense for me to continue to earn tax-free income abroad. In the meantime, my family can to reap all the benefits of being permanent residents. When I retire, one of them could sponsor me under the family reunification rules."

This strategy is no longer effective. First, you will be deemed Canadian resident for tax purposes if you have one or more "significant ties" or two or more "less significant ties" to Canada. Having a spouse and/or dependent children in Canada is considered a significant tie. Therefore, for tax purposes, you may be regarded as "tax resident" even if you never applied for immigration status, or relinquished it.

Secondly, if convicted of tax evasion, you are barred from applying for PR status for five years after all sanctions against you have ended. And other family members may, by way of their own tax returns, be deemed to be complicit in your "tax evasion strategy."

Third, if you are working in a jurisdiction that has an updated tax treaty with Canada, that country may be legally obligated to collect taxes on Canada's behalf, including seizing your assets in that country!

Let's imagine the situation of a permanent resident and his family who landed in Canada a few years ago. Shortly thereafter the father left his family to work tax-free in the United Arab Emirates.

Both he and his wife filed tax returns every year but, based on advice from other similarly situated permanent residents and friends, they did not report all of their non-Canadian income. However, the new UAE-Canada tax treaty will provide Canadian tax authorities with access to virtually all official documents filed with UAE authorities (employment contracts, personal sponsorship applications, loans, credit card applications, lease agreements, corporate filings, entry and departure dates, etc.). Canada and Kuwait have signed a similar treaty, and the Canadian government is now updating other treaties so that these provisions will eventually apply to Canadian permanent residents working in any of 76 jurisdictions with a tax treaty with Canada. The official purpose of these treaties is to "eliminate double taxation" but a secondary purpose is to "prevent fiscal evasion" and there is no doubt that they will be used for that purpose.

If you are living a lifestyle substantially richer than one that could be reasonably supported by the income claimed on your tax returns, you will be re-assessed in an "income/lifestyle" audit. Should the tax authorities' assessment be higher than the income previously declared, you will be required to pay the additional taxes and interest. And, if an applicable tax treaty permits it, Canada may enforce its assessment by seizing your assets in that country!

Recommendations:

1. If you are a permanent resident and eligible to apply for Canadian citizenship, do so without delay. However, ensure beforehand that all previously filed tax returns for you and your spouse fully disclose your non-Canadian source income.

2. Evaluate whether you and all family members will be able to succeed in your applications for a PR card.

3. If you and/or your legal counsel (and accountant) determine that you would be unable to successfully obtain a PR card, for whatever reason, identify those areas that require attention and take the necessary steps to rectify them on a proactive basis without delay (i.e. before the immigration or tax authorities come to the same conclusion!).

Foreigners Live in London Practically Tax-Free

By Mark Nestmann, *The Sovereign Individual*, November 2002

The United Kingdom is a "tax hell" for most of its residents—but not if you're a wealthy immigrant. Given sufficient assets and clever accountants, you can live in London, or anywhere else in the United Kingdom, practically tax-free.

This "resident but not domiciled" status is viewed with increasing disfavor by both leftist U.K. politicians and by European Union bureaucrats in Brussels. But for the moment, it survives.

This tax system is a relic of Britain's colonial past, and originally had nothing to do with taxes. As Britain created and administered its empire, millions of British subjects left to find fame and fortune in its colonies. But no matter how distant British subjects were from their mother country, they retained British domicile, unless they demonstrated clear intent to establish a permanent home, or domicile, overseas.

Conversely, individuals not born in Britain were not entitled to British domicile. This discrimination extended to individuals from British colonies relocated to Britain; even as residents, they continued as "non-domiciles."

It was not until 1914 that this arrangement came to have tax consequences. The Finance Act established the premise that all overseas income was taxable, whether or not it was actually conveyed ("remitted") to the United Kingdom. However, this premise applies only to individuals resident and domiciled in the United Kingdom. Non-domiciled residents of the United Kingdom ("nondoms") are taxed on foreign income only on a remittance basis. In addition, non-doms are exempt from inheritance tax on their non-U.K. property. However, individuals are deemed U.K. domiciled for inheritance tax purposes if they have been resident for 17 out of the preceding 20 tax years.

Since non-doms pay U.K. tax on income earned within the United Kingdom, as a practical matter, these benefits are limited to persons with substantial non-U.K. assets who can arrange their affairs so that all or most of their income originates outside the United Kingdom.

Even absent attacks from the left and from Brussels, the tax advantages for non-doms are not as straightforward as they might appear at first glance. To begin with, the Inland Revenue is constantly expanding the concept of "remittance." Transferring funds from a foreign account to the United Kingdom is obviously a remittance, but so is using a credit card in the United Kingdom if the bill will be paid outside the country. Borrowing on non-U.K. assets to fund a U.K. property purchase is also a remittance.

As a result of this fiscal regime, an estimated 60,000 wealthy foreigners have moved to the United Kingdom. Many of them have settled in London, where their obvious wealth and tax-free status has led to increasing publicity and criticism of what the press calls the non-domiciled "loophole," which is said to cost the Treasury US$3.2 billion annually. This has particularly been true since the Labour party assumed control of the U.K. government in 1997.

In 2001, the U.K. Treasury commissioned a study of the tax treatment of non-doms. The results of this study were "leaked" to the media in early 2002. While the current budget did not address the issue directly, the government is said to be considering an Internal Revenue proposal that individuals living in the United Kingdom for extended periods (possibly as few as four years) would lose the tax advantages of non-dom status after this period.

But what may finally end the happy circumstances in which non-doms live is the EU's continuing crackdown on "harmful tax practices" by its members. It is claimed by one authority that U.K. non-dom status is the #1 "harmful tax practice" that the EU has vowed to eliminate.

The EU Treaty ratified by the U.K. government requires member states "to take all requisite measures to prevent infringements of national law and regulations, in particular in the field of taxation." Depending on how this clause is interpreted in the future, it could potentially force the U.K. government to end or restrict non-dom status.

If you have several million dollars or more of accumulated wealth, sufficient to live off of without working, non-dom status may be worth investigating. If the rules are changed, they may not take effect for a few years. In addition, whatever new rules are enacted may not be retroactive and would apply only to new applications for non-dom status from a future date.

A U.K. tax attorney whose practice includes assisting individuals seeking non-domiciled residency is *James McNeile* of Farrer & Co. **Tel.:** +(44) 20-7242-2022. **Fax:** +(44) 20-7242-9999. **E-mail:** JDM@farrer.co.uk.

CHAPTER EIGHT
Offshore Tax Havens

Part One—Tax Havens Explained

Part Two—Havens Under Siege

For those who know the ocean or enjoy the beach, "offshore" may bring back pleasant memories of far-off vessels passing on a blue horizon, of a leisurely sail cutting through the waves in your own sturdy boat.

In this chapter "offshore" takes on a whole new meaning—a different, expanded definition that, once understood, potentially could change your life forever.

Here "offshore" refers to sovereign nations with laws that protect your financial privacy, your assets and your cash. Countries where the welcome mat is always out for foreign citizens weary of high taxes and government snoops back home.

In the abstract we explain how the offshore system operates, what is legal and what is not, and how you can use this system to your own advantage. We also give you an up-to-date battle report on the tax hungry, major nations' war against havens.

Part One—Tax Havens Explained

Why Go Offshore?

by John Pugsley, January 1999

True financial security must include: 1) the maximum possible tax avoidance allowed by law; 2) the greatest possible financial privacy; 3) the highest level of asset protection; and, 4) access to the most profitable investments available.

I often have said that voters in the wealthy industrialized democracies seek to transfer benefits to themselves at the expense of the successful and thrifty. This attack on affluent and productive individuals in the United States, Canada, Germany and the United Kingdom has led to a rising exodus of both assets and individuals to political environments offering greater asset protection, privacy and lower taxation.

Through taxation and regulation the executive branch of government excels in attacks on wealth, but the judicial system is now becoming an equal enemy of prosperity. Especially in the United States, courts are clogged with hundreds of thousands of civil suits demanding enormous sums for imagined or statutorily-concocted injuries such as sexual harassment or psychological discrimination. Contingent fee lawyers whip up billion dollar class action suits against persons or corporations deemed a ripe target, meaning one with enough ready assets to finance big judgments and outrageous jury awards.

It is a truism to say statist government has diminished personal liberty with its unchecked power of taxation. In the United States, the United Kingdom and Germany the effective rate of personal taxes far exceeds 50 percent of earnings. In some nations, such as France and Sweden, it is much higher. Business is taxed at even greater levels. And everyone, as consumers, pays the ultimate price imposed by taxation.

How can a person of wealth defend against such ferocious attacks?

As James Dale Davidson and Lord William Rees Mogg said in their book *The Sovereign Individual*, one cannot transport hard assets, farms or factories out of a high tax or politically oppressive jurisdiction. But the most important capital assets today are knowledge, experience and information which no political boundaries can contain.

Sovereign individuals understand these trends and take advantage of them. We chose our residence for its quality of life and will not be tied down by an accident of birth. We select haven nations for placement of our assets according to the relative safety and privacy such places guarantee by law. Those who move all or a portion of their assets offshore simply recognize reality, that government is engaged in a systematic destruction of its citizens' right to financial privacy, what's been called the "Nazification of the economy." Sadly, we must look to foreign lands for the sort of economic freedom once guaranteed by our homeland.

How to Choose an Offshore Haven
By John Pugsley, *The Sovereign Individual*, June 2003

Since its inception, the Sovereign Society has guided members through the minefields of international law, and this has chronicled the accelerating decline of financial privacy in many jurisdictions once considered secure, private havens for personal assets.

At the root of this pernicious erosion are the hyped-up "wars" on drugs, money laundering and terrorism. The war on drugs gave birth to money laundering laws, and together these legal weapons are being used to destroy privacy and bank secrecy. Rising terrorism (inspired by a rising resentment of American intervention in the politics of foreign nations) engenders the need for random searches, wiretapping and 24/7 surveillance.

Where two or three decades ago there were numerous haven nations where privacy was expected and delivered, the high-tax nations have pushed, cajoled and threatened until the field of choices has been dramatically reduced.

How do individuals interested in privacy and security choose the best haven for wealth?

To begin with, you should understand that each "offshore" haven is unique. A country that provides the best banking regulations won't necessarily be the best place for incorporating a business, just as the best jurisdiction for privacy won't necessarily be the best for an offshore trust. Yet, there are general guidelines for choosing an asset haven that apply across the board. The following are the more important considerations.

Is the haven a completely independent sovereign nation? Or is it a territory, dependency or colony of a larger country? While the government of a dependency or territory may enact favorable legislation to attract foreign investment, such legislation will be hostage to the political and economic environment prevailing in the mother country.

Nothing illustrates this point more than the recent events in the British Virgin Islands. An overseas territory of the United Kingdom, beginning in the late 1970s, the BVI, with U.K. encouragement and funding, developed one of the world's largest and most sophisticated offshore financial sectors. Indeed, it became second only to Hong Kong in the formation of international business companies, registering nearly 40,000 new corporations annually. With a land area smaller than Washington, D.C., and a population of 21,000, providing a home for almost 400,000 companies provided substantial revenues both to the government and the country's financial sector, along with ending the BVI's historical dependence on U.K. foreign aid.

A key provision of the law that made the BVI so attractive as a corporate domicile was that shares in an IBC could be issued in "bearer" form. This meant the actual ownership of the corporation could be kept confidential. However, beginning in the late 1990s, escalating pressure from the U.K. Home Office and international organizations threatened the BVI's ability to offer bearer shares and enforce other aspects of its laws protecting privacy and wealth. Indeed, the U.K. Home Office threatened to use an arcane provision of colonial law called an "Order in Council" to enact binding BVI legislation, over the heads of the local elected representatives, if the BVI government failed to dismantle its favorable laws on its own.

Faced with this overwhelming pressure, the BVI recently re-wrote their laws regarding IBCs. One of the casualties was the ability of IBCs to issue bearer shares.

The BVI is only one of the U.K.'s overseas territories. The others—Anguilla, Bermuda, the Cayman Islands and the Turks & Caicos Islands—were subject to similar pressure from the U.K. Home Office.

Closer to the United Kingdom itself are several jurisdictions with a different constitutional status than overseas territories, but still subject to substantial interference in their financial affairs by the U.K. government. These "Crown dependencies"—the Isle of Man, Jersey, Guernsey and Sark—have also been forced to dismantle many of their favorable laws designed to attract foreign capital.

Does the haven respect privacy? And is privacy built into its law? Under what circumstances can creditors or the government obtain information about your wealth, or even seize it? Financial privacy has gotten a bad reputation in recent years. The prevailing attitude is, "if you're not committing a crime, why do you need privacy?"

This attitude ignores the very real need for privacy in a nation such as the United States where there exist very few legislative protections for it. It is worth noting that a sue-happy lawyer or identity thief, armed with nothing more sophisticated than a personal computer, can in a few minutes unearth a great deal of financial information about whatever U.S. assets you own.

This is the reason why strong privacy laws are a must in any haven that you might consider. Some countries have a tradition of secrecy but no legal requirement enforcing it; others have laws that allow the local government access to information while pretending that the government is sworn to secrecy. Others have bank-secrecy laws but frequently ignore them, or have laws filled with exceptions.

Ideally, secrecy should be built into the legal code and violations should be prosecuted with civil or criminal sanctions. However, even in jurisdictions with the best privacy laws, it's foolish to violate tax or money-laundering laws of your home country. In their search for tax-evaders, big governments have a history of illegal espionage, bribery and coercion to get the information they seek.

Moreover, you may wake up one morning to find the haven nation's laws changed and your "secret" records in the hands of your home government. Make sure you comply with the laws in your home country!

From the standpoint of the tradition and legal basis for banking secrecy, the four countries that stand out are Austria, Liechtenstein, Luxembourg and Switzerland.

Austria has strict bank secrecy laws calling for the prosecution of any bank employee who divulges any information on a client's account, and its banking tradition is more than 200 hundred years old.

Liechtenstein has some of the strongest bank secrecy laws in existence. Since Liechtenstein is one of the five richest countries in the world in per capita income and personal wealth, it is unlikely to be swayed away from privacy by promises or threats.

Luxembourg is one of the fastest growing financial centers in the world and has seen a massive influx of capital in the last decade due to its liberal banking and tax laws. Although its secrecy laws only date back to the early 1980s, it has maintained a long tradition of banking confidentiality. Information will only be released to foreign governments if the depositor has been charged with a crime that is related to the account that is also a crime in Luxembourg.

Switzerland has been economically and politically stable for centuries, enjoys a low rate of inflation and the Swiss franc is one of the strongest currencies in the world. It remains the model from which all other financial centers are compared. Although Switzerland has succumbed to the pressure of the U.S. government to loosen its strict secrecy laws, for safe banking it still rates as one of the top havens.

How long a tradition has the haven had? A country like Switzerland with centuries of traditional respect and protection of privacy, or like Luxembourg with decades of stability, are unlikely to change for transient reasons. The longer and stronger the traditions of law and privacy, and the more stable the economy, the better chance that those traditions will be continued.

Political stability is a major consideration. During the last half of the 20th century, Hong Kong was a bastion of financial stability, growth and privacy. Hong Kong achieved this in spite of being a dependency of the United Kingdom. But when the U.K.'s lease on the territory ran out in 1997, control returned to China, casting a deep shadow of doubt about Hong Kong's future as an asset haven, a fact underscored by the continued exodus of wealth from the country.

Do the citizens support the haven's offshore status? In some havens, such as the Bahamas, the local citizens are not the primary beneficiaries of banking secrecy. Since taxes are low to non-existent and the local legal eagles have not evolved into predators, locals have little interest in privacy laws or bank secrecy. This contrasts with Switzerland, Austria and now Panama, where privacy laws and traditions affect a significant segment of the citizenry.

Is the haven important to your government? The United Arab Emirates, because it is a "friendly" nation in an unstable region, enjoys the favor of the U.S. government. Haven income is important to it and Washington won't want to lean too hard on it over a "non-strategic" issue. And, since the CIA uses Liechtenstein for its financial transactions, the U.S. won't seek to wipe out its haven status. Another example is Panama, with its strategically important canal linking the Atlantic and Pacific Oceans. The Cayman Islands, on the other hand, has little or no strategic value to Washington.

Does the haven wave a "red flag?" Public dealings with high-profile havens can raise a "red flag" in tax collector's offices around the world. The Cayman Islands, Switzerland and Liechtenstein are examples. Panama, Austria and Luxembourg are another step below that level. Bermuda is lower still, though it doesn't offer the secrecy the others do.

How efficient and convenient are the services? Are competent personnel available to serve your needs? How well do they speak how well do they speak English? How easy is it to visit the place? Nothing substitutes for personal contact with the people who are trusted with your assets. It's best to visit your money periodically, and so much the better if it's in a place that you enjoy visiting.

What taxes are levied on the haven's users? The first requirement of a haven is to offer capital preservation. Nonetheless, to include a haven country which scores heavily in capital preservation but which also has high withholding, corporate, estate or other taxes, is to ignore an important consideration.

As I've written in *Forbidden Knowledge*, true financial security must include: the maximum possible tax avoidance allowed by law; the greatest possible financial privacy; the highest level of asset protection; and access to the most profitable investments available.

Sovereign individuals select haven nations for placement of our assets according to the relative safety and privacy such places guarantee by law. Those who move all or a portion of their assets offshore simply recognize reality, that governments in the major nations are engaged in a systematic destruction of their citizens' right to financial privacy. Sadly, we must look to foreign asset havens for the sort of economic freedom once guaranteed by our homeland. The number of safe havens is dwindling, but they still exist.

Tax Havens & Offshore Financial Centers
by Denis J. Kleinfeld, JD, CPA, January 1996

Capital is flowing from the industrialized nations into the offshore world. This is occurring not because those in control of capital have any ideological, theological or political philosophy, but due to their desire to invest freely and with security. This is true of multinationals, small businesses and individuals alike.

Capital will always seek an environment where it can best be exploited. Pennies sitting in a piggy bank do no one any good. Those same pennies placed in an interest-bearing account in a bank benefit the owner of the pennies deposited, the bank which now has money to lend and borrowers who can use the capital for their enterprises. While the industrialized governments squander capital to the detriment of their economies, the offshore world applies capital for the betterment of all. Tax havens and financial centers play an integral part in the world's economic system by facilitating the efficient and effective movement of capital in response to market demands.

The offshore world provides those with capital with the necessary financial environment—an infrastructure of professionals and a panoply of financial services. Many simplistically define tax havens as being locations where money or income is deposited securely and in confidence under zero or low tax regimes. Others think of them as jurisdictions employing normal rates of taxation but otherwise providing preferential treatment to certain classes of income, or which may be exploiting a treaty network.

But tax havens and offshore centers can offer more than this. Each has characteristics marked by its own particular and pragmatic efforts to find workable means by which local government can promote and assist businesses to be prosperous and successful.

Offshore jurisdictions have benefitted from the phenomenal growth of demand for international trade, demand for international financing and the marvel of electronic communications. They exist because the costs outweigh the benefits for each participant in the system. Tax havens and financial centers have developed by establishing legal and economic environments which are highly desirable to their existing and potential clientele.

For comparison purposes the following are the predominant factors in comparing offshore tax haven jurisdictions:

1. A legal and regulatory environment which has been specifically established to benefit the

type of business being considered or sought.

2. A legal system which has demonstrated that property rights will be respected, obligations enforced and that the rule of law, rather than ideological fad, will prevail.

3. Modern electronic communications.

4. An infrastructure of professionals, financial institutions and support businesses that will be able to perform specifically needed functions or services properly and on a deadline.

5. Freedom from exchange control, unwarranted restrictions and unnecessary governmental regulations.

6. A political environment which is stable but realistically active.

7. Laws and traditions which respect confidentiality and privacy in business affairs.

8. Fulfilling individual requirements as to geographic location or time zones.

Formation of international business corporations has been the primary activity of tax havens. This has enabled them to further develop and market facilities for international finance, sales, royalties, licensing, banking, insurance, investment funds and many other services.

Trusts have followed in the wake of formation of companies. Individual owners of private companies needed to place the ownership of stocks and other assets in some vehicle for financial and estate planning reasons. As onshore legislation was developed to attack the deferral of tax by use of trusts, trusts evolved to serve additional legitimate business purposes such as holding insurance for buy-sell arrangements, pension schemes, investment funds, coordinating multi-jurisdictional investments, avoiding forced heirship rules and to meet new needs of their clients.

Multinational corporations focus on jurisdictions which provide a means to transmit capital, goods and services whether in the form of investment inventory or sale in a manner that incurs the least total aggregate taxation.

The traditional role of tax havens and financial centers is for the protection and conservation of wealth. The threat to individuals with retained assets has grown in the industrialized nations because of the extension of financial risk, new and novel theories of liability and new methods of government imposition or shifting of costs to the wealthy through legislation.

People who are tired of the effect of these "soak-the-rich" politics have sought the comfort of the offshore world. Tax havens have responded by the creation of an environment which can provide comfort and safety for the protection of assets. Recognizing a growing need in the capital market place represented by wealthy individuals who feared, quite wisely, the effective confiscation of their wealth, some of the tax haven jurisdictions have responded by modernizing their internal trust law to provide a legal environment to secure capital from claimants. Other competing jurisdictions are, at least, examining the possibility of establishing a similar legal base.

It is reasonable to expect that as the industrialized nations' societies continue to deteriorate because of poor governmental policies, those with wealth will increase the flow of money into the offshore arena to be protected. These funds represent a capital pool that can be invested on a diversified basis worldwide. Thus, the protection of assets is in keeping with the traditional exploitation of capital by providing economic resumes which are enjoyable and usable globally.

The tax havens and financial centers located around Europe, the Caribbean and elsewhere have vital and necessary functions for individuals, small businesses, multinational corporations and the industrialized states themselves. All are now independent. The jurisdiction which will best be suited for a particular economic activity will depend on numerous economic, tax, financial, legal, as well as practical factors.

Some offshore companies will serve in a passive manner, for instance as a holding company, owning patents or other intellectual property rights, or providing financing for subsidiary operations. Other companies will have a more active capacity, dealing with manufacturing, sales and distribution of products.

Certain jurisdictions will be ideal for base operations which will receive and hold income in a no tax or low tax environment. Other operations need a conduit company situated in a treaty jurisdiction that will receive funds and transmit them onward to a base company but obtain the benefit of reduced tax withholdings. For individuals, various jurisdictions will have desirable attributes to serve particular personal protection needs. Any comparison of jurisdictions is dependent solely on the objective being sought.

Without this vital offshore factor, the governmental policies of the industrialized nations would soon cause their own internal economies to be capital starved, potentially leading to economic collapse. The billions of dollars, pounds, francs, lira and other currencies that have flowed into the offshore world through tax havens and financial centers appear to be but a trickle to the billions more that are sure to follow.

Four Types of Tax Havens
by Robert E. Bauman, *Fundamental Tools of Wealth Protection*, 2001

Simply stated, a tax haven is any country whose laws, regulations, policies and, in some cases, treaty arrangements, make it possible for a foreign national to reduce overall personal or corporate tax burdens by voluntarily bringing one's self within the country's jurisdiction. Usually this is done by establishing a residence in that nation. This general definition covers all four major types of tax haven nations, each categorized by the degree of taxation imposed, and it's important to understand the differences.

No-Tax Havens

In what are known as "pure" or "no-tax havens," there are no income, capital gains, or wealth taxes, and a foreign national can quickly and easily incorporate, form a trust and register to do immediate business.

The government in a pure tax haven nation earns revenue from the volume of registration and annual maintenance fees paid by foreign corporations and trusts doing business within its borders. "No tax" means there is no tax levied on income or profits from corporate business operations, but there are minor taxes including stamp duties on documents of incorporation, charges on the value of corporate shares issued, annual registration fees, or other fees not levied directly on income.

Examples of this type of country include the British overseas territories of Bermuda, the Cayman Islands and the Turks and Caicos Islands, plus independent nations such as The Bahamas, St. Kitts and Nevis (primarily the latter of the two-island federation), all located in or near the Caribbean basin, and in the south Pacific, the Cook Islands and Nauru.

Foreign-Source Income Havens

These havens use a domestic "territorial" approach, taxing only income actually earned within the country. They exempt from tax any income earned from foreign sources involving no local "in-country" business activities-apart from simple housekeeping matters. Often there is no tax on income derived from the export of local manufactured goods, as compared to the domestic manufacture itself, which may be taxed. These nations also could be called "no-foreign-source income tax havens," and they are divided into two groups.

The first group allows a person or a corporation to do business both internally and externally, taxing only the income earned from internal domestic sources. These nations include Costa Rica, Ecuador, Guatemala, Honduras, Israel, the Philippines, Thailand and Sri Lanka.

The second group requires corporate organizers to elect at the time of incorporation whether the business will limit itself to domestic activity, with consequent local tax liabilities, or to do only foreign business that is exempt from taxation. Primary examples in this category are Panama, Liberia, Jersey, Guernsey, the Isle of Man and Gibraltar.

These countries are particularly well suited as a location for a US-owned holding company, foreign trading corporation, or a foreign investment corporation.

Tax Treaty Nations

The third class of nations are called "tax treaty nations" because their law does impose taxes on corporate or trust income, wherever earned worldwide. However, these governments have adopted reciprocal double-taxation avoidance agreements with other nations, especially ones with which they have extensive trade, such as the United States, France, Germany or the United Kingdom. These mutual agreements may reduce significantly the national withholding tax imposed on income derived from abroad by domestic corporations, usually giving full credit against domestic tax liability for taxes paid by a local business to a foreign government.

These nations may be less attractive as a base for an American seeking asset protection, since international tax treaties permit the free exchange of information between national taxing authorities, allowing far less financial privacy. Cyprus, the Netherlands, Belgium and Denmark are primary examples of tax treaty nations.

Special Use Tax Havens

In the fourth and last category are countries that impose most taxes with which Americans are all too familiar, but the government has a policy of granting special tax concessions, tax holidays or rebates to designated types of business enterprises they wish to attract and promote.

These concessions typically include corporate tax credits for job creation, tax exemptions for manufacturing and processing of exports, or special tax benefits for international business or holding companies, offshore banks, or other selected industries.

A primary example of a special use tax haven is the independent south Pacific nation of Samoa. All entities operating under its 1987 Offshore Banking, International Trust, and International Companies Act, and its 1988 International Insurance Act are exempt from Samoan income, stamp, and withholding taxes, and any other direct or indirect levies, as well as exchange and currency controls, foreign exchange levies, central bank restrictions, and domestic Samoan legislation.

Although the fact is largely unknown to their own citizens, both the United States and Canada offers such tax break incentives to foreigners who establish businesses within their borders, so long as certain minimal amounts are invested and local jobs result.

Tax Haven Legal Entities
The Tax Haven Report, 1997

Essential to successful use of a tax haven for tax reduction purposes is the creation of legal entities within the offshore nation that have these general characteristics:

1. The entities are separate and distinct from their creator in a way that guarantees the income derived from their assets cannot be considered part of his personal income.

2. The entities are created in, and are therefore "residents" of, a country where the tax situation is much better than in the creator's home country.

3. A creator can control these entities, their assets and income without incurring either personal tax or debt liabilities.

Such business entities exemplify the basic idea of separating ownership and control. Once one's cash or assets are vested in such an entity, he no longer has title to them. But since he has title to stock in the company, he has the power to make decisions about the ways its assets are used.

There are two basic forms of such entities: the corporation and the trust. We will discuss both in turn, because all the countries considered as possible tax havens allow at least one form or the other and most allow both. (There are additional hybrid business entities available in Liechtenstein.) It is very important the nature of corporations and trusts and all related concepts be clearly understood.

International Business Corporations

What is a corporation? To understand, it is important to reflect how the corporate form of business enterprise first came into being. The initial motivation had nothing to do with taxes but more with avoiding debts.

If a grocer owns his own store, any loan he takes out to buy stock for his shelves is his personal loan, his personal debt. The security for the loan, the assets that can be taken away from him and sold to cover the loan and repay the debtor, is all the grocer's personal assets, everything he owns. If he fails to repay a loan taken out for business purposes, his debtors can claim his TV set, house, car—everything. This means that if one runs a business as a personal property, he has unlimited debt liability; the business debts are its owner's debts. In the US, this personal form of business ownership is called a "sole proprietorship."

Because of this personal liability, the need arose to separate business debts from claims against personal property, avoiding the adverse consequences of business failures. The corporation was the answer. In the eyes of the law the formation of a corporation creates a new "legal person" insofar as liabilities are concerned. This legal person can assume its own debts and acquire its own assets. The assets may derive from the individual who establishes the corporation, and he then becomes liable for the debts of the company, but only to the extent of the assets expressly transferred to the corporation or committed to such a transfer. An act of government—the registration of the corporation—makes valid this "legal personification" and defends those with interests in the company from invasions of business debtors into their private lives.

Since economic growth required investment by many individuals and since most people were reluctant to take part if it involved unlimited personal liability, the idea of incorporation became widely accepted. It answered a need. Instead of becoming a partner in ownership of a business property (and thus a proportional direct owner of the business assets), one owned shares of stock.

Stocks are certificates of partial ownership in a corporation. The corporation is a legal person which owns its own assets and has its own liabilities. Owning the stock of the corporation does not mean owning its assets. The corporation has title to these. The stockholder has title to his stock.

A stockholder's percentage of ownership in a corporation equals the number of shares he holds divided by the total issued. The corporation may have a fixed authorized capital or, in some countries, a variable one. Say it can vary between $10,000 and $50,000. It may start, then, with 100 shares of $100 par value each. Each such share would then equal one percent control of the company. But then the company could expand its capital base by selling new shares up to the limit of $50,000. A $100 share would then represent only 0.2 percent control.

Another important distinction concerning shares of corporate stock is that between registered and bearer shares. A registered share has the name of its current owner printed on the certificate and in the official corporation record (the shareholders ledger). The record of registered shares is open to official inspection, and the owners of such stock are easily identified. A registered share thus has obvious drawbacks when privacy is important.

A bearer share belongs to whoever physically holds it; there is no name on it, and its sale is not logged anywhere. The sale of registered shares is always recorded and, depending on the corporation, may require the agreement of other shareholders. Bearer shares can be bought and sold in complete privacy without any third-party interference.

Bearer shares are not allowed in some tax havens. A major problem with bearer shares is that they can be stolen, and the owner has no means of proving ownership. In addition, unlike registered shares, which can be purchased at a percentage, bearer shares must usually be paid for in full.

It is possible to have the "best of both worlds" by buying registered shares at a percentage and having them registered in the name of a proxy. This reduces the capital requirements while at the same time providing privacy and security. A private contract can be arranged with the proxy that binds him to follow the real owner's instructions in all his actions as a stockholder. A proxy can be a real individual or an institution.

Corporation A can hold stock in Corporation B, serving as a "holding company." Holding companies are very popular in tax havens. Their owners' names are not registered. They can be used to absorb and reinvest returns on the shares they hold without tax liabilities; and they can be established in many countries with very low local tax liabilities, even if there are heavy local taxes on other types of corporations.

In some tax havens, names of persons associated with the corporation must be filed with their addresses: shareholders, ultimate-beneficiary share owners (in the cases where shares are held by proxies), directors, officers. Other countries may require a specification of the span of time the corporation is supposed to exist before liquidation. Sometimes the articles of association are required to be a part of the articles of incorporation. The articles of incorporation are usually approved and confirmed by a government official, the Registrar of Companies or something comparable. Most often, but not always, an announcement of the formation of a new corporation is required to be published in some official government gazette.

The articles of association must usually also be submitted to the government registrar. These articles represent the basic terms of a corporation's structure and direction. There are variations from country to country on the requirements. In some places the local law is rigid and detailed; in others it indicates broad outlines and certain specific restrictions. Thus the law may require that each corporation have a board of directors and that at least one director reside in the country where incorporation takes place.

The legal structure of a corporation is distinct, of course, from its operational structure. A large corporation may have branches, divisions, departments headed by managers or executives who may or may not be members of the board of directors. But all this vast structure need not be more than a tissue of technicalities if incorporation is accomplished in a tax haven.

If the local law requires three initial incorporators, these are supplied for a reasonable fee by the local law firm that handles the incorporation. These proxies can then either turn over their shares to the "real incorporator" after incorporation or continue to act on his behalf under a private contract. Similarly, the general meeting of stockholders can in some cases be no more than a meeting with the single majority stockholder in front of the bathroom mirror, with minutes duly recorded of course. If this is not good enough for the local law, a real local annual stockholders' meeting can be arranged by the corporate legal representative in the haven, with proxies provided for moderate fees.

The same sort of arrangements can be made to cover all requirements for local corporate officers and the like. The "ultimate owner" can run the company as he pleases, with all the legally formidable structure and rituals carried out by proxies.

It should be remembered the corporate legal form came into being for business purposes, not tax purposes. Corporations were invented to encourage capital investment in the form of ownership with limited debt liability. Since corporations are legal persons, government approval is required to form them and corporation laws, quite similar all over the world but with important place-to-place variations, have been enacted, establishing government control over the formation and operation of corporations.

Governments generally concede corporations require special tax treatment to avoid killing the goose that lays the golden egg. They cannot be taxed "progressively" as individuals are because the justification does not apply. If an individual has a large income he is "too rich" and the soak-the-rich mentality of modern welfare statism makes progressive taxation popular.

But a huge corporation with large gross profits can be owned by thousands of "little people." Progressive corporate taxation would wipe out the little guys' profits—hardly a politically popular consequence—and would discourage investment in corporations. Consequently with but two exceptions, corporate income taxes are assessed at flat rates, in most cases 40-50 percent of net profits. The exceptions are Switzerland and Liechtenstein. In these two nations, corporate-tax brackets are determined by the ratio between profit and authorized capital. For example, $100,000 made on an authorized capital of $1 million, a 10 percent yield, would be taxed at a higher rate than the same dollar profit on an authorized capital of $10 million, a one percent yield.

Corporate flat-rate taxes mean that incorporation can be used to reduce personal income tax burdens by shifting personal sources of income to the new corporation. This is a major reason for incorporation in a tax haven that has no taxes, or very low corporate taxes.

In sum, a tax haven corporation created by a shrewd investor can shift returns on investments from personal income, and thus save crippling home country personal income taxes. Even if the investments are in a high tax country, a tax haven corporation can reduce the total tax to as low as five percent. The profits can then be reinvested. If these fast-growing savings are repatriated to the investor's home country as dividends or as capital gains upon the liquidation of the corporation, the investor must then pay his country's taxes. Shrewd investors live off the income from their work and keep reinvesting the tax haven profits abroad, to be tapped later upon retirement or to be passed on to heirs.

Concerning the matter of inheritance, if the money is returned to the investor's home country while the investor is still alive, there will be a tax penalty in the form of high income or capital gains taxes and, at the investor's death, estate taxes and probate duties. If the tax haven company survives the investor, its stock is part of his estate and is subject to estate taxes and probate in his country. In both cases, if the tax haven investment is principally intended to benefit heirs, a tax haven trust is called for.

Trusts

Like corporations, trusts were originally spawned by non-tax considerations. A careful parent concerned about a frivolous child would transfer some of his wealth in trust using a contract (the trust deed or instrument) between himself (the settlor) and a trustee. The trustee could be counted on to manage and disburse the trust assets for the benefit of the child. The trust operates as a legally distinct entity, like a corporation, with its own assets and liabilities.

The trustee would invest the assets within limits expressed in the trust deed. He would pay the child, as trust beneficiary, a regular sum. The money distributed would include both the return on the investment of the trust principal, the original sum constituting the assets of the trust, as well as portions of the principal itself. The trust would be legally required to terminate at some point when all funds, principal, and return on principal, have been distributed to the beneficiary, less management expenses incurred by the trustee.

As you can see, a trust serves a role similar to that of a will with additional advantages because it allows:

1. Private disposal of assets separate from one's will, which must be made public.

2. Separation of designated assets from property for inheritance purposes before death, making these assets immune to further liabilities incurred by the trust creator. This is especially so if the trust is irrevocable, meaning the trust cannot be revoked and assets returned to the creator.

3. Competent professional management of trust assets.

4. The trustor to encourage aspects of a beneficiary's life by allocating benefits for certain specified purposes. This contrasts with a will, which transfers ownership but usually cannot establish total control over how transferred assets are used.

5. Avoidance of laws that direct how property must be divided.

The major disadvantages of a trust are irrevocability and the chance of trustee abuse. The latter can be avoided by a careful trust deed and trustee selection. In the case of professional trust companies, any temptation to abuse trustee powers is strongly moderated by the need to maintain a good professional reputation.

In many ways trusts are quite different from corporations. Usually, they need not be publicly recorded. A legal contract or trust instrument accompanied by transfer of the creator's assets to the trust fund establishes the trust. Under a trust:

1. The beneficiaries are "third parties" entitled to sue the trustee for violations of trust deed provisions but they are not parties to the original contract.

2. One party to the contract, the trust creator, usually has no official right to intervene in the management of the trust.

3. The trustee has full power to manage and distribute trust assets but may not have any personal interest in the trust.

The trust is an historical development of the "common law" arising from cases decided in the English courts rather than from statutes. It is recognized in the U.K. and all Commonwealth nations plus the United States. By comparison the "civil law" system dates back to the Roman empire, modernized by the French Code Napoleon and is accepted throughout continental Europe and its former colonies. The civil law is derived from explicit statutes with court precedents having a limited role. Some civil law countries have enacted laws authorizing common law trusts within a civil law framework. There are many common law tax havens in which to settle a trust, so there is no need to consider the civil law havens for this purpose.

What do trusts have to do with taxes?

To begin with, money given to a trust when the settlor is alive (a living trust) may be subject to a gift tax, but not to heavy estate taxes and probate duties. Thus, a living trust is often superior to a testamentary trust that is established by a will, because it avoids estate taxes and probate costs. Moreover, trust income is not usually taxable to the trustor. Nor is it taxable to the trustee, who derives no benefits from its growth (except his fees and expenses, which are tax deductible expenses of the trust). The beneficiaries, of course, cannot be taxed until they start receiving benefits. In the U.S. or U.K. a trust itself is subject to tax on its own income. But a trust located in a tax haven nation is not subject to tax and so can serve to reinvest all its income tax free, growing rapidly through this untaxed investment. Thus, a tax haven trust can do for one's heirs what a tax haven corporation can do for one's self.

Tax haven trusts can be used in conjunction with tax haven corporations. Instead of owning a holding company that owns stock and other investments, one can be a beneficiary of a trust established by a foreign holding company to hold its own stock. This and other double-tier structures are important when home-country tax provisions come into play.

Remember that trusts, unlike corporations, are almost never publicly disclosed entities. No official public record of their creation is published. No audited accounts go to anyone except the trustor and/or his beneficiaries. Such privacy allows decisions based on whatever considerations one chooses without unwanted publicity.

The Limited Liability Company

The real value of an LLC in tax haven planning is when one needs an entity that is taxed differently than a corporation, but is clearly incorporated and has limited liability. In some complex tax haven plans, it may also be possible to use differing tax treatments, for example, the investor's home country may tax the LLC as a corporation while the host country taxes it as a partnership, or vice versa. Such schemes need very careful review by qualified tax professionals.

Captive Insurance Companies

One of the hottest topics in boardrooms today is whether or not to climb onto the captive insurance bandwagon. Captives now number over 10,000. Many are located in Bermuda, The Bahamas, the British Virgin Islands, the Cayman Islands, Guernsey, and the Netherlands Antilles. Several billion dollars in premiums flow through Bermuda-based captive companies each year and the island is the major world base for such operations. Of the U.S. Fortune 500 companies, over half have captive insurance affiliates.

A captive insurance company is a company whose charter permits it to offer insurance to its parent or sister subsidiaries in return for premiums. Usually, this company is located offshore for tax savings. In almost every case, captives are started because of a general dissatisfaction with existing insurance coverage or costs.

A captive can provide insurance for risks which may not be normally insurable. For example, there is limited insurance available in the areas of labor strikes, defective product recall, patent infringement suits, etc. Loss experience ratings are based on the company's experience rather than being averaged with other companies that may have less stringent controls and are more prone to claims. Reduction of insurance costs is available as there is no sales force or overhead to pay for, no claims administration group, etc. Insurance company direct costs run around 20-50 percent compared to five percent for captives. Insurance income is earned on premiums by receiving commissions from reinsurance companies, which go to the captive rather than an outside insurance company.

The captive's prime advantage is to earn interest on capital and reserves, thus turning a business cost drain into a profit maker. The captive insurance can be used to enhance product acceptability. Instead of a product warranty, a $100,000 insurance policy against damage by the product may be more attractive to a manufacturer who knows claims will seldom, if ever, occur. More flexible settlement of damage claims is also possible. Insurance can be more acceptable than a company guarantee or promise to pay, as when a captive can provide sick leave insurance for employees in lieu of contract benefits a union demands.

Captives provide the opportunity of converting specific reserves to insurance costs at the parent level, thus converting post-tax reserves to pre-tax expenses. Examples would be reserves against product reliability or subsidiary debt, guarantees, etc. Captives allow lower costs derived from the realistic evaluation of exposure vis-a-vis existing premium/risk expenses. In countries with currency controls, a captive arrangement offers the ability to transfer normally non-convertible funds to a subsidiary as a genuine risk financing measure. Premium expense is generally deductible at the parent company level, but income earned on investment at the captive level is not taxable. Special rules apply for U.S. and Canadian companies. The lack of regulation of investments at the captive level means funds could, with prudence, be used to finance the needs of sister companies.

Premiums paid to a captive are generally deductible at the parent level. (U.S. and Canadian companies require special planning, but remember the tax advantages are merely a bonus to the captive idea.) Capital, reserves, and premiums are not taxed in most offshore locations. The success of a captive relies on good management not good luck. Top management must understand the long-term commitment to captive insurance. Bad risk assessment or a series of unlucky occurrences can cost a captive dearly in the early years. Annual premium costs alone are not criteria for establishing a captive. More importantly, a company needs a good spread of risks and low maximum loss potential.

Captive reserves may be invested in the money markets. Loans may be made to fund capital for the captive, or to provide premiums which must be paid in advance. Loans for claims payments may be made where assets are temporarily unavailable in the captive or the captive is involved in legal action. New banking relationships are available with the captive. Direct access to reinsurance companies throughout the world, instead of having to deal with a local insurance carrier, can be a major advantage. Added service may be offered to existing clients, such as a credit card or investment company offering free life insurance to its account holders. And this tax and cost savings captive insurance magic can only occur "offshore" in an established tax haven.

———◆———

Creating a Trust in a Tax Haven Nation
March 1996

If you are going to set up a trust in a tax haven, there are several important factors which must be considered to ensure the best possible service and convenience.

- *Language.* Are there going to be communication problems because of a language barrier? If English is your first language, you would be wise to consider an English-speaking haven. If this is not suitable, you could always choose a country where the main business language is English and is therefore widely understood by foreigners, such as Switzerland.

- *The time difference between your home country and your tax haven.* What happens if you need immediate communication at 2:00 P.M. only to find that it's midnight in your haven? Try to choose a haven within a similar working day time zone to your home.

- *Financial and political stability.* A haven will be of little use to you if civil war breaks out or the value of its currency goes through the floor.

- *Geography.* Will you require frequent personal contact with the foreign trustees in your haven? If this is likely, having a haven on the other side of the world is very inconvenient.

- *It is important the trustee understands your plans.* You are entrusting your wealth to a relative stranger. Although a trustee isn't going to run off with your money, it is important they understand your goals. Based on full understanding they can provide the most suitable arrangements to meet those goals.

- *The degree of confidentiality available.* For many this is not an issue. If it concerns you, make sure the haven has strong financial privacy laws and enforces them.

- *Mutual tax treaties.* If a haven is part of an effective bilateral tax treaty system, income can move into a treaty country with tax relief granted at the source and minimal or no taxes imposed in your tax haven country.

In addition to the above, there are other factors to be taken into account in relation to the actual formation of the trust:

- *If you need to move your trust to another jurisdiction, does your tax haven's laws permit a quick and easy transfer, or "portability," as it is called?* Make sure you will have power to convert to another jurisdiction should this become necessary.

- *If the law allows it, a local "protector" should be appointed to watch over the trustees on your behalf.* In addition, you should retain the power for yourself and the protector to remove and appoint trustees.

Depending on the haven country chosen, you may pay little or no taxes. Or there may be other attractive financial incentives. Here's a sample of havens that welcome trusts and corporations by imposing low or no taxes:

Anguilla—forming a trust for commercial purposes is permitted and it need not to be registered publicly, so privacy is a benefit. Appointment of a trust protector is acceptable. No taxes are imposed on trusts, however an annual registration fee for a trust or international business company (IBC) ranges from US$500 to US$1000 depending on circumstances.

The Bahamas—the Trusts Act 1989 allows a trust declaration provision that causes Bahamian law to govern all trust activity. This means disputes must be settled in The Bahamas and conflicting foreign court judgments receive little or no local recognition. This could be beneficial in a situation involving a U.S. community property claim or forced heirship laws. There are no trust taxes but a yearly registration fee is charged.

[**Ed. Note**: Extensive recent changes in Bahamian laws now make this nation far less attractive for any offshore financial activity.]

British Virgin Islands—no taxes apply to trusts when beneficiaries are not BVI residents. The law recognizes a "managing trustee" as the person responsible for trust decisions. Transfer of a BVI trust to another jurisdiction is possible. Property held in the BVI by a foreign or non-domiciled national is not taxed. If property is held by a company, there is no transfer or capital gains taxes imposed and transfer of shares is also tax exempt.

Under international pressure, most tax havens now actively enforce anti-money laundering laws. This does not necessarily dilute financial privacy laws. It does mean those haven nations with mutual legal assistance treaties with the U.K. and the U.S. will cooperate fully should a criminal investigation arise. Finally, remember to calculate carefully the expense of the creation of the offshore trust or corporation. In addition, take into account the annual fees for trustees and official registration.

The U.S. as an Offshore Tax Haven
by Robert Bauman, JD, & David Melnik, QC, *The Offshore Money Manual*, 2002

Few hard-pressed American taxpayers realize it, but the United States is a tax haven for foreign investors. There is a whole host of laws that provide liberal U.S. tax breaks that apply only to foreigners. While Americans struggle to pay combined taxes that rob them of more than 40 percent of their total incomes, careful foreign investors can and do make money in the United States tax free.

Even so, the U.S. is not a straightforward "no-tax" haven like Panama, even for foreigners. Instead, a haphazard array of complex provisions in the Internal Revenue Code, coupled with a host of international tax treaties, provide rich opportunities for the foreign investor. Assisting these investors is an elite group of high-priced American tax lawyers and accountants known as "inbound specialists." They specialize in structuring transactions to minimize taxes and maximize profits.

Q. *Why does the U.S. allow foreign investors to get off tax-free?*

A. The U.S. government desperately needs foreign investment.

The U.S. Treasury needs it to provide capital to bolster the national economy and, more importantly, to finance the huge government budget deficit. A large portion of foreign investment goes directly into short-and long-term U.S. Treasury securities. This enormous cash inflow keeps the government afloat from day to day. Billions of dollars of the much-talked-about national debt is owed directly to European and Asian investors. The communist government of the Peoples Republic of China is one of America's largest individual creditors by virtue of their investments in U.S. government debt securities.

One other scary fact: the annual interest paid on all this $5 trillion government debt now exceeds all other federal budget program costs, except the Defense Department. Some 38 percent of the entire budget for interest payments alone, and most of it goes to foreign investors. We're talking very big money here!

To give credit where it's due, foreign companies operating in the U.S. do pay corporate income taxes on some of their U.S. earnings. According to a November 1996 report by KPMG Peat Marwick, they pay plenty. Based on IRS data, taxes paid by U.S. subsidiaries of foreign-owned corporations surged to a record US$8.2 billion in 1993, from US$7.1 billion in 1992.

Q. *Do these foreign investors have power over the U.S.?*

A. You bet they do.

Congress recently imposed a 30 percent withholding tax on all interest payments to foreign residents and corporations doing business in the US. Foreign investors bluntly let it be known they would take their money elsewhere if the withholding tax remained. Not surprisingly, the IRC is now riddled with exceptions to the 30 percent tax.

The biggest U.S. tax break for many foreigners comes from a combination impact of domestic IRC provisions and the tax laws of the investor's own country. The United States taxes its citizens and residents on their worldwide income. But non-citizens and non-residents are allowed to earn certain types of income from within the U.S. tax free. As you can guess, droves of smart foreign investors take advantage of the situation.

Where There's a Will

Q. *Can Americans get in on this foreign investor tax-free gravy train?*

A. The answer is a qualified "yes."

In the right circumstances, a U.S. citizen or resident can benefit from this same tax-free income that makes so many foreign investors wealthy. The qualifying process is complex, so it's not for everyone, but the laws offer clear possibilities and you can exploit them.

The United Kingdom as a Tax Haven

by Nicholas Pullen, *The Sovereign Individual*, May 2001

The United Kingdom continues to crack down on tax avoidance by its own citizens and support the attack by the Organization for Economic Cooperation and Development on nations alleged to be engaged in "harmful tax competition." So it is richly ironic that the United Kingdom offers foreign individuals and companies tax incentives in a bid to attract them and their capital to U.K. shores. And as you'll learn in this column, the tax advantages aren't wholly confined to foreign individuals and entities.

Non-Domiciled U.K. Residents Live Practically Tax-Free

If you are a foreigner and qualify for U.K. residency, but are not U.K. domiciled, you are required to pay income tax only on U.K. source income and foreign source income "remitted" (transferred from abroad) to the United Kingdom. You are subject to capital gains tax only on assets remitted to the United Kingdom and to inheritance tax only on your U.K. assets. This tax break has made London the home of more expatriate millionaires then the rest of Europe's capitals combined.

If you neither live nor are domiciled in the United Kingdom, you can establish a trust there that avoids all U.K. income, capital gains and inheritance taxes. A U.K. tax practice that is familiar with this "London trust" strategy is *Morgan, Lewis & Bockius*. **Tel.:** +(44) 207 710-5500. **Link:** www.morganlewis.com/london.htm.

Pay as Little as 1 percent Tax on U.K. Corporate Profits

While the United Kingdom takes pains to avoid positioning itself as a "tax haven," its tax-advantaged corporate structures and its network of more than 100 tax treaties, the largest number of any nation, makes it very useful to international tax planners.

For companies requiring an EU base to register for value added tax, or for other purposes, the United Kingdom is a better option than most other EU countries. U.K. corporate tax rates are among the EU's lowest. Most U.K. companies pay tax at a bottom rate of 10 percent.

Companies with profits between £50,000 and £300,000 pay 20 percent. Profits above this threshold attract a rate of 30 percent. However, several structures can reduce this relatively low tax burden even further: Non-resident companies are not liable to tax on foreign source income; only

U.K. activity is taxable. This status requires that the company be managed and controlled from a country that has a U.K. tax treaty containing a "tie breaker clause." The U.K./Portugal tax treaty is suitable. A U.K. company managed and administered from Madeira would enjoy a respectable U.K. trading persona, but remain free from taxation on foreign source income in both countries.

U.K. international trading companies are useful both for tax avoidance and obtaining a U.K. persona. They involve a U.K. company established solely for international trading purposes acting as an agent on behalf of a foreign principal. All contracts, invoicing and general correspondence are executed in the U.K. company's name. This relationship need not be disclosed to any foreign tax department or foreign third parties.

There are two levels of tax avoidance:

1. The U.K. company retains only an agent's fee—typically 10 percent of each transaction. The remaining 90 percent of revenue may be paid to the offshore principal free from U.K. taxation.

2. The U.K. company is liable only for corporate tax of 10 percent on its own trading profits. The effective U.K. tax rate can be as low as 1 percent (10 percent of 10 percent).

The company must be owned by non-U.K. persons; managed outside the United Kingdom; and all trading operations must be conducted outside the United Kingdom.

International Holding Companies (IHCs) are efficient vehicles for the collection of foreign dividends. Profits remitted to a U.K. IHC receive a full credit against U.K. income taxes for any foreign tax paid before their arrival in the United Kingdom. If dividends have already been taxed at a rate equal to or higher than the applicable U.K. rate (20-30 percent), no U.K. tax will be payable on that income either upon arrival or subsequent distribution. However, sales of shares of U.K. IHCs are subject to capital gains tax.

U.K. companies may adopt IHC status if U.K. non-resident investors beneficially own at least 80 percent of the company. The identities of beneficial owners must be reported to the Inland Revenue and, if authorized by a U.K. tax treaty, this information may be passed on to foreign tax authorities.Seek advice from a professional international corporate tax planner before creating any corporate structure.

Tax Breaks for U.K. Residents

The U.K. government offers various relief to U.K. residents who invest in small and medium sized companies whose shares do not trade on a U.K. stock exchange.

Venture Capital Trusts (VCTs) are quoted investment vehicles introduced by the U.K. Treasury for investments of £3,000-£100,000 in the ordinary shares of companies not listed on a U.K. stock exchange. VCTs are eligible for an exemption from income tax on dividends. There is also an income tax deduction of 20 percent of your initial investment for the tax year in which you make it (provided you hold it for five years). Gains are exempted from capital gains tax on disposal of ordinary shares. You also defer tax on gains arising from the sale of any asset by sheltering them within a VCT. For further information contact: *The British Venture Capital Association.* **Tel.:** 0207 240 3846. **E-mail:** bvca@bvca.co.uk. **Website:** www.bvca.co.uk. Also consult booklet IR 169 available on the Inland Revenue's website: www.inlandrevenue.gov.uk/pdfs/ir169.htm.

Resources

- The Inland Revenue publishes a number of free guides of interest to anyone considering U.K. residency: IR20—Residents and non-residents (liability to tax in the United Kingdom) IR139 —Income from abroad (a guide to U.K. tax on overseas income) IHT18—Inheritance tax (foreign aspects) Request these from any local IR office or from http://www.inlandrevenue.gov.uk.

- For advice regarding U.K. residency and other immigration issues, contact: The Immigration Advisory Service, 190 Great Dover Street, London SE1 4YB, United Kingdom. **Tel.:** +(44) 207-357-7511. **Fax:** +(44) 207-403-5875.

Contacts

- A U.K. attorney who is available for consultation on tax and succession issues for non-domiciled residents is: *James McNeill*, Farrer & Co, 66 Lincoln's Inn Fields, London WC2A 3KG, U.K. **Tel.:** +(44) 207-242-2022. **Fax:** +(44) 207-917-7431. **E-mail:** jdm@farrer.co.uk.

- A company that can offer advice on the corporate structures discussed here is *Sovereign Corporate and Fiscal Services*. **Tel.:** +(44) 207 479 7070. **Fax:** +(44) 207 439 4436. **E-mail:** uk@sovereigngroup.com. **Link:** www.sovereigngroup.com.

———◆◆———

Part Two—Havens Under Siege

Big Government's War Against Harmful Tax Competition
by Mark Nestmann, *The Sovereign Individual*, January 1999

In recent months, world governments have unleashed a parade of special investigations, groundbreaking reports, and multilateral actions with a single goal severely curtailing or even wiping out the world's burgeoning offshore financial sector.

Three recent components of this war are the Organization for Economic Cooperation and Development's (OECD) report on tax competition; the Edwards Report on the Channel Islands and the Isle of Man; and the Cook Initiative on U.K. Overseas Territories, from U.K. Foreign Secretary Robin Cook.

The War on Drugs Begets the War on Tax Avoidance

In an April 1998 report entitled "Harmful Tax Competition," the OECD called for "severe countermeasures" against countries used by persons or companies trying to reduce taxes. The report proposes that domestic taxes be enforced internationally, using the anti-drug and anti-money laundering regime constructed in recent years as a model.

Many of us have long predicted that the "War on Drugs" was nothing more than a smokescreen to construct an international tax collection authority. We were right. Lost in the OECD's hand wringing over unfair tax competition is the fact that taxes are merely another cost of doing business. An individual or business that lowers its tax burden will be more successful than one that doesn't.

Wake Up, OECD: Marxism Doesn't Work!

In most OECD countries, a person or company pays tax according to their vulnerability to coercion by special interest groups that receive transfer payments according to their "needs." This is, of course, the Marxist model that was a colossal failure in the Soviet Union. Now the "kinder and gentler" version of Marxism that has flourished in the social democracies of western Europe and the United States for decades is also in collapse.

However, the OECD is not merely delusional, but also schizophrenic. At about the same time it released Harmful Tax Competition, it also published Policy Brief No. 9: Fostering Entrepreneurship. A key factor in fostering entrepreneurship, of course, is reducing regulatory and tax barriers to success. Once that is done, history has proven time and again that markets will establish themselves, a fact forgotten by the OECD.

OECD Members Lead in Harmful Tax Competition

The OECD defines a tax haven that conducts "harmful tax competition" as any nation that:

- Imposes nominal or no tax on income.

- Offers preferential treatment to certain types of income at no or low tax rates.

- Offers, or is perceived to offer, nonresidents the ability to escape taxes in their country of residence.

- Permits tax-related planning in activities that lack substantial economic (non-tax) advantages.

Under this definition, almost every OECD country is a tax haven. Indeed, OECD members Switzerland and Luxembourg, two of the world's largest offshore centers, refused to endorse the report.

Virtually every other OECD member uses tax competition to attract foreign investment or wealthy residents. For instance, the United States does not tax many types of income earned by nonresident investors. The United Kingdom and Ireland invite wealthy foreigners to live there, essentially tax free, through their "resident but not domiciled" rules. Even Germany has enacted recent legislation that makes it much more attractive tax wise for holding companies.

Economic Warfare

But the hypocrisy goes even deeper. While the OECD is prepared to tolerate tax competition among its members, it threatens "severe countermeasures" against nonmembers. It has in effect declared economic war against some of the world's most impoverished countries, that, in the absence of their offshore industries, would have few if any opportunities to advance economically.

The OECD campaign is a concerted effort by the world's richest nations to hamper the development of some of the poorest ones, disguised in the rhetoric of "fairness."

Big Government is Dying

The politicians governing the world's high tax democracies know that they cannot continue to tax and spend forever. But they will hang on to power until they are forced to abdicate because, to a politician, power is everything.

There will be major confrontations with "out of favor" offshore centers that do not at least pay lip service to the idea of applying anti-money laundering laws to tax crimes. Indeed, such a confrontation is already occurring in the U.K.'s Caribbean overseas territories.

The OECD Battle: Will David Slay Goliath?

by Daniel J. Mitchell, PhD, *The Sovereign Individual*, June 2001

Less than one year ago, it appeared that the Organization for Economic Cooperation and Development's assault on low-tax countries was going to be successful. Representing the world's most powerful nations, the OECD asserted that all jurisdictions had to participate in a global system of information exchange between tax authorities.

The Paris-based bureaucracy then put together a list of 41 nations and territories that it considered "tax havens," largely because of their low-tax policies and strong financial privacy laws. These regimes were threatened with financial sanctions unless they agreed to become vassal tax collectors for OECD nations. Six jurisdictions immediately capitulated, including Bermuda and the Cayman Islands, and it appeared that it would be only a matter of time before the rest surrendered their sovereign rights as well.

Yet Goliath has faltered. The American free-market community, led by the Heritage Foundation and the Center for Freedom and Prosperity, has mobilized in opposition to the OECD's proposed global network of tax police. Their efforts have resulted in nearly 50 members of the U.S. Congress sending letters of opposition to Treasury Secretary, Paul O'Neill. Virtually every pro-taxpayer organization has registered its opposition to the effort, and leading conservative voices such as *National Review*, the *Wall Street Journal*, and the *Washington Times* have condemned the initiative. This avalanche of antagonism can be viewed at the Center's website, www.freedomandprosperity.org.

The goal of this coalition is to convince the Bush Administration that tax competition should be encouraged, not condemned. And if the U.S. government decides not to support the OECD, it is believed that the OECD initiative will collapse. Not because Europe's welfare states will change their positions, but rather because it will make no sense for OECD nations to impose sanctions as such a step will simply drive more business to U.S. financial institutions.

The battle over tax competition, financial privacy and fiscal sovereignty has been a roller coaster contest. When the OECD first issued its 1998 report, *Harmful Tax Competition: An Emerging Global Issue*, it was generally ignored by low-tax nations. Many observers dismissed the report as wishful thinking by France and other high-tax, uncompetitive nations.

This cavalier attitude was a big mistake. The preponderance of left-of-center governments, combined with the inherent bias of the OECD's Fiscal Affairs Committee (representing tax-collection agencies from the member governments), created fertile ground for an unprecedented attack on low-tax nations. The 2000 report, *Towards Global Tax Cooperation*, identified 41 so-called tax havens and outlined a series of protectionist measures to be imposed against them unless they agreed to rewrite their tax and privacy laws according to OECD specifications.

The threat of a financial blockade was augmented by two other "name-and-shame" lists, one produced by an OECD-spinoff known as the Financial Action Task Force (allegedly concerned with money laundering) and the other produced by a G73 creation known as the Financial Stability Forum (supposedly concerned with the effect of "unstable" capital). Low-tax nations were placed on the defensive. Indeed, an OECD victory seemed a foregone conclusion.

Yet the last nine months have witnessed a tremendous counter-offensive. Supporters of tax competition have turned the tide. The bureaucrats in Paris are on the defensive. The Bush Administration ,during April's G7 meeting, blocked the inclusion of language endorsing the OECD initiative—a development of monumental proportions.

The OECD self-characterizes its campaign as a fight against "tax cheats." This reckless and inflammatory language is an attempt to mask the real issue.

Stripped of rhetoric, this is a battle between source-based (territorial) taxation versus residence-based (worldwide) taxation. The OECD avidly supports worldwide taxation, meaning that governments can collect tax on any income their taxpayers earn in other nations. But to tax income earned outside its borders, a government's tax collection agency must be aware of the income. Hence, the supposed need to eliminate financial privacy.

In contrast, under the territorial method of taxation, countries reserve the right to tax the income earned inside their borders, regardless of who earns the money; but they do not assert the right to tax income earned in other countries. While this seems to be a rather arcane debate, the choice has profound implications. For instance:

Tax competition. A territorial system promotes competition since investors and entrepreneurs can take advantage of lower tax rates by doing business in jurisdictions with pro-market tax systems. A worldwide system, by contrast, largely destroys competition as high-tax governments would have the right to export their tax burdens around the world.

Financial privacy. A territorial system is much more protective of financial privacy, particularly if combined with a withholding regime for jurisdictions that tax capital income. Taxpayers are not forced to divulge personal financial information to the government every year. By contrast, a system of information exchange necessarily means that at least two governments are privy to the most intimate financial details of a taxpayer's life.

Fiscal sovereignty. By definition, a territorial system does not create conflicts with other nations. Each country has the right to impose any and all taxes on any and all income earned inside its borders. Any income earned in other countries, however, is off limits.

Tax reform. A territorial system is conducive to fundamental tax reform. A flat tax, for instance, only taxes income earned inside national borders. A worldwide tax system, by contrast, is an impediment to tax reform. Indeed, many high-tax countries favor "information exchange" because it allows them to double-tax income that is saved and invested, a misguided practice that every major tax reform plan abolishes.

Needless to say, high-tax nations want worldwide taxation and low-tax nations prefer territorial taxation. In a just world, countries would be free to select the system that best promotes each nation's national interests. But because high-tax nations are finding it more difficult to enforce oppressive tax systems in a global economy, they are using the OECD to radically alter the rules of international commerce and taxation. For all intents and purposes, the OECD is seeking to criminalize territorial taxation.

It is never easy to predict the future, and it is especially risky to make any kind of definitive statement in an article that has even a small gap between when it is written (April 30, 2001) and when it is published. Nonetheless, it is now reasonable to believe that the OECD initiative will be defeated. The U.S. decision to block any pro-OECD language at the conclusion of April's G7 meeting was a pivotal occurrence.

This raises a rather interesting question. What will the OECD do if the United States refuses to participate in its proposed tax cartel? Because of pride and/or stubbornness, it is unlikely that the bureaucrats will retreat from their anti-tax competition initiative. The author's best guess is that the OECD will issue a report in July, as promised, listing "non-cooperative" regimes. Further, the report will probably suggest that these jurisdictions be progressively isolated from the global financial system. But everyone will realize that this is a pointless recommendation in the absence of U.S. support—and the report will gather dust.

This does not mean, however, that advocates of competition, privacy, and sovereignty have won the war. The OECD's "harmful tax competition" initiative is just one skirmish in an important battle, and the battle is just one episode in the ongoing war to preserve individual freedom against government. The European Union Savings Tax Directive, for instance, mimics the OECD in that all nations—even those outside the EU—would be expected to participate in global system of information exchange.

But if the OECD is defeated, it is a safe bet that the EU proposal also will fail. And if that happens, then governments will face tremendous pressure to lower tax rates and alleviate the punitive taxation of capital income. This approach is the fair and just way of encouraging greater compliance with tax laws.

The OECD House of Cards Collapses

by Mark Nestmann, *The Sovereign Individual*, August 2001

The headlines tell the story: "U.S., Allies to Ease Curbs on Offshore Tax Havens" (*Wall Street Journal*, June 15); "OECD Likely to Push Back Tax Haven Sanctions Deadline:" (*Bloomberg*, June 12); "U.S. wants "redirection" of OECD tax havens plan" (*AF News Service*, June 13).

What a difference a year makes!

A year ago we reported that the Organization for Economic Cooperation and Development (OECD) had published in June 2000 a report blacklisting 35 nations alleged to be possibly engaged in "harmful tax competition." A second report published that same month by the Financial Action Task Force, an OECD affiliate operating out of the OECD's office complex in Paris, blacklisted 15 jurisdictions alleged to not be doing enough to fight money laundering.

Former President Clinton's Treasury Secretary, Lawrence Summers, vigorously supported the OECD/FATF efforts. Gloating over the success the threat of blacklisting and economic sanctions had in persuading offshore centers to "voluntarily" cave in to demands for a global high-tax cartel,

Summers announced on May 21, 2000, that the campaign represented "an important milestone in the effort to ensure that the global mobility of capital does not subvert national interests" and that it was making "a contribution to preventing tax evasion and avoidance around the world." (Note Summers' deceptive words equating legal tax avoidance with illegal tax evasion.)

But in a very different statement a year later, incoming U.S. Treasury Secretary Paul O'Neill on May 10, 2001, proclaimed that the Bush Administration would not support the harmful tax competition initiative out of respect for other nations' rights to determine their own tax system. A month later, O'Neill ordered a review of U.S. anti-money laundering rules, planning an overhaul of an onerous system Bush officials call burdensome and ineffective.

The sudden shift in momentum has provoked shrill invective from the OECD/FATF and their collectivist apologists. French Finance Minister Laurent Fabius warned O'Neill that the U.S. retreat could doom the OECD's entire initiative. And seven former IRS commissioners attacked the Bush Administration position, writing in a letter to the *New York Times*, "We have never been closer to cracking down on tax abuse through the use of tax havens." And the *Times* itself criticized in an editorial those who wish to "sabotage domestic and international efforts to prevent criminals from laundering their profits."

With the defection of the United States, the OECD's largest member, the consensus that allowed the OECD/FATF anti-offshore vendetta to progress is dead. This was confirmed on June 15, when the OECD agreed to drop efforts to prohibit non-OECD countries from offering special tax breaks to foreign companies and investors.

Then on June 27, the OECD announced that it would delay imposing sanctions at least until 2003, and only against those jurisdictions that refused to hand over taxpayer data to other countries' authorities in specific cases. It also backtracked on its demand that offshore jurisdictions eliminate "ring-fencing"—having one set of laws for domestic investors and a more favorable set for offshore investors.

The new U.S. position also will frustrate the socialist dream of an EU-wide bank account information exchange between tax authorities. This would require unanimous agreement among all EU members. But Austria and Luxembourg have agreed to data exchange only if the United States, Switzerland and key offshore jurisdictions agree to participate by the end of 2002. Switzerland is standing firm on this issue, as are anti-OECD Republican leaders in the U.S. Congress.

In the meantime, the legitimacy of our concerns about indiscriminate information exchange is now being proven. Employees of Europol, the newly created EU police organ, are under investigation for corruption. On June 2, the Belgian press reported that Dutch police raided Europol offices and the home of a French police official following a trail of stolen money that allegedly terminates in Bermuda, one of the few offshore jurisdictions that have cooperated with the OECD. What happens when information is exchanged not only with EU countries, but also with totalitarian governments such as Iraq, Algeria, and Afghanistan?

But the throttling back of the OECD's harmful tax competition vendetta is only a temporary respite in the war on offshore freedom. There is no assurance that victory will be swift, or lasting. Thanks to the party switch of Vermont Senator Jim Jeffords, from Republican to Independent, the Democrats now hold a majority in the U.S. Senate. Carl Levin, the newly appointed chairman of the Senate Governmental Affairs Committee's investigative panel, says he will use his new power to scrutinize the actions of the Treasury.

We reported on Mr. Levin's campaign against offshore dealings in February 2001 when his subcommittee staff released an investigative report highly critical of so called "correspondent accounts" in U.S. banks. (These are "master" accounts set up in U.S. banks by offshore financial institutions on behalf of their clients, each of whom has a sub-account.)

Relying on the Senate testimony of informant and convicted felon John Mathewson, the former head of a Cayman bank, Levin's investigators concluded that correspondent accounts were hotbeds of laundering. Among other changes, Levin is pushing a measure to make the sub-accounts of correspondent accounts more vulnerable to civil forfeiture.

For the moment, though, the Bush Administration is standing firm. Treasury Secretary O'Neill has made it clear that the United States will support information exchange only when facts support investigating a particular individual for a specific crime or crimes.

The next few months promise a seesaw behind-the-scenes battle for influence in Washington, Paris and other world capitals. And also the welcome involvement of a new party to the discussion: the offshore jurisdictions themselves, which have belatedly recognized the threats to their existence the OECD and FATF represent. They have set up their own advocacy group, the International Tax and Investment Organization (ITIO). Among other requests, ITIO has pointedly asked the OECD to require its members to end the same types of tax incentives and secrecy provisions it tolerates in their own economies that the OECD is demanding blacklisted countries end.

This will never happen. The OECD's most powerful member, the United States, is also the world's largest tax haven, and the current strength of the U.S. dollar and indeed of the global economy is completely dependent on its economic strength. Ending its tax haven status, or disclosing the identity of foreign investors in U.S. banks to foreign tax authorities, as suggested in proposed regulations issued in the closing days of the Clinton Administration, would have catastrophic economic effects globally.

What, then, will happen? It is clear that offshore jurisdictions will remain free to set their own tax regimes. On the other hand, the OECD/FATF was successful in forcing offshore jurisdictions to implement "know-your-customer" rules, although the U.S. Congress has refused to enact such rules into law in the United States. It is unclear how widely information collected as a result of KYC rules will be shared.

The world remains years away from a comprehensive system of information exchange.

The bottom line: With the defeat of the OECD's high tax campaign, tax havens will continue to offer offshore investors tax free or very low tax status for foreigners using their services via trusts, international business companies and bank accounts. Now that the world knows that the OECD is a paper tiger, we predict these sovereign nations will defend their constitutional and statutory guarantees of financial privacy and their lucrative offshore financial centers. And The Sovereign Society will continue to promote their legitimate use for wealth preservation and international tax planning.

The Outlook for World Tax Competition
By Daniel J. Mitchell, *The Sovereign Individual*, February 2003

Against great odds, 2002 was a remarkably successful year. The White House decided to reject the European Union's (EU) proposed savings tax cartel.

The "harmful tax competition" scheme of the Organization for Economic Cooperation and Development (OECD) remains moribund. Supporters of tax competition even blocked a proposed IRS regulation that would force U.S. banks to put foreign tax law above American tax law. And most impressive of all, advocates of international fiscal competition managed to neutralize all efforts either to prohibit companies from re-chartering in jurisdictions with better tax laws or to subject them to fiscal protectionism if they made the decision to "invert."

But this does not mean that all the battles have been won. The EU, for instance, has announced that it will continue to push for the Savings Tax Directive. The OECD is still trying to bully low-tax jurisdictions. The IRS regulation could be finalized any day. And the American left intends to renew its campaign against corporate "inversions."

Unfortunately, there will never be a permanent (or at least long-term) victory in the battle for tax competition, financial privacy, and fiscal sovereignty until there is fundamental tax reform in the United States. Fortunately, there is growing evidence that the Bush Administration wants to reform the Tax Code. Proposals announced in January 2003 to reduce the double-taxation of corporate income are a sign that the White House understands the need to make America's tax code more competitive.

There is every reason to believe that victories will outnumber defeats in the coming year. Thanks to the efforts of groups such as the Center for Freedom and Prosperity, the coalition supporting tax competition gets stronger every day. Their efforts will be even more effective now that Republicans control the Senate.

EU Savings Tax Directive: The EU failed to achieve its primary tax harmonization goal. The EU Savings Tax Directive would have required low-tax jurisdictions to inform high-tax nations about the private financial affairs of selected non-resident investors, but the scheme required unanimous support from all member nations—a difficult hurdle. Moreover, Luxembourg, Austria and Belgium promised to veto the Directive unless the bureaucrats in Brussels could trick six non-EU nations (including the United States and Switzerland) into participating in the cartel.

Responding to a vigorous campaign organized by the Center for Freedom and Prosperity, the United States decided in July 2002 to oppose the EU scheme. The U.S. Treasury Department attempted to undermine this position, but separate announcements in September and October by two of President Bush's senior advisers removed any ambiguity. Perhaps more importantly, Switzerland held firm.

2003 Prognosis: The EU Directive is dead. Many EU member nations are secretly relieved that the proposal failed. The bureaucracy will continue to make noise, but there is almost no way to resuscitate the proposed cartel.

OECD Anti-Tax Competition Initiative: In response to its ill-conceived tax haven "blacklisting" initiative, the OECD persuaded many low-tax jurisdictions to promise changes to tax and privacy laws that will make it easier for high-tax nations to impose extra-territorial taxation. But the jurisdictions promised to implement these laws only if all OECD member nations agreed to the same misguided policies (the "level playing field"). This put the OECD in a difficult situation since the United States, the United Kingdom, Switzerland, and Luxembourg are "tax havens" according to the OECD's own criteria.

The collapse of the EU Savings Tax Directive means there is no "level playing field," but the OECD is still trying to force capitulation from low-tax jurisdictions. Fortunately, most low-tax jurisdictions have refused to implement the OECD wish-list, and two nations—Panama and Antigua—have sent letters to Paris explaining that they are no longer bound by the earlier commitment letters.

2003 Prognosis: The OECD "harmful tax competition" campaign will remain stalled. More low-tax jurisdictions will disavow their commitment letters.

IRS Interest Reporting Regulation: In the waning days of the Clinton Administration, the IRS proposed a regulation to force U.S. banks to report the interest paid to all non-resident aliens. This proposal drew heated opposition from both industry and the public policy community, and numerous members of Congress weighed in against the proposed regulation. About 18 months after the regulation was first proposed, the IRS was forced to withdraw the regulation.

But the IRS almost immediately re-issued the regulation after some cosmetic changes. Even worse, it appeared that certain segments of the financial services industry were tricked by the IRS bait-and-switch routine and planned to remain neutral, weakening the pro-tax competition coalition. Notwithstanding the odds, the Center for Freedom and Prosperity re-launched its battle against the regulation and was able to block the proposal. But this may only be a short-term victory. The Treasury Department is actively pushing the proposal—even though it puts the interests of foreign tax collectors above U.S. law and before the interests of the American economy.

2003 Prognosis: If the decision goes the wrong way, expect a legal challenge since the regulation contravenes existing.

Anti-Inversion Campaign: The United States has a worldwide tax regime that makes it difficult for U.S.-chartered companies to compete overseas. In an effort to remain competitive, some companies have chosen to re-incorporate (or invert) in jurisdictions such as Bermuda and the Cayman Islands. Some members of Congress sought to block inversions by introducing legislation that would treat these companies as U.S. taxpayers regardless of where they are chartered.

Other politicians sought to bar the companies from competing for government contracts. Because 2002 was an election year, it was widely believed that these protectionist proposals would be approved. But groups in favor of low taxation, particularly the Coalition for Tax Competition, worked very hard to explain that inversions were a way for American companies to compete on a level playing field. The companies keep their jobs and headquarters in America, but can compete overseas since they no longer have to pay an extra layer of tax to the IRS on income that is earned—and taxed—in other nations.

2003 Prognosis: The left will launch several legislative initiatives and may even succeed in attaching anti-inversion amendments to legislation. Such efforts will likely be emasculated during House-Senate conference committees.

International Tax Reform: The World Trade Organization has ruled several times that selected provisions of the internal revenue code are impermissible "export subsidies." Because the European Union (which brought the case) has the right to impose US$4 billion in "compensatory" tariffs if nothing happens, U.S. policy makers will almost surely change American tax laws. The best option is territorial taxation, the common-sense notion that foreign-source income is no longer subject to U.S. tax. This approach is WTO-compliant and is used by most nations.

2003 Prognosis: Legislation will be enacted that shifts America closer to a territorial system for corporate income.

The International Tax Collectors Fail for Now
By Mark Nestmann, *The Sovereign Individual*, June 2003

Throughout history, individuals have migrated to wherever their personal freedoms are maximized and the risk to themselves and their property are minimized.

In the 20th century, this migration assumed a new dimension, made possible by more efficient transportation and communications and by the ongoing transformation of major industrial nations to information and service economies.

Because skills and information are portable, governments risk losing their most productive citizens, and their assets, if they penalize these individuals through high taxes. And indeed, there is a global trend toward smaller government and lower taxes now taking place.

However, high-tax governments are conducting a coordinated, behind-the-scenes strategy to end the growing phenomenon of "tax competition." By far the most important effort along these lines is being carried out by the Organization for Economic Cooperation and Development (OECD). Ironically, the OECD's employees, working out of the organization's sumptuous headquarters in Paris, are, by international agreement, not subject to taxes on their income from the OECD.

Like any other form of competition, tax competition succeeds in keeping the price of a commodity—in this case, government services—down to the lowest level commiserate with the services received. Left to a free market, tax competition leads to smaller government and greater prosperity. This trend obviously terrifies the OECD.

In 1998, the OECD released a report entitled *Harmful Tax Competition: An Emerging Global*

Issue. The report committed the OECD to preparing a list of jurisdictions engaging what it called "harmful tax" and demanded that bank secrecy in low tax countries be dismantled to the extent that it applied to tax investigations by OECD countries.

The OECD's June 2000 report, *Towards Global Tax Cooperation*, identified 35 so-called taxes and outlined a series of protectionist measures to be imposed against them unless they agreed to rewrite their laws according to OECD specifications. Threatened sanctions included terminating tax treaties, ending tax credits and imposing extra domestic reporting requirements for persons or entities doing business in those countries.

The list of "tax havens" was released only four days after the publication of the Financial Action Task Force's blacklist of so-called "non-cooperative jurisdictions" in the global fight against money laundering . There is little doubt that the release of the lists was orchestrated to make the maximum impact on the affected jurisdictions.

The list would have even been longer, but days before its release, Bermuda, the Cayman Islands, Cyprus, Malta, Mauritius and San Marino capitulated and agreed in principle to open financial records for inspection by the tax collectors of other countries. Since then, some other targeted jurisdictions did the same: Aruba, Bahrain, Bermuda, the Cayman Islands, Cyprus, the Isle of Man, Malta, Mauritius, the Netherlands Antilles and the Seychelles.

Conspicuously absent from this list were the OECD's own tax havens of Luxembourg, Switzerland, the United Kingdom and the United States (the world's largest tax haven for non-U.S. resident investors).

The OECD gave the 35 jurisdictions until July 2001 to sign compliance agreements that would obligate each of them to bring their laws into line with standards set by the OECD. Seven jurisdictions refused to sign such an agreement and are now on an OECD blacklist: Andorra, Liechtenstein, Monaco, Marshall Islands, Liberia, Nauru, and Vanuatu. These jurisdictions still face the prospect of sanctions being imposed by OECD countries, although such sanctions are unlikely to be imposed anytime soon.

This is because while most offshore jurisdictions were coerced into signing agreements promising to curb "harmful tax competition," almost all of them included a "level playing field"clause in their commitment letter stipulating that they are not obliged to acquiesce to the OECD unless and until every OECD member nation agrees to obey the same practices. This will never happen, since the United States, under President Bush—the most powerful member of the OECD and the world's largest beneficiary of "tax competition"—specifically has rejected the OECD's demands.

In the wake of the events of Sept. 11, 2001, the OECD embarked on a shameful campaign to associate "harmful tax competition with terrorism. Gabriel Makhlouf, chairman of the OECD's Committee on Fiscal Affairs, urged offshore centers to "improve transparency" and "exchange of information." He warned again that countries that failed to roll back "harmful tax regimes" would face sanctions. Fortunately, this fallacious effort has been spectacularly unsuccessful.

U.S. Opposition Derails "Harmful Tax Competition" Campaign

Low tax jurisdictions found a powerful ally in the United States and the Bush administration, which in 2001, announced that the it would not support the OECD initiative out of respect for other nations' rights to determine their own tax system.

With the defection of the United States, the OECD's largest member, the consensus that allowed the OECD anti-tax competition vendetta to progress died. Therefore, the OECD had no choice but to drop efforts to prohibit non-OECD countries from offering special tax breaks to foreign companies and investors. It also backtracked on its demand that offshore jurisdictions eliminate "ring-fencing"—having one set of laws for domestic investors and a more favorable set for offshore investors. And it announced that it would no longer demand the right for tax authorities to conduct wholesale "fishing expeditions" into offshore accounts.

The shift by the United States to an adherent of tax competition is not out of any concern for the welfare of offshore financial centers, many of which have struggling economies that were staggered by the twin blows from the OECD and FATF. It is because the United States is itself the world's largest tax haven. With few exceptions, the U.S. government does not tax the investment income of foreigners and does not report this income to foreign governments. Low taxes and financial privacy have led to foreigners to invest more than US$9 trillion in the United States—investments the U.S. government is anxious to keep.

EU Backpedals on Savings Tax Initiative

It remains to be seen how the "harmful tax competition" campaign will be resolved. In early 2003, the OECD suffered another defeat when the European Union announced that it will permit three EU member nations with strict bank secrecy laws, Austria, Luxembourg and Belgium, to opt out of the requirement for exchange of information on tax matters with other EU members.

While most member states will begin sharing information in 2004, Austria, Luxembourg and Belgium will impose a withholding tax on non-residents' savings and hand back 75% of the proceeds to their countries of origin. The tax will start at 15% in 2004, rising to 20% in 2007 and to 35% by 2010. Crucially for the plan, both Switzerland and Liechtenstein, neither EU members, but both with significant numbers of EU depositors, have said they will go along with the deal if final details are satisfactory.

Like the OECD's harmful tax initiative, the EU savings tax initiative foundered in the face of official opposition from the United States. While the IRS had already proposed a limited form of tax exchange, in 2002 the Bush administration announced its opposition to the initiative and its refusal to cooperate with the EU's information exchange demands.

The EU savings tax initiative plan has serious flaws, the worst of which is that neither the United States nor Asian offshore centers have agreed to participate. This means that EU depositors seeking to avoid the withholding tax merely have to transfer funds outside the EU, Switzerland or Liechtenstein.

In addition, the deal has enraged offshore centers such as Panama and Antigua, which believe EU ministers are taking a lenient stance on tax havens within their own borders while demanding full cooperation from non-EU states. Several offshore jurisdictions have now informed the EU-dominated OECD that, given the exemptions provided Austria, Luxembourg and Belgium in the EU accord, they are no longer legally obligated to abide by their previous promise to dismantle "harmful tax practices."

Coping With Measures Aimed at Curbing "Tax Competition"

The Sovereign Society predicts that, in coming years, tax jurisdictions will be permitted to continue to attract offshore investors with no tax policies. Havens will be forced to accept reforms that allow exchange of tax and financial information in certain circumstances, particularly in the event of tax fraud. But this will be circumscribed by local judicial procedures that will insist on at least a modicum of due process before information is released.

We also believe that the EU withholding tax plan is not likely to go into effect in 2004 as scheduled. Look for continued delays in its implementation until the United States agrees to go along, a highly unlikely possibility given the U.S. dependence on trillions of dollars of inbound investments to finance its ballooning balance of trade deficit.

In the long run, the trend toward increased tax competition is unstoppable. However, it is possible that proponents of curbing tax competition may win some victories, particularly if some future U.S. government endorses the idea, as the did the Clinton administration (1992-2000).

Are U.K. Overseas Territories Safe Havens?
by Robert E. Bauman, JD, *The Sovereign Individual*, June 1999

Several of the world's leading offshore havens are not independent, but rather are part of what remains of the British Empire. As such, they remain under control of the Labour government in London.

Speaking of India's independence in 1945, Winston Churchill remarked that he had not become Prime Minister to "preside over the dissolution of the British Empire." Now, a half century later, with only remnants remaining and the Empire's final dissolution at hand, New Labourite Prime Minister Tony Blair deserves much of the credit for its final push into oblivion. That end could be marked by the possible independence of some of the U.K.'s Overseas (formerly known as "dependent") Territories ("OTs").

Independence, if it occurs, will be a reaction against the U.K.'s stiff-arm attitude toward its prosperous asset havens. Last year the U.K. Foreign Office ordered several of its OTs (Bermuda, the Cayman Islands, the Turks and Caicos Islands, the British Virgin Islands and Anguilla) to expand existing anti-money laundering statutes to include "all crimes." This would allow enforcement of foreign tax claims in these traditional havens that impose no taxes and don't even recognize tax avoidance (or "evasion") as a crime.

A second, even greater threat to the OTs is the possible intent of the Labour government to force the adoption of a 20 percent withholding tax on interest and other income earned by non-citizens. This scheme is part of the European Organization for Economic Cooperation and Development's (OECD) campaign against "harmful tax competition."

The OECD acknowledges that these asset havens are far more attractive to business than the high-tax socialist governments of Europe. In the 10-year period ending in 1995, the OECD estimates that over US$200 billion flowed into the OTs.

Of course, taxes and an end to financial privacy would spell the demise of these territories as tax and asset protection havens. They would become again, as they have been for most of their history, isolated island dots on the world map with little chance of economic self-sufficiency. Recognition of this fact has not been long in coming.

"They could kill some of these island governments," said Derek Sambrook, a former British offshore bank regulator, now in the offshore service business in Panama. "There are people who will go to Singapore, The Bahamas or Panama, knowing that if they do create income there, the government isn't obliged to report it to any foreign government."

The U.K. government also may be on shaky legal ground in making its demands. Edmund Bendelow, then president of the Offshore Institute claims, "The big issue is being lost. Under the UN and EU Human Rights Conventions you have a right to privacy." The *Wall Street Journal* noted that what U.S. and U.K. bureaucrats really want is "an aggressive push to get financial havens to release bank records to assist in tax evasion investigations."

Independence Is Legal—But Is It Viable?

Representatives of all of the OTs are now discussing a joint response to the U.K. anti-haven initiatives. Independence is probably not a real option for some, e.g., Anguilla or the Turks and Caicos, places that would find it very difficult to survive without ties to the "mother country." But independence is not out of the question for Bermuda and possibly the Cayman Islands, which are not dependent on handouts from the United Kingdom.

Unlike the United Kingdom, the constitutions of the U.K. Overseas Territories are written. They spring from the U.K. Statute of Westminster (1931). Each of these constitutions provides the Crown of the United Kingdom (the government, i.e., the majority party in the House of

Commons) the power to declare an emergency, overrule the will of the people and their governments and impose London's will on the hapless colonials.

Indeed, on March 17, 1999, U.K. Foreign Secretary Robin Cook issued an ultimatum in the House of Commons: January 1, 2000, is to be the deadline for stricter anti-laundering laws in the OTs. Otherwise, the U.K. government will act unilaterally to change local laws. A self-serving report from the U.K. Foreign and Commonwealth Office also criticized the OTs for being slow to adopt reforms. Without proof, it alleged that the OTs permit "vehicles to disguise money laundering and financial fraud"—meaning offshore trusts, international business companies and private bank accounts.

However, the Westminster system also confers on each territory the right to independence. Indeed, in a recent White Paper, the Labour government insists it remains "ready to respond positively when independence [is] the clearly and constitutionally expressed wish of the people."

That time has come to Bermuda. *The Bermuda Sun* reported on May 21, 1999, that, "If a referendum were to be held tomorrow, Bermuda would likely be headed for independence." In an island-wide poll conducted in mid-May, 53 percent of respondents supported independence, while 37 percent wanted closer ties with Britain. Ten percent were uncertain. That's a major change since 1995 when 75 percent of Bermudans voted "no" in an independence referendum. In the 2002 parliamentary elections, independence is likely to be the main issue that Bermudans will be asked to decide.

Bermuda, a long-time tax and banking haven, is a world-class financial center. The three local banks clear more than US$3 billion daily. The island is home to more than 8,000 "exempted companies," more than 600 "collective investment schemes" (mutual funds, unit trusts and limited partnerships). There are about 1,400 "captive insurance companies" with capital exceeding US$29 billion and total assets over US$76 billion.

Bermuda is also a center for offshore trust creation and management. There is no corporate income, gift, capital gains or sales taxes on non-citizens. The island's friendly, tax-neutral environment, established business integrity and minimal regulation have made its success.

Unlike the Cayman Islands or The Bahamas, Bermuda has no statutory bank secrecy laws officially protecting privacy. However, bankers have a common-law duty to respect the privacy of their customers and bank and government policies make it virtually impossible to obtain information in most cases. That requires a lengthy judicial process. A 1988 tax treaty with the United States allows for government exchange of limited information. Bermuda does have strict anti-money laundering laws.

Clearly, Bermuda has the financial infrastructure in place to become independent. Rumblings about possible independence began last fall when the mildly pro-independence Progressive Labour Party won control of parliament for the first time in decades. Walton Brown, who heads the independence effort, says it is inevitable. "Bermudans are beginning to appreciate that we really do a substantial amount on our own, that more importantly, Britain does very little on behalf of Bermuda, that we are capable of governing ourselves."

Leading Hamilton trust and asset protection attorney Gordon L. Hill, QC, told us he believes sentiment for independence "will grow rather than abate." He predicted, "If the United Kingdom has its way and imposes the EU 20 percent tax there will be a mass exodus of international business from Bermuda."

Calum Johnston, chief executive of Bermuda's Bank of NT Butterfield, put it more bluntly: "Bermuda is under attack. This U.K. move is very unfair." Johnston says business and government leaders are solidly united against the OECD's demands based on so-called "harmful tax competition." Most are convinced Bermuda is a target only because it imposes no personal income and corporate taxes. Eugene Cox, the Bermudan finance minister admits, "It could be destructive to us" if the U.K. forced taxes on the island.

[**Ed. Note**: Since the above was written the Progressive Labour government of Bermuda has shown no signs of pushing independence, even though they formally advocated that when last elected to office. Indeed, under pressure from London, tax free Bermuda has changed its laws to make foreign tax evasion a crime, allowing the U.S. and other governments to pursue its nationals and their assets located on the island. If you have bank deposits, investments, a trust or IBC in any of the U.K. overseas territories, consult your professional advisors to determine if your assets may be at risk. If so, you can relocate to an independent jurisdiction outside the U.K.'s control such as Panama or Nevis. If you are now considering a U.K. overseas territory as a base for your offshore business, get the latest, reliable information before you make a final decision.]

Are the Channel Islands & the Isle of Man Safe Havens?
by Robert E. Bauman, JD, *The Sovereign Individual*, August 1999

It's not just the United Kingdom's Overseas Territories that are seriously considering independence from London. Now some of the oldest parts of what was once the British Empire, the Crown Dependencies, are also in revolt.

"Bloody stupid," said attorney and tax planner Charles Cain, a leading offshore financial expert and editor of *Offshore Investment*. Mr. Cain spoke to me by phone from his office on the Isle of Man. His wrath was aimed at the shabby treatment by Tony Blair's New Labour government of the U.K.'s prosperous international asset havens, the Isle of Man and the Channel Islands. And at "nationalist socialists from the European loony left."

Mr. Cain's concern about these islands' future is shared by the vast majority of his fellow Manxmen (i.e., the 72,000 residents of the Isle of Man) and by the residents of the Channel Islands located off the coast of France: Jersey (85,000), Guernsey (60,000), Alderney (2,500) and Sark (600).

Islanders have a knack for forecasting heavy weather when landlubbers don't even see clouds gathering. These island residents harbor a common suspicion that New Labour is secretly negotiating away their unique financial status in exchange for EU tax concessions that favor the London financial markets.

Manx Home Affairs Minister Alan Bell warned months ago that the British government could sell out the island's interests, saying, "The Isle of Man and the Channel Islands may well be sacrificed to protect the greater good of the United Kingdom." Bell's warning came as some islanders argued the only answer might be independence.

Last February, the House of Keys, the lower house of the 1,000-year-old Manx parliament Tynwald (the world's oldest continuous parliamentary body), debated a motion calling for contingency plans for independence and for the Manx pound to be pegged to the U.S. dollar. The independence issue will be debated again later this year.

As in the U.K.'s Overseas Territories, a wave of independence sentiment is growing in the Crown Dependencies. "Channel Islands Face Tax Revolt" blared a *Sunday Telegraph* headline on June 20, 1999, as the London newspaper asked, "May we see the Channel Islands and the Isle of Man declaring their independence from Britain after 1,000 years?"

A prime cause for concern has been the recent secret deliberations of an EU tax committee chaired by the U.K. Treasury Minister Dawn Primarolo. She insists that any EU-wide tax code would not legally bind the Isle of Man or the Channel Islands, because the constitutional arrangement with the Crown Dependencies does not give the U.K. government jurisdiction over the islands' internal tax policy.

But fear persists in the islands. The *Isle of Man Examiner* (June 15, 1999) reported that Deputy Paul Le Claire is planning to raise independence as a proposition in Jersey's parliament, The States, later this year. Le Claire says all the Channel Islands should draw up contingency plans for independence from the United Kingdom.

Established Havens

For nearly half a century these islands have served as the U.K.'s own offshore tax and banking havens. Their offshore status serves as a convenient safety valve for English wealth. But investors come to these islands from all over the world, and official estimates put the assets maintained there as exceeding £400 billion/US$640 billion.

The islanders have fashioned their rocky coasts into a hospitable base for tens of thousands of trusts, various categories of "exempt" and "non-resident" companies (more than 100,000), insurance companies, mutual funds and offshore bank accounts. All three islands feature low taxes or no taxes and a strong tradition of privacy (although none of these havens has enacted bank secrecy statutes into law).

The bulk of the Isle of Man's financial industry is insurance-oriented, much of it linked to structured investments. Jersey and Guernsey specialize in offshore investment and mutual funds. All of the islands have many U.K. expatriates as clients, but also a global clientele including U.K. residents. And Americans can invest here in offshore funds to which they are denied access within the United States.

Free Capital in Jeopardy

Those financial freedoms are now in jeopardy. To understand the sense of alarm felt by residents of the Crown Dependencies and those that invest there, consider the following chain of events (indeed, residents of or investors in any offshore asset haven should feel the same alarm):

December 1, 1997. Finance ministers of the 15 EU nations agree on a "taxation code of conduct" that calls for a 20 percent withholding tax on all interest payments to foreigners and/or reporting of payments to the payee's home government. EU member states, including the United Kingdom, agree "to ensuring that these principles are adopted" in their dependent territories.

April 1998. The Organization for Economic Cooperation and Development (OECD) publishes *Harmful Tax Competition: An Emergency Global Issue.* The report blacklists 35 "tax havens" (12 more added later) alleged to "harm" high tax nations by levying low taxes or by imposing no taxes. The U.K. Crown Dependencies (and Overseas Territories) are on this tax list. An OECD "offshore initiative" to eliminate tax havens is launched.

June 1998. A United Nations conference claims the "enabling machinery" of international financial crimes is provided by offshore haven nations (trusts, international business corporations, privacy laws, private banking). Haven nations, it claims, are "an enormous hole in the international legal and financial system" that must be plugged. Conferees are warned that the world must stop "the use of sovereignty by some countries to give citizens of other countries a way around the laws of their own society." A UN "white list" of acceptable haven nations is proposed, with those nations given five years to conform to these principles.

November 1998. The OECD's Financial Action Task Force (FATF) says "transnational [money] laundering activity" is aided by the "outright refusal" of offshore financial centers to identify "the true owners or beneficiaries of foreign registered business entities-shell companies, international business companies, offshore trusts, etc." The FATF demands surrender of such information to foreign investigative agencies. A "black list" of uncooperative haven nations is proposed.

New Labour: Capitulate...or Else

The foregoing initiatives provide a backdrop for the U.K. government's attack on Crown Dependencies. While Thatcherite Conservatives controlled Parliament, U.K. tax havens were not considered a problem. But New Labour's 1997 sweep to power brought a dramatic change in London's attitude.

On January 20, 1998, what the *Daily Telegraph* termed "a comprehensive review of the financial regulations in the Channel Islands and the Isle of Man," was announced. The aim was "to curb any use of their banks and companies for laundering the proceeds of criminal activity." The result was the notorious "Edwards Report."

Nervous island officials tried to put the best face on its harsh recommendations. But the demand was for nothing less than the islands' voluntary surrender of the most attractive features on which their haven reputations are built. It called for special police financial crimes units to investigate money laundering, full cooperation with foreign police agencies and public revelation of the true owners of offshore companies registered in the islands. Full details of offshore trusts were also to be made available to investigators.

Before the Edwards Report, each of the islands had begun adopting or planning tougher new laws to accomplish many of these demands. Stepping up the pressure, Home Secretary Jack Straw threatened that if the island authorities did not quickly introduce the reforms themselves, Whitehall could intervene. Exactly how this could be done was left unsaid.

Crown Dependencies Outside U.K. & EU

While tougher financial regulation is indeed a major issue, the real fight is over potential new taxes imposed on the Crown Dependencies. And this raises a major constitutional issue: just how much right has the U.K. government to force its will on them?

The islands are not part of the United Kingdom. Jersey and Guernsey were originally part of the French Duchy of Normandy, when France conquered Great Britain at the Battle of Hastings in 1066. The British government bought the Isle of Man for £70,000 in 1765 in order to put an end to pirates using the island as their home base.

Based on their "ancient privileges," the islands have always governed their own internal domestic affairs, although laws enacted by the legislative assemblies are validated by Royal Assent—until now a pro forma procedure. While they are not part of the United Kingdom, the U.K. government is responsible for the islands' foreign relations and military defense.

In 1973, when the United Kingdom joined the European Union, the islands were allowed to remain outside of it. Their fiscal autonomy remained intact, including the sole right to levy their own taxes. Articles 25-27 and Protocol 3 of the 1973 U.K. Act of EU Accession only require the islands to impose the EU common external tariffs for imported goods from outside the European Union. Otherwise, the islands are excluded from other EU treaty requirements, including EU taxation rules.

Causing chronic ulcers for island politicians are repeated public demands by EU leaders to end their haven status. In early 1998, the Luxembourg budget minister said any EU tax system must have a withholding tax that would be "applicable in the dependent territories such as the U.K. Channel Islands." A year later, just as the new euro currency was launched, a German official confirmed the worst fears of island politicians, calling the Channel Islands a tax "loophole" that should be closed to protect the rest of Europe.

What does the future hold in this highly fluid and uncertain environment? If necessary, will the U.K. government use its EU veto power to protect the island's interests against a mandatory EU withholding tax? If such a tax is imposed, will the United States pressure the United Kingdom to "persuade" the islands to impose a similar tax for U.S. investors? These important questions remain unresolved.

We conducted an informal poll among 15 international asset protection lawyers as we went to press. For the moment, none recommends the Channel Islands as a suitable base for asset protection purposes. While opinion was divided on the Isle of Man (the experts view Manx insurance products as some of the best available), the majority urged caution until the outcome of EU tax negotiations and the Labour government's demands for new financial laws are finally known.

The End of Financial Privacy in U.K. Overseas Territories?

By Robert Bauman, *The Sovereign Individual*, June 2002

During its five years in power, Tony Blair's "New Labour" party has converted the United Kingdom into a police state with U.S. style asset forfeiture, lawyers and accountants forced to spy on clients and blanket police interception of e-mail and other electronic communications. Labour's newest plans are to curb trial by jury and abolish the 800-year-old rule against double jeopardy.

In tandem with its oppressive domestic financial policies, the Blair government has systematically imposed on its former empire a "new colonialism" that demands compliance with "tax harmonization" demands of the EU and the campaign against "harmful tax competition" carried out by the Organization for Economic Cooperation and Development (OECD).

The former empire comprises Britain's 13 far-flung overseas territories, many of which (with historical encouragement from successive British governments) have become flourishing offshore financial centers (including Bermuda, the Cayman Islands, the Turks & Caicos Islands, the British Virgin Islands and Anguilla).

The Blair government has similarly altered the relationship with the British Crown colonies (the Channel Islands of Jersey and Guernsey, Alderney and Sark and the Isle of Man)

New Labour's demands include four basic elements:

1. Complete "transparency," meaning an end to financial privacy and free government exchange of tax information;

2. An end to bearer shares and concealed beneficial ownership of trusts, international business corporations and bank accounts;

3. An end to "harmful tax competition," meaning repeal of any tax breaks for foreign persons or foreign entities doing business within a specific haven, and;

4. Strict "know your customer" and "suspicious activity" reporting (policies which have met with near universal acceptance in all U.K. havens).

If a haven fails to change it laws as ordered by London, Labour has invoked the ancient powers of Her Majesty, the Queen, through the arcane procedure of royal "Orders in Council" to repeal democratically adopted laws in U.K. overseas territories.

The process began in 1999 when the U.K. Foreign Office ordered several overseas territories to expand existing anti-laundering statutes to include "all crimes." The object was to allow enforcement of foreign tax claims in these havens that imposed no taxes, and where tax evasion was not even a crime.

Bermuda was the first to capitulate, when it changed its laws to allow enforcement of foreign tax laws within it borders. With a nervous eye on Washington, it also concluded a tax information exchange agreement (TIEA) with the United States.

The Cayman Islands also did as it was told and made foreign tax evasion a crime. In November 2000, it startled observers when it signed a TIEA with Washington that opens all financial records to IRS inspection, almost upon demand, although the agreement does not come fully into effect until 2006.

With this recent history, the latest statements from the British government are not reassuring. During a December 2002 EU debate over demands that Switzerland end its bank secrecy, British Chancellor Gordon Brown gave the EU "unequivocal assurance" that automatic, universal tax information exchange will be introduced in the U.K.'s Caribbean territories. He threatened: "If necessary, we will legislate directly," referring to the Orders in Council route.

The Channel Islands and the Isle of Man are historically self-governing Crown dependencies with the longstanding right to set their own tax policies. Through their U.K. association, the islands also enjoy some benefits of EU membership, although none of the islands is an official EU member. But in April 2002, Chancellor Brown threatened to impose new restrictions on British financial dealings with Jersey (and by implication, on other Crown dependencies), using new legislation that permitted the Treasury to impose special taxes on U.K. firms and controlled foreign companies located in offshore jurisdictions "where harmful tax practices are prevalent."

In the meantime, the EU and London continue to pressure Crown dependencies into ending all preferential tax treatment of offshore investors who use them for banking, trusts and international corporate business.

To counter these demands, in October 2002 the Isle of Man abolished all corporate taxes, a move quickly followed by Jersey and Guernsey. Such a no-tax policy continues the attractiveness of these havens to offshore business. At the same time it meets the EU/London demand for an end to tax preferences for foreign business.

But the Isle of Man, Jersey and Guernsey went a step further in 2002 on the issue of information exchange, each signing TIEAs with the United States. So much for financial privacy.

A year ago, Derek Sambrook, a member of the Sovereign Society Council of Experts and a distinguished former member of the British foreign service, noted that the British haven tax information exchange agreements with Washington "underscores the weakness of the dependencies. I witnessed the sell-out in Rhodesia. Whether its terrorists or taxes, when the U.K. lowers its flag in a colony the mess left behind has to be cleaned up by others." Referring to London's tax collecting goals, Mr. Sambrook said: "This will surely have profound consequences as the hunt for taxes continues. Offshore financial centers controlled effectively by Mr. Blair are very soft targets."

British Labour's renewed colonialism, indeed imperialism, could be countered if one or all of the overseas territories choose independence, as they have a right to do under the Westminster constitutions that are their basic law. But that requires local political leadership with a degree of courage that appears lacking in these abject colonial governments.

Undoubtedly this wholesale destruction by Labour of the best financial aspects of the British colonial territories will enhance the offshore standing of truly independent haven nations such as Switzerland, Austria, Luxembourg and Panama.

Where are the Real Money Laundering Havens?

By Mark Nestmann, *The Sovereign Individual*, November 2003

For over a decade, governments worldwide, along with organizations such as the Organization for Economic Cooperation and Development (OECD) and its bastard stepchild, the Financial Action Task Force (FATF), have conducted a full-court press on small offshore financial centers (OFCs) alleged to be "money laundering havens."

We have documented these efforts—the FATF's infamous "blacklist,"and, after the events of September 11, 2001, the notorious "USA PATRIOT Act," along with similar anti-OFC vendettas carried out in other high-tax countries.

The truth, however, is that there is far more money laundered in OECD member countries than in the OFCs that they are targeting. For proof, you need to read between the lines of the statistics trotted out to justify the crackdown on OFCs. For instance, the FATF quotes the World Bank as stating that between US$500 billion-US$1.5 trillion is laundered each year. But every U.S. government agency that has studied money laundering has concluded that OFCs do not attract a disproportionate share of laundered funds.

Instead, laundering predominates in the world's largest economies—all members of the OECD.

Indeed, about half of global money laundering activity is in the United States. The crackdown on OFCs due to their alleged involvement in "terrorism" doesn't hold water, either. To date, virtually all the funds used in last September's attacks on the United States have been traced to either OECD countries or in a handful of Islamic countries.

Why then, are the OECD, FATF and many governments trying to eliminate OFCs? The crackdown has very little to do with fighting money laundering or terrorism and everything to do with collecting taxes. As we've documented in recent issues, the OECD's spurious onslaught against OFCs alleged to engage in "harmful tax competition" has been completely discredited due to the refusal of the world's largest OFC—again, the United States—to participate in this effort. The FATF's vendetta against OFCs should also be discredited, for the same reason—its most important member is the single largest source of laundered funds.

There are signs that the attack against OFCs may abate, at least temporarily. This is due to infighting between the FATF and the largest (and by far the richest) of all "multilateral" organizations, the International Monetary Fund (IMF). Now, we are hardly fans of IMF taxpayer-financed bailouts of third-world countries. Indeed, IMF aid directly contributes to money laundering, since much of it, as U.S. Treasury Secretary Paul O'Neill recently observed, winds up stashed by the corrupt leaders of recipient governments in offshore bank accounts!

For months, the IMF and the FATF have been trying to forge a joint approach to fight terrorist financing, but the IMF's Board (some members of which are blacklisted countries) is now insisting on a year's moratorium on the FATF's next blacklist as the price of the IMF's co-operation. The FATF has responded by temporarily suspending its blacklist. OFCs can breathe a little easier, if not for long.

Since most laundering occurs in OECD countries, does that mean they should take even more draconian measures than they have already—more seizures, less financial privacy, more restrictions on cash transactions, etc.? Not at all. These approaches have been spectacularly unsuccessful. Indeed, the percentage of funds "laundered" in OECD economies is about the same today as it was two decades ago when the "War on Laundering" began.

What, then, is the answer to the laundering "crisis" in OECD countries? We have suggested that the real problem is that laundering laws are designed principally to punish crimes where there is no identifiable victim, such as drug offenses. Decriminalization or partial legalization would be far preferable from a civil liberties standpoint than providing governments even greater powers to incarcerate and seize property.

In contrast, where there is an identifiable victim of fraud or other wrongdoing, the legal tools needed for effective deterrence are already in place. They just need to be more effectively employed.

CHAPTER NINE
Very Special Places

The small nations and territories we name in this chapter each have a big business sense about what you need—expert banking, reliable professional assistance, instant worldwide communications and a well-developed code of laws to support high-stakes financial activity.

Not all offshore havens are equal. We tell you which ones are best and which to avoid. Here you will learn the secrets of the rich who are not, and do not wish to become, famous.

We show you ways and explain means so that you can join them offshore.

Good Places to Do Business
The Business Haven Report, 1997

What follows is a general description of the characteristics of those nations or territories that have tailored their laws to be hospitable to foreign businesses. Many of these areas also impose no taxes on foreign citizens who live in or have their businesses based in these states.

Imagine living in a large estate with servants to handle all the mundane chores. Imagine running your own business, setting your own hours, having plenty of money to do what you want when you want to do it. Imagine traveling and entertaining. Imagine being wealthy.

A dream? Not at all. A life like that is well within your reach if you are willing to work hard and make the right business choices. The first, and most important, decision is to locate your business in a nation that caters to international business—a "business haven" if you will. But what, exactly, is a business haven?

A business haven is a place—it may be a country or a region-where an individual, partnership, company, or corporation is given significant incentives to establish an active business. Because the government or ruling body of a business haven wants to attract new businesses, it offers the owners of businesses major advantages to locate their enterprises there. Such inducements might be tax-free situations, tax holidays (for example, several years tax-free for specific operations), long-term, low-interest loans for new businesses, reduced rents for factory space, or other vital benefits.

In addition to these factors, many business havens also offer well-educated, highly motivated workforces at compensation rates well below those of the major industrialized nations. Thus, low overhead coupled with major incentives results in increased profitability.

While some countries qualify as business havens because of their pro-business policies, in many cases a business haven may be found in a particular part of a country. Often these areas go by the name of "free zones" or similar designations. They are found throughout the world.

The opportunities are limited only by your imagination. Think of all the kinds of businesses citizens of industrialized countries take for granted, from fast-food restaurants to convenience stores, to telecommunications firms to small specialty manufacturers and quiet bed and breakfast resorts.

Countless businesses are candidates to start new or relocate in a business haven. Of course you would need to carefully scrutinize the business haven you are considering to make sure that the business you are proposing would be successful there, but if it's not, simply choose one that is or consider a different business haven.

However, a few words of caution are necessary.

1. Thoroughly research any business haven both for the inducements it offers and any potential drawbacks. Write to the embassy of the country or unit that oversees the business haven and ask for all the information they can send you. Many business havens have special agencies that act as liaisons between the government of the business haven and entrepreneurs or corporations that would like to establish a business there. These agencies can streamline paperwork and put you in touch with the people who will provide you with the facts you'll need to make a sound decision.

2. Visit the business haven before making any commitments. See if the facts you have learned hold up under personal investigation. See if you like the area and the lifestyle you will be living there.

3. Before signing any agreements, have your attorney review them carefully. Your attorney should have experience with international business relations. Don't agree to any contracts unless you are entirely satisfied. Remember: everything is negotiable. It won't hurt to ask.

4. Assess your potential overhead (be sure to include all your costs) and expected income carefully. Be certain that your venture is worth your investment of time and money.

5. If you are entering into the venture with partners, discuss their business attitudes and goals, and make sure that they match yours. It's not unusual for partners to find it more difficult to deal with each other than with the representatives of a business haven. This is especially true if your partner is from the country in which the business haven is located. Above all, remember that the choices you make in establishing a business will affect the business overall profitability. Decisions based on first-hand experience can be the difference between a business that achieves great success and one that remains mediocre in performance.

Business havens offer entrepreneurs and corporations a marvelous chance to begin an enterprise with significant economic incentives and advantages on foreign soil. If you wish to expand your business, start a new business, or begin a new life in a different part of the world, exploring the opportunities presented by business havens is an option you must consider.

The World's Best Asset Havens: #1 - Switzerland

by Robert E. Bauman, JD, *The Sovereign Individual*, May 2003

In preparing a survey of the world's top asset havens, we reviewed the laws, political stability, economic climate, tax situation and the overall "clout" in dozens of different jurisdictions.

We narrowed our choices down to four top jurisdictions: Switzerland, Panama, Liechtenstein and Hong Kong. Plus, we listed several havens as "honorable mention."

To evaluate each jurisdiction, we reviewed five factors:

* Government/political stability: How long has the current system of government been in place? Is the jurisdiction politically stable?

* Favorable laws, judicial system: How long a tradition has the haven had? Does its legal and judicial system have reputation for "fair play" with regard to foreign investors?

* Available legal entities: Does the jurisdiction have a large enough variety of legal entities to satisfy the average person seeking an estate planning or business solution?

* Financial privacy/banking secrecy: Does the jurisdiction have financial secrecy laws? How strictly are they applied? What exceptions to secrecy exist?

* Taxes: Does the haven impose taxes on foreign investors? How easily can these taxes be avoided legally? Are there tax treaties or tax information exchange agreements in effect?

Our winner in terms of the highest number of points achieved is Switzerland. However, because of the high minimum investments necessary to deal with most Swiss financial institutions, we believe that Panama provides a more practical offshore solution for most members of The Sovereign Society.

And the Winner is . . . Switzerland, Still the World's Best Money Haven!

In spite of the many compromises the Swiss have been forced to make under world pressures, Switzerland today still stands as the world's best all-around offshore banking and asset protection haven.

A Reputation to Uphold

A global survey of private banks published by Price Waterhouse Coopers (PWC), found that the major attraction for a bank's new customers is its reputation. Certainly, Switzerland's solid financial reputation is central to the claim that this mountainous nation serves as "banker to the world."

For 250 years, as European empires and nations rose and fell, Swiss topography and determination have combined to defend this Alpine redoubt, while maintaining more or less strict neutrality towards other nations.

In 1945, after the 20th century's second "war to end all wars," Swiss voters overwhelmingly rejected membership in the United Nations. It was not until 2002 that a bare majority backed U.N. membership.

In 1992 and 2001 national polls, Swiss voters also rejected membership in the European Union, rightly fearing EU bureaucratic interference with Swiss privacy and banking laws. A few years ago, a national ballot soundly rejected a specific proposal to ease Swiss bank secrecy laws.

After each of these national plebiscites, and during world recessions, even greater amounts of foreign cash flowed into Swiss banks, confirming the widespread notion that Switzerland is the place to safeguard cash and other personal assets. It is estimated that currently Swiss banks manage at least one third of all assets held offshore by the world's wealthy. As a safe haven for cash, Switzerland has become something of a modern cliche.

But in recent years, the nation's image as bankers to the world's rich has taken some severe hits. In 1998, Swiss banks paid US$1.25 billion into a fund for Holocaust survivors to settle claims made by World War II-era depositors and their heirs based on the banks' alleged collaboration with Nazi Germany.

Equally disturbing to privacy seekers is the major Swiss banks' surrender under pressure to demands of the U.S. Federal Reserve System. The 1998 merger of Swiss Bank Corp. and Union Bank of Switzerland creating UBS AG was approved by the U.S. Federal Reserve only after the banking giant agreed to provide U.S. regulators all information "necessary to determine and enforce compliance with ...[U.S.] federal law." No doubt, that means U.S. tax laws too. U.S. regulators had threatened to shut down the bank's extensive U.S. operations, and rather than defend their client's privacy rights, the bank compromised.

As a result, U.S. depositors considering Swiss banks should avoid UBS AG and any other Swiss bank with U.S. based branches, affiliates or banking operations, other than a mere "representative office."

Times Are Changing

Despite these privacy setbacks, the Swiss financial system, warts and all, still has plenty going for it. Unless there is a strong suspicion of criminal wrongdoing, under Swiss law it is still a crime for bankers to violate the secrecy of their clients. Most Swiss banks still refuse to expose records to foreign tax authorities, although UBS AG may not be able to resist such demands based on its agreement with the Feds.

But success can breed notoriety. Having a Swiss bank account today is a red flag for home country tax collectors. This is particularly true within the high-tax European Union. Plainclothes tax police from neighboring France stalk the streets of Geneva, recording French-registered auto license plates. They then call ahead to have the cars stopped and searched at the French border. France also systematically screens mail to and from Switzerland for magnetically striped checks. Two French tax officials were arrested for bribing a Swiss bank employee to provide computer tapes of client account data.

Although distance constraints force U.S. IRS agents to be somewhat less zealous than their French counterparts, U.S. nationals who visit Swiss banks regularly or receive business mail with Swiss postmarks may find themselves subjected to IRS audits. Then too, in 2003, a supplemental annex to the existing U.S.-Swiss tax treaty came into effect, which expands Swiss cooperation with the IRS—although "fishing expeditions" into Swiss accounts by U.S. tax authorities still aren't permitted.

The Very Special Swiss Franc

Switzerland's currency, the Swiss franc, generally has reflected the state of Swiss banking: strong, valuable and unaffected by inflation and stylish monetary fads.

Since 1971, the franc has appreciated nearly 300% against the U.S. dollar. U.S. owners of Swiss franc denominated assets have profited handsomely as a result. That profit came despite traditionally low Swiss interest rates and the bothersome 35% withholding tax on bank interest. In recent years, the value of the franc has fluctuated against the U.S. dollar, strengthening in the early 1990s, weakening from 1995-2001, and strengthening once again in the last two years.

The 1934 Bank Secrecy Law

The rise of Hitler and Nazi Germany in the early 1930s prompted the famous 1934 Swiss bank secrecy law that remains in force today. That law was an effort to stop Nazi agents from bribing bank employees for information about the accounts of German citizens and expatriates. The law protects foreign depositors from unwarranted intrusions into their bank privacy, although now it has been tempered in many important ways.

Swiss banks are prohibited from responding to inquiries about an individual account, whether from attorneys, credit rating services or foreign governments. The law punishes violations of bank secrecy with fines up to Sfr50,000 (US$33,000) and six months in prison. In most cases, the Swiss government cannot obtain information about an account without a court order. To obtain an order, investigators must demonstrate the probable violation of Swiss law and that there is reason to believe the particular account at issue is involved in that violation. Non-payment of taxes is not a crime in Switzerland, but "tax fraud" is, and, as you'll soon learn, that can be a rather elastic phrase.

In spite of its reputation for bank secrecy, in 1990 Switzerland was one of the first European countries to make money laundering a criminal offense. That law resulted in the demise of the famous Swiss compte anonyme, as the French-speaking Swiss termed it. Previously, it was possible to open a nominee account in which the identity of the beneficial owner need not be revealed to the bank.

Since 1994, a central office in Bern has been devoted exclusively to fighting organized crime. Mandatory "know your customer" guidelines are used by Swiss banks to investigate potential clients. Banks are particularly attentive to prospective clients that try to open an account with more than SFr25,000 in cash or its equivalent in foreign currency.

On April 1, 1998, a new and even stricter money laundering law took effect that transformed the face of Swiss banking in a fundamental way. Previously, bankers had the option of reporting suspicious transactions to police authorities. Now, under pressure from world governments pursuing corruption, drug cartels and organized crime, Switzerland requires banks to report suspicious transactions. Failure to report is a crime; bankers can now go to prison for keeping secret the names and records of suspect clients. In another era, not so long ago, they faced imprisonment for failing to keep such secrets.

Using these new statutes, in a few cases Switzerland has actually released information in circumstances not involving a crime under Swiss law. The Swiss government has proven itself willing to freeze assets before an individual is even charged with a crime if a foreign government can demonstrate "reasonable suspicion" that the accused engaged in criminal conduct. This is especially the case in high-profile drug or corruption cases.

Unfortunately for the Swiss, the government's money laundering investigations have become a national political issue. Several officials at the Bern office responsible for investigating money laundering have resigned to protest what they charged was lax enforcement of these laws. And outside pressure continues.

But there are limits to how far the Swiss will go. In 2001, the Swiss parliament rejected a new, even stricter laundering bill. And, the Swiss have successfully resisted enormous pressure from the G-7 nations and its public relations arm, the OECD, as well as the European Union, to further compromise banking secrecy. At issue was imposition on the Swiss of the EU's "savings tax directive" which aimed at free exchange among all EU governments of any EU citizen's investment and banking records. The intrusive plan was sold as an anti-tax evasion measure, but it would have ended all financial privacy.

World Class Banking System

Although Swiss banking privacy is legendary, secrecy is not the most important reason for Switzerland's success. Of far greater significance are the country's political, financial and economic stability and strength. Most of the world's largest companies and hundreds of thousands of honest, law-abiding foreigners bank with the Swiss. Indeed, Swiss banks manage over two trillion Swiss francs, approximately US$1.4 trillion! Even the international intermediary banking institution, the Bank for International Settlements, is located in Switzerland.

Switzerland is home to several hundred banks ranging from small private and regional banks to the two giants, Union Bank of Switzerland (UBS AG) and Credit Suisse. These major Swiss banks have branch offices in most of the world's financial centers, from New York to Panama.

Swiss banks are unequaled as a base for global investing. Opening a Swiss bank account can be a first move in developing a strategy of safety and international diversification. An individual, corporation, trust, foundation, pension plan or any other legal entity can open an account.

Swiss banks combine traditional banking with international brokerage and financial management. To guard against inflation or devaluation, Swiss bank accounts can be denominated in the currency you choose—Swiss francs, U.S. dollars or any major currency. An account opened in one currency can be switched to another denomination when the time is right for short-term profits or long-term gains and safety.

You can invest in certificates of deposit, U.S. and other national stocks, bonds, mutual funds and commodities; buy, store and sell gold, silver and other precious metals; and buy insurance and annuities.Swiss banks can act as your agent to buy and hold other types of assets. Of course, Swiss banks also issue international credit and ATM bank cards.

To some extent, "know your customer" rules have complicated the process of opening a bank account in Switzerland, and proof of identity and references are required. Bank officers speak several languages with English as a must. Swiss banks are equipped for fax, wire, e-mail or telex and instructions are carried out immediately. Or just phone your own personal banker who handles your account.

The biggest downside to banking in Switzerland is the high minimum deposits necessary at most banks. While only a few years ago, many banks were content with initial deposits of only a few thousand dollars, Switzerland's popularity among foreign investors, along with the cost of administering "know your customer" laws, has led to sharp increases in deposit minimums, which now average about US$100,000.

An option for smaller bank accounts can be found in banks run by the various Swiss "cantons," as the largely self-governing provinces are called. These banks offer full services, have relatively low minimum deposits and each cantonal government insures the deposits.

Strict Control, High Quality

Swiss banks have attained their unique position because of financial expertise, honesty, international capabilities and the high percentage and quality of their reserves, much of it in gold and Swiss francs. The Swiss financial industry is tightly regulated, with banks strictly supervised by the Federal Banking Commission (FBC).

Swiss law imposes stiff liquidity and capital requirements on banks. The complicated official liquidity formula results in some private banks maintaining liquidity at or near 100%, unheard of in other national banking systems. Every month, Swiss banks with securities investments must write the value of their holdings to market price or actual cost, whichever is lower. That assures no Swiss banks will have unrealized paper losses as often happens in other countries.

Swiss banks are also subjected to two regular audits. The first audit is to insure compliance with the Swiss corporation law. The second is the banking audit, conducted by one of seventeen audit firms specially approved by the FBC. These exacting audits provide the primary guarantee for Swiss bank depositors. Supervision and regulation of Swiss banking surpasses any other nation and the banks have comprehensive insurance to cover deposits, transfers, theft or abnormal losses. The Swiss reputation also rests on the fact that banks traditionally hold substantial unreported, hidden reserves.

The Fiduciary Investment Account

One popular Swiss account for foreign investors is the fiduciary account. A Swiss bank investment manager oversees the account, but all its investments are placed outside Switzerland, as the account holder directs. Funds that pass through the account are therefore not subject to Swiss taxes.

The two types of accounts are the fiduciary investment account and the fiduciary loan account. With the investment account, the bank places the client's funds as loans to foreign banks in the form of fixed-term deposits. In the loan account, the customer designates the commercial borrower.

Although the bank assumes no risk, it provides an important service by conducting a thorough investigation of the prospective borrower's credit credentials. Many international companies use fiduciary loans to finance subsidiaries.

There is an element of risk in making such loans. In the event of a currency devaluation, or the bankruptcy of the borrower, the lender can lose.

Discretionary Accounts

With over 250 years in the international portfolio management business, Swiss banks are among world leaders in investment management. Experienced money managers constantly analyze world markets, choosing investments with the greatest potential and a minimum of risk. Swiss banks offer a broad selection of investment plans diversified by industry, country, international or emerging markets. Outside financial managers can be employed to invest deposited funds and bank loans can be arranged for investment purposes.

These accounts are best managed by a private Swiss bank or alternatively, a Swiss portfolio manager. The Swiss invented what has come to be called "private banking." They honed private banking to a fine edge centuries before U.S. "cookie cutter" banks discovered the concept. With a private bank, you get personal contact and individual service. However, most private banks require an initial US$250,000 minimum investment and a personal introduction from a source well known to them.

The Swiss Alternative: Insurance

Switzerland is also a world-renowned center for insurance and reinsurance. Many Swiss insurance companies offer a broad range of financial services that in some cases approach the flexibility of a bank account. Indeed, many Swiss residents use their insurance company as their only financial institution.

Swiss insurance policies offer other important advantages:

- They generally offer higher interest rates than bank accounts.

- Unlike a bank account, they may be configured to offer significant asset protection

- Swiss 35% withholding tax on earned bank interest is not imposed on insurance accounts.

Note: Effective Feb. 9, 1998, amendments to U.S. tax law ended the tax deferral previously allowed on fixed annuity contracts issued by foreign insurance companies after April 7, 1995. All such annuity income must now be reported as part of taxable annual income. However, income from properly structured foreign variable annuities and life insurance contracts generally remains tax deferred.

Switzerland and Taxes

Switzerland is not a low-tax country for Swiss residents or companies, although tax rates are lower than in the EU. But foreign investors can avoid many local taxes by choosing certain types of investments that escape taxes.

By law, Swiss banks collect a withholding tax of 35% on all interest and dividends paid by Swiss companies, banks, the government or other sources. Foreign investors to whom this tax applies may be eligible for refunds of all or part of the tax under the terms of Switzerland's network of more than 50 tax treaties.

In addition, there are many legal ways to avoid Swiss taxes by investing in accounts structured for foreign investors. These include non-Swiss money market and bond funds, fiduciary precious metal accounts and other instruments. For instance, Switzerland imposes no taxes on dividends or interest from securities that originate outside Switzerland. For this reason, many Swiss banks offer investment funds with at least 80% of earnings in foreign investments or, even better, in money-market funds located in Luxembourg or Ireland.

Tax Treaties Abound

To reduce the possibility that Swiss citizens or companies might be subject to double taxation, the Swiss government has entered into a global network of more than 50 tax treaties.

Tax treaties, however, have the unfortunate by-product of eroding financial secrecy. It is not possible to claim a tax credit under a tax treaty without also revealing the income that was taxed. In addition, tax treaties have a dual purpose: they exist not only to help individuals and companies investing or doing business internationally to avoid double taxation, but also to facilitate information exchange between tax authorities.

The U.S.-Swiss tax treaty, which came into effect in 1997, is a case in point. While nonpayment of taxes is not a crime in Switzerland, Article 26 permits the two governments to exchange information about alleged tax fraud. It also allows authorities to transfer information that may help in the "prevention of tax fraud and the like in relation to taxes." IRS officials claim this expansive definition opens up previously secret Swiss bank information, streamlining Swiss judicial procedures for finding tax evaders. According to alarmists, this gives the U.S. government the right to access Swiss bank information when IRS agents utter the magic words, "tax fraud."

The Protocol accompanying the new treaty defines "tax fraud" as, "fraudulent conduct that causes or is intended to cause an illegal and substantial reduction in the amount of tax paid to a Contracting State."

However, a careful reading of Article 26 negates claims that the Swiss bank secrecy has now yielded to the demands of the IRS. In fact, the official "Comments on Article 26" states, "the New Treaty does not significantly modify the exchange of information clause that was applicable under the 1951 Treaty."

The U.S. undoubtedly presses hard to bend Swiss bank secrecy in specific cases. But this new treaty did little more than codify the Swiss view that bank secrecy should be waived only in extreme cases, and certainly not for unsubstantiated "fishing expeditions" launched by the IRS.

Tax Advantaged Residency

Although it is not generally known, for those who wish to retire in Switzerland, it is possible to negotiate a lump sum annual income tax payment (known as a forfait) with cantonal tax authorities. The more populous and popular cantons are likely to charge more, but the smallest, Appenzell, will settle for around Swf65,000 (US$45,000) per year, regardless of your actual income. The difficulty comes in obtaining a Swiss residency permit, an extremely scarce commodity. But if you are wealthy and offer proof of sufficient future income, you may qualify.

Contacts

Banks

- *Banque Union de Credit (BUC)*, Rue du Mont-Blanc 3, P.O. Box 1176, 1211 Geneva 1. **Tel.:** +(41) 22-732-7939. **Fax:** +(41) 22-732-5089.

- *Banque SCS Alliance*, 18 rue de Contamines, 1206 Geneva. **Tel.:** +(41) 22-346-1281. **Fax:** +(41) 22-346-1530. Director of Financiere for SCS Alliance in New York is Elisabeth Cerrone, Tel.: (800) 226-5727.

Private Banks

- *Bank Julius Baer*, Bahnhofstrasse 36, P.O. Box, CH-8010 Zurich **Tel.:** +(41) 1 228-5111. **Fax:** +(41) 1 211 2560. http://www.juliusbaer.com.

  U.S. Representative office: 251 Royal Palm Way, Suite 601, Palm Beach Fla. **Tel.:** +1 (407) 659-4440. **Fax:** +1 (407) 659-4744: Owned and managed by the founding family, this private bank serves clients with the same discretion it has offered for over a century. This is the place for those of great wealth who want a private relationship with sophisticated international bankers.

- *Banque Piguet & Cie SA*, rue de la Plaine, 14, CH-1400, Yverdon-Les-Bains, Switzerland. **Tel.:** +(41) 24-423-4300. **Fax:** +(41) 24-423-4308. Banque Piguet & Cie was founded in 1856 and is owned by Banque Cantonale Vaudoise, the fourth largest Swiss banking group. Throughout its 140-year history, Banque Piguet & Cie has specialized in private banking with the utmost in confidentiality, professionalism and personal service.

Financial Consultants

- *Robert Vrijhof*, partner, Weber, Hartman, Vrijhof & Partners Ltd., Zurichstrasse 110 B, CH-8134 Adliswil-Zurich. **Tel.:** +(41) 1-709-1115. **Fax:** +(41) 1-709-1113. This asset management company offers a wide range of services including investment counseling, formation of companies and trusts, estate planning and mergers and acquisitions. Rob Vrijhof serves on the Sovereign Society Council of Experts.

- *Marc Sola*, NMG International Financial Services Goethestrasse 22 8001 Zurich Switzerland. **Tel.:** +(41) 1-266-2141. **Fax:** +(41) 1-266-2149. E-mail: marcsola@nmg-ifs.com. Mr. Sola has extensive experience in Swiss life insurance and annuities, and serves on the Sovereign Society Council of Experts.

- *Christian Kälin*, Henley & Partners, Kirchgasse 24, 8001 Zurich Switzerland. **Tel.:** +(41) 1-267-6090. **Fax:** +(41) 1-267-6091. E-mail: chris.kalin@henleyglobal.com. Link: http://www.henleyglobal.com. Henley & Partners are specialists in tax advantaged residency and provide international tax planning services for private clients worldwide. Mr. Kälin serves on the Sovereign Society Council of Experts.

The World's Best Asset Havens: #2 - Panama
by Robert E. Bauman, JD, *The Sovereign Individual*, May 2003

Privacy and Profits in the World's Most Useful Asset Haven

Alone among current offshore tax havens, Panama combines maximum financial privacy, a long history of judicial enforcement of asset protection-friendly laws, strong anti-money laundering laws, tax exemptions for foreigners and, due to its unique historic relationship with the United States, a high degree of independence from outside pressures.

Along with the old millennium, 96 years of official United States presence in the Republic of Panama ended at midnight, Dec. 31, 1999. Panama finally got what its nationalistic politicians had demanded for much of the last century—full Panamanian control over its famous inter-oceanic Canal.

When most people hear "Panama," they think of the canal. But the country is not so well known for what it has become in the last three decades—after Miami, it is Latin America's second major international banking and business center, with strong ties to Asia, Europe and a special relationship with the United States that, however contentious, continues apace.

New Era?

Panama is rapidly attaining world-class tax haven status. Indeed, in many respects—financial privacy, solid asset protection and freedom from outside political pressures—Panama has moved to the head of the class.

However, Panama remains a third world country, with much of its population mired in poverty. In world rankings, Panama is classed as a middle-income country, with annual per capita income of US$3,000. But more than one million Panamanians, 37% of the people, live in poverty, half of those in extreme poverty, surviving on US$50 a month. This proportion has changed little since 1970, in spite of 5% average annual gross domestic product growth. The richest 20% of the population earns 60% of the country's annual income, while the poorest fifth earn just 2%, according to a

World Bank study.

Nevertheless, Panama is in much better shape financially than its Central American neighbors to the north, or Colombia to the south. Although economic growth has slowed in recent years, Panama still receives more than US$2 billion annually in foreign investments. For the last 45 years, inflation averaged only 2.4% per annum; during the 1990s barely exceeding 1% per year. Annual inflation has averaged 1.4% for the past 30 years, much lower than in the United States.

Then there is the wealth represented by the canal, generating nearly US$1 billion in annual revenues. While much of this income must be plowed back into maintenance, profits from the canal represent Panama's largest source of income. And in a move that could turn the current flow of 14,000 annual ship transits into a flood, the government is now planning to invest US$6 billion into widening the canal and building bigger locks.

There are also the thousands of acres of land from former U.S. military installations, prized real estate with an estimated value of US$4 billion. Admittedly, its distribution and privatization has been slow and marked by charges of corruption, but development of this property in the next few decades will undoubtedly bring significant benefits to Panama.

Panama Revisited

In 1999, I returned to Panama for the first time in 20 years. Since then, I have visited five more times.

It's a very different place than I remember during my many visits in the 1970s when I served in the U.S. House of Representatives as the ranking Republican on the Panama Canal subcommittee. My visits then were made during U.S. legislative implementation of the Carter-Torjillos treaty negotiations.

Upon my return, I marveled at the modern skyscrapers, first class hotels and restaurants, excellent digital Internet and other international communications, as well as the reduced U.S. ambiance. Downtown Panama City, the balmy, tropical capital on the southern, Pacific end of the Canal, suggests Los Angeles or Miami, except arguably more locals speak English here than in some parts of south Florida.

Yes, Panama also has a long history of government corruption that continues to this day. This hasn't seemed to affect the loosely regulated banking sector, but bribery, cronyism, nepotism and kick backs in government dealings regularly make headlines here. But isn't that true of the United States as well?

Privacy, Profits and No Taxes

In many ways, the Republic of Panama is ideally suited for the offshore investor who wants to enjoy the increasingly rare privilege of strong, legally guaranteed financial privacy and no taxes, either corporate or personal. Unlike Bermuda and the Cayman islands, Panama pointedly refused to sign the OECD memorandum of understanding that would have committed it to exchanging information with tax authorities in OECD countries.

According to Canada's Fraser Institute, Panama is near the top of the list of the world's freest economies, ranked eighth with Australia, Ireland, the Netherlands and Luxembourg. Panama has adopted more than 40 laws protecting foreigners' financial and investment rights, including the Investments Stability Law (Law No. 54), which guarantees foreign and local investors equal rights.

Panama's central location makes it a natural base for world business operations. Most importantly, and in spite of its history, Panama isn't directly under the thumb of the United States. And unlike the British overseas territories of Bermuda and the Cayman Islands, it isn't under the control of Tony Blair's Labourite Foreign Office in London.

Among the current 80 plus banks, the major players are the 58 multinational banks representing 30 countries that primarily conduct offshore business. They hold 72% of a reported total US$37 billion in total assets. Banking alone accounts for about 11% of Panama's GNP.

Nearly every one of the world's major banks has a full-service branch office in Panama, with representation from Japan, Germany, Brazil and the United States. Derek Sambrook, a veteran international bank regulator and trust expert based in Panama points out: "Brass plate banks represented by a law firm, for example, are not permitted in Panama and the 82 banks that do operate are fully staffed and functional. Compare that with the Cayman Islands that until recently had nearly 500 banks, but less than ten that are full-service retail banks."

Admittedly, it's taken time for the banking sector's reputation to recover from the aftermath of the 1988 U.S. military invasion ordered by former U.S. president George H.W. Bush. In the invasion's aftermath, under the direction of DEA and FBI agents, invading U.S. troops hauled away bank records alleged to show criminal conduct by the deposed president, Manuel Antonio Noriega and his regime. That Noriega had long been in the pay of the U.S. Central Intelligence Agency did not protect him when he outlived his usefulness.

Since then, Panama's bankers have been anxious to reassert the sanctity of their banking secrecy laws.

Reasserting Financial Privacy

Along with other established havens such as Luxembourg and Liechtenstein, Panama is one of the world's oldest tax havens, with legislation establishing tax advantages for corporations dating back to the 1920s.

A central part of the long tax haven tradition has been statutory guarantees of financial privacy and confidentiality. Violators can suffer civil and criminal penalties for unauthorized disclosure. There is no requirement to reveal beneficial trust or corporate ownership to Panama authorities and no required audit reports or financial statements. Bearer shares are still permitted.

Panama has no double taxation agreements and no tax information exchange agreements with other countries. Pressured by Washington to sign a TIEA with the United States, Panama has politely ignored such demands. In contrast, under American and British pressure in the last few years, numerous so-called "privacy" havens have capitulated, including The Bahamas, Bermuda, the Cayman Islands, the British Virgin Islands, the Isle of Man and the Channel Islands of Jersey and Guernsey.

This fact means that in U.S. government circles, a bank account in Panama raises immediate suspicion about the account holder. But that's also true of accounts in Switzerland, Liechtenstein and anywhere else that the IRS can't readily stick its official nose into private financial activity.

Still, Panama has made a significant effort to reform its banking system to minimize corruption and insure that banking secrecy can be lifted in criminal investigations. However, this occurred only after significant pressure from the international community. In June 2000, the OECD's Financial Action Task Force (FATF) placed Panama on a blacklist of 15 countries alleged to be tolerant of money laundering. In October 2000, Panama's Congress unanimously approved a strong anti-money laundering law in line with FATF recommendations. In June 2001, the nation was removed from the FATF blacklist. The new law covers all crimes and brings all financial institutions under the supervision of the government banking agency.

In contrast, Panama has stoutly resisted the OECD's demands for the imposition of taxes on foreign investors. In a ringing speech in late 2002, Panama's foreign minister denounced OECD "imperialism" and said flatly his nation will not bow to such outside pressures. Panama's defense of tax competition has created major opportunities for it. One opportunity comes from the EU decision in January 2003 to impose EU-wide withholding taxes on income from savings.2 Under the deal, the tax will start at 15% in 2004 and rise to 35% by 2010. All EU countries, and Switzerland, will impose this tax on deposits from all EU residents and companies.

The withholding tax agreement, if implemented as currently construed, will inevitably lead EU funds to non-EU financial centers that don't impose such taxes, and that don't routinely exchange financial information with tax authorities. Panama qualifies on both counts.

The Yankee Dollar

While "dollarization" is debated as a novel concept elsewhere in Latin America, since 1904 the U.S. dollar has been Panama's official paper currency.

Panama has no central bank to print money and as Juan Luis Moreno-Villalaz, an economic adviser to Panama 's Ministry of Economy and Finance recently noted: "In Panama... there has never been a systemic banking crisis; indeed, in several instances international banks have acted as the system's lender of last resort. The Panamanian system provides low interest rates, around 9% on mortgages and commercial loans. Credit is ample, with 30-year mortgages readily available. These are unusual conditions for a developing country and are largely achieved because there is no exchange rate risk, a low risk of financial crises, and ample flow of funds from abroad."

If Panama has a major financial worry, it is the government's deficit spending. In early 2003, Standard and Poor's reduced Panama's public bond rating from BB with a stable outlook, to BB with a negative outlook. In part, this was due to an accounting gimmick in which the government included Canal revenues when counting official income in order to make the deficit look smaller. (The Canal treaties forbid the mixing of Canal revenue with that of the Panamanian government).

Because of the declining quality of Panamanian government bonds, we don't recommend investing in them. But apart from this precaution, the fiscal status of Panama's government does not detract from its overall attraction as a premier offshore center.

Welcome Bankers

Panama grew as an international financial center after enactment of Decree No.c238 of July 1970, a liberal banking law that also abolished all currency controls. The law exempts offshore business in Panama from income tax and from taxes on interest earned in domestic savings accounts and offshore transactions. In 1999, a comprehensive new Banking Law was enacted that accelerated Panama's growth as a leading world offshore finance center.

The 1999 law uses the guidelines of the Basle Committee on Banking Supervision, requiring all banks with unrestricted domestic or international commercial banking license to maintain capital equivalent to at least 8% of total assets. Government investigative powers and tighter general controls were increased, bringing Panama in line with regulatory standards found in European and North American banking centers. Although confidentiality is reaffirmed in the new law, a prima facie case of illicit financial conduct can launch an investigation of possible criminal conduct. The law also permits foreign bank regulators to make inspection visits to any of their domestic banks with branches in Panama.

Panama's growing financial sector also includes an active stock exchange, captive insurance and re-insurance companies and financial and leasing companies.

Another major business and financial attraction at the Atlantic end of the Canal is the booming Colon Free Zone (http://www.zonalibre.com), a major tax-free transshipment facility, the second largest free trade zone in the world, after Hong Kong.

IBCs and Foundations

Panama has liberal laws favoring trusts, international business companies and holding companies. In 1995, it enacted Law No. 25, a new private foundation statute modeled after the popular Stiftung or family wealth protection and estate planning vehicle long used in Liechtenstein. That law allows the tax-free family foundation to be used for investment, tax sheltering, commercial business and private activity, with the founder retaining lifetime control. Foundation assets are not counted as part of the founder's estate for death tax purposes, and Panama does not recognize the often-restrictive inheritance laws of other nations.

Some argue that the Panamanian private foundation law is only a relatively untested clone of the Liechtenstein law. While it is true that the Panamanian law is much newer, the costs of operating a foundation in Panama are lower than they are in Liechtenstein. For South American clients and others from civil law backgrounds who are unfamiliar with the concept of an Anglo-American trust, a Panamanian private foundation often represents an ideal estate planning solution.

Panama's international business company (IBC) Law 32 of 1927, is modeled after the U.S. State of Delaware's corporation friendly statutes. There are about 350,000 IBCs registered in Panama, second only to Hong Kong's 400,000. A Panamanian IBC can maintain its own corporate bank account and credit cards for global management of investments, mutual funds, precious metals, real estate and trade. Tax-free corporate income can be spent for business purposes worldwide and using the Panama IBC allows avoidance of home country zoning, labor, manufacturing, warranty, environmental and other restrictions.

Leading Retirement Haven

Despite its relatively advanced industrial and financial infrastructure, Panama remains an affordable place in which to live. A live-in maid earns about US$120 a month; first-run movies cost US$1.50. Unlike much of Central America, Panama boasts a first class health care system with low costs compared to the United States. A doctor's office visit costs about US$15.

Because of Panama's geographical diversity, there is considerable climatic variation. Panama City, the historical and financial center, has a year-round tropical climate. Yet, only a few hundred miles away is a sub-tropical forest, with cascading waterfalls, mountainsides covered with flowers, and spring-like weather year-round.

There are also many low priced buys on condos and other real estate, particularly in Panama City and the surrounding areas, a byproduct in part of the U.S. government exodus.

The government makes retirement in Panama easy, and laws provide important tax advantages for foreigners who wish to become residents. The only significant requirements are good health and a verifiable monthly income of at least US$500. There are no local taxes on foreign income and you can import your household goods tax-free.

Contacts

Banks:

- *Banco Continental*, Banco Continental Tower, 50 Street & Aquilino De La Guardia Ave., Panama 6, Republic of Panama. **Tel.:** +(507) 215-7000. **Fax:** +(507) 215-7134

- *National Bank of Panama* (Banco Internacional de Panama), P.O. Box 11181, Panama 6, Republic of Panama. **Tel.:** +(507) 263-9000. **Fax:** +(507) 263-9514.

Trust companies:

- *Trust Services* SA. PO Box 6-3685, Estafeta El Dorado, Panama, Republic of Panama. **Tel.:** +(507) 269-2438 or +(507) 263-5252. **Fax:** +(507) 269-4922. **E-mail:** marketing @trustserv.com. **Link:** http://www.trustserv.com. Licensed in Panama since 1981, this respected firm specializes in offshore corporations and trust formation. Derek R. Sambrook, a member of the Sovereign Society Council of Experts, is a director of the firm.

Attorneys:

- *Rainelda Mata-Kelly*, P.O. Box 9012, Panama 6 (Bethania), Republic of Panama. Office Address: No. 414, 4th Floor, Balboa Plaza, Balboa Avenue, Panama 6, Republic of Panama. **Tel.:** +(507) 263-4305. **Fax:** +(507) 264-2868. **E-mail:** rmk@mata-kelly.com. **Link:** http://www.mata-kelly.com. Ms. Mata-Kelly specializes in Panamanian administrative, commercial and maritime law and assists clients with immigration, real estate, contracts, incorporation and other legal issues. She is a member of The Sovereign Society's Council of Experts.

Panamanian residency:

- *Greg Geurin*, c/o International Living (Panama), 17 Avenida Jose Gabriel Duque, La Cresta, Panama, Republic of Panama. **Tel.:** +(507) 264-2204. Mr. Guerin directs the operations of

International Living in Panama and has excellent contacts in the Panamanian legal and real estate communities.

On the Web:

- List of Panamanian embassies and consulates. Link: http://www.embassyworld.com.
- General Information on Panama. Link: http://www.panamainfo.com/english/index.htm.
- Panama Tax and Banking Laws. Link:
- Why Panama? Pensionados for retirees. Link: www.internationalliving.com/contadora/whypanama.html

---

The Island of Nevis: Airtight Privacy & Fast Service

Robert E. Bauman, JD, & David Melnik, QC, *Offshore Money Manual 2000*

Of all the places in the world now welcoming foreigners with guarantees of no taxes, complete financial privacy and statutory asset protections, Nevis stands out. Find out why.

If there is any one haven country that has all the things you need for smooth offshore financial operations, it's Nevis (pronounced KNEE-vis). Best of all, Nevis has a no-nonsense banking and business privacy law that even the U.S. government can't crack. Its pro-offshore laws have existed for almost two decades—so there is plenty of experience and precedent in the local courts—and the legislative assembly keeps the applicable laws current. There are well-established service companies that can do what you want, and many have U.S. offices for your convenience.

The "sovereign democratic federal state" of St. Christopher-Nevis (as its 1983 constitution ceremoniously describes it), has a governmental form and name almost larger than its population (45,000), and total land area (267 sq. km).

But this tiny West Indies island nation, known to the natives as "St. Kitts-Nevis," has become very prominent in certain exclusive international financial circles. That's because Nevis has no taxes, extremely user-friendly incorporation and trust laws, and an official attitude of hearty welcome to foreign offshore corporations and asset protection trusts.

The islands are located 225 miles east of Puerto Rico and about 1,200 miles south of Miami. Until their September 19, 1983, declaration of independence, both were British colonies. They are still associate members of the British Commonwealth and recognize Her Royal Highness Elizabeth II as the head of state. She still appoints a local Governor General. The elected unicameral Parliament sits in the capital of Basseterre on St. Kitts (population 35,000).

Nevis (pop. 10,000) also has its own Island Assembly, and retains the constitutional right of secession from St. Kitts. There are heated editorial demands for separation, but if it happens it will be bloodless. The Nevis independence movement became very active in August 1996, based on complaints of neglect by the federal government based on St. Kitts. As of this writing, the mini-country remains united.

Based on the Island Assembly's adoption of the Business Corporation Act of 1984, Nevis has an established, decade-long record of catering to foreign offshore corporations. The statute contains elements of Delaware's extremely liberal corporation laws, along with English commercial law. As a result, U.K. solicitors should have little fear about navigating its provisions.

The corporation statute allows complete confidentiality for company officials and shareholders. There is no requirement for public disclosure of ownership, management, or financial status of a business. Although they must pay an annual fee of US$450, international business corporations are otherwise exempt from taxes—no withholding, stamps, fees or taxes on income or foreign assets. Individually negotiated, government-guaranteed tax holidays are available in writing, provided the IBC carries on no business locally. Official corporate start-up costs can be under US$1,000, including a minimum capitalization tax of US$200 and company formation fees of US$600. These low government levies compare very favorably with those imposed by other corporate-friendly havens like the high profile, high-cost Cayman Islands.

There are no exchange controls and no tax treaties with other nations. As a matter of policy, the government will not exchange tax or other information with any other foreign revenue service or government. Principal corporate offices and records may be maintained by Nevis companies anywhere in the world the owners wish.

Nevis corporation law is almost unique in that it contains a very modern legal provision. It allows the international portability or transfer of an existing foreign company from its country of origin to the island. Known as the "re-domiciling provision," this allows the smooth and instantaneous transfer of an existing corporation from any nation and retention of its original name and date of incorporation. This is all done without interruption of business activity or corporate existence. The only requirement is the amendment of existing articles of incorporation to conform with local laws.

New company creation and registration is fast in Nevis. It's accomplished simply by paying the capitalization tax and fees mentioned earlier. Using Nevis corporate service offices in the U.S. (see the list below), your corporation or limited liability company can be registered and ready to do business within a few hours. You can do everything by phone, fax and wire. Your confirmation papers can be sent by courier to you overnight from Nevis. Formal incorporation documents must be filed within ten days of receiving the confirmation papers. Corporate service firms will assist you with ready-made paperwork.

Small wonder that in 10 years since the law's original adoption, thousands of foreign corporate owners have established their companies in Charleston, Nevis.

Asset Protection Trusts

Building on their reputation for statutory corporate cordiality, on April 28, 1994, the Island Assembly adopted the Nevis International Trust Ordinance, a comprehensive, clear and flexible asset protection trust (APT) law. This law is comparable—and in many ways superior—to that of the Cook Islands in the South Pacific, already well known as an APT world center. The new Nevis law incorporates the best features of the Cook Islands law, but is even more flexible. The basic aim of the law is to permit foreign citizens to obtain asset protection by transferring title to an APT established in Charleston, Nevis.

Nevis simply is taking advantage of the worldwide growth in medical, legal and professional malpractice law suits. Legislative and judicial imposition of no-fault personal liability on corporate officers and directors has become a nasty fact of business life. A Nevis trust places personal assets beyond the reach of foreign governments, litigious plaintiffs, creditors and contingency-fee lawyers.

Under the law, the Nevis judiciary does not recognize any non-domestic court orders regarding its domestic APTs. This forces a foreign judgment creditor to start all over again, retrying in Nevisian courts, with Nevisian lawyers. A plaintiff who sues an APT must first post a US$25,000 bond with the government to cover court and others costs before a suit will be accepted for filing. And the statute of limitations for filing legal challenges to a Nevisian APT runs out two years from the date of the trust creation. In cases of alleged fraudulent intent, the law places the burden of proof on the foreign claimant.

Nevis APT Formation

Nevis has an established international bar and local trust experts who understand and can assist in furthering APT objectives. The APT act has proven very popular, as a considerable number of trusts have been registered in Nevis.

Under the statute, the Nevis government does not require the filing of trust documents. They are not a matter of public record. The only public information you need to establish an APT is a standard form or letter naming the trustee, the date of trust creation, the date of the filing, and the name of the local trust company representing the APT. The only government fee is US$200 upon filing, and an equal annual fee to maintain the filing.

Broader Trust Powers

Under the provisions of the Nevis International Trust Ordinance, the same person can serve in the triple role of grantor, beneficiary and protector of the APT. This allows far greater control over assets and income than U.S. domestic law permits. Generally, American law forbids you to create a trust for your own benefit. The basic structure of a foreign asset protection trust differs little from an Anglo-American common law trusts.

The grantor creates the trust by executing a formal declaration describing the purposes, then transferring assets to be administered according to the declaration by the named trustees. Usually there are three trustees named, two in the grantor's country and one in Nevis, the latter known as a "protector." Named trust beneficiaries can vary according to the grantor's estate planning objectives, and under Nevis law the grantor may be the primary beneficiary.

Nevis requires the appointment of a trust protector who, as the title indicates, oversees its operation and ensures legal compliance. A protector does not manage the trust, but can sometimes veto actions. Nevis also allows a beneficiary to serve in the dual role as protector.

Tax & Legal Advantages for Americans

Under U.S. tax law, foreign asset protection trusts are "tax-neutral." They are considered domestic trusts, meaning income from the trust is treated by the IRS as the grantor's personal income and taxed accordingly. Because the grantor retains some control over the transfer of his assets to any foreign trust, including those established in Nevis, U.S. gift taxes can usually be avoided. Although Nevis has no estate taxes, U.S. estate taxes are imposed on the value of trust assets for the grantor's estate, but all existing exemptions for combined marital assets can be used.

One device a grantor may employ to retain optimal control of assets is to form a limited partnership, making the Nevisian trust a limited partner. This allows you to retain active control over all the assets you transfer to the Nevis trust/limited partner. It also protects trusts from creditors and other legal assaults.

Aside from the undoubted protection offered by the new Nevis International Trust Ordinance, this is a small nation with great economic and political stability, a highly reputable judicial system, favorable local tax laws, no language barrier and excellent international communication and financial facilities.

Contacts

- *Nevis Services Ltd.*, Suite 200, 125 Half Mile Rd., Redbank, NJ 08830 U.S.A. **Tel.**: +1 212 575 0818. **Fax**: +1 212 575 0812. Contact: Mario M. Novello, President.

- *Nevis Trust Ltd.*, Springate, Suite 100 West, Government Rd., Charleston, Nevis, West Indies. **Tel.**: +1 869 469 1017.

Belize: Polishing a Caribbean Gem

Robert E. Bauman, JD, *The Sovereign Individual*, June 2001

After Panama and Nevis, Belize is a close third for banking privacy, low and no taxes and a business-friendly government. It should be on everyone's list of possible offshore bases.

Belize is the only English-speaking country in Central America. Its mixed population of 200,000 includes descendants of native Mayans, Chinese, East Indians and Caucasians. Independent since 1981, its language came from its colonial days as "British Honduras." Situated south of Mexico and to the east of Guatemala, Belize is on the Caribbean seaboard. It has the largest barrier reef in the Western Hemisphere and great deep sea diving. To the east, there's a sprinkle of Caribbean tropical islands included within the nation's borders. American television viewers discovered Belize as the locale for the show "Temptation Island."

Belize retains many of the colonial customs and features familiar in places such as the Cayman Islands and Bermuda. The first settlers were probably British woodcutters who in 1638 found the valuable commodity known as "Honduran mahogany." Bananas, sugar cane and citrus fruit are principal crops. Like many small countries dependent on primary commodities, Belize recently recognized the benefits of introducing tax haven services to boost its income.

U.S. Nervous Over a Hot Haven

American government officials have gotten a case of nerves over Belize as a tax haven. They privately fear that the sleepy little capital town of Belmopan could become a prime site for U.S. tax evasion and money laundering.

In 1992, the Belize National Assembly enacted up-to-date legislation seeking to make the country a competitive offshore financial center. Drafters combed tax haven laws worldwide and came up with a series of minimal corporate and tax requirements which could well fit your business needs. The new laws include the Trust Act, which allows a high level of asset protection, great freedom of action by the trustee, and no taxes on income earned outside Belize. There is also a statute allowing the creation of international business companies, corporations which can be formed in less than a day for about US$700. You only need one shareholder and/or director, whose name can be shielded from public view.

Since 1990, when the International Business Companies Act became law, foreigners have registered about 4,000 IBCs. That's a relatively small number compared to a place like the Cayman Islands, but the number is growing. There are no local income taxes, personal or corporate, and no currency exchange control.

Belize City, the main center for business, has also seen major growth in the shipping registry business. This is also encouraged by a new law. Now in the works are laws favoring offshore insurance companies, limited liability partnerships, and banking. There are no anti-money laundering laws.

So far Belizean banking is tiny, but very secret by force of law. Deposits could soar quickly as even more new laws make this subtropical paradise the next "hot" international tax and asset haven. Privacy protection here rivals even that of air-tight Nevis.

BAI Corporation—A Big Presence

Visa credit cards are issued by Belize Bank Ltd., owned by Belize Corporation, a holding company with banking and financial services in Belize. BAI also has major stakes in local Belizean telecommunications, electricity, hotels, citrus and other industries. The principal owner of BAI is Michael Ashcroft, a British multimillionaire described by the *Wall Street Journal* as an "unconventional and sometimes controversial deal maker." BAI stock is publicly traded in the U.S. on the NASDAQ stock exchange. The Belize Bank is the largest commercial banking operation in Belize, and is a correspondent of the Bank of America.

Over the last decide the government of Belize has carefully and systematically established the nation as an offshore haven that welcomes foreign investment and foreign nationals. It has enacted a series of laws crafted to protect financial privacy and promote creation of offshore trusts and international business corporations (IBCs). It has in place one of the few available quick economic citizenship programs, plus an attractive special residency program aimed at retirement bound foreign citizens.

Having visited Belize for the first time a few months ago, I can attest that it's definitely "third world," but people are amazingly friendly and even ocean front real estate is still relatively cheap.

Belize is one of the few remaining independent nations proud to hold itself out as a tax and asset protection haven.

Belize's name was among the 35 nations that appeared on the "harmful tax competition" blacklist issued by the OECD in June 2000. This small eastern Caribbean country of 230,000 was accused of being a tax haven that had been "uncooperative" in the OECD's spurious global attack on tax evasion. "Cooperate or risk incurring unspecified international economic sanctions" was the OECD threat. With the 2002 change in political control in Washington, D.C., the subsequent abandonment of this OECD phony high tax campaign by the George W. Bush administration has all but ended the possibility of sanctions.

Largely because of its stringent anti-money laundering laws and strict enforcement, Belize escaped being tarred on the earlier June 2000 Financial Action Task Force (FATF) "dirty money" blacklist aimed at nations alleged to have been lax on combating money laundering crimes. Belize does not have an extensive banking establishment and very few banks, unlike the Cayman Islands or The Bahamas, but it does police carefully its banks and all their offshore transactions.

London Pressures

A member of the Commonwealth and a former British colony independent since 1981, Belize still has strong ties with London and is thus susceptible to U.K. Foreign Office pressures. British troops train here for tropical duty and the U.K. provides military aid because of a continuing boundary dispute with neighboring Guatemala.

In June 2000, shortly after the OECD tax blacklisting of Belize, London made known future aid of all kinds, including debt forgiveness, would depend in part on Belize's willingness to cooperate in modifying some of its tax haven attractions. The U.K. Labor government pointedly objected to certain tax breaks Belize had granted to billionaire Lord Michael Ashcroft, a major investor in Belize and a controversial British Conservative Party peer and former Tory treasurer. Ashcroft has extensive business holdings in Belize which he makes a second home away from London. At one point London suspended debt relief to Belize in response to Ashcroft's alleged tax breaks and those of other favored offshore investors in Belize.

In July 2000 Belize bowed to the pressure by promising to tighten, somewhat, its offshore regulations. Among changes considered, corporate bearer shares, which allow secrecy for true company owners and which can be transferred by mere possession of the share certificate, were partially neutralized. One plan under discussion would require the registered Belizean company agent to maintain actual possession of bearer share certificates. But bearer shares still remain legal for international business companies incorporated in Belize.

Belize Bank, controlled by Lord Ashcroft, is one of the local companies that performs bearer share services. His holding company, Carlisle Holdings, also has a stake in the registry of such companies. (Lord Ashcroft in the past had divided his time between homes in Belize and Florida, where he acted as official consular representative for Belize in the United States.)

Offshore Industry Expands

In spite of OECD and London carping, Belize's offshore industry continues to grow, providing offshore financial services to largely non-resident clientele. These services include international business company and offshore trust formation and administration; international banking services, including foreign currency bank accounts and international Visa cards; fund management, accounting and secretarial services; captive insurance, and ship registration.

A sympathetic government continues to work closely with the Belize Offshore Practitioners Association in drafting future legislation. Areas under consideration include offshore banking, captive insurance, limited duration companies, protected cell companies, limited partnerships, as well as other legal entities to expand further Belize's role as one of the few remaining independent nations offering offshore services.

Tax-Free Residency

A good example of Belize's welcome of offshore persons is the Retired Persons Incentive Act passed by the Belize parliament in 1999. This came into effect in 2000 and is implemented by the Belize Tourism Board. The program, which resembles the popular but now defunct *pensionado* program in Costa Rica, is designed to attract foreign retirees and foreign capital. (Panama has a similar program.)

Known as the "qualified retired persons" (QRP) program, the law offers significant tax incentives to those willing to become permanent residents (but not full citizens). The program is aimed primarily at residents of the U.S., Canada and the U.K., but is open to all.

A qualified retired person is exempted from all taxes on income from sources outside Belize. QRPs can own and operate their own international business based in Belize exempt from all local taxes. Local income earned within Belize is taxed at a graduated rate of 15-45 percent and QRPs need a work permit in order to engage in purely domestic business activities. For QRPs import duties are waived for personal effects, household goods and for a motor vehicle or other transport, such as an airplane or boat. There is no minimum time required to be spent in Belize and QRPs can maintain their status so long as they maintain a permanent local residence such as a small apartment or condo.

To qualify for the QRP program, an applicant must be 45 years of age or older and prove personal financial ability to support oneself and any dependents. A spouse and dependents (18 and younger) qualify along with the head of household at no extra fee cost. Initial fees for the program are US$700, plus $100 for an ID card upon application approval. Minimum financial requirements include an annual income of at least US$24,000 (or equivalent) from a pension, annuity or from other sources outside Belize. By the 15th of each month at least $2000 must be deposited in the QRP's Belize account, or by April 1st annually $24,000 must be placed in deposit.

For more information about the QRP Program, contact the following agencies: *The Belize Tourism Board*, New Central Bank Building, Level 2, Gabourel Lane, P.O. Box 325, Belize City, Belize. **Tel.**: +501 231-913. **Fax**: +501 231-943. **E-mail**: info@travelbelize.org. **Web**: www.travelbelize.org.

The Ministry of Tourism, Constitution Drive, Belmopan, Belize. **Tel.**: +501 823-393. **Fax**: +501 823-815. **E-mail**: tourismdpt@btl.net.

Conclusion

In spite of British, U.S. and OECD pressures, Belize is not about to enact income or corporate taxes that would drive away foreign investors and residents. In this relatively impoverished third world country, the offshore sector is a needed and highly valued source of foreign capital that has strong government support. Any modifications to offshore laws are likely to be minimal and mainly window dressing to mute foreign critics.

Belize certainly is not what the Caymans or The Bahamas used to be as an offshore haven, but neither has it sold out to outside pressure.

Contacts

- *Belize Economic Citizenship Program*, **Website**: www.visafree.com.
- *Avalon Trust Co. Ltd.*, PO Box 1113, Northern Hwy, Belize City, Belize. **Tel. and Fax**: +501 2 33338. **E-mail**: mscba@catsa.com.bz.
- *Bank of Belize Ltd.*, Belize City, Belize. **Tel.**: +501 2 72567.
- *Belize Corporate Services Center Ltd.*, 60 Market Square, PO Box 364, Belize City, Belize. **Tel.**: +501 2 72567. **Fax:** +501 2 77018. **E-mail**: bblbcsl@btl.net.
- *Official Registrar of IBCs*, PO Box 364, Belize City, Belize. **Tel.**: +501 2 72390. **Fax** +501 2 77018.
- *Central Bank of Belize*, PO Box 852, Belize City, Belize. **Tel.**: +501 2 77216. **Fax** +501 2

70221.

- *Belize Offshore Center*, 35 Barrack Rd., Belize City, Belize. **E-mail**: cititrust@offshore.com.bz, **Website**: www.belizeoffshore.com.

- *Belize Trust Company Ltd.* (BTCL), 60 Market Square, PO Box 364, Belize. **Tel.**: +501 2 72390. **Fax**: +501 2 77018.

- *KPMG Corporate Services*—Belize. **Website**: www.kpmgbelize.com.

The Bahamas: Offshore Haven No More
by Robert E. Bauman, JD, August 2001

Until 2000 The Bahamas was one of the leading offshore tax and asset havens for U.S. persons. Then the government, following demands of the OECD and FATF, adopted radical laws that have in effect called into serious question the future offshore financial role of the nation.

The Bahamas is just minutes from Miami by plane or a few hours by boat. A quarter of a million people live on 700 islands in this archipelago, the oldest offshore money haven in the Americas. An independent nation and member of the British Commonwealth since 1973, it began operating as a money haven in 1908 when the Royal Bank of Canada opened a branch in Nassau. Until the year 2000 The Bahamas stood out as one of the world's premier asset and tax haven nations. That is no longer true.

Since June 2000 the current Free National Movement (FNM) government in Nassau systematically has dismantled and diluted the islands' offshore legal framework that had been carefully designed to protect financial privacy and wealth in the islands.

This signal retreat from asset haven status by the FNM government was a defeatist response to the triple "honor" of being listed on all three blacklists issued by the FSF, FATF and the OECD. Respectively, The Bahamas was charged with damaging "international financial stability," being uncooperative in combating money laundering and engaging in "harmful tax competition," meaning levying no taxes. The groups threatened undefined "stern countermeasures" against The Bahamas if it failed to open bank and other financial records to foreign tax and criminal investigators and to make numerous other changes in its offshore laws.

Washington Pressure

Instead of fighting back and telling these outsiders to "buzz off," the FNM government rapidly pushed through parliament, over strong minority opposition, a host of statutory changes that substantially weakened the very financial privacy and asset protection that once attracted to the islands tends of thousands of offshore bank accounts, international business companies and asset protection trusts. These new laws admittedly were drafted with the direct assistance of "financial experts" from London and Washington. The FNM government also said it had accepted "a generous offer" of technical assistance from the U.S. Treasury Department.

Prime Minister Hubert A. Ingraham's defense was his belief that if The Bahamas desired the support and endorsement of the United States, the government had to comply "fully with the new internationally accepted practices now current in major financial centers in the developed world."

Within days of the release of the June 2000 FATF money laundering blacklist, in an obviously coordinated effort, the U.S. Treasury's Financial Crimes Enforcement Network (FinCEN) issued an advisory warning calling on all U.S. banks to give "enhanced scrutiny" to activity with The Bahamas that did not involve "established and adequately identified and understood, commercial or investment enterprises" in the islands. While such an advisory does not prohibit transactions with a nation, it creates a presumption that all dealings with them may be criminally suspect and it makes always cautious U.S. bankers very nervous.

Prime Minister Ingraham's initial reaction to the OECD-FATF blacklisting was a hat-in-hand pilgrimage to Canada and the United States. In Washington the Prime Minister met with Attorney General Janet Reno, and Secretary to the Treasury Lawrence Summers. Upon Ingraham's return there followed introduction in parliament of the first many laws described here.

This capitulation to Washington demands echoed a crisis in the early 1980s when the late Prime Minister Linden O. Pindling, accused of drug dealing, was confronted by an angry U.S. government that threatened sanctions against The Bahamas. Although Pindling was cleared, he was forced to grant U.S. law and drug enforcement officers diplomatic immunity and free passage through the archipelago, plus limited access to secret offshore banks of some accused criminals.

European Junket

As a preliminary to the government's legislative sellout of the offshore financial community, Ingraham in October, 2000 led a large delegation on a month long junket to OECD and FATF headquarters in Paris. Other stops included Madrid, Prague, Zurich and London.

According to the Prime Minister, the expedition's goal was to assure government officials, the private financial sector, the leaders of the OECD and FATF and the international community that The Bahamas intended to become "a reputable major finance center." Ingraham also asked the International Monetary Fund to perform an independent assessment of The Bahamas financial services sector.

In Paris The Bahamas' contingent visited the OECD headquarters to meet with Secretary General Donald Johnston, Fiscal Affairs Division leader Jeffrey Owens, and head of the Tax Competition Unit, Frances Horner. At the meeting, Johnston praised Ingraham for personally leading his delegation, saying he considered it evidence of The Bahamas "serious intention to co-operate with the OECD."

At one point the executive director of The Bahamas Financial Services Board told the press the government did not want the islands to be known as an "offshore tax haven" any longer, but rather as a "highly competitive, low tax international financial center." But the chairman of that board, Ian Fair, warned The Bahamas blacklisting was "a smoke screen for rich countries' concerns about competition from small offshore banking." Fair cautioned, "I think we have to be careful that we don't go too far."

Strong Opposition Fails

Progressive Liberal Party (PLP) opposition members accused the Prime Minister of selling out to the U.S. and to the OECD and of abandoning the offshore financial community.

In an initial response to the blacklisting, some few multinational banks and companies with branch offices in The Bahamas threatened to leave the islands, apparently concerned they might be tarnished by continued presence in an alleged "soft on money laundering" nation. This threat of "capital flight and isolation" from the global financial system was used by the government as justification to strengthen anti-money laundering laws and streamline the legal process by which foreign governments can now obtain records and evidence.

The PLP parliamentary opposition rightfully argued that repeal or change of most of the offshore laws that brought huge investments and assets to The Bahamas would indeed result in capital flight, as individual offshore bank accounts were closed and financial activity fled elsewhere. Dr. Peter Maynard, president of The Bahamas Bar Association charged that what the OECD and FATF demanded "would be disastrous, a total devastation of the financial sector. It will have an affect on the entire financial services sector and will mean many jobs lost." (Several months later the Bar association endorsed the government's actions). Of the 120,000-strong Bahamian work force, about 5,000 work in offshore banking and trust companies, accounting for an estimated 20 percent of the gross domestic product. (Largely due to increased offshore financial activity, the Bahamian economy grew by 40 percent from $3.2 billion in 1992 to $4.5 billion in 2000).

At one point PLP-opposing senators, who felt their concerns were being ignored by the government, walked out of a Senate debate on the Evidence Act. The government leader in the Senate, Dame Dr. Ivy Dumont, openly admitted the government was determined to end 20 years of official bank and financial secrecy in the islands in order to conform to "international norms." The Bahamas has "sought to preserve, defend and protect bank secrecy as enshrined in legislation in 1965 and strengthened in 1980 for as long as was possible and/or practical," Dumont said. "We did not wish to be amongst the first to move. In fact, we determined to be amongst the last and it might be said that we held the line to the end. Now is the end."

Sounding the retreat, Bahamas Finance Minister William Allen admitted: "We, as a sovereign nation, did not make a decision until we understood that we had no choice. We have to redefine The Bahamas because we recognize that the so-called tax havens will not be tolerated by the international community any longer."

Subsequently several banks and offshore financial firms have announced their departure, siting the new laws as reason for their exodus. In parliament Prime Minister Ingraham admitted that the crackdown would cause a loss of millions of dollars in annual revenue from the incorporation, registration and operation of international business corporations alone.

Bahamian PLP opposition members of parliament called on the government to resign over the OECD and FATF debacle, claiming that the blacklisting was directly related to the government's prolonged inability to deal with drug trafficking. Privately, Bahamian sources said government figures were implicated in numerous questionable, but highly profitable financial activities, a situation the U.S. was holding over their heads unless they acted as Washington demanded. Throughout recent months U.S. government representatives have hovered over Bahamian officials on Nassau, pressuring them with Washington's point of view.

New Laws, Amendments to Old Laws

Among the many new Bahamian laws, the Evidence Proceedings in Other Jurisdictions Act 2000 removed the requirement that requested evidence could not be released to another country until a court proceeding had begun in the requesting nation. Evidence can now be released for foreign preliminary investigations. This new law appears to permit Bahamian enforcement of U.S. civil forfeiture orders for the first time. The government also forced through another new law allowing it to confiscate cash and assets under a U.S.-style civil forfeiture procedure that permits freezing of bank and other accounts. Still another new law empowers Bahamian courts to extradite criminal suspects during investigations before trial. It should be noted that The Bahamas already had in force mutual legal assistance treaties with the U.S., U.K. and Canada.

Money Laundering

Existing anti-money laundering laws were toughened to make violations punishable by a possible sentence of 20 years in jail and/or a $100,000 fine for each instance. A new Currency Declaration Act requires reporting of all cash or investment transfers, in or out of the islands in excess of $10,000. The Central Bank also was given broad new powers to regulate offshore banks, their registration, operation and reporting. In a radical move, for the first time the new law allows foreign bank inspectors to conduct on-site and off-site examinations of the accounts in bank branches or subsidiaries located in The Bahamas.

Financial Police

The Bahamas also has created a new police financial intelligence unit modeled on the U.S. Treasury Financial Crimes Enforcement Network (FinCEN). Opposition members of parliament criticized the FIU's powers as far too broad, charging there are no provisions to prevent political "fishing trips" or "witch hunts" by government police. This unit can request ("order" might be a better word) a bank to freeze any funds suspected of being part of criminal activity for up to 72 hours while a secret "monitoring order" is sought by police to confiscate money or block transactions. In such cases all other financial confidentiality laws are waived. The FIU in early 2001 issued new U.S.-style rules requiring "suspicious activity reporting" by all financial institutions and "know your customer" rules are in the offing.

Know Your Customer

Still other laws for the first time require all banks to verify the true identity of customers for whom Bahamian intermediaries open accounts. Since early 2000 Bahamian banks have been using a special U.S. cash flow analysis software to detect possible money laundering. Offshore financial trustees and attorneys are now required to maintain records of beneficial owners of offshore trusts and international business corporations. Previously, professional attorney-client privilege rules prevented revealing such information.

The Prime Minister warned that any banks failing to comply with the new client identity laws would be placed on a government "must watch" list for FIU police scrutiny. In December 2000, for example, the government revoked the license of Surety Bank and Trust Co. Ltd. for failure to comply with new reporting rules. In March 2001 the government suddenly closed down the Suisse Security Banking & Trust, forcing it into receivership, a move that was challenged in court but upheld.

IBCs Under Fire

Until now IBCs have not been required to disclose the identities of shareholders or other detailed business information unless forced to do so by a court order. Now the right of IBCs to issue and use bearer shares has been repealed and all IBCs are required to submit to the government the true identities and addresses of directors. There are currently more than 106,000 international business corporations in The Bahamas, with about 16,000 added each year. Secrecy of ownership undoubtedly was a large factor in attracting these IBCs and now that has ended.

Taxes

The Bahamas levies no business or income taxes, although various registration and transfer fees amount to a tax estimated by some to approach 20 percent, depending on the nature of the transactions.

According to the current Bahamian government, as it has in the past, it will continue to refuse assistance to foreign governments seeking information about tax or other fiscal offenses under foreign law. However, the Nassau government announced it will negotiate a new "Tax Information Exchange Agreement" with the United States, which for the first time will allow exchange of information relating to both criminal and civil tax liability. In vain Washington had sought this agreement for 35 years.

[*Ed. Note*: In May 2003 the new government of the Bahamas announced that it was about to negotiate the TIEA with Washington, although it had won election in 2002 by opposing the prior government's offshore finance changes. The new government also stated its willingness to negotiate tax information exchange agreements with other nations.]

The Nassau government claimed in 2001 it does not plan to negotiate similar treaties with other countries but, unless political control of the government changes, the trend clearly is toward even greater government forced disclosure and an end to financial privacy. The government has admitted that Canada is seeking a similar tax treaty with The Bahamas.

The major demand of the OECD is that all offshore havens abolish the "no tax" preferences granted to offshore foreign investors. In OECD parlance this is known as "ring fencing." This is part of the so-called "unfair tax competition" about which the OECD loudly complains in its blacklisting. Bahamian sources insist that, in spite of all the other radical changes in local laws, taxes will not be imposed or increased on offshore investment. But based on recent events, in order to gain OECD approval there is no certainty about what the FNM government might do. There are reports of growing political unrest with Prime Minister Ingraham's government and what is viewed as his overboard appeasement of the U.S. and the OECE-FATF crowd.

Bahamian sources tell us any such tax attempt would be challenged in the courts as unconstitutional, and other laws may be similarly attacked in law suits to be filed. As we go to press some of the new law's provisions are being challenged by lawsuits and some provisions have been stayed by the courts pending are review on constitutional grounds.

New Laws Now In Force

Among the many new laws now in force are: Banks and Trust Companies Regulation Act 2000, Central Bank Act 2000, Criminal Justice (International Cooperation Act) 2000, Dangerous Drugs Act 2000, Financial and Corporate Service Providers Act 2000, Financial Intelligence Unit Act 2000, Financial Transactions Reporting Act 2000, International Business Companies Act 2000, Proceeds of Crime Act 2000, the Corporate Services Providers Act, the Mutual Legal Assistance (Amendment) Act, and the Prevention of Bribery Act (Amendment).

Conclusion

The government's surrender strategy obtained the removal of The Bahamas from the FATF blacklists in June 2001. In early 2001 FATF had deigned to identify The Bahamas as one of seven nations that it believed were taking "substantial steps" to comply with its demands, but FATF suggested more requirements may be forthcoming.

Our advice is to completely scratch The Bahamas off the list of offshore tax and asset haven nations. If you were thinking of using the islands as a base of offshore operation, forget it. If you have financial accounts or other interests located there, move them to a safe place. But there may be some attractive real estate deals in The Bahamas soon, as the exodus of the offshore community begins in earnest.

[**Ed Note:** In 2002 the FNM government was overwhelmingly defeated by the opposition PLP, and a new government headed by Prime Minister Perry Christie took office. In spite of promises to turn back the FNM laws, the PLP government has done virtually nothing to reform these Draconian laws and the offshore financial sector of the economy has taken a nosedive. Many offshore banks have closed down and millions of dollars in capital has fled to safer nations.]

Contacts

- *Securities Commission of The Bahamas*, Charlotte House, Charlotte St., PO Box N-8347, Nassau, The Bahamas. **Tel.:** +1 242 356 6291.

- *Banque SCS Alliance (Nassau) Ltd.*, Alliance House, East Bay Street, Nassau N.P., The Bahamas. **Tel.:** +1 242 394 6161. **Fax:** +1 242 394 6262. A Swiss private bank.

- *Graham, Thompson & Co, Attorneys.* P.O. Box N-232, Nassau, New Providence, The Bahamas. **Tel.:** 242 322 4130. **Fax:** 242 328 1069. **E-mail:** info@gtclaw.com. **Web:** www.grahamthompson.com.

- *McKinney, Bancroft & Hughes*, P.O. Box N-3937, Mareva House, 4 George Street, Nassau, The Bahamas. **Tel.:** (242) 322 4195-9 or 4214-5. **Fax:** (242) 328-2520. **E-mail:** mcbanhu@bahamas.net.bs.

- *International Trade & Investments Limited.* **Tel.:** +1 800 370 8921. **Fax:** +1 242 356 2037. **Contact:** Roy Bouchier, CEO.

- *The Central Bank of The Bahamas*, P.O. Box N-4868, Nassau, The Bahamas. **Tel.:** +1 242 322 2193/6. **Fax:** +1 242 323 7795.

The United Kingdom's Caribbean Overseas Territories
by Robert E. Bauman, JD, August 2001

Unsurprisingly, high finance generates more money than agriculture, tourism or fisheries combined, even in the tropics. Many of the sunny island nations of the Caribbean realized this economic fact and so purposefully transformed themselves into international tax and asset protection havens. If you make careful decisions about locating your business in this area, you can be a direct beneficiary of these insular transformations.

In a broad arc stretching southward from the mid-Atlantic to the Isthmus of Panama lies a string of countries (and a few woefully dependent British territories), that specialize in offshore banking and finance. Each offers varying degrees of financial privacy and friendly, no-tax relations with foreigners.

Each of the sovereign nations in this group is a member of the United Nations and the Organization of American States (OAS). Some are also members of the British Commonwealth, including the dependencies who by their U.K. association enjoy special participation rights in the European Union (EU). Most are members of the Caribbean Community (CARICOM), an area-wide economic and trading group of 14 nations.

Even as U.S. government agents have watched their every move, until now these small nations and dependencies have built a record of protecting the money, wealth and hard-earned assets of offshore persons from many nations.

Under the Gun

We said "until now" because circumstances are changing rapidly in this area, and not for the good in every case.

Anyone with investments, banking or offshore entities located in the U.K.'s "overseas territories"—Bermuda, the British Virgin Islands, the Cayman Islands, Anguilla and the Turks & Caicos Islands—should have serious concerns about the direction in which these (until now) asset havens seem to be headed. And if you're thinking of doing business here for the first time, think again.

In late 1998, the U.K. Foreign Office ordered these territories to amend local laws to permit the enforcement of foreign tax judgments, something none of them previously allowed. Since the U.K. clearly has ultimate jurisdiction over the territories, their only alternative to compliance with the U.K. demands is to declare independence from the U.K., a step none of them has been willing to take so far.

At least one U.K. territorial head of state minced no words about Tony Blair's Labor Party policy towards the overseas territories: "You have one option; independence or serfdom." The Chief Minister of the up-and-coming asset haven of Anguilla, Hubert Hughes, made this blunt statement in a letter to all Anguillan citizens in direct response to the U.K. Foreign Office demands.

Hughes said London was bestowing dictatorial powers on the official Crown-appointed governor who, with agreement of the U.K. Foreign Secretary, may now amend, veto or introduce legislation without consulting the Anguillan legislature. Similar directives now affect the other U.K. Caribbean dependent territories, including the Cayman Islands, British Virgin Islands, Montserrat and Turks and Caicos Islands. Representatives of these territories have talked about a joint response to the U.K., but independence is not likely to be on their agenda.

The U.K. claims it is acting to meet its obligation to comply with the EU's anti-money laundering directives, but the proposals, according to Minister Hughes, will effectively sink the fledgling international financial services industry there. The same may be true elsewhere. Hughes said the offshore business sector would be swamped in costly paperwork and, worse, lose the protection of strict financial secrecy laws. And offshore investors certainly don't want to do business in a place where their tax planning is likely to be challenged as "money laundering." This situation will be repeated in other Caribbean asset havens that choose to remain U.K. dependent territories.

Nor is independence a real option given the size of Anguilla or the smaller dependent territories, some of which, like the Turks and Caicos, would find it difficult to survive without ties to the "mother country." That cannot be said of places like Bermuda and the Cayman Islands that can stand on their own considerable financial feet, just as The Bahamas have done successfully since they became independent from the U.K. in 1973.

The written constitutions provided to U.K. asset haven dependent territories pursuant to the U.K.'s Statute of Westminster (1931) contain specific provisions allowing the British Crown (i.e., New Labor, the government of the moment), to bypass local legislatures by declaring an emergency and imposing its own rules. These extraordinary powers were invoked in the Caribbean area dependent territories in January 1998 after they initially refused London's demand to enact "all crimes" anti-money laundering statutes that would enforce foreign tax claims. These asset haven nations traditionally impose no significant taxes on income and do not recognize foreign tax avoidance or evasion as a criminal matter.

All four territories already had adopted tough money laundering laws modeled on the 1996 Cayman Proceeds of Criminal Conduct Law that permits enforcement of foreign confiscation orders in money laundering cases from "designated countries"—only the U.S. and the U.K. to date. However, contrary to U.K. demands, they all included in their statutes a "fiscal offense" exemption that precludes enforcement in case of tax and customs violations alleged by a foreign government.

[**Ed. Note**: Since this was written, the Cayman Islands, Bermuda, and the British Virgin Islands all announced agreement to sign official Tax information Exchange Agreements (TIEAs) with the United States. In various ways they have weakened financial privacy laws and bank secrecy to such a degree as to make them far less attractive as offshore asset protection havens. They are now being pressured by the British Labor government to impose taxes on foreign investors. If the U.K. OSTs comply with orders from London to impose such taxes, none of these jurisdiction will be able to claim any longer the status as "tax havens."]

In late 1998 the Cayman Islands government removed the fiscal offense exemption, but because of other related amendments, foreign tax enforcement powers are still in doubt. London says it expects all the territories to follow orders. Indeed, if acceptable legislation is not enacted, the U.K. Foreign Office expects the Crown-appointed governors to go right ahead and bypass the legislatures.

While the Caymans law now requires the government to have prima facie evidence of a crime in order to seize cash or property, there is little recourse for a falsely accused person. An innocent defendant is ineligible for compensation unless he can prove "serious default" on the part of prosecuting authorities. Cayman legal experts tell us this lack of restraint will result in the law being used oppressively for "fishing expeditions." The legal situation is virtually identical in the other U.K. territories.

In another turn of the screws, in March 1999 the U.K. government officially announced that January 1, 2000, is the deadline for financial law reforms in the 13 U.K. overseas dependent territories, including the Channel Islands, the Isle of Man, the Cayman Islands, Bermuda, the Turks and Caicos Islands, the British Virgin Islands and Anguilla. Foreign Secretary Robin Cook warned these areas must conform to "international standards" on money laundering, end strict financial privacy laws and cooperate with law enforcement authorities.

Cook reiterated that Britain has the power to act unilaterally to change local laws if necessary, and he promised that would be done if the territories resisted London's demands.

It appears to us that if these demands are met, the U.K. territories will have lost their highly valuable status as true asset havens. Our advice: If you are a foreign depositor or investor in one of these territories, consult your attorney to determine if your assets may be at risk. If so, relocate to a jurisdiction independent of the U.K., such as Panama or Nevis. If you are considering the U.K. territories as a base for your offshore business, obtain the very latest information before you decide.

Bermuda: No Longer the "Cadillac" of Offshore Banking
Robert E. Bauman, JD, August 2001

Bermuda as an asset and banking haven jurisdiction is not what it once was.

Bermuda is located in the mid-Atlantic, 750 miles southeast of New York City, 3,445 miles from London. The island (57,000 people, 21 square miles) has a long history as a tax and banking haven. This is a world-class financial outpost, not to mention a very pleasant place to visit or live in any season.

A self-governing British overseas territory, Bermuda is a major international financial center. In the early days, the focus was based largely on reinsurance companies. In fact, Bermuda still ranks right behind the U.S. and England in the field. There are now over 1,300 "captive insurance companies" registered in Bermuda with capital exceeding US$29 billion, and total assets over US$76 billion.

Bermuda imposes no corporate income, gift, capital gains, or sales taxes. The income tax is extremely low—11 percent on income earned from employment in Bermuda. More than 8,000 international business corporations call Bermuda home. They are drawn by the island's friendly, tax-neutral environment, established business integrity and minimal regulation. Over 60 percent of these companies operate as "exempted," meaning their business is conducted outside Bermuda (except for the minimal contacts needed to sustain an office on the island).

Bermuda is also home to more then 600 "collective investment schemes" (a popular British Commonwealth phrase for mutual funds, unit trusts and limited partnerships). Just like domestic funds, they offer pooled, diversified investments. Under the strong protective umbrella of the U.K. Copyright Act of 1965, also applicable in Bermuda, collective investment schemes with intellectual property and software interests increasingly use the island as a legal home port.

With a statutory structure for protection, Bermuda more recently has become a center for offshore trust creation and management. The island offers a wide variety of trusts to meet every need, including offshore asset protection.

The "jewel of the Atlantic" is also a great place to live, but a word about real estate restrictions. Demand is high and supply short. In general, non-Bermudians are permitted to own only one local property. Acquisition is allowed only after careful background checks (at least one bank reference, and two or more personal references). Out of 20,000 residential units on the island, only 250 detached homes and 480 condominiums qualify for non-Bermudian purchasers based on government set values. The price for a single home starts at US$1.5 million, US$375,000 for condos. Purchase licenses come from the Department of Immigration and take six months or more for approval. A fee based on purchase price is payable at settlement—20 percent for homes, 15 percent for condos.

Bermuda Banking

Such extensive worldwide finance and insurance activity requires a highly sophisticated banking system. Bermuda provides this with up-to-date services and fiber optic connections to the outside world. The three local banks clear over US$3 billion daily. In accordance with the Banking Act of 1969, no new banks can be formed or operate in Bermuda unless authorized by the legislature. The chances of that happening are slim to none. However, international banks may form exempted companies engaged in non-banking activities, and many have done so.

Bermuda's three banks follow very conservative, risk-averse policies. They hold an average of 85 percent of customer liabilities in cash and cash equivalents. For example, the Bermuda Commercial Bank recently had a weighted "risk-asset ratio" of 32 percent. Eight percent is the minimum required by Basil International Banking Agreement standards. Bank of Bermuda, founded in 1889, has assets exceeding US$5 billion and offices in George Town, Cayman Islands, Guernsey, Hong

Kong, the Isle of Man, Luxembourg and an affiliate in New York City. Butterfield Bank (founded in 1859) also has offices in all of those havens, except the Caymans. In 2001 the Bank of Bermuda, sued in U.S. district court in Miami, agreed to a multi-million dollar settlement to repay thousands of people swindled by a U.S. client of the bank.

The Bermuda dollar circulates on par with the U.S. dollar. U.S. currency is accepted everywhere. There are no exchange controls on foreigners or on exempt companies, which operate freely in any currency except the Bermuda dollar.

Unlike the Cayman Islands or The Bahamas, Bermuda has no bank secrecy laws officially protecting privacy, but bank and government policy make it virtually impossible to obtain information in most cases. To do so requires a lengthy judicial process. A 1988 tax treaty with the U.S. allows for governmental exchange of limited information in certain cases, but this treaty is now being renegotiated and will probably be much more liberal in information exchanges in the future. Bermuda does have strict anti-drug and general money laundering laws. On a comparative 1-to-10 international bank privacy scale, Bermuda ranks about five.

Foreign Tax Evasion a Crime

In August 1999, at a marathon adjournment session of Parliament, the Progressive Labor Party majority rolled over the minority United Bermuda Party in what one opposition leader charged was "imperious style." The PLP rammed through new proposals to toughen the provisions of the U.S.-Bermuda tax treaty and existing anti-money laundering laws, as well as financial management laws and rules governing the chartering and operation of banks and trust companies. These new laws were seen as Bermuda's calculated response to demands from the Foreign Office in London, and the OECD and FATF.

The rewrite of the U.S.-Bermuda tax treaty toughened the existing agreement at Washington's request. It clarified and expanded the types of information which Bermuda can now give the IRS "relevant to the determination of the liability of the [U.S.] taxpayer". For the first time Bermuda also permitted on site inspections of records by foreign tax authorities. The Proceeds of Crime Act fiscal offence list was broadened to include fraud. This criminalized acts which, even though committed overseas, would have been an offence if the same acts had occurred in Bermuda.

Most importantly, the fraudulent evasion of foreign taxes was a made a crime, a major reversal of prior Bermuda policy and law. This made Bermuda the first major tax haven and the first British overseas territory to pass such legislation.

Together these new laws allow the U.S. IRS and the U.K. Inland Revenue (as well as other nations' tax collectors) to pursue their alleged tax evading citizens with the assistance of Bermuda prosecutors and courts. The island already had legislation and agreements that enabled U.S. authorities and plaintiffs in civil court investigations to obtain information including those involving tax offenses. Subsequently there has been much controversy as to whether the new information exchange laws require exchanges retroactively dating back for more than three years. Prior Bermuda law allowed police to investigate allegations of money laundering, no matter how long ago it may have occurred.

Because of the large number of international companies that conduct insurance operations from Bermuda, the island does not rely as heavily on personal offshore services and banking as do most other havens. Bermuda legislators and the business establishment apparently calculated that any commerce lost in the offshore banking sector would be offset by increases in other sectors including insurance and e-commerce.

In 1999, 11,494 international businesses maintained registration in Bermuda, and 2,528 locally. Total income generated by international companies was $1.2 billion. Since 1999 there has been a marked increase in new incorporations. The number of business permits surged in 2000 as the island promoted itself as an e-commerce haven and opened its shores to licensed investment services providers for the first time. Bermuda has long been a haven for offshore businesses. There is no income tax in Bermuda and international companies pay vastly reduced corporate taxes compared to the United States and Europe. International companies spent $912.1 million locally in 1999, an increase of 20.2 percent over the $759 million recorded in 1998.

Business Unrest

In the summer of 2000 a number of problems caused publicized discontent within the offshore and expatriate community on the island. The government instituted new, more restrictive policies for expatriate work permits, alleging in the past native black Bermudians had been passed over for job openings and that a disproportionate number of foreigners held jobs, especially in the offshore financial sector. A few firms departed the island based on complaints about this new policy. The Bermuda Chamber of Commerce claimed real fears existed about the island's economic future in many areas of business, based on what some viewed as racial quotas.

One major issue was an increase of payroll taxes charged to all businesses on the island. All Bermuda companies now have to pay payroll tax of 12.75 percent on all salaries up to $250,000, and the parliamentary opposition charged this would drive away business.

Early Surrender to the OECD

Bermuda was one of only six offshore financial centers which gave a prior written pledge to the OECD before publication of its June 2000 blacklist of "harmful tax competition" nations. Each promised to meet OECD tax requirements in the future. Even after the 1999 adoption of criminal tax evasion and tax information exchange laws, Bermuda's tax agreement with the OECD was still a surprise.

Essentially the Bermuda government pledged to the OECD to exchange all tax information with other nations; to require local and international companies to file publicly audited annual accounts; to maintain its current tax system and to implement unspecified recommendations from an advisory committee of local persons by 2003 for the financial sector, and by 2005 for other businesses.

Bermuda also told the OECD it would allow IBCs to participate in previously sheltered but unnamed sectors of the economy. By year's end the so-called Bermuda "60/40 ownership rule" was relaxed. The rule had meant that any local company had to be owned by a 60 percent majority of Bermudians, the other 40 percent could be owned by foreign persons.

Clean Money

Not only did Bermuda evade the OECD hit list but it escaped the FATF list of jurisdictions alleged to indulge dirty money laundering through banking secrecy and lack of "transparency." Bermuda has only three banks and each has worked to maintain clean reputations, although several money laundering cases have occurred without any bank complicity.

The former Bermuda Financial secretary, Peter Hardy, argued that endorsement from the FATF and OECD "enables those major companies that want to set up in Bermuda to demonstrate they are, in fact, able to move to jurisdictions where international standards are upheld. We are able to say Bermuda is an upstanding and clean jurisdiction." And also a nation no longer able to guarantee financial privacy for those who do business on the island.

Somewhat defensively the Bank of Bermuda told its international clients that the bank did not see any major changes in the areas of exchange of information or transparency from the way Bermuda currently conducts business. In the main, Bermuda had to make the smallest number of changes in order to meet the OECD's guidelines and is already largely compliant with the OECD principles.

British Colonial Review

Until a few years ago Bermuda was a British "Crown colony," but that colonial sounding title gave way to "British Overseas Territory" (OST) for London's public relations purposes.

In 1999 Britain's Labor government offered the overseas territories full U.K. citizenship and the right to live and work within the U. K. and thus, within any European Union member nation. But in return, London demanded that OSTs end their established roles as offshore tax havens and that they impose strict laws against money laundering. Part of the demand was that the OSTs employ the best financial practices in their offshore sectors, principally meaning and end to offshore financial privacy.

An official British review by the international accounting firm KPMG examined Bermuda, the Cayman Islands, Anguilla, the British Virgin Islands, Montserrat, and the Turks and Caicos. It covered laws on banking, insurance, securities, IBCs and trusts, as well as financial regulatory authorities. It also looked at arrangements for international information exchanges and co-operation, as well as anti-money laundering rules.

As part of this review process a steady stream of Bermuda officials shuttled back and forth to London all during 2000, trying to influence a favorable report on the island's financial community. The Bermuda government issued claims that a newly "clean" Bermuda compared to "dirty" offshore havens would be a big draw for more respectable offshore business.

IRS Qualified Intermediary Status

The U.S. Internal Revenue Service, as of January 2001, forced foreign banks and financial institutions into the unwelcome role of IRS informants, a.k.a. "qualified intermediaries" (QI). On that date, U.S. persons holding U.S.-based investments purchased through offshore banks had a choice of either having banks report the holdings to the IRS, or having the bank withhold a 30 percent tax on all interest and dividends paid. To avoid either, the U.S. investor could liquidate his or her U.S.-based investments.

Foreign investments held offshore by U.S. persons are exempt from these new IRS rules. Bent on crushing possible tax evasion, in effect the IRS imposed extraterritorial tax enforcement burdens on foreign nations and their offshore banks. Both have been forced to meet IRS established anti-money laundering and "know your customer" standards in order to obtain "QI" status. Those who qualified got IRS "approved status," meaning the 30 percent tax on U.S. source income need not be withheld, and reduced tax rates can be applied under mutual double tax avoidance treaties.

But the IRS stamp of QI approval comes freighted with onerous conditions which end customer confidentiality for U.S. offshore investors. It also gives the IRS leverage over offshore nations when demanding exchange of tax and other financial information. Offshore banks may suffer U.S. financial sanctions if they don't tell the IRS who their U.S. customers are and what they are doing. Under the guise of enforcing American tax laws, the IRS has demanded and received imperial approval of foreign nations' banking rules and reporting requirements.

In October 2000 Bermuda became an approved jurisdiction of the U.S. IRS for tax reporting purposes. That meant that the island's banks, investment advisors and other financial services who deal in U.S. securities agreed to disclose to the IRS the names of their U.S. clients, or to impose a 30 percent withholding tax on investment income paid to such U.S. persons. This was said to show IRS approval of Bermuda's stricter know-your-customer and suspicious activity reporting rules.

A Wealth of Ambiguity

As 2001 dawned, Bermuda was in the midst of a mini-boom in offshore e-commerce as numerous web servers located their operations there, using new international fiber optic links to the U.S. and the world beyond.

Michael Allen of the *Wall Street Journal* reported: "There are serious questions about whether some of these structures would pass muster with the Internal Revenue Service and its foreign counterparts. But many accountants figure there's enough ambiguity in the industrial world's offshore tax codes that e-commerce companies could, at least theoretically, rack up tax-free profits for years before the authorities sort things out. The issues are often murkier than for a standard offshore tax shelter, because they involve technological innovations that the U.S. Treasury couldn't have antici-

.

pated when it began laying the ground rules for offshore taxation in the 1960s."

Bragging Rights

All this financial house cleaning and its strict new laws led Bermuda's Premier, Jennifer Smith, to claim in October that the island was now "the business leader among the British overseas territories." She claimed Bermuda would meet and exceed international demands for financial standards and regulation.

The British Westminster system confers an immensely important constitutional right on each U.K. overseas territory. While most Bermuda political leaders try to avoid mentioning the word, the only alternative to bowing down to London is to declare independence. Indeed, the Labor government insisted it remains "ready to respond positively when independence [is] the clearly and constitutionally expressed wish of the people."

Conclusion

Bermuda remains a good basic asset protection nation for location of offshore trusts and IBCs. But its new-found willingness to cooperate with tax-hungry governments in Washington and London has seriously diminished what was formerly a policy of strict financial privacy.

Contacts

Government

- *Bermuda Monetary Authority*, Burnaby House, 26 Burnaby St., Hamilton HM 11, Bermuda. **Tel.**: +441 295 5278.

Banks & Finance

- *Bank of Bermuda*, 6 Front Street, Hamilton 5-31, HM 111, Bermuda. **Tel.**: +441 295 4000.

- *Butterfield Bank*, 65 Front Street, P.O. Box HM 195, Hamilton HM, AX, Bermuda. **Tel.**: +441 295 1111. **Fax** +441 292 4365.

- *Bermuda Commercial Bank Ltd.* (founded in 1969); 44 Church Street, Hamilton HM 12, Bermuda; or PO Box HM 1748, Hamilton GX, Bermuda. **Tel.**: +441 295 5678. **Fax** +441 295 8091.

- *Royal Trust (Bermuda) Ltd.* (an exempt non-banking company and member of the Royal Bank of Canada Group) PO Box HM 2508-HM GX, 37 Church Street, Hamilton HM 12, Bermuda. **Tel.**: +441 292 4400. **Fax** +441 292 4070. **E-mail**: rt.bermud@lbl.bm.

- *Emerald Financial Ltd.* (financial consultants and stock brokers) Suite 341, #48 Par-la-ville Rd., International Center, Bermudiana Rd., Hamilton HM 11, Bermuda. **Tel.**: +441 292 3235. **Fax** +441 292 8087.

- *Lines Overseas Management Ltd.*, 73 Front St., PO Box 2908, Hamilton HM 12, Bermuda. **Tel.**: +441 295 5808. **Fax** +441 295 3343. **Telex**: 3240 LOM BA.

Trust Companies

- *SCS Trust, Ltd.* and *SCS Finance* (both subsidiaries of Banque SCS Alliance, Geneva). **Tel.**: +1 800 226 5727 (toll-free from the U.S. and Canada) or +441 296 0607. **Fax** +441 296 0608. Contact: Elisabeth Cirone.

Attorneys

- *Gordon L. Hill*, QC, Cox, Hallet & Wilkenson, Milner House, 18 Parliament St., PO Box HM 1561, Hamilton HM FX, Bermuda. **Tel.**: +441 295 4630. **Fax** +441 292 7880. **E-mail**: cw@cw.bm.

- *Appleby, Spurling & Kemp*, PO Box HM 1179, Hamilton HM EX, Bermuda. **Tel.**: +441 295 2244. **Fax** +441 292 8666.

Real Estate

- *Sinclair Realty Ltd.*, 2 Reid St. Penthouse, Hamilton HMLL, Bermuda. **Tel.**: +441 296 0278. **Fax**: +441 292 5932.

- *Castles Realty, Ltd.*, Somers Bldg., 15 Front Street, Hamilton HM AX, Bermuda. **Tel.**: +441 295 6565. **Fax:** +441 295 2323.

- *Rego Ltd.*, PO Box HM 169, Hamilton HM AX, Bermuda. **Tel.**: +441 292 3921. **Fax** +441 295 7464.

The Cayman Islands: No Taxes But Less Secrecy
by Robert E. Bauman, JD, August 2001

"The Cayman Islands is paradise for those whose money flows through tiny one-person offices or thick-carpeted, regal-seeming digs of lawyers and accountants. Their clients can protect their money from taxes because there are none. The Caymans are among the Caribbean's richest islands, though nothing of significance is grown or made here. They are rich because they make money on money."
—*Stephen Franklin, Chicago Tribune, April 8, 2000.*

That, sadly enough, was the old Cayman Islands, before it began its voluntary self-transformation into a potential acolyte of the Organization for Economic and Community Development (OECD) and the Financial Action Task Force (FATF).

And not all Caymans residents agree with what has happened here since June 2000. The OECD's argument is "nonsense," argued Michael Alberga, a Caymans lawyer with a long list of foreign clients. He accused the world's richest nations of practicing "economic terrorism" against economically weak places such as the Caymans. The Caymans are simply "practicing pure capitalism; few or no taxes and little regulation," he told the *Tribune* reporter.

Mr. Alberga was not the only one of the 33,000 residents of this British overseas territory who was disturbed by the OECD and FATF demands. In elections held on November 8, 2000, the Leader of Government, Truman Bodden, was defeated along with another minister who, with Bodden, led negotiations with the OECD. Voters ousted both in apparent anger over the government's OECD-demanded pledge to weaken financial privacy and banking secrecy laws that made the islands wealthy.

Capitalism has thrived here, to be sure. The Caymans was home, as of September 2000, to 57,900 international business companies (IBCs), 465 financial institutions including most of the world's top banks, 2,621 mutual funds, 114 trust companies, 541 insurance companies and thousands of closed-end and hedge funds, plus the latest financial schemes dreamed up by lawyers and savvy investors.

Measured in assets under management, the Caymans rank as the world's fifth-largest financial center behind New York, London, Tokyo and Hong Kong. Offshore business accounts for roughly 30 percent of the territory's gross domestic product of US$1.4 billion. Many of the world's most reputable companies do business through subsidiaries registered in the islands to take advantage of the favorable, tax free laws. And until a year ago, all these financial operations were conducted in statutorily guaranteed secrecy.

OECD-appeasing changes in financial laws and rules made here during the last year may not have hurt the islands' immediate financial standing. According to January 2001 information from the Monetary Authority, as of June 2000, total assets of Caymans banks stood at US$747.6 billion, a 50 percent growth over a 1996 figure of US$497 billion.

But that was before all the radical new policy changes began.

History

The Caymans are located 475 miles south of Miami and 200 miles north of Jamaica. The

Caymans tax haven tradition, strongly supported by the government, is a major factor in economic growth. One can fly to the Caymans from Miami or Kingston, Jamaica. There are adequate airmail, telephone, telex, and cable services.

Politically, the Caymans are a crown colony by choice. In 1962 when Jamaica became independent of Great Britain, the Caymans were a Jamaican dependency but decided by national referendum against independence. They decided instead to stay with "colonial imperialism" and stability.

The local population is a racial mix of 20 percent Europeans, 20 percent African and 60 percent racially mixed. Racial tension, prejudice and segregation have never been serious factors in the Caymans or its politics.

British common law modified by local legislation governs. Corporate legislation is modernized and efficient. Currency exchange controls are more relaxed than in Bermuda and The Bahamas, applying to local residents. A "nonresident" company doing business outside the islands can be formed and operate without exchange-controls. A broad range of high quality legal, banking, accounting, finance, and trust services is available.

The only sources of government revenue are stamp and import duties. An automatic no-tax guarantee of 20 years is granted to nonresident exempted corporations, and there is a 50-year no-tax guarantee to trusts. There is virtually no revenue department.

Incorporation is quick and easy. For an "ordinary corporation" a memorandum of association, involving three initial shareholders (or local proxies), is required. Upon payment of a registration fee, the Registrar of Companies issues an immediate certificate of incorporation. An annual corporation fee and information statement is required and these and other standard office services are supplied by an agent for a modest fee. Total costs of incorporation run about US$2,500—the only constant being the government fee, while the agent's fees vary. Annual maintenance averages about US$1,500.

A second category of "exempt corporation" is eligible for a 20-year no-tax guarantee. A company that trades outside the Caymans need not be "exempt." An exempt company can issue shares without par value, dispense with formal annual shareholder meetings, and maintain privacy since there are no listings in any official public records, including names of shareholders. Start-up costs and annual maintenance run about 50 percent higher. Even with these fees, a Caymans exempt company costs about the same as a Bermudian nonresident company, and apart from the above advantages, it can also issue bearer shares, and there is no extra charge in the form of stamp duties on the transfer of shares.

An exempt company can issue non-voting redeemable preference shares, which have liquidation priority over ordinary shares. Such shares are useful to finance the company while avoiding loans and keeping control of the company.

The common law tradition of the Caymans also allows trusts, and numerous trust companies compete for clients. Trust deeds require a stamp duty and a nominal fee for official recording. However, total formation costs for an average trust company can be as low as US$1,000. There are no trust limitations on sectors or beneficiaries and no taxes on trust profits. The trust counterpart of an exempt corporation, the exempt trust, has a 50-year guarantee against future taxes.

The Caymans offer a wide range of business activities and bank privacy is strongly guarded. A governmental official who breaches bank privacy can expect heavy fines and a prison term. Clearly, the Caymans are superior in many respects—future no-tax security, costs, easy incorporation, flexible corporate structure, privacy, immigration and land ownership. Very positive government support of the tax haven industry is a big plus.

Cayman's Careful Bankers

Regulation is tight and banking licenses are not easy to acquire. Under the 1986 Mutual Assistance Pact with the United States and other banking centers, only clean money is welcome in the islands. For example, when political problems arose after the U.S. invasion and arrest of former Panamanian President Manuel Noriega, many disreputable Panama-based banks seeking refuge in the Caymans found the door shut.

Major banks on the island include National Westminster of Britain, Canadian Imperial Bank, and the Royal Bank of Canada. All of these have U.S. branches or subsidiaries, and all might have to provide information to U.S. authorities. A better bet for total privacy is N T Butterfield & Son in George Town. It's a subsidiary of the N T Butterfield Bank of Bermuda.

Banking products available in Cayman range from Certificates of Deposit to money market accounts, from mutual funds to fiduciary services, from corporate formation to foreign exchange. Asset and portfolio management for high-net-worth individuals is growing. Investors increasingly conduct such business right on the island, instead of from a faraway base in London or New York.

U.S. Assault Goes Offshore

U.S. bank regulators, the IRS and the Drug Enforcement Agency (DEA) constantly make waves in the Caribbean. It often gets so bad that some islands fear they will be swamped. Pressure from their neighbor to the north has led offshore tax haven countries in the Caribbean to relax bank secrecy and agree to exchange tax information with the United States. In return, these countries occasionally obtain U.S. aid. Countries that have yielded to pressure—at least to some degree—include Panama, The Bahamas, the Netherlands, Antilles, Bermuda, and the Turks & Caicos Islands.

Under terms of the U.S.-Caymans treaty, U.S. authorities have wide access to the financial records of Cayman banks in criminal investigations. The attorney general of the Cayman Islands may order disclosure of confidential banking and corporate information to U.S. officials investigating matters that would constitute criminal activity under Cayman Islands law.

Caymans is one of the largest offshore financial service centers and remains attractive to money launderers because of its sophisticated banking services, tradition of bank secrecy, and the ease with which shell companies can be created. Shell companies are believed to play a significant role ... in money laundering; there are an estimated 26,000 companies which, along with several hundred banks, cannot be closely monitored given Cayman's resources.

The U.S. authorities do not have to obtain a court order in the Caymans to examine banking or corporate records. They need only show to the satisfaction of the Cayman Attorney General that the information being sought is relevant to a criminal investigation.

As a result, there has been considerable bank account movement out of the islands and into other havens, notably Switzerland. The figures of the Swiss National Bank show that enormous sums flow from sunny places—notably the Cayman Islands, The Bahamas, and Panama—into the Swiss banking system. Because these sites are used to create trusts, much of this money may not be fleeing the Caribbean pressures, but merely flowing through it.

Nonetheless, the British-ruled Cayman Islands is less susceptible to pressure from the U.S. than are some other banking havens. The British-dependent status hinders statistical accounting that shows the actual influx of money from the U.S. Secondly, the Caymans are not asking for aid under the so called U.S. "Caribbean Initiative." This program, and others like it, come with strings attached. Lastly, the U.S. Treasury's own report on tax evasion showed that the Cayman Islands were less likely to be used to hide drug money than were other banking havens in the Caribbean, such as Panama and The Bahamas.

Still, in September 1996, partly in an effort to please Washington officials, the Caymans enacted a tough new anti-money laundering law patterned after U.S. banking statutes. It outlaws acquiring, possessing, concealing, disguising or using property or proceeds of criminal conduct.

[**Ed. Note**: In 2002 the Cayman Islands signed a Tax information Exchange Agreement with the United States, an unimaginable action only a few years ago].

Sunshine & Banking

The Caymans have a number of major advantages over others in the tax and asset haven business. One is convenience; the islands are a short hop by plane from Miami, Houston or Atlanta. You can combine banking with fun tourism; the Seven-Mile Beach on Grand Cayman, for example, is a popular tourist destination. There are no currency exchange controls. You can direct dial from the United States. The Caymans do business from 9:00-5:00 in the U.S. Eastern Standard Time zone.

Only "Class A" banks, which have a high capital requirement, may take deposits. "Class B" banks on the Islands may only operate offshore from the Caymans. Moreover, they must be located in and use the administrative support of the Class A banks. This enables some control over their activities. All of the banks listed at the end of this chapter are either Class A banks, or Class B banks. [**Ed. Note**: In 2001 the Islands adopted a stringent new banking law that yanked the charters of any bank without a physical office and staff presence. Hundreds of banks went out of business.]

Talking Surrender

In February 2000 the rumor surfaced that the Cayman Islands government was secretly negotiating with the OECD and FATF. Discussion centered on Caymans' moves to stop foreign tax evasion and increase "transparency" of the islands' financial institutions. The islands' government was under obvious pressure to avoid threatened OECD/FATF blacklisting and possible sanctions. The *Financial Times* in London said the government might agree to increase co-operation in international efforts to crack down on criminal tax evasion, but only as part of a multilateral initiative that also would include agreement by competing tax haven nations.

Talks were also underway to expand existing mutual legal assistant treaties (MLAT) with the U.S. and the U.K. to include for the first time criminal tax evasion. The U.S. MLAT, which was signed in 1986 and ratified by the U.S. in 1990, already had been used 170 times to exchange information. Traditionally the Caymans had not viewed foreign tax evasion as a crime since its law imposed no income taxes.

Under pressure in 1998 the Caymans repealed a specific exemption in law that had until then prevented bank account freezes and forfeiture based on foreign government tax claims. London and Washington long had demanded repeal of this legal exemption for "tax offenses." Since non-payment of taxes is not a crime in the Caymans and local law had applied the principle of "dual criminality," that meant MLAT requests were honored only for alleged acts that were clearly criminal under Caymans law, as well as the law of the requesting nation.

As the law stands now, a Caymans court can confiscate all assets of a convicted person up to the amount by which he benefitted from the crime.

Caymans Agree to Surrender Financial Secrecy

Even though the Caymans were listed on the June 2000 FATF blacklist of nations allegedly soft on money laundering, on June 19 the Cayman Islands government proudly announced what its politicians repeatedly had said they would never do. They had reached an agreement with the OECD on the issue of future "transparency."

Thus the government officially embraced the OECD's demand for an end to Cayman's traditional bank and financial secrecy, guaranteeing it would provide financial information about Caymans clients to foreign tax collecting authorities. This Caymans "advance commitment" said that effective exchange of information on tax matters would begin by January 1, 2004 and be fully implemented after December 2005. In return for this major surrender, the OECD promised the Caymans would not appear on the OECD blacklist of tax havens allegedly engaged in "harmful tax practices" which was published on June 26, 2000.

This OECD promise proved useless when the United States, under a new president in 2001, forced an end to the phony OECD harmful tax competition campaign by refusing to go along. At this writing it is unclear whether the Caymans will now honor its OECD commitment on transparency, but local leaders will be hard pressed not to uphold banking secrecy which remains on the statute books. In fact, the Caymans high court has recently upheld these laws in the Ansbacher Caymans Bank case against demands of Irish tax collectors.

Within three weeks of the FATF report in June 2000, all the primary legislation necessary to address every one of the FATF's concerns was on the statute books. Within a further few weeks anti-money laundering rules were introduced to complete the legislative framework. The Islands now have a regime considerably tougher than that which exists in many of the FATF's 29 member countries.

The new laws allow the Cayman Islands Monetary Authority to obtain information on bank deposits and bank clients without a court order and ends restrictions on sharing information with foreign investigators. A new provision made it a crime to fail to disclose knowledge or suspicion of money laundering. Previously it had been a crime for financial sector workers to disclose any private financial information without a court order. The Caymans government even went so far as to guarantee that it would stop island financial services providers from "the use of aggressive marketing policies based primarily on confidentiality or secrecy."

One crucial OECD demand died in June 2001. That would have required the Caymans (and all other blacklisted haven nations), to abolish any preferential tax treatment accorded foreign business and investment, so-called "ring fencing." Fortunately for the Caymans and other tax havens, this June the Bush administration forced the OECD to abandon this high-handed demand, preserving the no tax appeal that has made the Caymans what it is today.

Recommendation

It now appears that the Caymans may not remain tax free, and as for its banking and financial secrecy, that is still very much an open question. That's especially so because of an apparent U.S.-OECD deal announced in early July which may subject offshore havens to economic sanctions starting in 2003 if they do not provide information to tax authorities in OECD countries seeking data in specific tax inquiries. To avoid being considered "uncooperative," governments would be expected to hand over taxpayer data to other countries' authorities in specific cases. They could not refuse a request for information on the ground that the alleged tax violation was not a crime under their own laws, as is the case in the Caymans.

If you value financial privacy and are considering or have financial dealings in the Cayman Islands, or any British overseas territory, including Bermuda, the Turks and Caicos Islands and Anguilla, plan accordingly.

Contacts

Banking

- *Cayman National Bank & Trust Co.*, PO Box 1097, Georgetown, Grand Cayman, BWI. **Tel.:** +1 345 949 4655. **Fax:** +1 345 949 7506. Cayman National issues its own MasterCard.

- *Cayman Securities Ltd.*, PO Box 275, Georgetown, Grand Cayman, BWI. **Tel.:** +1 345 949 7722. **Fax:** +1 345 949 8203. **E-mail:** d.markiuk@candw.ky/.

- *Midland Bank Trust Corp.* (Cayman) Ltd., PO Box 1109, Mary Street and Fort Street, George Town, Grand Cayman, BWI. **Tel.:** +1 345 949 7755. **Fax:** +1 345 949 7634.

Attorneys/Investment Advisors

- *Portfolio of Finance & Development*, Government Administration Bldg, George Town, Grand Cayman, BWI. **Tel.:** +1 345 949 7900. **Fax:** +1 345 949 9538. **Website:** www.businessmonitor.co.uk.

- *Goldman Sachs Trust Ltd.*, PO Box 896, Harbour Center, Second Floor, George Town, Grand Cayman, BWI. **Tel.:** +1 345 949 6770. **Fax:** +1 345 949 6773.

- *International Management Service Ltd.*, Box 61G, 3rd Floor, Harbour Court, Grand Cayman, BWI. **Tel.:** +1 345 949 4244. **Fax:** +1 345 949 8635.
- *Citco Fund Services Ltd.*, Corporate Center, West Bay Rd., PO Box 31106 SMB, Grand Cayman, BWI. **Tel.:** +1 345 949 3977. **Fax:** +1 345 949 3877.

The Spy Who Shagged the Caymans

by Robert E. Bauman, *The Sovereign Society Offshore A-Letter*, January 2003

Even in this age when Americans have been stripped nearly naked by the destruction of their right to financial privacy, consider what would be the public reaction to this scenario: the CIA is exposed as having had, for 10 years, a paid secret spy in a major U.S. bank who regularly reported to them on the accounts of private citizens.

Well, dear readers, that is exactly what was revealed last week in, of all places, The Cayman Islands, home to the fifth largest hoard of cash and assets (2001 est. $800 billion) in the world. Indeed, that ranking (after NYC, London, Tokyo and Hong Kong) will now dwindle even more rapidly after these shocking revelations.

A major anti-money laundering trial (Euro Bank) was abruptly aborted by the CI Chief Justice, who revealed that the head of the CI's Financial Reporting, Brian Gibbs, was a paid "mole" for MI-6, the British CIA. Gibbs, a former London police detective, had been paid monthly for 10 years to report to London whatever his spy masters demanded, under a supposedly secret intelligence operation, code named "Victory." It turned out that Gibbs, on London's orders, had destroyed evidence concerning the Euro Bank trial and may have wiretapped the Chief Justice's telephone.

As of 2001, the Caymans was home to 57,900 IBCs, 465 banks, including most of the world's top banks, 2,621 mutual funds, 114 trust companies, 541 insurance companies and thousands of hedge funds. Presumable many of these were the object of MI-6 spying, which reportedly was coordinated with the United States.

The chief justice said the territory's British appointed governor, its attorney general and the police chief were aware that Gibbs was a U.K. mole since the early 1990s, but elected CI government ministers were kept in the dark.

The Leader of Government, McKeeva Bush, was livid at the revelations, calling the U.K. government's secret conduct "shocking and reprehensible behavior." Bush charged that "the U.K. has a plan to destroy us" and that London had been waging "a cold war" against the islands' financial sector. Bush and four cabinet colleagues demanded that Gibbs and the islands attorney general resign. Shortly thereafter Gibbs and his family fled by plane to Miami, then to London. Baroness Amos, Under-Sec. for U.K. Caribbean Overseas Territories, rejected resignation demands, but said nothing about the Labor government's exposed spying.

In recent years, under London pressure, the Cayman Islands compromised their strict financial privacy laws. Last year they surprised many by signing a tax information exchange agreement with the U.S., as London demanded. Now it appears the government may face a class action suit on behalf of Euro Bank depositors. The solvent bank was forced into liquidation as a result of the charges, now dropped.

The islands' leader, Mr. Bush said recent developments have "shaken the very foundation of our partnership" with the United Kingdom.

There's a way out if Bush has the courage to pursue it. The Westminster constitution permits voluntary independence from Britain. That would end colonial control and, hopefully, clumsy Austin Powers spying.

The British Virgin Islands: Walking a Tightrope

by Robert E. Bauman, JD, August 2001

Among the U.K. overseas territories, the British Virgin Islands (BVI) is probably unlikely to break away from London. Its population and resources are small and British ties are seen as insurance of future prosperity, even at the price of going along with demands for tougher banking and incorporation laws.

The BVI benefit from being a British overseas territory, which allows them to dodge pressure from the U.S. government. Over the years BVI offshore companies have played a supporting role in scores of scandals, from Bank of Credit & Commerce International (BCCI), which formed companies here to further its financial intrigues, to the accused insurance-company swindler, American Martin Frankel, who used several BVI companies as fronts.

The BVI, even smaller than the Caymans (56 square miles of territory, population 22,000), currently has four banks: Chase, Barclays, Scotiabank of Canada, and First Pennsylvania. Only major international banks are granted banking licenses. Since adoption of the Mutual Funds Act of 1996, over 2,000 mutual funds have registered in the BVI.

Since 1984, a special BVI law has allowed quick and cheap formation of corporations to hold assets and execute offshore transactions. According to the *Wall Street Journal*, the incorporation business started in 1984, under guidance from the U.S. law firm Shearman & Sterling, and boomed in the late 1980s, when political instability in the region's incorporation leader, Panama, drove professionals and customers here. Offshore fees now account for about $75 million a year in government revenue, or more than half the total budget. Incorporation usually costs less than one thousand dollars, including a government fee of about $300.

These IBC operations are tax-free. That why the BVI was on the OECD's 35-nation blacklist of "harmful tax competition" places, since deflated by the Bush administration abandonment of this anti-tax haven campaign. (See Chapter 8.)

As of this writing BVI corporate registration is secret, and the identity of owners is not part of public record. That could change. In June 2000 the government announced it had agreed to an amendment to the Mutual Legal Assistance Treaty (MLAT) with the U.S. to allow IRS access to information relating to criminal tax investigations. This waived the then existing requirement of dual criminality under both U.S. and BVI law before information could be provide to U.S. investigators. The government pledged a "commitment" to addressing the opaqueness of IBCs by requiring names of directors to be recorded at the official Company Registry and restricting the mobility and anonymity of bearer sharers by requiring them to be deposited with licensed financial institutions.

In early 2001 the government began enforcement of a new anti-money laundering law, and gave the Director of Financial Services authority to assist foreign investigative bodies regarding criminal activities including money laundering.

Use of a standard BVI corporation can be more profitable than an IBC, particularly if one wants to take advantage of the BVI double tax treaties still in effect with Japan and Switzerland. The U.S. canceled a similar tax treaty over a decade ago. BVI companies are not subject to withholding tax on receipts of interest and dividends earned from U.S. sources.

After the demise of the U.S.-BVI tax treaty, the 1984 International Business Companies Ordinance was implemented. The new law led to a ballooning number of corporate registrations-from about 1000 when the law was passed, to nearly 10,000 today. Nowadays, corporations almost outnumber people in the BVI.

Contacts

- *Financial Services Dept.*, BVI Government, Road Town, Tortola, BVI. **Tel.**: +1 284 494 6430,

Fax: +1 284 494 5016. Website: www.bvi.org.

- *ILS Fiduciary Ltd.*, Suite 6, PO Box 3085, Mill Mall, Wickhams Cay 1, Road Town, Tortola, BVI. Tel.: +1 284 494 2999. Fax: +1 284 494 5076.

- *The AMS Group*, Creque Bldg, Upper Main St, PO Box 116, Road Town, Tortola, BVI. Tel.: +1 284 494 3399. Fax: +1 284 494 3041.

- *Harney Westwood & Riegels*, attorneys at law, Craigmuir Chambers, PO Box 71, Road Town, Tortola, British Virgin Islands. Tel.: (284) 494-2233. Fax: (284) 494-3547. E-mail: mail@harneys.com. Website: www.harneys.ac.psiweb.com.

British Destroyers

By Robert E. Bauman, *The Sovereign Society Offshore A-Letter*, April 2002

Among the principal reasons for the founding of the Sovereign Society five years ago was the perceived need for greater asset protection, better investment opportunities and a solid guarantee of financial privacy.

Then and now, a drastically restricted freedom climate in America dictated our conclusion that all of these traditional values were disappearing rapidly within the United States.

The Sovereign Society solution was, and remains, to go offshore.

In last five years The A-Letter has chronicled the sad decline of financial privacy in many jurisdictions once known as tax havens. We have assessed the causes, including the lost war on drugs, the tax collector mentality of the OECD, cloaked in FATF's anti-money laundering push, plus the Draconian laws imposed by thoughtless politicians myopically fighting their war against terror.

The United Kingdom stands out as one nation that has done much to destroy financial privacy, both at home and offshore. Under control of Tony Blair's so-called New Labor party, the Foreign Office has dismantled financial privacy in the British Overseas Territories; Bermuda, the Cayman Islands, and the British Virgin Islands. The same fate has been imposed on the Crown dependencies; the Isle of Man and the Channel Islands of Jersey, Guernsey and Sark, supposedly independent constitutional entities.

A prime example of this destruction of privacy was last week's announcement by the British Virgin Islands of the end of absolute privacy, until now accorded the 380,000 international business corporations (IBCs) registered there. The secrecy allowed until now by the BVI was a major factor in making it the second in the world in total number of IBCs, behind only Hong Kong.

The BVI parliament, on orders from London, has ended the use of corporate "bearer shares" which allow company ownership without registering the names of the actual owners. Secrecy could be pierced in criminal matters, but otherwise financial privacy prevailed.

In 1997 Sovereign Society Council of Experts member Derek Sambrook said that those who chose Panama as their offshore haven did so knowing "that the Panama secrecy laws will not be swept aside by a foreign country, whereas several prime offshore financial centers are dependent territories, thus constantly susceptible to compromise because of their dependence on a sovereign power with its own agenda of priorities."

The death of corporate financial privacy in the BVI proves his point once again. When you choose an offshore haven, keep that in mind.

The U.S. Virgin Islands—Little-Known Tax Haven

by Robert E. Bauman, JD, *The Passport Report, 2000*

Few people realize that corporate and individual residents of the U.S. Virgin Islands can live practically tax free. It requires an established residence and some paperwork, but it's the only tax haven available within the jurisdiction of the United States.

The Virgin Islands of the United States, as their name is officially styled, are constitutionally "an unincorporated territory" of the U.S.

After their discovery by Columbus in 1493, the islands passed through control by the Dutch, English and French. In 1666, St. Thomas was occupied by Denmark, which five years later founded a colony there to supply the mother country with sugar, cotton, indigo, and other products. By the early seventeenth century, Danish influence and control were established and the islands became known as the Danish West Indies. That political status continued until Denmark sold the islands to the U.S. for US$25 million in 1917.

The islands—St. Croix, St. Thomas, and St. John—have a strategic value for the U.S. since they command the Anegada Passage from the Atlantic Ocean into the Caribbean Sea as well as the approach to the Panama Canal. U.S. citizenship status was conferred on the islands' inhabitants in 1927. Although they do not vote in U.S. presidential elections, residents are represented by a non-voting delegate in the U.S. House of Representatives.

A Low-Tax Residence

The islands are administered by the U.S. Department of the Interior under the Basic Organic Act of 1954 and earlier statutes dating back to the Naval Service Appropriations Act of 1922 (48 USC 1397). The 1922 law provides, in part, "that the income tax laws in force in the United States shall be likewise in force in the Virgin Islands of the United States, except that the proceeds of such taxes shall be paid to the treasuries of said islands."

It is not widely known, but under a unique federal income tax arrangement applying only to the Virgin Islands, U.S. nationals who make the islands their main residence can enjoy substantially reduced taxes compared to other Americans. This makes the islands an offshore tax haven option for wealthy U.S. citizen-entrepreneurs and for foreign nationals seeking U.S. citizenship.

Unlike all other U.S. taxpayers, island residents and corporations pay federal taxes on their worldwide income to the Virgin Islands Internal Revenue Bureau (IRB), not to the U.S. Internal Revenue Service. Legal residents of the islands, those who are born there, or those who become naturalized U.S. citizens in the V.I., for purposes of U.S. federal gift and estate taxes, are not treated as residents of the U.S. Since the V.I. levies no estate or gift taxes, this means that upon death, the estates of such persons owe zero federal/state estate or gift taxes.

Special Business Incentives

To attract investment, the Virgin Islands Industrial Development Commission grants generous tax relief in the form of a 90 percent exemption on corporate federal taxes on all worldwide income. This tax holiday package, usually offered for a period of 10 to 15 years, with a possible five-year extension, is available to V.I. chartered corporations, partnerships, and limited liability companies.

Here's an example of how valuable this tax break can be, using a V.I. corporation we'll call "Worldwide, Inc." Worldwide, Inc. has a US$10 million international portfolio with a wide range of investments. Last year, Worldwide, Inc. did well and ended with net taxable income after all possible deductions of US$2 million.

U.S. mainland corporate tax computations based on $2,000,000 taxable income:

15% x $50,000 = $7,500

25% x $25,000 = $6,250

34% x $25,000 = $8,500

37% x $1,900,000 = $703,000

Total tax liability without exemption = $725,250

90% V.I. Exemption = -$675,000

Worldwide income net taxes owed = $50,250

If the principal shareholders of Worldwide, Inc. are V.I. residents, the V.I. tax laws allow each of them a 90 percent individual income tax exemption on income derived from corporate dividends.

If Worldwide, Inc. is a subchapter S corporation, owned by a single individual, the total income tax liability on US$2,000,000 at the maximum U.S. income tax rate would be US$79,200 (39.6% x 90% exemption). Because the V.I. imposes no territorial or local income taxes, the individual can keep US$1,920,800. In sharp contrast, if this investor was a U.S. mainland resident, he/she would owe the IRS US$792,000 in U.S. income taxes, plus any applicable state and local taxes which could amount to another US$200,000.

For the last 40 years, a few knowledgeable U.S. investors, with business activities ranging from petroleum production, aluminum processing, hotel and other tourism activities, banking, insurance, and other financial services have taken advantage of these very liberal V.I. tax laws. In 1998, 68 V.I. corporations with over 3,500 employees enjoyed these tax benefits.

The V.I. Government recently established a new precedent by granting the 90 percent tax exemption to a financial management company. The investing partners established a V.I. corporation to manage their worldwide assets. Each owner established bona fide V.I. residence by renting or buying a home or condominium, registering to vote in the V.I., and designating their stateside home as their secondary residence. The investors confirmed their new principal residence by canceling their stateside voter registration, their state and county homestead exemptions, and moving their business and personal affairs to the V.I.

There is no restriction against maintaining a second home elsewhere, either in or outside of the U.S., as long as a V.I. resident maintains a principal residence in the V.I. These fortunate people can live in a second home anywhere in the United States during spring, summer, and fall, then come home to the Virgin Islands for the winter, where they play golf, tennis, sail and swim, all under protection of the U.S. flag. In addition, they enjoy the unique and legal privilege of paying only 10 percent of what they would otherwise owe in federal income taxes.

Moving your residence to the V.I. is no more difficult than moving from one U.S. state to another. The V.I. has a well-developed infrastructure and judicial and legal system under the U.S. Constitution. The islands are served by the U.S. court system, postal service, currency, customs and immigrations laws. For any wealthy person considering U.S. naturalization, or any current U.S. citizen willing to relocate to a warmer climate to legally avoid burdensome taxes, this little known tax "loophole" certainly is worth exploring.

Contact

- *Henley & Partners AG*, Haus zum Engel, Kirchgasse 24, 8001 Zurich, Switzerland. **Tel.:** +(41) 1 267-6090. **Fax:** +(41) 1 267-6091. **E-mail:** zurich@henleyglobal.com. **Website:** www.henleyglobal.com.

The Cook Islands: Far Out

by Robert E. Bauman, JD, & David Melnik, QC, *Offshore Money Manual*

It is so far out in the south Pacific it's almost over the International Date Line and into tomorrow. But in the last 20 years these islands have become the home-away-from-home for billions of dollars worth of wealth. There is more here than just coconuts and white sandy beaches.

If you're researching the world of offshore asset protection, you'll soon hear all about the Cook Islands. Since the CI government first adopted a series of wealth and asset-friendly laws in 1981, the Cook Islands, though small in population and remote from the rest of the world, have come to play a significant role in offshore financial circles.

A broad net of 15 coral islands in the heart of the South Pacific spreads over 850,000 square miles. The islands occupy an area the size of India, but have a population (18,000 people) no bigger than a small town in Indiana. Indirectly, the islands are part of the British Commonwealth by virtue of their unique association with nearby New Zealand. From 1901 to 1965, this was a colony of New Zealand, and New Zealand still subsidizes the CI government. The islanders even retain NZ citizenship. The subsidy has become a sore point in both nations.

The Cook Islands offshore industry, says the government, was conceived in 1981 as the result of its official collaboration with the local financial services industry. There is a lot of overlap between the two groups. Financial services now rank second only to tourism in the economy. Despite some 50,000 visitors a year to the capital island, Rarotonga, the Cook Islands have remained largely unspoilt. Cook Islanders have their own language and enjoy a vigorous and diverse culture, though most also speak English.

This is a micro-state with macro aspirations, and the grasp may have exceeded the reach. Their checkered history of high finance has been marked by some pretty rancid scandals sponsored by fast-talking American, U.K. and New Zealand expatriates. Although perfectly legal, it's no secret that certain American asset protection attorneys play a large role in advising the government on asset protection issues, and actually draft statutes for the island's parliament.

Constantly teetering on the brink of bankruptcy, CI government debt exceeds NZ$250 million-this in a nation with a GDP of only NZ$175 million. Much of that debt stems from a failed Sheraton Hotel project fiasco involving government officials in the 1980s. Two-thirds of the work force is on the government payroll, financing an old-fashioned spoils and patronage system that would make an American big city political boss blush.

Tailored Wealth Protection

Whatever the politics, existing statutes meticulously provide for the care and feeding of international business companies (IBCs) including offshore banks, insurance companies and trusts. All offshore business conducted on the Cook Islands must be channeled through one of the five registered trustee companies. A comprehensive range of trustee and corporate services is offered for offshore investors. The government officially guarantees no taxes will be imposed on offshore entities.

Thousands of foreign trusts, corporations and partnerships are registered here, protected by an exceedingly strong financial privacy law. In 2000 the highest court here pointedly upheld these laws and refused to repatriate trust funds after being order to do so by a U.S. federal district court in Nevada in a case in which the U.S. government was the plaintiff.

The Development Investment Act requires all foreign enterprises (those with more than one-third foreign ownership) that want to do business to first obtain approval and register their planned activities with the Cook Islands Development Investment Board. There are various incentives and concessions for tariff protection, import duty and levy concessions, tax concessions by way of accelerated depreciation, allowance for counterpart training, and recruitment of Cook Islanders from overseas.

A leading New Zealand asset protection attorney, highly respected in the profession, told us that in spite of the Cook Islands' obvious fiscal problems, the government's tax and asset haven laws are likely to remain in place, even if New Zealand has to take control again (a prospect Wellington officials do not relish).

Contacts

Solicitors

- *Clarkes P.C.*, PO Box 123, Rarotonga, Cook Islands. **Tel.:** +682 24 567. **Fax:** +682 21 567 (or +682 25 567).

- *Miller Howard & Lynch*, PO Box 39, Panama, Rarotonga, Cook Islands. **Tel.:** +682 21 043. **Fax:** +682 21 143.

- *Stevenson Nelson & Mitchell*, PO Box 552, Avarua, Rarotonga, Cook Islands. **Tel.:** +682 21 080. **Fax:** +682 21 087.

- *Tim Arnold*, PO Box 486, Rarotonga, Cook Islands. **Tel.:** +682 23 565. **Fax:** +682 23 568.

- *Tony Manarangi*, PO Box 514, Rarotonga, Cook Islands. **Tel.:** +682 23 840. **Fax:** +682 23 843.

Accountants

- *Carolyn Short & Assoc.*, PO Box 632, Rarotonga, Cook Islands. **Tel.:** +682 24 530. **Fax:** +682 24 531.

- *Deloitte & Touche Tohmatsu*, PO Box 910, Rarotonga, Cook Islands. **Tel.:** +682 24 449. **Fax:** +682 23 449.

- *KPMG Peat Marwick*, PO Box 691, Rarotonga, Cook Islands. **Tel.:** +682 20 486. **Fax:** +682 21 486.

- *Michael A. Innes-Jones*, PO Box 910, Rarotonga, Cook Islands. **Tel.:** +682 24 449. **Fax:** +682 23 449.

- *Moore Stephens*, PO Box 67, Rarotonga, Cook Islands. **Tel.:** +682 22 371. **Fax:** +682 20 932.

- *Trends Limited*, PO Box 1040, Rarotonga, Cook Islands. **Tel.:** +682 20 537. **Fax:** +682 24 537.

Banking & Financial Services

- *Asiaciti Trust Pacific Ltd.*, Level 3, CIDB Bldg., PO Box 822, Rarotonga, Cook Islands. **Tel.:** +682 23 387 or 24 439. **Fax:** +682 23 385.

- *ANZ Banking Group Ltd.*, PO Box 907, Rarotonga, Cook Islands. **Tel.:** +682 21 750. **Fax:** +682 21 760.

- *Westpac Banking Corporation*, PO Box 42, Rarotonga, Cook Islands. **Tel.:** +682 22 014. **Fax:** +682 20 802.

- *Cook Islands Development Bank*, PO Box 113, Rarotonga, Cook Islands. **Tel.:** +682 29 341. **Fax:** +682 29 343.

- *Cook Islands Savings Bank*, PO Box TX, Rarotonga, Cook Islands, **Tel.:** +682 29 471. **Fax:** +682 20 471.

- *Southpac Trust Ltd.*, Centrepoint, Raratonga, Cook Islands. **Tel.:** +682 20 514. **Fax:** +682 20 667.

Real Estate

- *Cook Islands Commercial Realty Brokers Ltd.*, PO Box 514, Rarotonga, Cook Islands, **Fax:** +682 23 843.

U.S. Contacts

- *Michael G. Chatzky JD*, Chatzky & Associates, PC, 888 Prospect St., La Jolla, CA 92037 U.S.A. **Tel.:** +1 619 456 6085. **Fax:** +1 619 456 6099.

Andorra: Secret Tax-Free Mountain Redoubt

by Robert E. Bauman, JD, *The Passport Report*, 2000

It lies in a secret valley in one of the most stunning mountain ranges in Europe. It's a secluded medieval principality not governed by any European bureaucracy. For the few in the know, this picturesque valley, almost forgotten by the rest of the world, offers affordable crime-free, tax-free European living. The big secret is, you don't even need a permit to live there—you can just move in!

Andorra is an accident of geography. A small mountaintop principality located in the Pyrenees between France and Spain, it is hours away from the nearest airport in Barcelona. Much of the year the skiing is great, but the roads are covered with snow.

Andorra is also a blissful tax haven—no income, capital gains or inheritance taxes. No sales taxes or customs duties. There is a small local residence tax charged in most "parishes," as the unit of local government is called.

In 1992, absolute authority was withdrawn from the two princes who previously governed—a Spanish Roman Catholic bishop and the French head of state. The two now act as advisory figureheads of state. Their powers were reassigned to a legislative Council General whose electors are the 11,571 native-born citizens with Andorran parents. This electorate constitutes less than one-sixth of the total Andorran population. The total population includes 30,000 Spanish, with sizeable communities of Portuguese, French and English speakers.

Under Andorra's old constitution, what are called "passive residence permits" were handed out by designated personal representatives of the co-princes. Andorrans, with no control over this process, resented the permits given arbitrarily to politicians' friends and cronies. After the 1992 constitution, the new Council General blocked permits by refusing to pass on applications to the co-princes' representatives until a stricter immigration law was adopted. A tougher law on passive residence permits became final on June 30, 1995, and in 1997 permits again were issued.

Passive Residence

Residence, under Andorran law, is defined as a person's permanent principal residence. A second residence in Andorra does not alter an individual's domicile of origin for the purposes of home nation inheritance or estate taxes.

Those granted a passive residence in Andorra have the right to protection under the law, certain benefits from the health and social security system, the right to a driver's license and to own and register vehicles with resident plates. Residence does not confer the right to vote, either in local or national elections, nor does it allow local commercial activity, such as owning or running a business.

Come & Stay a While

An individual who is not a resident is considered a tourist. But there is no legal limit on the period of stay and tourists are permitted to rent or purchase a property for personal use for as long as they wish. Thus, it is easy to live in Andorra perpetual traveler-style even without an official residence permit. And there are ways to benefit from Andorran tax advantages, depending on the tax laws in your home nation or place of legal domicile. Questions on tax issues should be directed to your attorney or the financial services firm Servissim. (See below for contact details.)

There are two categories of residence permits, both difficult to obtain: 1) those that give the holder the right to work in Andorra, and; 2) those that do not allow work. Residence permits are issued for periods of four years and are renewable. Applications for permits should be submitted to the Office of Immigration in Andorra la Vella, the capital city (telephone: +376 826222).

A holder of a permit should spend at least six months annually in Andorra and have documented proof of that fact. Failure to meet this requirement can result in revocation of the permit.

The annual maximum quota for issuance of passive, non-work permits (passive residency permits) is now 200. The earlier each year one applies, the better the chance of obtaining one. Applications are considered without regard to nationality, race or religion, but the person must be at least 18 years of age.

Applicants must also show they, and their family, have "sufficient economic means" to reside in the Principality of Andorra without any professional or work activity on their part throughout the period of his passive residence.

"Sufficient Economic Means"

How much cash or assets does "sufficient economic means" require? An applicant must be able to demonstrate income of £16,000/US$24,000 per annum. A couple must be able to demonstrate combined income of £24,000/US$38,000. There is an additional income requirement if children are included on the application. Proof of annual income is sometimes waived if the applicant's net worth, as declared in a required confidential financial statement, is at the very high end. Obviously, the more wealth declared, the better the chance for a permit.

An applicant for passive residence must be able to prove he or she has in force public or private health insurance to cover illness, incapacity, and old age for him and those in his charge for the duration of his passive residence. Private insurance purchased from an Andorran insurer is more likely to be acceptable, the usual route since insurance can only be procured after a residence permit is granted.

The applicant must be able to show documentary evidence he is the owner or tenant of a house or apartment, or that he has initiated the process of acquiring or renting a dwelling within the Principality, which process must be concluded within a period of one year from the date of application. He must be able to prove neither he nor those in his charge have any previous penal criminal convictions. Some nations, including the U.K., do not issue such certificates, but a reference from a professional person of standing, such as a solicitor or attorney, usually is sufficient.

Each applicant must supply a non-interest bearing deposit of £16,000/US$24,000 for the principal applicant and £4,000/US$6,000 for each additional applicant (spouse/child) to the Institute National de Finances, the financial controls office. Deposits are returned in full at the end of residence. In addition, a new resident must pay an annual fee to cover the benefits he (and his family) receive from his residence in the Principality.

Andorran Citizenship

After 20 years of residence, whether passive or working, an individual can become a privileged resident. This stepped-up status allows activity in commercial matters on behalf of a maximum of one trading company, but does not confer the right to vote.

Under current law, any person in residence more than 25 years may acquire Andorran nationality after renouncing his previous nationality. Children born in Andorra of resident foreign parents may opt for Andorran nationality when they become 18 if they and their parents are still officially resident in Andorra. These applicants also must renounce any previous nationality.

Newly restrictive residency laws adopted in 1995 produced something unusual in Andorra—a national political debate involving residents and organizations that represent the major nationality groups on one side, and the politicians on the other. Complainers see the law as pushing many residents to leave and keeping others out. They cited Andorra's then-sluggish summer property market, blaming the slump on the new residence laws.

Local politicians, not used to public criticism, were unsettled by the protests, and revisions in the law produced the present annual quota of 200 available residency permits.

Contacts

- *Servissim*, Roc Escolla 3, 1A+B, Avinguda Meritxell 20, Andorra la Vella, Principat d'Andorra. **Tel.:** +376 860414. **Fax:** +376 863797. Servissim is a dependable relocation agent that provides, free of charge, a newsletter with information about the residency laws and changes that may occur.

- *Permanent UN Mission of the Principality of Andorra*, 2 United Nations Plaza, 25th Floor; New York, NY 10017 USA. **Tel.:** +1-212-750-8064. **Fax:** +1-212-750-6630. **Website:** www.andorra.ad/govern/.

- *Embassy of Andorra*, 30 Rue d'Astorg, 75008 Paris, France. **Tel.:** +33 1 40 06 03 30. **Fax:** +33 1 40 06 03 64.

- *Andorra Tourist Delegation*, 63 Westover Road, London SW18 2RF, U.K. **Tel.:** +44 181 874 4806. *Contact:* Director: Sra. Maria Rosa Picart.

Austria—Unique European Banking Secrecy
by Robert E. Bauman, May 2003

Strategically located on the eastern European border between former Cold War blocs, the Austrian Republic has long been a bastion of banking privacy. From 1945 to the Soviet Russian collapse in 1992, while the Soviet Union and the U.S. were locked in constant confrontation, this convenient banking haven served as a willing go-between used by both West and East.

When Austrian national banking laws were officially codified in 1979, the well-established tradition of bank secrecy was already two centuries old.

During this time Austrian bank secrecy and privacy produced two major types of so-called "anonymous accounts." These accounts usually required no account holder identification, no mailing address and no personal references. Just deposit funds and use the account as you pleased, all anonymously. Both the *Sparbuch* bank account and the *Wertpapierbuch* securities account have now been abolished, victims of the European Union's fixation with destroying financial privacy wherever possible.

Secrecy: It's the Law

Notwithstanding the demands of the EU, current Austrian bank secrecy laws forbid banks to "disclose or make use of secrets which have been entrusted or made accessible to them solely due to the business relationships with customers." This prohibition is waived only in criminal court proceedings involving "intentional fiscal violations [crimes], with the exception of fiscal petty offenses." The prohibition does not apply "if the customer expressly and in writing consents to the disclosure of the secret."

As an additional protection, the Austrian constitution includes a guarantee of banking and financial privacy. This protection can only be changed by a majority vote in a national referendum, a highly unlikely event. All major political parties support financial privacy as an established national policy of long standing.

No EU Information Tax Sharing

As a member of the European Union, Austria consistently mounted strong official opposition to EU plans for compulsory withholding taxes and financial information sharing. Defending the banking secrecy behind which its financial sector has prospered, Austria rejected any deal that would force it to exchange information on non-resident account holders. Austrian finance minister Karl-Heinz Grasser, said his nation would not agree to the proposed information exchange system unless and until other major offshore financial centers, including Switzerland, Luxembourg and those in the Caribbean accepted similar measures, an unlikely prospect that has yet to come about.

In late 2002, Austria was one of three EU nations exempted from an EU-agreed tax information sharing plan. (Belgium and Luxembourg were the other two.) All three nations, along with non-EU member Switzerland, declined to share tax information, but did agree to phase in over a period of years a 35% withholding tax on interest paid to nationals of other EU member states.

Foreign nationals of non-EU nations, including U.S. persons, are not subject to this withholding tax.

In 2000 the sanctimonious EU declared unofficial war on Austria. Self-righteous European Union politicians imposed an informal diplomatic boycott because they did not like the outcome of the Austrian elections. The Socialist rat pack dominating the fledgling European Union had decided to annul the election results of tiny (7 million) Austria.

The EU pols, gratuitously injecting themselves into domestic politics, objected to the formation of a coalition government in Vienna including the conservative People's Party of chancellor Wolfgang Schüssel and the nationalist Freedom Party, headed by the controversial Jörg Haider, governor of Carinthia.

Commented the *Daily Telegraph* in London: "This shunning of Austria is really just another excuse for the 'international community' to parade its conscience; as high-minded and ill-thought-out as the bombing of Kosovo and Serbia. No one objects to the presence of communists in Italy, and 80 million died in the last century, thanks to the tyranny of communism."

Despite such criticism, Austria's 14 EU partners imposed a 7-month freeze on high level diplomatic relations with Vienna. A surprisingly high number of Austrians, 67%, had voted in 1995 for EU membership. But within two years support for it had melted to little over 50%. But by June 2001 the ill-advised "boycott" had thoroughly discredited the EU in the opinion of most Austrians. This had the unintended result in strengthening Austrian resistance to EU demands for changes in the nation's strict financial and banking privacy laws. It also raised the specter of an eventual Austrian referendum on whether to end EU membership.

By early 2001 more than 100,000 Austrians had signed a petition for a referendum on whether to quit the European Union, obliging Parliament to discuss the issue within six months. The petition said the EU had stripped Austria of its sovereignty, undermined its policies and threatened its neutrality.

Austria's exemption in 2002 from the EU tax information sharing plan was in large part a triumph over the EU stupidity that had driven the nation away from the EU and its insensitive demands.

Stocks and Bonds

The Austrian stock market has had one of the world's best performance records in recent years. It has benefitted in part from the Eastern European expansion boom in the early 1990s after the Iron Curtain disintegrated.

Nonresidents are not subject to restrictions on securities purchased in Austria. They can be transferred abroad without restrictions or reporting. Nonresidents can purchase an unlimited amount of domestic and foreign bonds and stocks, on condition the money used for purchase is in either a foreign currency or euros. When securities are sold, the cash proceeds can be freely converted and exported without restrictions.

The Differential

Inevitably, Austrian tax authorities have found a way to profit from their attractive banking haven status. The government levies a 25% tax on the total bank account interest paid to the account holder. Foreigners can also avoid the 25% tax on bond interest, because there is no tax withheld if the bank account is held by a declared non-resident. Interest paid on investments in Austrian banks held in non-bearer form, such as certificates of deposit, is exempt from the withholding tax. Interest on convertible bonds, however, is subject to a withholding tax at 20%, withheld at the payment source.

Unfortunately, an American citizen bond holder is still subject to capital-gains tax in the U.S. on the full capital gain, despite the Austrian tax. A double-taxation treaty between the U.S. and Austria eases this hardship: if you file a request with the IRS (as authorized by this treaty), the

Austrian tax will be partly repaid, so the tax burden amounts to10%.

The other 10% can offset part of the U.S. capital-gains tax that would ordinarily be imposed. The double-taxation agreement does not apply to Austrian interest and dividends (as opposed to capital gains), which remain fully taxable in the U.S. Obviously, when you file to get relief from an Austrian capital-gains tax, you alert the IRS that you may be liable for taxes on dividends or bond interest in previous reporting periods.

Make Austria Your Home

Few people know it, but a wealthy foreigner who takes up residence in Austria can qualify for a unique tax break—100% of annual income completely free of taxes! This arrangement is ready and waiting at an obliging Ministry of Finance. This fact alone makes Austria the civilized European alternative to those hot, humid, out-of-the-way "tax free" banana republics.

If you decide to make it your home and transfer some of your assets there, you can apply to the Ministry of Finance for a little-known preferential tax treatment for new residents, called in German a *Zuzugsbeguenstigung*.

As a foreigner who is a new Austrian resident, you can qualify if:

1. You had no residence in Austria during ten years prior to your application;

2. You do not engage in any business activity within Austria;

3. You prove sufficient income from outside sources and agree to spend in Austria each year a minimum of US$70,000;

4. You have a place to live and intend to stay in Austria for at least six months (183 days) each year.

Meet all these conditions, and you may be able to live tax-free in Austria. All income from foreign pension or retirement funds, dividends and interest from foreign investments and securities or any offshore businesses, including passive income derived from licenses or patents outside Austria is tax-exempt.

Applying for a *Zuzugsbeguenstigung* requires filing forms at the Ministry of Finance. In most cases officials grant a tax break of at least 75% of potential tax liability, but a good local lawyer may be able to negotiate a 100% reduction. If you have foreign income taxable in your home country, and there is no double taxation agreement between Austria and your country, the Ministry of Finance may grant you a zero tax base, or a special circumstances ruling, but only after you establish your residence in Austria.

Consider the foreigner who uses Austria as his second residence, but not as the "center of his vital interests," (a phrase from Austrian tax law). He goes skiing for three or four weeks each year in Austria. His legal domicile (the place where he lives most of the time, and to which he eventually intends to return) is in another country. In his case, any Austrian source income is taxable in Austria, but all other income not earned in Austria is taxable in the country where he lives, his domicile. His exact tax status and obligations will be determined under the terms of a double taxation treaty that may exist between Austria and his country of domicile.

It's definitely a good deal worth considering.

Is Austrian Residence Status for Sale?

To be frank, yes, if you are a wealthy foreigner who is a reputable person, there will be few obstacles to becoming a resident. Residency gives you the best of both worlds: life in an extremely desirable location, but without the high taxes Austrian citizens must pay.

Once in residence, you could apply for citizenship, but that defeats the purpose. As an Austrian citizen, you'd be liable for full taxation. The only additional advantage would be having an Austrian passport and the right to purchase as much real property as you wish, which is otherwise very difficult for a foreigner merely residing in Austria.

Conclusion

We predict Austrian banking laws will remain secure and pretty much "as is," at least for the immediate future. The more outsiders try to pressure the government in Vienna, the more the Austrian people resent the interference in their internal affairs. We don't think this "Vaterland First" attitude will change any time soon. As a result, it's wise to keep Austria near the top of your potential banking list, especially if your major area of business interest is in eastern Europe and Russia.

Contact

Government:

- *Austrian Ministry of Finance*, Himinelpfortgasse 8, 1010 Vienna. **Tel**: +43 1 5143 30.

Banks:

- *Anglo-Irish Bank*, Rathaustrasse 20, Box 306, AlOll, Vienna, Austria. **Tel**.: +431-406-6161. **Fax**: +431-405 8142. **Contact**: Peter Zipper. The bank will accept a minimum account of $10,000, although smaller accounts are charged higher fees. This European bank offers the lowest fees we have encountered for arranging and purchasing European government CDs in most currencies.

- *Creditanstalt*, Schottengasse 6-8, 1030-Vienna, Austria. **Tel**.: +431-53-131.

- *Raiffeisen Zentralbank*, Anstadtpark, #9, 1030-Vienna,Austria. **Tel**.: +43-171-7070.

Safe Deposit Boxes:

- *Das Safe*, Auerspergstrasse 1, 1080 Vienna, Austria.

The World's Best Asset Havens: Liechtenstein
by Robert E. Bauman, JD, *The Sovereign Individual*, May 2003

World's Oldest and Most Exclusive Tax Haven

With asset protection laws dating from the 1920s, a host of excellent legal entities designed for wealth preservation, and strict bank secrecy guaranteed by law, this tiny principality has it all-plus continuing controversy about who uses it and why.

In the not so distant past one had to be a philatelist to know the Principality of Liechtenstein even existed. In those days, the nation's major export was exquisitely produced postage stamps, highly prized by collectors. Until the 1960s, the tiny principality, wedged between Switzerland and Austria, subsisted on income from tourism, postage stamp sales and the export of false teeth.

But in the last 50 years, its lack of taxes and maximum financial privacy propelled Liechtenstein to top ranking among the world's wealthiest nations. This historic Rhine Valley principality grew into a major world tax and asset haven, posting per capita income levels higher than Germany, France and the United Kingdom.

Tiny Liechtenstein (16 miles long and 3.5 miles wide, population 32,000) is nestled in the mountains between the Switzerland and Austria, has existed in its present form since January 23, 1719, when the Holy Roman Emperor Charles VI granted it independent status.

Absolute Monarchy

The government is a constitutional monarchy, with the Prince of Liechtenstein, Hans-Adam II, as head of state. Until recently, His Highness's power only extended to sanctioning laws passed by the popularly elected unicameral legislature, the Diet. For the most part, the Diet made the laws, negotiated treaties, approved or vetoed taxes, and supervised government affairs. Proposed legislation was frequently submitted directly to citizen referendum.

This system changed on March 16, 2003, when Hans-Adam II dropped his threat to leave the country after winning an overwhelming majority in favor of overhauling the constitution to give him more powers than any other European monarch. Liechtenstein's ruling prince now has the right to dismiss governments and approve judicial nominees. The prince may also veto laws simply by refusing to sign them within a six-month period.

Tempering this authority is the fact that the signature of 1,500 Liechtenstein citizens on a petition is sufficient to force a referendum on the abolition of the monarchy, or any other change in the law.

A Leading Financial Center

Liechtenstein's economy is well diversified, and it is one of the most heavily industrialized countries in Europe. Still, financial services provide some 40% of budget revenues, so anything that tarnishes its reputation is a major crisis. Its 16 locally owned banks, 60 lawyers and 250 trust companies employ 16% of the workforce, and its licensed fiduciary companies and lawyers serve as nominees for, or manage, more than 75,000 legal entities, most of them owned and controlled by non-residents of Liechtenstein.

Indeed Liechtenstein was one of the first nations in the world to adopt specific offshore asset protection laws, as far back as the 1920s.

Liechtenstein's unique role in international circles is not so much as a banking center, but as a tax haven. The nation acts as a base of operations for foreign holding companies, private foundations, family foundations and a unique entity called an Anstalt (Establishment). The banks and a host of specialized trust companies provide management services for thousands of such entities Personal and company tax rates are low, generally under 12% for local residents. Any company domiciled in Liechtenstein is granted total exemption from income tax if it generates no income from local sources.

Until recently, there was a near total absence of any international treaties governing double taxation or exchange of information. Most notable is a minor double-tax agreement with neighboring Austria, primarily to cover taxes on people who commute across the border for work.

Liechtenstein is independent, but closely tied to Switzerland. The Swiss franc is the local currency and in many respects, except for political independence, Liechtenstein's status is that of a province integrated within Switzerland. Liechtenstein banks are integrated into Switzerland's banking system and capital markets. Many cross-border investments clear in or through Swiss banks. Foreign-owned holding companies are a major presence in Liechtenstein, with most maintaining their accounts in Swiss banks.

Principality Under Attack

Until 2000, Liechtenstein had an impeccable reputation, perhaps overblown, with government regulators stressing the professional qualifications and local accountability of financial managers.

All that changed drastically in June 2000 when the Financial Action Task Force (FATF) named Liechtenstein as the sole European country on its list of 15 nations accused of failing to cooperate in the international fight against money laundering. Liechtenstein was forced to defend itself against charges of acting as banker to Central American drug lords, the Russian underworld and the Mafia. The threat of unspecified sanctions against Liechtenstein caused a sharp, but temporary slowdown in the inflow of funds as suddenly nervous foreigners avoided one of the world's most secretive tax havens.

In January 2001, Liechtenstein suffered another blow, when Liechtenstein Global Trust Bank (LGT Bank), owned by the family of Liechtenstein's ruling prince, was raided by agents investigating money laundering. Prince Hans Adam II admitted that plucky Liechtenstein was facing its most serious challenge since staving off invasion by Nazi Germany in World War II.

Liechtenstein's reaction to the blacklisting and the LGT scandal was very much in keeping with its history. Rather than overtly contest this designation, the monarchy worked through its own diplomatic and financial channels to quietly be removed. Liechtenstein hired a high-powered expert from Switzerland to see it through a difficult transition period as its banks, the country's main employers, suffered financial losses and an exodus of assets.

The strategy worked. In June 2001, Liechtenstein was removed from the FATF blacklist. However, the price was steep: it was forced to adopt tough new anti-money laundering laws that cover "all crimes;" create a Financial Intelligence Unit (FIU); impose much stricter "know your customer" and suspicious activity reporting laws; ease its historic, strict financial secrecy; and abolish the rights of trustees and lawyers not to disclose the identity of their clients to banks where funds are invested.

Liechtenstein's longstanding tax haven status was the source of a second major attack by the OECD, which in June 2000 placed the principality on its phony, 35-nation "harmful tax practices" blacklist. There it remains, along with the few jurisdictions that have refused to surrender to the OECD.

Secrecy Guaranteed By Law

Liechtenstein's secrecy statutes have historically been considered stronger even than those in Switzerland. The 2000 amendments to the money laundering laws weaken secrecy significantly, but Liechtenstein still boasts some of the strictest confidentiality statues in the world. While banks must now keep records of clients' identities, such records may not be made public. Secrecy also extends to trustees, lawyers, accountants and to anyone connected to the banking industry. All involved are subject to the disciplinary powers of Liechtenstein's Upper Court.

A court order is required to release an account holder's bank records. Creditors seeking bank records face a time-consuming and costly process. Liechtenstein is not obliged to honor a foreign court's request for information. Such requests might be approved if it can be shown that a clear violation of Liechtenstein law has occurred.

Big Bucks Banking

Liechtenstein's banks have no official minimum deposit requirements, but their stated goal is to lure high net-worth individuals as clients. Opening a discretionary portfolio management account generally requires a minimum of SFr 1 million. Trust and limited companies registered here must pay an annual government fee of either 0.1% of capital, or SFr 1,000 (whichever is higher). Most banks also charge an annual management fee of 0.5% of total assets under their supervision.

If you're considering opening a banking or investment account with a Swiss or Austrian bank, Liechtenstein is worth a comparative look. The principality has all the benefits of the other two nations, a strong economy, rock-solid (Swiss) currency, political stability, and ease of access, plus a few added attractions of its own. Unlike Switzerland, it has no double-taxation treaties, except with Austria. What's more, the government guarantees all bank deposits against loss, regardless of the amount involved. Numbered accounts are available for large investors.

Until very recently, Liechtenstein also had no information exchange agreements with any nation. But in 2002, bowing to U.S. pressure, it signed a Mutual Legal Assistance Treaty with the United States. The agreement, now under consideration by Liechtenstein's parliament, covers a broad range of mutually recognized crimes.

There is concern within Liechtenstein that the MLAT will open the door to "fishing expeditions" by U.S. tax authorities and compromise the "dual criminality" principal under which cooperation with authorities in other countries has previously required. However, the treaty gives Liechtenstein the right to refuse to disclose information that would require a court order to comply with, if a court order has not been obtained. If Liechtenstein defends its sovereignty by invoking this provision whenever the United States makes unreasonable demands under the treaty, the impact on otherwise law-abiding investors and businesses will be minimal.

Most observers doubt that Liechtenstein will surrender its financial privacy laws to appease the OECD demands for tax information exchange or the U.S. demands for unfettered access to financial records. That, and a certified history of excellent asset protection and banking, make this tiny Alpine redoubt one of our choices for offshore financial activity and estate planning.

Robert Vrijhof, senior partner in a leading Swiss investment firm, and a member of the Sovereign Society Council of Experts, does a lot of business in Liechtenstein on behalf of American and other foreign investors. He says he has seen a noticeable cleaning up of suspect practices, together with a new willingness to accommodate legitimate banking and investment. "Notwithstanding bad publicity, I recommend Liechtenstein unreservedly, if you can afford it."

Contacts

Banks

- *Centrum Bank*, AG Heiligkreuz 8, 9490 Vaduz. **Tel.:** +(423) 235-8585. **Fax:** +(423) 235-8686

- *LGT Bank in Liechtenstein*, Herrengasse 12, 9490 Vaduz. **Tel.:** +(423) 235-1122. **Fax:** +(423) 235-1522

- *Liechtensteinische Landesbank* AG, Städtle 44, 9490 Vaduz. **Tel.:** +(423) 236-8811. **Fax:** +(423) 236-8822

- *Neue Bank AG*, Kirchstrasse 8, 9490 Vaduz. **Tel.:** +(423) 236- 0808. **Fax:** +(423) 232-9260

- *Verwaltungs- und Privat-Bank* AG, Im Zentrum Aeulestrasse 6, 9490 Vaduz. **Tel.:** +(423) 235-6655. **Fax:** +(423) 235-6500

- *Vorarlberger Volksbank AG*, Heiligkreuz 42, 9490 Vaduz. **Tel.:** +(423) 237-6930. **Fax:** +(423) 237-6948

Trust Companies

- *First Advisory Group*, Aeulestrasse 74, 9490 Vaduz, Liechtenstein. **Tel.:** +(423) 236-0404. **Fax:** +(423) 236-0405

Financial Consultants

- *Robert Vrijhof*, partner, Weber, Hartman, Vrijhof & Partners Ltd., Zurichstrasse 110 B, CH-8134 Adliswil-Zurich. **Tel.:** +(41) 1-709-1115. **Fax:** +(41) 1-709-1113. This asset management company offers a wide range of services including investment counseling, formation of companies and trusts, estate planning and mergers and acquisitions. Rob Vrijhof serves on the Sovereign Society Council of Experts.

- *Marc Sola*, NMG International Financial Services Goethestrasse 22 8001 Zurich Switzerland. **Tel.:** +(41) 1-266-2141. **Fax:** +(41) 1-266-2149. E-mail: marcsola@nmg-ifs.com. Mr. Sola has extensive experience in Swiss life insurance and annuities, and serves on the Sovereign Society Council of Experts.

- *Christian Kälin*, Henley & Partners, Kirchgasse 24, 8001 Zurich Switzerland. **Tel.:** +(41) 1-267-6090. **Fax:** +(41) 1-267-6091. **E-mail:** chris.kalin@henleyglobal.com. **Link:** http://www.henleyglobal.com. Henley & Partners are specialists in tax advantaged residency and provide international tax planning services for private clients worldwide. Mr. Kälin serves on the Sovereign Society Council of Experts.

High Life in Monaco
The Monaco Report, 1995

This unique and ancient principality is not for everyone. If you want to make it your permanent home it helps to have more than a modest amount of money and an assured income for life. And it doesn't hurt to know the Prince and his royal family.

Monaco, in general, is for individuals who have already made their money: people who want to practice the art of living while others mind the store for them. Monaco is for individuals who want to spend time on the Riviera. If tax avoidance is the only goal, there are other places. Other cheaper places.

Monaco is home to all sorts. Celebrities, aristocrats and millionaires rub shoulders with pretentious society "wannabes." Not all the residents flash their money around. In fact, many residents are just upper-middle class people who have decided to retire in Monaco. They were drawn to the pleasant atmosphere, Mediterranean climate and leisure possibilities available. Monaco has all the facilities that wealthy people consider necessary. There are country clubs, health clubs, golf and tennis clubs. Indeed, Monaco may have a population of only 30,000 and an area of only 1.08 square miles, but it has all the services and cultural activities of a city the size of San Francisco.

There is no denying it. Monaco has a reputation for being horribly expensive. An American was once overheard asking his wife why Monaco is still above sea-level with the weight of all the residents' gold. In fact, the first few times you go out on the streets, you believe that everyone is in a competition. The How-Much-Gold-Can-You-Wear-Without-Falling-Over competition. Even on the beaches! Men and woman in bikinis, bathing costumes and gold jewelry.

Fortunately, not all of Monaco is like this. It is refreshing to see that a good bargain can still be found. Take food, for example. It is not difficult to spend US$25 on an elaborate buffet breakfast. But it is possible to be more adventurous. This morning your editor walked seven minutes downhill to the public market place in the Condamine district. I was overwhelmed by the choice of produce! Pates, olives, pickles, cold meats, flesh fruits. And the cheeses!

I put together a veritable feast and took it to the coffee bar which overlooked the market. For the price of a drink they gave me a knife and a table. I sat back with my baguette and let myself be entertained by the haggling, joking and market activities of a typical French village. One block and a hundred light years from the glitz! Five years ago I made a bet with a friend who claimed that he could survive a month in Monaco on less than US$15 per day. He actually won the bet.

Monaco has a legendary reputation. Prince Rainier III has worked hard to expand the scope of the country. The Principality is no longer a frivolous playground for the rich funded primarily through gambling proceeds. It is now a modern economy participating at a global level in a diverse range of sectors. The Principality has even weathered the recession well, far better than nearby Nice and Cannes. The level of employment has fallen to less than three percent in Monaco and only 700 from the 30,000 population were unemployed.

Undeniably there are tax benefits to be gained from a move to Monaco. The authorities do not like the Principality to be known as a tax haven. Perhaps they are wise not to attract the attention. It is, of course, a low-tax area rather than a no-tax area but, for all intents and purposes, it is still a haven. There are no direct, withholding or capital gains taxes for individuals of foreign nationality, except for the French who do not escape the clutches of the French fiscal system. There are registration taxes for the drawing up of documents but there are no real estate taxes. Even the French can benefit from this and that is why some French nationals choose to keep accommodation in the Principality.

There are corporate and banking advantages too. The hefty business profits tax is not too inspiring, but concessions for administrative and management enterprises are unquestionably attractive. Confidentiality is good as far as business records go and the same can be said for the banking services.

The tax benefits rate quite highly when compared to other havens. But some havens have no taxation at all and are much kinder to businesses. Likewise the banking services in Monaco are not as comprehensive as they could be. There are no numbered accounts and attempts are being made to loosen the banking secrecy rules which are currently in operation.

Monaco has a high profile. As all the world remembers, Grace Kelly, the star of such films as

High Noon and *Rear Window*, married Prince Rainier in 1956. The international spotlight followed her to the Principality where she remained until she died in a tragic car accident in 1982. Princess Grace is given a lot of the credit for sprucing up Monaco's image. Either you like a high profile or you don't. Supermodels Claudia Schiffer and Helena Christensen obviously don't seem to mind it. They were only two of the recent additions to the list of residents that already included Karl Lagerfeld, the fashion designer, and Helmut Newton, the photographer. Tenor Luciano Pavarotti and tennis great Boris Becker both call this home, although the respective Italian and German tax authorities have challenged this in court.

The Monaco lifestyle has much to offer. Some people even argue that finding entertainment in the Principality is cheaper than in London. Personally, I think that such people betray an ignorance of the great capital. But, there again, if they are comparing like with like, they are probably right. To tell the truth, there is no club in London as glamorous as Jimmy'z. No casino as opulent as The Casino.

This lack of variety could get under your skin after a while. Especially if you are a well-traveled, free-spirited individual who does not want to be tied down to one kind of experience. Most of us enjoy a bit of glitz and gold but in Monaco the people simply aren't relaxed about it. They're constantly looking over their shoulders to see what everyone else is wearing. It can all be a bit vulgar and artificial.

As for culture, Princess Grace worked hard to ensure that there is now a full program of events every year. Once again, though, one gets the feeling that there's something rather artificial about it all. In some venues there is no temperature regulation and it can become quite hot. Both the audience and the performers suffer on such occasions and the instruments even go out of tune! But most of the spectators don't seem to mind. Or perhaps they don't notice. After all, they are there to be seen, not to enjoy the music!

The public services are exceptional. Two warnings though. There are a lot of dogs in Monaco and where there are dogs there is dog waste. Passage through Monaco is often achieved on foot through beautifully lit marble-lined subterranean corridors. The presence of so much excrement amongst so much luxury is extremely offensive. Fortunately, efforts have been made to keep the otherwise immaculate streets and sidewalks free from such blemishes. In fact, a poop-scoop law has been now been introduced requiring that owners clean up after their dogs. Public scoopers were even introduced at one stage but it seems that many of them have disappeared. In short, it isn't as bad as it was but there's still too much.

Some people may find Monaco's police presence a little severe. The Principality has the lowest crime rate of any highly urbanized area in the world. This physical security is, of course, one of its great advantages. One of the reasons for this low crime rate is the closed circuit television (CCTV) which operates throughout Monaco. After all, no one's going to commit a crime if he knows it'll be recorded on tape. But not everybody sees CCTV as a harmless crime prevention device. Many simply do not feel relaxed knowing that they are being watched on some television in some control room. But CCTV is not a police tool restricted to Monaco. Most of the Western world is now using it. In the U.K., for example, CCTV has been installed in many major cities, apparently even behind two-way mirrors in some restaurants. This is not the time to argue the merits of such surveillance systems. For our purposes we must simply note that they exist in Monaco as they do in many other Western cities. There are, of course, areas of the world which do not suffer from this kind of surveillance and, if it is an important issue for you, you might feel more comfortable in such a place.

When contemplating a move to another country, it is important to consider its future. Can we make any predictions about Monaco? The Principality's residents are a mobile lot with younger single people staying as little as two years. As residents leave, replacements take their place. This will continue to happen. Monaco is not going to become a ghost town!

It is stable and any major changes are unlikely to come from inside. After all, the authorities like the way things are progressing. The Principality has escaped very lightly in the recession and the economy continues to grow at a very healthy rate. The aesthetically minded will be pleased to hear that the manic construction program of the last two decades has mellowed greatly. Quite simply, there's no more space. But the expansion into the sea continues. A new breakwater in the Condamine will protect its port, provide docking facilities and support 20,000 square meters of habitable space. An expansion of Fontvieille is also under way. It will reclaim for residential purposes a further 200,000 square meters from the sea.

In 1997, the Principality celebrated its 700th anniversary of life under the rule of the Grimaldi family. Prince Rainier III is now in his 70s. His children, of course, have wild reputations and the details of their private lives constantly appear in the gossip columns of the European press. Princess Caroline rose to prominence as the first topless princess and shocked Catholic Monaco with a divorce from her husband. Prince Albert is said to have been linked with over 120 women, including the actress Brooke Shields and, more recently, Claudia Schiffer. Princess Stephanie was not to be outdone by her brother and sister and chose a string of unsuitable partners. But these are their private lives and, if anything, shows how human they are. They are not aloof. Albert is likely to be a broad-minded ruler, in touch with the needs of both the economy and the people.

The Principality has offered financial and fiscal concessions for a long time. These have been restricted by the Conventions with France in 1963 and, more recently, by agreements with France after pressure from the EU. And here lies the major concern. Monaco isn't likely to initiate changes. But the rest of Europe, especially France who has always exhibited a jealous dog-in-the-manger attitude towards the Principality, might pressurize it into getting into line. This might be all the more valid if Monaco is unable to shake rumors associating it with the Mafia and money laundering activity.

If you're on the move already, stability may not be an important issue. However, you might be looking for a base and would do well to consider Monaco. The lifestyle is attractive but is not everybody's cup of tea. If you are contemplating a move purely for financial or fiscal reasons, you might, depending on your specific requirements, do better elsewhere.

If you do take up residence in Monaco you would be advised to keep only some pocket money for living expenses. Your assets should be kept somewhere else. Somewhere with better fiscal and financial concessions. Somewhere which has 100 percent stability with respect to those concessions.

Furthermore, if you do decide to move to Monaco, there are some further points to note. Make all your purchases before you go. All home furnishings and appliances can be found at tax-free ports like Jersey or Singapore. But make these purchases well in advance because, to be eligible for duty-free importation into Monaco, items must be listed upon your visa application as your household goods.

Once there, keep a low profile. Foreign nationals who are resident are afraid to make any public criticisms of the country. Why? If the authorities consider you a troublemaker, they can issue a 24 hour notice of expulsion. There's no one to appeal to and you'll be out the door.

If these last comments are a bit sobering, don't worry. Monaco is still one of the most prosperous little countries on the planet. Come and have fun!

Campione d'Italia: Where Taxes Are Non-Traditional

by Robert E. Bauman, JD, *The Passport Report*, 2000

Campione is a unique, semi-autonomous mountainside community located entirely within Switzerland, but under Italian political jurisdiction, at least in theory. As a separate enclave, it is not subject to any Swiss laws, taxes or tax treaties. Becoming a resident of Campione gives one all the advantages of being Swiss, but none of the disadvantages. No compulsory lifetime military summer camps, no heavy Swiss income taxes and none of the disadvantages of being outside the European Community. Media reports in 2001 that claimed Italian tax authorities were about to clamp down on Campione thankfully proved to be false.

Campione is a part of the European Union with all the EU benefits of passport-free, visa-free travel. Its citizens have the right to travel, work, engage in commerce or perform services anywhere in the EU. Although foreigners living in Campione (or in Italy) are technically subject to income tax on their worldwide income, most do not pay it and the government looks the other way. Hence, for foreigners living there, Campione has no income taxes since the local government taxes only income earned within the enclave.

At present any self-supporting person can legally buy or rent an apartment and live in Campione, simply by going there and making the arrangements. A domicile on a permanent, registered and legalized basis is yours. Anyone who becomes an official Campione resident is entitled to a Swiss driving license and Swiss motor vehicle license plates plus an Italian identity card. Since there is no border control between Campione and Switzerland, anyone in Campione has unlimited access to Switzerland and to Liechtenstein, with which the Swiss have a special free border, without the need to show identification documents.

The general requirements for a resident's card are the same as for Italy. If you would like to establish legal residence in Campione, get a *longue dude* visa for Italy from your nearest Italian consulate before arrival. No visa is needed for EC citizens, although they are supposed to register with the police.

Campione has a strange legal "limbo" status. For many centuries it was a papal state ruled benignly by the Pope. When the Swiss Federation was formed, Campione was a poor village half the size of New York City's Central Park, under the political rule of the Bishop of Milan. Later, when Italy took over the papal states, title passed to Italy, even though it was located entirely within Switzerland. Today neither the Italian nor Swiss government bothers the residents about taxes.

The Campionese own a gambling casino in which 500 locals work. Gambling revenues support perhaps the highest level of municipal services in the world, eliminating the need for local property taxes. Foreign gamblers pay for the local government budget and Rome also gets a cut. In return, Italy grants the locals privileges not enjoyed by other Italians, including freedom from currency reporting requirements, most taxes, regulations and many economic restrictions. There is a Swiss value added tax (VAT) of seven percent.

Another Campione secret is an unusual Mediterranean-type climate found only in the small Italian-Swiss province of Ticino, which surrounds Campione. Situated on lovely Lake Lugano and considerably lower in altitude than the rest of mountainous Switzerland, its token white sand beach supports a small grove of tropical palm trees. The mountain and lake scenery is breathtaking. The sub-Alpine climate and year-round temperature is exhilarating. A vibrant social and cultural life is a few minutes away in Lugano or Locarno by regular ferry boat. Take the superhighway due south from Campione and in 90 minutes you can hear the world's best grand opera at La Scala in Milan or visit the fabulous shops in the city Center.

There are hoards of bankers and stockbrokers locally in Lugano and Chiasso and the area rivals Zurich and Basle in proliferating financial services. Tokyo, London and New York financial news publications are available at many stands on the day of publication. Locally you can eat in several hundred ethnic gourmet restaurants and see first run English language films, in a movie palace from a bygone era. Most of the action is in Lugano, 10 minutes across the lake by *vaporetto* (bus boat) or over the mile-long causeway by car. Shopping, dining, night clubbing, golf, horses, tennis clubs, spectator sports are available. Modern hospitals and internationally known clinics attract the world's wealthy seeking a variety of cures. On issues of morality and personal eccentricity, local Italian Swiss are easy-going and more tolerant than their German-Swiss brothers 50 miles to the north.

Only a short drive from Italy, France, Austria, Liechtenstein and Germany, Campione is still a sleepy, peaceful and unspoiled tax haven. For retired individuals permanently moving to Campione and making it your home base is a good idea. You can live comfortably even luxuriously in Campione, the most climatically agreeable part of Europe, on just your tax savings alone.

With the casino as the major source of revenue for the Italian government, local citizens are in an enjoyable tax limbo between Switzerland and Italy. Neither Italian nor Swiss income tax collectors have yet bothered the Campionese. The Swiss legally cannot, and the Italians will not. Too many powerful people's investments would be harmed. Understand that this cozy arrangement is not sanctioned by law. It is the way things are done here.

Thus, Campione is not a tax haven sanctioned by law like Monaco or Andorra where no taxes are imposed. It is simply an odd place where the authorities find it convenient for a many reasons not to enforce tax collections on foreigners! In that sense, Campione is no different than the rest of Italy. A foreigner living anywhere in Italy without official residence status faces no harassment for taxes on non-Italian source income.

Foreigners are left alone as long as they remain "low profile." Italian tax collectors have enough problems dealing with their own 60 million tax evaders. Conventional wisdom in Rome is that rich foreigners are good for Italy. Tax them and they will leave. When the French government attempted to tax resident foreigners on their worldwide earned income, a mass exodus ensued. Thus despite the general anarchy that characterizes Italian government, sometimes correct decisions are made, especially if the decision is not to decide.

Contacts

- *Henley & Partners AG*, Haus zum Engel, Kirchgasse 24, 8001 Zurich, Switzerland. **Tel.:** +(41) 1 267-6090. **Fax:** +(41) 1 267-6091. **E-mail:** zurich@henleyglobal.com. **Website:** www.henley-global.com/campione.

Hong Kong: A Far East Offshore Haven Lives On

Even though it is now controlled for all purposes by the Communist government in Beijing, Hong Kong remains one of the freest jurisdictions with a strong set of common law based statutes governing banking and finance. Five years of Red rule has produced major compromises but on balance, Hong Kong remains relatively free, a reflection of Beijing's need for Hong Kong as its financial powerhouse. If you're doing business in Asia, this is the place to be.

In 1996, after 157 years as a British Crown Colony, Hong Kong was unchallenged as the world's richest city-state.

Known as a free market business haven, in 1996 its 6.4 million residents enjoyed a US$23,000 per capita GDP. In the last year of its independence from Communist China that per capita GDP figure was higher than in Germany, Japan, the U.K., Canada and Australia. At the time, the top income and corporate tax rate of 15% was one of the world's lowest.

It was a great place to do business, especially if Asia was your territory. Except for one major factor. On July 1, 1997, the United Kingdom surrendered its colonial control of Hong Kong to the sovereignty of Communist China.

The transfer came under a 1984 agreement engineered by then British prime minister, Margaret Thatcher. The peaceful handing over of a democracy to a Communist-controlled dictatorship was unprecedented in history. And the outcome has been far from pleasant in many respects, notwithstanding Ms. Thatcher's expressed hope at the time that this would mean "a new impulse toward freedom and democracy in China and the rest of Asia."

Anything but.

Uncertainty is now a way of life in Hong Kong. That, despite the fact that Communist Chinese rule has not been nearly as oppressive as feared, and the city's democratic forces have made good showings in legislative elections. But Beijing has systematically clamped down on previously existing civil rights, including a free press, the right of assembly, freedom of religion and many aspects of due process under British common law, both civil and criminal.

The Communist Chinese government in Beijing promised to honor its 1984 commitment to allow Hong Kong a free, 50-year dual political/economic existence. This was the so-called "one country, two systems" theory.

Once Beijing gained power, it let the world know Hong Kong was no longer the full-fledged democracy it became in its waning British colonial days. The elected legislature was abolished by Communist China, replaced by handpicked agents with a new electoral system rigged to favor Beijing. Instead of its former status as a international financial center, Hong Kong is moving towards a status not unlike other Chinese cities, albeit a very important one.

This anti-democratic trend was accented in 2002-2003 with the introduction of new Beijing-backed laws that appeared to limit further existing civil rights. Critics of the legislation may have overstated the threat to civil liberties, which most observers said were likely to remain essentially intact for the foreseeable future.

Current political realities suggest that Beijing will restrain itself. As long as Red China hopes for peaceful reunification with the Chinese Republic on Taiwan, it has to maintain a more or less hands-off policy towards Hong Kong to demonstrate to the world that Thatcher's "one country, two systems" still works. Taiwan had over $80 billion invested on the mainland in 2002 and Taiwan's exports to mainland China and Hong Kong totaled US$40.82 billion in 2002, up 28.7% from the previous year. In 2002, mainland China and Hong Kong took up 31.2% of Taiwan's total exports, much higher than the 20.5% posted by the U.S.

It's The Economy, Stupid

But in 2003 Hong Kong was still suffering from one of its worst recessions since the city-state began compiling annual economic statistics in 1961, and probably the worst since the end of World War II in 1945. In 1998 the local GDP fell 5.1% and has declined every year since.

A few years ago Hong Kong was the world's fifth largest banking and foreign exchange center, seventh largest trading power, and the world's busiest container port. With low taxes and an established English common law system, international banking and business flowed in, sure of stability and a high degree of financial privacy. Business was booming then. Today the economy is struggling back to its feet, weighted down with a huge government budget deficit, steep declines in once soaring real estate prices and huge bank loan defaults.

Worse still, this city once known as the laissez fare capital of business, is run by a government beholden to the Communist rulers in Beijing and its own rich cronies among the Hong Kong tycoons that dominate the local economy. Beijing's handpicked government repeatedly has intervened to prop up the failing economy in ways that favored the real property-owning tycoons. The worst example was the government purchase of US$15 billion worth of Hong Kong stocks in a vain effort to stem the free fall of the Hang Seng, the Hong Kong stock market. That did major damage to the city's official reputation as a hands-off friend of free enterprise.

But Hong Kong is proof that "money talks." China has too much invested in Hong Kong to destroy it all in a fit of rigid political ideology. Today 30% of Hong Kong bank deposits are Chinese and China accounts for 22% of all its foreign trade, including cross border trade, 20% of the insurance business and over 12% of all construction. More than 2,000 Chinese-controlled entities now do business in Hong Kong, many of them "red chip" stocks, the value of which have declined steeply in the last year.

Red China has long employed Hong Kong as a convenient financial window to the West. It was their banker, investment broker and go-between in what is now a multi-billion annual trade flow. In the past 15 years, some US$150 billion of foreign direct investment has flooded into China —three fifths of which came from, or through, Hong Kong. But with the coming of the Asian recession that began to change. For the first time in a decade, 1997 saw direct foreign investment drop to US$30 billion, from a high of $42 billion in 1996. It declined still further in 1998. But with a potential 1.2 billion Chinese consumers, foreign investment will continue and likely grow again. A Rand study projected that mainland China's GDP will be about US$12 trillion by 2015, a number comparable to the GDP of the United States. In spite of all its troubles, in the Chinese GDP has grown at an amazing rate.

China's economy is already enormous. In current 2003 dollar terms, its GDP is the sixth largest in the world, just smaller than France's. In terms of purchasing-power parity, after adjusting for price differences between economies), it is second only to the United States with an 11.8% share of world GDP. Its growth rate is extraordinary. 2002's official figure of 8% made it the most dynamic large economy in the world by far.

China, including Hong Kong, already imports more from the rest of Asia than does Japan. In 2001, China's exports rose by 23% to $266 billion and accounted for 4.4% of all world exports. That is the highest level they have ever reached, but it is still a long way off Japan's record (of 10.1% of world exports) in 1986. It is even below Japan's figure for 2001 of 6.6%. China's trade surplus in 2001 increased to over $30 billion, 2.9% of GDP. Data from the Ministry of Foreign Trade and Economic Co-operation showed Hong Kong invested US$19.17 billion in mainland China in 2002, more than any other source.

Despite their wrong-headed attitudes regarding Hong Kong democracy, the leaders of the People's Republic of China realize that they have an enormous vested interest in Hong Kong's economic health. They want Hong Kong to keep running at full steam, but on their own terms.

World-Class Financial Sophistication

In a strange twist of world economic fate, the recent clamp down by the European Union and the OECD on tax havens in the West operates to the benefit of the remaining true tax havens such as Hong Kong and Panama. Another factor; wealthy account holders from the Middle East started shifting cash towards Asia from Europe and the United States in the wake of the September 11, 2001, terror attacks.

Hong Kong is still regarded by foreign firms as a highly advantageous location from which to do business. In early 2003 over 77% of foreign firms based in Hong Kong surveyed said they felt that it was an advantageous location for them, due to advanced telecommunications networks, a free trade environment, low tax system and high standard of regulation, all cited as beneficial factors. On an industry basis, according to the survey results, the financial services sector was the most positive overall.

One major attraction for offshore business has been Hong Kong's 16% business tax rate, raised to 17.5% in 2003. Faced with recession, years of declining revenue and a major budget deficit, in 2003 the government increased from15% to16% the ceiling for taxes on personal income and unincorporated businesses. The so-called property tax (actually a tax on rental income, taxed separately from the former, the equivalent of the US property tax called "rates") was raised from 15% to 16%.

Hong Kong's status as one of the world's top trading centers for stocks, bonds, commodities, metals, futures, currencies, personal and business financial operations long has meant that such transactions could be conducted there with a high degree of sophistication. That's still true, and the city's 154 licensed banks hold nearly US$300 billion in deposits. Hong Kong-based fund managers, analysts, and traders—like their counterparts in London or New York—remain in close contact with local and international markets.

In early 2003 *China Daily* news service reported that 30 major financial services and real estate ventures were joining the176 other mainland companies (as of October 2002) which so far had opted for the Hong Kong as the location for their initial public offerings.

But Hong Kong is no longer the free-for-all market of old, where insider trading, self-dealing and other illegal practices were commonplace. After severely tightening financial laws in recent years, local regulators continue to press to meet higher world standards. There have been significant reforms in laws governing stocks, bonds, banking, mutual and hedge funds. A strict anti-money laundering law is in place and enforced with vigor. But there is evidence that the widespread corruption that infects mainland China's economy is spreading to Hong Kong. That's another good reason to be wary about doing business here.

Hong Kong as a Business Base

In Hong Kong there is no specific legal recognition of what usually is called an international business corporations (IBC) or offshore company. The basic Hong Kong corporate legal principle applied to taxes is territoriality of profits. If profits originate in there or are derived from Hong Kong, then profits are subject to local tax. Otherwise they are tax free, regardless of whether the company is incorporated or registered there.

Interestingly, IBCs and all other foreign corporations generally are able to open a Hong Kong bank account without prior registration under the local business statute. This can save charges for auditing and annual report filing, and removes the annoyance of having to argue with the Inland Revenue Department about the territoriality of the business. On the other hand, one must be careful not to transact any taxable local business, because doing that without local registration is against the law. In cases where local business does occur, tax authorities generally are lenient, usually requiring local registration and payment of unpaid tax. But in some cases IBCs have been forced to register as a listed public company at considerable expense.

Hong Kong offshore companies require by law a local resident company secretary, who usually charges about US$500 per year for filing a few documents with the Company Registry. Annual auditing by a CPA starts from about US$500 for companies with few transactions, and can easily reach ten times as much for a mid-size and operational offshore trading company.

Doing Business in Hong Kong

Until now, Hong Kong's banking laws did not permit bank regulators to give information about an individual customer's affairs to foreign government authorities, except in cases involving fraud. But Hong Kong has never had specific banking secrecy laws such as many asset and tax haven nations enjoy.

As a matter of local custom, Hong Kong banks have always requested a judicial warrant before disclosing records to any foreign government. Access is much easier for the local government, but there are no double-taxation agreements with countries different from the People's Republic of China. A mutual legal assistance treaty (MLAT) with the United States was signed in 1998 and came into force in 2000. Text: http://travel.state.gov/hong_kong_legal.html.

New anti-money laundering laws and "know your customer" (KYC) rules have made the opening of bank accounts for IBC's much more difficult. Accounts applicants must declare to the bank the "true beneficiary" of an IBC or a trust with supporting documentation. Documentary proof must be shown for all corporate directors and shareholders of the registering entity and any other entities that share in that ownership.

In What Direction?

Many "experts" thought Hong Kong's powerful business taipans would use their considerable financial muscle to temper the worst excesses the Communist might impose. Instead, Beijing recruited these money musclemen onto its own team with offers of favorable treatment. One of the business elite's own leaders, Tung Chee-hwa, now is in his second term of office, has five years behind him as head of Hong Kong's "Special Administrative Region" government—unhappy years in the view of many locals.

If you do intend to make Asia your investment target, keep in mind lessons other foreigners have already learned "the hard way."

Pick your Asian business partners (and investments) carefully, avoiding the inefficient Chinese state enterprises. Stick to those with solid basics like marketing, distribution and service. Guard technology from theft. And remember, a series of small ventures gets less government attention and red tape than big showcase projects that often produce demands for graft. Many foreign investors have been burned by crooked bookkeeping, few shareholder controls, sudden government rule changes and systemic corruption. Only recently, as the nation's economy has become more Westernized, has Beijing finally begun to address the need for laws guaranteeing the right for citizens and foreigners to own and transfer private property. So in dealing with China, remember "Caveat emptor!"

And keep a sharp eye not on the government's hype, but on what's really happening in China.

All this uncertainty means that offshore financial activities by foreign citizens can prosper, but without immediate assurance of success. Unless the New China is definitely your sphere of intended business activity, you may want to look elsewhere in Asia for your financial haven.

Communist Connections

For non-Chinese wishing to conduct business in China, another, perhaps more secure option is to open a bank account at the Hong Kong branch of the Bank of Communications (BC).

Headquartered in Beijing, BC provides good openings to the mainland. Unlike the Bank of China, it has no U.S. branches subject to the kind of U.S. government investigative pressures that have been brought against other Hong Kong banks, such as Standard Chartered. The Bank of China is also in a weakened state.

The Bank of Communications is likely to resist any U.S. pressure to lift bank secrecy practices. There are U.S. banks in Hong Kong, but when you open an account in one of those institutions, they demand a signed waiver allowing secrecy to be lifted at the request of U.S. authorities. That is a good argument for going Communist when banking in Hong Kong, or at least banking non-American.

Beware of Hong Kong's best-known bank, Hongkong & Shanghai Banking Corp. (HSBC). Thanks to its purchase of Marine Midland, the well-known New York bank, part of its diversification away from Hong Kong, it now is subject to pressure from American authorities. It is also under the regulatory gun of the U.K. where it has a major base. 44% of the bank's business comes from the U.K. and Europe, 38% from Asia and 18% from the Americas. HSBC Holdings PLC, the bank's London based parent, has made the conglomerate ever more global, marketing its New York ties and its control of the British Bank of the Middle East and Seoulbank in Korea as one big world banking system. HSBC now is be listed on the New York Stock Exchange and thus is under the US SEC's thumb. With operations in 79 nations, Hong Kong, where it began, has become far less important to the global HSBC.

Hong Kong Contacts:

Government:

- *Hong Kong Official Government site:* http://www.info.gov.hk/eindex.htm.
- *Hong Kong Economic and Trade Offices.* http://www.hongkong.org/.

Banks:

- *Bank of Communications*, Hong Kong Branch, 20 Pedder Street, Central, Hong Kong. **Tel.:** 2841 9611 / 2973. **Fax:** 2810 6993. **Website:** http://www.bankcomm.com.hk/e_sme.htm.
- *Hongkong & Shanghai Banking Corp.*(HSBC), 29 Queen's Road Central, Central HSBC Premier Center, Central District, Hong Kong Island. **Tel:** [852] 2847 7388. **Fax:** [852] 2877 6301. **Website:** http://www.hsbc.com.hk/hk/.
- *Rabobank*, 2 Exchange Square, Central, Hong Kong. **Tel.:** (852) 2103 2000. **Fax:** (852) 2530 1728.

Attorneys

- *Johnson, Stokes & Masters*, 16th-19th Floors, Prince's Building, 10 Charter Road, Central Hong Kong. **Tel.:** (852) 2843 2211. **Fax:** (852) 2845 9121. **E-mail:** jsm@jsm-law.com. **Website:** http://www.ceoffice.org.uk.

- *Maples & Calder Asia*, 1504 One International Finance Center, 1 Harbor View Street, Hong Kong. **Tel:** (852) 2522-9333. **Fax:** (852) 2537-2955. **E-mail:** hkinfo@maplesandcalder.com. **Website:** http://www.maplesandcalder.com/.

Corporation & Trust Services:

- *Offshore Incorporations Ltd.*, Hong Kong Office: 9th Floor, Ruttonjee House 11 Duddell Street Central Hong Kong. **Tel.:** (852) 2521 2515. **Fax:** (852) 2810 4525. **E-mail:** info@offshore-inc.com. **Website:** http://www.offshore-inc.com. *Taiwan Office: Offshore Incorporations Ltd.* 3F, 121, Minsheng East Road, Sec. 3 Taipei 105 Taiwan, R.O.C. **Tel.:** (886) 2 2718 2222. **Fax:** (886) 2 2719 7651. **E-mail:** taiwan@offshore-inc.com. *Singapore Office: Offshore Incorporations (S.E.A.) PTE Ltd* 80 Raffles Place #16-20 UOB Plaza 2 Singapore 048624. **Tel.:** (65) 6438 0838. **Fax:** (65) 6438 2023. **E-mail:** singapore@offshore-inc.com.

- *OCRA (Hong Kong) Limited.* **Website:** http://www.ocra-worldwide.com/offices/officespopup/hongkong.html. **Tel.:** + 852 2522 0172. **Fax:** + 852 2521 1190. **E-mail:** ocra@ocra-asia.com.

- *Sovereign Trust (Hong Kong) Ltd.* Suites 1601-1603, Kinwick Centre 32 Hollywood Road, Central Hong Kong. **Tel.:** +852 2542 1177. **Fax:** +852 2545 0550. **E-mail:** hk@SovereignGroup.com. **Website:** http://www.sovereigngroup.com/worldwideoffices/hongkong.asp.

For More Information:

- *Hong Kong Trade Development Council*, provides economic and trade information. http://www.tdc.org.hk.

A Very New South Africa
by Robert E. Bauman, JD, *The Sovereign Individual*, May 2003

Cape Town, South Africa: By the time you read this I will have returned to the United States, but as I write I am in Muizenburg, in the Western Cape province. This is a beach community south of Cape Town, where my son, Ted, and his family live. We're only a few score miles from the southern tip of the African continent at the Cape of Good Hope, where the cold waters of the south Atlantic blend with the warmer Indian Ocean.

At the end of March, I enjoyed my fourth visit to South Africa since 1976, when I first visited as a Member of the U.S. Congress from Maryland. For that trip (not at taxpayers expense), I was blasted by an editorial in The Baltimore Sun complaining that I should have boycotted the then apartheid Nationalist Party government. That I openly opposed that dreadful system didn't matter to the Sun, which accompanied their blast with a cartoon showing "B'wana Bauman's Safari"-me riding atop a smiling Republican elephant. The caption reads: "Gosh, I feel right at home!" I proudly have it framed in my study.

Truth be told, I do feel right at home whenever I visit South Africa, now and then.

Thank God, this beautiful land and its wonderful people were able to work out their racial differences in peace-a miracle when you study the tortured history of this nation.

A Major Attitude Change

During my most recent visit to South Africa, I traveled from Pretoria and Johannesburg to

Cape Town, almost a thousand miles by auto. I met Sovereign Society members at an informal reception at the Groot Constantia Jonkershuis Museum in one of the Cape province's loveliest and most historic areas. I also visited with Frikki Botha, an old friend who served with distinction as South Africa's ambassador to the United States and Japan, and as Deputy Minister of Foreign Affairs as well.

A bit of history: after the British seized the Cape of Good Hope in 1806, many of the original Dutch settlers (the Boers) trekked north to found their own republics. The discovery of diamonds (1867) and gold (1886) spurred great wealth and immigration from Europe.

The Boers were defeated in the Boer War (1899-1902) in which British atrocities against the Boers gave a foretaste of 20th century military horrors to come. The resulting Union of South Africa eventually imposed a policy of apartheid; a strict segregation of the black, white and colored races. By 1995, apartheid ended and black majority rule under Nelson Mandela and the African National Congress (ANC) began.

During my 1995 visit, I recall there was a palpable sense of doom among many white South Africans. (Whites now number five million out of a total population of 45 million, with about three million mixed race "coloreds" and 37 million blacks). Long accustomed to total control of all aspects of South Africa, (maintained by an often brutal police state), many whites believed their lives and fortunes to be in jeopardy.

Thousands left their native land, contributing to a "brain drain" that cost the nation much needed professional talent and leadership.

Talking with whites here in 2003, I find general praise for the black-led government that, after two national elections, is in the firm majority control of the African National Congress. There are bitter differences on specific matters, and great fear because of serious crime problems, but overall there is agreement that the nation is slowly headed in a direction in which all races can live and prosper.

Economic Surprises

Under white rule, the ANC was a party of often violent, always revolutionary outcasts. Its leaders, such as Nelson Mandela, were imprisoned and exiled. When the ANC took over after the first "one person-one vote" democratic elections in 1995, with South African Communist Party support, many in the West feared the worst. Instead, the ANC has steered a relatively moderate course, mixing a small measure of free market economics with a gradual move away from the old Nationalist Party's economic policies, which in many respects were fascist and statist.

At first, the ANC imposed strict financial controls to prevent a cash and asset drain that easily might have matched the brain drain. But the government is slowly freeing the economy from central control. For instance, it has long since abolished the "dual rand" system that had established two controlled currencies, one domestic and one for foreign trade.

Recently, exchange controls were lifted further, allowing more offshore investment and granting tax amnesty for South Africans willing to repatriate offshore funds. Thus domestic corporations now can invest more freely abroad, and a tax amnesty for those who secretly moved funds offshore could attract billions of repatriated rands, in violation of foreign exchange and tax laws.

South Africa has developed an established and diversified manufacturing base that has demonstrated resilience and the potential to compete in a global economy. However, with an unemployment rate running close to 40%, the nation continues to face serious economic problems. But business confidence is boosted by improved import and export volumes, a rising rand, plus increased retail sales and manufacturing output.

For foreign investors considering South Africa, real estate remains a bargain along with selected shares of gold and other mineral producers. Real estate sales are booming, especially for expensive waterfront properties in the Cape Town area.

Oceanfront estates with pools and outbuildings go for a fraction of what they cost in Florida or California. But prices are rising rapidly: one South African told me that luxury home prices were going up so rapidly that "anyone who doesn't get in soon will miss the boat."

A Bright Future

If you have never visited South Africa, I strongly recommend that you do so. For tourists, this nation presents some of the most beautiful scenery in the world. For careful investors there are true bargains. And for those seeking a place to retire or establish a second home, the possibilities are endless.

A Tale of Two Asian Havens

by Mark Nestmann, *The Sovereign Individual*, August 2003

Thailand and Singapore are close geographically, share a hot, humid climate, and both are popular destinations for expatriates. Beyond these superficial similarities, however, the two countries are very different.

Thailand: Laid Back, Inexpensive

If you're looking for a laid-back and inexpensive tropical lifestyle largely free of "Big Brother," in an environment friendly to westerners, Thailand is worth considering. The official language is Thai, although English is widely spoken, particularly in the major cities.

In the Thai language, the word Prathet Thai (Thailand) is literally translated "land of the free."

And freedom is a big reason why Thailand is a popular expat destination.

The only country in Southeast Asia that was never conquered by Europeans, Thais don't generally have the anti-western attitudes that prevail in some other Asian countries. And Thailand, with its overwhelmingly homogenous Buddhist population, has suffered little of the ethnic, racial and religious strife that plagues many countries in the region.

The Thai "live and let live" attitude is exemplified in the heart of Bangkok, Thailand's capital and largest city. People fish in the river that runs through the heart of Bangkok and elephants walk down the boulevards. As writer Harold Stephens explains, "Anything can happen in Bangkok, and does."

Tourists from most western countries, including all EU nations, the United States and Canada, can visit Thailand for up to 30 days as tourists, without obtaining a visa.

The cost of living is very reasonable—in part a consequence of a collapse in the value of the Thai currency, the baht, in 1998. Indeed, you can still rent a nicely furnished room in Bangkok for B3,000 (about US$70)—per month. Want something a little larger? No problem—the going rate for a two-bedroom townhouse is only about B8,000/mo. (US$190).

Thailand is a shopper's paradise, with superb woven goods, silks, gemstones and amazingly

intricate wooden carvings all specialties. Food is plentiful, cheap and extremely good. Excellent health care is available at rock-bottom prices. And there remains a fascination among native Thais of westerners.

Be wary of Thailand's dark side, though. In recent months, Thai police have compiled lists of alleged drug dealers (and others) and engaged in brutal arrests and, in some cases, alleged killings of these individuals.

Another downside of Thailand is that it isn't a hot place to invest right now. This wasn't always true—in the go-go 1990s, Thailand was considered one of the Asian "tigers" and its stock market boomed. Today, the SET index remains 70% below its 1995 peak. Thailand's entire stock market cap is less than US$40 billion, less than one big U.S. company. Despite these depressed values, investors should be careful before picking up Thai shares. Neil George, a member of the Sovereign Society Council of Experts recently issued a "sell" recommendation on the Thai Fund (NYSE: TTF).

One Thai investment that might be worthwhile, according to expat Paul Terhorst, is real estate. Purchase of property in Thailand by foreigners is severely restricted, but many expats own condos in Bangkok and in the beautiful northern city of Chiang Mai. You can buy a beautifully furnished condo in Bangkok for under US$100,000. But with rentals so inexpensive, real estate still seems overpriced.

Sound worth a look? Here's a rundown on the requirements to live in Thailand.

If you want to work in Thailand—and just about any native speaker of English can easily support themselves teaching English at one of Bangkok's many foreign language schools—you must obtain a non-immigrant visa category B (business visa) before entering the country. This is valid for 90 days but can be extended up to a year. This visa also permits you to eventually apply for permanent residence in Thailand and, after 10 years, Thai citizenship.

There are many other categories of visas, including investment visas for qualified investors.

Application can be made to the Board of Investment or the Immigration Department.

Unfortunately, the granting of work permits and the extension of business visas can be a lengthy process. However, persons who are sponsored by a Thai employer may receive a work permit and immigration extension in three hours at the "One Stop Service Center" upon completion of the proper application.

Thailand also welcomes self-supporting retirees. You must obtain a certificate that you are in good health; have no criminal record; and have sufficient income to support yourself in Thailand. This is currently defined as having B800,000 (US$19,300) in a Thai bank account or a monthly income of B65,000 (US$1,560).

The Thai tax system is relatively simple, although Thailand is not a tax haven. However, offshore income not remitted to Thailand is not subject to income tax. If you spend more than 180 days in Thailand in a calendar year, you are considered resident for tax purposes. All earned income derived from Thai employment is subject to Thai personal income tax. You must also pay income tax on foreign source income remitted to Thailand. U.S. citizens living in Thailand who are subject to double taxation can obtain relief under the U.S.-Thailand tax treaty.

For More Information

Thailand Board of Investment. **Link**: http://www.boi.go.th/

One Stop Service Center. This government office provides expedited services to obtain a permit to live in Thailand, but only to foreigners sponsored by a Thai employer. Address: 207 Rachadapisek Road, 3rd Floor, Bangkok, Thailand. **Tel.:** +(66) 2-693-9333-9.

Immigration attorneys

Most large international law firms in Thailand don't deal with immigration matters but *Changmai Law Services* does. Refreshingly, this firm even posts its fees on the Internet. The cost for a retirement visa, for instance, is B8,000 (US$190). **Link**: http://www.chiangmailaw.com.

Escape Artist Thailand. Links to articles about living and investing in Thailand. **Link**: http://www.escapeartist.com/Thailand/Thailand.html

Singapore: World's Most Efficient Expatriate Haven

In contrast to laid-back Thailand, the tiny island of Singapore is rigorously efficient. It's also one of the world's cleanest places with an extremely efficient infrastructure and high quality of life.

The price for this efficiency, though, is one of the highest costs of living in the world, along with a hefty dose of Big Brother. Singapore's modern history began in 1819 when Sir Stamford Raffles claimed Singapore for the British Crown and the East India Tea Company. Since then,

Singapore has built on that infrastructure to become one of the most technologically advanced societies in the world, with an excellent communications system, political stability and a disciplined work force. And in 1965, Singapore achieved independence and is now a bustling city-state of nearly five million inhabitants.

Due to the British legacy, English became the language of business and administration, and remains today the common language spoken and understood by nearly everyone in Singapore. (The other three official languages are Malay, Mandarin and Tamil).

While the island has no mineral wealth, it does have a superb deep-water port and a strategic location along one of the world's busiest sea-trading routes. Today, Singapore is the world's busiest port, with over 600 shipping lines, and is a center of shipbuilding, ship-repair and oil-rig building. It is also a huge oil refining and oil distribution center, a major supplier of electronic components and a major player in the Asian financial services industry.

For the most part, foreign investors are welcomed, although all foreign investment requires government approval. In addition, non-Singapore citizens may not own equity interests in local banks and the ownership of newspapers is subject to legislative control. Other sectors where foreign investments are limited include telecommunications, broadcasting and property ownership. Another factor making Singapore competitive is low taxes. The top personal and corporate income tax rate is 22% and the government plans to cut both tax rates to 20% by 2005. Singapore also has tax treaties with most major countries to avoid double taxation. This makes it a suitable base for multinational corporations with operations in high-tax countries. As a "treaty haven," Singapore permits multinationals to form entities there through which profits can flow and qualify for lower withholding rates under its treaty network. As a result, Singapore is a popular base of operations forintermediary holding, finance and licensing companies.

Tax incentives are also available for export-oriented businesses and other sectors the Singapore government wishes to encourage. These incentives have the effect of reducing tax even further. Singapore also has a 10% tax rate for trust companies and for managing, servicing or underwriting foreign securities issued from Singapore by non-residents. Non-resident depositors pay no withholding tax on income or dividends earned in Singapore bank accounts or offshore funds purchased through Singapore. And like Thailand, foreign income that is not remitted to Singapore is not subject to personal or corporate tax.

Because of its prosperity and the high wages paid, Singapore has become a haven for well-educated immigrants. The government has an open immigration policy and seeks qualified foreign workers in many different fields, including banking, finance, biomedical sciences, communications, education, electronics, engineering, healthcare and information technology.

Wealthy retirees, particularly from Asia, also use Singapore as a residential haven due to its territorial tax system. Residency permits may be purchased for approximately US$800,000. After a period of residency ranging from two to six years, it is possible to obtain Singapore citizenship and passport. The shorter two-year expedited citizenship is available to individuals that the government classifies as "professionals, entrepreneurs, skilled personnel and other qualified persons." Otherwise, you must reside in Singapore for six years before you can obtain citizenship and passport.

That's the good news about Singapore. The bad news is that Singapore is one of the world's most regimented societies. Political opposition to the ruling party is strictly regulated. Both the print media and the Internet are heavily censored, and the death penalty is mandatory for drug trafficking, murder, treason and certain firearms offences. Even the use of computer encryption is restricted; police have the power to fine and imprison computer users that do not provide encryption keys or the plain text of encrypted files or communications to authorities.

All cars and motorcycles in Singapore must be equipped with a special transmitter, which beams information to authorities on the location of the vehicle. Possession of a national ID card equipped with digital thumb prints is mandatory. By 2008, Singapore plans a transition to the world's first entirely cashless society, where coins and bills are replaced entirely by electronic money transactions, all Instantly linked to government databases.

These innovations have undoubtedly lowered crime and made Singapore a cleaner and more efficient society. This is undoubtedly an attraction for some, but not for those individuals looking for a haven that, above all, respects civil liberties.

To travel to Singapore, you don't need a visa if you're from the United States or a EU country. You can stay from 14-31 days, depending on what country you're from, and extensions are available.

For More Information

Singapore Economic Development Board. "EDB acts as catalyst and facilitator to nurture a vibrant, self-sustaining enterprise ecosystem, a conducive total environment for startups and companies of all sizes." **Link:** http://www.sedb.com/edbcorp/index.jsp.

Singapore Tax Authority. Complete information about taxation in Singapore. **Link:** http://www.iras.gov.sg/

Immigration and Checkpoints Authority. Complete information on immigration, residency and citizenship in Singapore. **Link:** http://app.ica.gov.sg/index.asp.

Summary of Singapore tax incentives. **Link:** http://www.kpmg.com.sg/services/sg_tax_incentives/sg_tax_eei.pdf

Legal representation in Singapore. *David Chong,* 6 Temasek Boulevard, #09-04 Suntec Tower 4, Singapore 038986, Singapore. **Tel.:** +(65) 6224-0955. **Fax:** +(65) 6538- 6585. **E-mail:** dclaw@singnet.com.sg.

Escape Artist Singapore. Many links to articles about living and investing in Singapore. **Link:** http://www.escapeartist.com/singapore/singapore.html.

CHAPTER TEN
Personal Privacy

When you read this chapter your blood may boil as you discover the enormous degree to which your personal privacy has been compromised by big government, big business and big banking.

The right to privacy is not even mentioned in the U.S. Constitution. But to survive in a modern world where most of us are forced to live in financial glass houses, maximum privacy is essential.

In this chapter, we reveal the cold, hard facts about how anti-privacy forces try to strip you of your wealth, constantly engaged in stealthy dirty work done without your knowledge or consent. Nothing is sacred any more-not your mail, your phone calls, or even your Internet surfing. Unless you take the precautions we describe, you may be naked before the world.

The War Against Privacy
by John Pugsley, *The Sovereign Individual*, August 1999

The chairman of the Sovereign Society looks at threats to privacy and concludes those of us who refuse to be stripped bare by government must continue to fight for our right to be left alone.

Like you, I am distressed at the amount of information about my private affairs that is collected, archived and traded by business. Even more so, I am outraged about the covert surveillance of my financial and personal life that is carried out by government. The decision of my wife and I to move offshore was strongly influenced by our desire to protest the destruction of personal privacy in the United States. While we're not doing anything that we know to be illegal, we don't like being spied on.

I'm a bit embarrassed to admit that when I was young I was a spy for the U.S. government. Sort of. In the 1950s, I was drafted into the Army and served my two years as a "Morse Code Interceptor." My job was to sit at my short-wave radio and listen for encrypted Morse-code messages being transmitted by government agencies and military units throughout Europe, Russia and the Middle East. I eavesdropped on the British, the French, the Germans, the Israelis, the Russians and anyone else who was using the airwaves. Eight hours wearing headphones and typing out an endless series of scrambled letters wasn't the sexy side of espionage, but I was definitely a spy.

In those days, despite the fact that all governments monitored each other's radio traffic and everyone knew that everyone did it, covert surveillance of neighbor nations was illegal according to international treaties. As one British gentleman had sniffed, "Gentlemen do not read other gentlemen's mail." As recently as 40 years ago, it was presumed that even governments had the right to privacy. My, how times have changed.

Today, governments have dropped the pretense. Government-to-government espionage is an enormous industry. Neither the public nor governments see any moral issue relative to government espionage, notwithstanding the hullabaloo Congress and the media make of special cases such as the theft of U.S. nuclear secrets by the Chinese. Friendly nations still fuss a bit when their allies are found snooping, but no one sees any moral issue involved in spying on friend or foe.

Spying on private citizens, however, is another matter. One of the major issues being debated today is the extent to which individuals have a right to privacy. Privacy is losing. Governments and businesses are both aggressively accumulating immense data banks on private citizens. Most data is gathered by assembling information given out by the person in the normal course of daily activities, such as making a credit card purchase, registering a car, applying for insurance, etc. A growing amount, however, is gathered by covert means. For example, it is probable that the U.S. National Security Agency records and scans every long-distance phone call, fax, and e-mail sent or received in the United States. In addition, all financial transactions conducted through commercial financial institutions are recorded and open to scrutiny by the Feds.

Surveillance is even further advanced in Europe. Over 150,000 cameras throughout the United Kingdom transmit round-the-clock images of public areas to 75 constabularies. The United States isn't far behind. Big Brother really is watching.

Nor is lobbying likely to turn this trend around. I agree with author David Brin who argues that cameras on every lamppost are coming, as surely as the new millennium. They can't be stopped by all the agitation, demonstration or legislation we can muster. Although we might delay the growth of government surveillance by blocking this bill or that law, the public is overwhelmingly convinced that government needs to snoop in order to catch criminals. It's hard to conceive that most people miss the irony. "I'm from the government, and I'm here to help—by watching you."

It seems probable that the vestiges of privacy that citizens still cling to will become extinct in the not-too-distant future. While privacy advocates still refer to the "right" to privacy, that concept is likely soon to become as passe as the old belief that sovereign governments shouldn't spy on one another. The masses are being brainwashed into believing that there is no moral case for a right to privacy.

How tragic. The moral right to privacy is so clear. The late physicist and teacher Andrew Galambos argued that all conflicts were property conflicts and could be quickly resolved with what he referred to as the "universal can-opener," which was to simply ask the question, "Whose property is it?" Applying Galambos' argument, the privacy issue boils down to a question of property rights. Does information about your personal life belong to you, to someone else, or to everyone? Are your affairs your property or public property?

In private financial dealings, we take it for granted that revelations we make to our banker or broker do not then become his property, to be given out or sold at his discretion. In this light, we take it for granted that our private communications and activities are our property and morally can be used only with our consent. How can it be otherwise?

The moral rights to property and privacy do exist. The problem facing the sovereign individual is how to defend privacy in a world that believes otherwise. This is an ongoing task for anyone seeking to become a sovereign individual and one of the major issues of our lifetimes.

Surveillance? Who Cares?

By John Pugsley, *The Sovereign Individual*, December 2002

Does anyone really care that they are being watched by the government?

As I sat in the boarding area waiting for my flight to be called, I found myself studying the faces of fellow passengers. Light ones, dark ones, speckled, hairy and hairless, long noses or petite, balanced and lopsided, densely made up or freshly scrubbed.

I wasn't the only one in the room looking at faces. The surveillance camera sat there taking in the same facial nuances. Was it piping its pictures to a government computer where facial recognition software was looking for matches? I wondered if anyone else among the passengers had any thought about being watched, either by the cameras or me.

Surveillance is everywhere. Airports. Train stations. Malls. Department stores. Although private owners install many surveillance cameras, increasingly they are installed by local, state and federal agencies.

And cameras are just one means of surveillance. More insidious are the covert eavesdropping techniques of telephone, e-mail and fax wiretaps ordered by federal and state authorities. They jumped 20% in the past two years, with more to come. In the aftermath of the September 11 attack, roughly half of America's states introduced electronic surveillance bills.

What do Americans think about this? The majority thinks it's just keen.

A Harris Poll released October 3, 2001, showed that 86% of the more than 1,000 adults polled supported the use of facial-recognition technology; 63% supported expanded camera surveillance on streets and public places; 63% supported monitoring of Internet discussions and chat rooms; and 54% supported more monitoring of cell phones and e-mails.

Another poll recently conducted by ABCNEWS.com asked, "Do you personally feel that the government's anti-terrorism efforts are intruding on your civil liberties?" Eighty percent of respondents said no, the government efforts were not impinging on their freedoms.

Why are we not surprised? The vast majority of Americans have no clear sense of the meaning of "civil liberties." For an intrusion to gain the attention of the average citizen, a SWAT team must be knocking at the door. With the exception of the inconvenience of having your shoes sniffed at the airport, snooping goes unnoticed.

Most people think their civil rights are unaffected by the new surveillance laws because most of them have not felt any effect. While their phones may be tapped and their images scrutinized as they walk through the mall, they sense nothing. Even most of us who are sensitive to the erosion of privacy feel no immediate consequences. Yet.

It's akin to Frederick Bastiat's parable of "that which is seen and that which is not seen" in economic events. The passerby sees the bakery window broken by a vandal, and thinks of the good fortune of the glazier whose business will profit from making a new one. The observer even thinks that this will be good for the community, as the glazier will then spend his profits with the tailor for a new suit, and the good fortune will trickle down. What is not seen, of course, is that the poor baker must now spend the money he had saved for a new suit on a new window, and that the community, in toto, is poorer by the amount of property destroyed.

So it is with the average individual regarding the loss of privacy. What is seen is the added security from terrorists (a negligible if not completely imaginary security, to be sure). What is not seen is the dramatically lowered security from the threat of government (an extremely real threat).

History testifies that a citizen's risk from street crime or terrorism pales in comparison to the numbers killed by authoritarian governments. As noted by R. J. Rummel in his sobering book, *Death by Government*, "The mass murder of their own citizens or those under their protection or control by emperors, kings, sultans, khans, presidents, governors, generals, and other such rulers is very much part of our history." In the 20th century alone he tallies 169,202,000 murdered by government. Yet the masses continue to believe that government is there to protect them.

When younger, I was certain that all individuals were educable, and that they could easily be convinced of their own right to the fruits of their labors. After all, it's obvious, isn't it? From there it should be simple to prove that the state is an imposter posing as their protector.

Alas, it's not so. The masses do not change their views simply through logical persuasion. They are more attracted to bread and circuses (or baseball and sitcoms in today's world) than to critical thinking. There is little hope that the masses will suddenly awaken to the danger of omnipotent government, so the cameras and wiretaps will undoubtedly proliferate.

The real question facing those of us seeking to become sovereign individuals is how to best insulate ourselves from popular ignorance and the concomitant threat to our personal liberty. History suggests the answer is for individuals to continuously search for our own personal security.

As for changing the course of society, the best way to change the direction of a running herd is not to try to convince them they're heading toward danger, but to run in the right direction yourself, and have confidence that by protecting yourself you'll set an example. The thoughtful members of the crowd will follow you.

Meanwhile, technology in the form of the expanding Internet and science in the form of the biology of human behavior will, hopefully, awaken the younger generations to the ultimate destiny of the species, which is individual sovereignty.

Your Privacy in Danger
February 1998

A new European Commission report has uncovered one of the biggest and most secretive intelligence projects ever conceived. The project in question is nothing less than the development of a global surveillance system by the U.S. government.

The dramatic report, *Assessing the Technologies of Control*, is the work of the European Parliament's Civil Liberties Committee. It states that American listening stations in Europe, manned by U.S. personnel, eavesdrop on innumerable messages "routinely and indiscriminately." It is the first official acknowledgment of a spy system designed to eavesdrop on European citizens—a system able to scan every e-mail and fax you send, and every phone call you make.

All telecommunications—faxes to banks, telephone calls to brokers and e-mail to loved ones—are now subjected to an unprecedented degree of scrutiny. The right to communicate freely and privately with whomever you wish—a fundamental of life in a democracy—has disappeared.

Warnings about U.S. eavesdropping have previously come from several quarters. In 1995, *Wired U.K.* magazine suggested that although America's shadowy National Security Agency (NSA) is forbidden in law from spying on U.S. citizens on home soil, NSA sites in Britain can evade domestic U.S. legislation. *Wired* also claimed that one particular NSA base in the U.K., known as Menwith Hill, "could easily listen to U.K. citizens as well." They reported that a growing number of commentators believed government authorities were "systematically trawling the entire phone system." And in 1997, German magazine *Der Spiegel* claimed top secret bases were intercepting the innocent, everyday communications of civilians in a number of EU countries.

Those fears have now been borne out. The Civil Liberties Committee report reveals an unprecedented intelligence gathering system being used to spy on private citizens all around the planet. The revelations will remind many privacy advocates of the words of one U.K. cryptography expert, Ross Anderson. Commenting on the increasingly electronic nature of our daily transactions, he once raised the specter of a "surveillance society in which authority will know our every details of our lives. Even Hitler and Stalin couldn't have dreamt of that." That society is already with us.

No Privacy Anywhere

The eavesdropper placed firmly in the frame is the NSA. Established by presidential decree 36 years ago without Congressional debate, its existence was only admitted in recent years.

The report says, "Within Europe, all e-mail, telephone and fax communications are routinely intercepted by the United States National Security Agency (NSA)..." Key to the power of the listening system is the cooperation between governments, and the sharing of information. The U.S. spy network relies upon a 1948 pact called the U.K.-U.S.A. agreement. This agreement was designed to intercept targets such as Russian radio transmissions. Other signatories to the agreement—dubbed a "charter for snooping" by one U.K. newspaper—were the U.K., New Zealand, Australia and Canada.

Since the creation of the eavesdropping pact, astounding leaps in technology have allowed governments to develop their activities into the largest intelligence-gathering system ever created. And to then, turn it on the taxpayers who funded it.

The Hills Are Alive

The reports' authors have also confirmed that the secret Menwith Hill base is vital to the listening system. They write that the NSA system works by listening to public communications in Europe and then "transferring all target information...to Fort Meade (Maryland, U.S.A.) via the crucial hub at Menwith Hill..."

Menwith Hill is actually the world's largest spy base. And despite the end of the Cold War, it just keeps growing. Situated in the Yorkshire countryside, near the town of Harrogate, it is conspicuously absent from public maps. Approximately 1,200 U.S. personnel busy themselves around the clock capturing, labeling and circulating ordinary civilian communications. The local landscape is peppered with vast golf ball structures know as "radomes." These contain the NSA's eavesdropping satellite dishes.

Although Menwith is the largest Big Brother listening station, it is by no means the only one. The report states that a whole chain of bases around the global is eavesdropping for the U.S. authorities. The stations are believed to be targeting Intelsat communications satellites. These relay millions of faxes, e-mail and phone conversations every day. The overall result is to provide the U.S. and its allies with a virtual stranglehold on communications all around the planet.

And when the global listening system is included with other information gathering systems, such as official databases, camera networks and phone tapping and metering, a picture of a previously unimaginable infrastructure emerges. One that can watch, record and profile every area of a person's life, in the name of national security.

ECHELON

The ambitious goal of monitoring communications around the globe has been made possible by high-tech artificial intelligence programs, running on super-computers. These scrutinize hundreds of thousands of real-time private messages simultaneously. For many years now anecdotal evidence has pointed to the existence of such a system. Significantly, the report also recognizes its existence. Its name is ECHELON. The Euro-report states, "The ECHELON system works by indiscriminately intercepting very large quantities of communications and then siphoning out what is valuable using artificial intelligence aids... to find key words." It goes on to say, "...unlike many of the electronic spy systems developed during the Cold War, ECHELON is designed for non-military targets: governments, organizations and businesses in virtually every country."

ECHELON works by sucking up vast quantities of civilian communications and examining them for words of "interest" to national governments. Each country has created a list or "dictionary" of names, phrases and locations. The software scans for these and singles out references to them. The nature of ECHELON is to be totally indiscriminate. Your messages are being searched for subject words and place names, even if your telephone number or e-mail address does not appear on a government wanted list.

If your message happens to include subject words of interest to the government, however innocent, it may be recorded, tagged and passed to the requesting agency for further investigation. Each listening base is believed to have copies of other countries' dictionaries, so every tentacle of the system knows what the others are looking for, and can feed it on.

Eavesdropping: A Global Standard

Ironically, as Euro MPs document the erosion of privacy by unaccountable government agencies, the U.K. government has talked of incorporating the European Convention of Human Rights. The Convention accords privacy and free speech as equal rights.

Euro-politicians have also worked hard to poke their noses into your e-mail and faxes. In November 1993, the EU's Council of Justice and Home Affairs met in Brussels to discuss "the interception of telecommunications." The horrifying result was a resolution calling upon an "expert group to compare the requirements of members states with those of the FBI."

Two years later, a memorandum was produced by the 15 EU member states. It spoke of the need for "international interception standards" to "fight organized crime and for the protection of national security." U.K. pressure group Statewatch labeled the document an "EU-U.S. plan for global telecommunications surveillance." But Minister Michael Hower saw things differently. He told a House of Lords committee that the memorandum was "not a significant document."

Privacy Solutions

Big Brother's grip on world telecommunications is clearly tight. So what steps can you take to ensure you aren't innocently caught in the crossfire from the "wars" against drugs and money laundering, or investigated in the name of "national security?"

Anonymity. Randomly chosen public payphones and a handful of coins remain the fastest way to regain anonymity. Do not select payphones at airports, seaports, rail stations or areas of ill repute. These may be monitored with wiretaps as well as cameras. Airports are a source of enormous temptation as their facilities often boast user-friendly data-ports for the traveler's PC. You may find a direct hotline to Big Brother. Assume the worst about our telecommunications, and act accordingly.

Encryption. The EC study can only support the belief that the final hope of communications privacy in the twenty-first century lies in the widespread use of encryption. The belief is best exemplified in the words of the privacy advocate and NSA critic, John Gilmore, who once commented, "We aren't going to be secure in our persons, houses, papers and effects unless we get a better understanding of cryptography." The world's most popular encryption program is called Pretty Good Privacy, or PGP. You can use it to make your e-mail and your computer files virtually unreadable. Download it for free at www.pgpi.com. A program called PGPFone enables you to have an encrypted telephone conversation with a fellow PGPFone user over the Internet. U.S. and Canadian residents can download the PGPFone from web.mit.edu/network/pgpfone.

But the final word on the topic of cryptography must go to the NSA itself. Although the U.S. government fears the global use of encryption, it has now lifted most of the export restrictions it once placed on encryption products.

One of its spokesmen revealed an interesting aspect of policy. He said, "We have always supported the use of cryptographic products by U.S. businesses operating domestically and overseas to protect their sensitive and proprietary information." EU citizens who believe good things ought to be shared may wish to act upon that ringing endorsement of encryption.

Global Surveillance Exposed

by Mark Nestmann, *The Sovereign Individual*, August 1999

"There was of course no way of knowing whether you were being watched at any given moment. How often, or on what system, the Thought Police plugged in on any individual wire was guesswork. It was even conceivable that they watched everybody all the time—You had to live— did live, from habit that became instinct—in the assumption that every sound you made was overheard—every movement scrutinized."
~George Orwell, 1984

The world of Winston Smith, George Orwell's protagonist in *1984*, was one of surveillance-a constant, all-encompassing surveillance; one in which every whisper, every liaison, indeed, every thought was subject to monitoring.

In a world where free markets and free ideas have supposedly triumphed over totalitarianism, global surveillance appears unlikely, even surreal. But today's surveillance infrastructure, although far more covert than that of 1984, is in many ways more comprehensive. Justified at its creation to "fight Communism," this infrastructure is today used to monitor political dissidents, civil libertarians and gather commercial intelligence for government-favored enterprises.

Constructed in near-total secrecy, it was not until late 1999 that governments officially acknowledged that this infrastructure existed, ending five decades of official denials.

All Communications Monitored

It began at the end of World War II. To more effectively fight the "Cold War," the five major English-speaking democracies—the United States, the United Kingdom, Canada, New Zealand and Australia—signed a secret treaty agreeing to share "signals intelligence" or in the jargon of military intelligence, "SIGINT." The 1947 agreement was code-named "U.K.-U.S.A."

In the ensuing decades, the participating governments set up a global network of listening posts—more than 2,000 in all—capable of monitoring any information transmitted over wire and (especially) through the air. Voice, data, teletype, fax transmissions, and telephone beeper signals are all vulnerable. So are mobile radio systems, local area network communications, radio PBXs and cordless and cellular telephones.

Speaking of the capabilities of this network, the U.S. House Government Operations Committee concluded in an unpublished report released in 1976:

> [Messages monitored by the NSA are] processed through computers that are programmed to isolate encrypted messages, as well as messages containing "trigger" words, word combinations, entities, names, addresses and combinations of addresses. The intercepted messages that are in code or cipher are, whenever possible, solved. These messages and messages selected by "target procedures" are then inspected by human analysts. Messages which the NSA electronically scans and judges to be of no interest to the NSA or its consumers [i.e., other federal agencies]-annually accounting for tens of millions of communications of U.S. citizens-are not considered by the NSA to have been intercepted or acquired.

Given these capabilities, it was perhaps inevitable that political leaders sought to use the network for non-military purposes. The domestic intelligence activities of the NSA were highlighted in 1976 hearings before the Senate Intelligence Committee. Witnesses described initiatives such as Project Minaret, in which the NSA monitored political dissidents and Project Shamrock, in which from 1945 to 1975 the NSA inspected daily all overseas cables. According to the Committee's final report, Shamrock was the "largest governmental interception program affecting Americans, dwarfing the CIA's mail opening program by comparison."

Tapping the Internet

More than 20 years after the NSA's domestic spying activities were documented, new reports surfaced describing how the global surveillance infrastructure was now being used-a decade after the end of the Cold War—to monitor the activities of human rights organizations and for economic intelligence.

In 1998, Nicky Hager's *Secret Power* claimed that the U.K.-U.S.A. agreement had been implemented in a global surveillance network called ECHELON. The network monitors communications satellites, undersea telephone cables and microwave transmission towers in dozens of countries, among other sources. According to Hager, in ECHELON:

> Every word of every message intercepted at each station gets automatically searched . . . keywords include such things as the names of people, ships, organizations, country names and subject names. They also include the known telex and fax numbers and Internet addresses of any individuals, business, organizations and government offices that are targets.

Hager's book documents how ECHELON interconnects the surveillance network's listening stations and allows them to function as components of an integrated whole. An individual station's computer contains not only its parent agency's chosen keywords, but also has lists entered in for other agencies.

Are You Under Surveillance?

Also in 1998, the European Parliament's Scientific and Technological Options Assessment (STOA) committee published a landmark study on advances in surveillance technology. The report confirms that "within Europe, all e-mail, telephone and fax communications are routinely intercepted by the U.S. National Security Agency." STOA further revealed that ECHELON monitors primarily non-military targets. For instance, it states that in June 1992, a group of current "highly placed [U.K.] intelligence operatives" spoke to the *London Observer*, confirming that U.K. intelligence agencies had monitored the communications of charitable organizations, including Amnesty International and Christian Aid. According to the report, "with no system of accountability, it is difficult to discover what criteria determine who is not a target."

Despite the outrage this report caused, the European Parliament approved its own Euro-surveillance initiative that in many respects will have similar capabilities to ECHELON.

Australia, Canada Admit Global Surveillance

In March 1999, Australia became the first country to officially acknowledge its participation in ECHELON. In a letter to Channel 9's Sunday television program, Martin Brady, director of the Australian Defense Signals Directorate (www.dsd.gov.au), stated that the DSD "does cooperate with counterpart signals intelligence organizations overseas under the U.K.-U.S.A. relationship."

The Channel 9 report focused on how the ECHELON system was being transformed into an economic intelligence network. There are few legal limits on the government gathering economic intelligence in most countries. U.S. and Australian law permits it if other countries or their exporters are perceived to be behaving unfairly. The United Kingdom has no legal restraint on the practice.

According to Mike Frost, a former Canadian intelligence agent interviewed for the program, "ECHELON is a total, complete invasion of an individual's privacy." To circumvent national laws prohibiting domestic intelligence agencies from spying on their own citizens, according to Frost, the intelligence agencies involved in ECHELON ask each other to spy on their own citizens. "They circumvent their own legislation by asking the other countries to do it for them." Among the Canadian targets that Frost asked other countries to monitor was the wife of the late Prime Minister Pierre Trudeau.

When the Australian report aired, Canada acknowledged the existence of its own communications monitoring network. It confirmed that the Communications Security Establishment collects and analyzes foreign communications.

Interception Capabilities 2000

Also in 1999, a report entitled *Interception Capabilities 2000* was approved by STOA. The report contains near-encyclopedic coverage of the monitoring capabilities of the world's intelligence services—from radio transmission to microwaves to satellites. Among the revelations, the Clinton Administration ordered the systematic tapping of undersea communications cables by nuclear-powered submarines.

The report also reveals that NSA had developed systems to collect, filter and analyze the forms of fast digital communications used by the Internet. Because most of the world's Internet capacity lies within the United States or connects to the United States, many communications in cyberspace will pass through intermediate sites within the United States. Communications from Europe to and from Asia, Oceania, Africa or South America normally travel via the United States.

The report contains additional confirmation of commercial intelligence gathering efforts through ECHELON. For instance, in 1995, the NSA monitored all the faxes and phone calls between the European consortium Airbus, the Saudi national airline and the Saudi government. It found that Airbus agents were trying to bribe a Saudi official. It passed the information to U.S. officials pressing the bid of Boeing and McDonnell Douglas Corp., which triumphed in the US$6 billion competition.

While the official position of the U.S. government continues to be that ECHELON does not exist, the overwhelming volume of documentary evidence published made this position untenable.

In response, Congress has demanded information on ECHELON. An amendment attached to the Intelligence Authorization Act requires the NSA to prepare a report on ECHELON for Congress. The report is to describe the legal standards employed by the NSA in conducting SIGINT activities, including electronic surveillance. But the NSA rejected the request, stating that the requested files are held by its general counsel and thus subject to attorney-client privilege. As of March 2001, the impasse continues.

This debacle has had one fortuitous outcome: it has led most European countries to loosen restrictions on encryption technology, the most effective way to foil surveillance on the scale of ECHELON. For instance, France, which had previously banned effective encryption, has lifted that restriction. European businesses now are particularly conscious of the threat of industrial espionage courtesy of ECHELON.

Unprotected Wealth is a Target

ECHELON demonstrates how a global surveillance network purportedly created to gather military intelligence can be used against political opponents or civil liberties groups. But the network is also now being used for another purpose—to target property to be seized in "economic emergencies" and in cases of money laundering. Indeed, the U.S. Treasury's Financial Crimes Enforcement Network (FinCEN) was created for this express purpose.

Because FinCEN was established as a unit of the U.S. Treasury, NSA intelligence could be combined with domestic sources of information, including information from the Federal Reserve and the Treasury's own databases, which included various types of financial, tax, and customs information. It also meant the merger of foreign and domestic intelligence.

FinCEN takes information gleaned from NSA's monitoring of bank wire data and other intelligence sources to develop money laundering intelligence—with virtually no oversight. Indeed, FinCEN is exempt from the Freedom of Information Act, the Right to Financial Privacy Act and other legislation that would otherwise permit a subject of its investigation to verify the accuracy of the information it collects.

FinCEN is also part of a global network of more than 50 financial intelligence units (FIUs) that share information, although the network does not appear to be as advanced as ECHELON. According to FinCEN, FIUs are funded with the proceeds of the assets they identify for confiscation.

A global network of FIUs funded with forfeited assets creates a global network of bounty hunters with ever-expanding authority to seize "suspect assets." Seizures of narcotics, gambling equipment, nuclear materials, child pornography and other illegal commodities generate no revenues for law enforcement. But seizing agencies keep up to 100 percent of the seized proceeds of the sale of such commodities, along with all property "involved in" such transactions. Some of this bounty is now shared with FIUs.

It is inconceivable that a global network of FIUs operating under these incentives, with continuous input from ECHELON, will not be used for political purposes, private gain or be vulnerable to penetration by hackers. Information theft is already endemic in other "secure" government databases. The apparent theft of U.S. nuclear weapons technology by China is only the one example.

If rogue scientists sell information and services to selected bidders, why should FinCEN and its affiliate FIUs be expected to operate differently? Certainly, drug kingpins would pay dearly for access to FIU databases. Knowing what information FIUs have on their assets and laundering techniques, not to mention those of their competitors, would be extremely valuable.

Of course, FinCEN and affiliate FIUs will also be expected to generate revenues beyond their operating costs. Now that most countries have enacted "all crimes" laundering legislation, all income allegedly generated or otherwise tainted by criminal activity is fair game. Increasingly, with the removal of "fiscal exemption" clauses in anti-laundering laws worldwide, this will include legitimate funds moved offshore in violation of tax or exchange control laws.

Defensive Strategies

The reality of global surveillance must be taken into account by anyone seeking privacy or asset protection; civil libertarians; and by any company developing high-technology products. But despite the high volume of communications signals relayed by satellite and microwave, a great many communications—both local and domestic long distance—can't be intercepted without a direct wiretap. And, adds Canadian ex-spook Mike Frost, there's a problem sorting and reading all the data. While ECHELON can potentially intercept millions of communications, there aren't enough analysts to sort through everything.

In addition, you can employ simple strategies that can frustrate the operations of this network:

Use voice communication. The technical capabilities to listen in to voice communications are less advanced than those available to tap data. Frost describes NSA computers that can "listen" to telephone calls and recognize keywords. However, voice recognition computers that can listen in to a large volume of telephone calls simultaneously don't appear to yet be available, he says, although according to other predictions, by 2005, this technology may be in place. For the moment, telephone calls are more secure from ECHELON monitoring than e-mail, fax or other computer-generated communication.

Use encryption. The easiest targets for ECHELON are unencrypted data streams. Merely taking the precaution of using off-the-shelf software such as PGP (www.pgpi.com) to secure e-mail makes it virtually impervious to being read. It remains extremely important, however, to guard your private key(s) and pass phrase(s).

Ways to Protect Internet Anonymity
by Mark Nestmann, *The Sovereign Individual*, June 1999

"The real world is routinely anonymous. When you drive down the street, typically there is no one photographing your license plate, no one keeping track of where you park and how long you stay. What's unusual about the Internet is that everything is by default logged and tracked. What's aberrant is not the presence of anonymity on the Internet, but that you have to take special steps to achieve it."
~Lance Cottrell, CEO, Anonymizer.com

*"If you're serious about prosecuting crime on the global
communications infrastructure, you have to have traceability."*
~Philip Reitinger, U.S. Department of Justice

Many people assume that since they don't physically interact with anyone on the Internet, their actions are private. They aren't. Without taking precautions to preserve your anonymity, every time you log on, you leave a calling card that reveals your present location, what kind of computer you have and, potentially, other details about your identity and viewing habits.

Why be anonymous? There are many reasons:

- To avoid "Trojan Horse" programs that hackers can infect your PC with that secretly take it over and relay everything you do on it to a thief or an investigator;

- To browse without giving up personal information to marketers;

- To avoid malicious websites that can actually steal confidential files off your PC;

- To avoid spam, the bulk-mail advertising pitches that advertisers send to e-mail addresses they have captured;

- To post messages using a pseudonym to avoid the permanent archiving of news group postings under your real name; and

- To chat online without revealing your real identity.

Internet anonymity is under attack in the courts. In the United States, a growing number of corporations have issued subpoenas to Internet Service Providers (ISPs) and operators of online message boards seeking to identify and locate individuals who posted material that the companies find objectionable. This tactic can be used to intimidate potential critics into silence and destroy the anonymity that has contributed to the Internet's explosive growth.

However, the stakes in the cyber-privacy war are now, literally, a matter of life and death. In 1999, during the conflict in Kosovo, several persons who reported Serb atrocities on the web later vanished. Serb authorities used telephone records and records maintained by ISPs to identify and track them.

How to Protect Your Internet Privacy

- Use computers in public accommodations for Internet access or use a machine dedicated only for this purpose. Don't keep confidential files—especially your PGP private keys—on this machine.

- Open an anonymous e-mail account at www.hushmail.com. Free encrypted Hushmail can be sent to other Hushmail users. This service, based outside the United States, is much more private and more secure than other free, but much better known, services such as www.hotmail.com, http:www.juno.com, or www.bigfoot.com.

- Beware of sending attached files that might contain remnants of earlier versions. This is the case, for instance, with Microsoft Word. Moreover, if a file itself contains identifying characteristics (such as in Office 97), an anonymous e-mail program won't strip them out.

- Install virus detection software such as that sold by McAfee (www.mcafee.com) or Norton (www.symantec.com).

- Obtain anonymous dial-up service through the Anonymizer or another ISP that will allow you to anonymously prepay for service.

- Encrypt sensitive e-mail and files using PGP 6.5 or a similar program.

- Keep sensitive files on a floppy disk, never on your hard drive.

- Securely delete files you're finished using with PGP 6.5 or a similar program.

- At the end of each computer session, turn off your computer, then turn it back on and wipe the free space on your PC's hard disk with PGP 6.5 or a similar program.

- Do not register Windows 98 or any other software online.

- Use pseudonyms, but don't count on them to always be effective. For example, defense contractor Raytheon sued nearly two dozen employees for posting pseudonymous messages about the company. Yahoo (www.yahoo.com), which ran the message service, was forced to reveal their identities in response to a subpoena.

- Don't execute programs or files from anyone you don't trust. This is the most frequent way that viruses and similar malicious programs are spread.

- Don't buy a PC equipped with a Pentium III or IV processor. Instead, purchase a PC with a processor manufactured by Advanced Micro Devices (AMD) (www.amd.com).

Achieving Untraceable Telecommunications
By Mark Nestmann, *The Sovereign Individual*, January 2003

In the name of fighting "crime" and "terrorism," many governments have ratified laws and treaties that obligate telecommunications providers to build surveillance technologies into their networks. Other initiatives require telecom companies to turn over customer records to authorities with a lower burden of proof than previously required, or allow them to "voluntarily" turn them over if they suspect wrongdoing.

To actually listen in on telephone conversations or read the contents of e-mail messages, law enforcement agencies in the United States and most other Western countries must still obtain a search warrant approved by a judge, based on probable cause that the subject under investigation is involved in illegal (not necessarily terrorist) activity.

But obtaining information on "traffic data"—the origination or destination number or e-mail address of phone calls and e-mails—is much easier. And in the case of e-mail and text-messaging systems, it is hard to review only traffic data and not also the content of the messages.

In most countries, law enforcement only needs to stipulate that such data is relevant to a criminal investigation. Customer payment records—finding the identity behind an e-mail address—generally don't require a warrant, either.

In the United States, such inquiries have increased by a factor of five since the events of September 11, 2001.

Representatives at Yahoo, one of the largest U.S.-based online services, say that the typical subpoena now asks for much more information; not just user-account information, but details about subscribers' Internet use, billing and credit-card history.

Technology has also expanded the reach of information that can be subpoenaed. For instance, a subpoena to a cellular service provider now can request data on every call made in a certain time range in a certain geographical location.

The most important surveillance initiatives in recent years have been:

- *The Communications Assistance for Law Enforcement Act* (CALEA). This 1994 U.S. law requires telecommunications companies to install secret "back doors" in their equipment to facilitate surveillance.

- *Regulations of Investigatory Powers Act* (RIP). This 2000 U.K. law requires all major U.K. Internet Service Providers (ISPs) to route all data passing through their networks to a monitoring center at the headquarters of the British intelligence service, MI-5. It permits police to obtain customer account data, billing information, telephone dialing records, lists of e-mail messages sent or received or web sites visited based on the orders of a senior law enforcement officer. It also requires PC users to release their encryption keys on demand.

- *The Council of Europe Cybercrime Treaty.* Designed to fight computer crime, this treaty, now signed by dozens of countries, requires ISPs to maintain logs of users' activities for up to seven years and to keep their networks "tappable." The equivalent of the treaty in the physical world would be to require valid return addresses on all postal mail, installing cameras in all phone booths and making all currency traceable. It remains to be seen whether the U.S. Senate will ratify this Convention, which appears to violate several provisions of the U.S. Constitution.

- *The USA PATRIOT Act.* This law makes it possible for federal law enforcement agencies to obtain e-mail message "header" information (i.e., obtain source, destination and subject line information) and web browsing patterns without a wiretap order. It is no longer necessary to prove that the information is relevant to a criminal investigation. What's more, law enforcement may obtain access to subscriber data without subpoenas if they "reasonably believe that (it's) an emergency involving danger of death or serious physical injury."

- *EU: One-year mandatory record keeping of all telecommunications traffic proposed.* In June 2002, the EU allowed member states to require that Internet providers retain traffic and the geographical location of all people using any electronic communications device. The initiative would override a 1997 Privacy Directive stipulating that traffic data (covering phones, mobiles, e-mails, faxes and Internet usage) could only be retained for billing purposes after which it has to be erased. So far, only Spain has acted, adopting a one-year data retention requirement.

- *The Homeland Security Act.* This recently enacted U.S. statute lowers the burden for telecommunications providers to notify law enforcement of their suspicion of criminal activity by a customer from a "reasonable belief" test to a "good faith" provision. It also permits disclosure to "any federal, state or local governmental entity," not just law enforcement agencies. This will allow the IRS or any other government agency access to these records if they can persuade them that there is an "emergency," which need not involve an "immediate danger."

Countermeasures: Traceless Telephone Calls

The mass surveillance engendered by these initiatives will be effective only at keeping tabs on the law-abiding public. Anyone who wants to secure privacy in their communications can still cover their tracks by using the techniques discussed in this article.

Here's a rundown of measures you can still legally take to protect yourself from telephone surveillance:

- *Use public telephones.* Use a network of pay phones, not just one. Unfortunately, many payphones no longer accept incoming calls. Have persons you wish to call page you when they are ready to receive your call. Then call back from a public telephone to a pre-arranged number. Professional investigators may anticipate your use of pay phones, so avoid using the most convenient ones. Many public telephones in major cities and at airports, train stations, etc. are under continuous closed-circuit television surveillance. Timed film footage is increasingly being matched to "suspicious" calls on public phones. Phones in rural or isolated areas are free from this threat. Use cash to pay for your calls. Alternatively, buy pre-paid phone cards (see below), which are available in over 100 countries.

- *Obtain an anonymous voice mailbox.* This is a great way to have a "local" phone number without obtaining local service. You can retrieve messages from any touch-tone phone. Find a company that doesn't require identification and permits you to prepay for service at least a year in advance. This way, they will not need to send correspondence to the "temporary" address you (should) leave with them.

- *Obtain anonymous telephone service.* In the United States, for about a 50% premium over the local Bell provider, you can obtain local phone service without a credit check and in many cases without showing proof of identify. While such companies target persons with poor credit, the service is attractive to privacy-seekers. You simply provide the company your "name," the address at which you wish service to be connected, and pay the hook-up fee. One provider of this service is 1-800-RECONEX: (800) 732-6639.

- *Make anonymous long-distance calls.* Avoid the revealing "call detail" on your local telephone bill of long-distance calls dialed by setting up a separately billed account for such calls. Even better, use prepaid calling cards. Now available in more than 100 countries, you can purchase such cards almost anywhere—at convenience stores, post offices, vending machines, etc. Do not use a "rechargeable" card that allows you to add value to the card with a credit card or debit card. This compromises privacy, although less so if you're using a card issued by an off-shore bank. The only way that "you" can be linked to a prepaid card is if calling records indicate that the card was accessed from your home or business telephone number. To protect your privacy, dial from a public phone or through an operator.

- *Purchase anonymous cellular service.* This is possible by pre-paying for the service. In the United States, one of the most popular services is called Cricket. For US$32.95 a month, you obtain unlimited local phone service. And you can purchase pre-paid long distance service for eight cents per minute. Many other services permit you to set up service with no credit check, no contract and no ID. In Canada, nationwide prepaid cellular service is available from Rogers AT&T (www.cellphones.ca/rogers/rog8381.html), among other sources. In the United Kingdom, you can purchase a cell phone almost anywhere without revealing your identity. To pay for your calls, purchase "scratch cards" from most post offices or newsstands. Calls cost around 50p/minute; less if you purchase a larger block of time.

- *Obtain a pager anonymously.* A pager is useful if you want to keep your location or phone numbers private. Like cellular phones, pagers can be obtained for one-off payments with no contracts, no ID requirements, no monthly bills, and no credit checks. Unfortunately, availability is diminishing, a consequence of text messaging services now available with many cellular phones.

- *Obtain an anonymous fax number.* If your voice mail provider offers a fax option, you can program the system to have the faxes sent to a local office services store. Or have them delivered to you via e-mail. J2.com (www.j2.com/free/free.asp) and eFax (www.efax.com) provide Internet and e-mail based services that allow you to receive voice mail messages and faxes via e-mail. You can view your faxes on your PC, print them to your PC's printer and forward them via e-mail to anyone else equipped with the appropriate fax viewing software. When you sign up, you will be asked for your name, street address, home telephone number, e-mail address, etc., but this data does not appear to be verified. One customer tells me he signed up as "Harry Houdini." You must use a valid e-mail address, but the address may be an anonymous one set up through www.hushmail.com or a similar service.

- *Consider telephone encryption.* Several companies manufacture telephones that encrypt conversations so that a would-be eavesdropper will hear only inaudible static. An encrypted telephone is required at each end of the telephone conversation. If you choose this option, everyone with whom you wish to communicate securely will need to be equipped with the same model of encrypted telephone as the one you are using. Manufacturers include Starium (www.starium.com) and TCC (www.tccsecure.com).

- *Conduct secure voice communication through your PC.* This requires a computer, an Internet telecommunications package such as VocalTec's Internet Phone (www.eurocall.com), PGP (www.pgpi.com) and a good sound card. Your receiving partner must have the same set-up. The configuration is best left to an expert to install. Another option, again requiring expert assistance to install, is pgpFone (http://web.mit.edu/network/pgpfone).

- *Other practical solutions for telephone anonymity.* When purchasing pre-paid telephones or services, it is wise to "blend in" as a "typical" user; someone who has not established credit, or has poor credit. Never make your "privacy" motives apparent.

In addition, combine these strategies for maximum effectiveness. Never use your home or office telephone for "controversial" calls. Keep an anonymous cell phone in reserve, and use it when you need to make a confidential call. While authorities can now pinpoint the location of a cell phone call, if they can't identify its owner, this information is of little value. Use a pre-paid calling card to make longer-duration confidential calls from a payphone.

Can criminals use these methods? Of course. But so can law-abiding persons who believe, as I do, that they have a right to privacy and freedom from surveillance.

U.S. Authorizes Back Door "Roving Wiretaps"
The Sovereign Individual, December 1998

If you're the U.S. Attorney General, head of the U.S. Department of Justice, and you can't persuade legislators to openly pass laws that curtail civil liberties, you have another option: Hide the same laws in other, less controversial legislation. Wait until that law has passed both the House and the Senate and is sent to a conference committee to iron out minor differences between the two versions. Persuade the conferees to insert the controversial provision into the conference bill. Then quietly pass the revisions without public debate.

This was the back-door approach used by the Department of Justice in 1984 to bring about the largest expansion in civil forfeiture laws in U.S. history. And in 1998 it repeated the performance. Without debate or notice, U.S. lawmakers approved a proposal long sought by the FBI that dramatically expanded the authority of police to conduct "roving wiretaps"—i.e., tapping any and all phones potentially used by a criminal suspect. (Congress rejected this very same idea when the matter was openly debated as part of the1996 Anti-Terrorism bill).

The law, which allows police to tap any telephone used or located near a wiretap target, was added to the Intelligence Authorization Conference report during a closed-door meeting. Then, without debate, both the House and Senate approved it.

Previously, police had to demonstrate that a target was switching telephones for the specific purpose of avoiding surveillance. Now, they need only show that the target of a wiretap's actions could have the effect of thwarting interception from a specific facility.

When the FBI originally requested roving wiretap authority, it acknowledged that less than one percent of the conversations it recorded were relevant to its investigations. In other words, 99 percent of the time, police are listening in on irrelevant conversations. The vast majority of these conversations involve participants neither suspected nor accused of any wrongdoing. Roving wiretap authority will make it even more likely innocent third parties will be drawn into the government's surveillance net.

Say, for instance, you're unknowingly meeting with the target of a roving wiretap in your home or office. Your phone number is added to the list of target phones, not for a single day, but potentially for as long as the investigation continues—perhaps weeks, months or years.

Investigators are supposed to ignore conversations that are not directly relevant to the authorized wiretap. But of course they don't. The safest course of conduct: Don't say anything on a telephone that you don't want to hear played back in a courtroom.

The United States: An Informer's Paradise
by Robert E. Bauman, JD, December 1997

Most Americans know little or nothing about the widespread domestic use of police Informants—and few government and police officials are willing to talk openly about this big, dirty secret. For people outside the U.S., an accurate knowledge about how the U.S. government uses informants in its international operations is essential to avoid entrapment and worse. What happens in the U.S. has a disturbing tendency to be exported elsewhere. It could be you being investigated or charged with crimes you didn't commit because an informant pointed the finger at you.

Increasingly informants are being used by U.S. police agents in so-called "white collar" international business and finance cases. "Money laundering" is one of the favorite charges pursued. Shrouded in secrecy, informers don't want publicity about their nasty work. They want lenient treatment for past crimes, money rewards and sometimes revenge.

Despite constant government efforts to keep the public in the dark, the bright sunlight of publicity has exposed the squirming mass under the rock. In numerous U.S. money laundering cases, informants have played an important role.

It's Happening in America

The growing informant scandal is so serious it prompted federal appeals court judge Stephen S. Trott of Boise, Idaho, head of the Criminal Division of the U.S. Department of Justice under President Reagan, to warn, "The integrity of the criminal justice system is at stake. There needs to be better control and supervision of informants." He said the current use of informants "... reminds me of a movie I saw in which the characters played a game they called TEGWAR—an acronym for 'The Exciting Game Without Any Rules.'"

And yet, in the wake of the 1995 Oklahoma City bombing, President Clinton quickly demanded that Congress pass legislation greatly increasing police wiretapping, FBI surveillance and the expanded use and protection of government informants. According to press reports, a key part of what the President wanted was a national network of paid informants, or so-called "human intelligence sources." Fortunately, congressional civil rights advocates, on the left and right, managed to thwart the worst excesses Clinton wanted, but many of his dubious proposals found their way into law under the guise of "anti-terrorism"controls.

15,000 "Wild, Out-of-Control" Informants

Michael Levine, a retired 25-year veteran of both U.S. Customs and the Drug Enforcement Agency (DEA), estimates there are currently at least 15,000 informers on federal payrolls, not counting many thousands more paid by state and local police. His estimate does not include more than 10,000 informants who claim money rewards each year for reporting fellow taxpayers to the IRS, or the nearly 1,000 so-called "controlled informants" the IRS pays to inform on others, some of them tax accountants. For example, for the fiscal year ending September 30, 1996, the IRS paid informants US$3.5 million, nearly double what it paid for the previous year.

Levine, retired in 1990, charges that informants, earning three or four times more in government pay than the DEA and FBI agents who are supposed to be their bosses, have literally taken over most criminal investigations. Says Levine, "Our rights as citizens and the U.S. Constitution are now in the hands of 15,000 wild, out-of-control informants. If you get in their way they will take you down, and government agents are ignorant enough or lazy enough to let them do "

Protests Are Few

In this era of sound bites and media-oriented "get tough on crime" politics, few elected officials dare to decry loss of constitutional protections. U.S. Representative Henry J. Hyde is an exception. In the 1996 book *Forfeiting Our Property Rights* (Cato Institute, Washington D.C.), the Chairman of the House Judiciary Committee attacked government use of "an army of well paid secret informers," whom he described as "a motley crew of drug pushers, ex-cons, convicts, prisoners and other social misfits."

Hyde stated bluntly: "They have a strong incentive to lie, and they often do. Informants, by their very nature, are not normal, gainfully employed, honest, upright citizens. Rather they are, or have been, involved in drug or other serious criminal activity, and their motivation is to save their own skins."

Typical is the 1996 New York federal district court case in which Emad A. Salem, the unsavory main government witness in New York's World Trade Center terrorist bombing conspiracy trial, admitted he lied, testifying he was promised more then US$1 million by the government for his assistance as the principal informer in the case. Similarly, informants in the Miami federal case against ex-Panama dictator Manuel Noreiga were paid over US$4 million and spared hundreds of years of potential prison time.

Informing—A Big Business

Individual informants do receive princely sums from the U.S. Treasury, a grotesque example of tax dollars at work. Like U.S. lawyers, informers are sometimes paid on a contingency fee; the total value of property they finger for successful forfeiture determines how much money the government pays into their personal bank accounts. So-called "cooperating witnesses" receive 25 percent of the value of property seized by the government in any one case, with a maximum cap of US$250,000.

A U.S. House Committee on Government Operations report in August 1992 showed how well informers are doing for themselves, revealing that in 1990-91, the Justice Department paid 65 informants more than $100,000 each, 24 were paid between $100,000 and $250,000, and eight got over $250,000 each.

Secrecy Is the Rule

Although the Sixth Amendment, part of the U.S. Constitution's Bill of Rights, guarantees an accused person the right "to be confronted with the witnesses against him," courts have held this is not absolute and usually applies at trial, but not always in preliminary stages of investigation and indictment. These rulings supporting the so-called "informant's privilege," allow secret accusers to avoid risk of exposure by having to testify in public. Instead, a police officer seeking a search warrant simply repeats before a magistrate, or testifies before a grand jury about what he was told by "a reliable informant."

The highly unfair result: most criminal defendants never find out who accused them of wrongdoing, unless prosecutors decide an informant's testimony at trial is essential to convict. Prosecutors, police and federal agents defend this system, arguing informants are indispensable in organized crime, terrorism and white-collar crime cases.

It's the War on Drugs, Stupid!

The driving force behind the massive use of informants during the last decade has been the much-touted "war on drugs." Informants are often the key to drug arrests and property confiscation under civil asset forfeiture laws, a valuable cash cow for police. Law enforcement officials keep most of the cash and property seized, and the funds go directly into police budgets, salaries and other perks.

In the case involving the alleged murder by Mexican nationals of DEA agent Enrique Camarena in Mexico, yet to go to trial, as of 1994 the government had paid US$2.7 million to informants. One of these, Rene Lopez-Romero, allegedly involved in the 1984 kidnapping and murder of four American missionaries in Guadalajara, receives US$3,000 monthly until the trial, and another Camarena case informant got US$909,862 stemming from yet another case in which he gave information.

Phantom Police Informers

In his book, *The Best Defense*, Harvard law professor Alan Dershowitz offers some little-known rules he says "govern the justice game in America today." Rule IV is, "Almost all police lie about whether they violated the Constitution in order to convict 'guilty defendants.'"

That is certainly accurate when it comes to the use and/or manufacture of police informers. It is now commonplace for police lacking a "reliable informant" on which to base a request for a search or arrest warrant, to invent them. Lying by police to support questionable criminal charges against suspects has gone on for years in New York City, according to a report of the Mayor's commission investigating police corruption. After 1993-94 hearings, the Mollen Commission concluded New York police routinely made false arrests, invented informers, tampered with evidence and committed perjury on the witness stand. "Perjury is the most widespread form of police wrongdoing," the report stated, noting it even has a well-known nickname among the court house cognoscenti— "testilying."

Early on the morning of October 2, 1992, millionaire Donald Scott was shot to death by a member of a 27-man police drug squad as they broke into his rural ranch home. A subsequent five-month investigation by the Ventura County district attorney found police had lied to a judge to obtain the search warrant, based on a false tip by an informant that Scott was growing marijuana. The report also concluded police hoped to confiscate Scott's ranch and turn it over the National Park Service, a federal agency to which Scott has repeatedly refused to sell his land. No charges were brought against the police, nor was anyone disciplined about Scott's death.

America Under Surveillance

The official incompetence, corruption and criminal conduct associated with informants might be understandable if these were isolated examples, but such events are widespread. Studies show the major groups who suffer as a result are African-Americans, Latinos, Arabs and Asians, including international travelers.

In 1992 in the Memphis, Tennessee, airport, 75 percent of the travelers stopped by police on informant tips were black, yet only four percent of the flying public is black. CBS television's "60 Minutes" reporters checked out DEA airport operations in New York, Atlanta and other cities, with a well-dressed black male undercover reporter buying a plane ticket with cash. Within minutes of each purchase, DEA agents accosted the reporter and confiscated all his money; ticket clerk-informers turned him in on the spot every time.

DEA operates permanent surveillance in designated hotels in New York, Miami, Los Angeles and other cities considered scenes of likely drug activity. Hotel employees are paid to act as informers and report "suspicious" guests and people with too much or too little luggage, guests who pay room bills in cash or make multiple long distance phone calls.

Threat To Civil Liberties

Congressman Hyde believes "most Americans don't realize the extent to which our constitutional protections have been violated and diminished in recent years." Neutral observers, libertarians like the Cato Institute, political conservatives like Hyde and Judge Trott, have joined with liberals and others on the left like Professor Dershowitz and Philip S. Gutis, media relations director of the American Civil Liberties Union (ACLU). They believe unchecked police informant use constitutes a serious danger to individual liberty.

While the public only learns about major informant cases that go wrong, there are thousands of accused persons fingered by a "friend" for a crime they did not commit. Carefully controlled use of informants has a place in proper law enforcement, but what kind of justice is it when prosecutors boast of charges against a businessman whose employee or associate settles a score with an anonymous accusation of criminal conduct?

Betrayal is an essential element in the government police-informant game, but the repeated betrayal of basic constitutional principles guaranteeing our freedom is the real menace to society. In a 1928 dissent in an early wiretapping case, the late Supreme Court Justice Louis D. Brandeis warned: "The greatest dangers to liberty lurk in the insidious encroachment by men of zeal, well-meaning but without understanding." U.S. government agents may boast of cleverly turning criminals into instruments of law enforcement, but in this crude process law officers have become willing co-conspirators in crime—and too often, criminals themselves.

Using Attorney-Client Privilege Effectively
by Mark Nestmann & Robert E. Bauman, JD, *The Sovereign Individual*, August 1999

It's an established right recognized and protected by law. But unless you understand how it works and exercise that right, your private business could become a matter of public record.

In the United States it's known as the "attorney-client privilege." In the United Kingdom, it's called the "solicitor client privilege." At times, you may hear it referred to as an "attorney's duty of confidence."

In each instance, the phrase describes a long-established rule that establishes a legal and ethical duty binding an attorney not to divulge confidential communications from a client. It also gives a client the right to refuse to disclose, and to prevent others from disclosing, "confidential communications" between the client and his attorney.

Attorney-client privilege has evolved as a means to encourage clients to make complete disclosure when seeking legal advice, without fear that their attorney might inform others. It encompasses verbal and written communications, including letters, records, an attorney's notes, research, and the legal work product developed for a client.

Effective use of this privilege is crucial to preserve the privacy of any asset protection plan, estate plan or any other confidential legal matter. And when "going offshore" requires professional legal assistance, you should understand what this privilege means and how to use it.

Your attorney cannot divulge information protected by the privilege unless you give your consent or he is so ordered by a court. To gain this protection, it is always best to establish a formal representation agreement with an attorney before discussing confidential matters.

Exceptions & Waivers

Attorney-client privilege is narrower than generally perceived. For example, your identity and fee arrangements are not protected. In addition, an attorney, as a licensed member of the bar, is an "officer of the court." While your attorney must pursue your best interests, his actions are constrained by professional rules of conduct. For instance, your attorney cannot knowingly assist you in perpetrating a fraud or other illegal act.

If your attorney delegates responsibilities to others, usually the privilege extends to these persons as well. Typically, this may include other lawyers in the firm, a secretary or non attorney associates. But the privilege does not attach to work an attorney does at the direction of another person on your behalf, such as your accountant.

The privilege is also waived if you disclose information your attorney conveyed to you in confidence or that you conveyed to him. If you hire an attorney to prepare a legal opinion, your engagement letter should stipulate that release of the opinion letter does not waive your privilege concerning any other communications between you. Include a statement to this effect with any information you might disclose about your estate or asset protection plan.

To guard against waiver, it is best not to discuss legal matters with a spouse or business partner, unless you are confident the relationship will remain permanent. Many states recognize a "spousal privilege" that allows a wife or husband called as a witness to refuse to answer questions relating to communications between them. However, this protection is dissolved by divorce and does not extend to unmarried partners.

Offshore Privilege Limited

In the United States, an attorney has no duty to disclose to authorities suspicion that a client may have engaged in criminal activities. However, he must report immediately any knowledge of a client's planned future criminal acts.

In contrast, solicitors and attorneys in the United Kingdom, Switzerland and some other countries are required to notify police if they suspect a client may be engaged in certain illegal activities relating to "money laundering." A similar Canadian requirement is now pending.

In the United Kingdom, this includes any suspicion that a client may be evading taxes. In 1993 U.K. barristers and solicitors were forced to serve as the government's "independent financial investigators" under the terms of the Criminal Justice Act and Money Laundering Regulations that came into force then. The law states that any such disclosure "will not be treated as a breach of the solicitor's duty of confidence."

These rules by extension apply in principle to attorneys practicing in all U.K. Overseas Territories. However, many of the OTs, including the Cayman Islands and Bermuda, have enacted similar local laws, as have the Crown Dependencies of Jersey, Guernsey and the Isle of Man.

Since 1998 attorneys in Switzerland who act as asset managers have been required to notify a central authority if they suspect a client is engaged in money laundering. But an attorney asset manager need not notify authorities of suspected money laundering after an initial contact with a prospective client, if that individual is not accepted as a client. Swiss attorneys acting in other capacities are not subject to these rules.

Compromised Privilege

The attorney-client privilege can be compromised in numerous other ways. As an "anti-money laundering" tactic, U.S. law is unique in requiring attorneys to report to the government one or more "related" cash payments made to them by a client that, in aggregate, exceeds US$10,000. Courts have consistently upheld these requirements as superceding attorney-client privilege.

In the United States and elsewhere the attorney-client privilege does not apply where:

- You involve your attorney in a criminal conspiracy, even if the attorney isn't aware of it. This may include efforts to defeat a judgment or hide assets from legitimate creditors.

- Your attorney becomes an informant against you.

- You sue your attorney and the attorney in good faith releases documents in his own defense.

- You file bankruptcy and the court-appointed trustee waives the privilege.

- The government serves your attorney with a valid warrant allowing eavesdropping on conversations between you and your attorney.

- Your attorney is under criminal investigation and his files are subpoenaed by a grand jury.

The privilege may be partially waived if:

- A person who is not a client of the attorney participates in a conversation between you and your attorney.

- A court issues a subpoena to your attorney to obtain your name and address or to review your fee arrangements.

- Your attorney possesses documents relating to your case that he did not prepare.

- Your attorney prepares your income tax return.

- You testify under oath that you are acting on the advice of your attorney.

- You review privileged documents prior to testifying concerning those documents.

High-Tech Risks Abound

Modern technology may compromise attorney-client privilege. According to the American Bar Association, "confidential" communications between an attorney and client via e-mail are protected by the privilege. But e-mail is easily monitored. The solution is to encrypt confidential messages with encryption software such as PGP or a similar program.

Similarly, it is illegal to monitor cellular or cordless telephone calls, but these electronic communications often travel via unencrypted radio waves and are easily monitored. This security problem is so serious that state bar associations have warned attorneys that use of unencrypted cellular or cordless phones to discuss sensitive client matters may violate attorney client privilege. The solution is to use only the latest generation of 900-MHZ cordless phones and digital cellular phones that digitally encrypt transmissions sent through the air.

Another new threat to attorney-client privilege lies in the American Bar Association proposal to end the nationwide prohibition against lawyers forming partnerships with non-lawyer professionals such as accountants, psychologists, psychiatrists or even social workers. If this is allowed and a psychologist refers a client to an attorney within the same firm, it is unclear whether attorney-client privilege would apply. If an attorney referred a client to an associated psychologist, it is possible-but not assured-that the consultation would be protected by attorney-client privilege. Similar mixed professional partnerships are already commonplace in Europe.

Attorneys Under Attack

The worldwide proliferation of tough anti-money laundering and civil forfeiture laws has placed attorneys "under the gun." As a potential client, you must be aware of these challenges.

In the United States, attorneys face possible "criminal liability" just for providing alleged "routine legal services." They are advised by a former federal prosecutor to "conduct client conferences as if each client is an undercover agent or a government informant (as he or she may be)." The risk is illustrated by the conviction of a California attorney whose prosecution was based solely on routine legal services for a client who later testified against him in exchange for a reduced sentence.

To avoid criminal liability, some attorneys in the United States insert language in offshore asset protection instruments that eases compliance with certain forfeiture or repatriation orders. An asset protection guidebook recommends insertion of language defining circumstances under which trustees of "asset protection trusts" must convey trust assets to U.S. regulatory agencies.

Attorneys "Know Thy Client"

We have discussed "know your customer" requirements that U.S. based offshore financial planners must follow to avoid criminal liability for their actions. Similar precautions now apply to U.S. based attorneys and increasingly to attorneys in other countries. An attorney's main defense against civil or criminal liability for subsequent wrongdoing by a client is to obtain full facts about a client and his finances. If you contact an attorney for such advice, expect a thorough grilling about your personal and professional background and your offshore motives.

Conversely, you should make an effort to "know your lawyer." Call the bar offices to determine if an attorney is a member in good standing of the state and local bar. Inquire whether he has been the subject of bar disciplinary actions—usually a matter of public record. Check court calendars to see if an attorney has been a defendant in civil cases or has judgments recorded against him. This information is available through your local clerk of court's office or with help from a private investigator.

Make the Most of It

You can strengthen your own attorney-client privilege protection by using a domestic attorney working in tandem with another attorney located offshore in the haven nation where you plan to do business. You retain the offshore attorney, who in turn retains an attorney in your home country to assist him. Under this plan, the foreign attorney is the client of the domestic attorney. For example, your offshore attorney can establish a foreign asset protection trust, working with a domestic attorney to insure compliance with domestic tax and reporting requirements.

Even if a domestic creditor pierces the attorney-client privilege between the offshore and domestic lawyers, the most he could learn would be the name and address of the offshore lawyer and the fee arrangements. This dual strategy obviously adds additional costs, but it can be a very powerful enhancement of attorney-client privilege.

Attorney-Client Privilege Under Siege
By Robert E. Bauman, JD, *The Sovereign Individual*, August 2003

On June 19, 2003, a U.S. District Court judge in Chicago ordered one of the largest U.S. law firms to disclose to the Internal Revenue Service the names of about 700 clients who received tax shelter advice from attorneys at the firm.

The IRS has in recent years greatly increased its use of such "John Doe" summonses. Beginning in 2000, it employed them when seeking information on thousands of holders of offshore bank account credit cards from American Express, VISA and MasterCard. But the IRS has reportedly never used this highhanded tactic against a law firm.

The law firm, Jenkens & Gilchrist, one of the nation's largest, has refused to comply with the unprecedented court order, saying it will fight it all the way to the U.S. Supreme Court. "Americans have a right to consult with an attorney in confidence, and only the clients themselves can waive that right," a spokesman for the firm said, adding that it expected the courts to uphold its position. The IRS position, of course, is that it is seeking evidence about tax shelters which it alleges are illegal.

Why Attorney-Client Privilege is so Important

In The United States, Canada, the United Kingdom and other common law nations, attorney-client privilege describes a well-established, traditional right. It encompasses the ethical duty of an attorney or solicitor not to divulge to others confidential communications with a client. It also includes the client's right to refuse to disclose, and to prevent others from disclosing, such confidential communications with his or her attorney.

This important rule evolved as a means to encourage clients to make full disclosure to an attorney when seeking legal advice, without fear that the legal advisor would inform others. To do less might well hamper preparation of the client's case, or prevent the attorney from giving the correct advice.

In the Chicago case, acting as prior judge and jury, the IRS simply branded certain types of tax avoidance shelter plans (called COBRA) as illegal. It alleged the law firm was offering advice about these supposedly "illegal" plans. That speculation, said the IRS, supposedly gives it the right to see COBRA client files. IRS officials said the transactions, which allegedly took place between 1998 and 2003, generated phony paper losses of about US$4 million each, or about US$2.4 billion in all.

If the IRS is successful in its demands against Jenkens & Gilchrist, there will remain almost no confidentiality for tax attorneys and their clients. A simple statement from the IRS that it believes a certain tax shelter or other plan to be "abusive" will open the files of any client who may have discussed the plan with a lawyer, whether or not he adopted the plan as his own personal or business tax strategy.

This radical new course of judicial activism is the easy way out for the IRS. In the past, the agency had to proceed against a taxpayer individually, proving that his or her tax plan was somehow illegal or had been used in an abusive way. Now, if the IRS position is upheld, the agency can simply speculate that certain groups of people are engaging in alleged illegal tax avoidance schemes and grab their lawyers' files.

In one sense, no one should be surprised that the IRS, backed by the U.S. Department of Justice, is playing this sort of legal hardball. Only a few years ago, the FBI raided the law offices of several criminal defense attorneys in south Florida that represented accused drug kingpins. Grabbing files and computers, the attorneys themselves eventually were indicted and some convicted of "conspiring" with their clients, a far cry from simply "representing" them.

Anti-money laundering laws and more recently, anti-terrorism laws, have also been used to force attorneys to report "suspicious activities" of clients, with mixed results. It has always been a requirement that attorneys report a client's pending or planned future criminal acts, if the lawyer is aware of them. An attorney cannot knowingly assist a client in committing fraud or a criminal act. Indeed, attorneys today are wary of positioning themselves so as to be accused of any criminal conduct by a client who may sell out the lawyer in negotiations with prosecutors. "Know your client" is a modern attorney's watchword and guide.

But when a tax attorney discusses a tax avoidance plan with a client (which is 100% legal), and the client later adopts the approach based on that competent legal advice, that cannot, in my view, justify waiving attorney-client privilege. This does not constitute criminal conduct, but rather the normal practice of law.

How to Preserve Attorney-Client Privilege

These recent events mean you must take great care when hiring a tax or any other attorney.

Don't discuss confidential matters until you conclude a representation agreement in writing.

This serves as the benchmark when privilege attaches and begins to run.

In some cases, it is best to have your domestic tax attorney hire an offshore trust attorney to handle matters in a foreign tax haven or other nation. This dual arrangement can add another protective layer of attorney-client privilege.

In the United States, an attorney has no duty to report that a client may have in the past been engaged in illegal conduct. However, in the United Kingdom, Switzerland and some other nations an attorney must report suspicion of money laundering. In the United Kingdom, this includes reporting of suspected illegal tax evasion. Canadian attorney-client privilege is now under revision, with the government demanding to know all. This means you must find out about the status of attorney-client privilege in any offshore nation where you may decide toemploy an attorney.

It's your privilege. Protect it—and yourself.

Your Privacy Is Compromised in the U.S. Mail
December 1997

The U.S. Congress imposed a government monopoly over first class mail delivery in 1872. This monopoly facilitates surveillance by requiring the delivery of most correspondence by a single carrier. While it ordinarily requires a search warrant to open first-class mail, the monitoring and opening of mail without a search warrant by police, intelligence agencies and the U.S. Postal Service is legal or condoned under various circumstances. For instance, all packages sent from "source areas for the distribution of narcotics and/or controlled substances" might be inspected by drug-sniffing dogs. Court testimony from federal agents indicates that every major city in the United States is considered such a "source area."

The Postal Service also sells change-of-address information to direct marketing companies (and provides it to government agencies) and has an established intelligence unit to target for surveillance persons engaged in "suspicious mailing patterns." Mail surveillance programs carried out by or with the cooperation of the Postal Service include mail covers, intelligence agency "mail taps," and opening of mail.

Mail Covers

The monitoring of mail by a government agency is a "mail cover." The mail is only monitored, not opened; no warrant is required. The investigating agency records the address, sender, return address, meter number, place and postmark date and class of mail for all mail delivered to the target address.

Mail covers can be extended indefinitely. International correspondence is a frequent target of mail covers. In the 1960s, the IRS photocopied all correspondence between Switzerland and the United States. It matched the postal codes on the envelopes with the names and addresses of Swiss banks and audited persons who had received correspondence from these banks. Many account holders were subsequently prosecuted for income tax evasion.

Intelligence Agency Mail Taps

The courts have ruled that opening mail requires probable cause of criminal wrongdoing. But according to testimony before Congress from Professor Mel Crain of San Diego State University, while employed by the CIA, "I found myself extensively involved in mail tapping of American citizens. The letters were opened, reproduced, and sent on their way without interrupting mail flow or their opening in any way being detected."

Targets were chosen, according to the National Center for Security Studies, "on [the agents'] own interpretation of current events" This operation was curtailed in the 1970s in the wake of the Watergate scandal, although unofficial reports of illegal mail opening by U.S. intelligence agencies continue. In the meantime, the CIA built a database of 1.5million persons whose names were listed in the illegally opened correspondence. Portions of this list may have been merged with the CIA's DESIST anti-terrorist database.

The FBI also illegally opened mail during this period from a list of about 600 "subversives," mostly opponents of the War in Vietnam. However, only about 25 percent of the mail that was opened came from persons on this list. As with the CIA, individual FBI agents used their "judgment" to determine what other mail to open.

Opening of Mail

The Postal Service may allow mail to be detained while a law enforcement agency decides if it has probable cause to examine the contents. However, the definition of probable cause is remarkably broad, as the following example, taken from documents filed in federal court, demonstrates:

The Chicago division of the U.S. Postal Inspection Service has implemented an Express Mail Profile program at the air mail facility at Chicago O'Hare International Airport. This program consists of a physical profile of express mail parcels which have been mailed to or from locations within the Northern District of Illinois. Targets were cities and/or areas of the United States which have been identified by law enforcement personnel as being source areas for the distribution of narcotics and/or controlled substances.

After the packages are identified, they are placed in front of DEA dogs trained to sniff out the smell of drugs. If the dogs "alert" to the presence of drugs, the packages are then opened for inspection. Should drugs be found, the package is delivered to the address, and the recipient arrested. The positive reaction of the dogs, according to the affidavit, provides probable cause for the packages to be opened. Many packages opened contain no drugs, only cash, which in some cases may be seized if it contains narcotics residues. Packages may then be re-sealed and delivered to the addressee with no indication a search has occurred.

Mail Drops

Mail drops or mail receiving services are available in many countries. A mail drop may facilitate privacy when receiving or sending sensitive correspondence, but may be compromised. International investors can use mail drops outside their domestic jurisdiction to defeat mail covers of their international correspondence.

Law enforcement agencies associate mail drops with criminal activity. Some advertisements for mail drops in privacy-oriented publications are a ploy to get your name and address, which is cross-referenced with lists of missing or wanted persons. This is known as "reverse skip tracing."

Instant Mail Privacy Techniques
August 1998

Your mail is confidential. It contains private personal and financial information. If it falls into the wrong hands this information will be abused or used against you to damaging effect. Imagine if a statement from your offshore bank fell into the clutches of a tax office informant—paid to provide names of possible tax evaders. You may have made all necessary legal declarations and complied with all reporting requirements—but you will be drawn under the microscope nevertheless. If the authorities even suspect you of a financial misdemeanor, your life will be thoroughly scrutinized for evidence.

Now, imagine if a desperate opportunist acquired the same statement. Avaricious litigants work on a deep pocket principle. Only those with wealth worth pursuing through the courts will be pursued. If you've got visible wealth, such as a good-sized offshore bank account, you might find yourself hauled through the courts on trumped up charges. You have a choice: mount an expensive defense or forfeit the case to the litigant. Whatever you do, you lose.

Misappropriation of your mail can have devastating personal and financial effects. Yet we all entrust a great deal of sensitive information to domestic and international postal systems, sometimes on a daily basis. We receive financial statements from banks, credit card companies, loan companies, stores, car dealers, insurers and pension funds. We write letters to family and friends, sometimes committing intimate thoughts and details to paper. We pay bills through the post. Products, publications and information are requested, ordered and delivered through the post. We deal with government and the authorities via the post system.

Imagine all the data you send and receive through the post being read and noted by an unknown individual or institution before being delivered—a blackmailer looking for evidence of an affair, exotic recreational activities or financial wrongdoing; a private investigator compiling a profile of you and your life for an aggressive and determined business competitor; a thief hoping to find out if you're going away so he can burgle your house and belongings without fear of disturbance. If any of these parasites do get you in their sites, your mail will be vulnerable to their attentions unless you take immediate precautions—now.

Introduce the following safeguards to strengthen your mail privacy and to alert you to interference with items you send or receive through the post:

- *Try to be alert to when sensitive mail arrives each month.* Know when your bank statement should arrive. Know when your credit card bill is due. Phone bills, store accounts, utility bills—all should be anticipated. That way if there is a delay, for whatever reason, you know about it immediately. Enter the projected dates into your diary. Tick off each item as it arrives. By keeping tabs on your mail, you will be instantly aware of any unusual patterns which develop, and which may indicate interception or redirection of your mail. If you think your mail is being interfered with, contact the relevant postal authorities immediately.

- *Simple and quick precautions can make an envelope extremely difficult for a tamperer to access.* The gum on envelopes can't always be trusted. A strip of Scotch tape should be used to doubly secure envelope flaps. Any attempt to remove the tape will damage the envelope and will be instantly noticeable. The tamperer will have to send the envelope on to you untouched or risk exposing his interest.

- *Professional mail tamperers have chemical sprays in their arsenal.* These are used on envelopes to make them translucent, enabling snoops to read fragments of correspondence through the envelope. To protect against any such weapon, wrap all mail contents in a sheet of silver foil or black carbon paper to foil attempts to read them.

- *Steaming open envelopes is an amateur tactic, one the professionals don't need to resort to. But that doesn't mean an amateur won't.* You need to guard against the possibility. When completing envelopes use ink that isn't water resistant. Steam will make the ink run, alerting the recipient to the interference. You could ask correspondents to use the same tactic when writing to you.

- *When sending mail, don't put your address, the sender address, on the back of any envelope.* Doing this enables observers to connect you with whomever you're corresponding as their name and address appears on the front. This seemingly insignificant detail could be used by observers and investigators to establish further lines of enquiry against you.

- *Don't send valuables through the post.* Telltale signs are a temptation to dishonest mailmen, postal workers and even complete strangers at the recipient's end. Birthday and Christmas cards are obvious risks, easily recognizable and often accompanied by cash. One not so obvious indication, the presence of a staple in an envelope, often indicates the presence of a check. Checks reveal bank account numbers, card numbers, bank details, a signature, a creditor and often an accompanying statement revealing further account numbers and related details—useful to thieves, fraudsters, profilers and other observers. Leave checks loose and avoid using staples.

- *Beware of courier services such as FedEx or UPS.* All these services give the courier the right to inspect the contents of your package, with or without cause. In practice, private couriers are even less protective of customer privacy than national postal authorities. Some delivery services routinely cooperate with police requests to search packages, while other require police to obtain valid search warrants. Alternatively, use a private courier to hand-deliver important and sensitive correspondence on your behalf.

- *To protect your identity and to make it difficult for investigators to spot your mail in the system, ask correspondents to send your mail to "the Occupant" or "Resident."* Alternatively, use an alias, either of an individual or a company. Using an alias is not illegal unless it is adopted in order to defraud. An alias also keeps your real name of databases and mailing lists.

- *E-mail can be encrypted so only the sender and intended recipient can access them.* Use encrypted e-mail wherever possible in place of the ordinary postal system. Where it isn't possible, you and your correspondents should use pre-determined codes to similarly defend ordinary mail. Create your own codes and keep them private. Only you and your correspondents should know how the code is constructed and how it can be deciphered.

- *Don't hand write envelopes.* Use typed address labels. Vary the type of label you use and the typeface. Offer expert observers nothing that makes it easier for them to recognize and intercept your post. Handwriting and repetitive behavior are distinct and recognizable to specialists. Vary the type and size of envelopes you use. Don't use the same pen consistently. Don't use a franking machine you can be connected with; use stamps. When you post the items, use a selection of different post boxes.

- *Ideally, for optimum security, open and start using a mail drop today.* A mail drop enables you to receive mail at (and often send it from) an address which is totally unconnected with you. Mail originating from and arriving at a mail drop, especially if you use an alias, is unlikely to attract the attention of anybody watching mail connected to any of your known addresses. Unfortunately, it is no longer possible in the United States to open a mail drop address privately without giving your true name and physical address to the mail drop operator, who in turn must give it to government inspectors upon request.

- *Sensitive mail should be received at a mail drop not at known addresses most vulnerable to mail tamperers.* Financial communications, sensitive personal correspondence, and international mail should be received at and sent from (many mail drops will agree to forward mail on your behalf) your mail drop.

Open an account with a mail drop in the next town, or even the next country, for an additional layer of security. Collect the mail in person to avoid revealing your home or business address to the mail drop operator. Pay cash; leave no paper trail connecting you to the mail drop in any way. Don't phone the mail drop from your home. The calls you make will show up on your phone records and can be obtained by amateur and professional investigators looking into your background and activities. Use a payphone to talk to your mail drop. Change mail drops regularly.

For Privacy, You Need a Mail Drop
PT2, 1997

For some individuals, using an address other than one's own—a mail drop—somehow may seem wrong. The term "mail drop," first popularized in spy novels, describes a process for sensitive communication by one intelligence agent to another using a so-called "dead drop," perhaps a hollow tree or a trash bin. That sort of clandestine gimmick is not feasible for receiving mail with the help of a national postal service.

A commercial mail drop operation is a physical address recognized by the postal service—either a post office box or a street address where they will deliver mail. This address is controlled by persons who, for a fee receive, keep or forward mail according to the wishes of customers who do not physically reside on the premises.

These services are legal businesses that comply with all requirements of the country's postal system for delivering mail. In the U.K., mail is delivered to any post office box number or street address indicated on an envelope, regardless of the name of the addressee. Some other national postal services only will deliver mail to a named recipient who is known to live at the address to which mail is sent. For this reasons if you use a name other than your own be sure the staff at your mail drop are informed before the mail arrives. Otherwise, it may be returned or refused.

Mail drops exist to make money, charging a fee for receiving and distributing mail to individuals willing to pay for the service. In spite of free home delivery of mail, many people pay to receive mail at an address other than that at which they actually live. Standard mail delivery practice means mail is simply shoved through a door or stuffed into a mailbox. Anyone can look at these envelopes and their return addresses with possibly unwanted consequences for the intended recipient of the mail. Government agents regularly monitor all international mail, particularly that which originates in well-known tax haven nations. Without opening mail, these snoops can gain information which may be used to justify an investigation.

Any individual can be the subject of official mail surveillance for any reason, often suspected tax evasion. Agents can obtain bank names, making it much easier to place a lien on an account, even one located in a tax haven.

Open a "Branch" Office

Business corporations also benefit by using mail drops that appear to be a branch office or even the head office of the company. This fits in with the fact mail drops also provide telephone answering and fax forwarding services. In such cases the mail drop acts as agent for the company, all quite legal. Some countries do not accept a post office box number as a corporate address. Instead, a mail drop provides a real address that does qualify and costs far less than rent for even the smallest office. Mail drops can screen your location, its address can be printed on corporate checks and it can accept express courier packages that cannot be delivered to post office boxes. If you or your company moves, you can continue to receive mail at the same commercial mail drop.

In summary, there are four basic reasons to use a mail drop:

1. To receive mail in one's own name in a discreet fashion while preventing unwanted visits by clients, salesmen and other correspondents.

2. To receive mail in a name other than your own.

3. To keep physical distance between oneself and people and companies from whom one receives mail.

4. To incorporate a company without renting a office.

Any large daily newspaper has classified ads for such services in the business services section. Daily the *International Herald Tribune* carries ads from mail drops located all over the world. Such services are priced at double or triple the rates charged by similar local services. You can also find them in the Yellow Pages.

The modern world is far from an ideal place. Honesty and integrity do not immunize from annoyances and danger. It is wise put distance between yourself and potential harm. If you seriously want to protect yourself and your privacy, you must take prudent counter-measures well before they are ever necessary. Commercial mail drop operations provide an excellent vehicle for protection in the form of an alternative address. It is much like an unlisted telephone number.

The steps to follow are:

• Choose a reliable, reasonably-priced mail drop convenient to your home or office.

• Pick the name or names you wish to use when receiving mail.

• Establish a mail pick-up procedure.

• If you wish greater privacy, don't give your true name or address to the mail drop operators.

• Send the mail drop your own test mailings to make sure everything is working properly.

[**Ed. Note**: Regulations now require all U.S. persons opening accounts at mail drops to present positive identification and complete forms verifying under penalty of perjury identification details. In addition, it is no longer possible to identify a mail drop address as a "suite," although you may still designate your box number with the pound sign (#).]

Protect Your Medical Privacy
January 1997

Medical files are incredible concentrations of information: marital status, religion, social security number, genetic data and lifestyle. We look at the American scene; the picture in countries where debate is less open may be even grimmer. Privacy is vital to health care, but people are not asking necessary questions: How do I stop abuses? What is in my records? Can I correct information?

Threats to medical privacy are numerous. The greatest fear involves patients becoming reluctant to receive treatment. Then there are the risks of the loss of insurance (companies may check records before approving treatment or extending coverage), and employment.

Many have discovered that errors in files can ruin careers and finances by costing them a job, some form of license, or insurance cover. Even if information is accurate, there is the danger that someone might draw false inferences. Imagine your boss read your records and decided you are not up to the job.

There are short-term worries—how safe is the information from hackers who sell information to private investigators and business rivals? And long term concerns—could Big Brother find new uses for this information such as monitoring individuals?

The issue has been on the agenda following the 1997 U.S. healthcare bill. This provided for a new centralized computer network, but not the safeguarding of privacy. The effects of the Health Insurance Portability Act were to: 1) create a centralized national medical file data bank that will not have privacy standards set down for three and a half years; 2) make the reporting of medical information to a new national computer network mandatory; 3) increase the number of bureaucrats with access to your records.

The provisions relating to fraud have been botched. The confiscation of property is now mandated for health care crimes. Doctors and patients can receive five years in jail for making a false statement to a health care plan, or omitting to provide a health care investigator with information. The result is distrust between doctor and patient. Little will be revealed by the patient and even less will be recorded by the doctor.

Issues of access, meanwhile, are very important, whether they are authorized users abusing their positions or illegal access persons exploiting inadequate controls. For example:

- In Maryland, clerks were arrested for selling thousands of confidential files or taking bribes.

- In Florida, a state employee used records on HIV patients to screen out potential partners.

- It has been known for criminals to try to get passwords to file data banks in their search for the addresses of victims. This happened in Boston with a convicted rapist.

One reason for the erosion of privacy is computerization. The authorities rush to collect more data and store it in as small as a space as possible, making mistakes more likely. Information is networked allowing access anywhere, anytime. This causes the demand for information to increase, and gives the government excuses to create yet more databases.

A case in point is that of Maryland, where the Health Care Access and Cost Commission (HCACC), and the Health Services Cost Review Commission (HSCRC) are collecting huge amounts of information. Medical claim payers have been passing claims to a government department. Vermont, Washington, North Dakota, Minnesota, Kentucky and Iowa are following suit or look set to do so. Soon, whenever a claim is submitted the government will ask the carrier for many pieces of information, including:

- Your diagnosis and treatment
- Your social security number
- The location of your doctor's office.

The motivation is that of managing doctor's fees. The government feels that the doctor should have more than your welfare in mind when he decides on treatment. Another factor is how many people have had a particular procedure lately. Bureaucrats will know what your doctor is doing, allowing them to curb "unnecessary" costs. Your doctor could be made to think again about that scan, even if you are the one who will be footing the bill.

The claims have been going into the Maryland Department of Health and Hygiene's Medical Care Database. The data undergo basic encryption, and the whole process has occurred without either the consent or the notice of the citizens involved. Organizations that have objected include the Maryland Psychiatric Societies, Maryland Medical Society, American Civil Liberties Union and the Maryland Mental Health Association.

The HCACC agreed to eliminate data such as the patient's date of birth and race. But this was a token gesture. All the HCACC has to do is compare the data tapes it has with the HSCRC's. It is this body's records that have been causing most concern. Their tapes contain a massive amount of information, some of which goes out of date quickly, such as provisional diagnosis. Incredibly HSCRC wants to collect more data. It boasts that it has suffered no leaks. That means so far no leak has been found and reported. The more data collated the greater the probability of a breach of privacy. Once breached, it can never be returned.

The excuses just get weaker. They claim that names and addresses are being removed before entering the database. Such claims are simply public relations stunts, because whether the names are removed or not, anonymity cannot be guaranteed. Other public databases, like Lexis-Nexis, can be used in a simple cross-referencing exercise to restore names. But even nightmarish cost control exercises could be conducted anonymously.

Our advice? When citizens sign up for care-private or government—they sign away their privacy on the first visit to a doctor. This is done when they sign a "blanket waiver" authorizing the release of information. Often there is no choice, but ask if you have to sign. It might be possible to edit the waiver to say what you are releasing. The Medical Information Bureau (MIB) holds 12 million records. Discover which insurance companies have reports about you. Get a copy of your file for approximately US$10 (telephone +1 617 426 3660).

Communicate your concerns. Ask about your doctor's privacy protocol. You may be able to use something other than your social security number as an identifier on your records.

Pay cash for services you want to keep private. If you pay cash, you also may not be required to present positive identification. In addition, don't ask insurance companies for reimbursement of procedures you don't want them to know about.

Proposed medical privacy regulations issued in the waning days of the Clinton Administration were supposed to protect medical privacy, but instead, carve out wide exceptions for marketing purposes and government monitoring. In early 2001 the Bush Administration placed the new regulations on hold.

As usual, when it comes to medical privacy, you can't count on the government to protect you. You have to learn to protect yourself.

[*Ed. Note*: In 2003 a new U.S. "medical privacy" law took effect. While it supposedly guards an individual's medical records from improper use, it also ratifies a host of government and private uses of such data without a patient's consent. Opponents of the law charge that it does little to protect patient privacy.]

———◆—◆———

Identity Theft: Ways to Protect Yourself
By Mark Nestmann, *The Sovereign Individual*, March 2003

*"He that filches from me my good name robs me of that which
not enriches him and makes me poor, indeed."*
—Iago in Shakespeare's "Othello"

Each year, a staggering number of Americans—between 700,000 and 1.1 million—have their good name stolen by "identity thieves." Complaints about identity theft nearly doubled in 2002 as the fast-growing crime topped the U.S. government's list of consumer frauds for a third consecutive year.

Expatriates and others away from home for extended periods are particularly vulnerable. Nor is the problem limited to the United States—in recent months, gigantic ID thefts have been uncovered in Canada and in Russia.

If you're an American, all someone needs to impersonate you is your name and Social Security number (SSN), plus one or two other easy-to-find pieces of information such as your birth date, mother's maiden name or residential address. Millions of people have access to this information. Anyone you've ever borrowed money from probably has a record of your SSN. Under federal law, banks and brokers must keep your SSN on file. Employers must have it to withhold Social Security taxes. Other businesses can ask for it at their discretion, and many do—doctors, hospitals, utility companies, insurance companies, etc.

Most ID theft victims are liable for no more than US$50 per fraudulent account. But a much larger loss is denial of credit and employment, or even arrest, as impostors misuse their identities.

Many victims spend thousands of dollars in legal fees and spend years cleaning up the mess. Nor is it practical to count on help from police. Because ID theft victims often live outside the state, or even the country, where the theft occurs, investigations often hit jurisdictional "brick walls." Preventing identity theft is much easier than recovering from it after it occurs.

Why Expatriates are Vulnerable

Because they may not check their mail frequently, expatriates and others away from home for extended periods are especially vulnerable to ID theft. ID thieves begin by filing a change-of-address form with the Postal Service to forward your correspondence to a new address. Of particular interest is correspondence from banks, brokers, credit card companies, etc. They use these account numbers to buy goods or services on your credit. They open new credit card accounts, using your name, birth date and SSN.

ID thieves may order checks or debit cards and use them to drain your bank account, or open new accounts and write bad checks. They can also set up phone or cellular service, take out auto loans, make false insurance claims or even file for bankruptcy—all under your name.

None of these activities will necessarily come to your attention, because the person conducting these transactions is supposedly "you." Indeed, your first inkling of a problem may come when you are detained or arrested at a U.S. border crossing.

Identity Theft—How It's Done

Most ID thefts are "inside jobs." The perpetrator has access to credit or other records useful for ID theft. Members of fraud rings continually seek to employment at with access to such data, often as temporary workers or cleaning staff.

Other common sources of ID theft include:

- *Duping a person out of information required for ID theft.* One clever scam involves falsified tax forms purportedly from the IRS to gather private data.

- *Dumpster/mailbox diving.* ID thieves examine discarded trash and unlocked mailboxes for credit card and bank statements or pre-approved offers of credit.

- *Burglary and robbery.* A wallet, purse, glove compartment or file cabinet can be a gold mine for ID thieves.

- *Someone you know.* Family members, household employees and visitors to your home can pilfer to confidential documents.

- *Computer hacking.* It is relatively simple for someone to hack into an unsecured home PC or business computer to retrieve personal information: addresses, credit card numbers, etc.

Make Yourself a "Hard Target"

No magic bullets exist to prevent ID theft, because it's such a simple crime to commit. However, by adhering to the following suggestions, you'll become a "hardened target" to impersonation.

Basic strategies:

1. *Check your credit reports at least once a year from all three major credit bureaus.* Make sure it includes only those extensions of credit you've authorized. (1) TransUnion, WATS: (800) 888-4213; fraud division (800) 680-7289. Link: www.tuc.com. (2) Experian, WATS: (888) EXPERIAN; fraud division (888) 397-3742). Link: www.experian.com. (3) Equifax, WATS: (800) 685-1111, fraud division (800) 525-6285. Link: www.equifax.com.

2. *Never disclose personal information unless you have initiated the contact.* Identity thieves often pose as bank representatives or government employees to obtain your SSN, mother's maiden name or financial account information.

3. *Guard your SSN.* Don't disclose it unless you are applying for credit, dealing with the IRS or

the Social Security Administration or (in some states) applying for a driver's license. Never have your SSN imprinted on stationary or checks. Don't carry any document in your wallet or glove compartment that lists your SSN. Keep the card itself in a safety deposit box.

4. *When using a credit card, don't let it out of your sight.* This guards against an employee surreptitiously reading the information in the card's magnetic stripe using a device called a "skimmer." If you can't keep watch on your credit card during the entire transaction, use cash.

5. *Pay attention to billing cycles.* A missing bill could mean a thief has taken over your account and changed your billing address.

6. *Put passwords on your credit card, bank and phone accounts to prevent unauthorized changes of service.* Avoid easy-to-learn passwords; e.g., your birth date, the last four digits of your SSN, etc.

7. *Use credit cards wisely.* Minimize the number that you carry and keep the lowest credit practical credit limits. Cancel inactive accounts; unused accounts still appear on your credit report, and can be used by thieves.

8. *Guard your residential address.* Use a post office box or mail receiving service to receive your mail. Ask companies that provide services at your residential address to bill to a secured address.

9. *Buy a crosscut shredder.* Bank and credit-card statements, receipts, old tax forms, pre-approved offers of credit, etc. should go into it.

10. *Get off commercial mailing lists.* Write to the Direct Marketing Association's Mail Preference Service, P.O. Box 9008, Farmingdale, N.Y. 11735 and ask to be removed from all commercial mailing lists.

11. *Opt out of pre-approved credit card offers.* Call 1 (888) 5OPT OUT. You will need to disclose your SSN to use this free service.

12. *Lock up sensitive information.* Keep credit card records, bank records, etc. in a locked safe bolted, or even better, embedded, in the floor.

13. *Use common sense.* If it seems too good to be true, it probably is.

14. *Learn more about ID theft.* Reliable sources of free information include: (1) *Identity Theft Resource Center.* **Link**: www.idtheftcenter.org. (2) *Privacy Rights Clearinghouse.* **Link**: www.privacyrights.org. (3) *Federal Trade Commission.* **Link**: www.consumer.gov/idtheft.

Advanced Strategies: The preceding strategies are sufficient for most members. However, expats and anyone else scoring higher than 50 points on our ID theft vulnerability quiz (see below) should seriously consider taking the following additional precautions. Downside: The advanced strategies may lead to inconvenience, particularly if you need credit quickly.

1. *Notify credit bureaus and card issuers not to authorize credit extensions over the phone.* This forces credit card issuers to obtain written authorization before they give someone a card in your name. Also, it gives you a sample signature to compare to your own.

2. *Consider a credit monitoring service.* Providers include: (a) *Identity Fraud Inc.* **Link**: www.identityfraud.com. (b) *Privista.* **Link**: www.privista.com. (c) *Privacy Guard.* **Link**: www.privacyguard.com.

3. *"Freeze" your credit report.* This service, only available in California, prevents lenders and financial institutions from accessing your credit report without your express permission. Once an account is frozen, you are given a personal identification number. The frozen credit report then can only be "thawed" if you contact the credit-reporting agency and provide the PIN.

What to Do If You Suspect ID Theft

1. *Call the three credit bureaus.* Place a "fraud alert" on your file and have them send you copies of your reports. Review them for fraudulent activity or inaccuracies.

2. *Contact local law enforcement.* They must take a report and give you a copy of it, although they may not have the resources to investigate. You'll need the report to "prove" to credit grantors that you reported a crime to authorities.

3. *Notify creditors who have opened fraudulent accounts in your name.* Start with a phone call and follow up with a certified letter. Request copies of all application and transaction information.

4. *Notify your bank.* If necessary, cancel your checking and savings accounts and obtain new account numbers.

5. *Contact the FTC's Identity Theft Hotline* at 1(877) ID-THEFT. **Link:** www.ftc.gov.

A Test to Protect Yourself from ID Theft

Are you at risk for ID theft? Take this quiz (adapted from one at www.privacyrights.org) to learn how vulnerable you are.

1. I receive frequent offers of pre-approved credit (5 points). Add five points if you don't shred these offers before discarding them.

2. I carry my Social Security card in my wallet or glove compartment (10 points). Add 10 points if you carry your driver's license, military ID or any other documents containing your SSN there.

3. My driver's license has my SSN printed on it (10 points).

4. I receive mail in an unlocked mailbox (5 points).

5. I use an unlocked mailbox to drop off outgoing mail (10 points).

6. I do not shred banking and credit information when I discard it (10 points).

7. I provide my SSN whenever asked (10 points). Add 5 points if you provide it orally without checking who might be listening.

8. I use my SSN as an employee or student ID number (5 points).

9. I have my SSN printed on my employee badge that I wear at work or in public (10 points).

10. I have my SSN and/or driver's license number printed on personal checks (10 points).

11. I am listed in a Who's Who guide (5 points).

12. I have not ordered a copy of my credit report in at least two years (20 points).

13. I do not believe that people would look in my trash looking for credit or financial information (10 points).

14. My name is listed in U.S. credit bureau files and I live outside the United States (15 points).

100+ points: High risk. Carefully follow the precautions listed in the accompanying article to reduce your vulnerability.

50-100 points: Average risk; higher if you have good credit.

0-50 points: Low risk. Keep up the good work and don't let your guard down now.

How to Take Back Your Personal & Financial Privacy
By Mark Nestmann, *The Sovereign Individual*, September 2002

In the ongoing "War on Terror," privacy has been one of the major casualties.

We often have documented the erosion in privacy as justified by the fight against terrorism, tax evasion and money laundering. But there remain state-of-the-art strategies that go a long way toward minimizing intrusions into your personal and financial affairs.

Perhaps the most powerful plan ever devised to preserve privacy is the "five flags" strategy:

Flag #1. Obtain citizenship and passport from a country that does not tax non-residents on their worldwide income. Almost every country qualifies in this regard, with the notable exception of the United States.

Flag #2. Form a company in a country that does not tax business income earned outside that country. Most offshore centers qualify.

Flag #3. Obtain legal residency in a country that taxes only income generated within that country, not foreign income. Belize, Croatia, Grenada, Malta and Panama are such jurisdictions.

Flag #4. Place your wealth in asset havens with strict bank secrecy laws that can only be penetrated in a criminal investigation, and that do not liberally exchange data with foreign revenue authorities. Liechtenstein, Panama, and Switzerland are such jurisdictions.

Flag #5. Spend your time in whatever countries you enjoy the most, taking care not to stay long enough to become legally resident there and thus possibly subject to tax on your worldwide income.

The selection of each of these centers of activity depends upon your own unique needs and desires. Which country offers the lowest costs, best deal, best climate, and the most fun? Which country offers the greatest advantages for those particular activities that you find most desirable? And, as the "War on Terrorism" turns increasingly into a war on civil liberties, which countries offer both a reasonable degree of security while preserving individual freedoms, including the all-important right to personal and financial privacy?

Five Steps to Privacy

Using the criteria listed above, how might you best take advantage of the five flags strategy? Here are some suggestions:

1. *Internationalize your investments.* An essential part of the five flags strategy is geographical diversification. It is much easier to move assets across borders than to physically relocate. The first step you should take to fulfill this strategy is to open a bank or investment account outside your own country. Austria, Panama and Switzerland are all acceptable jurisdictions. The Sovereign Society has Offshore Convenient Account relationships with banks in Austria, Panama and Denmark.

Most OECD countries tax worldwide income, so if you live in an OECD country, this strategy generally won't provide any tax benefits. Nor will it provide any asset protection benefits, although it will have the privacy advantage of taking your assets off the domestic "radar screen."

With simple refinements, you can combine international investments with tax and asset protection advantages. For instance, U.S. persons who purchase a properly structured offshore variable annuity will obtain tax deferral on the build-up in value of the investments inside the annuity. In addition, the laws of many offshore jurisdictions protect the insurance policies from creditor claims. In this regard, Switzerland perhaps has the strongest asset protection laws of any jurisdiction.

2. *Internationalize your sources of income.* As your overseas investments grow in value, they will hopefully appreciate in value and/or generate income. But an even better way to integrate the five flags strategy into your own life is to form and operate an international business.

The "secret" to creating any business is to "turn your passion into profit." For instance, international investment advisor Gary Scott tells the story of a woman who publishes a calendar each year with pictures of horses she photographs all over the world. Horses are this woman's passion. She loves her business because it allows her to see and ride horses all over the world.

Finding a local business partner greatly increases your chances for success. It can also provide privacy, asset protection and tax advantages. Lawsuits are much less common overseas than in the United States. And when you earn income and keep profits overseas, these funds are both off the "radar screen" and isolated from legal attack. Moreover, your business, income and assets are also safer if diversified in more than one country and currency.

Finally: Active overseas businesses owned by 50% non-U.S. business partners, when correctly structured, can defer all U.S. taxation...sometimes forever!

How should you structure your business? There are two primary options: organize it as a foreign corporation or as a foreign partnership. A corporation is a separate "tax person" and may permit you to defer paying tax in your country of residence on corporate income. But the rules are extremely complex, particularly if you are a U.S. citizen and resident. If so, you will generally obtain more favorable tax results if you elect to have your business taxed as a partnership. This choice avoids many "tax land mines" in the U.S. "controlled foreign corporation" (CFC) laws, but also eliminates the possibility of tax deferral on foreign income.

Because of the complexity of these rules, consult with a qualified international tax planner before forming your international business.

3. *Obtain legal residency outside your own country, preferably in a jurisdiction that does not tax foreign income.* Such "territorial" taxation means that the income from your foreign business(es) will not be subject to local taxes. If you are a U.S. citizen, becoming a non-U.S. resident will not relieve you of the obligation to pay U.S. taxes, although the first US$80,000 of your earned income will not be subject to U.S. tax. What's more, if you are a non-U.S. resident, it is easier to justify a claim that your non-U.S. business is not controlled from the United States, thus making your foreign business income less likely to be subject to U.S. taxation.

4. *Obtain alternative citizenship and passport.* Having a second passport provides several important benefits. Perhaps the most important is "travel insurance." For instance, when Iraq invaded Kuwait and precipitated the Gulf War crisis, many western passport carriers trying to flee Iraq were not allowed to leave. Instead they were taken hostage and moved to installations that were likely bombing targets.

However, a few westerners were able to leave unmolested because they could present Iraqi border guards with passports from small, innocuous countries of no strategic consequence or propaganda value to Saddam Hussein.

The easiest way to obtain an alternative passport is to take advantage of your ancestry, marriage or religious affiliation, any of which can lead to the expedited granting of citizenship by another country. In Ireland, for instance, persons with at least one Irish grandparent qualify for Irish citizenship and passport.

Another option is to purchase economic citizenship from one of the two countries—Dominica and St. Kitts-Nevis—that still offer it. This is the fastest way to obtain alternative citizenship, as approval can be obtained in only a few months. However, it costs US$50,000 or more to obtain economic citizenship, so this is not a strategy for everyone.

5. *"Disconnect" from the tax system of your native country.* For residents of most countries, all that is necessary to avoid income tax liability there is to demonstrate a prolonged period of non-residency; ordinarily, one or two years. Avoiding capital gains tax liability often requires a longer period of non-residency.

Avoiding estate tax liability may require that you obtain a new domicile. We all begin life with a domicile of origin; ordinarily, the country in which we are born. To change domicile, you must first change residence and then indicate your new domicile of choice by establishing as many connections as possible to your new home and disconnecting from your domicile of origin. For instance, you could purchase property in your domicile of choice, obtain a driver's license there, and purchase a burial plot there, while severing these connections in your domicile of origin.

U.S. citizens must go even further to disconnect from the American tax system; they must give up their U.S. citizenship. There are many "tax land mines" involved in eliminating these tax liabilities. For this reason, consult with a qualified international tax planner before you assume that you are no longer subject to tax in your old "home."

Obviously, there are many variables involved in this strategy.

The Five Flags Strategy vs. the "PT" Strategy

In 1989, "Bill Hill" (a nom de plume) wrote a book entitled *PT* that he claimed provided "a coherent plan for a stress-free, healthy and prosperous life without government interference, taxes or coercion." PT stands for many things: a PT can be a "Prior Taxpayer," "Permanent Tourist," "Practically Transparent," "Privacy Trained," etc.

This libertarian manifesto claims that you can live tax-free, out of reach of Big Brother, by "living nowhere." The essential elements of this strategy involve moving out of whatever high-tax jurisdiction you currently live in and begin roaming the world, never staying in one place long enough to become subject to its jurisdiction.

You also have no real home, must give up most of your possessions and be prepared to instantly move from wherever you have made your temporary resting place at the first sign of trouble from the authorities. Harry Schultz, who coined the term "PT," recommends "keeping a packed suitcase."

The five flags strategy was a cornerstone of maintaining a PT lifestyle. Yet there were important shortcomings in Hill's recommendations. According to immigration attorney and Council of Experts member David Lesperance: "Everyone should be aware that unless they acquire a new domicile and a new residence, the country that they have left would consider that their previous residence and domicile were never severed as no new 'tax home' was established. In other words, getting rid of indicia of residence in one jurisdiction is not enough to sever residence. You must re-acquire these indicia in another jurisdiction."

Among other implications, this means that persons who live full time on a yacht and simply wander from country to country have not established a new tax home and may remain subject to taxes in their former residence.

The crucial difference between the five flags strategy we have outlined and that described in *PT* is that our approach involves relocating to a new "tax home," rather than simply wandering from place to place. However, you are free to arrange your affairs so that your new tax home need not actually levy any kind of tax on your income.

Moreover, there are several countries, among them Belize, Croatia and Malta, that do not require persons legally resident there to actually reside there full time. With proper planning, you can live practically full-time on your yacht (or wherever else you want) while being legally tax-resident in a low-tax or zero-tax jurisdiction!

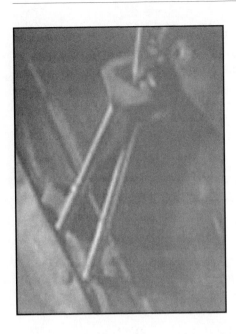

CHAPTER ELEVEN
Personal Security

Here we explain how the personal safety of people of wealth can be compromised. Kidnapping is not just for government officials anymore. You and your family could be the target of terrorists willing to use you as pawns to obtain cash.

But don't despair. In these pages, the experts tell you exactly how to protect your cash, your family and yourself.

Protect Your Wealth by Keeping a Low Profile
by Nicholas Pullen, April 1998

There is an old Chinese proverb: The nail that sticks out is the first to be knocked down. In the modern world it is the wealthy who must make sure they don't stand out. That's because in today's world, it is distinctly dangerous to be wealthy, outstanding and successful. Your wealth—the fruit of your talents and creativity, the reward for hard work and sacrifice—exists in an increasingly hostile and unstable climate. In today's world, wealth and those who have accumulated it are used for target practice. If you have visible wealth, you are a visible target—easily hit. If you don't take adequate precautions it may only be a matter of time before you show up on some predator's radar screen. There is no shortage of predators out there constantly looking for an opportunity to get their hands on your wealth.

Big Government: In the first instance, your wealth is aggressively targeted by tax-hungry governments. Poor performing economies, sprawling bureaucracies and wasteful welfare programs don't come cheap. To foot the bill, governments and their tax officials expend huge resources in an effort to turn as much of your private wealth as possible into government wealth. The U.S. government is particularly aggressive in its pursuit of private wealth. It actually has a policy directing its investigative agents and prosecutors to actively seek out high-profile and successful people. More is likely to fall from a wealthy man's pockets when he is turned upside down and shaken than a poor man's. Unfortunately, other western governments are following suit.

Deep-Pocket Litigation: The growing litigation culture directly threatens the wealthy. Courts in the U.S. increasingly operate on a deep-pocket theory—like star struck puppies, other western nations are again following suit.

As far as the "justice" system as the twenty-first century is begins, if you've got cash—you're fair game. Unscrupulous litigants can, quite literally, select affluent targets at their leisure and then make speculative claims, spurious allegations, allude to imagined grievances and point to exaggerated or non-existent damages in the hope of being awarded a bumper payout from a jury.

This is the age of the litigation lottery. More and more greedy and malevolent individuals are finding it pays to play. For wealthy people who must pay to launch defenses against spurious lawsuits or be found guilty by default (and face a heavy fine and possibly worse), the situation isn't particularly encouraging.

Sharks Always Circling: Finally, as outlined in an example below, the world is full of unscrupulous individuals who are only too keen to launch predatory attacks on the wealthy. Those in most danger from the criminal classes —robbers, con men, fraud artists and other parasites—are those wealthy individuals who haven't taken sufficient precautions to protect themselves from opportunists. Unprotected rich people are little more than sitting ducks just waiting to be bagged.

Blend In: The key to successful wealth defense is the adoption of a low profile lifestyle. Blend into the background and avoid being noticed. If predators don't see you, it is highly unlikely they'll be able to single you out for attack. If the nail isn't standing out for all to see, there is no opportunity to hammer it.

It's extremely foolhardy for high net worth individuals to adopt a high profile. It is suicidally reckless to make ostentatious displays of success and wealth. Tax investigators, opportunist litigants and parasites spend their whole lives looking for just these signs of excess—the signs of an ideal target. And, once they've spotted wealth, they never stop thinking of methods to separate it from its owner. Parasites are all around. Constantly watching and listening, unseen in the shadows, waiting for the chance to strike.

Aim For Invisibility

Sensible people, as well as striving to be invisible to all governments, must also strive to be invisible to those they encounter on a casual basis in day to day life—these people can be as dangerous as your government. Invisibility means not attracting the attention of anybody—your neighbors, the people with whom you work, the girl at the check-out register, the authorities—anybody.

By adopting a few low-profile methodologies you'll give yourself the type of insurance you can't buy from some slick talking guy in a suit.

- *Blend in like a chameleon.* Appear normal. Don't do anything that sets you apart from the crowd. In a nutshell, invisibility is the art of appearing as the gray man. Who is the gray man? He's Mr. Average. Unspectacular. Unworthy of note. Unlikely to attract attention. Unlikely to stand out to predators.

- *Adopt an air of genteel poverty or modest success.* Dress down. Don't be outspoken—this attracts attention. Appear humble. Arrogance breeds resentment. Fade into the background. Don't strive to be the center of attention.

- *Don't be the local celebrity.* Shun media exposure. Don't have your photograph leaping out of the newspapers. Keep your activities cloaked in privacy. It may seem like fun to be the life and soul of the community but it can prove expensive. Learn to distrust publicity. Lose your ego. It's better than losing your wealth to a malicious litigant who takes a speculative potshot.

- *Don't spend money recklessly.* This gets you noticed. Great rolls of notes and lavish spending sprees breed resentment. Don't be a big shot at the casino. Avoid lavish displays.

- *Don't drive top-of-the range, luxury vehicles or exotic sports cars.* Tax men in particular notice these status symbols with alarming regularity. They often log the details and launch investigations into the registered owners on the basis of their sightings.

- *Avoid gold or platinum credit cards.* Even to the uneducated eye these signal money. Stick with the standard issue card.

- *Be seen to live comfortably. Not ostentatiously.* Palatial homes equipped with all the latest security systems invite closer attention. A comfortable, discreet home doesn't get noticed. A comfortable home doesn't invite speculation or investigation.

- *Avoid strutting around town like a peacock dripping with gold jewelry.* Similarly, you may love your wife or girlfriend but bedecking her with diamonds and pearls means she will be an irresistible lure to predators for more than one reason.

- *Avoid any situation where you may be likely to come under the scrutiny of any authority figure, official representative or police officer.* These are the very last people you want taking an interest in your affairs and activities. The best way of avoiding them permanently is never to arouse their curiosity. Observe all laws, even minor ones. Don't get into arguments. Don't annoy your neighbors. Live the life of an ordinary, moderately successful, law-abiding citizen and you're likely to be left alone.

- *Keep your mouth shut.* Never tell anybody your business. Never mention your wealth, activities or any success you have enjoyed. Loose lips sink ships. More people have fallen foul of their own slack jaws than for any other reason. Today's friend, wife, lover or colleague is tomorrow's government informer. Trust no one. If nobody knows your business, they can't tell anybody about it.

- *Sometimes it is helpful to appear slightly stupid.* A little play-acting and a little misinformation means many predators will pass you by. Feigned stupidity is an excellent smokescreen.

Remember, there is always someone watching, listening and waiting. There is always someone waiting for an opportunity to strike. A scrap of information, a glimpse of wealth, and the sharks will circle. Your wealth is their target. Take steps to protect it—adopt a low profile today.

Four Steps to a Low Profile
by Patrick O'Connor, *You Are the Target*, 1997

None of us can afford the luxury of being indifferent to security in this day and age. Indifference means your head could wind up on the criminal chopping block. We must realize that we are the only certain guardians of our own and our family's security. Others will take care of themselves—or perhaps be making plans to "take care of us" in a most undesirable way.

STEP 1: Always Be Security Conscious

Behavior that is unthinking or born of a momentary personal arrogance destroys sound personal security procedures. The approach to security should be as professional and business-like as the approach to a chosen career. That is the only reasonable way to guard against harm to yourself and your family or loss of your personal and business assets.

Explore the positive steps that can and should be taken to reduce your personal target profile. Begin by developing a low personal profile. Remember collaboration with the enemy is one of the worst offenses and when you advertise your target potential, that is exactly what you are doing. Obviously, if your life attracts the media, a low personal profile may be difficult or impossible to achieve. Moderate behavior is the key to an effective low personal profile. Develop a list of things that call attention to yourself in public and eliminate them. We all developed habits that call unnecessary attention to ourselves.

STEP 2: Avoid the Habitual & Routines

This is one of the most important aspects of personal security. Studies of rapists, muggers, assassins, robbers and kidnappers prove the incredible dangers posed by their victims' habits. Living in a predictable way can be the perfect scenario for predatory criminals.

You can alter your routine. Do grocery shopping with your spouse on Wednesday if the usual day is Saturday. At work vary your lunch time and the place you eat. Reporting to your office every day at the same time is a common error. When leaving home, notify a trusted person of your destination and make arrangements for a second phone call to verify arrival.

Arrange code words to alert your wife or a friend of trouble by phone. In the office, adopt silent emergency signals. The cash room of a major department store has a code system by which a supervisor regularly greets employees with a cheery "Hello." The response must be a bright, "Hello, Mr. Powers." If the response is anything else, the supervisor takes immediate emergency measures.

Whether your car is parked in a public place or in a locked garage it is a target for bombing, bugging or disabling. Transmitters can be attached in seconds. These can emit a signal picked up and traced over several miles. An explosive device can be clamped to the underside a car in seconds. A cellular phone should be installed in your car so you can summon help or report trouble. After looking for bugs and explosives, check tires, lights, the horn and be sure your petrol tank is full and not leaking. A flat tire or a slow leak can place you in a critical and vulnerable position.

It is imperative to avoid anyone who may be following you. Professional followers have a number of techniques designed to fit specific needs. They may use several vehicles including helicopters. Changing taxis and often doubling back on yourself can throw off pursuers off your tail. If you are in your car and feel threatened by followers, lead them into a congested traffic area if possible, stop the car, get out and walk away quickly leaving the car where it is.

Police say victims of crimes are often accomplices in their own demise. Private security consultants caution customers that imprudent or showy conduct is the catalyst in random criminal activity. Your safety checklist should include a check of cosmetic features. Do you consistently overdress for surroundings? Do you wear inappropriate or unnecessary jewelry? These are signposts to criminals seeking a target. Avoid flashing inordinate amounts of cash or wallets filled with credit cards. Carry only cash you need and don't flash a roll of bills. Use the credit card you need and keep the others safely concealed. A minimum conscious effort provides great personal security by denying criminals information.

Personal conversation should be guarded in public. If you maintain a moderate appearance and conservative conduct, why negate it all with loose conversation. Professional criminals make an excellent living capitalizing on overheard conversations.

STEP 3: Avoid Dangers, Known & Unknown

Strangers about which we know little or nothing should be assumed to be dangerous until proven otherwise. That sounds stringent until examined under the light of effective security. It doesn't offend anyone and it keeps us from compromising ourselves by keeping people at a safe arm's length until their background and character are known to us.

The same approach is correct for strange places, venues about which we know little or nothing. They are the types of places that we find ourselves at an unguarded moment. When there is even the slightest doubt about a place, avoid it. There never is a good reason for putting yourself in an area of potential jeopardy.

STEP 4: Make Your Home Secure

Every residence should be penetration proof. Only residents should be able to come and go at will. This means there must be a security system and security procedures which will vary with single-or multi-unit dwellings.

Family Security Protection Check Points

by Patrick O'Connor, *You Are the Target*, 1997

Practical things you can do now—today—to protect your family, at home and away at school. What to tell your children. Plus a school security check up.

Security Begins at Home

- Be certain outside doors, window, and screens, especially those in children's rooms, are securely locked.

- Keep children's room doors open so you can hear any unusual sounds; or install an intercom or video camera system in their rooms.

- Make sure your residence is not readily accessible from the outside and that the alarm system is functional.

- Never leave young children unattended at home or anywhere else. Be certain they are always in the care of a responsible person.

- Instruct your family and domestic staff that doors and windows must be locked and that strangers are never to be admitted.

- Instruct young children how to telephone the police and test their knowledge with a trial call.

- If you leave pre-teenage children at home with a sitter at night, keep the house well lit inside and out.

- During an extended absence, avoid indications you are away. Close garage doors and cancel newspaper delivery. Install day-night, light-sensitive controls on appropriate light systems.

- Never advertise family activity routines. To acquaint themselves with a family's habits, would-be intruders often have victims under surveillance prior to acting.

- Instruct your family, especially the children, your staff and business associates never to provide information to strangers.

- Avoid providing personal details in response to inquiries from publications such as business directories, social registers, or community directories. Always demand a caller's identification and double-check by calling them back at their office before talking at length.

Security Tips to Tell Your Children

- Always travel in groups or pairs.

- Walk along heavily traveled streets and avoid isolated areas whenever possible.

- Refuse automobile rides from strangers and never go with strangers anywhere on foot. Never accept any gifts, food, candy, drinks, or money from strangers. Refuse requests for help from strangers.

- Use municipal or private play areas with recreational activity supervision by responsible adults and readily available police protection.

- Immediately report anyone who molests or annoys you to the nearest person of authority.

- Never leave home or a hotel without telling you parents where you are going and who will be with you.

- Instruct your children never to disclose your residential address without your permission, especially over the Internet.

Minimum Security Rules for Your Child's School

- Never release a child except to his/her parents during school hours. A teacher or school official must confirm parents approval before release of a child to any person other than the parent.

- Confirm the caller's identity when phone requests are made concerning a child's activity or a request is made that the child be permitted to leave during school hours. If a parent calls, check the request by a return telephone call and have the child positively identify the parent's voice. When appropriate, the caller should be asked identifying questions such as the child's date of birth, courses being studied, names of teachers and classmates and other facts known only to the parents. When in doubt, do not release the child.

- Be alert to suspicious persons loitering in or near school buildings or grounds. If such persons can provide no logical explanation for their presence, notify police immediately. Obtain the identity and full description of the suspect person.

- School personnel must ensure that adult supervision is provided in schools and recreational areas at all times.

Security Questions for Your Child's School Administrator

- Are thorough background checks done before hiring school staff, including maintenance people?

- While children are in school is a qualified nurse on duty at all times?

- Describe procedures followed when a child is injured at school. How is parental notification given?

- To what hospital is a child transported in the event of injury?

- What police and fire station has supervision over the school?

- How many and what kind of security personnel are available on the school premises? Where is their office?

- Is a special background check made on all security personnel before hiring?

Security Checklists for Business People
by Patrick O'Connor, *You Are the Target*, 1997

Service, manufacturing or retail, every business has its soft spots and choke points. Do you know where your business vulnerabilities are? The four most common targets for security violations:

- Your physical person
- Your loved ones, including family, home and possessions
- Your business
- Your employees

The two most serious challenges to security:

- Your own indifference
- Hostile outside forces

The two guiding principles when considering security:

- Eliminate all vulnerabilities.
- Never knowingly create or invite a threat.

Security check points for service-oriented businesses:

- Keep a minimum amount of cash on hand.
- Keep all valuable papers and records in a secure place within a restricted area.
- Release papers and records only on a qualified and controlled basis. Pin-point responsibility at all times.

- Screen all visitors and potential clients within a reception area separate and apart from work and office areas.
- Designate specific responsibility for day-end premises lock up.
- Periodically test premises and telephones for electronic spying apparatus.
- Caution employees to avoid shop talk outside the office except in controlled business situations.
- Screen new employees thoroughly and avoid the use of temporary help for confidential or critical assignments.
- Provide intelligent security when the premises are vacant.

Additional security check points for manufacturing businesses:

- Assign portable equipment and collect it daily.
- Keep a running inventory of raw materials.
- Distribute raw materials on a sign-out basis.
- Maintain daily inventory records of manufactured goods in a secure place.
- Promulgate and enforce specific entrance and departure procedures for all employees.
- Adopt responsibility and assignment rules for stationary machinery.
- Have uniformed security personnel on duty and highly visible at all times.

Additional check points for retail businesses:

- Display expensive items in the most controlled manner possible.
- Make frequent but irregularly-timed bank deposits depending on cash-flow.
- Employ uniformed store guards.
- Keep inventories well secured.
- Establish individual responsibility for cash drawers.

Learn to Read People
PT2, 1997

A little intuition and practical savvy can help you avoid some of life's worst pitfalls—other human beings bent on making trouble for you. You can stop them before they even start if you know how to read the telltale signs.

People who are born and live in other cultures have unique ways of expressing themselves through body language. Before traveling internationally, always familiarize yourself with local customs in the countries you will visit. As Groucho Marx used to say, "When in Rome, do as the Romanians do!" Every good guide book contains an introductory lesson on possibly offensive body language to be avoided. Fail to heed such useful advice and you may cause a social crisis that not only deeply offends local people but also brings unwanted negative attention to yourself.

Once while visiting the Temple of the Emerald Buddha in Bangkok, one of Thailand's most holy shrines, I saw a woman insult every Thai within sight. She accomplished this when she sat in front of the statue of Buddha with the soles of both of her feet pointing directly at the shrine. In Thailand, it is highly insulting to show anyone the soles of your feet, much less Buddha. Thais present angrily whispered among themselves, until someone finally asked the woman to leave the shrine. Her ignorance had transformed the traditionally friendly Thais into menacing adversaries. She is probably still wondering what all of the fuss was about.

As in Thailand, the soles of your feet are an insult in most Arab nations. In many Moslem countries, a man who sits with crossed legs is indicating he is gay. Finger signs mean different things in different places. Making a circle by putting your forefinger and thumb together means "perfect" or "thanks" in most countries. In Greece, however, it invites homosexual advances. The two-finger sign ("bull") that expresses disbelief in the U.S., in Italy is a private signal that the wife of a man with whom the signal sender is speaking is having an extramarital affair.

In any country a good indication of a conversation partner's honesty of expression can be seen in his or her body language. Read some books on this subject if you are frequently involved in conferences where clues to the true feelings of your opponents or colleagues may be helpful. Someone who fidgets while talking is probably nervous. If one stands with arms crossed over the chest it may mean a negative or defensive attitude, even more so if a person sits with arms crossed on the chest. When you learn how to read others, you also learn how not to reveal your own attitudes through body language.

Reading facial expressions is more tricky. People are usually more aware and in control of their facial expressions than of their body language. As a defense mechanism some people constantly present a poker face to the world. A hint: someone who is less than truthful may respond to an accusation with a fleeting facial expression of feigned surprise or astonishment. If the look lasts a bit too long, he's probably a phony. Test yourself on this in a mirror. The insincerity revealed is quite obvious once you attuned to its meaning.

So when you go abroad, learn how to look before you leap.

10 Mistakes to Avoid When World Traveling
by Paul Terhorst, December 1997

Don't believe all those old wives tales about travel precautions you've heard repeatedly. Take it from a veteran traveler who learned the truth from hard experience.

After 16 years living and investing all over the world I thought I could be most helpful to you by exposing some bad advice you may hear—advice that travel agents, credit card vendors, tour guides, innkeepers and others want you to hear because it's in their interest.

Below are the Ten Worst Offshore Travel Tips—advice you're likely to hear about traveling and investing abroad that you can feel comfortable ignoring.

1. *The American Express Card, Don't Leave Home Without It.* An ad campaign for American Express many years ago and bad advice. One time I was in London during a period of stable exchange rates. I charged several items each day on a Diners, American Express, Visa, and MasterCard. When I got the bills back in the U.S., I checked the exchange rates. Diners, Visa, and MasterCard were all close. But American Express stepped three percent on every exchange rate. Why pay American Express three percent of your monthly expenditures? I tore up the card.

2. *Don't Drink the Water.* This tip is okay as far as it goes. But then the guidebooks remind you that "water" includes ice, and advise you not to put ice in drinks. This is an example of "developed-world-centric" thinking. In rich countries bars and restaurants buy ice machines and connect them to the tap water. But in Third World countries bars and restaurants buy their ice from ice plants. I've been in some of those ice plants, and in each case the host has pointed out the water purifier. The last thing these ice people want is dirty water jamming up their plant. So the ice is probably okay. On a hot day you're probably running a greater risk of dehydration than you are of getting sick from eating ice.

3. *Buy Cheap Countries.* This is bad advice and the reason why is quite complicated. It sounds reasonable enough—buy low, sell high, right? Why shouldn't you buy cheap countries? Well, first of all, when I say cheap, I don't mean stocks are cheap, but that the country is cheap to you—the visitor. A beer or a taxi ride or a local hotel room is cheap. The only way a country can be cheap, with

only a few exceptions that I can think of, is to have an undervalued currency. So cheap means a foreign currency is cheap.

So why is expensive good and cheap bad? Because of a paradigm shift. The old model, most notably in Japan and western Europe, particularly Germany, in the 1950s, was to undervalue the currency. That way those countries could produce things cheaply. Years later, after booming export-led growth and the expansion of internal markets, the market revalued those currencies.

The new paradigm today is to skip directly to the expensive currency phase. To heck with building factories, taking advantage of low-cost labor, improving manufacturing techniques, becoming the low-cost producer, and then watching your currency go up in value. In every case—Brazil, Argentina, Russia, Hungary—countries which have overvalued their currencies, or revalued their currencies, have met with initial success under this new paradigm:

- Inflation disappeared.

- Money poured in from Wall Street and western Europe.

- Stock markets soared.

- Real estate and other assets soared.

So why am I telling you all this? Because PTs are in a unique position to take advantage: PTs travel and they have money to invest in speculative, turnaround situations. As a PT all you need to do is note when a given country becomes very expensive, very quickly. There's your opportunity. Expensive is good, cheap is bad.

So where's the next opportunity likely to be? Well, it's got to be a cheap country right now: Indonesia, the Philippines, even Burma or Vietnam, none of which are tied to the old model, are viable possibilities. Here's what I'm saying—but don't be premature—wait until these countries purposefully and dramatically overvalue their currency. Bide your time, continue your travels. Keep your eye out for newly expensive, especially very expensive places. When you see a big change... there's your opportunity. This is the new paradigm and you can do very well from it.

4. *Pack Your Fodor's Guide.* Over the years, I think I've seen all the guidebooks and the best for travelers are the Lonely Planet guide book series. I'm talking here about travelers versus tourists. I define "travelers" as people who move around within the country at large rather than within carefully defined, guided, tourist groups. Lonely Planet guidebooks have the best maps, details on transportation, and lists of hotels in all price ranges.

They're very specific. For example, they tell you precisely how to take the train from Bangkok to Chiang Mai in Thailand. Go to the station, through the black door on the right, to the left toward a desk marked "Foreigners." Believe me this depth of illumination can help you avoid all sorts of confusion and mistakes.

Contact Lonely Planet Publications, Barley Mow Center, 10 Barley Mow Passage, London W4 4PH U.K., telephone +44 181 742 3161, fax +44 181 742 2772. Or visit the Lonely Planet website at www.lonelyplanet.com.

5. *Avoid Countries in Turmoil.* No one went to Iraq during the Kuwaiti war. Then again, I guess not many people go to Iraq under any circumstances. But deciding whether or not to go to a country in turmoil depends on the turmoil. If you're in a country shortly after a coup, for example, you're safer than any place on earth. After many years being around it, my view is that turmoil is good. It's exciting and provides all kinds of benefits to the traveler who's in a position to take advantage.

For example, in 1989 I was in Argentina, a country in turmoil with massive inflation. I got up one morning and decided to buy a pair of leather Adidas tennis shoes. I had seen the shoes the day before at 2,000 pesos. With the peso at 100 to the dollar, that was about US$20, a good price. By the time I got to the store the peso was at 200, so the shoes were now only US$10. The merchant guaranteed the 2,000-peso price for an hour while I raced downtown to change money. By the time I got to the exchange dealer the peso was at 500. The shoes wound up costing only US$4.

6. Check Home for Messages Every Now and Again. Calling home is old fashioned. Computers, e-mail and the Internet provide the modern traveler with a direct line to the wider world. Using the Internet you can have your messages forwarded to you. You can operate bank and broker accounts and check that transactions were recorded properly. You can purchase plane tickets. During 1995-96, Vicki and I were on the go for over a year. All the while we were in constant touch, via e-mail, with family and friends. I don't think we would have been comfortable traveling for that long without having our small computer along.

7. Enjoy Exotic, Native Culture in Tahiti. The principal argument I have with this advice is that Tahiti is one of the world's most expensive tourist destinations. Now you may have your own reasons for going to Tahiti. But westerners, in general, are terrified of visiting inexpensive countries. Tourism to Mexico plummeted after the 1994 devaluation. Travel agents and airlines are already bracing for a huge drop in tourism to Thailand and Malaysia this season, because of the devaluations there.

Why do people avoid countries that become cheap? They feel uncomfortable. They assume they can't get the luxury they want. They don't know how to tip, think that they're unfairly taking advantage, whatever. There's no reason for this. Visit countries when you want to go, whether they're cheap or not. If a country is cheap—you can take advantage and cut some deals. In the South Pacific, consider going to Bali, Malaysia, or Fiji instead of the much more expensive Tahiti.

8. Beware of Dictatorships or Corrupt Countries. When I first moved to Argentina in 1981, it was a military dictatorship. People in the U.S. were screaming about lack of rights. But the streets of Buenos Aires were safe. I'm not supporting dictatorships. But dictatorships are often very safe for tourists. Under a military dictatorship the guys in the streets with the guns are often protecting you. Another point here: there seems to be little correlation between investment results and whether a country is a dictatorship or not, or whether it's very corrupt or not.

9. Take Traveler's Checks. They're Safer Than Cash. They're also expensive and obsolete. It's difficult to replace them, unless you have a purchase voucher, and if your checks are lost in your luggage, the purchase voucher is often lost too. But that's if you lose them. If you don't lose them, you're sure to get a lousy exchange rate and pay exchange fees. You're sure to have to present your passport to cash them.

A better way to travel is with plastic—cash machine cards, credit cards. ATMs work just as well in Thailand or Argentina as they do at home. They also have higher limits on withdrawals, charge no exchange fees, and offer very favorable exchange rates. Personally, I prefer debit cards. With these you can go into a bank and get more money than from the machines, and you don't pay the cash advance fee credit cards charge.

10. If You Get in Trouble Abroad, Get Help from the U.S. Consulate. One specific piece of advice for Americans-avoid U.S. consulates. Remember: the people there don't work for you. They work for the government of the United States. And like all government types they have only contempt for those who propose making work for them.

If you're in trouble abroad, the person to ask for help is the owner of your hotel or apartment-hotel. He's a big man in town, because he owns significant real property, and you're his customer. He probably speaks some English. He's working for you, your interests coincide, you both want to get you out of trouble. If you must go to a government office, use the British or Canadian consulates. They speak English and for some reason seem to have a more compassionate attitude toward needy travelers than their U.S. counterparts.

Finally, I want to leave you with the sense that life is an adventure, and that travel, and living abroad, and investing abroad are part of that adventure, and a wonderfully exciting part.

What You Don't Know About Foreign Laws Can Hurt You

By Mark Nestmann, *The Sovereign Individual*, 2002

As if increasing threats against English-speaking tourists aren't bad enough, there's an often overlooked threat when you travel internationally: that of being arrested or even jailed for something that's perfectly legal where you live.

Here's a rundown of some laws of which you should be aware. But for the most definitive information, consult the embassies or consulates of the countries to which you will be traveling to learn more about what regulations might apply.

Credit cards. In some countries (Greece is one), you can be arrested for over-extending the credit limit on your credit card. Make certain you have adequate credit limits before you leave.

Vehicles. Be careful how you drive and, if you rent a vehicle, where you drive it. In some countries—Mexico is one—even a passenger of a vehicle involved in an accident may be temporarily detained, and occasionally, even jailed. Make certain that you obtain temporary auto insurance. In Mexico, you can be arrested if you don't have it. If you rent a vehicle, it may be illegal to leave the country where you rented it. In Austria, for instance, drivers attempting to enter countries listed as "prohibited" on the car rental contract may be arrested, fined and even charged with attempted auto theft.

GPS devices. The use of global positioning system devices is subject to special rules and regulations in many countries. In 1997, a U.S. citizen was imprisoned in Russia on charges of espionage for using a GPS device to confirm proper operation of newly installed telecommunications equipment. While he was released after 10 days, using a GPS device in a manner deemed to compromises Russian national security can result in a 20-year prison term.

Cellular telephones. Many countries require a permit to import a cellular telephone. Russia again has some of the strictest laws. To obtain permission to bring in a cellular telephone, you must sign an agreement for service from a local cellular provider. That agreement and a letter of guarantee to pay for the cellular service must be sent to a government agency, along with a request for permission to import the telephone. In Panama, a government granted phone monopoly will require you to rent a cell phone while there.

Laptop computers. Laptops are commonplace these days, and most countries permit you to freely cross a border with one in your possession. There may be restrictions on how you use your laptop, particularly if you plug it in to the national telecommunications system. For instance, some countries that monitor telecommunications prohibit the use of encryption programs. Others permit laptops to be imported, but will confiscate them when you leave the country, particularly if the laptop contains encryption software or software that uses encryption, which is standard in all Internet browsers.

Prescription drugs. Bringing a sufficient quantity of prescription drugs into a country for your use while you are there is almost never a problem. But this is not always the case; in Bahrain, for instance, you must obtain a license from the Health Ministry to import prescription drugs. Even if imported pharmaceuticals are permitted, keep your medication in its original container and carry a copy of your prescription with you. For more information, see www.medicine-gallery.com/ restrictions.html.

Firearms. Bringing a firearm (and in some cases merely ammunition) across an international border can result in a long prison sentence and the confiscation of the luggage, vehicle or boat in which it was found. In Mexico, for instance, dozens of Americans are incarcerated for the crime of bringing a licensed U.S. firearm into the country. In several cases, the firearms were even declared to the border inspector—but the persons carrying it were still arrested, tried and imprisoned.

If you are arrested or detained in a foreign country, you can usually turn to your local embassy or consulate for at least limited assistance. Most countries, including the United States, have ratified the Vienna Convention on Consular Relations, which requires ratifying states to permit consular officers to have access to imprisoned nationals of their country. The Convention also provides that the foreign law enforcement authority shall inform the local consulate or the arrest of a national "without delay" (no time frame specified), if the national requests such notification.

Consular services available to prisoners generally include: visiting the prisoner as soon as possible after notification of the arrest; providing a list of local attorneys to help the prisoner obtain legal representation; providing information about judicial procedures in the foreign country; notifying family and/or friends, if authorized by the prisoner; relaying requests to family and friends for money or other aid; providing loans to destitute prisoners; arranging dietary supplements; and arranging for medical and dental care if not provided by prison. For more information, see http://travel.state.gov/arrest.html.

Ways to Make Travel More Private
By Mark Nestmann, *The Sovereign Individual*, November 2002

When you travel, from the time you book your ticket to the time you return home, computers, sensors, transmitters and cameras surround you, all collecting data. Much of this data collection is supposedly justified to fight the "War on (Some) Terrorists;" all of it is intrusive.

Monitoring is most pervasive if you're traveling by air, but governments also monitor travel by rail, bus and even private vehicles, with the United States (as usual) leading the way. Meet the wrong "profile," have the wrong passport stamp or make the wrong comment to a security guard, and you could be fined or even land in prison.

There are still ways to make traveling more private, although the era of anonymous travel is mostly over. Here are suggestions to increase travel privacy.

• *Pay cash (except for air travel).* Cash is untraceable, but if you purchase your airline tickets with cash, this automatically marks you for further attention.

• *Small is beautiful.* Fly on small airlines. Rent vehicles from small local operators. Stay in small local hotels. Avoid rental and hotel chains that will keep records of your stay in a database that is often posted to a national or international computer system.

• *Don't get your passport stamped.* This may require a special request to customs officials, which may or may not be honored. Some countries (Cuba and Switzerland are two) do not automatically stamp passports.

• *Beware of importing electronic equipment without prior authorization.* In most countries, it's perfectly legal to bring cellular telephones and laptops in for your personal use, but not always. For instance, in Russia, the unauthorized importation of a cellular telephone is a criminal offense.

• *Consider indirect routing.* If your final destination is a country that you'd rather not have identified in computerized records, don't fly there, but to a nearby country. Then take a train or rent a car to your final destination. Example: Fly to Germany to visit Switzerland, Liechtenstein, Austria or Luxembourg.

• *Consider air charters or private planes.* Air charter and general aviation companies rarely search their passengers or inspect their luggage. However, tickets can cost ten times or more as much as tickets on commercial airlines. Since October 2002, U.S. air charter companies operating planes heavier than 95,000 pounds (about 130 seats) have had to comply with the same security regulations as commercial airlines. Smaller charters will not be required to comply with these regulations. In Europe, the cutoff is 100,000 pounds.

Tips for Clearing Airport Security

• *Check your luggage and minimize carry-ons.* Avoid carrying on sharp objects or anything that could be used as a weapon. Wear non-metallic clothing and tennis shoes, not leather shoes. Place any metal items you bring with you in your carry-on luggage that is x-rayed. Items that commonly set off the detectors include cell phones, car alarm transmitters, pagers, key rings, watchbands, pens, coins, glasses, metal buckles and candy wrapped in foil.

• *Do not lock checked luggage.* Airline and security personnel are notorious for stealing cash and other valuable items from checked luggage. But new rules allow security personnel to search your luggage without asking you open it for them.

• *Don't interfere with a search or even raise your voice.* Assaulting a screener is a federal crime in most countries. In the United States, assault is defined as including fear of imminent physical assault. Under the new Aviation and Transportation Security Act, it carries a penalty of up to 10 years in prison, a fine, or both. Yelling at the screener could land you in federal prison!

• *Keep batteries in your laptop.* If you carry on your laptop, you may be asked to "boot it up" at security. Be sure to charge your battery.

• *Keep controversial reading material in your checked luggage.* Or leave it at home. In several cases, individuals carrying books with provocative titles or illustrations in carry-on luggage have not been permitted to board their flight. In one case, when security personnel discovered a book by Karl Marx in a passenger's carry-on luggage, they arrested him! "After September 11, you can't travel with books like this," said the arresting officer.

Private Rail, Bus and Auto Travel

All forms of ground transportation are much more private than air transportation. Amtrak, the U.S. rail carrier now requires a photo ID to board its trains. Bus carriers on some interstate routes now require photo ID as well. Outside the United States, air and bus travel is more private except when crossing borders, other than EU borders across which IDs are no longer systematically checked.

• *To avoid showing up in rental car databases, rent from a small, local firm.* If you rent a car in most countries, you will need to show a driver's license (or international driving permit) and credit card. Do not list your home address on the agreement—use a mail receiving service instead. (This address should match that on your driver's license.) Read the agreement to make certain that your rental vehicle will not be tracked by a GPS satellite, as is becoming increasingly more common.

• *Avoid toll roads.* If you must use them, pay tolls with coins, never with an automated payment voucher system.

• *Don't volunteer information.* Finally, and most important: the best way to protect your privacy, at home, in the air or on the road, is to maintain a private attitude. Never give out your Social Security number (or its equivalent if you're not a U.S. resident). When in doubt—try to "blend in" with the crowd and keep your mouth shut!

Do terrorists use these techniques to avoid detection? Perhaps. But "terrorism" is now so broadly defined that anyone who participates in a concerted effort to effect political change can arguably be labeled as a terrorist. Don't let "fear of terrorism" prevent you from protecting your privacy!

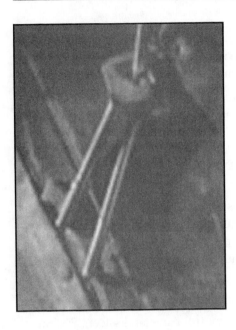

CHAPTER TWELVE
Technology

One of the waning century's great futurists, Peter F. Drucker, author and lecturer, notes that the next information revolution is well underway and yet most people don't even realize it.

It's not just a revolution of digital technology, machines, techniques, software or speed, he says. It is a revolution in concepts. The last 50 years witnessed a major revolution centered on data collection, storage, transmission, analysis and presentation. The next revolution, already begun, is about the meaning of information, its use and purpose.

And in the economic world, Drucker argues, the concept, the purpose, the new function of free enterprise must be the creation of value and wealth. That can only be done by understanding and using the amazing amounts of information now at hand in all fields—medicine, education, business and finance.

A major element in the successful creation of value and wealth is your own personal ability to communicate, instantly and anywhere, with full confidence in your privacy. In a world full of snoops and terrorists, privacy is paramount. Here we tell you how to defend your wealth and your life.

That requires a working knowledge of computers, fax machines, encryption, cryptography, the Internet, digital communication and tech systems that change daily.

How to Make Your PC "Disappear"
By Mark Nestmann, *The Sovereign Individual*, February 2003

Your PC is under attack from governments and private intelligence-gatherers.

Dozens of governments have ratified laws and treaties that obligate telecommunications providers to build surveillance technologies into their networks. Industrial espionage is at an all-time high as intelligence agencies offer their services to private enterprise. Some of the largest and most-technologically savvy corporations in the world have been victims of such surveillance—Microsoft, for instance.

You should therefore assume that every time you send or receive e-mail or connect to the Internet, hackers will monitor your communications and try to extract information from your hard disk. Here I provide you with more than a dozen easy, yet vital, steps you can take to build a privacy "toolkit" to overcome such surveillance so that your PC literally disappears off the Internet, thereby permitting virtually untraceable communications.

Step 1: Set Up Your PC for Privacy

Using two PCs instead of just one provides an excellent boost to security. If the security of your "online" system is breached, the confidential data on your "offline" system remains intact.

Every time you connect to the Internet, a hidden partition in your hard disk may be remotely activated and information transmitted to persons unknown. The only way to deal with this vulnerability is to use a two-PC setup or a hard-switched or removable "C" hard disk with its own operating system installed.

Use one hard disk for high security purposes, the other for routine tasks. Keep the data on the high security drive "encrypted" with a program such as Pretty Good Privacy (www.pgpi.com) except when you're actually using it. When you want to copy programs or files to your offline system—after testing them on the online machine—back them up and restore them on the main one using a rewriteable CD-ROM. Programs like pcAnywhere (www.symantec.com/pcanywhere) also work, but in addition to being a security risk in their own right, can facilitate the transfer of viruses or other malicious programs to your offline system.

If using a two-PC system isn't practical for you, consider the following precautions:

Disguise your "online identity." In Windows systems, go to the control panel and select "System properties" to review registration data. The "General" tab contains the registration information. This information is recorded in the Windows registry and the only practical way for a non-programmer to change it is by reinstalling Windows. Use the same precautions for your applications software.

Physically disconnect your PC from the telephone line or cable modem when you're not online. These connections carry plenty of energy to manipulate chips in your modem, activating programs that can activate the next time your computer is turned on.

Disable unnecessary "bindings." Windows systems have multiple levels of "connectivity" that most users don't need. Disable the ones you don't use, following the instructions at http://grc.com/su-bondage.htm.

Minimize or turn off the Windows "swap file." Data can be recovered from the "swap file" Windows writes to your hard disk. Use Windows help to search for "virtual memory" and follow the prompts to manage virtual memory. Start with 100 megabytes and adjust to zero or as close to zero for your programs to run properly. Set the same "maximum" and "minimum" figures. Whatever size you specify, you must have at least 50 megabytes additional disk space free.

Disable "universal plug and play (UPnP)." This is a networking standard designed to make different manufacturer's networking equipment, software and peripherals compatible with one another. Unfortunately, the Windows implementation of UPnP contains security flaws so serious that the FBI issued a warning in advising consumers to disable it. A free utility program to do so available at http://grc.com/UnPnP/UnPnP.htm.

Disable printer and file sharing. Bring up "My Computer" on your desktop. Right click on the name of each hard disk. Select "properties," then "sharing." Click "not shared" for each hard drive.

Wipe "free disk space" regularly. Forensic analysis of the unused "free disk space" on your hard disk can reveal traces of incompletely deleted files and a great deal of additional information you might prefer to keep private. Run at least weekly a utility such as the one in Windows versions of PGP (www.pgpi.com) that permits you to wipe free disk space. Also run the Windows "DEFRAG" facility at least weekly.

Preserve e-mail privacy. The most important precautions are to close the "preview pane" in your e-mail program; turn off "active scripting" (instructions at www.europe.fsecure.com/virus-info/u-vbs); and to send and receive e-mail in "plain text" format, not HTML (instructions at www.expi-ta.com/nomime.html).

Step 2: Practice "Safe Surfing"

Minimize your online sessions. The fewer sites you visit and the shorter the time you are online, the less likely it is that you'll encounter a rogue web site that will copy files from your hard disk.

Obtain anonymous Internet dial-up service. In the United States, two Internet Service Providers (ISPs) that permit prepaid anonymous dial-up accounts are Anonymizer (www.anonymizer.com/services/dialup.shtml) and Cyberpass (www.cyberpass.net). In most other countries, anonymous dial-up service is not available. However, if you use a small ISP, the risk of monitoring is reduced. For instance, in the United Kingdom, only ISPs with more than 10,000 users are monitored.

Beware of "always-on" Internet connections. High-speed cable or DSL connections have much higher security risks than dial-up connections. A continuous Internet connection makes it easier for a person running a "packet sniffer" to monitor the data flowing between the Internet and your PC.

Step 3: Use Privacy Enhancing Software

Use your "proxy servers." A proxy server is a computer between your browser and the web page that you are visiting. When you type in a web page address, your browser passes the address to the proxy server and the proxy server retrieves the page. This protects your privacy because all the web site sees is the proxy; you remain invisible. A good choice for a proxy server is WebWasher (www.webwasher.com).

Use browser-scrubbing software. Your web browser keeps detailed logs of everything you do on the Internet. To eliminate these logs, use a program such as NSClean (for Netscape) or IEClean (for Internet Explorer). Both are available from www.nsclean.com.

Use anti-virus and firewall software. Good choices are AVG 6.0 (anti-virus) from www.grisoft.com and ZoneAlarm 3.0 (firewall) from www.zonelabs.com. A properly functioning firewall will insure that there is no evidence of your PC even existing when you connect to the Internet! To test the "stealthiness" of your PC, run the programs at http://grc.com/x/ne.dll?bh0bkyd2.

Use Trojan-detecting software. It's remarkably easy for a hacker to install a program on your PC to secretly record everything you do on it. BOClean is a utility designed to detect and deactivate such "back door" or "Trojan Horse" software (www.nsclean.com).

Use encryption software. Monitoring e-mail communications is easy, thanks to the fact that PC communications pass through multiple computers on the way to their destinations. Using encryption software creates an armored envelope around your e-mail messages (or the files on your PC) that can be defeated only with great effort or if you make a significant error. I recommend PGP for this purpose (www.pgpi.com).

Use "spyware" detection software. Many free or low cost programs downloaded from the Internet secretly install software on your PC that monitors your online activities, then reports them back to the software manufacturer. To detect and remove such "spyware," install a program such as Ad-aware. (www.lavasoftusa.com or www.lavasoft.de).

Step 4: Use Someone Else's PC

If you're a frequent PC user, you'll probably need to configure your own PC for the most private communications possible. But if you only use a PC occasionally, or are traveling, you may need to use someone else's PC to surf or send and receive e-mail.

However, don't use your PC at work for this purpose—it may be booby-trapped. Indeed, about one-third of U.S. companies monitor their employees' Internet use, and such monitoring is increasing in other countries as well.

Instead...go to your local library. Most public libraries in the United States and Canada have free Internet service. You may have to sign in, but you probably won't have to show an ID (although this is now starting to change, allegedly as an anti-terrorist measure).

Find a PC with a floppy disk drive, or a CD-ROM drive. Upload encrypted messages you've prepared in advance to your account with an anonymous e-mailer such as www.hushmail.com. Copy any encrypted messages you receive to your floppy disk. Decrypt them later on your own computer.

Unfortunately, this strategy is becoming more risky. For instance, the USA PATRIOT Act permits the FBI to obtain records of library patrons, including their PC use, without a warrant. Library PCs may also be "bugged." PCs in smaller branch libraries are much less likely to be monitored than in larger libraries.

Commercial PC services and cyber-cafes are also widely available. I've never been asked for an ID, although you will have to sign in and possibly leave a security deposit. For a list of more than 5,000 cyber-cafes in over 140 countries, see www.cybercaptive.com.

However, you have no assurance when using a "public" PC that the network it uses is secure. For this reason, sending encrypted messages and browsing through a "proxy server" is doubly important. In addition, when you use a public PC, your web surfing may be tracked by a network monitor and evaluated against a list of key words or phrases that if triggered will alert law enforcement. If you can't visit chat forums or certain web sites, the network is probably using monitoring or screening software.

You should also assume that any online search engine such as Google.com (my favorite) has the same capability. In China, the Internet police (now more than 40,000 officers strong) make arrests based on certain words used in e-mails or typed into search engines.16 You should assume police in other countries have similar capabilities. If you search for phrases like "enriched plutonium" AND "triggering device," an alarm may go off in a network administrator's office—or at the local FBI office.

You may also be being monitored via closed circuit television every time you go to a public location such as a library or office services store. Your arrival time might later be estimated based on the time you logged on to the Internet. Film from the estimated time of arrival may be examined to identify your face. A face can be matched against a database of more than 60 million faces in less than a second!

For all these reasons, use multiple locations if you use public PCs for Internet access. Finally, remove your "tracks" from whatever browser you use when you leave. This requires installing a browser cleansing program such as NSClean, running it, then uninstalling it. However, most public PCs do not permit users to install or run software not already on the system. You'll probably need to manually delete your online trail. This data is ordinarily maintained in a subdirectories named "archive," "cache," e-mail" and "news," etc. in the Netscape or Internet Explorer program directory. Locate these files on your own PC using a program such as NSClean or IEClean so you know where to look. Also, delete all files in the Windows "temp" subdirectory and with the extension "*.tmp." By taking these steps, you will have achieved greater security than the vast majority of Internet users.

Most hackers, upon discovering that your PC is operating in "stealth mode" will move on to less well-secured PCs. And even if they don't, following these precautions will make it virtually impossible for them to break in.

Protect Your Laptop Computer from Theft
by Matthew Dyke, April 1998

For many PTs, the portable PC is the ultimate source of independence. Despite his globetrotting lifestyle, the PT, thanks to his portable PC, can operate businesses from multiple jurisdictions, communicate with friends, family and colleagues via fax, e-mail and voice mail, all at the touch of a button; maintain encrypted data; gain instant access to a staggering range of services and information on the World Wide Web—and all this from any location in the world, free from problems created by government and bureaucrats "back home."

For the Sovereign Individual/PT a laptop is essential equipment—opening up new worlds, real and virtual, of opportunity and liberty. A portable PC/laptop is a symbol of the very independence and mobility it makes possible. Unfortunately, it isn't just PTs who realize the value of laptops. Your portable PC is the target of choice for today's opportunist thieves. Thieves know a leading laptop can cost £4000/US$6400. They also know that the data contained on a laptop's hard drive may be even more valuable.

Con men, business rivals, bureaucrats, tax collectors, blackmailers and vindictive ex-partners could all potentially profit from the data stored on your laptop's hard drive. Damage can be long-lasting. Confidential, irreplaceable, sensitive information stored on stolen laptop can return to haunt you years later.

And the more information your laptop holds, the more it can lose. Consider the laptop stolen from Visa International's San Mateo, California, office in 1996. It held information on 314,000 credit card accounts. Imagine the effect that kind of sensitive information could have in the wrong hands.

Crime statistics tell an incredible story:

- Insurance agents Safeware, Inc. reported that in 1996 one in every 14 laptops was stolen. That's 265,000 laptops—a figure up 39 percent from 1995.
- The Computer Security Institute says 57 percent of high-tech crimes reported by businesses involved stolen laptops.

The Airport Hustle

The most dangerous environment for your laptop is, without doubt, the airport. USA Today reported that a staggering 10 percent of all laptop thefts occur in airports. And particularly dangerous is the x-ray machine. The problem lies not in the machine itself, but clever thieves operating nearby at security gates and baggage checkpoints.

An Internet security alert warned of an alarming scam, first spotted at Brussels Airport in Belgium. A thief clears security just ahead of his victim. He pauses at the other end of the x-ray machine. A second thief waits for the target laptop to be placed on the conveyor belt. He then steps in front of the victim (who has just placed his laptop on the belt) and intentionally triggers the metal detector. Now that airport officials are paying attention to him, the thief's accomplice empties his pockets and removes his jewelry . . . very slowly. This distraction and delay allows the first thief (still waiting at the end of the conveyor belt) to collect the laptop as it exits the security machine and make good his escape. In a matter of seconds your laptop has disappeared—perhaps permanently.

How To Thwart The Airport Thieves

- Don't put luggage on the conveyor belt until you are at the front of the line, and you know you are the next person going through the metal detector.
- Watch the conveyor belt and the passengers on the other side of the machine very carefully.
- The longer your computer is on the conveyor belt the more vulnerable it is. If you're traveling with company, send your companion through first. Have them pick up your laptop as soon as it clears the x-ray equipment.
- Single travelers should wait for the PC to enter the x-ray machine before walking through the metal detector.
- If you set off the metal detector and are called back by airport officials, demand that a member of the airport staff safeguard your laptop before you walk through again.

Extra vigilance in such busy surroundings is absolutely vital. But how else can you protect your laptop from thieves? There are three good ways:

1. You can deter thieves with locking cables and alarms.

2. You can minimize the damage suffered if a machine is taken by using passwords, security software, file backup services, encryption and insurance.

3. Finally, you can recover machines with tracking systems.

Step 1: Deterring Thieves, The Lock Down

Laptop owners often hear the golden rule—never leave your laptop unattended. But this isn't always possible—especially if your laptop is an older, heavier machine which is difficult to constantly move around with your person.

So how can you protect your hardware while you are elsewhere? One method is to attach your laptop to something difficult or impossible to move, such as furniture or household pipes using a "hardware deterrent"—usually a long steel cable, similar to those used to secure bicycles. Owners of the latest big brand laptops may not realize that their model may have a special "security slot" built in that can secure such locking cables. Security cables may not make your machine totally thiefproof, but they will slow down opportunists who may well prefer to move on to safer, quicker, unsecured pickings elsewhere.

Alarm Systems

The second deterrent is the sonic alarm. These systems use distance detectors to sense when you and your laptop are parted. The shrieking blast should make any thief drop his booty. It is important that you remember to arm and disarm the system. One drawback is that the alarm is not very low profile. But drawing a little attention to yourself may be preferable to losing your laptop and sensitive data. Once you've acted to deter thieves from grabbing your prized portable, think about ways to minimize the damage if a particularly enterprising thief does find a way around your safeguards.

A system called Trackit (www.trackitcorp.com) uses distance detectors—one for the laptop and one for you to carry—to sense when you and your laptop become separated. If you travel more than 40 feet away from your laptop, the alarm sounds.

Step 2: Limiting Damage From Loss of Passwords, Encryption

Password protection is a basic first step in preventing a thief who gets hold of your hardware from getting access to your sensitive data too. Create different passwords to authorize boot-up and entry into programs. Pick passwords that are difficult to guess. Random letters and numbers are better than the name of your wife and child, for instance. Directories can be encrypted and password-protected automatically. The boot lock function prevents anyone using the hard disk, even if they try to boot-up from the floppy drive.

On the subject of encryption, some PTs worry about the legality of leaving the U.S. with encryption software, especially PGP software. The answer is that the U.S. government has removed most export restrictions on encryption, although it remains illegal to import encryption technology into countries the United States has an arms embargo against, such as Cuba or Iraq.

Back-Up Files Over The Net. The best way to minimize the damage and inconvenience caused by the loss of a laptop is to have a file backup system in place. Many savvy computer users no longer back up critical files manually. Instead, they routinely use an on-line system that backs up for you.

Insurance: It is vital you consider insurance coverage—for laptops, coverage against loss and damage. Find out if your laptop is covered by your current residential, business or travel insurance policies. Consider insuring your PC separately. Remember to ask your insurer if owners using anti-theft systems receive reduced premiums.

Step 3: Recovering Your Machine

If you do lose a laptop, is there anything that can be done to trace it? The answer is yes, if you act in advance. There are several companies that offer a service in which you purchase tracking software that you install on your laptop. Every time you log on to the Internet, the software calls up the service to make certain that an alert hasn't been issued that the laptop hasn't been stolen. If it has, you alert the service and it then traces the originating phone number and reports it to police.

These services use toll-free numbers to defeat caller ID blocking. But this means that they are not effective outside the country in which they are purchased. Moreover, they obviously compromise your privacy as well since every time you log in your location is revealed. Two such services are CompuTrace (www.computrace.com) and CyberAngel (www.sentryinc.com).

Consider biometric access. You can now purchase equipment that insures that only you can log on to your laptop. This is done in most cases with a fingerprint scanner. Compaq Computer makes a fingerprint scanner that costs $180 and fits any notebook computer. The device, made by Identix (www.identix.com) comes on a card that plugs directly into the side of the computer.

Not recommended: The Cyber Group Network Corporation has developed technology that it claims will allow you to locate a stolen computer, remotely retrieve information from it, and then destroy it. I don't recommend it because of the potential that a hacker might use it to maliciously destroy your company's laptops. Nor am I reassured by the company's claim that the patent pending technology that makes all this possible is being developed at a top-secret location identified only as "Area 74."

Mobile computing means risks, but these risks can be minimized. Nightmares can be avoided. With a little technology and common sense, your laptop—and you—can be secure.

They're Spying on Your PC

by Mark Nestmann, *The Sovereign Individual*, December 1998

We have consistently warned that only with special precautions can you maintain any practical level of privacy on the Internet. Many reports indicate that if anything, we understated the threat.

Researchers discovered flaws in Microsoft Internet Explorer that permit web sites to examine the contents of users' computers. In addition, software has also become available that can be surreptitiously delivered and installed on your PC to make available to eavesdroppers every file on your PC and every keystroke you make.

The Internet Explorer flaw causes version 4.01 to upload a file when a browser visits a malicious web site containing instructions written in a programming language called "JavaScript." The person writing and posting the script needs to know the specific location and name of a user's file in order to retrieve it. But many sensitive files, including your e-mail messages, are kept in common locations under default and widely known filenames. The Windows registry file is also kept in a common location and, if stolen, will reveal information about the location of other files.

The vulnerability is tied to new interactive features that were made part of Internet Explorer 4.0. Earlier versions of Microsoft's browser don't have this problem.

While Microsoft has now introduced a "fix" for the problem, it's also easy to defeat if you browse using the Anonymizer—www.anonymizer.com. This is still good advice, despite assurances from Microsoft that Internet Explorer is "safe." (A similar flaw was uncovered more than a year ago in Netscape Navigator and Netscape Communicator. Netscape reportedly has fixed the problem.)

Other powerful tools for surreptitiously examining the contents of your hard disk—and more—have also become available. The best known program is "Back Orifice," released in August 1998 by a hacking group known as the "Cult of the Dead Cow" (www.cultdeadcow.com). The program, which can be delivered as an attachment to an e-mail message, is a "back door" into Windows 95 and 98 that allows a remote user to log your keystrokes, download your files, steal your passwords, etc. There have been at least 200,000 downloads of Back Orifice since August 3, 1998, according to information posted on this web site. Several commercial programs also log keystrokes, including WinWhatWhere (www.winwhatwhere.com).

The best way to avoid having Back Orifice or similar programs clandestinely installed on your computer system is to not execute any attached files e-mailed to you except from trusted sources.

The capabilities of Back Orifice are well documented, but those of another powerful tool for surreptitiously intercepting data are shrouded in secrecy. Called DIRT (Data Interception and Remote Transmission), this program from Codex Data Systems (www.thecodex.com) is available only to law enforcement and the military. Investigators need only know your e-mail address to secretly install the program. Once they do, investigators can read your documents, view your images, download your files and intercept your encryption keys. DIRT was developed to assist police in child porn investigations, but its use will surely be expanded to include watching tax avoiders, privacy seekers and other "enemies of the state."

The only ways to defend against programs such as DIRT are to use a public-access machine for your online use, or to use a system dedicated ONLY to online use, upon which you do not keep confidential files-or your PGP private keys.

<hr />

The Encryption Battle: Money & Power
by Robert E. Bauman, JD, January 1998

In *Wired* magazine ("I Encrypt, Therefore I Am," November 1997), John Browning explained how the same computer software that digitally certifies ownership, also allows completely private electronic financial transfers. And this system offers another tantalizing prospect—the power of each person to protect every aspect of his or her personal privacy—credit, health records banking—by limiting personal identity to nothing more than a unique digital signature. Merchants need never know your name when your card instantly confirms the cash.

The software system is called "encryption" and if you've avoided it so far, don't any longer. For newcomers, it's simple: encryption software scrambles (encrypts) digital information—money, documents, pictures—into mathematically coded messages for electronic transfer or storage. Sent over the Internet, or any capable wire, cable, telephone or satellite system, the recipient at the other end unscrambles (decodes) it. Both parties hold "keys" that allow only them to access the information. Without these keys the code cannot be broken, not even with the most powerful computers working non-stop for years on end.

It's government's worst fear: millions of computers linked worldwide, electronic banking and on-line investment accounts, "smart card" money and easily available encryption. As one astute observer says, "You get untraceable banking and investment, a black hole where money can hide and be laundered, not just liar conglomerates or drug cartels, but for anyone."

You can see why bureaucrats are frantic. The freedom potential of this new money system runs counter to all the Big Brother policies that have bled taxpayers and stifled prosperity for decades. Two centuries ago Mayer Amschel Rothschild (1743-1812), founder of the famous continental banking dynasty, defined power. "Give me control over a nation's currency, and I care not who makes its laws." Soon each of us will have that potential power.

Princes & People

Top-secret spy agencies like the U.S. National Security Agency (NSA) and the U.K.'s Government Communications Headquarters (GCHQ) have used encryption for decades. Banks use it for obvious reasons.

But now unbreakable encryption software is available to anyone for free on the Internet, or for sale at computer stores. The most secure program is called Pretty Good Privacy, or PGP.

Jean Guisnel, in his fascinating *Cyberwars: Espionage on the Internet* asserts what most have suspected. Government agencies, like the NSA and GCHQ, have spied on private citizens for years without legal authority. And on royals too, as Prince Charles and the late Princess Diana bitterly discovered. The ironic contradiction of such a mentality is lost on these police spies. Their fervent desire is to serve and protect and to do so they will use any means. Such as the war on drugs, money laundering, terrorism, pornography and perverts, all scare tactics the U.S. government uses to oppose encryption.

In September 1995, U.S. FBI director Louis Freeh claimed a "public safety" issue, saying private data encryption that impedes the police "will not be tolerated." Just before the U.S. Congress adjourned in 1998, Freeh almost got his wish. But a committee of the U.S. House rejected "key escrow"—a plan to give government access to encrypted data in any computer without the owner's knowledge.

The issue will come up again. An almost identical plan for keys to be held by trusted third parties has been advocated in the U.K. The IRS is demanding access to computer databases so it can calculate every taxpayer's annual income tax.

The U.S. Treasury Department's Financial Crimes Enforcement Network Unit (FinCEN) wants a "Deposit Tracking System" (DTS) that will permit government to track all bank account deposits and withdrawals in real time.

A host of rules issued under the Bank Secrecy Act has turned U.S. banks into informers and the definition of criminal "money laundering" now includes almost every conceivable financial transaction.

The 1994 Digital Telephony Act is forcing phone companies to install special eavesdropping equipment so police can monitor every phone call-and every transmission of computerized data.

As this new world financial system grows, the basic issue is clear: what takes precedence - individual liberty or "state security" as defined by the police? Big Brother's plan to use the monetary system to pry into private lives is well-advanced. Encryption can make certain privacy wins over tyranny.

Resources

- PGP can be downloaded for free from the PGP website at www.pgpi.com.
- Philip Zimmerman, the author of PGP, has written *The Official PGP User Guide* published by MIT Press. To order in the U.S. **Tel.:** +1 617 625 8569. **Fax:** +1 617 625 6660. For MIT Press in Europe: **Tel.:** +44 171 306 0603. **Fax:** +44 1781 306 0604. Or visit MIT Press bookshop on the web at mitpress.mit.edu/bookstore.
- Further Information see: *Crypto*, by Steven Levy (Viking Penguin, 2000), *Cyberwars: Espionage on the Internet* by Jean Guisnel (Plenum Press, New York, 1997); *The Future of Money in the Information Age* by Alan Greenspan (Chairman, U.S. Federal Reserve Board), 1997, The Cato Institute, Washington, D.C. (Cato Books, tel: 800 767-1241).

PGP Cryptography Means Computer Privacy
Computer Privacy Report, 1998

PGP, Pretty Good Privacy, is a high-security cryptographic software application that allows people to exchange files or messages with privacy, authentication and convenience. No secure channels are needed to exchange keys between users, which makes PGP much easier to use. This is because PGP is based on a powerful technology called "public key" cryptography. With it, you can communicate securely over a network or on the Internet with other people without having to meet beforehand to exchange secret passwords!

PGP is shareware so it's free. It can be downloaded from the Internet at www.pgpi.com. It's a program that gives your electronic mail privacy by encrypting it so that nobody but the intended recipient can read it. When encrypted, the message looks like a meaningless jumble of random characters. PGP can resist even the most sophisticated forms of analysis aimed at cracking encrypted text.

PGP can also apply a unique digital signature to a message without encrypting it. This is normally used in public postings where you don't want to hide what you are saying, but rather want to allow others to confirm the message is authentic—that it actually came from you. Once a digital signature is created, it is impossible for anyone to modify either the message or the signature without the modification being detected by PGP.

While PGP is easy to use, you should become thoroughly familiar with its options before using it to send messages.

Phil Zimmermann, the author of PGP, explains why he created the program: "People want their privacy very badly." PGP has spread like a prairie fire, fanned by countless people who fervently want their privacy restored in the information age. Today, human rights organizations are using PGP to protect their people overseas. Amnesty International uses it. The human rights group in the American Association for the Advancement of Science uses it. Some Americans don't understand why I am concerned about the power of government. But talking to people in eastern Europe, you don't have to explain it to them. They already get it—and they don't understand why we don't."

PGP will encrypt files so not even super-computers can decrypt them. You write e-mail on a word processor, encrypt it using someone's public key and send it off. They use their private key to decrypt it. Public keys are just that—public. Give yours out freely. Once a person encrypts a message with your public key, not even they can read it again. Only you can, using your private key.

You should encrypt your e-mail for the same reason you don't write all your correspondence on the back of a postcard. E-mail is actually far less secure than a letter sent through the postal system. When using the post you put your letter in an envelope to conceal it from casual snooping. Take a look at the printed "header" area of an e-mail message you received and you will see it has passed through numerous nodes on its way to you. Each node gives an opportunity for copying and snooping.

Encryption should in no way imply illegal activity. It is simply intended to keep personal information private. If you are not a politician, research scientist, investor, CEO, lawyer, celebrity, libertarian in a repressive society, investor, or person having too much fun, and you do not send e-mail about your private sex life, financial/political/legal/scientific plans, or gossip then maybe you don't need PGP. But at least realize that privacy has nothing to do with crime. And privacy, is in fact, what keeps the world from falling apart.

Public & Private Keys

In conventional cryptosystems, such as the U.S. Federal Data Encryption Standard (DES), a single key is used for both encryption and decryption. This means that a key must be initially transmitted via secure channels so that both parties have it before encrypted messages can be sent over insecure channels. This may be inconvenient. If you have a secure channel for exchanging keys, then why do you need cryptography in the first place?

In public key cryptosystems, everyone has two related complementary keys, a publicly revealed key and a secret key. Each key unlocks the code that the other key makes. Knowing the public key does not help you deduce the corresponding secret key. The public key can be published and widely disseminated across a communications network. This protocol provides privacy without the need for the same kind of secure channels that a conventional cryptosystem requires. Anyone can use a recipient's public key to encrypt a message to that person, and that recipient uses their own corresponding secret key to decrypt that message. No one but the recipient can decrypt it, because no one else has access to that secret key. Not even the person who encrypted the message can decrypt it.

Message authentication is also provided. The sender's own secret key can be used to encrypt a message, thereby "signing" it. This creates a digital signature on a message, which the recipient (or anyone else) can check by using the sender's public key to decrypt it. This proves that the sender was the true originator of the message, and that the message has not been subsequently altered by anyone else, because the sender alone possesses the secret key that made that signature. Forgery of a signed message is not feasible, and the sender cannot later disavow his signature.

These two processes can be combined to provide both privacy and authentication by first signing a message with your own secret key, then encrypting the signed message with the recipient's public key. The recipient reverses these steps by first decrypting the message with their own secret key, then checking the enclosed signature with your public key. These steps are done automatically by the recipient's software.

Don't Respond to This E-Mail Message!
by Mark Nestmann, *The Sovereign Individual*, February 2004

If you receive an e-mail from a bank, securities broker or Internet Service Provider accounts asking for confidential information, don't respond to it before you follow the precautions I give in this article. The e-mailer may not be who he pretends to be and you could find yourself bilked out of thousands of dollars, or your identity stolen.

In November 2003, you may have received an e-mail message, purportedly from e-gold, an online provider of a gold-backed electronic currency. The message, sent to millions of PC users, instructed the recipient to log into their e-gold accounts to verify or update information by clicking on a link in the message.

The message, however, wasn't really from e-gold. And if you clicked on the link, it didn't take you to the e-gold Web site. Instead, it took you to a fraudulent Web site, designed to trick you into revealing your e-gold account number and passphrase. After entering this information, you were told that you had successfully updated your account. What you weren't told is that by entering this information, the operator of the fraudulent Web site had everything needed to log on to your e-gold account on the real e-gold Web site and clean it out.

The e-gold scam is only the latest episode in an e-mail crime wave known as "phishing" or "carding" and uses disguised messages to deceive recipients into disclosing their account numbers, passwords, credit card numbers, Social Security numbers and other sensitive information. They include:

• The AOL customer services scam. In July 2003, the U.S. Federal Trade Commission settled a case against a 17-year-old boy who sent millions of spam messages to PC users telling them they needed to update their AOL billing information. The message threatened customers with a cutoff of their service and a $50 cancellation fee if they did not respond. Recipients were told to click on a link that supposedly connected them to the "AOL Billing Center." However, the link actually took them to a fake Web page that contained the AOL logo, and, to lend authenticity, links to actual AOL Web pages. The fake page contained a questionnaire where browsers were instructed to enter their credit card numbers, Social Security numbers and other confidential data – more than enough information to steal their identity.

• The Best Buy "fraud alert" scam. In another July 2003 incident, electronics retailer Best Buy became the victim of a similar scam. Millions of PC users received an e-mail message ostensibly alerting them to theft of their credit card numbers and asking them to click on a link to Best Buy's fraud department. The link directed the user to a fake Web page, which contained a form asking for sensitive personal information.

Such "phishing expeditions" have also involved the impersonation of Web sites from e-bay, PayPal, CitiBank and dozens of other companies. Phishing is effective because e-mail messages can be sent in the form of a Web page complete with embedded graphics that permit senders to hide a fraudulent Web site address inside a legitimate looking link. In the e-gold scam, for instance, the Web site address listed in the e-mail was e-gold's legitimate address: www.e-gold.com. But if clicked on this link, instead of going to the e-gold Web site, you were taken to a fake Web site with a very similar address.

How to Avoid Being a Victim of a Phishing Expedition

Fortunately, by taking a few simple precautions, you can avoid these scams:

1. Never click hypertext links in HTML formatted e-mail to access any online account. Instead, manually type in a link you know is correct. Or contact the company cited in the e-mail using a telephone number or Web site address you know to be genuine.

2. Before entering your account details, make certain you are on a secured Web page (begins with https://, not http:// and displays a "lock" icon on your browser's status bar). Pfishing scams don't generally use secured Web pages.

3. Verify that the "site certificate" is legitimate. In most browsers, you will receive a warning message if the certificate is outdated or uncertified.

4. Be alert to misspellings or other telltale signs that the site to which you're being directed is not genuine. For instance, in the AOL scam, the e-mail header showed that the "AOL Billing Services Team" was using an old version of AOL software. In addition, the subject line contained a misspelling.

5. Turn off HTML-formatted e-mail. This will protect you not only from phishing but a host of other nasties that are typically delivered through HTML enabled messages, including viruses and remote administration programs that can literally take over your PC. Unfortunately, the most popular e-mail program, Microsoft Outlook, doesn't offer this capability except in its newest versions.5 However, an add-on program for Outlook called "No HTML" provides this capability. For more information on No HTML, see http://ntbugtraq.ntadvice.com/default.asp?sid=1&pid=55&did=38.

6. Turn off the "preview pane" in your e-mail program. In most programs, this is performed by clicking on "view" and then following the prompts.6

7. If you receive an e-mail message phishing for information, report it to www.antiphishing.org. The operators of this Web site try to track down the originators of phishing scams as they are occurring. This is critical because the Web sites designed for collecting personal information in phishing attacks are often only in place for a few days.

Finally: Phishing is not limited to the Internet. Telephone phishing scams are also common. Be particularly suspicious if you receive a call from someone alleging to represent your Internet Service Provider or a government agency seeking information about credit card numbers, SSNs, etc. Instead, contact the company or government agency at the phone number listed in correspondence you've previously received.

Electronic Re-mailers: Key to E-mail Privacy
by Matthew Dyke, March 1998

As e-mail becomes a part of everyday life it's easy to forget the dangers involved. Your e-mail address is more than just a local postbox. It identifies you and your opinions to the world at large. Unlike phone calls, copies of e-mail can last indefinitely, sitting in a server's electronic archives long after you sent them. If government agents or private investigators get their hands on that data they can easily use it for whatever they wish. There is a way around this potential rape of your privacy.

Re-mailers Defined

Whereas encryption scrambles the actual message before you send it, Internet re-mailers are an intermediary stop on the Internet that simply strips off your name and address (the header on an e-mail message). Only then is your message forwarded to its final destination. Many popular re-mailers are free of charge, but e-cash may one day enable re-mailers to start charging—anonymously—for their services.

Why You Need A Re-mailer

The Net has always been a haven for those who believe free speech requires the right to privacy and anonymous expression. Re-mailers reinforce these rights. They can be a vital lifeline for people living in a nation under the "wrong" government, who wish to talk about the authorities' excesses or express minority viewpoints in the face of injustice and intolerance.

Re-mailers are also a great way to research information unobtrusively. They are ideal for accessing data for business or personal purposes without attracting attention from competitors, snoops or opportunistic would-be litigants searching for possible "deep pocket" defendants. And, if you wish to express opinions or communicate ideas anonymously, then re-mailers are ideal.

Using encryption software prevents eavesdroppers from reading the content of your messages. But without a re-mailer, snoopers still can see that two e-mail addresses have engaged in communication—even if they cannot decipher what was said. But just establishing the existence of that e-mail connection may be enough to cause further surveillance or to instigate an investigation.

The best way to thwart any investigation into your personal e-mail communications is to send encrypted messages through re-mailers. You can, if you so choose, identify yourself in the encrypted part of the message. Similarly, you and the people you communicate with can work out identification codes in advance as an extra level of security.

Many e-mail programs add a signature to messages automatically. Remember to disable this function when sending private messages. Many people have come unstuck by not remembering to take this precaution. Instead of being anonymous their messages are more like postcards advertising the sender to any silent watchers.

Anonymity Defined

Net users often refer to all re-mailers as "anonymous." This is a misleading and potentially dangerous interpretation. There are actually two classes of re-mailers—pseudo-anonymous (sometimes referred to as pseudonymous) and anonymous. Only the second makes your messages truly anonymous and gives you the highest level of protection.

Pseudo-Anonymous Re-mailers

If you wish to send an e-mail message without the recipient knowing your identity, you send the message not to your intended recipient but to a pseudonymous re-mailer instead. The re-mailer removes the header, replaces it with its own artificial address, then sends it on to its ultimate destination. The re-mailer sends you confirmation of the transmission.

If the recipient wants to respond to your "anonymous" message, the re-mailer receives the reply on your behalf, matches it to your artificial and real addresses and forwards it to you. This creates a privacy problem with pseudo-anonymous re-mailers because your true e-mail address is directly linked to your re-mailer address. A record of this link then exists as a clear electronic trail that snoopers can follow. Your anonymity is only as strong as the integrity and security of the re-mailer operators.

In 1997, one of the most popular re-mailers of this type located in Finland closed down voluntarily because he felt he could no longer guarantee the security of his clients. Finnish authorities successfully pressured him for the identity of one particular client who was accused of criminal activity.

Anonymous Re-mailers

These re-mailers are best for sensitive personal and commercial communications. The main advantage of anonymous re-mailers over their pseudo counterparts is that they remove your true e-mail address from messages without adding an artificial replacement.

The downside is that recipients can't reply to messages sent in this manner. But that is a small price to pay to ensure you are leaving absolutely no electronic trail whatsoever. With a little organization, there doesn't have to be any drawback at all. Pre-arranged, encrypted code names enable recipients to identify message senders. They can then send replies to your real address—using the re-mailer to protect their own identity.

You can further protect your anonymity by routing messages through a chain of re-mailers. The first re-mailer is the only one to know your true identity. The last re-mailer is the only one to know the message's final destination. Those in between know neither. Using this chain method means that, even if one re-mailer's security has been breached, your anonymity stands a strong chance of remaining intact.

Mixmasters for U.S. & Canada

The safest re-mailers are known as Mixmasters. The crucial difference is that it isn't possible to send normal e-mail through these re-mailers until you download special software from their Internet website, ftp://ftp.obscura.com/pub/no-export. This allows you to write messages in a special secure format before sending them to your re-mailer. Unfortunately, U.S. government encryption restrictions apply because Mixmaster uses RSA encryption that can only be legally downloaded by users in the U.S. and Canada.

One good Mixmaster re-mailer is mix@anon.les.mit.edu. For more information, U.S. and Canadian users can send a message to this address with the words "re-mailer-help" in the subject box.

Re-mailing At Web Sites

Some Internet websites now offer re-mailer interfaces that allow you to type your message at the site rather than compose your message offline. An example is the Global Internet Liberty Campaign at www.gilc.org/speech/anonymous/re-mailer.html.

The Three Step Start:

- First, decide the level of security and re-mailer type you need. If you require replies make sure your recipient has a way of responding.

- Second, find out which re-mailers are presently on-line. Re-mailers rely on the goodwill of their administrators and they tend to come and go. A list of active and reliable re-mailers can be found at www.cs.berkeley.edu/~raph /re-mailer-list.html.

- Third, contact the re-mailers, read instructions they send and enjoy your new-found electronic anonymity.

Re-mailers are a vital defense against violations of your e-mail privacy. As the Internet grows the number of people using it to investigate others increases as well. That why using re-mailers is so very important.

Resources

- Arnoud Englefriet's Galactus site is a guide to computer privacy: www.stack.nl/~galactus/re-mailers/index-cpunk.html.

- If you want to use pseudonymous re-mailers to create a new identity, visit the John Doe home page at www.cix.co.uk/~net-services/jd.htm.

Cover Your Internet Trail
April 1997

Anonymous e-mail addresses and re-mailers, multiple e-mail addresses, pseudonyms—all are useful in muddying-up your electronic tracks, but these devices don't alter the fact that privacy on the Internet is non-existent—unless you make it so. Visit an Internet web site, however fleetingly, and the site's monitors detect some facts about you, usually your e-mail address, even if you don't fill in requested information blanks.

Cookies are small binary files a web site injects into your computer as evidence you have visited the site. They appear as a file in your browser and allow the site to ID you the next time you visit. They are used to send unwanted e-mail, sell things or build demographics about visitors to a web site.

Reject "cookies" by all means. Set your Netscape or Microsoft Internet Explorer browser security settings to warn you when they appear, giving you the option to reject them. Go to your Windows 95 or 98 search ("find") facility and key in "cookies" to see of any have gotten onto your hard drive. You can then delete them.

Some browsers automatically create a history of all URLs you visit on the Internet, making it easy for anyone with access to your computer to discover where you have been. Two software packages are available to erase the URL trails. First is IEClean, for use with Internet Explorer and Netscape browsers. You can download it from www.nsclean.com. The same source offers a neat program for maintaining your privacy while downloading from web sites. NSClean shields your e-mail address from view and protects against tracing devices. It's not free but it is low cost and a value for the price.

Remember: If you download from any web site, especially those not well-known, you risk downloading viruses as well. It pays to install strong anti-virus software on your computer and to keep it upgraded to guard against the many new virus patterns that appear constantly.

Appendices

Appendix I
Author Biographical Sketches

Robert E. Bauman JD, is a member of the District of Columbia bar and a former state senator and member of the U.S. House of Representatives from Maryland. He is a graduate of Georgetown University's Edmund A. Walsh School of Foreign Service and the GU Law Center. He is the author of *The Gentleman from Maryland* (Hearst Book Publishing, NY 1985), *How to Lawyer-Proof Your Life* (Shot Tower Press, Boca Raton, FL, 1995), *The Complete Guide to Offshore Residency, Dual Citizenship and Second Passports* (The Sovereign Society, 2002), co-author of *The Offshore Money Manual 2000* (The Sovereign Society, 1999) and editor of *Forbidden Knowledge* (Agora International, 2003). His writings have appeared in the *Wall Street Journal, The New York Times, National Review* and other publications.

Michael Checkan is President of Asset Strategies International, Inc. (ASI) in Rockville, Maryland, and is a member of The Sovereign Society's Council of Experts. Contact Michael or his business partner, Glen O. Kirsch, by toll free **telephone:** (800) 831-0007, **fax:** +1 (301) 881-1936 or **e-mail:** rcheckan@assetstrategies.com.

Doug Casey, a graduate of Georgetown University (1968), is best known for his books: *The International Man, Crisis Investing, Strategic Investing* and *Crisis Investing For The Rest Of The 90s*. He writes *International Speculator*, a monthly investment advisory focusing on precious metals, stocks, commodities and real estate. PO Box 8978, Aspen, CO 81611 USA. **Tel.:** +1 970 923 2062. **Fax:** +1 970 923 2064.

J. Richard Duke, J.D., L.L.M., is an international tax and asset protection attorney. His practice is in the areas of international and domestic tax, estate planning and asset protection planning (wealth preservation and wealth protection planning), international business tax planning and structuring of offshore and onshore entities and trusts. **E-mail:** richard@assetlaw.com. **Link:** www.assetlaw.com.

Selwyn Gerber, CPA, is the joint managing partner of Primeglobal LLC, Beverly Hills Cal. USA, which specializes in the design of tax-efficient asset protected structures and principal protected investment programs. **Tel.:** +1 (310) 432-4382. **E-mail:** sg@primeglobal.com. **Link:** http://www.primeglobal.com.

J. Orlin Grabbe, PhD, is a leading expert in financial data encryption systems and on international finance. His textbooks are used at universities worldwide. He is author of *International Financial Markets*, and is an internationally recognized derivatives experts and writes about cryptology, banking security and digital cash. **Link:** http://www.xs4all.nl/~kalliste/.

Douglas Hendler is a lawyer practicing corporate commercial law with the firm of Armel, Gray LLP in Toronto, Ontario, Canada. He has been a member of the Ontario bar since 1973 and the New York bar since 1984. He has BA from McGill University, Montreal, a law degree from the University of Toronto. **Tel.:** +1(416) 362-1400. **E-mail:** dhendler@armelgray.com. His address is Armel, Gray LLP, 390 Bay Street, Suite 500, Toronto, Ont. Canada, M5H 2Y2.

Ron Holland, an independent financial consultant, is a member of the Sovereign Society Council of Experts. He has authored numerous books and reports on global investing, retirement planning and wealth protection. **Tel.:** +1 (888) 550-8779. **Fax:** +1 (828) 681-8412. **E-mail:** ronholland@compuserve.com. **Website:** www.ronholland.com.

Vernon K. Jacobs, CPA, is a certified public accountant and tax advisor to The Sovereign Society. He provides tax services for U.S. persons with offshore investments or entities and for non-U.S. persons who have U.S. tax obligations. Jacobs is editor of the e-letters *Global Asset Protection* and *Offshore Tax Strategies* (with Richard Duke). **E-mail:** jacobs@offshorepress.com. **Website:** www.offshorepress.com.

Christian H. Kalin is a director and partner of Henley & Partners AG in Zurich, Switzerland, and a member of the Sovereign Society Council of Experts. **Contact:** Henley & Partners AG, Haus zum Engel, Kirchgasse 24, 8001 Zurich, Switzerland. **Tel.:** +41-1-267 60 90. **Fax:** +41-1-267 60 91. **E-mail:** c.kalin@henleyglobal.com. Website: www.henleyglobal.com.

Denis A. Kleinfeld, CPA, JD, is a member of the Florida and Illinois bars and a principal in the Kleinfeld Law Firm, Miami, Florida. Suntrust International Bldg., One SE Third Ave., Suite 1940, Miami, FL 33131. **Tel.:** (305) 375-9515. **Fax:** (305) 358-6541. **E-mail:** deniskleinfeld@kleinfeld.com or messagectr@kleinfeld.com. He is a recognized expert with an international practice in personal and corporate tax planning and wealth protection planning. He graduated from the U. of Illinois (1967) with a BS in accountancy and from the Loyola (Chicago) U. School of Law (1970). Prior to private practice, he served four years as an attorney in the Estate and Gift Tax Division of the IRS.

Marshall J. Langer, JD, is co-author of *U.S. International Taxation and Tax Treaties* (Matthew Bender Inc., New York) and author of several books, including *The Tax Exile Report*. He is also a member of The Sovereign Society's Board of Advisors. Contact Mr. Langer c/o Shutts & Bowen, 43 Upper Grosvenor Street, W1X 9PG U.K. **Tel.:** +(44) 171 493 4840. **Fax:** +(44) 171 493 4299. **E-mail:** mjlanger@aol.com.

David Lesperance, Barrister & Solicitor, is Chief Legal Counsel to Global Relocation Consultants S.A., a consultancy that specializes in the integration of immigration and citizenship, offshore trusts and tax planning. He is also a member of the Sovereign Society Council of Experts. Contact: David S. Lesperance, c/o Global Relocation Consultants S.A. 84 King Street West, Suite 202, Dundas, Ont., Canada L9H 1T9. **Tel.:** +1 (905) 627-3037. **Fax:** + 1 (905) 627-9868. **E-mail:** dsl@globalrelocate.com.

Bill McCord, CFP, is a certified financial planner (CFP) with a doctorate in education from Syracuse University. He is the author of *Better Than Gold: An Investor's Guide to Swiss Annuities*. He specializes in tax-protected financial planning and investments. **Tel.:** (719) 630-7747, Colorado Springs, Colorado, USA.

Donald MacPherson, JD, an attorney in Phoenix, Arizona, is a board certified specialist in both criminal law and tax law, a U.S. Military Academy (West Point) graduate and former Green Beret officer. He has authored books including *Tax Fraud and Evasion: The War Stories*. He represents offshore clients including those with foreign trusts, corporations, IBCs. **Website:** www.beatirs.com. **Tel.:** 1-800 232-8477.

David Marchant is an investigative journalist and a licensed private investigator in Florida. He owns Miami-based Offshore Business News & Research Inc., which publishes two newsletters, Offshore Alert and Inside Bermuda. Contact: OBNR, 123 SE. Third Avenue, Box 173, Miami, FL

33131, U.S.A. **Tel.:** +1 (305) 372-6267. **Fax:** +1 (305) 372-8724. **E-mail:** info@offshorebusiness.com. **Website:** www.offshorebusiness.com.

David Melnik, JD, Queen's Counsel, of Toronto, Canada, serves dual roles as a member of The Oxford Club's Board of Governors and Director of the Oxford Club Wealth Protection Program. He headed his own law firm (1962-76), then became chief executive officer of Vanguard Trust Ltd. of Canada. He also served as policy advisor to the Premier of the Province of Ontario. He taught at the University of Toronto and York University in their Masters in Business programs. Mr. Melnik serves as a director of several U.S. and Canadian corporations and also lectures worldwide. He is co-author of *The Offshore Money Manual* (The Sovereign Society, 1999) and of *Your Money and Your Life* (The Oxford Club, 1999).

Vincent H. Miller is founder and current president and chief executive officer of ISIL. He is also a member of the Sovereign Society Council of Experts. **Contact:** International Society for Individual Liberty, 836-B Southampton Rd., #299, Benicia, CA 94510 U.S.A. **Tel.:** +1 707 746 8796. **Fax:** +1 707 746 8797. **E-mail:** isil@isil.org. **Website:** www.isil.org.

Daniel J. Mitchell is the McKenna Senior Fellow in Political Economy in the Thomas A. Roe Institute for Economic Policy Studies at the Heritage Foundation, Washington, D.C. He is a leading expert on domestic and international tax policy. **E-mail:** dan.mitchell@heritage.org.

Mark Nestmann, editorial director of the Sovereign Society Ltd., has a BS from Denison University (1977). He has edited several publications; *The Sovereign Individual* (1998-present); *Asset Protection International* (1997-1998); *Low Profile* (1992-1995); *The Oxford Club Communiqué* (1986-1992). He is author of numerous books on privacy, asset protection and taxation. He is president of The Nestmann Group, Ltd.2303 N. 44th St. #14-1025, Phoenix, AZ 85008 USA. **Tel./Fax:** +1 (602) 604-1524. **E-mail:** assetpro@nestmann.com. **Website:** www.nestmann.com.

Kathleen Peddicord is the publisher of *International Living*, one of the oldest newsletters focusing on expatriate lifestyles. She has more than 14 years experience investigating real estate investments throughout the world. She is located in Waterford, Ireland. **E-mail:** 102503.353@compuserve.com

Nicholas Pullen writes widely on offshore opportunities and individual liberty. His latest book is *The Internationalist Blueprint*. Nicholas Pullen's *Offshore Opportunities Letter* is published monthly. **E-mail:** prometheus.press@virgin.net.

John Pugsley is Chairman of the Sovereign Society and author of many books on economics, investing and politics. His first book, *Common Sense Economics* (1974), sold over 150,000 hardcover copies and predicted the inflation that followed U.S. abandonment of the gold standard in the early 1970s. In 1980, his second best seller, *The Alpha Strategy*, warned against coming U.S. deficits, giving investors a practical plan for self-protection. For a decade beginning in 1988, he published *John Pugsley's Journal*, a newsletter of political, economic and investment ideas.

Eric Roseman is editor of *Global Mutual Fund Investor*, a monthly newsletter focusing on global asset allocation strategies, contrarian mutual funds and equity recommendations. He is president of Emerald Analytical Services, Inc., which specializes in global asset allocation and portfolio management. Two Westmount Square, Suite 1802, Westmount, PQ H3Z 2S4 Canada. **WATS:** 1 (877) 989-8027 (US and Canada). **Tel.:** +1 (514) 989-8027. **Fax:** +1 (514) 989-7060. **E-mail:** enr@qc.aibn.com. **Website:** www.eas.ca.

Derek R. Sambrook is a Fellow of the South African Institute of Bankers and a Registered Trust & Estate Practitioner in the United Kingdom. He is a partner of Trust Services, S.A., specialists in offshore corporations and trust formation, based in Panama. His practical experience spans more than 35 years and includes experience as an official offshore bank and insurance regulator for the United Kingdom. **Contact:** Trust Services, S.A., P.O. Box 0832-1630, World Trade Center, Panama, Republic of Panama. **Tel.:** +(507) 269-2438 or +(507) 263-5252. **Fax:** +(507) 269-4922 or (507) 269-9138. **E-mail:** marketing@trustserv.com. **Website:** www.trustserv.com.

Gary Scott has been an international economic writer and investment consultant for 30 years, with 23,000 readers in 82 countries. He is editor of *World Reports*, and can be reached at: International Service Center, PO Box 157, Lansing, NC 28643, U.S.A. **Fax:** +1-336-384-1577. **E-mail:** info@garyascott.com. **Website:** http://www.garyascott.com.

Marc-AndrÈ Sola is Managing Partner, NMG International Ltd., Zurich, Switzerland and a member of The Sovereign Society's Council of Experts. Before joining the Zurich subsidiary of the worldwide NMG-Group, he was the Managing Director of a US.-registered international investment advisory firm in Switzerland. This firm advised over 25,000 clients from more than 40 countries in the fields of banking and insurance. Sola attained his law degree from the University of Zurich and can call upon a global network of financial specialists and money managers. **Contact:** Marc-AndrÈ Sola, NMG International Financial Services, Ltd. **Tel.:** +(41) 1 266 21 41. **Fax:** +(41) 1 266 21 49. **E-mail:** marcsola@nmg-ifs.com. **Link:** www.nmg-ifs.com.

Dr. Erich Stoeger is Chairman of EurAxxess, a global financial services company in Switzerland. For more information call the toll free line: 1 (800) 331-0996 or e-mail info@euraxxess.com. **Website:** www.euraxxess.com.

John Sturgeon, JD, is an American lawyer who advises clients on their offshore moves and assists them in reorganizing their business and personal lives. **Tel.:** +44 1624 617050. **Fax:** +44 1624 617051. **E-mail:** dakota@enterprise.net.

Paul Terhorst was a successful CPA for Peat Marwick, an international accounting firm. At 33, he was making about $125,000 a year. He was able to retire at age 35. His book, *Cashing in on the American Dream—How to Retire at Age 35* (Bantam Books, 1988), tells how he did it. **Link:** http://www.geocities.com/TheTropics/Shores/5315/.

Appendix II
Offshore Websites

I. Best Offshore & Privacy Internet Web Sites:

The Sovereign Society—http://www.sovereignsociety.com

Asset Protection Guide—http://www.assetprotection.com

Best of the Web offshore links—http://www.Taxup.com

Center for Freedom & Prosperity—http://www.freedomandprosperity.org

Country Profiles—http://www.infoplease.com/countries.html

Current news articles (1800 sources)—http://w.moreover.com

Electronic Privacy Information Center—http://www.epic.org

Embassy World—http://www.embassyworld.com

Escape Artist—http://www.escapeartist.com

Financial Times Expat Page—http://news.ft.com/home/us

Financial web links—http://www.financialfind.com

Expat Forum—http://www.expatforum.com

Immigration & residency—http://www.henleyglobal.com

Mark Nestmann's Asset Protection—http://www.nestmann.com

Offshore news and information—http://www.tax-news.com

Pretty Good Privacy—http://www.pgpi.com

Reference sources portal—http://www.refdesk.com/instant.html

U.K. Foreign Office country profiles—http://www.fco.gov.uk/travel

Vern Jacobs' Research Press—http://www.offshorepress.com

II. Banking & Currency

Central, South America & Caribbean Banks—http://www.orcc.com/index.asp

Currency Converter & Financial Forecasts—http://www.oanda.com

Currency Converter & Exchange Rates—http://www.xe.net/ucc/

Interactive Investor Funds (U.K.)—http://www.iii.co.uk

International Company Services—http://www.icsl.com

NatWest Offshore Expat Banking Services—http://www.natwestoffshore.com

III. Other Offshore Web Sites:

Directories:

AAA Directory World Banks—http://www.aaadir.com

European Business Directory—http://www.europages.com

International Fax & Business Directories—http://www.infobel.com/World

ISI Emerging Markets—http://www.securities.com

Worldwide Yellow Pages—http://www.worldyellowpages.com

World Telephone Directories—http://www.infobel.com/teldir

Other Links:

Law, Lawyers and Governments of the World—http://www.hg.org/govt.html

Central Intelligence Agency (World Fact Book)—http://www.odci.gov

Electronic Embassy—http://www.embassy.org

Emerging Markets Companion—http://www.emgmkts.com

Times of London—http://www.thetimes.co.uk

Financial Times Group—http://news.ft.com/home/us

Gray's Inn U.K. Tax Barristers—http://www.taxbar.com

International Monetary Fund (IMF)—http://www.imf.org

Investment Center Switzerland—http://www.locationswitzerland.ch

Language Dictionaries Online—http://www.yourdictionary.com

Lex Mundi World Legal Network—http://www.hg.org/currwr.html

Liechtenstein News—http://www.news.li

Mondex International—http://www.mondex.com

Morgan Stanley Capital International—http://www.msci.com

New York Times—http://www.nytimes.com

Offshore conferences—http://www.shorex.com

Swiss News Agency—http://www.swissinfo.org

U.S. State Dept. Country Notes—http://www.state.gov/www/background_notes/index.html

Vern Jacobs Asset Protection Newsletter—http://www.rpifs.com/lawsuits

Vern Jacobs Offshore Web Forum—http://www.rpifs.com/rpifs/apfhelp.htm

Vern Jacobs Global e-commerce—http://www.rpifs.com/offshore

Vern Jacobs Offshore Tax Strategies—http://www.rpifs.com/taxhelp

World Citizen Foundation—http://www.worldcitizen.org

Wall Street Journal—http://www.wsj.com

Emerging Market Indexes:

Indexes, Morgan Stanley Capital International—http://www.msci.com

Closed-end Funds:

Bloomberg Personal (market data, comment & real estate)—http://www.bloomberg.com

Appendix III
Glossary

acceptance: Unconditional agreement by one party (the "offeree") to the terms of an offer made by a second party (the "offeror"). Agreement results in a valid, binding contract.

arbitrage: Buying the securities in one nation, currency or market and selling in another, to take advantage of the price differential.

asset protection trust (APT): An offshore trust which holds title to and protects the grantor's property from all claims, judgements and creditors, especially because it is located in a country other than the grantor's home country.

attachment: The post-judicial civil procedure by which personal property is taken from its owner pursuant to a judgement or other court order.

basis: The original cost of an asset, later used to measure increased value for tax purposes at the time of sale or disposition.

bearer share/stocks: A negotiable stock certificate made out only to "bearer" without designating the shareowner by name. Such shares are unregistered with the issuing company and dividends must be claimed by "clipping coupons" and presenting them for payment.

beneficiary: One designated to receive income from a trust or estate; a person named in an insurance policy to receive proceeds or benefits.

bequest: A gift of personal property by will; also called a "legacy."

capital gain: The amount of profit earned from the sale or exchange of property, measured against the original cost basis.

captive insurance company: A wholly owned subsidiary company established by a non-insurance parent company to share ("spread") insured risks of the parent and other associated companies.

civil suit: A non-criminal legal action between parties relating to a dispute or injury seeking remedies for a violation of contractual or other personal rights.

civil law: The body of law based on the Justinian Code of Roman law and adopted as the basis of law in most non-English-speaking nations in Europe and Latin America.

common law: The body of law developed in England from judicial decisions based on customs and precedent, constituting the basis of the present English, British Commonwealth and US legal systems. See "equity."

community property: In certain states, property acquired during marriage jointly owned by both spouses, each with an undivided one half interest.

contract: A binding agreement between two or more parties; also the written or other evidence of an agreement.

corporation: A business, professional or other entity recognized in law to act as a single legal "person," although composed of one or more natural persons, endowed by law with various rights and duties including the right of succession.

corpus: The property owned by a fund, trust or estate, also called the "principal."

creator: See "grantor."

creditor: One to whom a debtor owes money or other valuable consideration.

debtor: One who owes another (the "creditor") money or other valuable consideration, especially one who has neglected payments due.

decedent: A term used in probate to describe a deceased person.

declaration: A formal statement in writing of any kind, often signed and notarized, especially a document establishing a trust; also called an indenture or trust agreement.

deed: A formal written document signed by the owner conveying title to real estate.

domicile: A person's permanent legal home, as compared to a place that may be only a temporary residence. Domicile determines what law applies to the person for purposes of marriage, divorce, succession of estate at death and taxation.

equity: A body of judicial rules developed under the common law used to enlarge and protect legal rights and enforce duties while seeking to avoid unjust constraints and narrowness of statutory law; also, the unrealized property value of a person's investment or ownership, as in a trust beneficiary's "equitable interest;" also the risk sharing part of a company's capital, referred to as "ordinary shares."

estate: Any of various kinds or types of ownership a person may have in real or personal property; often used to describe all property of a deceased person, meaning the assets and liabilities remaining after death.

estate tax: Taxes imposed at death by the US and most state governments on assets of a decedent, except on the first US$600,000 in value which is exempt.

exchange controls: Government restrictions imposed on dealings in a national or foreign currency.

executor: A person who manages the estate of a decedent, also called an "executrix" if a female, "personal representative," "administrator," or "administratrix."

exemption: In tax law, a statutorily defined right to avoid part or all of certain taxes; also the statutory right granted to a debtor in bankruptcy to retain a portion of his or her real or personal property free from a creditor's claims.

expatriation: The transfer of one's legal residence and citizenship from one's home country to another country, often in anticipation of government financial restrictions or taxes.

family partnership (also "family limited partnership"): A legal business relationship created by agreement among two or more family members for a common purpose, often used as a means to transfer and/or equalize income and assets among family members so as to limit individual personal liability and taxes; see "partnership" and "limited partnership."

fiduciary: A person holding property in trust for another, as a trustee, guardian or executor of an estate.

flight capital: Movement of large sums of money across national borders, often to escape high taxes or pending political or social unrest.

future interest: An interest in property, usually real estate, possession and enjoyment of which is delayed until some future time or event; also, futures, securities or goods bought or sold for future delivery, often keyed to price changes before delivery.

gift tax: US tax imposed on any gift made by one person to another person annually in excess of US$10,000.

grantor: A person who conveys real property by deed; a person who creates a trust, also called a trust "donor," "settlor," or "trustor."

grantor trust: As used in US tax law, an offshore trust, the income of which is taxed by the IRS as the personal income of the grantor.

gross estate: The total value for estate tax purposes of all a decedent's assets, as compared to "net estate," the amount remaining after all permitted exemptions, deductions and taxes owed.

guardianship: A power conferred on a person, the "guardian," usually by judicial decree, giving them the right and duty to provide personal supervision, care and control over another person who is unable to care for himself because of some physical or mental disability.

haven or haven nation: A country where banking, tax, trust and corporation laws are specially designed to attract foreign persons wishing to avoid taxes, or protect assets.

indices of ownership: Factors indicating a person's power over, therefore ownership, especially of trust property, including the power of revocability.

income beneficiary: The life tenant in a trust.

incorporation: The registration and qualification process by which a corporation is formed under law.

indemnity: An agreement by which one promises to protect another from any loss or damage, usually describing the role of the insurer in insurance law.

inheritance tax: A tax imposed by many nations on the amount a person receives from a decedent's estate, rather than on the estate itself.

insider dealing: Illegal conduct entailing use of nonpublic, confidential information about a company's status to influence purchase or sale of its corporate shares, usually for the manipulator's personal benefit.

international business corporation (IBC): A term used to describe a variety of offshore corporate structures, characterized by having all or most of its business activity outside the nation of incorporation, maximum privacy, flexibility, low or no taxes on operations, broad powers and minimal filing and reporting requirements.

insurance: A contract or "policy" under which a corporation, known as an "insurer," undertakes to indemnify or pay a person, the "insured," for a specified loss in return for the insured's payment of a "premium."

irrevocable trust: A trust which, once established by the grantor, cannot be ended or terminated by the grantor.

joint tenancy: A form of property co-ownership in which parties hold equal title with the right of survivorship; a "joint tenancy by the entireties" is a similar tenancy reserved to husband and wife.

judgement: An official and authenticated decision of a court.

jurisdiction: The statutory authority a court exercises; also a word used to describe the geographic or subject matter area over which a government or court has power.

last will and testament: A written document in which a person directs the post mortem distribution of his or her property. State law governs the specific requirements for a valid will.

legal capacity: The competency or ability of parties to make a valid contract, including being of majority age (18 years) and of sound mind.

life insurance trust: An irrevocable living trust that holds title to a policy on the grantor's life, proceeds from which are not part of the grantor's estate.

life estate: The use and enjoyment of property granted by the owner to another during the owner's life, or during the life of another, at the termination of which, title passes to another known as the "remainderman."

limited partnership: A partnership in which individuals known as "limited partners" have no management role, but receive periodic income and are personally liable for partnership debts only to the extent of their individual investment.

marital deduction: The right of the surviving spouse under US law to inherit, free of estate taxes, all property owned at death by the deceased spouse.

marriage: The legal and religious institution whereby a man and woman join in a binding contract for the purpose of founding and maintaining a family.

money laundering: The process of concealing the criminal origins or uses of cash so that it appears the funds involved are from legitimate sources. A crime in most major nations.

mutual legal assistance treaty (MLATs): Bilateral treaty between nations governing cooperation in international investigations of alleged criminal conduct; the US has many such treaties, especially with offshore haven countries.

numbered bank account: Any account in a financial institution that is identified not by the account holder's name, but a number, limiting knowledge of the owner to a few bank officials. Law in many nations protects the privacy of such accounts and account holders. Often associated with Swiss banking, these accounts are available in many other asset haven nations.

offer: A written or verbal promise by one person (the "offeror"), to another (the "offeree"), to do or not to do some future act, usually in exchange for a mutual promise or payment (consideration). See "acceptance" and "contract."

option: A contract provision allowing one to purchase property at a set price within a certain time period.

partnership: An association of two or more persons formed to conduct business for mutual profit. See "limited partnership."

policy: In insurance law, the contract between insurer and insured; see "insurance."

power of attorney: A written instrument allowing one to act as agent for another, the scope of agency power indicated by the terms, known as "general" or "limited."

preservation trust: Any trust designed to limit a beneficiary's access to income and principal.

primary residence: Especially in tax law, a home place, as compared to a vacation or second home; see "domicile."

probate: A series of judicial proceedings, usually in a special court, initially determining the validity of a last will and testament, then supervising the administration or execution of the terms of the will and the decedent's estate.

property: Anything of value capable of being owned, including land (real property) and personal property, both tangible and intangible.

protector: In offshore haven nations, a person appointed by the grantor of an offshore trust, who has the duty of overseeing the trustee's activities.

quit claim deed: A deed transferring any interest a grantor may have in real property without guarantees of title, if in fact any interest does exist.

real estate: Land and anything growing or erected thereon or permanently attached thereto.

real estate investment trust (REIT): An investment fund in trust form that owns and operates real estate for share holding investors who are the beneficiaries.

remainder: In testamentary law, the balance of an estate after payment of legacies; in property law, an interest in land or a trust estate distributed at the termination of a life estate. The person with a right to such an estate is the "remainderman."

rescind: Cancellation or annulment of an otherwise binding contract by one of the parties.

residence: a place where one actually lives as compared to a domicile which is a place of a temporary sojourn. See "domicile."

revocable trust: A living trust in which the grantor retains the power to revoke or terminate the trust during his or her lifetime, returning the assets to themselves.

right of survivorship: An attribute of a joint tenancy that automatically transfers ownership of the share of a deceased joint tenant to surviving joint tenants without the necessity of probate.

signature trust: A bank account established by a person who gratuitously adds to the account the name of another person, who, as a result, may be the beneficiary of what is an implied trust.

spendthrift trust: A restricted trust created to pay income to a beneficiary judged by the trust grantor to be too improvident to handle his or her own personal economic affairs.

tenancy by the entireties: A joint tenancy between husband and wife, with the right of survivorship.

trust: A legal device allowing title to and possession of property to be held, used, and/or managed by one person, the "trustee," for the benefit of others, the "beneficiaries."

unit trust: In the U.K. and Commonwealth nations, the equivalent of the investment fund known in the US as a "mutual fund."